The Waite Group's

Visual Basic® 6
Database
How-To

Eric Winemiller
Jason Roff
Bill Heyman
Ryan Groom

SAMS

A Division of Macmillan Computer Publishing
201 West 103rd St., Indianapolis, Indiana, 46290 USA

Visual Basic® 6 Database How-To

Copyright © 1998 by Sams Publishing

International Standard Book Number: 0-57169-152-9

Library of Congress Catalog Card Number: 98-84684

Printed in the United States of America

First Printing: August 1998

00   99   98   4   3   2

Trademarks

Warning and Disclaimer

EXECUTIVE EDITOR
Brian Gill

ACQUISITIONS EDITOR
Ron Gallagher

DEVELOPMENT EDITOR
Chris Nelson

MANAGING EDITOR
Jodi Jensen

SENIOR EDITOR
Susan Ross Moore

COPY EDITORS
Sarah Burkhart
Kate O. Givens
Krista Hansing
Molly Schaller

TECHNICAL EDITOR
John Del Buono

SOFTWARE DEVELOPMENT SPECIALIST
John Warriner

EDITORIAL ASSISTANT
Carol Ackerman

PRODUCTION
Marcia Deboy
Michael Dietsch
Jennifer Earhart
Cynthia Fields
Susan Geiselman

CONTENTS AT A GLANCE

INTRODUCTION   **1**

CHAPTER 1:   **ACCESSING A DATABASE WITH BOUND CONTROLS** 3

CHAPTER 2:   **ACCESSING A DATABASE WITH DATA ACCESS OBJECTS** 55

CHAPTER 3:   **CREATING QUERIES WITH SQL** 127

CHAPTER 4:   **DESIGNING AND IMPLEMENTING A DATABASE** 229

CHAPTER 5:   **MICROSOFT ACCESS DATABASE** 297

CHAPTER 6:   **CONNECTING TO AN ODBC SERVER** 365

CHAPTER 7:   **SQL SERVER DATABASES AND REMOTE DATA OBJECTS** 427

CHAPTER 8:   **USING ACTIVEX DATA OBJECTS** 481

CHAPTER 9:   **MICROSOFT DATA REPORT** 553

CHAPTER 10:   **SECURITY AND MULTIUSER ACCESS** 647

CHAPTER 11:   **THE WINDOWS REGISTRY AND STATE INFORMATION** 753

CHAPTER 10:   **ACTIVEX AND AUTOMATION** 789

CHAPTER 13:   **ADVANCED DATABASE TECHNIQUES** 907

APPENDIXES

APPENDIX A: **SQL REFERENCE** 939

APPENDIX B: **DATA ACCESS OBJECT REFERENCE** 953

APPENDIX C: **REMOTE DATA OBJECT REFERENCE** 971

APPENDIX D: **ACTIVEX DATA OBJECTS REFERENCE** 983

APPENDIX E: **A SHORT INTRODUCTION TO VISUAL BASIC OBJECTS** 993

INDEX   **1001**

CONTENTS

INTRODUCTION 1

CHAPTER 1
ACCESSING A DATABASE WITH BOUND CONTROLS 3

1.1   Browse a recordset using bound controls 8
1.2   Validate data entered into bound controls 12
1.3   Allow users to undo changes they've made in bound controls 16
1.4   Add and delete records using bound controls .20
1.5   Create and use bound lists 28
1.6   Display many detail records for a single master record 36
1.7   Change data in data-bound grid cells from code 42
1.8   Gracefully handle database errors 46

CHAPTER 2
ACCESSING A DATABASE WITH DATA ACCESS OBJECTS 55

2.1   Browse and update records by using Data Access Objects 59
2.2   Validate data entered into Data Access Objects 75
2.3   Allow users to undo changes they've made in Data Access Objects 79
2.4   Add and delete records by using Data Access Objects 82
2.5   Use unbound controls to update fields in Data Access Objects 91
2.6   Find records by using index values in Data Access Objects 97
2.7   Determine how many records are in a dynaset- or snapshot-type recordset . . .106
2.8   Handle Data Access Object errors 110
2.9   Access Excel worksheets by using Data Access Objects 116

CHAPTER 3
CREATING QUERIES WITH SQL 127

3.1   Create recordsets by selecting records from single tables 133
3.2   Select unique field values in a SQL query 140
3.3   Use variables and Visual Basic functions in a SQL query 145
3.4   Use wildcards and ranges of values in a SQL query 150
3.5   Define and use a parameter query 155
3.6   Create recordsets by joining fields from multiple tables 159
3.7   Find records in a table without corresponding entries in a related table 163
3.8   Retrieve information such as counts, averages, and sums and display it by
        binding it to a Data control 167
3.9   Create a recordset consisting of records with duplicate values 172
3.10   Use Visual Basic functions within a SQL statement 177

3.11   Make bulk updates to database records 181
3.12   Create and delete tables 185
3.13   Append and delete records 199
3.14   Create a new table with data from existing tables 210
3.15   Modify a table's structure 215
3.16   Create a crosstab query 225

CHAPTER 4
DESIGNING AND IMPLEMENTING A DATABASE 229

4.1   Create a new database 232
4.2   Define tables and fields 237
4.3   Define the primary key and other indexes 258
4.4   Define relations between tables 274
4.5   Use the Jet database engine to enforce business rules 288

CHAPTER 5
MICROSOFT ACCESS DATABASES 297

5.1   Determine the number of records in a table and the table's creation and
      last-modified dates 301
5.2   Attach a table from another database file 308
5.3   Import a text file 317
5.4   Save graphics in a database file 335
5.5   Make sure that an operation involving multiple tables is not left partially
      completed 341
5.6   Compact a database or repair a corrupted database 351
5.7   Use parameter queries stored in Microsoft Access databases 355

CHAPTER 6
CONNECTING TO AN ODBC SERVER 365

6.1   Use the ODBC Administrator to maintain data sources 377
6.2   Use ODBC with the Visual Basic Data control 380
6.3   Create an ODBC-accessible data source by using `RegisterDatabase` 385
6.4   Prevent the login dialog box from being displayed when I open an
      ODBC database 393
6.5   Determine what services an ODBC server provides 403
6.6   Use ODBCDirect to connect to database servers 422

CHAPTER 7
SQL SERVER DATABASES AND REMOTE DATA OBJECTS 427

7.1   Browse a SQL Server database by using the RemoteData control 433
7.2   Add and delete records in a SQL Server database by using the
      RemoteData control 437

7.3   Connect to a SQL Server database by using Remote Data Objects 442

7.4   Browse records in a SQL Server database by using Remote Data Objects 445

7.5   Add, update, and delete records in a SQL Server database by using
Remote Data Objects 452

7.6   Execute a SQL Server stored procedure by using Remote Data Objects 464

7.7   Execute a parameterized SQL Server stored procedure with
Remote Data Objects 468

7.8   Handle Remote Data Objects errors 473

CHAPTER 8
USING ACTIVEX DATA OBJECTS 481

8.1   Browse a SQL Server database with the ADO Data control 486

8.2   Create and delete records in a SQL Server database using the
ADO Data control 489

8.3   Retrieve results from a SQL Server using ActiveX Data Objects 493

8.4   Alter data using ActiveX Data Objects 496

8.5   Perform a transaction using ActiveX Data Objects .507

8.6   Execute a SQL Server stored procedure using ActiveX Data Objects 512

8.7   Execute a parameterized SQL Server stored procedure with
ActiveX Data Objects 516

8.8   Create and modify SQL Server objects with ActiveX Data Objects 520

8.9   Execute batch updates with ActiveX Data Objects .523

8.10   Make remote updates to data with ActiveX Data Objects 528

8.11   Build a middle-tier business object using ActiveX Data Objects 531

8.12   Incorporate a business object into Microsoft Transaction Server 542

8.13   Handle ActiveX Data Objects errors 547

CHAPTER 9
MICROSOFT DATA REPORT 553

9.1   Create a report using Microsoft Data Report Designer 563

9.2   Add Calculated Fields to my Microsoft Data Report 567

9.3   Select whether the Microsoft Data Report will be displayed, printed,
or exported using Visual Basic code 572

9.4   Have Visual Basic generate a Microsoft Data Report based on criteria
I choose 579

9.5   Determine which records will be printed using Crystal Reports 582

9.6   Create subtotals and other calculated fields using Crystal Reports 591

9.7   Control the order in which records will be printed using Crystal Reports 605

9.8   Print labels using Crystal Reports 609

9.9   Create and print form letters using Crystal Reports .613

9.10 Print field data without extra spaces between the fields using
Crystal Reports 622

9.11 Prevent blank lines from being printed when a field contains no data using
Crystal Reports 627
9.12 Create cross-tab reports with Crystal Reports 634
9.13 Generate reports using user-entered variables 638

CHAPTER 10
SECURITY AND MULTIUSER ACCESS 647

10.1 Open a database so that others can't access it while the user is
working with it 651
10.2 Open a table so that others can't access it while the user is working with it . . .658
10.3 Work with locked records 667
10.4 Work with secured Microsoft Access database files 677
10.5 Assign permissions for database objects 686
10.6 Change ownership of database objects 701
10.7 Change or delete database passwords 706
10.8 Use a single password for data access for all users 712
10.9 Add new users to a system database 719
10.10 Define new groups in a system database 725
10.11 Add users to groups and delete users from groups 731
10.12 Track user activity in a database 738
10.13 Create and use an encrypted database 745

CHAPTER 11
THE WINDOWS REGISTRY AND STATE INFORMATION 753

11.1 Enter and retrieve Windows Registry entries from Visual Basic 757
11.2 Put data access-related information into an application's section of the
Registry 763
11.3 Determine which database and report-related files need to be distributed
with my applications 772
11.4 Tune the Jet database engine through Windows Registry entries 780
11.5 Tune the ODBC engine using Windows Registry entries 784

CHAPTER 12
ACTIVEX AND AUTOMATION 789

12.1 Use ActiveX Automation to edit pictures, documents, and spreadsheets
embedded in an application's database 797
12.2 Provide access to database files through a private class module 805
12.3 Publish my ActiveX private class so that others can use it 822
12.4 Provide controlled access to an encrypted, password-protected database
using an ActiveX EXE server 825
12.5 Use Microsoft Access as an ActiveX server to print reports from Visual Basic . .832
12.6 Use Microsoft Access queries containing user-defined functions from
Visual Basic 835

CONTENTS

12.7   Convert database data to a spreadsheet form that can be used to edit and analyze data 845
12.8   Include an editable report writer in a Visual Basic application 854
12.9   Work with the Windows Registry for my ActiveX classes 865
12.10 Create my own custom data control 867
12.11 Create my own data bound control 891
12.12 Use the DataRepeater control with custom Data Bound controls 901

CHAPTER 13
ADVANCED DATABASE TECHNIQUES .907

13.1   Search for database records by using a Soundex algorithm 910
13.2   Back up selected database objects at a set schedule 914
13.3   Replicate a database by using the Jet engine 923
13.4   Omit specified objects from replicas 932
13.5   Create a nonreplicated version of a replicated database 935

APPENDIX A
SQL REFERENCE 939

APPENDIX B
DATA ACCESS OBJECT REFERENCE 953

APPENDIX C
REMOTE DATA OBJECT REFERENCE .971

APPENDIX D
ACTIVEX DATA OBJECTS REFERENCE 983

APPENDIX E
A SHORT INTRODUCTION TO VISUAL BASIC OBJECTS 993

INDEX 1001

ABOUT THE AUTHORS

Eric Winemiller is a principal software developer for Visteon Corporation in Maitland, Florida, where he builds BackOffice- and Visual Basic–based medical applications. The project he helped develop for Orlando Health Care Group and Visteon Corporation placed 10th in Info World's 1995 Top 100 client server sites. Eric has previously published in *Visual Basic Developer*, *SQL Server Professional*, and the *Visual Basic 5 SuperBible*. He has a bachelor's degree in computer science from the University of Central Florida. His family considers the Commodore 64 they gave him for his 13th birthday the best 200 bucks they ever spent. In his spare time he can be found trying to be a digital artist, puttering around his wood shop, or renovating his old house. He can be reached at `winemill@visteon.com`.

Jason T. Roff currently works for Isogon Corporation, a company that provides asset management solutions to Fortune 500 companies. Here he develops C/C++ client/server applications that are designed to run on heterogeneous networks. Jason holds a bachelor's degree from the University at Albany, New York, in computer science with applied mathematics. Jason can be reached at `jroff@earthlink.net`.

Bill Heyman specializes in custom software development for Windows 98 and Windows NT in Visual Basic, C++, and Java. As founder and president of Heyman Software, Inc., Bill uses his skills and experience to engineer innovative software for his clients. He can be reached at `heyman@heymansoftware.com` and `http://www.heymansoftware.com/~heyman/`.

Ryan Groom has been a computer addict since getting a Commodore 64 for Christmas back in 1985. After graduation he started work for a local school board where he cut his teeth on various computer topics from administering OS/2 and Novell servers to creating attendance management software. In 1996, he co-founded Gulliver Software in Saint John, New Brunswick, Canada. Gulliver Software develops Internet-based software, including its retail package Gulliver's Guardian, an Internet filtering suite for families. Currently Ryan (and Gulliver Software) is working with National Electronic Technologies on a releasing a public Internet access terminal called VideoNet. Ryan can be reached at `ryan@gulliver.nb.ca`, or you can visit him at `http://www.gulliver.nb.ca` or `http://www.natel.ca`.

DEDICATION

To my parents, who got me started down the path.

Eric Winemiller

To my sister Tammi, who has put up with all my beatings, has kept all my secrets, and can drink me under the table. I love you.

Jason Roff

To my parents, for giving me an Apple II+ and the start to a wonderful career.

Bill Heyman

For Kristy. Our new life has just begun.

Ryan Groom

ACKNOWLEDGMENTS

I want to thank my wife Judy for again putting up with the grumpy foul beast who possesses me when I don't get enough sleep. I would also like to thank the Clinical and Clinical beta teams at Visteon who had to put up with that same beast.

Eric Winemiller

I would like to thank everybody at Macmillan who was gracious enough to give me another opportunity to do what I love, write. I would especially like to thank Brian Gill, Ron Gallagher, and Chris Nelson. I would also like to thank my other half, Kimberly, for putting up with many nights of not seeing me so that I could work to finish projects such as this book. I love you so very much, and I cannot wait to spend the rest of my life with you.

Jason Roff

I want to extend my thanks to the kind folks at Macmillan Computer Publishing for assisting me in contributing to this book. In addition, I would like to acknowledge the continuing love and support that my wife, Jodi, and toddler daughter, Cassie, give to me. Certainly I would not be where I am today without them.

Bill Heyman

To the staff at Macmillan Computer Publishing for providing the opportunity and patience for allowing me write about one of my favorite topics. It is very fulfilling to not only to be involved in such an exciting industry but also to have an opportunity to create documentation that may let others understand a topic I so enjoy. The gang at Gulliver Software and National Electronics for providing a fun and innovative atmosphere in which to work. Rory, a brother in arms, "You know what I mean, man!" Mom, Dad, Michael, and Peter, for your eternal support for every step I take. Steven and Dawn for providing a great get away from the woes of computerdom. Kristy, only with your support, patience, and understanding can any project be completed.

Ryan Groom

TELL US WHAT YOU THINK!

As the reader of this book, *you* are our most important critic and commentator. We value your opinion and want to know what we're doing right, what we could do better, what areas you'd like to see us publish in, and any other words of wisdom you're willing to pass our way.

As the Executive Editor for the Programming team at Macmillan Computer Publishing, I welcome your comments. You can fax, email, or write me directly to let me know what you did or didn't like about this book—as well as what we can do to make our books stronger.

Please note that I cannot help you with technical problems related to the topic of this book, and that due to the high volume of mail I receive, I might not be able to reply to every message.

When you write, please be sure to include this book's title and author as well as your name and phone or fax number. I will carefully review your comments and share them with the authors and editors who worked on the book.

Fax: 317-817-7070
Email: prog@mcp.com
Mail: Executive Editor
          Programming
          Macmillan Computer Publishing
          201 West 103rd Street
          Indianapolis, IN 46290 USA

INTRODUCTION

About This Book

Since version 3, Visual Basic has been the tool of choice for database programmers everywhere. First came DAO with version 3, RDO with version 4, and then the ability to build robust ActiveX components in version 5. With each successive version, Microsoft adds more functionality to make database programming easier for you.

Visual Basic's powerful database feature set has continued to grow with version 6. New tools and technologies like ADO, OLE-DB, and the Microsoft Data Reporter vie for your attention. What does it all mean, what can it do for you, and most importantly, how do you quickly get up to speed?

That's why this book was created. *Visual Basic 6 Database How-To* gives an in-depth view of each major method of data access, with real-life examples with which to work. Like all books in the successful How-To series, *Visual Basic 6 Database How-To* emphasizes a step-by-step problem-solving approach to Visual Basic programming. Each How-To follows a consistent format that guides you through the issues and techniques involved in solving a specific problem. Each section contains the steps to solve a problem, as well as a discussion of how and why the solution works. In most cases, you can simply copy the provided code or objects into your application and be up and running immediately. All the code described in the book is available on the accompanying CD-ROM.

The book's concepts and examples are useful to Visual Basic programmers of all skill levels. Each How-To is graded by complexity level, with information on additional uses and enhancements to fit your needs exactly. Additionally, each chapter contains an introduction that summarizes each How-To and covers the chapter's techniques and topics so that you can zero in on just the solution you need without having to go through hundreds of pages to find it.

What You Need to Use This Book

You need Visual Basic 6, Professional or Enterprise Edition. This book was written using Visual Basic 6 Enterprise Edition, but most sections will work with the Professional Edition. Many of the sections will also work with Visual Basic 5, but specific references to menu selections and windows may have changed between versions. You may have to improvise the How-To's to make the samples work with Visual Basic 5.

Most chapters avoid using controls or tools not included with Visual Basic 6, Professional or Enterprise Edition. However, much of Visual Basic's strength is its extensibility using third-party tools and controls. You are encouraged to explore third-party offerings; they can often cut significant time from the development cycle.

CHAPTER 1

ACCESSING A DATABASE WITH BOUND CONTROLS

1

ACCESSING A DATABASE WITH BOUND CONTROLS

How do I...

1.1   Browse a recordset using bound controls?

1.2   Validate data entered into bound controls?

1.3   Allow users to undo changes they've made in bound controls?

1.4   Add and delete records using bound controls?

1.5   Create and use bound lists?

1.6   Display many detail records for a single master record?

1.7   Change data in data-bound grid cells from code?

1.8   Gracefully handle database errors?

The Microsoft Jet database engine, supplied with Visual Basic, gives you the ability to access many types of databases—Microsoft Access databases; other PC-based databases such as dBASE, FoxPro, Paradox, and Btrieve; and any relational database that supports the open database connectivity (ODBC) standard. Visual Basic provides two basic techniques for working with the Jet database engine: the data control and the data access objects (DAO). The data control requires less code, but data access objects are much more flexible. This chapter shows you how to use the data control to perform common database operations. Chapter 2, "Accessing a Database with Data Access Objects," describes the use of data access objects.

VISUAL BASIC TERMINOLOGY PRIMER

If you're new to database programming, many Visual Basic terms might be new to you. Visual Basic works with all databases through a *recordset* consisting of all the records in a table or all the records satisfying a particular Structured Query Language (SQL) SELECT statement. A SELECT statement asks the database to retrieve specified database fields from one or more database tables in which record fields meet certain criteria. SQL itself is discussed in Chapter 3, "Creating Queries with SQL."

The programmer's interaction with the user is through *visual controls* placed on the form for data entry, command buttons, menus, labels, list boxes, and so on. The most common controls are *text boxes* for entering data, *command buttons* for getting the program to do useful work, *menus*, and *labels* to describe the other controls. *List boxes* and *combo boxes* allow the program to provide the user with multiple selections for text entry.

Most visual controls, including text, list, and combo boxes, can be *bound* to a data source for automatic display of data or have a special *data-bound* version. *Binding* is the process of connecting the data in a visual control to a field in a recordset. The most common binding method is the *data control*. The data control has a visual interface to support data movement through the records and a recordset object to manage the interface to the database engine. The data control *component* also supports several *methods* and *properties* for programmatic or design-time control. A component is simply a "piece part" used to build a Visual Basic application. A method is equivalent to a function call to the component to get the component to do useful work. A property is a data element of the component that helps control its behavior. For example, the data control has a DatabaseName property to tell it where the database can be found and a Move method to move the visual control around on the form. In addition, the data control *exposes* all the methods and properties of its contained recordset object.

All examples in this chapter use existing Microsoft Access database files delivered with Visual Basic (later chapters demonstrate how to create a database with Visual Basic). The techniques, however, apply to all the databases that Visual Basic can access through the Jet engine. In addition, the Enterprise Edition *remote data control* uses very similar techniques for direct use with ODBC databases. The remote data control bypasses the Jet engine and usually delivers faster performance than access through the Jet engine.

1.1 Browse a Recordset Using Bound Controls

One of the most fundamental operations in database work is the user's ability to browse through records in an existing database and modify data. In this How-To, you'll use the data control, bind its fields to some text boxes, and write one line of executable code to browse a database.

1.2 Validate Data Entered into Bound Controls

People make data entry errors, and an industrial-strength application anticipates and traps those errors before the data entry errors corrupt the integrity of the database. This How-To shows how to trap and respond to entry errors when you're using the data control and bound visual controls.

1.3 Allow People to Undo Changes They've Made in Bound Controls

Sometimes people catch their own mistakes. In this How-To, you'll learn how to enable them to undo those mistakes when the application uses the data control.

1.4 Add and Delete Records Using Bound Controls

A database is fairly useless without some means of adding and deleting records. In this How-To, you'll see how to add and delete records with bound controls.

1.5 Create and Use Bound Lists

One way to reduce data entry errors—and make people's lives a bit easier—is to provide people with lists from which they can choose appropriate values for database fields. Visual Basic 6 provides the DBCombo and DBList controls that make this easy to do. In this How-To, you'll use the DBCombo control to display suggested field values.

1.6 Display Many Detail Records for a Single Master Record

Frequently, you need to work with related records at the same time in a master-detail relationship. You might want to show an invoice header and all its detail lines or show all the orders for a particular product. This How-To shows how the DBGrid control can place multiple detail records on a form for each master record.

1.7 **Change Data in Data-Bound Grid Cells from Code**

The master-detail grid looks great, but some applications require the capability to expand and edit grid data from the main form. This How-To walks through a form that edits `DBGrid` data from the form's code.

1.8 **Gracefully Handle Database Errors**

Whenever you're working with disk files, unanticipated errors can occur. Your Visual Basic database program should handle errors gracefully. This How-To shows how.

FINDING THE SAMPLES

All the How-To's in this book are on the accompanying CD-ROM. After you install the source code, you will find a directory for each chapter; and within each chapter directory there is a directory for each How-To. The steps of each How-To start with an opportunity to preview the completed How-To from your installation directory. If you decide to work through a How-To in its entirety, we assume that you are working in a separate work area on your computer.

COMPLEXITY
BEGINNING

1.1 How do I...
Browse a recordset using bound controls?

Problem

I need to see the records in a database, but I don't want to write a lot of code. How can I do this with Visual Basic?

Technique

The Visual Basic data control object, in conjunction with data-bound controls, allows you to browse records in a supported database without writing a single line of code.

To use the data control, place it on your form and set two properties: `DatabaseName`, which specifies the database to which it will be linked, and `RecordSource`, which designates the source of data within the database. Add a text box to your form for every database field you want to access from the `RecordSource`, and bind each text box to the data control object and `RecordSource` field.

COMPATIBLE DATABASES

Databases that are compliant with the Visual Basic data control—and with Visual Basic data access objects, discussed in Chapter 2—include Microsoft Access, dBASE, FoxPro, Paradox, Btrieve, and any other database products that support the ODBC standard. Most relational database products for desktop systems and multi-user systems support ODBC. The examples throughout this book use Microsoft Access databases, except for those in Chapters 6, "Connecting to an ODBC Server," and 7, "SQL Server Databases and Remote Data Objects," which relate specifically to other database products. Virtually all the examples in the book (except for those in Chapters 6 and 7) can be applied to any of the database products.

When you work with Microsoft Access databases, `DatabaseName` is the name of a Microsoft Access database file. When you work with other database products, what constitutes "the database" depends on the type of database—for dBASE, Paradox, and FoxPro databases, for example, `DatabaseName` is the name of the directory in which data files are stored. `RecordSource` can also be a table or a SQL `SELECT` statement. Microsoft Access also allows you to specify the name of a query stored within the database as the `RecordSource`.

The data control not only provides the link between your form and the database, but it also provides tools for navigating through the database. Figure 1.1 shows a data control. The Next Record and Previous Record buttons move you through the database one record at a time. The First Record and Last Record buttons move you quickly to the beginning or end of the database.

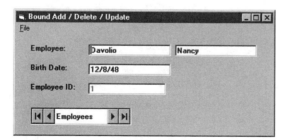

Figure 1.1 The data control.

Steps

To preview this How-To, open the project BrowseBound.VBP in the `Chapter01\HowTo01` directory. Change the `DatabaseName` property of the data control `datEmployees` to point to the copy of NWind.MDB installed on your system (probably in the directory where VB6.EXE is installed). Then run the project. The form shown in Figure 1.2 appears. Use the buttons on the data control to view records in the Titles table of NWind.MDB.

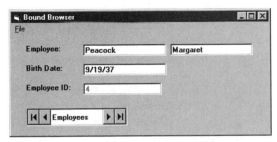

Figure 1.2 The Bound Browser form.

1. Create a new project in your work area called BrowseBound.VBP. Use Form1 to create the objects and properties listed in Table 1.1, and save the form as BrowseBound.FRM. Substitute the path to your copy of NWIND.MDB for the DatabaseName property of datEmployees.

Table 1.1 Objects and properties for the Bound Browser form.

OBJECT	PROPERTY	SETTING
Form	Name	Form1
	Caption	"Bound Browser"
Data	Name	datEmployees
	Caption	"Employees"
	DatabaseName	"D:\Program Files\Microsoft Visual Studio\VB6\NWIND.MDB"
	RecordSource	"Employees"
TextBox	Name	txtEmpLastName
	DataField	"LastName"
	DataSource	"datEmployees"
TextBox	Name	txtEmpFirstName
	DataField	"FirstName"
	DataSource	"datEmployees"
TextBox	Name	txtBirthDate
	DataField	"BirthDate"
	DataSource	"datEmployees"
TextBox	Name	txtEmployeeId
	DataField	"EmployeeID"
	DataSource	"datEmployees"
	Enabled	False

OBJECT	PROPERTY	SETTING
Label	Name	Label1
	Caption	"Employee:"
Label	Name	Label2
	Caption	"Birth Date:"
Label	Name	Label3
	Caption	"Employee ID:"

2. Use the Visual Basic Menu Editor to create the menu shown in Table 1.2.

Table 1.2 Menu specifications for the Bound Browser.

CAPTION	NAME	SHORTCUT KEY
&File	mnuFile	
----E&xit	mnuFileExit	

3. Enter the following code as the **Click** event for **mnuExit**:

```
Private Sub mnuFileExit_Click()
    Unload Me
End Sub
```

How It Works

When the application starts, the data control opens the NWind.MDB database, creates a recordset from the Titles table, and displays values from the first record of the recordset in the form's bound controls. A *recordset* is a Visual Basic object used to manipulate the contents of a database. *Bound controls* are visual interface controls such as text boxes that people can see on the screen but that are also linked, or bound, to fields managed by a data control's recordset. Recordsets provide methods for moving between records, as well as for adding, updating, and deleting records. When users click on one of the data control's record navigation buttons, the data control positions the record pointer to the selected record and updates the bound controls with the values from the new record.

Under the covers, the data control is working hard. You see a screen form with text boxes. Figure 1.3 shows the main interactions between bound text boxes, the data control, and the data control's recordset. Every time the data control moves to a different record, it checks for changed data between the bound controls and the recordset fields. If changes are found, the data control moves the data to the fields and performs an automatic update to the recordset and the underlying database. Finally, the data control retrieves the desired record from the database and copies the field data to text controls for display. In the remainder of this chapter, you'll explore the data control's events and methods to build solid applications with very little work.

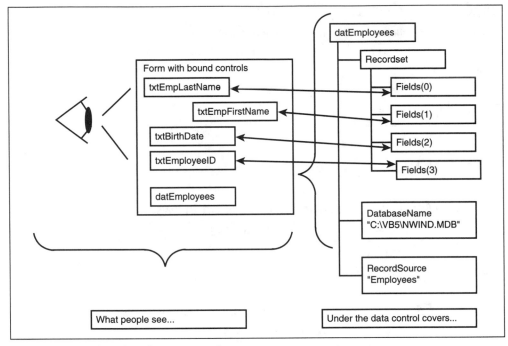

Figure 1.3 Under the data control's covers.

Comments

This is truly code-free development. The only executable line of code closes the application. However, this is a very limited application; there's no way to validate entries, add records, or delete records. To perform these operations, some code is necessary—not a lot of code, but some code nonetheless. The following How-To's show how to add these functions to this simple beginning.

COMPLEXITY
BEGINNING

1.2 How do I...
Validate data entered into bound controls?

Problem

The data control and bound controls provide low-code database access. But I need to verify that entered form data is valid before I update the database. How can I check entered data when I'm using bound controls?

Technique

Each time you change the current record in a recordset attached to a data control—by moving to a different record, deleting the current record, or closing the recordset—Visual Basic triggers the data control's **Validate** event. You can write an event subroutine to check any changes made to data in bound controls.

The **Validate** event subroutine receives two arguments:

✔ **Action**, an integer which describes the event that caused the **Validate** event.

✔ **Save**, a Boolean value that is **True** if data in any bound control has changed and **False** if the data hasn't changed.

In your event subroutine, you can check the value of **Save**. If it is **True**, you can then check each entry to verify that it falls within the bounds of what is legal in your application. If any entry is not legal, you can set the **Action** argument to the built-in constant **dbDataActionCancel**, which cancels the event that caused the **Validate** event. For example, if the **Validate** event was triggered by clicking on the data control to move to a different record, setting **Action** to **dbDataActionCancel** cancels the **Move** event and leaves the data control positioned on the original record. Your **Validate** event subroutine should also display a problem message so that the entry can be corrected.

Steps

Open the project ValidateBound.VBP in the **Chapter01\HowTo02** directory to preview the results of this How-To. Change the **DatabaseName** property of the data control **datEmployees** to point to the copy of NWind.MDB installed on your system (probably in the directory where VB6.EXE is installed). Then run the project. A form similar to that shown previously in Figure 1.2 appears. Use the buttons on the data control to view records in the Employees table of NWind.MDB. Select all the text in the Employee and Birth Date boxes and delete it; then try to move to another record. You'll see an error message like the one shown in Figure 1.4, informing you that you must enter a last name, first name, and birth date. Choose the File | Exit menu option to close the project.

1. Create a new project called ValidateBound.VBP in your work area. Use **Form1** to create the objects and properties listed earlier in Table 1.1, and save the form as ValidateBound.FRM. (Note that this is the same form used for How-To 1.1.) Substitute the path to your copy of NWind.MDB for the **DatabaseName** property of **datEmployees**. Use the Visual Basic Menu Editor to create the menu shown earlier in Table 1.2.

2. Add the file clsUtility.cls to your project from the **Chapter01\HowTo02** directory by selecting Project | Add File from the main menu or by pressing Ctrl+D on the keyboard. Use the File common dialog to select the file.

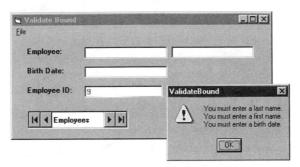

Figure 1.4 The Validate Bound form.

3. Add the following code to the declarations section of **Form1**. The Utility class is used to tie **MsgBox** strings together in a common place.

```
Private Utility As New clsUtility
Private mblnValidationFailed As Boolean
```

4. Enter the following code into **Form1** as the **Validate** event for the **datEmployees** data control. This code checks to make sure that valid data have been entered into all controls. If there are any invalid data, the subroutine displays an error message, cancels the **Validate** event, and sets the form-level variable **mblnValidationFailed** to **True**.

```
Private Sub datEmployees_Validate(Action As Integer, Save As
Integer)
    Dim strMsg As String
    Dim enumMsgResult As VbMsgBoxResult

    If Save = True Or Action = vbDataActionUpdate _
            Or Action = vbDataActionUnload Then
        ' One or more bound controls has changed or the form
        ' is being unloaded, so verify that all fields have
        ' legal entries. If a field has an incorrect value,
        ' append a string explaining the error to strMsg and
        ' set the focus to that field to facilitate correcting
        ' the error. We explain all errors encountered in a
        ' single message box.
        strMsg = ""
        If txtEmpLastName.Text = "" Then
            Utility.AddToMsg strMsg, _
                "You must enter a last name."
            txtEmpLastName.SetFocus
        End If
        If txtEmpFirstName.Text = "" Then
            Utility.AddToMsg strMsg, _
                "You must enter a first name."
            txtEmpFirstName.SetFocus
        End If
        If Not IsDate(txtBirthDate.Text) Then
            Utility.AddToMsg strMsg, _
                "You must enter a birth date."
```

```
            txtBirthDate.SetFocus
        Else
            If CDate(txtBirthDate.Text) >= Date Then
                Utility.AddToMsg strMsg, _
                    "Birth date must be in the past."
                txtBirthDate.SetFocus
            End If
        End If

        If strMsg <> "" Then
            ' We have something in the variable strMsg, which
            ' means that an error has occurred. Display the
            ' message. The focus is in the last text box where
            ' an error was found.
            MsgBox strMsg, vbExclamation
            ' Cancel the Validate event
            Action = vbDataActionCancel
            ' Deny form Unload until fields are corrected
            mblnValidationFailed = True
        Else
            mblnValidationFailed = False
        End If
    End If
End Sub
```

5. Enter the following code into **Form1** as the **Unload** event. If the **Validate** event has set the **UpdateCancelled** flag, this procedure cancels the **Unload** event.

```
Private Sub Form_Unload(Cancel As Integer)
    ' Don't allow the unload until the data is validated.
    If mblnValidationFailed Then Cancel = True
End Sub
```

6. Enter the following code as the **Click** event for **mnuExit**:

```
Private Sub mnuExit_Click()
    Unload Me
End Sub
```

How It Works

Each time the **Validate** event is called, the contents of the controls are checked to make sure that they contain valid data. If they do not, the **Validate** event is cancelled. This prevents the record from being saved with invalid data. The validation event procedure makes use of a "helper" utility class to append multiple messages from each error check to the displayed results. Displaying all validation errors at once is a good design technique because it reduces frustration for the user.

When the form is unloaded, the contents of bound controls are automatically saved through the data control. And that means that the **Validate** event gets called. If a control has invalid data, the **Validate** event is cancelled, but that does not in itself cancel the `Form Unload` event. Therefore, the `Validate` event sets a form-level flag variable, `mblnValidationFailed`, which the `Form Unload` procedure checks. If `mblnValidationFailed` is true, the `Form Unload` event is cancelled and the application does not terminate.

Comments

The validating browse form helps control data entry errors, but it is unforgiving without a cancellation option to undo form changes. After a field has been changed on this form, valid data must be entered before the user can change records or exit the application. Clearly, there should be a better way—and there is.

COMPLEXITY
BEGINNING

1.3 How do I...
Allow users to undo changes they've made in bound controls?

Problem

I want my form to have the capability to undo changes made to a record before the record is saved. How can I accomplish this when I'm using bound controls?

Technique

Your form gains the capability to undo changes to the current record by using the `UpdateControls` method of the data control. This method causes Visual Basic to reread the current record from the database file and refresh the value of each bound control with the respective field value from the database. Simply execute this method and any bound control changes are overwritten with the original data from the database.

Steps

Open the project UndoBound.VBP to preview this How-To. Change the `DatabaseName` property of the data control `datEmployees` to point to the copy of NWind.MDB installed on your system (probably in the directory where VB6.EXE is installed). Then run the project. The form shown in Figure 1.5 appears. Use the buttons on the data control to view records in the Employees table of NWind.MDB. Make a change in a record. Before you move to another record, select Edit | Undo. You'll see your changes "backed out" of the form.

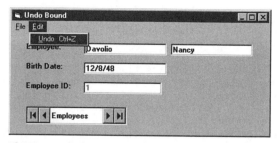

Figure 1.5 The Undo Bound form.

1. Create a new project called UndoBound.VBP. Use **Form1** to create the objects and properties listed earlier in Table 1.1, and save the form as UndoBound.FRM. (Note that this is the same form used for How-To's 1.1 and 1.2.) Substitute the path to your copy of NWind.MDB for the **DatabaseName** property of **datEmployees**. Use the Visual Basic menu editor to create the menu shown in Table 1.3.

Table 1.3 Menu specifications for UndoBound.FRM.

CAPTION	NAME	SHORTCUT KEY
&File	mnuFile	
----E&xit	mnuFileExit	
&Edit	mnuEdit	
----&Undo	mnuEditUndo	Ctrl+Z

2. Add the file clsUtility.cls to your project from the **Chapter01\HowTo03** directory by selecting Project | Add File from the main menu or by pressing Ctrl+D on the keyboard. Use the File common dialog to select the file.

3. Add the following code to the declarations section of **Form1**:

```
Private Utility As New clsUtility
Private mblnValidationFailed As Boolean
```

4. Enter the following code into **Form1** as the **Validate** event for the **datEmployees** data control. (Note the changes from How-To 1.2 highlighted in bold.) This code checks to make sure that valid data have been entered into all controls. If there are any invalid data, the subroutine displays an error message and asks for an OK or a Cancel response. An OK response cancels the **Validate** event and sets the form-level variable **mblnValidationFailed** to **True**. A Cancel response retrieves the database values to the bound form controls and backs out the changes.

```
Private Sub datEmployees_Validate(Action As Integer, Save As
Integer)
    Dim strMsg As String
```

continued on next page

continued from previous page

```
Dim enumMsgResult As VbMsgBoxResult

If Save = True Or Action = vbDataActionUpdate _
        Or Action = vbDataActionUnload Then
    ' One or more bound controls has changed or the form
    ' is being unloaded, so verify that all fields have
    ' legal entries. If a field has an incorrect value,
    ' append a string explaining the error to strMsg and
    ' set the focus to that field to facilitate correcting
    ' the error. We explain all errors encountered in a
    ' single message box.
    strMsg = ""
    If txtEmpLastName.Text = "" Then
        Utility.AddToMsg strMsg, _
            "You must enter a last name."
        txtEmpLastName.SetFocus
    End If
    If txtEmpFirstName.Text = "" Then
        Utility.AddToMsg strMsg, _
            "You must enter a first name."
        txtEmpFirstName.SetFocus
    End If
    If Not IsDate(txtBirthDate.Text) Then
        Utility.AddToMsg strMsg, _
            "You must enter a birth date."
        txtBirthDate.SetFocus
    Else
        If CDate(txtBirthDate.Text) >= Date Then
            Utility.AddToMsg strMsg, _
                "Birth date must be in the past."
            txtBirthDate.SetFocus
        End If
    End If

    If strMsg <> "" Then
        ' We have something in the variable strMsg, which
        ' means that an error has occurred. Display the
        ' message. The focus is in the last text box where
        ' an error was found
        enumMsgResult = MsgBox(strMsg, _
                        vbExclamation + vbOKCancel +
                        vbDefaultButton1)

        If enumMsgResult = vbCancel Then
            ' Restore the data to previous values using the
            ' data control
            datEmployees.UpdateControls
            ' Allow form unload.
            mblnValidationFailed = False
        Else
            ' Cancel the Validate event
            Action = vbDataActionCancel
            ' Deny form unload until fields are corrected
            mblnValidationFailed = True
        End If
    Else
```

```
            mblnValidationFailed = False
        End If
    End If
End Sub
```

5. Enter the following code into **Form1** as the **Unload** event. (This code is the same as that for the identically named procedure in How-To 1.2.) If the **Validate** event has set the **UpdateCancelled** flag, this procedure cancels the **Unload** event.

```
Private Sub Form_Unload(Cancel As Integer)
    ' Don't allow the unload until the data is validated or the
    ' update is cancelled
    If mblnValidationFailed Then Cancel = True
End Sub
```

6. Enter the following code as the **Click** event for **mnuEditUndo**:

```
Private Sub mnuEditUndo_Click()
    ' Undo all pending changes from form by copying recordset
    ' values to form controls
    datEmployees.UpdateControls
End Sub
```

7. Enter the following code as the **Click** event for **mnuExit**. (This code is the same as that for the identically named procedure in How-To 1.2.)

```
Private Sub mnuExit_Click()
    Unload Me
End Sub
```

How It Works

The **mnuEditUndo_Click** procedure allows for removing any pending changes from the database by using the data control's **UpdateControls** method. This method takes the copy of the field data from the data control's recordset and "updates" the displayed bound controls. Remember from Figure 1.3 that there are constantly two copies of all data in a data control application—the copy on the screen fields (in the bound controls) and the copy in the data control's recordset fields. Data is moved from the bound controls to the recordset fields during an update but only after validation is successful. So no matter how much the data on the screen has changed, nothing happens until the recordset gets updated. (In this application so far, a recordset is updated only when the data control is moved from one record to another.)

Another useful enhancement in this version of the program is the use of a Cancel response from the validation error message box to refresh the screen display automatically without making the user make a menu selection. Figure 1.6 shows the modified error message box. If the response indicates a cancellation, the validation is cancelled and the data values are restored from the database to the bound controls.

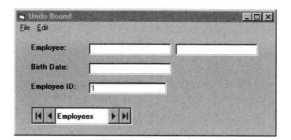

Figure 1.6 The Cancel button added to an error message box.

The validation event procedure (in step 4) makes extensive use of Visual Basic constants such as `vbDataActionCancel` and `vbCancel` rather than numeric constants to improve the ability of programmers to understand the code. Values for constants can easily be found by pressing the F2 key from within Visual Basic to bring up the Object Browser window from which constants can be copied and pasted into your code. Declaring `enumMsgResult` as a `VbMsgBoxResult` type shows the use of strong typing to help make the program's meaning clearer to subsequent programmers.

Comments

Even though you can update, validate, and undo changes to your employee records, you still can't hire or fire anyone with the information you have so far. Let's complete the core application by adding the add and delete functions.

COMPLEXITY
BEGINNING

1.4 How do I...
Add and delete records using bound controls?

Problem

How do I add and delete records when I'm using bound controls?

Technique

To add a record to the recordset of a data control, use the **AddNew** method of the recordset established by the data control. Visual Basic sets all bound controls to their default values (as determined by the table definition in the database you're accessing) and makes the new record the current record. After all data has been entered into the bound controls, Visual Basic creates a new record in the table and fills it with the values from the controls. Visual Basic knows that data entry is complete when you move to a different record, you add another new record, or your code executes the recordset's **Update** method. All records get added to the end of the data control's recordset.

If you make changes to an existing record and then unload the form, Visual Basic automatically updates the recordset with your changes. When you add a record, enter data into the record, and then either add another record or move to an existing record, Visual Basic automatically saves the new record. However, if you add a record, enter data into the new record, and then unload the form—before you move to another record—Visual Basic does not automatically save the new record. If you want to save the new record, you can invoke the **Recordset** object's **Update** method from the form's **Unload** event. The **Update** method saves the data in the form's bound controls to the corresponding fields in the recordset.

To delete the currently displayed record from the database, use the data control recordset's **Delete** method. Visual Basic deletes the current record from the database. It does not, however, move to a new record or update the controls. You must do this through your code by using one of the four **Move** methods: **MoveFirst**, **MoveLast**, **MovePrevious**, or **MoveNext**. If you do not move to a new record after executing the **Delete** method, there will be no current record. Visual Basic will, therefore, generate an error when you try to perform any operation on the current record.

Steps

Preview the project AddDeleteBound.VBP. Change the **DatabaseName** property of the data control **datEmployees** to point to the copy of NWind.MDB installed on your system (probably in the directory where VB6.EXE is installed). Then run the project. The form shown in Figure 1.7 appears. Select Data | Add Record. Enter some representative values into the fields. Move to another record or select Data | Save Record from the main menu. Move to the last record in the recordset by clicking the >| button on the data control. You should see the record you just added. Select Data | Delete Record. Move to the last record in the recordset again. The record you added should be gone.

1. Create a new project called AddDeleteBound.VBP. Use **Form1** to create the objects and properties listed earlier in Table 1.1, and save the form as AddDeleteBound.FRM. Substitute the path to your copy of NWind.MDB for the **DatabaseName** property of **datEmployees**. You might find it easier to start from the UndoBound.VBP form from How-To 1.3. Use the Visual Basic menu editor to create the menu shown in Table 1.4.

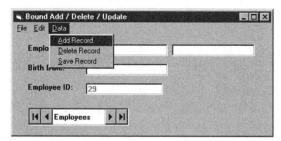

Figure 1.7 The Bound Add/Delete/Update form.

Table 1.4 Menu specifications for the Bound Add/Delete form.

CAPTION	NAME	SHORTCUT KEY
&File	mnuFile	
----E&xit	mnuFileExit	
&Edit	mnuEdit	
----&Undo	mnuEditUndo	Ctrl+Z
&Data	mnuData	
----&Add Record	mnuDataAdd	
----&Delete Record	mnuDataDelete	
----&Save Record	mnuDataSave	

2. Add the file clsUtility.cls to your project from the **Chapter01\HowTo03** directory by selecting Project | Add File from the main menu or by pressing Ctrl+D on the keyboard. Use the File common dialog to select the file.

3. Add the following code to the declarations section of **Form1**:

```
Private Utility As New clsUtility
Private mblnValidationFailed As Boolean
```

4. Add the following code as the **Validate** event of the data control **datEmployees**. (This code is the same as that for the identically named procedure in How-To 1.3, except for the code in bold.) The **Validate** event is called every time the current record changes, when the form is unloaded, and when the **Update** method is invoked. This procedure verifies that all entries meet the requirements of the application when data in bound controls have been changed. If an entry is incorrect, the routine cancels the **Validate** event and sets the form-level flag variable **mblnValidationFailed**.

```
Private Sub datEmployees_Validate(Action As Integer, _
        Save As Integer)
    Dim strMsg As String
    Dim enumMsgResult As VbMsgBoxResult

    If Save = True Or Action = vbDataActionUpdate _
    Or Action = vbDataActionUnload _
    Or Action = vbDataActionAddNew Then
        ' One or more bound controls has changed or the form
        ' is being unloaded, so verify that all fields have
        ' legal entries. If a field has an incorrect value,
        ' append a string explaining the error to strMsg and
        ' set the focus to that field to facilitate correcting
        ' the error. We explain all errors encountered in a
        ' single message box.
        strMsg = ""
        If txtEmpLastName.Text = "" Then
            Utility.AddToMsg strMsg, _
                "You must enter a last name."
            txtEmpLastName.SetFocus
        End If
        If txtEmpFirstName.Text = "" Then
            Utility.AddToMsg strMsg, _
                "You must enter a first name."
            txtEmpFirstName.SetFocus
        End If
        If Not IsDate(txtBirthDate.Text) Then
            Utility.AddToMsg strMsg, _
                "You must enter a birth date."
            txtBirthDate.SetFocus
        Else
            If CDate(txtBirthDate.Text) >= Date Then
                Utility.AddToMsg strMsg, _
                    "Birth date must be in the past."
                txtBirthDate.SetFocus
            End If
        End If

        If strMsg <> "" Then
            ' We have something in the variable strMsg, which
            ' means that an error has occurred. Display the
            ' message. The focus is in the last text box where an
            ' error was found
            enumMsgResult = MsgBox(strMsg, _
                    vbExclamation + vbOKCancel + vbDefaultButton1)

            If enumMsgResult = vbCancel Then
                ' Restore the data to previous values using
                ' the data control
                datEmployees.UpdateControls
                mblnValidationFailed = False
            Else
```

continued on next page

continued from previous page

```
                           ' Cancel the Validate event
                           Action = vbDataActionCancel
                           ' Deny form Unload until fields are corrected
                           mblnValidationFailed = True
                    End If
             Else
                    ' Allow form unload
                    mblnValidationFailed = False
                    ' Disable the Save menu
                    mnuDataSave.Enabled = False
             End If
      End If
End Sub
```

5. Enter the following code as the `Click` method of the Edit | Undo menu item. If the user chooses Undo while adding a new record, the subroutine uses the Recordset object's `CancelUpdate` method to cancel the pending `AddNew` operation. If the user clicks the menu item while editing an existing record, the procedure updates the form's controls by filling them with the current values from the recordset.

```
Private Sub mnuEditUndo_Click()
       ' Undo all pending changes from form by copying recordset
       ' values to form controls
       datEmployees.UpdateControls

       If datEmployees.Recordset.EditMode = dbEditAdd Then
              ' Disable the menu save and cancel the update
              datEmployees.Recordset.CancelUpdate
              mnuDataSave.Enabled = False
       End If
End Sub
```

6. Add the following code as the `Click` event of the Data menu's Add Record item. This subroutine uses the `Recordset` object's `AddNew` method to prepare the form and the recordset for the addition of a new record.

```
Private Sub mnuDataAdd_Click()
       ' Reset all controls to the default for a new record
       ' and make space for the record in the recordset copy
       ' buffer.
       datEmployees.Recordset.AddNew

       'Enable the Save menu choice
       mnuDataSave.Enabled = True

       ' Set the focus to the first control on the form
       txtEmpLastName.SetFocus
End Sub
```

7. Add the following code as the **Click** event of the Data menu's Delete Record item. The procedure confirms that the user wants to delete the record and then deletes it. It then ensures that the record pointer is pointing at a valid record.

```
Private Sub mnuDataDelete_Click()
    Dim strMsg As String

    'Verify the deletion.
    strMsg = "Are you sure you want to delete " _
            & IIf(txtEmpLastName.Text <> "", _
                txtEmpLastName.Text, _
                "this record") & "?"
    If MsgBox(strMsg, vbQuestion + vbYesNo + vbDefaultButton2) = _
        vbYes Then

        ' We really want to delete
        datEmployees.Recordset.Delete

        ' Make a valid record the current record and
        ' update the display.
        datEmployees.Recordset.MoveNext

        ' If we deleted the last record, move to the new last
        ' record because the current record pointer is not defined
        ' afterdeleting the last record, even though EOF is
        ' defined.
        If datEmployees.Recordset.EOF Then
        datEmployees.Recordset.MoveLast
    End If
End Sub
```

8. Add the following code as the **Click** event of the Data menu's Save Record item. The Save Record subroutine uses the **Update** method of the **Recordset** object to write the values in the form's bound controls to their respective fields in the recordset. The **If** statement prevents a recordset **Update** without a preceding **AddNew** or **Edit**.

```
Private Sub mnuDataSave_Click()
    ' Invoke the update method to copy control contents to
    ' recordset fields and update the underlying table
    datEmployees.Recordset.Update
    If datEmployees.Recordset.EditMode <> dbEditAdd Then
        ' If we added move to the new record
        datEmployees.Recordset.MoveLast
    End If
End Sub
```

9. Add the following code as the **Click** event of the File menu's Exit item. (This code is the same as that for the identically named procedure in How-To 1.2.)

```
Private Sub mnuFileExit_Click()
    Unload Me
End Sub
```

10. Add the following code as the form's **Unload** event. If the data currently in the bound controls is invalid, the procedure cancels the **Unload** event. If the data is valid and an add-record operation is in progress, the code invokes the **Update** event to save the data.

```
Private Sub Form_Unload(Cancel As Integer)
    ' Don't allow the unload until the data is valid or the
    ' update is cancelled
    If mblnValidationFailed Then Cancel = True
End SubEnd Sub
```

How It Works

Including record addition and deletion has made the data control program more complex, but it now looks like a real database application. A Data menu allows the user to explicitly control the data control's recordset activities through the appropriate click procedures. The **Data Add Record** procedure (step 6) adds a new, blank record to the data control's recordset. The data control is automatically positioned on the new record. The **Data Save** procedure (step 8) updates the recordset and moves to the last record (the new record) if the current action is a record addition. The Data Save Record menu choice is also managed explicitly by the program during record additions to provide clear feedback from the programmer about what is happening within the program.

Notice in the record deletion processing (step 7) that you have to manage the deletion of the last record carefully because the recordset object does not handle all changes without an error. In particular, deleting the last record can leave the recordset with "No current record." In this state, any update actions (potentially caused by a record movement) can cause an error in your application.

RUNTIME ERRORS

You should also note that you will receive a runtime error if you attempt to delete certain default records contained in the Employees database. The Employees table has a relationship with the Orders table within the same database, and the employee records you cannot delete have at least one entry in the Orders table. A runtime error will occur if you delete an employee record that has other data in the database because you would have entries in the Orders table that do not have a corresponding Employees record—which would result in a loss of data integrity in the database. To properly delete these records, you must delete the corresponding data in any other tables in the database. Refer to How-To 4.4 for information on defining and using relations between tables.

Comments

A Visual Basic data control maintains a record pointer into its `RecordSource`. The record pointer keeps track of where you are within the `RecordSource`. It always points to the current record—except when you move past the end or the beginning of the `RecordSource`.

You can move past the end of the `RecordSource` by clicking the Next Record button when the record pointer is positioned on the last record; similarly, you can move past the beginning of the `RecordSource` by clicking the Previous Record button when you are on the first record. The record pointer then points at a special location, known as the end of file (EOF) or the beginning of file (BOF). When you are on EOF or BOF, there is no current record. If you try to delete or edit the record when you are on EOF or BOF, Visual Basic generates an error message. EOF and BOF are useful when you use data access objects for checking to see when you've reached the end or beginning of a `RecordSource`; but when you use the data control, you generally don't want to stay on EOF or BOF.

For this reason, Visual Basic gives you a choice of what to do when your data control reaches EOF or BOF. You execute this choice by setting the `BOFAction` and `EOFAction` properties. The possible settings for each property are shown in Table 1.5.

Table 1.5 The `EOFAction` and `BOFAction` properties of the data control.

PROPERTY	DESCRIPTION	RESULT
BOFAction	0 - MoveFirst (default)	Positions the record pointer on the first record.
	1 - BOF	Positions the record pointer on BOF.
EOFAction	0 - MoveLast (default)	Positions the record pointer on the last record.
	1 - EOF	Positions the record pointer on EOF.
	2 - AddNew	Adds a new record at the end of the
		RecordSource and positions the record pointer on it.

The Visual Basic data control does not handle empty recordsets well; trying to move to another record generates an error. The only thing you can do with a bound, empty recordset is to add a new record. When you open an empty recordset, its EOF property is initially set to `True`. If you have the data control's `EOFAction` property set to `AddNew`, when you open an empty recordset Visual Basic immediately adds a record. This is a low-cost, no-code way to prevent empty recordset errors when working with bound controls.

COMPLEXITY
INTERMEDIATE

1.5 How do I...
Create and use bound lists?

Problem

Many tables in my database have fields that are related to other tables. I need to restrict entry into these fields to values that exist in the related tables. At the same time, I'd like to make it easy to select valid entries for these fields. How do I accomplish this when I'm using bound controls?

Technique

Assume that you have a warehouse application. You have two tables: Products and Categories. The Products table defines available products:

```
ProductID
ProductName
SupplierID
CategoryID
QuantityPerUnit
UnitPrice
UnitsInStock
UnitsOnOrder
ReorderLevel
Discontinued
```

The Categories table defines product categories and is related to the Products table via the `CategoryID` field:

```
CategoryID
CategoryName
Description
Picture
```

You have a form that displays basic product information from the Products table and its related category. Because almost everybody has trouble remembering customer ID numbers, you want to provide the capability to designate the category by name. With a **DBCombo** or **DBList** control, people can choose a category name and have the control insert the category ID number corresponding to that category name into the Products table.

The **DBList** and **DBCombo** controls both display values in a list format. The **DBList** control creates a list box, with several lines always visible. The **DBCombo** control can create a drop-down list. They are both bound controls. Unlike with most bound controls, however, you bind them not to a single data control but to two data controls. The first data control maintains the recordset represented by the form as a whole—the data records you are browsing or editing. The second data control refers to the validation recordset, the recordset that is displayed in the list box or combo box. (You normally make the second data control—the data control that displays the values in the list—invisible, because people do not need to access it.)

In the example, one data control is linked to the Products table—the table into which category ID numbers are inserted. The other data control is linked to the Categories table—the source of the list. The table that is the source of the list must include both the information to be displayed (in this case, the information in the `CategoryName` field) and the value to be inserted into the other table (in this case, the `CategoryID`).

You link the `DBCombo` or `DBList` control to its recordsets by setting five properties. Two properties describe the recordset to be updated; they are shown in Table 1.6. The other three properties define the recordset that makes up the list; these appear in Table 1.7.

Table 1.6 DBList/DBCombo properties that describe the recordset to be updated.

PROPERTY	DESCRIPTION	
DataSource	Name of the data control with the recordset to be updated	Data1
DataField	Name of the field to be updated	[company]

Table 1.7 DBList/DBCombo properties that create the list.

PROPERTY	DESCRIPTION	
RowSource	Name of the data control that provides the values to display in the list	Data2
ListField	Name of the field with the values to display in the list	[company]
BoundColumn	Name of the field with the value to be inserted in the table being updated	[company]

↳ Data1

DBCOMBO STYLE

If you set the `Style` property of the `DBCombo` control to 2 (Dropdown List), the control acts exactly like a `DBList` control—except, of course, that it displays only a single item until you drop it down. You can't add new items to the list through the control.

If you want to give the user the opportunity to add new items, set `Style` to 0 (Dropdown Combo) or 1 (Simple Combo). Your code must handle the addition of the user's entry to the underlying row source; the control does not do this automatically for you.

Steps

Open the project ListBound.VBP to preview this How-To. Change the **DatabaseName** property of the data control **datEmployees** to point to the copy of NWind.MDB installed on your system (probably in the directory where VB6.EXE is installed). Then run the project. The form shown in Figure 1.8 appears. Select Data | Add Record, and enter some representative values into the fields. Use the drop-down list to enter the publisher. When you move to another record, your new record is automatically saved.

1. Create a new project called ListBound.VBP. Use **Form1** to create the objects and properties listed in Table 1.8, and save the form as LISTBND.FRM. Substitute the path to your copy of NWind.MDB for the **DatabaseName** property of **datEmployees** and **datPublishers**.

Table 1.8 Objects and properties for the Bound Lister form.

OBJECT	PROPERTY	SETTING
Form	Name	Form1
	Caption	" Bound Lister "
Data	Name	datProducts
	Caption	"Products"
	DatabaseName	"D:\Program Files\Microsoft Visual Studio\VB6\Nwind.mdb"
	RecordSource	"Products"
Data	Name	datCategories
	Caption	"Categories"
	DatabaseName	"D:\Program Files\Microsoft Visual Studio\VB6\Nwind.mdb"
	RecordSource	"Categories"

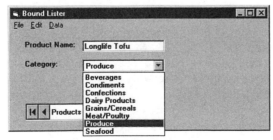

Figure 1.8 The Bound Lister form.

OBJECT	PROPERTY	SETTING
TextBox	Name	txtProductName
	DataField	"ProductName"
	DataSource	"datProducts"
DBCombo	Name	dbcCategory
	BoundColumn	"CategoryID"
	DataField	"CategoryID"
	DataSource	"datProducts"
	ListField	"CategoryName"
	RowSource	"datCategories"
Label	Name	Label2
	Caption	"Category:"
Label	Name	Label1
	Caption	"Product Name:"

2. Use the Visual Basic menu editor to create the menu shown in Table 1.9.

Table 1.9 Menu specifications for the Bound Lister.

CAPTION	NAME	SHORTCUT KEY
&File	mnuFile	
----E&xit	mnuFileExit	
&Edit	mnuEdit	
----&Undo	mnuEditUndo	Alt+Backspace
&Data	mnuData	
----&Add Record	mnuDataAdd	
----&Delete Record	mnuDataDelete	
----&Save Record	mnuDataSave	

3. Add the following code to the declarations section of **Form1**:

```
Private Utility As New clsUtility
Private mblnValidationFailed As Boolean
```

4. Add the following code as the **Validate** event of the data control **datProducts**. (This code is very similar to the **Validate Event** code for How-To 1.4 with the exceptions of data control name and actual field-checking logic.) The **Validate** event is called every time the current record changes, when the form is unloaded, and when the **Update** method is invoked. This procedure verifies that when data in bound controls have been changed, all entries meet the requirements of the application. If an entry is incorrect, the routine cancels the **Validate** event and sets the form-level flag variable **mblnValidationFailed**.

```
Private Sub datProducts_Validate(Action As Integer, Save As
Integer)
    Dim strMsg As String
    Dim enumMsgResult As VbMsgBoxResult

    If Save = True Or Action = vbDataActionUpdate _
    Or mblnValidationFailed Or Action = vbDataActionAddNew Then
        ' One or more bound controls has changed or a previous
        ' validation failed, so verify that all fields have legal
        ' entries. If a field has an incorrect value, append a
        ' string explaining the error to strMsg and set the focus
        ' to that field to facilitate correcting the error. We
        ' explain all errors encountered in a single message box.
        strMsg = ""
        If txtProductName.Text = "" Then
            Utility.AddToMsg strMsg, _
                "You must enter a Product name."
            txtProductName.SetFocus
        End If

        If strMsg <> "" Then
            ' We have something in the variable strMsg, which
            ' means that an error has occurred. Display the
            ' message. The focus is in the last text box where an
            ' error was found
            enumMsgResult = MsgBox(strMsg, vbExclamation + _
                vbOKCancel + vbDefaultButton1)

            If enumMsgResult = vbCancel Then
                ' Restore the data to previous values using the
                ' data control
                datProducts.UpdateControls
                mblnValidationFailed = False
            Else
                ' Cancel the Validate event
                Action = vbDataActionCancel
                ' Deny form Unload until fields are corrected
                mblnValidationFailed = True
            End If
        Else
            mblnValidationFailed = False
        End If
    End If
End Sub
```

5. Enter the following code as the `Click` method of the Edit | Undo menu item. (This code is very similar to that for the identically named procedure in How-To 1.4, except for the reference to a different data control.) The procedure updates the form's controls by filling them with the current values from the recordset. If the user chooses Undo while adding a new record, the subroutine uses the `Recordset` object's `CancelUpdate` method to cancel the pending `AddNew` operation and turns off the data save menu item.

```
Private Sub mnuEditUndo_Click()

    ' Undo all pending changes from form by copying recordset
    ' values to form controls
    datProducts.UpdateControls

    If datProducts.Recordset.EditMode = dbEditAdd Then
        ' Disable the menu save and cancel the update
        datProducts.Recordset.CancelUpdate
        mnuDataSave.Enabled = False
    End If

End Sub
```

6. Add the following code as the `Click` event of the Data menu's Add Record item. (This code is very similar to that for the identically named procedure in How-To 1.4.) This subroutine uses the Recordset object's `AddNew` method to prepare the form and the recordset for the addition of a new record. It also enables the Data | Save menu.

```
Private Sub mnuDataAdd_Click()

    ' Reset all controls to the default for a new record
    ' and make space for the record in the recordset copy
    ' buffer.
    datProducts.Recordset.AddNew

    'Enable the Save menu choice
    mnuDataSave.Enabled = True

    ' Set the focus to the first control on the form
    txtProductName.SetFocus
End Sub
```

7. Add the following code as the `Click` event of the Data menu's Delete Record item. (This code is very similar to that for the identically named procedure in How-To 1.4.) The procedure confirms that the user wants to delete the record, deletes the record, and then ensures that the record pointer is pointing at a valid record.

```
Private Sub mnuDataDelete_Click()
    Dim strMsg As String

    'Verify the deletion.
    strMsg = "Are you sure you want to delete " _
            & IIf(txtProductName.Text <> "", _
            txtProductName.Text, _
                "this record") & "?"
    If MsgBox(strMsg, vbQuestion + vbYesNo + vbDefaultButton2) = _
        vbYes Then

        ' We really want to delete
        datProducts.Recordset.Delete

        ' Make a valid record the current record and update the
        ' display.
        datProducts.Recordset.MoveNext

        ' If we deleted the last record, move to the new last
        ' record because the current record pointer is not defined
        ' after deleting the last record, even though EOF is
        ' defined.
        If datProducts.Recordset.EOF Then
        datProducts.Recordset.MoveLast
    End If
End Sub
```

8. Add the following code as the **Click** event of the Data menu's Save Record item. (This code is very similar to that for the identically named procedure in How-To 1.4.) The **Save Record** subroutine uses the **Update** method of the **Recordset** object to write the values in the form's bound controls to their respective fields in the recordset.

```
Private Sub mnuDataSave_Click()

    ' Invoke the update method to copy control contents to
    ' recordset fields and update the underlying table
    datProducts.Recordset.Update
    If datProducts.Recordset.EditMode <> dbEditAdd Then
        ' If we added move to the new record
        datProducts.Recordset.MoveLast
    End IfEnd Sub
```

9. Add the following code as the **Click** event of the File menu's Exit item. (This code is the same as that for the identically named procedure in How-To 1.4.)

```
Private Sub mnuFileExit_Click()
    Unload Me
End Sub
```

10. Add the following code as the form's **Unload** event. (This code is the same as that for the identically named procedure in How-To 1.4.) If the data currently in the bound controls is invalid, the procedure cancels the `Unload` event.

```
Private Sub Form_Unload(Cancel As Integer)

    ' Don't allow the unload until the data is valid or the
    ' update is cancelled
    If mblnValidationFailed Then Cancel = True
End Sub
```

How It Works

When the form is loaded, the combined actions of `datCategories` and `dbcCategories` fill the Category combo box with a list of category names from the Categories table in NWind.MDB. When a category is chosen from the list, the category ID associated with the chosen category is inserted into the `CategoryID` field in the Products table.

Unlike the unbound list box and combo box controls, their bound cousins `DBList` and `DBCombo` do not have a `Sorted` property. If you want to provide a sorted list, therefore, you must make sure that the recordset providing the list itself is sorted on the appropriate field. You can accomplish this by setting the `RecordSource` property of the data control named in the `DBList` or `DBCombo`'s `RowSource` property to a SQL statement with an `ORDER BY` clause. In the example cited in the "Technique" section of this How-To, you could provide a sorted list of customers by setting the `RecordSource` property of the data control to this:

```
SELECT * FROM Categories ORDER BY CategoryID
```

With `DBList` and `DBCombo`, you can designate how the list reacts to characters typed at the keyboard when the control has the focus. If the control's `MatchEntry` property is set to `vbMatchEntrySimple`, the control searches for the next match for the character entered using the first letter of entries in the list. If the same letter is typed repeatedly, the control cycles through all the entries in the list beginning with that letter. If you set the `MatchEntry` property to `vbMatchEntryExtended`, the control searches for an entry matching all the characters typed by the user. As you type additional characters, you are further refining the search.

Comments

The `DBCombo` and `DBList` controls are powerful additions to your programming arsenal, but be careful about the performance implications in everyday use. Each `DBCombo` and `DBList` control requires a data control, and the data control is a fairly large bit of code. In one experiment, replacing eight `DBCombo` controls with plain `Combo Box` controls loaded from a database reduced the form load time by more than 40%.

COMPLEXITY
INTERMEDIATE

1.6 How do I...
Display many detail records for a single master record?

Problem

I want to display product inventory and order detail information for a displayed product. How do I build a form to display "master-detail" information showing products and order quantities?

Technique

A "master-detail" display is frequently used to show a hierarchical relationship between two tables such as invoice headers and invoice lines. In this How-To, you build a form to display all the orders for a particular product.

Assume you have a warehouse application. The Products table contains the following fields:

```
ProductID
ProductName
SupplierID
CategoryID
QuantityPerUnit
UnitPrice
UnitsInStock
UnitsOnOrder
ReorderLevel
Discontinued
```

The Order Details table defines the quantity of the product included on each order:

```
OrderID
ProductID
UnitPrice
Quantity
Discount
```

You have a form that displays product and stock information together with order quantities for the displayed product. This master-detail relationship requires two data controls to display a single product and multiple order lines.

The master data control has a recordset tied to the Products table, and the detail recordset is tied to the Order Details table. Master table information is usually displayed in text boxes or other appropriate controls; detail information is displayed in a **DBGrid** control.

The **DBGrid** control displays multiple rows from a recordset in a scrolling table that looks much like a spreadsheet. The **DBGrid** control allows recordset scrolling, column width changes, display formatting, and other useful capabilities. It is most useful as a display-only tool, but the **DBGrid** control can provide recordset maintenance functions as well. Table 1.10 describes important properties that control **DBGrid** runtime behavior.

Table 1.10 Important **DBGrid** design-time properties.

PROPERTY	DESCRIPTION
AllowAddNew	Controls ability to add new records (default is False)
AllowDelete	Controls ability to delete records displayed by the grid (default is False)
AllowUpdate	Controls ability to update records through the grid (default is True)
ColumnHeaders	Controls display of column headers (default is True)

You specify a recordset at design time for **DBGrid** so that you can design the initial column layout and formatting. The **DBGrid** control can retrieve the field names from a linked recordset at design time to populate the initial column display. You then edit the column properties to set headers, formats, and default values.

Steps

Open the project GridLister.VBP to preview this How-To. Change the **DatabaseName** property of the data controls **datProducts** and **datOrderDetails** to point to the copy of NWind.MDB installed on your system (probably in the directory where VB6.EXE is installed). Then run the project. The form shown in Figure 1.9 appears. Navigate through the records using the product data control. Observe how the order detail information changes. Experiment with the grid's sliders to control the data display. Use the mouse to select rows or columns. Drastically change a column's display width, and observe how the horizontal scrollbar appears and disappears.

1. Create a new project called GridLister.VBP. Use **Form1** to create the objects and properties listed in Table 1.11 and save the form as GridLister.FRM. Substitute the path to your copy of NWind.MDB for the **DatabaseName** property of **datProducts** and **datOrderDetails**.

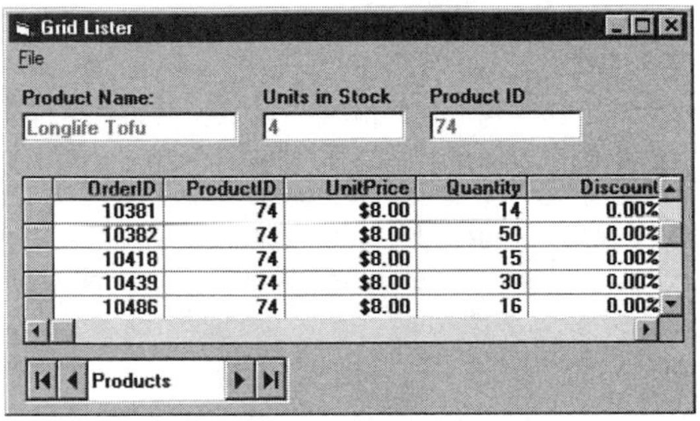

Figure 1.9 The Grid Lister form.

Table 1.11 Objects and properties for the Grid Lister form.

OBJECT	PROPERTY	SETTING
Form	Name	Form1
	Caption	"Grid Lister"
TextBox	Name	txtProductName
	DataField	"ProductName"
	DataSource	"datProducts"
TextBox	Name	txtUnitsInStock
	DataField	"UnitsInStock"
	DataSource	"datProducts"
TextBox	Name	txtProductId
	DataField	"ProductID"
	DataSource	"datProducts"
Data	Name	datProducts
	Caption	"Products"
	Connect	"Access"
	DatabaseName	"D:\Program Files\Microsoft Visual Studio\VB6\Nwind.mdb"
	RecordSource	"Products"
Data	Name	datOrderDetails
	Caption	"Order Details"

OBJECT	PROPERTY	SETTING
	DatabaseName	"D:\Program Files\Microsoft Visual Studio\VB6\Nwind.mdb"
	RecordSource	"Order Details"
	Visible	False
DBGrid	Name	dbgOrderDetails
	AllowAddNew	False
	AllowDelete	False
	AllowUpdate	False
	DataSource	"datOrderDetails"
Label	Name	Label1
	Caption	"Product Name:"
Label	Name	Label2
	Caption	"Units in Stock"
Label	Name	Label3
	Caption	"Product ID"

2. Use the Visual Basic menu editor to create the menu shown in Table 1.12.

Table 1.12 Menu specifications for the Grid Lister.

CAPTION	NAME	SHORTCUT KEY
&File	mnuFile	
----E&xit	mnuFileExit	

3. Use the DBGrid design-time controls to define the columns. Right-click the grid to display the menu shown in Figure 1.10, and then select the Retrieve Fields option. The DBGrid column information will be retrieved from the datOrderDetails recordset. Right-click the DBGrid again and select Edit to make on-screen modifications to column widths and row heights.

4. Right-click the DBGrid and select the Properties menu item to adjust the column formats. Figure 1.11 shows the Columns tab of the DBGrid design-time properties page.

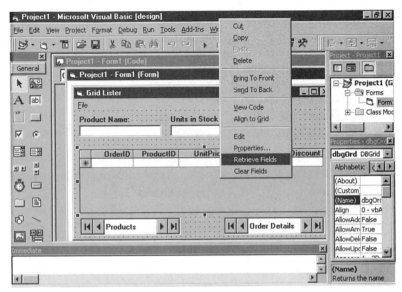

Figure 1.10 The DBGrid right-click design-time menu.

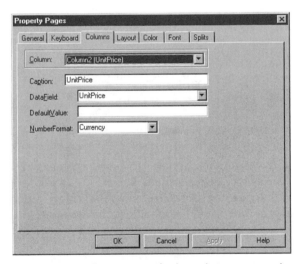

Figure 1.11 The DBGrid design-time properties.

5. Add the following code to the **Reposition** event of the data control datProducts:

```
Private Sub datProducts_Reposition()
    Dim strSql As String

    If datProducts.Recordset.RecordCount = 0 Then
        ' Don't re-query the Order Details if there are
```

```
                        ' no products displayed.
                        Exit Sub
                    End If

                    ' Re-query the Order Detail grid by SQL SELECT statement.
                    ' The WHERE clause picks up only the order details for
                    ' the displayed product.
                    strSql = "SELECT * FROM [Order Details] WHERE ProductID = " _
                        & datProducts.Recordset.Fields("ProductID")

                    ' Assign the desired SQL statement as the record source.
                    datOrderDetails.RecordSource = strSql

                    ' Re-query the database to bring new data to the recordset.
                    datOrderDetails.Refresh

                    ' Set the default value for ProductID for any possible future
                    ' Order Details inserts to the displayed product ID.
                    dbgOrderDetails.Columns("ProductID").DefaultValue = _
                        datProducts.Recordset.Fields("ProductID")

                End Sub
```

6. Add the following code as the `Click` event of the File menu's Exit item. (This code is the same as that for the identically named procedure in How-To 1.5.)

```
Private Sub mnuFileExit_Click()
    Unload Me
End Sub
```

How It Works

When the form is loaded, the `datProducts` data control retrieves the first Products record and fires the `Reposition` event. The event procedure creates a SQL statement to query only those order detail records you want to see by using a `WHERE` clause.

```
SELECT * FROM [Order Details] WHERE ProductID = <displayed product ID>
```

When the data control is refreshed, the `DBGrid` is populated with only the order detail records for the displayed product. A more complicated SQL statement (see Chapter 3, "Creating Queries with SQL") could also retrieve the order number and customer information for display on the form.

Comments

`DBGrid` is a powerful control well worth exploring in the Visual Basic 6 help files and books online. It provides powerful display capabilities as well as add, update, and delete capabilities. When your program is running, users can resize columns and rows to suit their display needs.

The **DBGrid** is also useful as the display for a master query in any database that requires logical partitioning. A multiple warehouse inventory application might use a **DBGrid** to select a "master" warehouse before browsing through "detail" items in order to limit inventory item display to a particular location. Logical partitioning is often required in service bureau applications to prevent making incorrect changes to a customer's account. Telephone companies and Internet service providers frequently need to see individual accounts but restrict the view to a particular corporate customer. **DBGrid** can help partition at the high level and provide "drill-down" capability through hierarchies.

COMPLEXITY
INTERMEDIATE

1.7 How do I...
Change data in data-bound grid cells from code?

Problem

I want to display product inventory and order detail information; I also want to restrict editing to the quantity-ordered information. How do I edit a single **DBGrid** cell?

Technique

Assume you have the same warehouse application as you did in How-To 1.6. Product information and order detail information are stored in two different tables, the structures of which are also shown in the preceding How-To. You have a form that displays product and stock information together with order quantities for the displayed product. Your management team wants to have a secure editing function to allow adjustment of order quantities for particular products.

The **DBGrid** control can allow data updates, but all columns shown on the grid then become available for updates. You don't want to let the warehouse supervisor adjust prices or discounts—only the order quantity. You will have to directly manipulate the **DBGrid** cells to update the order quantity only.

Steps

Open the project GridChange.VBP. Change the **DatabaseName** property of the data controls **datProducts** and **datOrderDetails** to point to the copy of NWind.MDB installed on your system (probably in the directory where VB6.EXE is installed). Then run the project. The form shown in Figure 1.12 appears. Navigate through the product records and observe how the order detail information changes. Highlight an order detail row, enter a new quantity in the text box, and press the Change Qty command button. The quantity will be updated in the DBGrid control and the underlying recordset and database table.

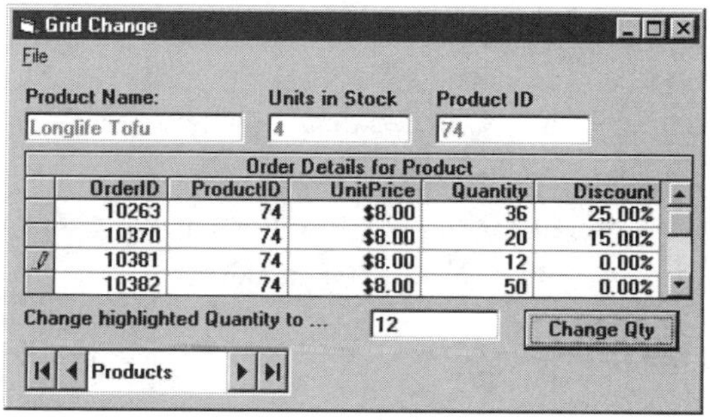

Figure 1.12 The Grid Change form.

1. Create a new project called GridChange.VBP. Use **Form1** to create the objects and properties listed in Table 1.13, and save the form as GridChange.FRM. Substitute the path to your copy of NWind.MDB for the **DatabaseName** property of **datProducts** and **datOrderDetails**.

Table 1.13 Objects and properties for the Grid Lister form.

OBJECT	PROPERTY	SETTING
Form	Name	Form1
	Caption	"Grid Lister"
TextBox	Name	txtProductName
	DataField	"ProductName"
	DataSource	"datProducts"
TextBox	Name	txtUnitsInStock
	DataField	"UnitsInStock"
	DataSource	"datProducts"
TextBox	Name	txtProductId
	DataField	"ProductID"
	DataSource	"datProducts"
TextBox	Name	txtChangeQuantity
	DataField	" "
	DataSource	" "
Data	Name	datProducts
	Caption	"Products"
	Connect	"Access"

continued on next page

continued from previous page

OBJECT	PROPERTY	SETTING
	DatabaseName	"D:\Program Files\Microsoft Visual Studio\VB6\Nwind.mdb"
	RecordSource	"Products"
Data	Name	datOrderDetails
	Caption	"Order Details"
	DatabaseName	"D:\Program Files\Microsoft Visual Studio\VB6\Nwind.mdb"
	RecordSource	"Order Details"
	Visible	False
DBGrid	Name	dbgOrderDetails
	AllowAddNew	False
	AllowDelete	False
	AllowUpdate	False
	DataSource	"datOrderDetails"
Label	Name	Label1
	Caption	"Product Name:"
Label	Name	Label2
	Caption	"Units in Stock"
Label	Name	Label3
	Caption	"Product ID"

2. Use the Visual Basic menu editor to create the menu shown in Table 1.14.

Table 1.14 Menu specifications for the Grid Lister.

CAPTION	NAME	SHORTCUT KEY
&File	mnuFile	
----E&xit	mnuFileExit	

3. Use the DBGrid design-time controls to define the columns. Right-click the grid to display the menu shown earlier in Figure 1.10, and then select Retrieve Fields. The DBGrid column information will be retrieved from the datOrderDetails recordset. Right-click the DBGrid again and select Edit to make on-screen modifications to column widths and row heights.

4. Right-click the DBGrid and select the Properties menu item to adjust column formats.

5. Add the following code to the `Reposition` event of the data control `datProducts`. The `Reposition` event is called when the current record changes. To handle this event, query the database for the new data.

```
Private Sub datProducts_Reposition()
    Dim strSql As String

    If datProducts.Recordset.RecordCount = 0 Then
        ' Don't re-query the Order Details if there are
        ' no products displayed.
        Exit Sub
    End If

    ' Re-query the Order Detail grid by SQL SELECT statement.
    ' The WHERE clause picks up only the order details for
    ' the displayed product.
    strSql = "SELECT * FROM [Order Details] WHERE ProductID = " _
        & datProducts.Recordset.Fields("ProductID")

    ' Assign the desired SQL statement as the record source.
    datOrderDetails.RecordSource = strSql

    ' Re-query the database to bring new data to the recordset.
    datOrderDetails.Refresh

    ' Set the default value for ProductID for any possible future
    ' Order Details inserts to the displayed product ID.
    dbgOrderDetails.Columns("ProductID").DefaultValue = _
        datProducts.Recordset.Fields("ProductID")

End Sub
```

6. Add the following code as the `Click` event of `cmdChangeGridCell`. This code validates the entered amount as a positive number and updates the displayed grid cell.

```
Private Sub cmdChangeGridCell_Click()
    ' Change the selected grid cell value to the entered value
    If Not IsNumeric(txtChangeQuantity.Text) Then
        MsgBox "Change quantity must be a positive number", _
            vbInformation
    ElseIf CInt(txtChangeQuantity.Text) < 0 Then
        MsgBox "Change quantity must be a positive number", _
            vbInformation
    Else
        dbgOrderDetails.Columns("Quantity").Text = _
            txtChangeQuantity.Text
    End If

End Sub
```

7. Add the following code as the **Click** event of the File menu's Exit item. (This code is the same as that for the identically named procedure in How-To 1.5.)

```
Private Sub mnuFileExit_Click()
    Unload Me
End Sub
```

How It Works

When the Change Qty button is pressed, the event procedure validates the entered number and updates the cell value in the grid. The heart of the code is the following statement:

```
dbgOrderDetails.Columns("Quantity").Text = txtChangeQuantity.Text
```

The data contents of the **DBGrid** control can be addressed directly, just as the data contents of any other visual control can be. The currently selected grid row is available to have its columns directly manipulated by code. The data control will update the recordset field and table when the record pointer is repositioned.

Comments

Another useful **DBGrid** trick with a bound grid is to make the data control visible and allow recordset movement with the data control. The **DBGrid** control automatically shows database positions. It can also be used as a record selector because it can function as a multicolumn list box.

COMPLEXITY
INTERMEDIATE

1.8 How do I...
Gracefully handle database errors?

Problem

When I access a database through Visual Basic, I have limited control over the environment. A user might move a database file or another program might have made unexpected changes to the database. I need my programs to be able to detect errors that occur and handle them in the context of the program. How do I accomplish this task with Visual Basic?

Technique

When an error occurs during execution of a Visual Basic program, control passes to error-handling logic. If you have not made provisions in your program to trap errors, Visual Basic calls its default error-handling process. When a compiled Visual Basic program is running, the default error-handling process displays a message describing the cause of the error—sometimes a helpful message, but often not—and terminates the program.

That's never a good solution, but fortunately Visual Basic gives you a choice. You can build error-trapping and error-handling logic into your Visual Basic code. Every Visual Basic program should make provisions for trapping and handling errors gracefully, but it's especially important in database work, in which many potential error conditions can be expected to exist at runtime.

Trapping Errors

Visual Basic error-trapping is accomplished through the **On Error** statement. When an **On Error** statement is in effect and an error occurs, Visual Basic performs the action specified by the **On Error** statement. You therefore avoid Visual Basic's default error-handling behavior.

An **On Error** statement is "in effect" when it has been executed before the occurrence of the error in the same function or subroutine where the error occurred or in a function or subroutine that called the function or subroutine where the error occurred. For example, assume that you have these five subroutines (subroutines are used here for the example; exactly the same principles apply for functions):

```
Sub First()
    .
    .
    .
    Second
    Third
    .
    .
    .
End Sub

Sub Second()
    'On Error Statement here
    .
    .
    .
End Sub

Sub Third()
    'On Error Statement here
    .
    .
    Fourth
    Fifth
    .
    .
    .
End Sub
```

continued on next page

continued from previous page

```
Sub Fourth()
    .
    .
    .
End Sub

Sub Fifth()
    'On Error Statement here
    .
    .
    .
End Sub
```

The subroutine `First` calls the subroutines `Second` and `Third`. The subroutine `Third` calls the subroutines `Fourth` and `Fifth`. `Second`, `Third`, and `Fourth` have `On Error` statements; `First` does not. If an error occurs during the execution of `First`, Visual Basic will use its default error handling because no `On Error` statement has been executed. This will be true even after the calls to `Second` and `Third` have completed; the `On Error` statements in `Second` and `Third` have no effect on the procedure that calls them.

If an error occurs during the execution of `Second`, Visual Basic will take whatever action is specified by the `On Error` statement at the beginning of `Second`. Likewise, if an error occurs during `Third`, the error handling specified by `Third` applies.

What happens if an error occurs during `Fourth`? There is no `On Error` statement in `Fourth`. However, because `Fourth` is called by `Third`, and because there is an `On Error` statement in `Third` (that is executed before `Fourth` is called), an error in `Fourth` will cause the error handling specified by the `On Error` statement in `Third` to execute.

`Fifth` is also called by `Third`, but `Fifth` has an `On Error` statement of its own. If an error occurs in `Fifth`, the error handling specified in its local `On Error` statement overrides that specified in `Third`'s.

The `On Error` **Statement**

These are the two forms of the `On Error` statement that you will use routinely:

```
On Error Goto label
```

```
On Error Resume Next
```

The `On Error Goto label` form tells Visual Basic this: When an error occurs, transfer execution to the line following the named label. A label is any combination of characters that starts with a letter and ends with a colon. An error-handling label must begin in the first column, must be in the same function or subroutine as the `On Error` statement, and must be unique within the module. In the code that follows the label, you take whatever action is appropriate to deal with the specific error that occurred. Most of the time, you will use the `On Error Goto label` form of the `On Error` statement because you normally want to respond to errors in a predetermined way.

`On Error Resume Next` tells Visual Basic this: If an error occurs, simply ignore it and go to the next statement you would normally execute. Use this form when you can reasonably expect an error to occur but are confident that the error will not cause future problems. For example, you might need to create a temporary table in your database. Before you create the temporary table, you need to delete any existing table with the same name, so you execute a statement to delete the table. If you try to delete a table that does not exist, Visual Basic will create an error. In this case, you don't care that the error occurred, so you insert an `On Error Resume Next` statement before the delete table statement. After the delete table statement, you would probably insert an `On Error Goto label` statement to restore the previous error-handling routine.

Determining the Error Type

Errors generated by Visual Basic or the Jet database engine are associated with error numbers. There are hundreds of error types, each with a specific error number. When an error occurs, Visual Basic puts the error number into the `Number` property of the `Err` object. You can determine the error that occurred by looking at that property.

After you know the error type, you can take a specific action based on that information. This is most often accomplished through a `Select Case` statement.

Assume that your application will be used in a multiuser environment and that you need to trap errors caused by more than one user working with the same record at the same time. (A full list of trappable data access object errors can be found in Visual Basic Help file JetErr.HLP, located in the VB6 Help directory.) In your error-handling routine, you might include code similar to what's shown in Listing 1.1.

Listing 1.1 Multiuser error handler.

```
Select Case Err.Number

    Case 3197

        ' Another user has updated this record since the last time
        ' the Dynaset was updated. Display a meaningful error message
        ' and give the user the chance to overwrite the other user's
        ' change.

        strMsg = "The data in this record have already been modified "
        strMsg = strMsg & " by another user. Do you want to overwrite "
        strMsg = strMsg & " those changes with your own?"

        If MsgBox(strMsg, vbQuestion + vbYesNo + vbDefaultButton2) = vbYes Then
                ' The user said yes, so reexecute the Update method.
                ' This time it should "take."
```

continued on next page

continued from previous page

```
                Resume

        Else

                ' The user said no, so refresh the dynaset with the
                ' current data and display that data. Then display a
                ' message explaining what's happened.

                rs.Requery
                DisplayRecord
                strMsg = "The current values of the record are now displayed."
                MsgBox strMsg, vbInformation

                ' Exit from the procedure now to bypass the code after
                ' the End Select statement.

                Exit Sub

        End If

    Case 3020

                ' The user clicked Update without previously having clicked
                ' Edit. The default error message is "Update without AddNew
                ' or Edit." Create an error that is more meaningful in the
                ' current context. (The message gets displayed after the
                ' End Select statement).

                strMsg = "You must click Edit before you click Update!"

    Case 3260

                ' Another user has the page locked. Create a meaningful
                ' message. (The message gets displayed after the End Select
                ' statement.)

                strMsg = "Locking error " & Str$(Err) & " on Update."
                strMsg = strMsg & " Optimistic locking must be enabled!"

    Case Else

                ' An unanticipated error, so just pass through Visual Basic's
                ' message.

                strMsg = Err.Description

End Select

        MsgBox strMsg, vbExclamation
```

Determining the Error Location

If your error handler needs to determine where in the code the error occurs, you can use old-fashioned line numbers. When an error occurs, the built-in **Erl** function returns the line number of the line that generated the error. If the line that generated the error has no number, the `Erl` function returns the line number of the most recent numbered line. If there are no numbered lines preceding the line that caused the error, `Erl` returns 0.

THE Err OBJECT

The `Err` object incorporates the functionality of the `Err` statement, `Err` function, `Error` statement, `Error` function, and `Error$` function from earlier versions of Visual Basic. (These older techniques are still supported for purposes of backward compatibility in Visual Basic 6.0.)

Terminating an Error Handler

Error handling code must terminate with a statement that clears the error. If it does not, the error handler itself will generate an error when it reaches the next `End Sub`, `End Function`, or `End Property` statement. The statements listed in Table 1.15 are those that clear an error.

Table 1.15 Statements that clear an error.

STATEMENT	EFFECT
Resume Next	Resumes execution at the line that follows the line that generated the error
Resume	Reexecutes the line that generated the error
Resume label	Resumes execution at the line following the named label
Resume number	Resumes execution at the line with the indicated number
Exit Sub	Exits immediately from the current subroutine
Exit Function	Exits immediately from the current function
Exit Property	Exits immediately from the current property
On Error	Resets error-handling logic
Err.Clear	Clears the error without otherwise affecting program execution
End	Terminates execution of the program

OPENING NWIND.MDB FOR HOW-TO'S

In many of the How-To's that use data access objects to work with NWIND.MDB, you will see directions to add READINI.BAS to the project. (READINI.BAS is a module that is installed in the main VB6DBHT directory.) In the code for the project you will see the following lines:

```
' Get the database name and open the database.
strName = strNWindDb()
Set db = DBEngine.Workspaces(0).OpenDatabase(strName)
```

continued on next page

continued from previous page

strNWindDb() is a function in READINI.BAS that reads the VB6DBHT.INI file and returns the fully qualified filename (that is, the directory, path, and name) of NWIND.MDB. The code assigns that fully qualified filename to the string variable strName and uses strName as the argument to the OpenDatabase method.

Steps

Open and run the project Errors.VBP. Three errors will occur in succession. For each, the message box reporting the error gives you the error number, error description, and line number where the error occurred. Figure 1.13 shows the first of these errors.

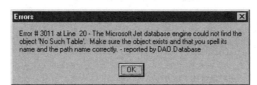

Figure 1.13 One of the errors.

1. Create a new project called Errors.VBP. Use **Form1** to create the objects and properties listed in Table 1.16, and save the form as Errors.FRM.

Table 1.16 Objects and properties for the Errors form.

OBJECT	PROPERTY	SETTING
Form	Name	Form1
	Caption	"Errors"

2. Add the file READINI.BAS to your project from the **Chapter01\HowTo08** directory.

3. Add the following code as the **Load** event of **Form1**. This code generates three errors:

✔ Line 20 generates an error because there is no such table as No Such Table.

✔ Line 40 generates an error because there is no such field as **No Such Field**.

✔ Line 60 generates an error because the **Year Published** field requires a numeric value.

Each error causes execution to branch to the label LoadError. The code beginning with LoadError displays an informative message and then executes a Resume Next. The Resume Next transfers execution back to the line following the line that caused the error.

```
Private Sub Form_Load()
    Dim dbErrors As Database
    Dim strDbName As String
    Dim rsTest As Recordset
    Dim strTmp As String

    On Error GoTo LoadError

  ' Get the database name and open the database.
    strDbName = strNWindDb()   ' NWindPath is a function in
                               ' READINI.BAS
10  Set dbErrors = DBEngine.Workspaces(0).OpenDatabase(strDbName)

    ' This statement will cause an error, because there's no such
    ' table as No Such Table.
20  Set rsTest = dbErrors.OpenRecordset("No Such Table", _
        dbOpenTable)

    ' There is a table named Products, so this one should work.
30  Set rsTest = dbErrors.OpenRecordset("Products", dbOpenTable)

    ' There's no such field as No Such Field, so here's another
    ' error.
40  strTmp = rsTest![No Such Field]

    ' This causes an error because UnitPrice only takes currency
    ' values.
50  rsTest![UnitPrice] = "XYZ"

    ' Finally!
60  End

Exit Sub

LoadError:
    MsgBox "Error #" & Str$(Err.Number) & _
            " at Line " & Str$(Erl) & _
        " - " & Err.Description & " - reported by " & Err.Source
Resume Next

End Sub
```

How It Works

This simple example merely shows the error-handling logic that is possible using Visual Basic. The key to this sample is the use of the MsgBox function to show the various Err Object properties on the screen. Meaningful error handling has to be written into your application as you discover the most common problems with your applications.

Comments

As you work with DAO, be forewarned that you might get some unexplainable errors. You can't assume that anything as complex as the data control will always behave the way you would have written it, so you sometimes have to learn parts of the data control's behavior through a process of discovery. The best way to trap elusive errors is to eliminate controls from your form and code from your program until the errors stop occurring. The last thing deleted before the program works again is, no matter how unlikely, the part of the code or control causing the problem. The multiple cascading of events between the data control, its recordset object, and your event handlers can have unforeseen consequences that result in inexplicable errors. The most common of these data control errors is referencing invalid recordset fields during a reposition event because the recordset has moved to the "No current record" area.

CHAPTER 2

ACCESSING A DATABASE WITH DATA ACCESS OBJECTS

2

ACCESSING A DATA-BASE WITH DATA ACCESS OBJECTS

How do I...

2.1 Browse and update a recordset with Data Access Objects?

2.2 Validate data entered into Data Access Objects?

2.3 Allow users to undo changes they've made in Data Access Objects?

2.4 Add and delete records by using Data Access Objects?

2.5 Use unbound controls to update fields in Data Access Objects?

2.6 Find records by using index values in Data Access Objects?

2.7 Determine how many records are in a dynaset- or snapshot-type recordset?

57

2.8 Handle Data Access Object errors?

2.9 Access Excel worksheets by using Data Access Objects?

The Data control provides a means of quickly developing database applications with little or no code, but it limits your access to the underlying database. The Microsoft Jet database engine exposes another method of working with databases: Data Access Objects (DAO). Although using DAO requires more coding than using the Data control, it offers complete programmatic access to everything in the database, as well as significantly greater flexibility. This chapter shows you how to use Jet Data Access Objects to perform common database operations.

All the examples in this chapter use Microsoft Access (.MDB) database files. The Jet engine can also access other PC-based databases such as dBASE, FoxPro, Paradox, and Btrieve, as well as Open Database Connectivity (ODBC) data sources. The techniques shown can be used with any database that Visual Basic can access through Jet. Chapter 6, "Connecting to an ODBC Server," and Chapter 7, "SQL Server Databases and Remote Data Objects," show how to access ODBC and SQL Server databases.

2.1 Browse and Update a Recordset with Data Access Objects

Browsing and updating records are two of the most basic database operations. In this How-To, you will use unbound controls and Data Access Objects to browse and update a recordset.

2.2 Validate Data Entered into Data Access Objects

Users make data entry errors, and robust applications anticipate and trap those errors. This How-To shows how to trap and respond to user errors when you're using Data Access Objects.

2.3 Allow Users to Undo Changes They've Made in Data Access Objects

Users expect to be able to undo changes they make while they are working. In this How-To, using Data Access Objects and unbound controls, you will learn how to enable users to undo changes.

2.4 Add and Delete Records by Using Data Access Objects

Inserting and deleting records are common database activities. In this How-To, you will learn to use Data Access Objects to add and delete records.

2.5 Use Unbound Controls to Update Fields in Data Access Objects

Simple text boxes are not the only user interface tools available when you're using unbound controls. In this How-To, you will build a generic form that can run an ad hoc query, display the results, and enable the user to select a record.

2.6 Find Records by Using Index Values in Data Access Objects

Indexes can substantially speed up access to records. This How-To shows how you can leverage indexes for performance.

2.7 Determine How Many Records Are in a Dynaset- or Snapshot-Type Recordset

If you need to know how many records are in your recordset, this How-To will show you how to get that number.

2.8 Handle Data Access Object Errors

Although Jet is a robust database engine, many things can go wrong when working with a database. This How-To shows you how to handle Data Access Object errors gracefully.

2.9 Access Excel Worksheets by Using Data Access Objects

An interesting capability of the Microsoft Jet engine is used to access Excel worksheets. In this How-To, we view and manipulate an Excel worksheet as if it were an ordinary database file.

COMPLEXITY
BEGINNING

2.1 How do I...
Browse and update records by using Data Access Objects?

Problem

Bound recordsets with Data controls are fine for many purposes, but the Data control has significant limitations. I can't use indexes with bound controls, and I can't refer to the Data control's recordset if the Data control's form is not loaded. How can I browse a recordset without using bound controls?

Technique

Visual Basic and the Microsoft Jet database engine provide a rich set of Data Access Objects that give you complete control over your database and provide capabilities beyond what you can accomplish with bound controls.

If you've worked with other databases, and in particular Structured Query Language (SQL), you might be accustomed to dividing the database programming language into Data Definition Language (DDL) and Data Manipulation Language (DML). Although Jet provides programmatic access to both structure and data, DAO makes no clear distinction between the two. Some objects, such as the **Recordset**, are used strictly for data manipulation, whereas others, such as the **TableDef** object, act in both data definition and data manipulation roles. Figure 2.1 shows the DAO hierarchy.

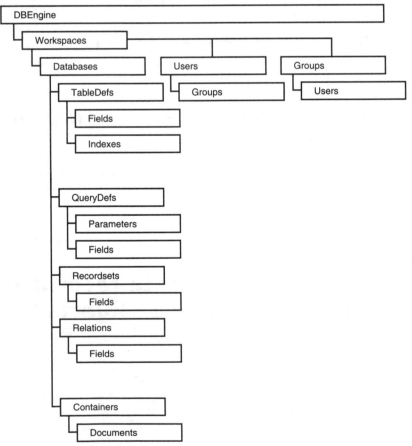

Figure 2.1. The Data Access Object hierarchy.

In most cases, you will be using DAO to manage data. There are four general types of data operations:

- ✔ Retrieve records
- ✔ Insert new records
- ✔ Update existing records
- ✔ Delete records

DAO provides the recordset object for retrieving records and both the recordset object and the `Execute` method for inserting, updating, and deleting records.

Before you can do anything useful with DAO, you must open a database. In most cases, this is as simple as using the `OpenDatabase` method of the default workspace. The following code fragment shows some typical code used to open an Access .MDB file and create a recordset:

```
' Declare database variable
Dim db As Database
Dim rs As Recordset

' Open a database file and assign it to db
Set db = DBEngine.Workspaces(0).OpenDatabase(App.Path & "\MyDB.MDB")

' Create a recordset
Set rs = db.OpenRecordset("MyQuery", dbOpenDynaset, , dbOptimistic)
```

If you are working with a secured database, you will need to take a few extra steps to provide a valid username and password to the database engine so that a secured workspace object can be created. Refer to Chapter 11, "The Windows Registry and State Information," for more information.

Moving Within an Unbound Recordset

When you use the Data control on a bound form, you rarely have to code in order to move operations. The user clicks on the navigational buttons, and the Data control executes a move internally. Only in the case of a delete do you need to code a move operation (see How-To 1.4).

When you use unbound controls, you must refresh the data displayed on the form with your code. The recordset object provides four methods to facilitate this task: `MoveFirst`, `MovePrevious`, `MoveNext`, and `MoveLast`.

When you use `MovePrevious`, you should always check to make sure that the movement has not placed the record pointer before the first record in the recordset. Do this by checking the value of the recordset's `BOF` property. If `BOF` is `True`, you're not on a valid record. The usual solution is to use `MoveFirst` to position the pointer on the first record. Similarly, when you use `MoveNext`, you should check to make sure that you're not past the last record in the recordset by checking the **EOF** property. If **EOF** is **True**, use **MoveLast** to move to a valid record. It's also a good idea to ensure that the recordset has at least one record by making sure that the value of the recordset's **RecordCount** property is greater than zero.

Updating Records

You can update the values in table-type or dynaset-type recordsets. Updating records in a recordset is a four-step procedure:

1. Position the record pointer to the record you want to update.

2. Copy the record's values to an area of memory known as the copy buffer by invoking the recordset object's **Edit** method.

3. Change the desired fields by assigning values to the **Field** objects.

4. Transfer the contents of the copy buffer to the database by invoking the recordset object's **Update** method.

Steps

Open and run the project HT201.VBP. The form shown in Figure 2.2 appears. Use the navigation buttons at the bottom of the form to browse through the records in the recordset. You can change the data by typing over the existing values.

1. Create a new project called HT201.VBP. Use **Form1** to create the objects and properties listed in Table 2.1, and save the form as HT201.FRM.

Table 2.1. Objects and properties for *Form1*.

OBJECT	PROPERTY	SETTING
Form	Name	Form1
	Caption	Unbound Browser
CommandButton	Name	cmdMove
	Caption	¦<
	Index	0
CommandButton	Name	cmdMove
	Caption	<
	Index	1
CommandButton	Name	cmdMove
	Caption	>
	Index	2

OBJECT	PROPERTY	SETTING
CommandButton	Name	cmdMove
	Caption	>¦
	Index	3
TextBox	Name	txt
	Index	0
TextBox	Name	txt
	Index	1
TextBox	Name	txt
	Index	2
TextBox	Name	txt
	Index	3
Label	Name	Label1
	Caption	&Title
Label	Name	Label2
	Caption	&Year Published
Label	Name	Label3
	Caption	&ISBN
Label	Name	Label4
	Caption	&Publisher ID

2. Create the menu shown in Table 2.2.

Table 2.2. Menu specifications for *Form1*.

CAPTION	NAME	SHORTCUT KEY
&File	mnuFile	
----E&xit	mnuFileExit	
&Data	mnuData	
----&Save Record	mnuDataSaveRecord	Ctrl+S

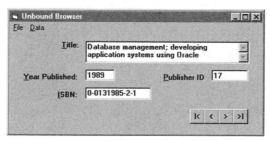

Figure 2.2. The Unbound Browser form.

3. Add READINI.bas to your project. READINI.bas looks for a file named VBDBHT.ini in the Windows directory with the following text:

```
[Data Files]
BIBLIO=<path to biblio directory>
```

The path should point to the Chapter 2 subdirectory of the directory where you installed the files from the CD setup program. The standard module uses the `GetPrivateProfileString` API function to obtain the path to the sample database.

You can also use the copy of `Biblio.mdb` that was installed with Visual Basic, although it is possible that there are differences in the file. If your copy has the same database structure, you can update the .ini file to point to your existing copy and delete the copy in the Chapter 2 subdirectory.

4. Add a class module to the project, name it `CTitles`, and save the file as HT201.CLS.

5. Add the following code to the declarations section of `CTitles`. Several private variables are declared, including database and recordset object variables, a flag to track changes to the record, strings to hold the property values, and public enumerations for record movement and class errors.

```
Option Explicit
' The CTitles class provides a light wrapper
' around the database and record for the
' Titles table in the Biblio database

' Note: It's up to the client to save

' Database and recordset objects
Private mdb As Database
Private mrs As Recordset

' Flags
' dirty flag
Private mblnIsDirty As Boolean

' Fields
' title
Private mstrTitle As String
' year - note use of string for
' assignment to text box
Private mstrYearPublished As String
' ISBN number
Private mstrISBN As String
' PubID - also a string
Private mstrPubID As String

' Move method constants
Public Enum CTitlesMove
    FirstRecord = 1
```

```
        LastRecord = 2
        NextRecord = 3
        PreviousRecord = 4
End Enum

' Error constants
' Note: RaiseClassError method provides the strings
' because you cannot assign a string to an Enum
Public Enum CTitlesError
    ErrInvalidMoveType = vbObjectError + 1000 + 11
    ErrNoRecords = vbObjectError + 1000 + 12
End Enum
```

ENUMERATIONS

Enumerations are a feature in Visual Basic that enables you to define publicly available constants within a class module. If you did any work with class modules in Visual Basic 4.0 or earlier, you might have been frustrated by the need to provide a standard "helper" module for any class that used public constants. This type of workaround has been replaced with public enumerations. Note, however, that you can assign only long integer values in an enumeration. No means exist for making strings or other types of constants public in classes.

6. Add the following code to the `Class_Initialize` and `Class_Terminate` event procedures in `CTitles`. `Class_Initialize` opens the database and creates a recordset, generating an error if no records exist. `Class_Terminate` closes the object variables opened by `Class_Initialize`.

```
Private Sub Class_Initialize()
    ' open the database and recordset

    Dim strDBName As String

    ' Get the database name and open the database.
    ' BiblioPath is a function in READINI.BAS
    strDBName = BiblioPath()
    Set mdb = DBEngine.Workspaces(0).OpenDatabase(strDBName)

    ' Open the recordset.
    Set mrs = mdb.OpenRecordset( _
        "Titles", dbOpenDynaset, dbSeeChanges, dbOptimistic)

    ' Raise an error if there is no data
    If mrs.BOF Then
```

continued on next page

continued from previous page

```
              RaiseClassError ErrNoRecords
         End If

         ' fetch the first record to the properties
         GetCurrentRecord

End Sub
Private Sub Class_Terminate()
' cleanup - note that since a Class_Terminate error
' is fatal to the app, this proc simply traps and
' ignores any shutdown errors
' that's not a great solution, but there's not much
' else that can be done at this point
' in a production app, it might be helpful to log
' these errors

    ' close and release the recordset object
    mrs.Close
    Set mrs = Nothing
    ' close and release the database object
    mdb.Close
    Set mdb = Nothing
End Sub
```

7. Add the private `RaiseClassError` method to `CTitles`. This is a simple switch that sets the `Description` and `Source` properties for errors raised by the class.

```
Private Sub RaiseClassError(lngErrorNumber As CTitlesError)
' Note: DAO errors are passed out as-is

    Dim strDescription As String
    Dim strSource As String

    ' assign the description for the error
    Select Case lngErrorNumber
        Case ErrInvalidMoveType
            strDescription = "Invalid move operation."
        Case ErrNoRecords
            strDescription = _
                "There are no records in the Titles table."
        Case Else
            ' If this executes, it's a coding error in
            ' the class module, but having the case is
            ' useful for debugging.
            strDescription = _
                "There is no message for this error."
    End Select

    ' build the Source property for the error
    strSource = App.EXEName & ".CTitles"

    ' raise it
    Err.Raise lngErrorNumber, strSource, strDescription
End Sub
```

8. Add the `GetCurrentRecord` method. This procedure fetches the data from the recordset and writes the values to the private module-level variables used by the property procedures.

```
Private Sub GetCurrentRecord()
' Get current values from the recordset

    ' a zero length string is appended to
    ' each variable to avoid the Invalid use of Null
    ' error if a field is null
    ' although current rules don't allow nulls, there
    ' may be legacy data that doesn't conform to
    ' existing rules
    mstrISBN = mrs![ISBN] & ""
    mstrTitle = mrs![Title] & ""
    mstrYearPublished = mrs![Year Published] & ""
    mstrPubID = mrs![PubID] & ""
End Sub
```

9. Add the private `UpdateRecord` method. This procedure writes the module-level variables to the recordset. The error handler in this procedure clears any changes that were made to the field values.

```
Private Sub UpdateRecord()
' DAO Edit/Update
On Error GoTo ProcError

    ' inform DAO we will edit
    mrs.Edit
    mrs![ISBN] = mstrISBN
    mrs![Title] = mstrTitle
    mrs![Year Published] = mstrYearPublished
    mrs![PubID] = mstrPubID
    ' commit changes
    mrs.Update
    ' clear dirty flag
    mblnIsDirty = False

    Exit Sub

ProcError:
    ' clear the values that were assigned
    ' and cancel the edit method by
    ' executing a moveprevious/movenext
    mrs.MovePrevious
    mrs.MoveNext
    ' raise the error again
    Err.Raise Err.Number, Err.Source, Err.Description, _
        Err.HelpFile, Err.HelpContext
End Sub
```

10. Add the `Property` Let and `Property` Get procedures for the `Title`, `YearPublished`, `ISBN`, and `PubID` properties of the class. The `Property`

Get procedures simply return the values of the module-level variables. The Property Let procedures assign the new values to the module level variables and set the mblnIsDirty flag.

```
Public Property Get Title() As String
    Title = mstrTitle
End Property

Public Property Let Title(strTitle As String)
    mstrTitle = strTitle
    ' set the dirty flag
    mblnIsDirty = True
End Property

Public Property Get YearPublished() As String
    YearPublished = mstrYearPublished
End Property

Public Property Let YearPublished(strYearPublished As String)
    mstrYearPublished = strYearPublished
    ' set the dirty flag
    mblnIsDirty = True
End Property

Public Property Get ISBN() As String
    ISBN = mstrISBN
End Property

Public Property Let ISBN(strISBN As String)
    mstrISBN = strISBN
    ' set the dirty flag
    mblnIsDirty = True
End Property

Public Property Get PubID() As String
    PubID = mstrPubID
End Property

Public Property Let PubID(strPubID As String)
    mstrPubID = strPubID
    ' set the dirty flag
    mblnIsDirty = True
End Property
```

11. Add the IsDirty Property Get procedure. This property returns the current value of the mblnIsDirty flag. Note that this is a read-only property. There is no corresponding Property Let procedure.

```
Public Property Get IsDirty() As Boolean
' pass out the dirty flag
    IsDirty = mblnIsDirty
End Property
```

12. Add the Move method. This method moves the current pointer for the recordset based on the lngMoveType parameter. The values for lngMoveType are defined by the CTitlesMove enumeration in the header section. This method is a simple wrapper around the various move methods of the underlying recordset object.

```
Public Sub Move(lngMoveType As CTitlesMove)
' Move and refresh properties

    Select Case lngMoveType
        Case FirstRecord
            mrs.MoveFirst
        Case LastRecord
            mrs.MoveLast
        Case NextRecord
            mrs.MoveNext
            ' check for EOF
            If mrs.EOF Then
                mrs.MoveLast
            End If
        Case PreviousRecord
            mrs.MovePrevious
            ' check for BOF
            If mrs.BOF Then
                mrs.MoveFirst
            End If
        Case Else
            ' bad parameter, raise an error
            RaiseClassError ErrInvalidMoveType
    End Select

    GetCurrentRecord
End Sub
```

MORE ON ENUMERATIONS

Declaring the lngMoveType parameter as CTitlesMove instead of as a long integer illustrates another benefit of using enumerations. If a variable is declared as the type of a named enumeration, the code editor provides a drop-down list of available constants wherever the variable is used.

13. Add the SaveRecord method. This method tests the mblnIsDirty flag and updates the current record if necessary.

```
Public Sub SaveRecord()
' save current changes

    ' test dirty flag
    If mblnIsDirty Then
        ' update it
        UpdateRecord
    Else
        ' record is already clean
    End If
End Sub
```

14. Add the following code to the declarations section of **Form1**. A private object variable is created for the **CTitles** class, as well as constants for the control arrays and a status flag used to prevent the **txt_Change** events from writing the property values in the class during a refresh of the data.

```
Option Explicit

' CTitles object
Private mclsTitles As CTitles

' These constants are used for the various control arrays
' command button constants
Const cmdMoveFirst = 0
Const cmdMovePrevious = 1
Const cmdMoveNext = 2
Const cmdMoveLast = 3
' text box index constants
Const txtTitle = 0
Const txtYearPublished = 1
Const txtISBN = 2
Const txtPubID = 3

' refresh flag
Private mblnInRefresh As Boolean
```

15. Add the **Form_Load** event procedure. **Form_Load** creates the **mclsTitles** object and loads the first record. If an error occurs, the error handler displays a message and unloads the form, which terminates the application.

```
Private Sub Form_Load()
' create the mclsTitles object and display the first record
On Error GoTo ProcError
    Dim strDBName As String

    Screen.MousePointer = vbHourglass

    ' create the CTitles object
    Set mclsTitles = New CTitles

    ' fetch and display the current record
    GetData

ProcExit:
    Screen.MousePointer = vbDefault
    Exit Sub

ProcError:
    ' An error was generated by Visual Basic or CTitles.
    ' Display the error message and terminate gracefully.
    MsgBox Err.Description, vbExclamation
    Unload Me
    Resume ProcExit
End Sub
```

16. Add the `Query_Unload` event procedure. This saves the current record before unloading the form. If an error occurs, the error handler gives the user the option of continuing (with loss of data) or returning to the form.

```
Private Sub Form_QueryUnload(Cancel As Integer, UnloadMode As
Integer)
On Error GoTo ProcError

    Screen.MousePointer = vbHourglass

    ' save the current record
    mclsTitles.SaveRecord

ProcExit:
    Screen.MousePointer = vbDefault
    Exit Sub

ProcError:
    ' an error here means the record won't be saved
    ' let the user decide what to do
    Dim strMsg As String

    strMsg = "The following error occurred while _
            "attempting to save:"
strMsg = strMsg & vbCrLf & Err.Description & vbCrLf
    strMsg = strMsg & "If you continue the current operation, " _
    strMsg = strMsg & "changes to your data will be lost."
    strMsg = strMsg & vbCrLf
    strMsg = strMsg & "Do you want to continue anyway?"

    If MsgBox(strMsg, _
        vbQuestion Or vbYesNo Or vbDefaultButton2) = vbNo Then
        Cancel = True
    End If
    Resume ProcExit
End Sub
```

17. Add the `cmdMove_Click` event procedure. This event saves the current record, requests the record indicated by the `Index` parameter from the `mclsTitles` object, and refreshes the form.

```
Private Sub cmdMove_Click(Index As Integer)
' move to the desired record, saving first
On Error GoTo ProcError

    Screen.MousePointer = vbHourglass

    ' save the record
    mclsTitles.SaveRecord

    ' move to the indicated record
    Select Case Index
        Case cmdMoveFirst
```

continued on next page

continued from previous page

```
                mclsTitles.Move FirstRecord
            Case cmdMoveLast
                mclsTitles.Move LastRecord
            Case cmdMoveNext
                mclsTitles.Move NextRecord
            Case cmdMovePrevious
                mclsTitles.Move PreviousRecord
        End Select

        ' refresh display
        GetData

ProcExit:
    Screen.MousePointer = vbDefault
    Exit Sub

ProcError:
    MsgBox Err.Description, vbExclamation
    Resume ProcExit
End Sub
```

18. Add the `txt_Change` event procedure. This event writes the control values to the properties unless the `mblnInRefresh` flag is set. The flag tells the event procedure that the form is being refreshed and that the property values in `mclsTitles` do not need to be set.

```
Private Sub txt_Change(Index As Integer)
' update property values if required
On Error GoTo ProcError

    Dim strValue As String

    Screen.MousePointer = vbHourglass

    ' fetch the value from the control
    strValue = txt(Index).Text

    ' check first to see if we're in a GetData call
    ' assigning the property values while refreshing
    ' will reset the dirty flag again so the data will
    ' never appear to have been saved
    If Not mblnInRefresh Then
        ' update the clsTitles properties
        Select Case Index
            Case txtTitle
                mclsTitles.Title = strValue
            Case txtYearPublished
                mclsTitles.YearPublished = strValue
            Case txtISBN
                mclsTitles.ISBN = strValue
            Case txtPubID
                mclsTitles.PubID = strValue
        End Select
    End If
```

```
ProcExit:
    Screen.MousePointer = vbDefault
    Exit Sub

ProcError:
    MsgBox Err.Description, vbExclamation
    Resume ProcExit
End Sub
```

19. Add the `mnuFileExit_Click` event. This procedure unloads the form. The rest of the unload logic is contained in the `QueryUnload` event procedure.

```
Private Sub mnuFileExit_Click()
    ' shut down
    ' work is handled by the Query_Unload event
    Unload Me
End Sub
```

20. Add the `mnuData_Click` and `mnuDataSaveRecord_Click` event procedures. The `mnuData_Click` event toggles the enabled flag for the `mnuDataSaveRecord` menu control based on the `IsDirty` flag of the `mclsTitles` object. The `mnuDataSaveRecord_Click` procedure saves the current record.

```
Private Sub mnuData_Click()
' set enabled/disabled flags for menu commands
On Error GoTo ProcError

    Screen.MousePointer = vbHourglass

    ' save enabled only when dirty
    mnuDataSaveRecord.Enabled = mclsTitles.IsDirty

ProcExit:
    Screen.MousePointer = vbDefault
    Exit Sub

ProcError:
    MsgBox Err.Description, vbExclamation
    Resume ProcExit
End Sub

Private Sub mnuDataSaveRecord_Click()
On Error GoTo ProcError

    Screen.MousePointer = vbHourglass

    ' save it
    mclsTitles.SaveRecord

    ' refresh display
    GetData
```

continued on next page

continued from previous page

```
ProcExit:
    Screen.MousePointer = vbDefault
    Exit Sub

ProcError:
    MsgBox Err.Description, vbExclamation
    Resume ProcExit
End Sub
```

21. Add the private `GetData` procedure. `GetData` is used to refresh the controls based on the property values in `mclsTitles` and sets the `mblnInRefresh` flag so that the properties aren't changed again by `txt_Change`.

```
Private Sub GetData()
' display the current record

    ' set the mblnInRefresh flag so that the txt_Change event
    ' doesn't write the property values again
    mblnInRefresh = True

    ' assign the values to the controls from the properties
    txt(txtTitle).Text = mclsTitles.Title
    txt(txtYearPublished).Text = mclsTitles.YearPublished
    txt(txtISBN).Text = mclsTitles.ISBN
    txt(txtPubID).Text = mclsTitles.PubID

    ' clear the refresh flag
    mblnInRefresh = False
End Sub
```

How It Works

When the form loads, it creates the object variable for the `CTitles` class and displays the first record. The user can navigate among the records by clicking the move buttons, and the logic in the form and the `CTitles` class saves changes if the record is dirty.

With placement of the data management logic in the class module and the user interface logic in the form, a level of independence between the database and the user interface is created. Several different forms can be created that all use the same class without duplicating any of the data management logic. Additionally, changes made to the underlying database can be incorporated into the class without requiring changes to the forms based on it.

Comments

The beauty of encapsulating all the data access code in a class module isn't fully revealed until you have an application that enables the user to edit the same data using more than one interface. If, for example, you display a summary of detail records in a grid and also provide a regular form for working with the same data, most of the code for managing that data will be shared in the class modules.

Each form that presents the data will only need to have code that controls its own interface.

COMPLEXITY
BEGINNING

2.2 How do I...
Validate data entered into Data Access Objects?

Problem

I need to verify that data entered is valid before I update the database. How can I do this with Data Access Objects and unbound controls?

Technique

Databases, tables, and fields often have various business rules that apply to the data. You can apply rules by writing code to check the values of the data in unbound controls before you write the changes to the underlying tables.

Class modules are most often used to handle the data-management logic for unbound data—adding a layer of separation between the database schema and the user interface logic. Normally, class modules should not handle any user interaction (unless, of course, the class is specifically designed to encapsulate user interface components), so instead of generating messages, classes raise errors if a validation rule is violated. The error is trapped by the user interface and handled in whatever manner is appropriate.

Steps

Open and run HT202.VBP. Tab to the Year Published text box, delete the year, and attempt to save the record. Because the Year Published is required, an error message is displayed, as shown in Figure 2.3. Experiment with some of the other fields to examine other rules and the messages that are displayed.

Figure 2.3. The Validating Browser form.

1. Create a new project called HT202.VBP. This project adds to the project developed for How-To 2.1 by adding validation code to the **CTitles** class module. The form and the READINI.bas module for this project are unchanged from the previous How-To, with the exception of the form caption, which was changed to Validating Browser. Changes to the class module are shown in the steps that follow.

2. Add the following code to the declarations section of the class module. The modified enumeration, shown in bold, defines the errors that can be raised by the class. The rest of the declarations section is unchanged from the previous How-To.

```
Option Explicit

' The CTitles class provides a light wrapper
' around the database and record for the
' Titles table in the Biblio database

' Database and recordset objects
Private mdb As Database
Private mrs As Recordset

' Flags
' dirty flag
Private mblnIsDirty As Boolean

' Fields
' title
Private mstrTitle As String
' year - note use of string for
' assignment to text box
Private mstrYearPublished As String
' ISBN number
Private mstrISBN As String
' PubID - also a string
Private mstrPubID As String

' Move method constants
Public Enum CTitlesMove
    FirstRecord = 1
    LastRecord = 2
    NextRecord = 3
    PreviousRecord = 4
End Enum

' Error constants
' Note: RaiseClassError method provides the strings
' because you cannot assign a string to an Enum
Public Enum CTitlesError
    ErrMissingTitle = vbObjectError + 1000 + 1
    ErrMissingYear = vbObjectError + 1000 + 2
    ErrMissingISBN = vbObjectError + 1000 + 3
    ErrInvalidYear = vbObjectError + 1000 + 4
    ErrMissingPubID = vbObjectError + 1000 + 5
```

```
        ErrNonNumericPubID = vbObjectError + 1000 + 6
        ErrRecordNotFound = vbObjectError + 1000 + 10
        ErrInvalidMoveType = vbObjectError + 1000 + 11
        ErrNoRecords = vbObjectError + 1000 + 12
    End Enum
```

3. Modify the `RaiseClassError` procedure, as shown. This is a simple switch that sets the `Description` and `Source` properties for errors raised by the class. Several new cases in the `Select Case` block are dedicated to assigning descriptions to validation errors.

```
Private Sub RaiseClassError(lngErrorNumber As CTitlesError)
' Note: DAO errors are passed out as-is

    Dim strDescription As String
    Dim strSource As String

    ' assign the description for the error
    Select Case lngErrorNumber
        Case ErrMissingTitle
            strDescription = "The Title is required."
        Case ErrMissingYear
            strDescription = "The Year Published is required."
        Case ErrMissingISBN
            strDescription = "The ISBN number is required."
        Case ErrInvalidYear
            strDescription = "Not a valid year."
        Case ErrMissingPubID
            strDescription = "The Publisher ID is required."
        Case ErrNonNumericPubID
            strDescription = "The Publisher ID must be numeric."
        Case ErrRecordNotFound
            strDescription = "The record was not found."
        Case ErrInvalidMoveType
            strDescription = "Invalid move operation."
        Case ErrNoRecords
            strDescription = _
                "There are no records in the Titles table."
        Case Else
            ' If this executes, it's a coding error in
            ' the class module, but having the case is
            ' useful for debugging.
            strDescription = "There is no message for this error."
    End Select

    ' build the Source property for the error
    strSource = App.EXEName & ".CTitles"

    ' raise it
    Err.Raise lngErrorNumber, strSource, strDescription
End Sub
```

4. Add the `IsValid` property. This property takes an optional argument, `blnRaiseError`, which defaults to `False` and controls the procedure logic.

If the flag is **True**, an error is generated when a validation rule is violated. Code within the class sets the flag to **True** so that errors are raised when rules are violated. Forms would normally ignore this optional parameter and simply test for a **True** or **False** value in the property.

```
Public Property Get IsValid _
    (Optional blnRaiseError As Boolean = False) As Boolean
' test the data against our rules
' the optional blnRaiseError flag can be used to have the
' procedure raise an error if a validation rule is
' violated.

    Dim lngError As CTitlesError

    If mstrISBN = "" Then
        lngError = ErrMissingISBN
    ElseIf mstrTitle = "" Then
        lngError = ErrMissingTitle
    ElseIf mstrYearPublished = "" Then
        lngError = ErrMissingYear
    ElseIf Not IsNumeric(mstrYearPublished) Then
        lngError = ErrInvalidYear
    ElseIf mstrPubID = "" Then
        lngError = ErrMissingPubID
    ElseIf Not IsNumeric(mstrPubID) Then
        lngError = ErrNonNumericPubID
    End If

    If lngError <> 0 Then
        If blnRaiseError Then
            RaiseClassError lngError
        Else
            IsValid = False
        End If
    Else
        IsValid = True
    End If
End Property
```

5. Modify the **SaveRecord** method to call **IsValid**. This method tests the **mblnIsDirty** flag and updates the current record if necessary. Before **UpdateRecord** is called, the procedure calls the **IsValid** procedure, setting the **blnRaiseError** parameter to **True** so that any rule violations are raised as errors in the form. The only difference between this version of **SaveRecord** and the version shown in How-To 2.1 is the call to **IsValid** and the relocation of the call to **UpdateRecord** so that it is called only if **IsValid** returns **True**.

```
Public Sub SaveRecord()
' save current changes

    ' test dirty flag
    If mblnIsDirty Then
```

```
                          ' validate, raise an error
                          ' if rules are violated
                          If IsValid(True) Then
                              ' update it
                              UpdateRecord
                          End If
                      Else
                          ' record is already clean
                      End If
                  End Sub
```

How It Works

Data validation logic is handled entirely within the `CTitles` class—no special coding is required in the form beyond the normal error handlers that trap errors and display a simple message about the error. The rules applied for validation can be as simple or as complex as the application requires.

Only minor modifications to the class were required to implement data validation. The error enumeration and the corresponding `RaiseClassError` procedure were expanded to include validation errors, the `IsValid` procedure was added to perform the validation tests, and a few lines of code were changed in the `SaveRecord` procedure.

Comments

Not all database rules require you to write code to perform data validation. The Jet database engine can enforce some—or possibly all—of your rules for using the properties of tables and fields or relational constraints. How-To 4.5 shows you how to use these objects and properties to supplement or replace validation code.

COMPLEXITY
BEGINNING

2.3 How do I...
Allow users to undo changes they've made in Data Access Objects?

Problem

Users sometimes make data entry errors while working. How can I allow users to undo changes they've made to data in unbound controls using Data Access Objects?

Technique

A few additional lines of code in the class module handling data management for your database can implement an undo feature. Because data is not updated in bound controls until you explicitly update it with your code, you can restore the original values by reloading them from the underlying recordset. The class module handles restoring the original values from the recordset and assigning them to the property values. The form only needs to read the data from the property procedures and write the property values to the controls.

Steps

Open and run the project HT203.VBP and the form shown in Figure 2.4 appears. Change the data in any control on the form, and use the Undo command on the Edit menu to restore the original value.

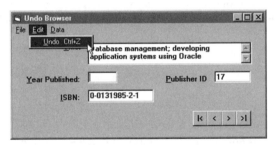

Figure 2.4. The Undo Browser form.

1. Create a new project called HT203 .VBP. This project is based on the example developed for How-To 2.1 and also includes the READINI.bas module and CTitles.cls module. Menu controls and supporting code have been added to the form developed for How-To 2.1 to support the undo operation, and a public method has been added to the class module. If you have worked through How-To 2.1, you can copy or modify your existing files. If not, refer to the steps in that example to create the foundation for this project.

2. Change the caption of Form1 to Undo Browser, and add the menu shown in Table 2.3.

Table 2.3. Menu specifications for the Edit menu.

CAPTION	NAME	SHORTCUT KEY
&Edit	mnuEdit	
----&Undo	mnuEditUndo	Ctrl+Z

> **NOTE**
>
> By convention, the Edit menu is placed to the immediate right of the File menu.

3. Add the mnuEdit_Click and mnuEditUndo_Click events to Form1. The mnuEdit_Click event checks the current record state and toggles the **enabled** property of the mnuEditUndo control based on the value of the IsDirty property of mclsTitles. The mnuEditUndo_Click procedure calls the UndoRecord method of the mclsTitles object and refreshes the form. This is the only new code in the form.

```
Private Sub mnuEdit_Click()
' enable/disable undo command based on current dirty flag
On Error GoTo ProcError

    Screen.MousePointer = vbHourglass

    ' toggle based on dirty flag
    mnuEditUndo.Enabled = mclsTitles.IsDirty

ProcExit:
    Screen.MousePointer = vbDefault
    Exit Sub

ProcError:
    MsgBox Err.Description, vbExclamation
    Resume ProcExit
End Sub

Private Sub mnuEditUndo_Click()
' undo changes
On Error GoTo ProcError

    Screen.MousePointer = vbHourglass

    ' undo changes
    mclsTitles.UndoRecord

    ' refresh the display
    GetData

ProcExit:
    Screen.MousePointer = vbDefault
    Exit Sub

ProcError:
    MsgBox Err.Description, vbExclamation
    Resume ProcExit
End Sub
```

4. Add the `UndoRecord`method to the `CTitles` class. `UndoRecord` clears the `mblnIsDirty` flag and restores the original values from the recordset to the private variables used for the property procedures by calling the `GetCurrentRecord` procedure.

```
Public Sub UndoRecord()
' clear changes and refresh properties

    ' clear dirty flag
    ' but do not clear new flag
    mblnIsDirty = False
    ' refresh the current values from the recordset
    GetCurrentRecord
End Sub
```

How It Works

Each of the property procedures that represent fields in the `CTitles` class sets the module-level `mblnIsDirty` flag. This flag is then used to toggle the **enabled** property of the Undo command on the Edit menu. When the user selects **Undo**, the form calls the `UndoRecord` method of the class and refreshes the controls on the form. The `UndoRecord` method needs only to restore the private module-level variables with the data that is still unchanged in the recordset.

Comments

The standard TextBox control supports a field level undo capability with the built-in context menu. By adding some code, you could also implement a field-level **undo** command for any field you display, regardless of the type of control that is used.

COMPLEXITY
BEGINNING

2.4 How do I...
Add and delete records by using Data Access Objects?

Problem

Viewing and editing existing records are only half of the jobs my users need to do. How do I add and delete records using unbound controls and Data Access Objects?

Technique

The recordset object provides the `AddNew` and `Delete` methods for inserting and deleting records. When you are using unbound controls on a form, adding a record is a five-step process:

1. Clear (and if necessary save) the current record so that the user can enter data for the new record.

2. Call the `AddNew` method of the recordset.

3. Write the values from the controls to the `Fields`.

4. Call the `Update` method of the recordset.

5. Restore the record pointer to the newly added record.

Deleting a record is a two-step process:

1. Call the `Delete` method of the recordset.

2. Move to a valid record and display it.

ADD AND DELETE USER INTERFACES

Microsoft Access and (if properly configured) the Data control enable users to add new records by navigating to the end of the recordset and clicking the Next Record button. Although this two-step procedure might seem obvious to most programmers and database developers, it is not at all obvious to most users. Users will be looking for something clearly labeled as a command that will give them a new record with which to work. Rather than emulate this confusing idiom, this example uses a New Record command on the Data menu.

The same reasoning applies to deleting records. Provide a clearly labeled menu command or button the user can click to perform a delete.

In short, don't aggravate your users by burying common operations with obscure procedures in the interface.

Steps

Open and run the project HT204 .VBP. To add a new record, select the Data | New Record menu command, as shown in Figure 2.5. To delete a record, choose the `Delete Record` command.

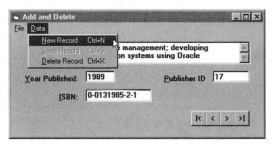

Figure 2.5. The Add and Delete form.

1. Create a new project called HT204.VBP. This project is based on the example developed for How-To 2.1. Only the changes to that project are described here. Refer to the steps in the original project for the complete details of creating the form, the `CTitles` class module, and the READINI.bas module.

2. Change the caption of `Form1` to Add and Delete, and add the New Record and Delete Record commands (shown in bold) to the Data menu, as shown in Table 2.4.

Table 2.4. Menu specifications for *Form1*.

CAPTION	NAME	SHORTCUT KEY
&File	mnuFile	
----E&xit	mnuFileExit	
&Data	mnuData	
----&New Record	**mnuDataNewRecord**	**Ctrl+N**
----&Save Record	mnuDataSaveRecord	Ctrl+S
----&Delete Record	**mnuDataDeleteRecord**	**Ctrl+X**

3. Modify the `Form_Load` event procedure to enable the user to create a new record if the table is empty when the form is initially loaded. Only the code in the error handler has changed.

```
Private Sub Form_Load()
' create the mclsTitles object and display the first record
On Error GoTo ProcError

    Dim strDBName As String

    Screen.MousePointer = vbHourglass

    ' create the CTitles object
    Set mclsTitles = New CTitles
```

```
        ' fetch and display the current record
        GetData

ProcExit:
    Screen.MousePointer = vbDefault
    Exit Sub

ProcError:
    ' An error was generated by Visual Basic or CTitles.
    ' Check for the "No Records" error and if so
    ' just provide a new record.
    Select Case Err.Number
        Case ErrNoRecords
            mclsTitles.NewRecord
            Resume Next
        Case Else
            ' Some other error
            ' Display the error message and terminate gracefully.
            MsgBox Err.Description, vbExclamation
            Unload Me
            Resume ProcExit
    End Select
End Sub
```

4. Add the event procedures for mnuData_Click and its submenu items mnuDataNewRecord_Click, mnuDataSaveRecord_Click, and mnuDataDeleteRecord_Click. The mnuData_Click event toggles the enabled flag for the mnuDataSaveRecord menu control based on the IsDirty flag of the mclsTitles object. The mnuDataNewRecord_Click event calls the NewRecord method of the mclsTitles object. The mnuDataSaveRecord_Click procedure saves the current record by calling the mclsTitles.SaveRecord method. The DeleteRecord method of mclsTitles is called by mnuDataDeleteRecord_Click. A special trap is used in the error handler. If the delete leaves the recordset empty, a new record is created.

```
Private Sub mnuData_Click()
' set enabled/disabled flags for menu commands
On Error GoTo ProcError

    Screen.MousePointer = vbHourglass

    ' save enabled only when dirty
    mnuDataSaveRecord.Enabled = mclsTitles.IsDirty

ProcExit:
    Screen.MousePointer = vbDefault
    Exit Sub

ProcError:
    MsgBox Err.Description, vbExclamation
    Resume ProcExit
End Sub
```

The mnuData_Click event procedure is unchanged from the example in How-To 2.1.

```
Private Sub mnuDataNewRecord_Click()
' set up a new record
On Error GoTo ProcError

    Screen.MousePointer = vbHourglass

    ' save existing first
    mclsTitles.SaveRecord

    ' get a new record
    mclsTitles.NewRecord

    ' refresh display
    GetData

ProcExit:
    Screen.MousePointer = vbDefault
    Exit Sub

ProcError:
    MsgBox Err.Description, vbExclamation
    Resume ProcExit
End Sub

Private Sub mnuDataSaveRecord_Click()
On Error GoTo ProcError

    Screen.MousePointer = vbHourglass

    ' save it
    mclsTitles.SaveRecord

    ' refresh display
    GetData

ProcExit:
    Screen.MousePointer = vbDefault
    Exit Sub

ProcError:
    MsgBox Err.Description, vbExclamation
    Resume ProcExit
End Sub

Private Sub mnuDataDeleteRecord_Click()
' delete the current record
On Error GoTo ProcError

    Screen.MousePointer = vbHourglass
```

```
                mclsTitles.DeleteRecord

                ' refresh display
                GetData

        ProcExit:
                Screen.MousePointer = vbDefault
                Exit Sub

        ProcError:
                Select Case Err.Number
                    Case ErrNoRecords
                        ' last record was deleted
                        ' Create a new record
                        mclsTitles.NewRecord
                        Resume Next
                    Case Else
                        ' inform
                        MsgBox Err.Description, vbExclamation
                        Resume ProcExit
                End Select
        End Sub
```

5. Revise the declarations section of **CTitles** to include the new **mblnIsNew**
flag, shown in bold in the following listing. This flag is **True** if the current
data is a new record and **False** if it is an existing record.

```
Option Explicit

' The CTitles class provides a light wrapper
' around the database and record for the
' Titles table in the Biblio database

' Note: It's up to the client to save

' Database and recordset objects
Private mdb As Database
Private mrs As Recordset

' Flags
' dirty flag
Private mblnIsDirty As Boolean
' new record flag
Private mblnIsNew As Boolean

' Fields
' title
Private mstrTitle As String
' year - note use of string for
' assignment to text box
Private mstrYearPublished As String
```

continued on next page

continued from previous page

```
' ISBN number
Private mstrISBN As String
' PubID - also a string
Private mstrPubID As String

' Move method constants
Public Enum CTitlesMove
    FirstRecord = 1
    LastRecord = 2
    NextRecord = 3
    PreviousRecord = 4
End Enum

' Error constants
' Note: RaiseClassError method provides the strings
' because you cannot assign a string to an Enum
Public Enum CTitlesError
    ErrInvalidMoveType = vbObjectError + 1000 + 11
    ErrNoRecords = vbObjectError + 1000 + 12
End Enum
```

6. Create the **AddNewRecord** method. This sub does the real work of inserting the record into the database. First the **AddNew** method is called, then the values from the properties are written to the fields, and finally the **Update** method is called to commit the changes. After a record is inserted using **AddNew** and **Update**, the current record is undefined. Setting the recordset's **Bookmark** property to the special **LastModified** bookmark restores the current record pointer to the new record.

```
Private Sub AddNewRecord()
' DAO AddNew/Update

    ' inform DAO we are going to insert
    mrs.AddNew
    ' write the current values
    mrs![ISBN] = mstrISBN
    mrs![Title] = mstrTitle
    mrs![Year Published] = mstrYearPublished
    mrs![PubID] = mstrPubID
    ' update the record
    mrs.Update
    ' return to the new record
    mrs.Bookmark = mrs.LastModified
    ' clear new flag
    mblnIsNew = False
    ' clear dirty flag
    mblnIsDirty = False
End Sub
```

7. Add the `IsNew` property. This flag indicates whether the current record is a new record (one that has not been added to the recordset) by returning the value of the private `mblnIsNew` flag.

```
Public Property Get IsNew() As Boolean
' pass out the new flag

    IsNew = mblnIsNew
End Property
```

8. Add the `NewRecord` method. This method clears the current values of the private variables used for the field properties and sets the `mblnIsNew` flag used by the `IsNew` property.

```
Public Sub NewRecord()
' clear the current values for an insert
' NOTE: the flags work so that if a new
' record is added but not changed, you
' can move off of it or close with no
' prompt to save

    ' assign zero-length strings to the properties
    mstrISBN = ""
    mstrTitle = ""
    mstrYearPublished = ""
    mstrPubID = ""
    ' set the new flag
    mblnIsNew = True
End Sub
```

9. Add the `DeleteRecord` method. `DeleteRecord` calls the `Delete` method of the recordset object and then uses the `MovePrevious` method to reset the current record to a valid record pointer. If `MovePrevious` takes the recordset to `BOF` (before the first record) a `MoveFirst` is executed.

```
Public Sub DeleteRecord()
' DAO delete

    ' delete the record
    mrs.Delete
    ' clear new and dirty flags
    mblnIsDirty = False
    mblnIsNew = False

    ' reposition to a valid record
    mrs.MovePrevious
    ' check for BOF
    If mrs.BOF Then
        ' could be empty, check EOF
        If Not mrs.EOF Then
            mrs.MoveFirst
        Else
```

continued on next page

continued from previous page

```
                    ' empty recordset, raise error
                    ' the client must decide how to
                    ' handle this situation
                    RaiseClassError ErrNoRecords
            End If
        End If

        GetCurrentRecord
    End Sub
```

10. Add the `SaveRecord` method. This method tests the `mblnIsDirty` flag and updates the current record, if necessary. If the record is new, the data is committed to the table using the `AddNewRecord` procedure. Existing records are updated using the `UpdateRecord` procedure.

```
Public Sub SaveRecord()
' save current changes

    ' test dirty flag
    If mblnIsDirty Then
        ' test new flag
        If mblnIsNew Then
            ' add it
            AddNewRecord
        Else
            ' update it
            UpdateRecord
        End If
    Else
        ' record is already clean
    End If
End Sub
```

How It Works

The `CTitles` class handles all the data processing with the database engine and provides a lightweight wrapper around the `AddNew`, `Update`, and `Delete` methods of the `Recordset` object. The form exposes these features in the user interface by providing menu commands for each data operation and handling save and error trapping logic.

Encapsulating all the recordset management logic in the class module means that all that code can be easily reused in other forms based on the same data.

Comments

A complete application might not necessarily have a one-to-one correspondence between tables and class modules. The classes should reflect the object model for the application and its data, not the database schema itself. The database underlying a complex application might have tables that are not reflected in the object model, such as tables used only for supplying lookup values to lists, or tables that are not directly represented, such as junction tables in many-to-many relationships.

COMPLEXITY
INTERMEDIATE

2.5 How do I...
Use unbound controls to update fields in Data Access Objects?

Problem

Using Data Access Objects to build data entry forms with unbound controls works well in most situations, but sometimes the data is difficult for the user to work with. I need to extend the user interface of my application to provide alternative methods of finding and choosing records.

Technique

The nature of database applications is that users must often deal with less-than-obvious values, such as foreign keys and coded data. Instead of forcing the user to remember arbitrary key values and data codes, you can alter the user interface to provide lists of values rather than simple text boxes.

> **NOTE**
> Chapter 4, "Designing and Implementing a Database," discusses foreign keys and table relationships.

Foreign key values can represent a special problem because the lookup tables for the keys are often quite large. Populating a list with all the available values can seriously damage the performance of the application. Additionally, because this is such a common operation, a generic tool for working with this type of data saves significant coding effort.

Using a simple form and a ListView control, you can build a generic tool that can display the results of an ad hoc query and return a key value for the record selected by the user.

Steps

Open and run the project HT205.VBP. Select Data|Find Publisher and enter SAMs. Click OK to display the results. The form shown in Figure 2.6 appears.

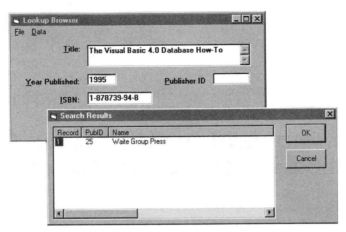

Figure 2.6. The Lookup Browser form.

1. Create a new project called HT205 .VBP. This example extends the project developed for How-To 2.1 to provide a means for the user to search for an identifier value for a publisher. Refer to the steps in How-To 2.1 for complete details on building the base application. Only the changes to the original project are shown in the steps that follow.

2. Change the caption of Form1 to Lookup Browser. Modify the Data menu as shown in Table 2.5, adding the Find Publisher command (shown in bold).

Table 2.5. Menu specifications for *Form1*.

CAPTION	NAME	SHORTCUT KEY
&File	mnuFile	
----E&xit	mnuFileExit	
&Data	mnuData	
----&Save Record	mnuDataSaveRecord	Ctrl+S
----&Find Publisher	**mnuDataFindPublisher**	**Ctrl+F**

3. Add the following code to Form1 as the mnuDataFindPublisher_Click event. This event uses an input box and the FSearchResults form to build and display the results of an ad hoc query. The user is prompted to enter all or part of the name of a publisher. The value entered is used to build a SQL statement that is passed to the FSearchResults form. The FSearchResults form handles the balance of the selection process and sets its KeyValue property before it returns control to the mnuDataFindPublisher_Click event.

```
Private Sub mnuDataFindPublisher_Click()
' Use the FSearchResults form to find a pub id
On Error GoTo ProcError

    Dim strPrompt As String
    Dim strInput As String
    Dim strSQL As String
    Dim fSearch As FSearchResults

    strPrompt = "Enter all or the beginning of _
                "the publisher name:"
    strInput = InputBox$(strPrompt, "Search for Publishers")
    If strInput <> "" Then
        ' search
        strSQL = "SELECT * FROM Publishers " & _
            "WHERE Name LIKE '" & strInput & "*';"
        Set fSearch = New FSearchResults
        ' Note: Search method does not return
        ' until the user dismisses the form
        fSearch.Search "PubID", strSQL, Me
        If Not fSearch.Cancelled Then
            txt(txtPubID).Text = fSearch.KeyValue
        End If
    End If

ProcExit:
    ' release the search form reference
    Set fSearch = Nothing
    Exit Sub

ProcError:
    MsgBox Err.Description, vbExclamation
    Resume ProcExit
End Sub
```

4. Create a new form, name it **FSearchResults**, and save the form. Table 2.6 shows the objects and properties for the form.

Table 2.6. Objects and properties for the *FSearchResults* form.

OBJECT	PROPERTY	VALUE
ListView	Name	lvwResults
	View	3 - lvwReport
	LabelEdit	1 - lvwManual
CommandButton	Name	cmd
	Index	0
	Caption	OK
	Default	True

continued on next page

continued from previous page

OBJECT	PROPERTY	VALUE
CommandButton	Name	cmd
	Index	1
	Caption	Cancel
	Cancel	True

5. Add the following code to the declarations section of **FSearchResults**. The two constants are used for the index to the CommandButton control array. The **mblnCancelled** flag is used to indicate that the user chose the Cancel button. The **mvntKeyValue** holds the value (typically the primary key field, but any field can be specified when the **Search** method is called) for the key field. The **mintItemIdx** holds the index into the **SubItems** collection of the ListView control for the key value.

```
Option Explicit

' This form will run an ad hoc query and
' display the results in the list view control

' command button array constants
Const cmdOK = 0
Const cmdCancel = 1

' cancel property
Private mblnCancelled As Boolean
' selected key value
Private mvntKeyValue As Variant
' subitem index for key value
Private mintItemIdx As Integer
```

6. Add the **cmd_Click** event procedure for the CommandButton control array. This event procedure sets the private flag indicating whether the user chose OK or Cancel and hides the form. Because the form is displayed modally, control returns to whatever procedure created the form after this procedure exits.

```
Private Sub cmd_Click(Index As Integer)

    If Index = cmdOK Then
        mblnCancelled = False
    Else
        mblnCancelled = True
    End If

    Me.Hide
End Sub
```

7. Add the `lvwResults_ItemClick` event procedure. When Visual Basic fires the `ItemClick` event for a ListView control, it passes the clicked `ListItem` object as a parameter. The `mintItemIdx` variable set by the `Search` method is used to retrieve the value of the key field from the `SubItems` collection and assign it to the `mvntKeyValue` variable, where it can be read by the `KeyValue` property procedure.

```
Private Sub lvwResults_ItemClick(ByVal Item As ComctlLib.ListItem)
On Error GoTo ProcError

    mvntKeyValue = Item.SubItems(mintItemIdx)

ProcExit:
    Exit Sub

ProcError:
    MsgBox Err.Description, vbExclamation
    Resume ProcExit
End Sub
```

8. Add the `Cancelled` and `KeyValue` property procedures. Each procedure returns the values assigned to the module-level variables. These properties are checked by the procedure that created the instance of the form to see what button the user chose and the key value of the record selected.

```
Public Property Get Cancelled()
    Cancelled = mblnCancelled
End Property

Public Property Get KeyValue() As Variant
    KeyValue = mvntKeyValue
End Property
```

9. Add the following code to `FSearchResults` as the `Search` method. The method takes three parameters: a key field name used to return a value in the `KeyValue` property, a SQL statement used to create the list of results, and a parent form reference used by the `Show` method. The method builds the results list by first creating a recordset object based on the SQL statement provided. If there are records to display, it iterates the `Fields` collection of the recordset to generate a set of column headers for `lvwResults` (determining the index of the key field in the process). After the column headers for the list have been created, the method enters a `Do` loop and iterates the records in the recordset. For each record, the fields are iterated and their values are placed into the appropriate `SubItem` of the ListView. In addition to the list of fields, the `lvwResults` ListView control shows the ordinal position in the results for each record.

```vb
Public Sub Search( _
    strKeyField As String, _
    strSQLStatement As String, _
    frmParent As Form)
' run the specified query and populate the
' listview with the results

    Dim strDBName As String
    Dim lngOrdRecPos As Long
    Dim db As Database
    Dim rs As Recordset
    Dim fld As Field

    strDBName = BiblioPath()
    Set db = DBEngine(0).OpenDatabase(strDBName)
    Set rs = db.OpenRecordset(strSQLStatement, _
        dbOpenDynaset, dbReadOnly)

    ' test for no records
    If Not rs.EOF Then
        ' create the ordinal position column
        lvwResults.ColumnHeaders.Add , "Ordinal", "Record"
        ' set width
        lvwResults.ColumnHeaders("Ordinal").Width = 600
        ' create the columns in the listview
        For Each fld In rs.Fields
            lvwResults.ColumnHeaders.Add , fld.Name, fld.Name
            ' best guess column width
            lvwResults.ColumnHeaders(fld.Name).Width _
                = 150 * Len(fld.Name)
            If fld.Name = strKeyField Then
                ' mark the item index for later retrieval
                mintItemIdx = fld.OrdinalPosition + 1
            End If
        Next    ' field
        ' populate the list
        Do
            ' increment the ordinal position counter
            lngOrdRecPos = lngOrdRecPos + 1
            ' add the item
            lvwResults.ListItems.Add _
                lngOrdRecPos, , CStr(lngOrdRecPos)
            ' add the fields to the rest of the columns
            For Each fld In rs.Fields
                lvwResults.ListItems(lngOrdRecPos). _
                SubItems(fld.OrdinalPosition + 1) = _
                fld.Value & ""
            Next    ' field
            ' go to next record
            rs.MoveNext
        Loop While Not rs.EOF
        ' clean up
        rs.Close
        Set rs = Nothing
```

```
            db.Close
            Set db = Nothing

            ' show modally
            Me.Show vbModal, frmParent
        Else
            ' no data, treat as a cancel
            mblnCancelled = True
            MsgBox "No matching records found.", vbInformation
            Me.Hide
        End If
    End Sub
```

How It Works

The **FSearchResults** form provides a generic tool for running an ad hoc query, displaying its results, and returning a key value selected by the user. The benefit of using a generic search form is that the form can be easily reused in any situation in which this type of lookup is required. This form can be added with minimal impact on the original design or performance of the main data entry form, but it still provides the user with a more advanced method of entering the **PubID** foreign key field.

The form works by filling a ListView control using a completely generic population routine in the **Search** method. When the user selects a record and dismisses the form by clicking OK, a private module-level variable retains the selected item, which can then be read from the **KeyValue** property.

Comments

Over time, you might build a significant library of generic components such as this lookup form. If the tools are properly designed and not coupled too tightly to any particular application or database, you might be able to bundle them together in an ActiveX DLL, which can then be included in future applications without having to return to the source code.

COMPLEXITY
BEGINNING

2.6 How do I...
Find records by using index values in Data Access Objects?

Problem

I know that indexes can be used to speed up database operations. How can I take advantage of indexes in my application?

Technique

When a table-type recordset has a current index (either the primary key or another index you have designated), you can use the `Seek` method to find records based on the indexed values. To use the `Seek` method, provide it with an argument that matches each field in the index. When the `Seek` method executes, if it finds at least one record matching the index values, it positions the record pointer to the first matching record and sets the `NoMatch` property of the recordset to `False`. If `Seek` does not find a matching record, it sets the `NoMatch` property to `True`; the current record is then undefined, which means that you can't be sure where the record pointer is pointing.

When you use `Seek`, specify not only the values for the key index fields but also the comparison criterion that `Seek` is to use. You provide the comparison criterion as the first argument to the `Seek` method, and you provide it as a string value. In the majority of cases, you will specify that `Seek` is to match the index value exactly; you do this by specifying a comparison criterion of =. You can also specify < > for not equal, > for greater than, < for less than, >= for greater than or equal to, or <= for less than or equal to.

Steps

Open and run the project HT206.VBP. Use the Index command on the Data menu to select the ISBN index. Browse forward in the recordset a few records, and copy the ISBN number from the form to the clipboard. Using the MoveFirst button, return to the first record; then select Data|Seek to display the input box shown in Figure 2.7. Paste the value you copied into the input box, and click OK. The record with the matching ISBN number is displayed.

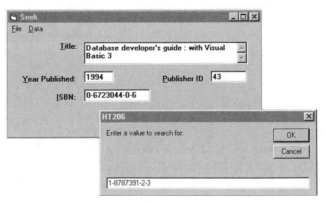

Figure 2.7. The Seek form.

1. Create a new project called HT206 .VBP. This example adds the capability to find records using the **Seek** method to the basic browser application developed in How-To 2.1. The form and class module contain minor changes and some added code to support the **Seek** operation. The READINI.bas module is unchanged. Only the code that has been added or modified for this project is shown in the steps that follow.

2. Change the caption of **Form1** to Seek, and modify the Data menu as shown in Table 2.7. The Index command, its submenu items, and the Seek command (all shown in bold) are new in this project.

Table 2.7. Menu specifications for Form1.

CAPTION	NAME	SHORTCUT KEY
&File	mnuFile	
----E&xit	mnuFileExit	
&Data	mnuData	
----&Save Record	mnuDataSaveRecord	Ctrl+S
----&Index	mnuDataIndex	
--------&ISBN	mnuDataIndexName	
--------&Title	mnuDataIndexName	
----S&eek	mnuDataSeek	

3. Modify the declarations section of **Form1** as shown. Index constants have been added for the **mnuDataIndexName** control array.

```
Option Explicit

' CTitles object
Private mclsTitles As CTitles

' These constants are used for the various control arrays
' command button constants
Const cmdMoveFirst = 0
Const cmdMovePrevious = 1
Const cmdMoveNext = 2
Const cmdMoveLast = 3
' text box index constants
Const txtTitle = 0
Const txtYearPublished = 1
Const txtISBN = 2
Const txtPubID = 3

' index constants
Const idxISBN = 0
Const idxTitle = 1

' refresh flag
Private mblnInRefresh As Boolean
```

4. Modify the mnuData_Click event procedure to toggle the enabled flag for the mnuDataSeek menu control if an index has been chosen.

```
Private Sub mnuData_Click()
' set enabled/disabled flags for menu commands
On Error GoTo ProcError

    Screen.MousePointer = vbHourglass

    ' seek enabled only if index is set
    If Len(mclsTitles.IndexName) Then
        mnuDataSeek.Enabled = True
    Else
        mnuDataSeek.Enabled = False
    End If

ProcExit:
    Screen.MousePointer = vbDefault
    Exit Sub

ProcError:
    MsgBox Err.Description, vbExclamation
    Resume ProcExit

End Sub
```

5. Add the following code to Form1 as the mnuDataIndexName_Click and mnuDataSeek_Click events. The mnuDataIndexName_Click procedure assigns the index to use for the Seek operation and manages the check marks on the menu. The mnuDataSeek_Click procedure prompts the user for search criteria and attempts to locate the value provided by calling the Seek method of mclsTitles.

```
Private Sub mnuDataIndexName_Click(Index As Integer)
' set the current index
On Error GoTo ProcError

    Screen.MousePointer = vbHourglass

    ' set the index
    Select Case Index
        Case idxISBN
            ' assign the index
            mclsTitles.Index = IndexISBN
            ' set up menu check marks
            mnuDataIndexName(idxTitle).Checked = False
            mnuDataIndexName(idxISBN).Checked = True
        Case idxTitle
            ' assign the index
            mclsTitles.Index = IndexTitle
            ' set up menu check marks
```

```
                    mnuDataIndexName(idxTitle).Checked = True
                    mnuDataIndexName(idxISBN).Checked = False
            End Select

            ' refresh display
            GetData

    ProcExit:
            Screen.MousePointer = vbDefault
            Exit Sub

    ProcError:
            MsgBox Err.Description, vbExclamation
            Resume ProcExit

    End Sub

    Private Sub mnuDataSeek_Click()
    ' seek a record
    On Error GoTo ProcError

            Dim strMsg As String
            Dim strResult As String

            Screen.MousePointer = vbHourglass

            ' prompt for a value
            strMsg = "Enter a value to search for:"
            strResult = InputBox$(strMsg)

            ' seek for the record
            mclsTitles.SeekRecord strResult

            ' refresh display
            GetData

    ProcExit:
            Screen.MousePointer = vbDefault
            Exit Sub

    ProcError:
            MsgBox Err.Description, vbExclamation
            Resume ProcExit

    End Sub
```

6. Modify the declarations section of the **CTitles** class to include the new enumeration for the index and to modify the error enumeration for new error messages.

```
Option Explicit

' The CTitles class provides a light wrapper
' around the database and record for the
' Titles table in the Biblio database

' Database and recordset objects
Private mdb As Database
Private mrs As Recordset

' Fields
' title
Private mstrTitle As String
' year - note use of string for
' assignment to text box
Private mstrYearPublished As String
' ISBN number
Private mstrISBN As String
' PubID - also a string
Private mstrPubID As String

' Move method constants
Public Enum CTitlesMove
    FirstRecord = 1
    LastRecord = 2
    NextRecord = 3
    PreviousRecord = 4
End Enum

' Index constants
Public Enum CTitlesIndex
    IndexISBN = 0
    IndexTitle = 1
End Enum

' Error constants
' Note: RaiseClassError method provides the strings
' because you cannot assign a string to an Enum
Public Enum CTitlesError
    ErrRecordNotFound = vbObjectError + 1000 + 10
    ErrInvalidMoveType = vbObjectError + 1000 + 11
    ErrNoRecords = vbObjectError + 1000 + 12
    ErrInvalidIndex = vbObjectError + 1000 + 13
End Enum
```

7. Change the `Class_Initialize` procedure so that a table-type recordset is created rather than a dynaset-type recordset. Only the table-type recordset supports the `Seek` method. The only thing required to change to a table-type recordset is to change the `dbOpenDynaset` constant to `dbOpenTable`.

```
Private Sub Class_Initialize()

    ' open the database and recordset

    Dim strDBName As String

    ' Get the database name and open the database.
    ' BiblioPath is a function in READINI.BAS
    strDBName = BiblioPath()
    Set mdb = DBEngine.Workspaces(0).OpenDatabase(strDBName)

    ' Open the recordset.
    Set mrs = mdb.OpenRecordset( _
        "Titles", dbOpenTable, dbSeeChanges, dbOptimistic)

    ' Raise an error if there is no data
    If mrs.BOF Then
        RaiseClassError ErrNoRecords
    End If

    ' fetch the first record to the properties
    GetCurrentRecord

End Sub
```

8. The `RaiseClassError` procedure has had new sections added to the `Select...Case` block for the newly added errors.

```
Private Sub RaiseClassError(lngErrorNumber As CTitlesError)
' Note: DAO errors are passed out as-is

    Dim strDescription As String
    Dim strSource As String

    ' assign the description for the error
    Select Case lngErrorNumber
        Case ErrRecordNotFound
            strDescription = "The record was not found."
        Case ErrInvalidMoveType
            strDescription = "Invalid move operation."
        Case ErrNoRecords
            strDescription = "There are no records " _
                & "in the Titles table."
        Case ErrInvalidIndex
            strDescription = "Invalid Index Name."
        Case Else
            ' If this executes, it's a coding error in
            ' the class module, but having the case is
            ' useful for debugging.
```

continued on next page

continued from previous page

```
                    strDescription = "There is no message for this error."
        End Select

        ' build the Source property for the error
        strSource = App.EXEName & ".CTitles"

        ' raise it
        Err.Raise lngErrorNumber, strSource, strDescription
End Sub
```

9. Add the `IndexName` and `Index` properties. The `IndexName` property is used to determine the current index for the recordset. The `Index` property changes the index based on the value provided in the `lngIndex` parameter.

```
Public Property Get IndexName() As String
    IndexName = mrs.Index
End Property

Public Property Let Index(lngIndex As CTitlesIndex)
' unlike the field values, this is validated when assigned
    Dim vntBookmark As Variant

    ' save a bookmark
    vntBookmark = mrs.Bookmark
    ' assign the index
    Select Case lngIndex
        Case IndexISBN
            mrs.Index = "PrimaryKey"
        Case IndexTitle
            mrs.Index = "Title"
        Case Else
            ' invalid, raise an error
            RaiseClassError ErrInvalidIndex
    End Select

    ' return to old record
    mrs.Bookmark = vntBookmark
End Property
```

10. Add the `SeekRecord` method. This method stores a bookmark and seeks for the value passed in the `strValue` parameter. If a matching record is found, it is fetched. If no matching record is found, the saved bookmark is used to restore the record pointer to the original position.

```
Public Sub SeekRecord(strValue As String)
' seek to the indicated record based on the current index

    Dim vntBookmark As Variant
```

```
    ' mark the current record
    vntBookmark = mrs.Bookmark
    ' seek, the first operator is the comparison,
    ' the following represent the field(s) in the index
    mrs.Seek "=", strValue
    ' check for match
    If Not mrs.NoMatch Then
        ' found it, now fetch it
        GetCurrentRecord
    Else
        ' not found, return to prior location
        mrs.Bookmark = vntBookmark
        ' raise the not found error
        RaiseClassError ErrRecordNotFound
    End If
End Sub
```

How It Works

The **Seek** method takes two or more parameters. The first parameter specifies the comparison operator (normally =), and the following parameters are the values for the fields in the index. The **Index Property Let** procedure in the **CTitles** class enables you to assign the current index for the recordset, and **SeekRecord** searches for a value. Both procedures use bookmarks to store records and, if necessary, return to the original record.

Comments

You cannot set indexes or use the **Seek** method with dynaset- or snapshot-type **Recordset** objects. To find a record in a dynaset or snapshot recordset, use one of the **Find** methods: **FindFirst**, **FindNext**, **FindPrevious**, or **FindLast**. Because these methods do not use indexes, they are much slower than **Seek** operations with table-type recordsets. You also cannot use **Seek** on remote server tables because these cannot be opened as table-type recordsets.

In most cases, it is much faster to create a new dynaset- or snapshot-type recordset than to use either a **Find** or the **Seek** method. You do this by building a SQL statement that includes a **WHERE** clause specifying the records you want to retrieve. If the database engine can find a useful index for the query, it uses that index to speed up the query.

See Chapter 3, "Creating Queries with SQL," for details on creating SQL statements, and Chapter 4, "Designing and Implementing a Database," for more information on choosing and defining indexes.

COMPLEXITY
BEGINNING

2.7 How do I...
Determine how many records are in a dynaset- or snapshot-type recordset?

Problem

I need to know how many records are in a recordset I've created. For table-type recordsets, this is easy—I just use the value of the RecordCount property. But when I try this with a dynaset- or snapshot-type recordset, I can't predict what value will be returned. Sometimes it's the correct count, while other times it's not. How can I reliably determine the number of records in a dynaset- or snapshot-type recordset?

Technique

The system tables in a Microsoft Access database include information about the number of records in every table in the database. As records are added or deleted, the table is continuously updated by the Jet engine. You can determine the number of records in the table at any time by checking the RecordCount property of the TableDef. Unlike a table, dynaset- and snapshot-type recordsets are temporary recordsets. You can't obtain a record count by checking a TableDef.

You can retrieve the RecordCount property of a dynaset- or snapshot-type recordset, but the value it returns depends on several factors in addition to the number of records actually in the recordset. The only way the Jet engine can determine how many records are in a dynaset- or snapshot-type recordset is by counting them. To count them, the Jet engine has to move through the records, one by one, until it reaches the end of the recordset. When the Jet engine creates a dynaset- or snapshot-type recordset, however, it does not automatically count the records because counting the records in a large recordset could take a long time. If you retrieve the RecordCount property immediately after you create a dynaset- or snapshot-type recordset, therefore, you're guaranteed to get back one of two values: 0 if the recordset is empty or 1 if the recordset has at least one record.

To get an accurate count, your code must tell the Jet engine to count the records. Do this by executing the recordset's MoveLast method. After a MoveLast, you can retrieve the RecordCount with the confidence that the value is accurate. In the case of a dynaset-type recordset, if you add or delete records, the Jet engine keeps track of them for you, and any subsequent looks at RecordCount will give you the correct current count.

Steps

Open and run the project HT207.VBP. You will see the form shown in Figure 2.8. This form shows the number of records in the BIBLIO.MDB Authors table. The first box reports the number of records reported immediately after Authors is opened as a table-type recordset. The second box shows the number of records reported immediately after a dynaset is opened with the SQL statement SELECT Au_ID FROM Authors—a statement that returns a dynaset consisting of the entire table, the same set of records that are in the table-type recordset reported in the first box. The third box shows the record count from the dynaset after its MoveLast method has been used. Note that the first and third boxes have the same number (which might be different on your system) The second box, reporting the dynaset record count before the MoveLast, shows a count of 1.

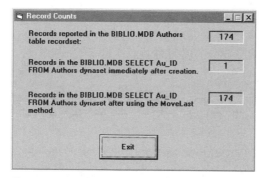

Figure 2.8. The Record Counts form.

1. Create a new project called HT207 .VBP. Create the objects and properties listed in Table 2.8, and save the form as HT207.FRM.

Table 2.8. Objects and properties for *Form1*.

OBJECT	PROPERTY	SETTING
Form	Name	Form1
	Caption	Record Counter
CommandButton	Name	cmdExit
	Cancel	True
	Default	True
	Caption	Exit
Label	Name	lblTable
	Alignment	2 (Center)
	BorderStyle	1 (Fixed Single)

continued on next page

continued from previous page

OBJECT	PROPERTY	SETTING
Label	Name	lblDynasetCreate
	Alignment	2 (Center)
	BorderStyle	1 (Fixed Single)
Label	Name	lblDynasetMoved
	Alignment	2 (Center)
	BorderStyle	1 (Fixed Single)
Label	Name	Label1
	Caption	Records reported in the
		BIBLIO.MDB Authors table
		recordset:
Label	Name	Label2
	Caption	Records in the BIBLIO.MDB SELECT
		Au_ID FROM Authors dynaset
		immediately after creation.
Label	Name	Label3
	Caption	Records in the BIBLIO.MDB SELECT
		Au_ID FROM Authors dynaset after
		using the MoveLast method.

2. Add READINI.BAS to your project.

3. Add the **Form_Load** event procedure. **Form_Load** opens the database, opens table and dynaset recordsets, and gets record counts for both recordsets. It then uses **MoveLast** to go to the end of the dynaset and gets the record count again. Finally, **Form Load** inserts each of the record counts into Label controls on the form.

```
Private Sub Form_Load()
On Error GoTo ProcError

    Dim strDBName As String
    Dim strSQL As String
    Dim db As Database
    Dim rsTable As Recordset
    Dim rsDynaset As Recordset

    ' Get the database name and open the database.
    ' BiblioPath is a function in READINI.BAS
    strDBName = BiblioPath()

    Set db = DBEngine.Workspaces(0).OpenDatabase(strDBName)
    Set rsTable = db.OpenRecordset("Authors", dbOpenTable)
    lblTable = rsTable.RecordCount

    strSQL = "SELECT Au_ID FROM Authors"
    Set rsDynaset = db.OpenRecordset(strSQL, dbOpenDynaset)
```

```
        lblDynasetCreate = rsDynaset.RecordCount
        rsDynaset.MoveLast
        lblDynasetMoved = rsDynaset.RecordCount

ProcExit:
    On Error Resume Next
    ' clean up
    rsDynaset.Close
    rsTable.Close
    db.Close
    Exit Sub

ProcError:
    MsgBox Err.Description
    Resume ProcExit
End Sub
```

4. Insert the following code as the `Click` event of `cmdExit`:

```
Private Sub cmdExit_Click()
    Unload Me
End Sub
```

How It Works

The table-type recordset enables you to check the `RecordCount` property immediately after it is created, but with a snapshot- or dynaset-type recordset, you must first access all the records before you can obtain an accurate count. This is typically done via the `MoveLast` method.

Comments

One common reason for wanting an accurate record count is to use the count as the control for a `For...Next` loop to cycle through the entire recordset, as in this code fragment:

```
myRecordset.MoveLast
n = myRecordset.RecordCount
myRecordset.MoveFirst
for i = 1 to n
    ' do something
    myRecordset.MoveNext
next i
```

The difficulties with getting and keeping accurate record counts make it inadvisable to use code like this—especially in shared data environments where the record count of a table can change the instant after you retrieve it. This fragment illustrates a more reliable way to accomplish the same goal:

```
myRecordset.MoveFirst
Do While Not myRecordset.EOF
    ' do something
    myRecordset.MoveNext
Loop
```

This loop executes until the last record in the recordset has been processed (when `myRecordset.EOF` becomes `True`), and it does not depend on a potentially unstable record count.

COMPLEXITY
INTERMEDIATE

2.8 How do I...
Handle Data Access Object errors?

Problem

When I access a database through Visual Basic, I have limited control over the environment. A user might move a database file, or another program might have made unexpected changes to the database. I need my programs to be able to detect errors that occur and handle them in the context of the program. How do I accomplish this task with Visual Basic?

Technique

When an error occurs in a Visual Basic program, control passes to error-handling logic. Unless you have enabled an error handler, Visual Basic uses its default handler, which displays a message about the error—one that is sometimes useful, but often not—and terminates the application.

Clearly, the default handling is not acceptable. Fortunately, Visual Basic provides tools that you can use to build your own error traps and handlers. Although any Visual Basic application should trap and handle runtime errors, it is especially important in database applications in which many error conditions can be expected to occur. Visual Basic error-trapping is enabled with the `On Error` statement. The `On Error` statement takes two basic forms:

```
On Error Goto label
```

```
On Error Resume Next
```

In the first form, when a runtime error occurs, Visual Basic transfers control of the application to the location specified by *label*. In the second form, Visual Basic continues execution with the line following the line in which the error occurred. When an error trap is enabled and an error occurs, Visual Basic performs the action indicated by the most recent `On Error` statement in the execution path. Listing 2.1 shows a hypothetical call tree and several variations of how error handlers are enabled and activated.

Listing 2.1. Trapping errors.

```
Sub SubA()

    ...other code
    SubB
```

```
End Sub

Sub SubB()
On Error Goto ProcError

  SubC

ProcExit:
    Exit Sub

ProcError:
    MsgBox "Error: " & Err.Number & vbCrLf & Err.Description
    Resume ProcExit

End Sub

SubC

    ...other code
    SubD

End Sub

SubD()
On Error Resume Next

    ...code

End Sub
```

Understanding the path of execution in this code fragment is important to comprehending how error handlers are activated:

✔ In SubA no error handler exists. If an error occurs before the call to SubB, Visual Basic's default handler displays a message and terminates the application.

✔ SubB uses the On Error Goto form. If an error occurs in this routine, control is transferred to the statement following the ProcError label.

✔ SubC has no error handler. However, when it is called from SubB, the error handler in SubB is still enabled, so an error in SubC also transfers control to the statement following the ProcError label in SubB.

✔ SubD uses the On Error Resume Next form. If an error occurs in this procedure, code within the procedure needs to detect and handle the error.

WARNING

Errors in Class_Terminate events and most form and control events are fatal to your application if untrapped, so it is especially important that you include error-handling logic in these procedures.

Errors generated by Visual Basic and by components of an application—including the Jet database engine—are associated with error numbers. You can obtain the error number, which tells you the nature of the error, by reading the **Number** property of the **Err** object. You can read additional information about the error from the **Description** property. After you know the type of error, you can take appropriate action to handle it. This is typically done with a **Select Case** block.

NOTE

For backward compatibility, Visual Basic still supports the outdated Err and Error statements and functions. However, any new code should use the Err object.

The code fragment in Listing 2.2 illustrates how you might handle some common errors that occur in a multiuser environment. (See Chapter 11, "The Windows Registry and State Information," for a complete discussion of working with a multiuser database application.)

Listing 2.2. Error handling.

```
Sub DAOCode()
On Error Goto ProcError

    ...code

ProcExit:
    Exit Sub

ProcError
    Dim strMsg As String
    Select Case Err.Number
        Case 3197
            ' Another user changed the data since the last time
            ' the recordset was updated
            strMsg = "The data in this record was changed by " & _
                "another user." & _
                vbCrLf & "Do you want to overwrite those changes?"
            If MsgBox(strMsg, vbYesNo or vbQuestion or vbDefaultButton2) _
                = vbYes Then
                ' VB only generates the error on the first attempt
                ' Resume re-executes the line that caused the error
                Resume
        Else
                ' refresh the existing data
                rs.Requery
                DisplayData
                Resume ProcExit
            End If
        Case 3260
            ' locked by another user
            strMsg = "The record is currently locked by another user."
            ' control continues at end of block
```

```
        Case Else
            ' default
            strMsg = "Error: " & Err.Number & vbCrLf & Err.Description
    End Select

    MsgBox strMsg, vbExclamation

    Resume ProcExit
End Sub
```

An error handler must execute a statement that clears the error. Table 2.9 list the methods of clearing an error.

Table 2.9. Statements that clear an error.

STATEMENT	EFFECT
Resume	Re-executes the line that generated the error
Resume Next	Resumes execution at the line that follows the line that generated the error
Resume label	Resumes execution at the line following the named label
Resume number	Resumes execution at the line with the indicated number
Exit Sub	Exits immediately from the current subroutine
Exit Function	Exits immediately from the current function
Exit Property	Exits immediately from the current property
On Error	Resets error-handling logic
Err.Clear	Clears the error without otherwise affecting program execution
End	Terminates execution of the program

ERRORS IN CLASS MODULES

It is good programming practice to separate data management code in class modules from user interface code in forms. To maintain this separation, it is important that you do not simply display a message if an error occurs in a class module. Two types of error situations can occur in a class module.

A class can detect an error condition (such as the violation of a validation rule). In this case, the class module should call the Raise method of the Err object and set the Number, Description, Source, and—if a help file is available—the appropriate help properties.

A class can also trap errors raised by the database engine. These can be much more difficult to handle. The sheer number of possible errors makes it impractical in most applications to reassign and describe these errors, so most applications simply regenerate them.

In either case, the code in the class module should, if possible, attempt to correct the error before raising it.

Steps

Open and run the project HT208.VBP. Three errors will occur in succession. For each, the message reporting the error gives you the error number, error description, and line number where the error occurred. Figure 2.9 shows the first of these errors.

Figure 2.9. The HT208 error message.

1. Create a new project called HT208.VBP. Use **Form1** to create the objects and properties listed in Table 2.10, and save the form as HT208.FRM.

Table 2.10. Objects and properties for *Form1*.

OBJECT	PROPERTY	SETTING
Form	Name	Form1
	Caption	Errors

2. Add the file READINI.BAS to your project.

3. Add the following code as the **Load** event of **Form1**. This code generates three errors. Line 20 generates an error because there is no such table as **No Such Table**. Line 40 generates an error because there is no such field as **No Such Field**. Line 60 generates an error because the **Year Published** field requires a numeric value. Each error causes execution to branch to the label **LoadError**. The code beginning with **LoadError** displays an informative message and then executes a **Resume Next**. The **Resume Next** transfers execution back to the line following the line that caused the error.

```
Private Sub Form_Load()
On Error GoTo ProcError

    Dim db As Database
    Dim dbName As String
    Dim rs As Recordset
    Dim s As String

    ' Get the database name and open the database.
    ' BiblioPath is a function in READINI.BAS
  5 dbName = BiblioPath()
```

```
10   Set db = DBEngine.Workspaces(0).OpenDatabase(dbName)

20   Set rs = db.OpenRecordset("No Such Table", dbOpenTable)
30   Set rs = db.OpenRecordset("Titles", dbOpenTable)
40   s = rs![No Such Field]
50   rs.Edit
60   rs![Year Published] = "XYZ"
70   rs.Update
80   End
Exit Sub

ProcError:
    MsgBox "Error: " & Err.Number & vbCrLf & _
        "Line: " & Erl & vbCrLf & _
        Err.Description, vbExclamation
Resume Next
End Sub
```

NOTE

Line numbers are used here to help illustrate the error handler.
Few programmers actually use them in production code, although
they can be helpful for debugging.

How It Works

When Visual Basic encounters a runtime error, it transfers control of the
application to the error-handling code you specify by using the `On Error`
statement. You have a choice of inline handling using `On Error Resume Next` or
centralized handling using `On Error Goto`. Either way, it's up to you to
determine the type of error generated and the appropriate action to take for that
error.

ERRORS COLLECTION

It is possible for a single statement in DAO code to generate
several errors. You can examine these errors by iterating the DAO
Errors collection, as shown in the following code fragment:

```
For Each Error In Errors
    Debug.Print Err.Number & " - " & Err.Description
Next ' Error
```

Comments

Hundreds of potential runtime errors can occur in a Visual Basic application,
and you are unlikely to be able to anticipate all of them. With experience and
careful coding, you can be prepared for the most common problems, but you
should expect that from time to time your application will encounter a situation
for which you did not explicitly plan. In this situation it is important for your

general error-handling code to offer as much information as possible to the user and to provide the opportunity to correct the problem.

You might also find it useful to write errors to a log file. Examining an error log provides you with information you can use to build more robust error-handling procedures.

COMPLEXITY
INTERMEDIATE

2.9 How do I...
Access Excel worksheets by using Data Access Objects?

Problem

I have Excel worksheets that my company created. I need to incorporate this data into my own applications. I want to both display and manipulate the data from these Excel worksheets. How do I work with these Excel files in my Visual Basic projects?

Technique

By using the Microsoft Jet engine, you can access Excel worksheets as if they were actually Access databases. As with accessing other types of ISAM files with the Jet engine, there are a few restrictions with accessing Excel worksheets:

✔ You cannot delete rows.

✔ You cannot delete or modify cells that contain formulas.

✔ You cannot create indexes.

✔ You cannot read encrypted Excel files, even when using the correct password (**PWD** parameter) in the **Connect** string.

You can add records to a worksheet or edit standard cells (those without formulas).

When opening an ISAM database with the **OpenDatabase** method, you must provide a valid ISAM type. In addition to this, if you want to use the first row of the Excel document as field names, you can specify a parameter **HDR** equal to **Yes**. (**HDR** stands for header.) If you set **HDR** to **No**, the first row of the Excel worksheet is included as a record in the recordset, as in this example:

```
Set db = DBEngine.Workspaces(0).OpenDatabase("C:\VB6DBHT\" & _
                          "CHAPTER02\HowTo09\WidgetOrders.XLS", _
                          False, False, "Excel 8.0; HDR=NO;")
```

Notice that when accessing Excel worksheets, unlike with other ISAM formats, you must specify the filename in the **OpenDatabase** method.

When opening a recordset from an Excel ISAM, you must specify the sheet name as the recordset name, followed by a dollar sign ($), as in this example:

```
WorkSheetName = "Sheet1"
Set rs = db.OpenRecordset(WorkSheetName & "$", dbOpenTable)
```

Here, **rs** is a recordset variable.

Steps

Open and run the ExcelDAO project. You should see a form that looks like the one shown in Figure 2.10. This application enables you to view a Microsoft Excel worksheet file in a ListView control. If you click the Add or Edit buttons, the form expands so that you can edit the contents. Clicking OK or Cancel when editing a record either saves or discards your changes, respectively. By clicking the View in Excel button, you can view the worksheet in Microsoft Excel (assuming that you have Microsoft Excel; it is not included on the distribution CD-ROM with this book). If you make changes in Excel and click the Refresh button on the form, the ListView control repopulates with the updates.

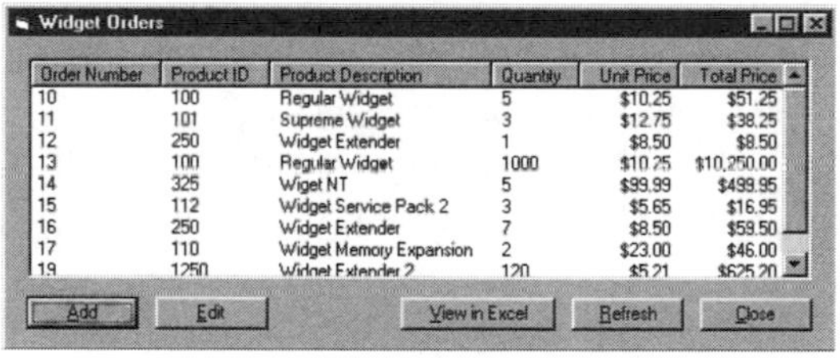

Figure 2.10. The ExcelDAO project.

1. If you have not already installed the Excel IISAM, reinstall Visual Basic with the Custom Setup option, and specify the Excel IISAM in setup.

2. Create a new project and call it ExcelDAO.

3. Go to the Project|Components menu item in Visual Basic, and select Microsoft Windows Common Controls 6.0 from the list. This selection enables you to use the ListView common control that comes with Windows 95.

4. Add the appropriate controls so that the form looks like that shown in Figure 2.11.

5. Edit the objects and properties of **Form1**, as shown in Table 2.11, and then save it as **frmWidgetOrders**.

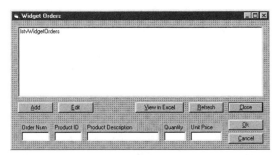

Figure 2.11. The ExcelDAO form in design mode.

Table 2.11. Objects and properties for the Widget Orders project.

OBJECT	PROPERTY	SETTING
Form	Name	frmWidgetOrders
	Caption	Widget Orders
	Height	3390
List view	Name	lstvWidgetOrders
	View	3 'vwReport
Command button	Name	cmdAdd
	Caption	&Add
Command button	Name	cmdEdit
	Caption	&Edit
Command button	Name	cmdView
	Caption	&View in Excel
Command button	Name	cmdRefresh
	Caption	&Refresh
Command button	Name	cmdClose
	Caption	&Close
	Cancel	True
	Default	True
Command button	Name	cmdOk
	Caption	&Ok
Command button	Name	cmdCancel
	Caption	&Cancel
Text box	Name	txtOrderNum

OBJECT	PROPERTY	SETTING
Text box	Name	txtProductID
Text box	Name	txtProductDesc
Text box	Name	txtQuantity
Text box	Name	txtUnitPrice
Label	Name	lblOrderNum
	Caption	Order Num
Label	Name	lblProductID
	Caption	Product ID
Label	Name	lblProductDesc
	Caption	Product Description
Label	Name	lblQuantity
	Caption	Quantity
Label	Name	lblUnitPrice
	Caption	Unit Price

6. Enter the following code in the declarations section of your project. The variables and constants included here are form level and can be accessed by any code within this form. The integer, m_nState, holds the value of one of the two constants defined. This variable states whether the user has selected to add a new record or edit the current one. The m_oSelItem object variable of type ComctlLib.ListItem is an object that holds the value of a selected item in the list view. The last two variables hold the path, filename, and worksheet name of the Excel file to be used in this project.

```
Option Explicit

' form-level variables used to hold the database and recordset

Private db As Database
Private rs As Recordset

' form-level constant values used to indicate the current state

Private Const ADD_RECORD = 0
Private Const EDIT_RECORD = 1

' form-level variables used to save the current state, and
' selected list item
```

continued on next page

continued from previous page

```
Private m_nState As Integer
Private m_oSelItem As ComctlLib.ListItem

' form-level variables used to store the file path and sheet name
' of the Excel file used in the app

Private m_sFilePath As String
Private m_sSheetName As String
```

7. Add the following code to the **Form_Activate** event to get the path and filename of the Excel XLS file to be used. This information is stored in the form-level variable **m_sFilePath**. The worksheet name is stored in the **m_sSheetName** form-level variable. Finally, the **PopulateListView** routine is called. The file is opened and read here.

```
Private Sub Form_Activate()
    ' allow app to paint screen
    DoEvents

    ' get paths and names of files used in app
    m_sFilePath = DataPath & "\Chapter02\WidgetOrders.xls"
    m_sSheetName = "Sheet1$"

    ' populate the list view control
    PopulateListView
End Sub
```

8. Add the following code to clear the text boxes and display the lower portion of the form for editing, or in this case, adding a new record. The last line of code sets the **m_nState** variable to **ADD_RECORD**, indicating that the user is adding a new record.

```
Private Sub cmdAdd_Click()
    ' clear all the text boxes
    txtOrderNum = ""
    txtProductID = ""
    txtProductDesc = ""
    txtQuantity = ""
    txtUnitPrice = ""

    ' show the bottom of the form and set the state to add so we
    ' know how to save the record later

    ShowBottomForm
    m_nState = ADD_RECORD
End Sub
```

9. The **cmdEdit_Click** event is used when the user wants to edit the current record. The database will already be open from the **PopulateListView** routine. This event walks through each record in the recordset until the selected item's order number matches the record's order number. After the record is found, the text boxes on the lower portion of the form are populated with the values in the corresponding fields. The **Total Price** field is left out because we will calculate it ourselves from the given information. After the text boxes are populated, the form is lengthened by the call to **ShowBottomForm**, and the **m_nState** variable is set to **EDIT_RECORD**, indicating that the user has chosen to edit the current record.

```
Private Sub cmdEdit_Click()
    ' we cannot use indexes with Excel files, so we must
    ' transverse the recordset until the record matches the
    ' selected item, then populate the text boxes with the records
    ' values
    With rs

        .MoveFirst

        While (.Fields("Order Number") <> m_oSelItem.Text)
            .MoveNext
        Wend

        txtOrderNum = .Fields("Order Number")
        txtProductID = .Fields("Product ID")
        txtProductDesc = .Fields("Product Description")
        txtQuantity = .Fields("Quantity")
        txtUnitPrice = .Fields("Unit Price")
    End With

    ' show the bottom of the form and set the state to editing so
    ' we know how to save the record later
    ShowBottomForm
    m_nState = EDIT_RECORD
End Sub
```

10. With the **cmdView** command button, the user can view the worksheet used in this project in Excel. To enable the user to view the file in Excel, the database must be closed first. This is done by setting the **rs** and **db** objects to nothing. The **Shell** command then calls Excel with the **m_sFilePath** variable, which holds the path and filename of the Excel worksheet. The **ExcelPath** function is included in the **ReadINIFile** module installed from the distribution CD-ROM.

```
Private Sub cmdView_Click()
    ' set the recordset and database to nothing because Excel will
    ' not be able to successfully open the file if not
    Set rs = Nothing
    Set db = Nothing

    ' open Excel with the file
    Shell ExcelPath & " """ & m_sFilePath & """", vbNormalFocus
End Sub
```

11. If the user edits the worksheet in Excel while the Widget Orders project is open, the changes will not be apparent in the application. Use the Refresh button to repopulate the information from the worksheet. Enter the code for `cmdRefresh_Click`:

```
Private Sub cmdRefresh_Click()
    ' force a repopulation of the list view (use when the user has
    ' made changes in Excel to the file)
    PopulateListView
End Sub
```

12. Now enter the following code for the Close button and the `Form_Unload` event to successfully end the application:

```
Private Sub cmdClose_Click()
    ' always use Unload Me instead of End
    Unload Me
End Sub

Private Sub Form_Unload(Cancel As Integer)
    ' it is good practice to set all objects to nothing
    Set m_oSelItem = Nothing

    ' this is equivalent to closing the recordset and the database
    Set db = Nothing
    Set rs = Nothing
End Sub
```

13. The OK button is used to save the information after a user has edited the current record or added a new one. The event can determine the proper recordset method to use from the `m_nState` variable, either `AddNew` or `Edit`. The information for each field is saved, and the `Total Price` field is calculated from the `Unit Price` and the `Quantity`. After the save, the list view is repopulated, and the bottom of the form is hidden from the user. The code for the button is as follows:

```
Private Sub cmdOk_Click()

    ' edit or add new is confirmed, save the values of the text
    ' boxes this would be a good place to code validation for each
    ' field
    With rs

        If (m_nState = ADD_RECORD) Then
            .AddNew
        Else
            .Edit
        End If

        .Fields("Order Number") = txtOrderNum
        .Fields("Product ID") = txtProductID
        .Fields("Product Description") = txtProductDesc
        .Fields("Quantity") = txtQuantity
        .Fields("Unit Price") = txtUnitPrice
        .Fields("Total Price") = txtUnitPrice * txtQuantity
```

```
            .Update
        End With

            ' repopulate the listview with the changes; then hide the
            ' bottom of the form
        PopulateListView
        HideBottomForm
    End Sub
```

14. The `cmdCancel_Click` event simply hides the bottom half of the form so that the user cannot edit the record. Because the recordset has not been set to `AddNew` or `Edit` yet, we need do nothing further.

```
Private Sub cmdCancel_Click()
    ' edit or add new was canceled, hide the bottom of the form
    HideBottomForm
End Sub
```

15. The following routines show the bottom of the form, hide the bottom of the form, and set the `Enabled` property of all input controls but the ListView to the appropriate state:

```
Private Sub ShowBottomForm()
    ' lengthen the height of the form and enable the proper
    ' controls
    Me.Height = 4350
    SetObjects False
End Sub

Private Sub HideBottomForm()
    ' shorten the height of the form and enable the proper
    ' controls
    Me.Height = 3390
    SetObjects True
End Sub

Private Sub SetObjects(StateIn As Boolean)
    ' set Enabled property for controls on top of form
    cmdAdd.Enabled = StateIn
    cmdEdit.Enabled = StateIn
    cmdRefresh.Enabled = StateIn
    cmdView.Enabled = StateIn
    cmdClose.Enabled = StateIn

    ' set Enabled property for controls on bottom of form
    txtOrderNum.Enabled = Not StateIn
    txtProductID.Enabled = Not StateIn
    txtProductDesc.Enabled = Not StateIn
    txtQuantity.Enabled = Not StateIn
    txtUnitPrice.Enabled = Not StateIn
    cmdOk.Enabled = Not StateIn
    cmdCancel.Enabled = Not StateIn
End Sub
```

16. The `PopulateListView` routine is the core of this project because it opens the database and sets the worksheet to a recordset. This routine also reads the database `TableDefs` collection to define the column headers for the list view, as well as populate the entire list view with the recordset. This first part of the routine adds a column for each field in the `TableDefs(m_sSheetName).Fields` collection. The second part of the routine steps through each record in the recordset and adds a list item for each record. Enter the code for the `PopulateListView` routine:

```
Private Sub PopulateListView()
    Dim oField As Field
    Dim nFieldCount As Integer
    Dim nFieldAlign As Integer
    Dim nFieldWidth As Single
    Dim oRecItem As ListItem
    Dim sValFormat As String

    ' this might take a noticeable amount of time, so before we do
    ' anything change the mouse pointer to an hourglass and then
    ' hide the bottom of the form
    Screen.MousePointer = vbHourglass
    HideBottomForm

    ' open the database (this might already be open; however, if
    ' the user has just started the app or selected the 'View in
    ' Excel' button, then the database and recordset would be set
    ' to nothing
    Set db = OpenDatabase(m_sFilePath, False, False, _
        "Excel 8.0;HDR=YES;")
    Set rs = db.OpenRecordset(m_sSheetName)

    With lstvWidgetOrders
        ' clear the list view box in case this is a refresh of the
        ' records
        .ListItems.Clear
        .ColumnHeaders.Clear

        ' using the For Each statement as compared to the For To
        ' statement is technically faster, as well as being
        ' easier to understand and use
        For Each oField In db.TableDefs(m_sSheetName).Fields

            ' align currency fields to the right, all others to
            ' the left
            nFieldAlign = IIf((oField.Type = dbCurrency), _
                              vbRightJustify, vbLeftJustify)

            ' our product description field is text, and the
            ' values in this field are generally longer than their
            ' field name, so increase the width of the column
            nFieldWidth = TextWidth(oField.Name) _
                          + IIf(oField.Type = dbText, 500, 0)
```

```
                              ' add the column with the correct settings
                              .ColumnHeaders.Add , , oField.Name, _
                                                   nFieldWidth, _
                                                   nFieldAlign

                Next oField
            End With

            ' add the records
            With rs
                .MoveFirst

                While (Not .EOF)

                    ' set the new list item with the first field in the
                    ' record
                    Set oRecItem = lstvWidgetOrders.ListItems.Add(, , _
                        CStr(.Fields(0)))
                    ' now add the rest of the fields as subitems of the
                    ' list item
                    For nFieldCount = 1 To .Fields.Count - 1

                        ' set a currency format for fields that are
                        ' dbCurrency type
                        sValFormat = IIf(.Fields(nFieldCount).Type = _
                                     dbCurrency, _
                                        "$#,##0.00", _
                                        "")

                        ' set the subitem
                        oRecItem.SubItems(nFieldCount) = _
                                     Format$("" & .Fields(nFieldCount), _
                                     sValFormat)

                    Next nFieldCount

                    .MoveNext
                Wend
            End With

            ' by setting the last record item to the selected record item
            ' form variable, we can assure ourselves that a record
            ' is selected for editing later
            Set m_oSelItem = oRecItem

            ' remember to set object variables to nothing when you are
            ' done
            Set oRecItem = Nothing
            Set oRecItem = Nothing

            Screen.MousePointer = vbDefault
        End Sub
```

How It Works

In this project, an Excel worksheet file is opened and used to create a recordset object to populate a ListView control. The code for accessing the recordset is the same as that of accessing Microsoft Access databases, using **AddNew** and **Edit** to alter the underlying ISAM data file. However, Excel worksheet rows cannot be deleted; therefore, the **Delete** method of a recordset is unavailable.

In the **PopulateListView** routine, the project uses the **TableDef** object of the database object to access the table definition of the Excel worksheet. Within this object, there is a collection of fields through which the project loops, adding a column header for each, using the fields' **Name**, **Width**, and **Align** properties.

After the column header collection of the list view is populated with the field names in the Excel worksheet, the ListView control is populated with the records. Accessing these records is the same as accessing other Jet database records. A list item is set for each record with the first field of the record. After this, the subitems of the list item are populated with the remaining fields in the current record.

This application also uses a trick to gain more space when necessary. The form is elongated when either the Add button or the Edit button is clicked, allowing room for a record editing area. After the record is saved or canceled, the form resumes its normal size.

Another feature of this project is that the user can view the worksheet in Excel by using the **Shell** method to start another application. By using this option, the user can load a worksheet, edit its changes, and then switch to Excel to see the results. Even if the user changes the worksheet within Excel while the project is still running (as long as the file is saved and the user clicks the Refresh button), the ListView control will be repopulated with the correct, up-to-date information.

Comments

It is possible to open ranges of an Excel worksheet using the Microsoft Jet Engine. To do this, replace the worksheet name in the **OpenRecordset** method with the range of cells you want returned, as in this example:

```
Set rs = db.OpenRecordset("B1:H12")
```

In this example, *"B1:H12"* is the range on which you want to create a recordset, from the specified Excel worksheet.

CHAPTER 3

CREATING QUERIES WITH SQL

3

CREATING QUERIES WITH SQL

How Do I...

3.1 **Create recordsets by selecting records from single tables?**

3.2 **Select unique field values in a SQL query?**

3.3 **Use variables and Visual Basic functions in a SQL query?**

3.4 **Use wildcards and ranges of values in a SQL query?**

3.5 **Define and use a parameter query?**

3.6 **Create recordsets by joining fields from multiple tables?**

3.7 **Find records in a table without corresponding entries in a related table?**

3.8 **Retrieve information such as counts, averages, and sums and display it by binding it to a Data control?**

3.9 **Create a recordset consisting of records with duplicate values?**

3.10 **Use Visual Basic functions within a SQL statement?**

3.11 Make bulk updates to database records?

3.12 Create and delete tables?

3.13 Append and delete records?

3.14 Create a new table with data from existing tables?

3.15 Modify a table's structure?

3.16 Create a crosstab query?

The Structured Query Language (SQL) is a standard language for defining and manipulating relational databases. Virtually all relational database products on the market today support SQL. The Jet database engine, the heart of Visual Basic and Microsoft Access, uses SQL as its primary definition and manipulation method.

For truly flexible, powerful database programming, SQL is a vital element. You *can* work with Visual Basic databases without SQL, of course; the Jet database engine provides a robust set of objects and capabilities to enable you to accomplish in Visual Basic almost anything you could accomplish in SQL.

Because of the versatility of the Jet database engine, the benefits of SQL are not readily apparent. To help you visualize the power that SQL can add to your database applications, examine the following example. Assume that you want to delete all the records with a **ShipmentDate** earlier than January 1, 1993, from the Orders table in your ACCOUNTS.MDB database. Your program could delete the records this way by using Jet Data Access Objects (commonly known as **DAO** objects):

```
Dim dbfAccounts as Database
Dim recOrders as Recordset
Set dbfAccounts = DBEngine.Workspaces(0).OpenDatabase("ACCOUNTS.MDB")
Set recOrders = dbfAccounts.OpenRecordset("Orders", dbOpenTable)
If recOrders.RecordCount > 0 Then
    recOrders.MoveFirst
    Do Until recOrders.EOF
        If recOrders("ShipmentDate") < #1/1/1993# Then recOrders.Delete
        recOrders.MoveNext
    Loop
End If
recOrders.Close
dbfAccounts.Close
```

Now, examine the following SQL example. (For an explanation of the **dbfAccounts.Execute** statement in this example, see How-To 3.13.)

```
Dim dbfAccounts as Database
Set dbfAccounts = DBEngine.Workspaces(0).OpenDatabase("ACCOUNTS.MDB")
dbfAccounts.Execute("DELETE Orders.* FROM Orders " & _
                    "WHERE Orders.ShipmentDate < #1/1/1993#")
dbfAccounts.Close
```

Both examples achieve the same result. However, the SQL result not only uses less code but also, in most cases, provides faster results than the Jet database example. The first example, employing Data Access Object (DAO) techniques, is forced to retrieve the entire table and then check each record one by one, deleting it if necessary. The second example, however, selects, checks, and deletes in one step, allowing the database, rather than Visual Basic, to manage the deletion.

Although the prospect of learning another language might be disquieting, you'll find that you can accomplish most SQL programming tasks with a very basic level of SQL training. The How-To's in this chapter illustrate the most important SQL statements and techniques. Furthermore, if you have a copy of Microsoft Access, you don't need to *learn* SQL to *use* SQL in Visual Basic. Access can write even the most difficult SQL for you by way of the various query design tools and wizards packaged with the application.

3.1 Create Recordsets by Selecting Records from Single Tables

The **SELECT** statement is the basic building block for retrieving records from a database with SQL. In this How-To, you'll learn how to create a **SELECT** statement that specifies fields, records, and a sort order.

3.2 Select Unique Field Values in a SQL Query

The **SELECT** statement normally returns one record for every record in the source table that meets the designated criteria. This How-To shows you how to modify the basic **SELECT** statement to ensure that the resulting recordset contains no duplicated records.

3.3 Use Variables and Visual Basic Functions in a SQL Query

The choice between SQL and regular Visual Basic code is not an either-or proposition. You can combine Visual Basic variables with SQL statements to create a powerful data management environment. In this How-To, you'll extend the basic **SELECT** statement with variables.

3.4 Use Wildcards and Ranges of Values in a SQL Query

Much of the power of SQL comes from the many ways you can specify recordsets. This How-To demonstrates the use of wildcards and the **Between** operator in SQL **SELECT** statements.

3.5 Define and Use a Parameter Query

The optimization process Microsoft Access uses on queries is more effective if the query is stored in the database and used multiple times. That can be difficult, however, when the query's parameters change often. A parameter query can bridge that difficult gap to give you both speed and flexibility, with remarkable ease of programming. This How-To demonstrates how to create and use a parameter query involving a single parameter.

3.6 Create Recordsets by Joining Fields from Multiple Tables

A properly designed relational database splits data into multiple tables and then relates those tables through key fields. Visual Basic SQL can "cement" fields from multiple tables together into dynaset- and snapshot-type recordsets. This How-To shows the technique for joining fields from multiple tables into unified recordsets through SQL INNER JOIN operations.

3.7 Find Records in a Table Without Corresponding Entries in a Related Table

You might need to identify records that have no corresponding entries in a related table—perhaps you're looking for Customer table records with no records in the Orders table, for example. This How-To shows how to use a SQL OUTER JOIN statement to locate these orphans.

3.8 Retrieve Information such as Counts, Averages, and Sums and Display It by Binding It to a Data Control

Sometimes you don't need the records themselves, just some statistics on records that meet certain criteria. This How-To shows you how to use SQL aggregate functions in SELECT statements to retrieve record counts, averages, sums, and other statistics.

3.9 Create a Recordset Consisting of Records with Duplicate Values

It's often useful to find duplicated values in a table—for example, you might want to find all cases in which the same customer was invoiced more than once on the same day. This How-To shows how to find the duplicate values in a table.

3.10 Use Visual Basic Functions Within a SQL Statement

Although SQL is a flexible and powerful method of database manipulation, sometimes you need extra power. Access and Visual Basic can make use of Visual Basic functions directly in a SQL query, ensuring your complete control over your data. This How-To illustrates how to employ Visual Basic functions in a SELECT query.

3.11 Make Bulk Updates to Database Records

In addition to SELECT statements, which retrieve recordsets from a database, SQL also provides a rich set of action statements. Action statements let you modify the contents of database tables. In this How-To, you'll see how to change values in existing records through SQL.

3.12 Create and Delete Tables

You can use SQL to create empty tables with a list of fields you specify. You can also use SQL to delete tables from your database. This How-To shows you how to accomplish both of these operations.

3.13 Append and Delete Records

Another type of action statement enables you to create a recordset and then append the records in that recordset to an existing table. In this How-To, you'll see how to accomplish this useful task, as well as how to delete records from a table.

3.14 Create a New Table with Data from Existing Tables

SQL action statements can also create new tables from records in existing tables. In this How-To, you'll create a new table from a recordset that you specify through SQL.

3.15 Modify a Table's Structure

SQL's capabilities don't stop at data manipulation. The data definition capabilities of SQL allow a great deal of control over a database's structure, as well as its data. This How-To demonstrates several ways a table can easily be modified with SQL statements.

3.16 Create a Crosstab Query

A crosstab report allows data to be cross-indexed in a compact, spreadsheet-like format. Once a difficult report to design, crosstab reports are now quick and easy. In this How-To, you'll receive an introduction in the ways of crosstab query design.

COMPLEXITY
BEGINNING

3.1 How do I...
Create recordsets by selecting records from single tables?

Problem

I want to select a subset of the records in a table, based on criteria I specify. I don't need to see all the fields for each record, but I do want to specify the order in which the records appear. How can I accomplish this task in Visual Basic by using SQL?

Technique

You create recordsets from data in tables through the SQL **SELECT** statement. You can embed the SQL statement in your Visual Basic code, or you can use it as the **RecordSource** for a Data control.

The SQL SELECT Statement

A basic single-table SQL **SELECT** statement has four basic parts, as shown in Table 3.1. Parts 1 and 2 are required in every **SELECT** statement. Parts 3 and 4 are optional. If you omit Part 3, the record-selection criteria, your recordset will consist of all the records in the table. If you omit Part 4, the sort order, the records will be ordered as they are in the table.

Table 3.1. The four parts of a basic SQL *SELECT* statement.

PURPOSE	EXAMPLE
1. Specify which fields you want to see	`SELECT [Name], [Telephone]`
2. Specify the table	`FROM [Publishers]`
3. Specify the record-selection criteria	`WHERE [State] = "NY"`
4. Specify the sort order	`ORDER BY [Name]`

Combining the four example lines in the table produces this complete SQL **SELECT** statement:

```
SELECT [Name], [Telephone] FROM [Publishers] WHERE [State] = "NY" ORDER BY [Name]
```

This example is from the BIBLIO.MDB database supplied with Visual Basic. This database has a table named Publishers. Among the fields in the Publishers table are `Name`, `Telephone`, and `State`.

In the example, the field names and the table name are surrounded by square brackets, and the text `NY` is enclosed within quotation marks. These syntax requirements help the Jet database engine interpret the SQL statement. Table 3.2 lists the enclosure syntax requirements for SQL statements.

Table 3.2. The enclosure syntax requirements for SQL statements.

ELEMENT	ENCLOSURES	EXAMPLES	WHEN REQUIRED
Numeric data	None		
Text data	Single or double	`"NY" or 'NY'`	Always quotation marks
Date data	Pound signs	`#6/11/1996#`	Always
Field names	Square brackets	`[Name], [Zip Code]`	When name has spaces or punctuation
Table names	Square brackets	`[Publisher Comments]`	When name has spaces or punctuation

CAPITALIZATION DOESN'T MATTER

In the Table 3.1 example, the SQL keywords (SELECT, FROM, WHERE, and ORDER BY) appear in capital letters. This is a convention, and it is completely optional. Neither Visual Basic nor the Jet database engine cares about the capitalization of SQL keywords or about the capitalization of table names and field names.

Note that in the example from Table 3.1, the field and table names do not require brackets because all the names consist of a single word with no spaces or punctuation characters. The brackets are optional when there are no spaces or punctuation.

Multiple Fields and Multiple Criteria

If you need more than one field in the returned recordset, specify the fields by separating the field names with commas. Do the same to designate multiple-field sorts. The following example returns three fields sorted first by the **State** field and then by the **City** field:

```
SELECT [Name], [City], [State], FROM [Publishers]
ORDER BY [State], [City]
```

Specify multiple criteria through the **AND** and **OR** keywords. Assume that you have a table consisting of invoices with the fields shown in Table 3.3.

Table 3.3. Fields for a hypothetical Invoices table.

FIELD	TYPE
Invoice Number	Numeric
Issue Date	Date
Amount	Currency
Customer Number	Numeric

You want to create a recordset consisting of invoices to customer number 3267 that were dated on or after August 1, 1995. Your SQL **SELECT** statement might look like this:

```
SELECT [Invoice Number], [Issue Date], [Amount] FROM [Invoices]
WHERE [Customer Number] = 3267 AND [Issue Date] >= #8/1/95#
ORDER BY [Issue Date]
```

Notice the use of the greater-than-or-equal-to operator (>=) in that statement. SQL comparison operators mimic those available in Visual Basic. Also notice that because the customer number is a numeric field, not a text field, the customer number is not enclosed in quotation marks.

In another situation, perhaps you want to find all invoices issued to customers 3267 and 3396. Your statement might be this:

```
SELECT [Invoice Number], [Issue Date], [Amount] FROM [Invoices]
WHERE [Customer Number] = 3267 OR [Customer Number] = 3396
ORDER BY [Issue Date]
```

You can combine **AND** and **OR** to select the invoices to customers 3267 and 3396 that were issued on or after August 1, 1995:

```
SELECT [Invoice Number], [Issue Date], [Amount] FROM [Invoices]
WHERE ([Customer Number] = 3267 OR [Customer Number] = 3396)
AND [Issue Date] >= #8/1/95# ORDER BY [Issue Date]
```

In the last example, the **OR**'d criteria are enclosed in parentheses. You do this to specify to the Jet engine the order in which it should evaluate the criteria. In this situation, "the **OR**s go together." You want to select the invoices that were sent to both customers after the specified date.

Using SQL Statements with the Data Control

When you use the Data control, you set the control's **RecordSource** property to specify the records that the control will display. The **RecordSource** property can be set to a table, to a stored query, or to a SQL **SELECT** statement. When you use a SQL **SELECT** statement as the **RecordSource**, you can specify records within a table by criteria you specify, and you can specify the order in which the records are presented. Because you cannot use indexes with the Data control, the ability to define the sort order is an important one.

Using SQL Statements with OpenRecordset

The **Database** object includes a method called **OpenRecordset**, with which you can create a dynaset or snapshot by using a SQL statement as the first argument. The SQL statement must be in the form of a string (that is, enclosed in quotation marks).

Assume that you have declared **dbfTemp** to be a **Database** object and **recTemp** to be a **Recordset** object and that you have set **dbfTemp** to point to a database. You can then create the recordset with the following statement (the statement must be all on one line, of course):

```
Set recTemp = dbfTemp.OpenRecordset("SELECT [Name], [Telephone] FROM [Publishers]
➥WHERE [State] = 'NY' ORDER BY [Name]")
```

After this statement has executed, **recTemp** represents a set of records that meet the criteria specified in the SQL statement. You can use any of the **Recordset** object's methods to work with these records.

Notice in the previous example that because the entire SQL statement is enclosed in double quotation marks, the text data within the SQL statement requires single quotation marks. If the text being enclosed contains single quotation marks, you should use a pair of double quotation marks. For example, assume that you are looking for records in which the company name is Joe's Beanery. The **WHERE** clause in your SQL statement would be this:

```
WHERE [Company Name] = "Joe's Beanery"
```

You can also assign the **SELECT** statement to a string variable and then use the string variable as the argument to the **OpenRecordset** method. Assume that **sqlStmt** has been declared as a string and that the following assignment statement appears all on one line:

```
sqlStmt = "SELECT [Name], [Telephone] FROM [Publishers] WHERE [State] = 'NY'
➥ORDER BY [Name]" Set recTemp = dbfTemp.OpenRecordset(sqlStmt)
```

Because SQL statements can get very long—and you can't use Visual Basic's line-continuation feature in the middle of a quoted string—assigning SQL statements to strings often produces more readable code. You can build the string with the concatenation operator:

```
sqlStmt = "SELECT [Invoice Number], [Issue Date], [Amount] FROM [Invoices]"
sqlStmt = sqlStmt & " WHERE ([Customer Number] = 3267 OR [Customer Number] = 3396)"
sqlStmt = sqlStmt & " AND [Issue Date] >= #8/1/95# ORDER BY [Issue Date]"
Set recTemp = dbfTemp.OpenRecordset(sqlStmt)
```

Steps

Open the project SELECT1.VBP. Change the **DatabaseName** property of the Data control **Data1** to point to the copy of BIBLIO.MDB installed on your system (probably in the directory where VB6.EXE is installed). Then run the project. The form shown in Figure 3.1 appears. Scroll the top list to see the publishers in the database. Scroll the bottom list to see the titles in the database.

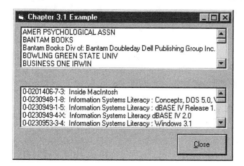

Figure 3.1. The SQL Select Form.

1. Create a new project called SELECT1.VBP. Use **Form1** to create the objects and properties listed in Table 3.4, and save the form as SELECT1.FRM.

Table 3.4. Objects and properties for the Simple SELECTer form.

OBJECT	PROPERTY	SETTING
Form	Name	Form1
	Caption	Chapter 3.1 Example
CommandButton	Name	cmdClose
	Caption	Close
	Default	True
ListBox	Name	lstTitles
Data	Name	dtaData
	Caption	dtaData
	RecordSource	SELECT [Company Name] FROM
		[Publishers] WHERE STATE =
		'NY' ORDER BY [Company Name]
	Visible	False
DBList	Name	dlstPublishers
	RowSource	dtaData
	ListField	Company Name

2. Add the following code to the declarations section of Form1. Ensure that your BIBLIO_PATH constant points to the location of your copy of BIBLIO.MDB, shipped with Visual Basic.

```
Option Explicit

'Change the following to point to your copy of BIBLIO.MDB.
Private Const BIBLIO_PATH = _
"D:\Program Files\Microsoft Visual Studio\VB6\Biblio.MDB"
```

3. Add the following code to the **Load** event of **Form1**. The **Form_Load** event will set the **dtaData** Data control's **DatabaseName** property, allowing it to retrieve data. Then, a snapshot-type **Recordset** object containing records from the Titles table where the [**Years Published**] field is equal to **1993** or **1994** is created, and the titles are added to the **lstTitles** list box. More detail about types of recordsets is provided in Chapter 2, "Accessing a Database with Data Access Objects."

```
PPrivate Sub Form_Load()
    Dim dbfBiblio As Database, recSelect As Recordset
    Dim strSQL As String

    'Set up the error handler.
    On Error GoTo FormLoadError

        'Get the database name and open the database.
        dtaData.DatabaseName = BIBLIO_PATH
        dtaData.Refresh
```

```
            Set dbfBiblio = _
    DBEngine.Workspaces(0).OpenDatabase(BIBLIO_PATH)

            'Open a snapshot-type recordset on the [Titles] table,
            ' selecting only those titles published in 1993 or 1994,
            ' sorting by the ISBN number. Note the use of the line
            ' continuation character (_), used throughout the
            ' examples, to make code more readable. " & _
            strSQL = "SELECT [Title], [ISBN] FROM [Titles] " & _
                "WHERE [Year Published] = 1993"
    Or [Year Published] = 1994 " & _
                "ORDER BY [ISBN]"

            'Create the recordset.
            Set recSelect = dbfBiblio.OpenRecordset(strSQL, _
                dbOpenSnapshot)

            'Iterate through the recordset until the end of the file
            '(EOF) is reached.  Display each record in the unbound
            'list box lstTitles.
            If recSelect.RecordCount > 0 Then
                recSelect.MoveFirst
                Do Until recSelect.EOF
                    lstTitles.AddItem recSelect![ISBN] & ":  " & _
                    recSelect![Title]
                    recSelect.MoveNext
                Loop
            End If
        Exit Sub

    FormLoadError:
        'If an error occurs, display it with a MsgBox command.
        MsgBox Err.Description, vbExclamation
        Exit Sub
    End Sub
```

4. Add the following code to the Click event of cmdClose. The code in the cmdClose_Click event will end the application.

```
    Private Sub cmdClose_Click()
        End
    End Sub
```

How It Works

This How-To displays two lists, each showing the records in a recordset generated by a SQL **SELECT** statement. The top list is a **DBList** control bound to the Data control **dtaData**. The SQL statement that generates the recordset is supplied as the **RecordSource** property of the Data control. The bottom list is an unbound `ListBox`. Its recordset is generated by the `OpenRecordset` method called from the `Form_Load` event.

Comments

As basic as the code for this example might seem, it becomes the foundation for data access in Visual Basic using SQL. No matter which method you use (Data controls, Data Access Objects, or some of the other methods this book explores), SQL is the foundation on which these methods stand.

COMPLEXITY
BEGINNING

3.2 How do I...
Select unique field values in a SQL query?

Problem

I know that records in my table contain duplicate values in a particular field. How can I create a list of the unique values in the field?

Technique

By default, a SQL statement returns one row for each row in the table that meets the criteria specified in the statement's `WHERE` clause. If this action results in duplicate rows, these duplications are reproduced in the output recordset. For example, assume that your company provides products in several colors but uses the same product number for all colors of an otherwise identical product. You might have a [Products] table with this structure:

```
Product Number        Color
AGD44523              Green
AGD44523              Red
AGD44527              Red
```

You have two records with the [`Product Number`] field equal to `AGD44523`, each with a different entry in [`Color`]. Query the table with this SQL statement:

```
SELECT [Product Number] FROM [Products]
```

Included in your resulting recordset will be two identical rows, each with the value `AGD44523`.

Perhaps you want a list of unique product numbers, with no duplication. You can tell the Jet engine to filter duplicates out of the resulting recordset by inserting the keyword `DISTINCT` immediately after the word `SELECT`. You would rewrite your SQL statement like this:

```
SELECT DISTINCT [Product Number] FROM [Products]
```

That statement would result in a recordset with just one occurrence of the value AGD44523.

WHICH IS FASTER: SQL OR PROCEDURAL?

The question "Is SQL or the procedural approach faster when interfacing with the database?" is a complex one. In most cases, SQL methods will be faster than traditional procedural approaches. If an operation is time critical, it will probably be profitable to benchmark both the SQL approach and the procedural approach before making a decision on which to use in your production code.

An important class of exceptions to the generalization that "SQL is usually faster" is random access into an indexed table using the Seek method when each Seek operation is followed by operations on a small number of records. This code fragment provides an example:

```
Set recSelect = dbfTest.OpenRecordset("MyTable", dbOpenTable)
recSelect.Index = "MyIndex"
recSelect.Seek "=", intSomeValue
If Not recSelect.NoMatch Then
    ' Perform an action on the record sought
End If
' If needed, perform another Seek, or close the recordset and
' move on.
```

In such cases, the traditional procedural methods are usually faster than SQL statements.

Steps

The BIBLIO.MDB database (supplied with Visual Basic) contains multiple publishers from the same state. Open the project SELECT2.VBP and run it. Initially, the list box on the form is blank. Click the Show All button, and the form then appears as shown in Figure 3.2; notice the occurrence of multiple CA entries. Click the Show Unique button, and the form appears as shown in Figure 3.3, with only one entry for each state.

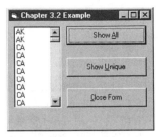

Figure 3.2. The SQL Select Unique form after the Show All button is clicked.

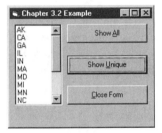

Figure 3.3. The SQL Select Unique form after the Show Unique button is clicked.

1. Create a new project called SELECT2.VBP. Use **Form1** to create the objects and properties listed in Table 3.5, and save the form as SELECT2.FRM.

Table 3.5. Objects and properties for the Distinct SELECTer form.

OBJECT	PROPERTY	SETTING
Form	Name	Form1
	Caption	Chapter 3.2 Example
CommandButton	Name	cmdClose
	Caption	&Close Form
CommandButton	Name	cmdShowUnique
	Caption	Show &Unique
CommandButton	CommandButton	cmdShowAll
	Caption	Show &All
Data	Name	dtaData
DBList	Name	dlstData
	DataSource	State
	RowSource	dtaData

2. Add the following code to the declarations section of `Form1`:

```
Option Explicit

'Ensure that the following points to your copy of BIBLIO.MDB.
Private Const BIBLIO_PATH = _
"D:\Program Files\Microsoft Visual Studio\VB6\Biblio.MDB"
```

3. Add the following code to the `Click` event of `cmdShowAll`. This code builds a SQL statement that creates a recordset with one record for every [Publishers] table row with a non-NULL [State] field and passes the SQL statement to the `RefreshControls` subroutine.

```
Private Sub cmdShowAll_Click()
    Dim strSQL As String

    'Perform the simple SELECT query.  Note the lack of the
    'DISTINCT keyword (see the cmdShowUnique_Click event
    'for more info.)
    strSQL = "SELECT [State] FROM [Publishers] " & _
        "WHERE [State] IS NOT NULL " & _
        "ORDER BY [State]"

    'Set the RecordSource and refresh the Data control and
    'DBList control
    RefreshControls strSQL
End Sub
```

4. Add the following code to the `Click` event of `cmdShowUnique`. This code builds a SQL statement that creates a recordset with one record for every unique value in the [State] field of the [Publishers] table and passes the SQL statement to the `RefreshControls` subroutine.

```
Private Sub cmdShowUnique_Click()
Dim strSQL As String

    'Perform the SELECT DISTINCT query.
    'Since the DISTINCT keyword is present, only
    'the first instance of a given [State] value is represented
    'in the result set.
    strSQL = "SELECT DISTINCT [State] FROM [Publishers] " & _
        "WHERE [State] IS NOT NULL " & _
        "ORDER BY [State]"

    'Set the RecordSource and refresh the Data control and
    'DBList control
    RefreshControls strSQL
End Sub
```

5. Create the `RefreshControls` subroutine by entering the following code into `Form1`. This routine assigns the SQL statement received as the argument to the `RecordSource` property of the Data control. It then refreshes the Data control and the bound list box.

```
Private Sub RefreshControls(strSQL as string)
    dtaData.RecordSource = strSQL
    dtaData.Refresh
    dlstData.Refresh
End Sub
```

6. Add the following code to the Click event of cmdClose:

```
Private Sub cmdClose_Click()
    End
End Sub
```

How It Works

The RecordSource property of the Data control dtaData is set to an empty string in the Properties window. At form load, therefore, the Recordset object of dtaData will be empty, and it will remain empty until the RecordSource property is set to something that will return a valid recordset and the Data control is refreshed. Because the DBList control is bound to the Data control, it will be empty while the Data control remains empty.

The Click routines of cmdShowAll and cmdShowUnique both perform the same basic function: They build a SQL statement to select the [State] field from the [Publishers] table and then pass the SQL statement to the RefreshControls subroutine. The difference in the Click routines is that cmdShowUnique includes the DISTINCT keyword in its SELECT statement and, therefore, returns only one record for each unique [State] value in the table.

Comments

In addition to the DISTINCT keyword described in this How-To, the Jet database engine also supports DISTINCTROW operations. When you use DISTINCTROW rather than DISTINCT, the database engine looks not only at the fields you've specified in your query but at entire rows in the table specified by the query. It returns one record in the dynaset for each unique row in the table, whether or not the output recordset row is unique.

Here's a simple example to illustrate the difference. Assume that the table [Cities] consists of these records:

```
CITY          STATE
Chicago       IL
Rockford      IL
Madison       WI
Madison       WI
Dubuque       IA
```

Here are two SQL queries:

```
SELECT DISTINCT [State] FROM [Cities]

SELECT DISTINCTROW [State] FROM [Cities]
```

The first SQL statement would return the following recordset. The DISTINCT statement ensures that each row in the output recordset is unique.

```
IL
WI
IA
```

The second SQL statement would return the following recordset. The IL entry appears twice because there are two unique records in the underlying table with a value of IL in the [State] field. The WI entry, on the other hand, appears only once because there is only one unique record in the underlying table.

```
IL
IL
WI
IA
```

In a well-designed database, a table will have no duplicate records because each record will have a primary key, and primary keys are by definition unique. If you have primary keys on all your tables, therefore, you have no need for DISTINCTROW.

COMPLEXITY
INTERMEDIATE

3.3 How do I...
Use variables and Visual Basic functions in a SQL query?

Problem

SQL SELECT statements are useful tools. But if I have to hard-code the criteria into the statement, it limits my flexibility because I can't change the criteria at runtime. I'd like to be able to use variables in the criteria clauses of my SELECT statements or—even better—use Visual Basic functions that return values. How can I accomplish this?

Technique

The SQL statement that you pass to the OpenRecordset method of the Database object or that you assign as the RecordSource property of a Data control is a string. Because it is a string, you can insert the values of variables into it using Visual Basic's concatenation operator. You can use the same technique to insert the value returned by a call to a function (a built-in Visual Basic function or one you write yourself) into the string.

Steps

Open the project SELECT3.VBP and run the project. The form shown in Figure 3.4 appears. Scroll the top list to see the publishers in the database. Click on a publisher, and the titles for that publisher appear in the bottom list. Enter a year in the Year Published box, and click on a publisher to restrict the display to titles published by a specific publisher in a specific year.

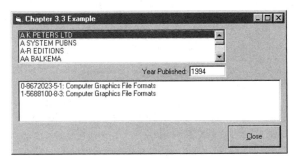

Figure 3.4. The Variable SELECTer form at startup.

1. Create a new project called SELECT3.VBP. Use **Form1** to create the objects and properties listed in Table 3.6, and save the form as SELECT3.FRM.

Table 3.6. Options and properties for the Variable SELECTer form.

OBJECT	PROPERTY	SETTING
Form	Name	Form1
	Caption	Chapter 3.3 Example
CommandButton	Name	cmdClose
	Caption	Close
	Default	True
ListBox	Name	lstTitles
Data	Name	dtaData
	Caption	dtaData
	RecordsetType	Snapshot
	RecordSource	SELECT [Company Name] FROM
		[Publishers] ORDER BY
		[Company Name]
	Visible	False
DBList	Name	dlstPublishers
	RowSource	dtaData

OBJECT	PROPERTY	SETTING
	ListField	Company Name
Label	Name	lblYearPublished
	AutoSize	True
	Caption	Year Published:
TextBox	Name	txtYearPublished
	Text	""

2. Add the following code to the declarations section of **Form1**:

```
Option Explicit

Private Const BIBLIO_PATH = _
"D:\Program Files\Microsoft Visual Studio\VB6\Biblio.MDB"
Dim dbfBiblio As Database
```

3. Add the following code to the **Load** event of **Form1**:

```
Private Sub Form_Load()
On Error GoTo FormLoadError
        'Set the Data control and load the Database object
        'dbfBiblio.
        dtaData.DatabaseName = BIBLIO_PATH
        dtaData.Refresh
        Set dbfBiblio =
DBEngine.Workspaces(0).OpenDatabase(BIBLIO_PATH)
    On Error GoTo 0
Exit Sub

FormLoadError:
    MsgBox Err.Description, vbExclamation
    Exit Sub
End Sub
```

4. Add the following code to the **Click** event of **dlstPublishers**:

```
Private Sub dlstPublishers_Click()
Dim recSelect As Recordset
    Dim strSQL As String
    Dim intYearPublished As Integer

    On Error GoTo PublishersClickError
        'Clear the list box
        lstTitles.Clear

        'Confirm that the year is numeric; if so, set the
        'intYearPublished variable to its numeric value.
        If IsNumeric(txtYearPublished) Then intYearPublished = _
            Val(txtYearPublished)
```

continued on next page

continued from previous page

```
'Build the SQL statement
strSQL = "SELECT [Title], [ISBN] FROM [Titles] " & _
    "WHERE [PubID] = " & GetPubID()

'If the year published selection is greater than zero,
'modify the SQL to search for it.
If intYearPublished > 0 Then
    strSQL = strSQL & " AND [Year Published] = " & _
            intYearPublished
End If

'Sort the results by the ISBN number.
strSQL = strSQL & " ORDER BY [ISBN]"

'Get the recordset from our SQL statement.
Set recSelect = dbfBiblio.OpenRecordset(strSQL, _
            dbOpenSnapshot)

'If we have obtained results, add the ISBN
'and Title fields to the list box.
If recSelect.RecordCount > 0 Then
    recSelect.MoveFirst
    Do Until recSelect.EOF
        lstTitles.AddItem recSelect![ISBN] & ": " _
        & recSelect![Title]
        recSelect.MoveNext
    Loop
End If
    On Error GoTo 0
Exit Sub

PublishersClickError:
    MsgBox Err.Description, vbExclamation
    Exit Sub
End Sub
```

When the user clicks on a publisher name, this subroutine opens a snapshot-type **Recordset** object created from the Titles table, selecting only those titles published by the selected publishing company and, if the user has entered a publication year in **txtYearPublished**, in the designated year. It sorts the records in the snapshot by the ISBN number.

The **WHERE** clause in the SQL statement includes the value returned from the function **GetPubID**. **GetPubID** returns a numeric value corresponding to the Publishers table's **PubID** field for the currently selected publisher in **dlstPublishers**. Its value can be inserted into the SQL string by concatenating the function call to the string.

If the user has entered a publication year into **txtYearPublished**, its value is assigned to the numeric variable **yrPublished** and then inserted into the SQL string by concatenating the variable **yrPublished** to the string. Note that both values added to the string (the return value of GetPubID and the value of yrPublished) represent numeric fields in the database. Therefore, neither value is delimited by quotation marks in the SQL statement.

5. Create the following function in Form1. This function creates a recordset consisting of the PubID field of the record from the Publishers table with the company name value of the current selection in the dlstPublishers list. (This code assumes that each record in Publishers has a unique company name.) It then returns the value of that PubID field. In the SQL statement, the value dblPublishers.Text is used as the criterion of the WHERE clause. Because this value is a string (text) value, it must be delimited by quotation marks in the SQL statement. A single pair of double quotation marks—one at the beginning of the variable name and one at the end—won't do because the entire SQL statement is in quotation marks. You could use single quotation marks, like this:

```
strSQL = strSQL & " WHERE [Company Name] = '" & dblPublishers.Text _
    & "'"
```

This would work if you could be sure that the value dblPublishers.Text would never include an apostrophe. But because you can't be sure of that (in fact, BIBLIO.MDB does contain one publisher, O'Reilly & Associates, with an apostrophe), a double quotation mark is the safest course.

```
Function GetPubID() As Long
Dim recPubID As Recordset
    Dim strSQL As String

    'This subquery, once constructed, selects the publisher ID
    'given a company name.
    strSQL = "SELECT [PubID] FROM [Publishers] " & _
        "WHERE [Company Name] = """ & dblPublishers.Text & """"

    'Construct the recordset from our SQL statement.
    Set recPubID = dbfBiblio.OpenRecordset(strSQL, dbOpenSnapshot)

    'If we have a record, get the ID.  If not, return zero.
    If recPubID.RecordCount > 0 Then
        GetPubID = recPubID![PubID]
    Else
        GetPubID = 0
    End If
End Function
```

6. Add the following code to the Click event of cmdClose:

```
Private Sub cmdClose_Click()
    End
End Sub
```

How It Works

When the form loads, it opens the database by setting the value of the **Database** object variable **dbfBiblio** to BIBLIO.MDB. The **Publishers** list is a bound list and is filled on startup by the records specified in the **RecordSource** property of **Data1** (see How-To 3.1 for a discussion of this bound list and Data control). The **Titles** list is initially empty, and it remains so until the user clicks on the name of a publisher. Then the **dlstPublisher_Click** event code fills the **Titles** list with the titles published by the selected publisher. It does this by building a SQL statement that includes the **PubID** of the selected publisher. If the user enters a year in the Year Published text box, its value is appended to the **WHERE** clause as an additional criterion.

Because the **dlstPublishers** list does not include the **PubID** field, its **Click** event needs to retrieve the value of the **PubID** field for the selected record. It does this by a call to the **GetPubID** function. **GetPubID** returns a numeric value, which is inserted directly into the SQL string.

Comments

You can also use built-in Visual Basic functions in your SQL statement. The functions are evaluated at runtime and their return values inserted into the SQL statement passed to the Jet engine. For example, if you have an integer variable named **intIndex**, you could use the built-in **Choose** function to build a SQL statement like this:

```
strSQL = SELECT * FROM Orders WHERE [Delivery Service] = '" & _
Choose(intIndex, "Speedy", "Rapid", "Quick", "Rabbit", "Tortoise") & "'"
```

COMPLEXITY
BEGINNING

3.4 How do I...
Use wildcards and ranges of values in a SQL query?

Problem

I need to create recordsets where the records returned fall within a range of values or contain certain text strings. How can I do this with SQL?

Technique

You might need to create recordsets that consist of records that fall within a range of values. Or perhaps you need to create recordsets consisting of records in which a given field contains a certain text string. You can accomplish both of these tasks with SQL.

Finding Records Within Criteria Ranges

You can use the standard comparison operators to find records that have a field value within a range of values. For example, to find all records in the Invoices table with `Invoice Date` values between January 1, 1996, and January 15, 1996, you can use this statement:

```
SELECT * FROM [Invoices]
WHERE [Invoice Date] >= #1/1/1996# AND [Invoice Date] <= #1/15/1996#
```

As an alternative, you can use the SQL `Between` operator. This statement returns the same recordset as the preceding one:

```
SELECT * FROM [Invoices]
WHERE [Invoice Date] Between #1/1/1996# AND #1/15/1996#
```

Using Wildcards in String Criteria

You can find records containing designated strings of text within text fields by using the wildcard characters * and ? with the SQL `Like` operator. The asterisk matches any combination of characters. The question mark matches a single character.

This statement retrieves all records that have the `Company` field beginning with `mcgraw`:

```
SELECT * FROM [Publishers] WHERE [Company] LIKE "mcgraw*"
```

This statement retrieves all records with the last name `Hansen` or `Hanson`:

```
SELECT * FROM [Authors] WHERE [Last Name] LIKE "hans?n"
```

You can use more than one wildcard character in a string. This statement retrieves all the records in which the `[Company Name]` field includes the word `hill`:

```
SELECT * FROM [Publishers] WHERE [Company Name] LIKE "*hill*"
```

Steps

Open and run the project SELECT4.VBP. The form shown in Figure 3.5 appears. Enter `*visual basic*` in the text box labeled Title Includes Text, and click the Look Up button. Enter **1992** and **1993** in the Published Between boxes, and click Look Up again. Delete the values from the Published Between boxes; then change the entry in the Title Includes Text box to `visual basic*` and click Look Up. Change the text in the Title Includes Text box to `*visual basic` and click Look Up.

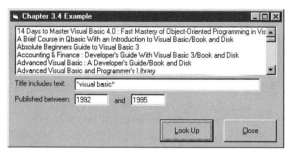

Figure 3.5. The Wildcard SELECTer form on startup.

1. Create a new project called SELECT4.VBP. Use **Form1** to create the objects and properties listed in Table 3.7, and save the form as SELECT4.FRM.

Table 3.7. Options and properties for the Wildcard SELECTer form.

OBJECT	PROPERTY	SETTING
Form	Name	Form1
	Caption	Chapter 3.4 Example
ListBox	Name	lstTitles
TextBox	Name	txtPartialTitle
TextBox	Name	txtStartYear
TextBox	Name	txtEndYear
Label	Name	lblPartialTitle
	AutoSize	True
	Caption	Title includes text:
Label	Name	lblStartYear
	AutoSize	True
	Caption	Published between:
Label	Name	lblEndYear
	AutoSize	True
	Caption	and
CommandButton	Name	cmdLookup
	Caption	&Look Up
	Default	True
CommandButton	Name	cmdClose
	Caption	&Close

2. Add the following code to the declarations section of **Form1**:

```
Option Explicit

Private Const BIBLIO_PATH = "D:\Program Files\Microsoft Visual
Studio\
➥VB6\Biblio.MDB"
```

3. Add the following code to the **Click** event of **cmdLookup**. This sets the values of the three variables to be inserted into the SQL statement to the contents of the three text boxes. It uses the **IIf** function to set the variables to default values if a text box is blank or if one of the Year text boxes contains a nonnumeric value. It then builds the SQL statement, inserting the variable values into the **WHERE** clause, opens the recordset, and fills the list with the recordset contents. (See How-To 3.3 for a discussion of using Visual Basic variables in SQL statements.)

```
Private Sub cmdLookup_Click()
Dim dbfBiblio As Database, recSelect As Recordset
    Dim strName As String, strSQL As String
    Dim strTitleText As String, strStartYear As String, strEndYear
As String

    On Error GoTo LookupError
        'Clear the list box
        lstTitles.Clear
        'Construct the search strings, using wildcards where
        'appropriate. For example, if the txtPartialTitle field is
        'blank, the * wildcard is substituted.
        strTitleText = IIf(txtPartialTitle <> "", _
                    txtPartialTitle, "*")
        strStartYear = IIf(IsNumeric(txtStartYear), _
                    txtStartYear, "1")
        strEndYear = IIf(IsNumeric(txtEndYear), _
                    txtEndYear, "9999")

        'Open the database
        Set dbfBiblio = _
            DBEngine.Workspaces(0).OpenDatabase(BIBLIO_PATH)

        'Build the SQL statement, substituting our search strings,
        'built above, in the appropriate locations.
        strSQL = "SELECT [Title] FROM [Titles] " & _
            "WHERE [Title] LIKE '*" & strTitleText & "*' " & _
            "AND [Year Published] BETWEEN " & strStartYear & _
            " AND " & strEndYear & _
            " ORDER BY [Title]"

        'Construct the SQL statement.
        Set recSelect = _
            dbfBiblio.OpenRecordset(strSQL, dbOpenSnapshot)
```

continued on next page

continued from previous page

```
                         'If we get results, load the Title field of each record
                         'into the list box.
                         If recSelect.RecordCount > 0 Then
                             recSelect.MoveFirst
                             Do Until recSelect.EOF
                                 lstTitles.AddItem recSelect![Title]
                                 recSelect.MoveNext
                             Loop
                         End If
                     On Error GoTo 0
                 Exit Sub

                 LookupError:
                     MsgBox Err.Description, vbExclamation
                     Exit Sub
                 End Sub
```

4. Add the following code as the `Click` event of `cmdClose`:

```
Private Sub cmdClose_Click()
    End
End Sub
```

How It Works

The true action of this sample application occurs in the `cmdLookup_Click` event. After clearing the contents of the `lstTitles` list box, the code uses the values supplied in the text boxes to construct a SQL statement to run against the `dbfBiblio Database` object. If records were retrieved after the statement was run with the `OpenRecordset` method, the `lstTitles` list box would be populated with the contents of the `[Title]` field from each record.

Comments

A Visual Basic database stores a date field as a number. In the `WHERE` clause of a SQL statement, you can treat it like a number; using the `Between` operator or comparison operators like ≥ or ≤ returns the results you would expect.

However, you can treat the date field like text in the `WHERE` clause of a SQL statement. This method enables you to use wildcard characters for any of the three values in a standard date.

For example, this `WHERE` clause returns all records with an invoice date in January 1996:

```
WHERE [Invoice Date] LIKE "1/*/1996"
```

The following `WHERE` clause returns all records with an invoice date in 1996:

```
WHERE [Invoice Date] LIKE "*/*/1996"
```

Notice that when you use the `Like` operator and wildcard characters, you delimit the date with quotation marks—not pound signs. Quotation marks tell the Jet database engine, "Treat this date like a string." The pound signs tell it, "Treat this date like a number."

COMPLEXITY
BEGINNING

3.5 How do I...
Define and use a parameter query?

Problem

I need to create recordsets with search criteria based on a parameter that will change often and reload quickly each time the parameter changes.

Technique

Normally, when using SQL to search for a specific value or values, you would specify which values you wanted in the statement. For example, to retrieve names and telephone numbers from the [Publishers] table in which the [State] field was equal to "NY", you would use this SQL statement:

```
SELECT [Name], [Telephone] FROM [Publishers] WHERE [State] = "NY" _
    ORDER BY [Name]
```

But this limits you. If you wanted all the names and telephone numbers from a different state, you would create a new query. There is, however, a faster way. A *parameter query* is a special SQL query in which replaceable parameters are used. Think of a parameter in SQL as a variable in Visual Basic. This allows your query to be flexible, and it also allows an increase in performance because the SQL precompiler doesn't have to completely build a new query every time you change a parameter.

To use a parameter in your SQL statement, you first have to specify the parameter—like declaring a variable in Visual Basic. You do this in the **PARAMETERS** section of your query, which usually precedes the **SELECT** statement. The declaration, as in Visual Basic, consists of a name and a data type, although the data types vary slightly from the names you might be accustomed to in Visual Basic. The **PARAMETERS** section is separated from the **SELECT** section by a semicolon (;) so that the SQL precompiler can tell the difference between the two sections.

To rewrite the preceding query for use with parameters, you might use something like this:

```
PARAMETERS prmState String; SELECT [Name], [Telephone] FROM [Publishers] _
    WHERE [State] = [prmState] ORDER BY [Name]
```

The parameter is substituted for the search value but in all other respects does not alter the SQL statement.

Steps

Open and run the project SELECT5.VBP. The form shown in Figure 3.6 appears. Enter NY in the State Abbreviation text box and click Search. Enter any other value in the State Abbreviation text box and click Search again.

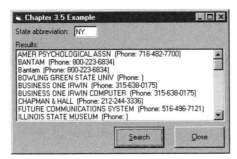

Figure 3.6. The SQL Parameter Query form on startup.

1. Create a new project called SELECT5.VBP. Use Form1 to create the objects and properties listed in Table 3.8, and save the form as SELECT5.FRM.

Table 3.8. Options and properties for the Parameter SELECTer form.

OBJECT	PROPERTY	SETTING
Form	Name	Form1
	Caption	Chapter 3.5 Example
Label	Name	lblParameter
	Caption	State abbreviation:
TextBox	Name	txtParameter
Label	Name	lblResults
	Caption	Results:
ListBox	Name	lstResults
CommandButton	Name	cmdSearch
	Caption	&Search
CommandButton	Name	cmdClose
	Caption	&Close

2. Add the following code to the declarations section of Form1:

```
Option Explicit

Private Const BIBLIO_PATH = _
        "D:\Program Files\Microsoft Visual Studio\VB6\Biblio.MDB"
Private mdbfBiblio As Database, mrecSelect As Recordset, _
        mqdfTemp As QueryDef
```

3. Add the following code to the Load method of Form1. The CreateQueryDef method is used on the database to create a QueryDef object, which will hold the parameter query. Later, the QueryDef will be used to create a recordset for display.

```
Private Sub Form_Load()
    'Open a Database object first - the familiar BIBLIO.MDB
        Set mdbfBiblio = _
            DBEngine.Workspaces(0).OpenDatabase(BIBLIO_PATH)

    'Use the CreateQueryDef method to create a temporary QueryDef
    'object that will store our parameter query.  The best way to
    'use a parameter query in DAO is with the QueryDef object.
    Set mqdfTemp = mdbfBiblio.CreateQueryDef("")

    'Set the SQL property to our parameter query SQL statement.
    mqdfTemp.SQL = "PARAMETERS pstrState String;SELECT " & _
        "[Name],[Telephone] " & _
        "FROM [Publishers] WHERE [State] = [pstrState] " & _
        "ORDER By [Name]"
End Sub
```

4. Add the following code to the Click event of cmdSearch. Now that you have a possible value for your parameter, you reference the pstrState parameter of the QueryDef object you created in the Form_Load routine. Then, using the QueryDef, you create a recordset. Now, the best part of this is when you change the parameter; instead of recreating the recordset, you use the Requery method provided by the Recordset object. Using this method is much faster because the recordset has an existing connection to the database and has its SQL already defined; you're just changing a parameter.

```
Private Sub cmdSearch_Click()
    Dim lstrTemp As String

    'Set the parameter to the contents of our text box
    mqdfTemp![pstrState] = txtParameter.Text

    'If we haven't run this query yet, we'll need to
    'create it.  If we have, we don't need to create it,
    'just to requery it.
```

continued on next page

continued from previous page

```
            If mrecSelect Is Nothing Then
                Set mrecSelect = mqdfTemp.OpenRecordset()
            Else
                mrecSelect.Requery mqdfTemp
            End If

            'Clear the list box
            lstResults.Clear

            'Populate the list box with names & phone numbers
            If mrecSelect.RecordCount > 0 Then
                mrecSelect.MoveFirst
                Do Until mrecSelect.EOF
                    lstResults.AddItem mrecSelect![Name] & "  (Phone: " _
                        & mrecSelect![Telephone] & ")"
                    mrecSelect.MoveNext
                Loop
            End If
        End Sub
```

5. Add the following code to the **Click** event of **cmdClose**:

```
        Private Sub cmdClose_Click()
            End
        End Sub
```

How It Works

When the application is started, Form1 loads. The **Form_Load** event creates a **Database** object instance and then uses object's **CreateQueryDef** method to create a temporary **QueryDef** object. At this point, your parameter query is created by placing the SQL statement for the query into the SQL property of the newly created **QueryDef** object.

When the **cmdSearch_Click** event is triggered, you first populate the **QueryDef**'s **Parameter** object with information from the **txtParameter** field. Then the routine checks whether the **Recordset** object it's about to populate is set to **Nothing**. If so, the query hasn't been run yet, so the routine constructs a **Recordset** object by running the **OpenRecordset** method from the **QueryDef** object. If not, it uses the **Requery** method, which simply re-executes the query without having to make a new connection to the database, compile the SQL, and so on.

After it does so, if the query has returned records, the **lstResults** list box is populated with the information.

Comments

One of the benefits of using a parameter query is the **Requery** method. The **Requery** method allows you to re-issue a query with different parameters; Microsoft Access will actually reuse the existing connection, running the query faster. Also, the optimization engine built into Jet works best on static SQL (that is, SQL stored in the database, as opposed to the SQL statements stored in code), so you can get even more benefit from the use of a parameter query that is saved to a Microsoft Access database. For more information on how to use a stored parameter query, examine How-To 5.7 in Chapter 5, "Microsoft Access Database."

COMPLEXITY

INTERMEDIATE

3.6 How do I...
Create recordsets by joining fields from multiple tables?

Problem

I've designed my database using good relational database design principles, which means that I have data in multiple tables that are related through key fields. How can I use SQL to return recordsets with data from multiple tables in each recordset record?

Technique

In BIBLIO.MDB, the Publishers table contains information about publishers, and the Titles table contains information about titles. Each publisher is assigned a unique publisher ID, which appears in the **PubID** field in the Publishers table. In the Titles table, the publisher is indicated by the publisher number as well as in a field named **PubID**. Figure 3.7 shows this relationship. If you were using procedural coding and wanted to find the name of the publisher of a given title, you would find the title in the Titles table, store the value of the **PubID** for that title, and then find the matching **PubID** in the Publishers table.

This job is a lot easier with SQL. When you have a link like the one in Figure 3.7, you can use the keywords **INNER JOIN** in the **FROM** clause of a SQL **SELECT** statement to create a single recordset with fields from both tables. To continue the example, you could create a recordset with the **Title** field from the Titles table and the **Name** field from the Publishers table with this SQL statement:

```
SELECT Titles.Title, Publishers.Name
FROM Publishers INNER JOIN Titles ON Publishers.PubID = Titles.PubID
```

In a single-table **SELECT** statement, the **FROM** clause is simple—it just gives the name of the table. A multitable statement **FROM** clause consists of one (or more) subclauses, each based on an **INNER JOIN**. The syntax of each **INNER JOIN** is as follows:

```
<table 1 name> INNER JOIN <table 2 name>
ON <table 1 linking field name> = <table 2 linking field name>
```

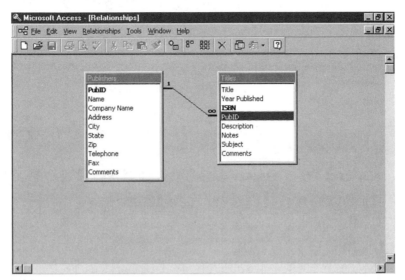

Figure 3.7. The BIBLIO.MDB Publishers and
Titles table relationship.

Note that the field names in both the SELECT clause and the FROM clause are fully qualified with their table names, with the period operator separating the table name from the field name. Strictly speaking, this is necessary only when both tables have fields with identical names. In the example, the table names are required in the FROM clause because both tables have a field named PubID; they are optional in the SELECT clause because only the Titles table has a field named Title and only the Publishers table has a field named Name. It's good practice, however, to fully qualify all field names in multitable SQL statements. This not only makes the code easier to interpret but also makes it less likely that your code will be broken by subsequent changes to the structure of the database.

MULTIFIELD JOINS

It's quite common to have relationships based on multiple fields within each table. For example, assume that you have an Employees table and an Hours Worked table. You identify each employee by two fields, [Last Name] and [First Name]. These two fields appear in each table and are used to link Employee records to Hours Worked records.

Code these multifield joins by creating an INNER JOIN subclause, with multiple ON expressions tied together with the AND keyword. Each ON expression links one pair of common fields. The FROM clause you'd use to link the tables in the example would be this:

```
FROM Employees INNER JOIN [Hours Worked]
ON Employees.[Last Name] = [Hours Worked].[Last Name]
AND Employees.[First Name] = [Hours Worked].[First Name]
```

Steps

Open the project SELECT6.VBP. The form shown in Figure 3.8 appears. Use the
Data control's record navigation buttons to page through the records in the
recordset.

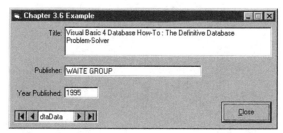

Figure 3.8. The SQL Inner Join form on startup.

1. Create a new project called SELECT6.VBP. Use Form1 to create the objects
and properties listed in Table 3.9.

Table 3.9. Options and properties for the INNER JOINer form.

OBJECT	PROPERTY	SETTING
Form	Name	Form1
	Caption	Chapter 3.6 Example
TextBox	Name	txtYearPublished
	DataField	Year Published
	DataSource	dtaData
TextBox	Name	txtPublisher
	DataField	Name
	DataSource	dtaData
TextBox	Name	txtTitle
	DataField	Title
	DataSource	dtaData
CommandButton	Name	cmdClose
	Caption	&Close
Data	Name	dtaData

continued on next page

continued from previous page

OBJECT	PROPERTY	SETTING
	Caption	dtaData
	RecordSource	SELECT DISTINCTROW Titles.Title,
		Publishers.Name, Titles.[Year
		Published] FROM Publishers INNER
		JOIN
		Titles ON Publishers.PubID =
		Titles.PubID ORDER BY
		Titles.Title
Label	Name	lblYearPublished
	AutoSize	True
	Caption	Year Published:
Label	Name	lblPublisher
	AutoSize	True
	Caption	Publisher:
Label	Name	lblTitle
	AutoSize	True
	Caption	Title:

2. Add the following code to the declarations section of **Form1**:

```
Option Explicit

Private Const BIBLIO_PATH = _
"D:\Program Files\Microsoft Visual Studio\VB6\Biblio.MDB"
```

3. Add the following code as the **Load** event of **Form1**:

```
Private Sub Form_Load()
    'Set the DatabaseName for the Data control.
    dtaData.DatabaseName = BIBLIO_PATH
End Sub
```

4. Add the following code as the **Click** event of **cmdClose**:

```
Private Sub cmdClose_Click()
    End
End Sub
```

How It Works

This program makes use of the innate capabilities of bound controls (discussed in more detail in Chapter 1, "Accessing a Database with Bound Controls") to illustrate the use of an **INNER JOIN**. When the program is started, the **Form_Load** event will set the **DatabaseName** property of the **dtaData** Data control to the location of BIBLIO.MDB. At this point, the `dtaData` Data control will run the SQL statement stored in its `RecordSource` property. The Data control will then handle the rest.

Comments

The `INNER JOIN` can be extremely useful in databases, but don't go "whole hog" with it. The more tables you add to a `JOIN`, no matter what type, the slower the SQL statement will execute. Consider this a database developer's maxim: Retrieve only the data you need; if you don't need it, don't include it. That goes for `JOIN`s as well. If you don't need the table, don't `JOIN` it.

COMPLEXITY
ADVANCED

3.7 How do I...
Find records in a table without corresponding entries in a related table?

Problem

I have an Orders table and a Customers table, related on the `Customer Number` field. I'd like to find all the customers who have not placed an order in the past six months. How can I do this?

Technique

The `INNER JOIN`, discussed in the preceding How-To, allows you to find all the records in a table that have matching records in another table, when the two tables are related on a key field and when "matching" means that values in the key fields match. SQL also provides an outer join, which lets you list all the records in one of the related tables whether or not they have matching records in the other table.

For example, assume that you have two tables, Customers and Invoices, with these entries:

Customers Table		Invoices Table		
Customer Number	Customer Name	Customer Number	Invoice Date	Invoice Amount
100	ABC Company	102	12/12/1996	$589.31
101	MNO Company	100	12/15/1996	$134.76
102	XYZ Company	102	12/22/1996	$792.13

Create a recordset using the following SQL statement with an `INNER JOIN` in the `FROM` clause:

continued on next page

continued from previous page

```
SELECT Customers.[Customer Name], Customers.[Customer Number],
    Invoices.[Customer Number], Invoices.[Invoice Date],
    Invoices.[Invoice Amount]
FROM Customers INNER JOIN Invoices
ON Customers.[Customer Number] = Invoices.[Customer Number]
ORDER BY Customers.[Customer Number], Invoices.[Invoice Date]
```

Executing that statement returns this recordset:

	Customers		Invoices		
Customer Name	Customer Number	Customer Number	Invoice Date	Invoice Amount
ABC Company	100	100	12/15/1996	$134.76
XYZ Company	102	102	12/12/1996	$589.31
XYZ Company	102	102	12/22/1996	$792.13

MNO Company, customer number 101, would not appear at all in the recordset because there are no records in the Invoices table for customer number 101, and an **INNER JOIN** returns only records with matching key field values in both tables. But see what happens when you change the join type in the **FROM** to a **LEFT JOIN**, one of the two types of outer joins:

```
SELECT Customers.[Customer Name], Customers.[Customer Number],
    Invoices.[Customer Number], Invoices.[Invoice Date],
    Invoices.[Invoice Amount]
FROM Customers LEFT JOIN Invoices
ON Customers.[Customer Number] = Invoices.[Customer Number]
ORDER BY Customers.[Customer Number], Invoices.[Invoice Date]
```

Executing this SQL statement returns this recordset:

	Customers		Invoices		
Customer Name	Customer Number	Customer Number	Invoice Date	Invoice Amount
ABC Company	100	100	12/15/1996	$134.76
MNO Company	101			
XYZ Company	102	102	12/12/1996	$589.31
XYZ Company	102	102	12/22/1996	$792.13

The recordset consists of all the records that the **INNER JOIN** version produced, and one additional record for each record in the table on the left side of the **FROM** clause that has no matching records in the table on the right side of the **FROM** clause.

LEFT JOINS AND RIGHT JOINS

There are two outer joins: LEFT JOIN and RIGHT JOIN. The *direction* of the join refers to the relative position of the table names in the FROM clause of the SQL statement. A LEFT JOIN returns a record from the table on the left side of the FROM clause, whether or not a matching record exists on the right side. A RIGHT JOIN returns a record from the table on the right side of the FROM clause, whether or not a matching record exists on the left side. These two FROM clauses, therefore, have identical results:

```
FROM Customers LEFT JOIN Invoices
```

```
ON Customers.[Customer Number] = Invoices.[Customer Number]

FROM Invoices RIGHT JOIN Customers
ON Invoices.[Customer Number] = Customers.[Customer Number]
```

The "missing" fields on the right side of the recordset all have the value **NULL**. You can use this fact to modify the SQL statement to select only the records from the left table that do not have matching records in the right table:

```
SELECT Customers.[Customer Name], Customers.[Customer Number],
    Invoices.[Customer Number], Invoices.[Invoice Date],
    Invoices.[Invoice Amount]
FROM Customers LEFT JOIN Invoices
ON Customers.[Customer Number] = Invoices.[Customer Number]
WHERE Invoice.[Customer Number] IS NULL
ORDER BY Customers.[Customer Number], Invoices.[Invoice Date]
```

This statement returns the following recordset:

Customers		Invoices		
Customer Name	Customer Number	Customer Number	Invoice Date	Invoice Amount
MNO Company	101			

The field used in the **WHERE** clause can be any field from the right-side table because all right-side fields will be **NULL** when there is no record to match a left-side table record.

Steps

Open the project SELECT7.VBP. The form shown in Figure 3.9 appears. The list shows all the publishers in the Publishers table that do not have entries in the Publisher Comments table.

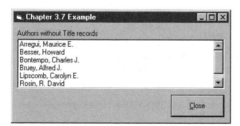

Figure 3.9. The SQL Left Join form on startup.

1. Create a new project called SELECT7.VBP. Use **Form1** to create the objects and properties listed in Table 3.10.

Table 3.10. Options and properties for the Outer JOINer form.

OBJECT	PROPERTY	SETTING
Form	Name	Form1
	Caption	Chapter 3.7 Example
Data	Name	dtaData
	Caption	dtaData
	RecordSource	SELECT Publishers.[Company Name]
		FROM Publishers LEFT JOIN
		[Publisher Comments] ON
		Publishers.PubID = [Publisher
		Comments].PubID WHERE [Publisher
		Comments].PubID IS NULL ORDER BY
		[Company Name]
	Visible	False
DBList	Name	dlstAuthors
	RowSource	dtaData
	ListField	Author
CommandButton	Name	cmdClose
	Caption	&Close
Label	Name	lblAuthors
	Caption	Authors without Title records:

2. Add the following code to the declarations section of **Form1**:

```
Option Explicit

Private Const BIBLIO_PATH = _
"D:\Program Files\Microsoft Visual Studio\VB6\Biblio.MDB"
```

3. Add the following code to the **Load** event of **Form1**:

```
Private Sub Form_Load()
    'Set the DatabaseName of the Data control.
    dtaData.DatabaseName = BIBLIO_PATH
End Sub
```

4. Add the following code as the **Click** event of **cmdClose**:

```
Private Sub cmdClose_Click()
    End
End Sub
```

How It Works

The `dtaData` recordset is built by the following SQL statement:

```
SELECT Publishers.[Company Name]
FROM Publishers LEFT JOIN [Publisher Comments]
ON Publishers.PubID = [Publisher Comments].PubID
WHERE [Publisher Comments].PubID IS NULL
ORDER BY [Company Name]
```

The WHERE clause of that SQL statement creates a LEFT JOIN between the left-side table (Publishers) and the right-side table (Publisher Comments). Ignoring the WHERE clause for a moment, this LEFT JOIN would create a snapshot with one record for each record in the Publisher Comments table, plus one record for every record in the Publishers table that does not have a matching record in Publisher Comments.

The WHERE clause eliminates from the snapshot all records in which there is a Publisher Comment, because the `[Publisher Comments].PubID` field will not be NULL where there is a record in Publisher Comments. For snapshot records created by records in Publishers without matching records in Publisher Comments, `[Publisher Comments].PubID` is NULL; the WHERE clause causes these records to be included in the output snapshot.

Comments

Like the INNER JOIN, explained in the preceding How-To, this can be a powerful tool if used well. You should experiment with the behavior of all sorts of joins—you might be surprised at what you get. Use this How-To's code as a basic example, and go from there, trying out different SQL joins to get a feel for what to expect with other SQL queries involving JOIN statements.

COMPLEXITY

INTERMEDIATE

3.8 How do I...
Retrieve information such as counts, averages, and sums and display it by binding it to a Data control?

Problem

I'd like to extract descriptive statistics about the data in a table (for example, averages and sums or numeric fields, minimum and maximum values, and counts of records that meet certain criteria). How can I use SQL to accomplish this task?

Technique

SQL includes a rich set of aggregate functions—functions you can embed in SQL statements to return descriptive statistics about the data in your database. Table 3.11 lists the aggregate functions available and shows what each function returns. Note that all functions ignore NULL values in the recordset.

Table 3.11. SQL aggregate functions.

AGGREGATE FUNCTION	RETURNS
Sum	Sum of the values in a designated numeric field
Avg	Average of the non-NULL values in a designated numeric field
Count	Count of non-NULL values in one or more designated fields
Min	Minimum value in a designated numeric or text field
Max	Maximum value in a designated numeric or text field
First	Value of a designated field in the first record in the recordset
Last	Value of a designated field in the last record in the recordset
StDev	Sample standard deviation of the non-NULL values in a designated field
StDevP	Population standard deviation of the non-NULL values in a designated field
Var	Sample variance of the non-NULL values in a designated field
VarP	Population variance of the non-NULL values in a designated field

The syntax for using these functions in the SELECT clause of a SQL statement is the same for all functions:

```
<functionname>(<fieldname>) AS <outputfieldname>
```

The `<fieldname>` is the name of the field in the table whose records you are examining. The `<outputfieldname>` is the name you give to the result column in the recordset created by the SQL statement. The two field names must be different, and the `<outputfieldname>` cannot duplicate the name of a field in any table referenced in the SQL statement.

For example, assume that you want to get a total of the Invoice Amount field for all Invoice Table records with Invoice Dates between January 1, 1996, and January 31, 1996. Your SQL statement could be this:

```
SELECT SUM([Invoice Amount]) AS SumOfInvoices
FROM Invoices
WHERE [Invoice Date] BETWEEN #1/1/1996# AND #1/31/1996#
```

That statement would return a recordset consisting of one record with one field, with a field name of SumOfInvoices. The field's value would be the total of all the invoices between the specified dates.

You can include more than one aggregate function in a SQL statement. The following statement would return a single record with two fields, SumOfInvoices and AverageInvoice. SumOfInvoices would be the sum of all invoices for the designated customer. AverageInvoice would be the average invoice amount for that customer (disregarding any fields for which the Invoice Amount is NULL).

```
SELECT SUM([Invoice Amount]) AS SumOfInvoices, AVG([Invoice Number])
        as AverageInvoice
FROM Invoices
WHERE [Customer Number] = 12345
```

Steps

Open the project SELECT8.VBP. The form shown in Figure 3.10 appears. The labels on the form show several statistics about the authors in the Authors table of BIBLIO.MDB.

Figure 3.10. The SQL Aggregate form.

1. Create a new project called SELECT8.VBP. Use **Form1** to create the objects and properties listed in Table 3.12. Save the form as SELECT8.FRM.

Table 3.12. Options and properties for the Author Statistics form.

OBJECT	PROPERTY	SETTING
Form	Name	Form1
	Caption	Chapter 3.8 Example
Data	Name	dtaData
	Caption	dtaData
	RecordSource	SELECT Count(*) AS
		CountOfAuthor, Avg([Year Born])
		AS [AvgOfYear Born], Min([Year
		Born]) AS [MinOfYear Born],
		Max([Year Born]) AS [MaxOfYear
		Born] FROM Authors
	Visible	False
	RecordsetType	Snapshot

continued on next page

continued from previous page

OBJECT	PROPERTY	SETTING
CommandButton	Name	cmdClose
	Cancel	True
	Caption	&Close
	Default	True
Label	Name	dlblCount
	BorderStyle	Fixed Single
	DataField	CountOfAuthor
	DataSource	dtaData
Label	Name	dlblMin
	BorderStyle	Fixed Single
	DataField	MinOfYear Born
	DataSource	dtaData
Label	Name	dlblMax
	BorderStyle	Fixed Single
	DataField	MaxOfYear Born
	DataSource	dtaData
Label	Name	dlblAvg
	BorderStyle	Fixed Single
	DataField	AvgOfYear Born
	DataSource	dtaData
Label	Name	lblCount
	AutoSize	True
	Caption	Number of authors:
Label	Name	lblMin
	AutoSize	True
	Caption	Earliest year born:
Label	Name	lblMax
	AutoSize	True
	Caption	Latest year born:
Label	Name	lblAvg
	AutoSize	True
	Caption	Average year born:

2. Add the following code to the declarations section of `Form1`:

```
Option Explicit
```

```
Private Const BIBLIO_PATH = _
"D:\Program Files\Microsoft Visual Studio\VB6\Biblio.MDB"
```

3. Add the following code to the **Load** event of **Form1**:

```
Private Sub Form_Load()
    'Set the DatabaseName of the Data control.
    dtaData.DatabaseName = BIBLIO_PATH
End Sub
```

4. Add the following code as the **Click** event of **cmdClose**:

```
Private Sub cmdClose_Click()
    End
End Sub
```

How It Works

The Data control creates a one-record recordset with this SQL statement:

```
SELECT Count(*) AS CountOfAuthor, Avg([Year Born]) AS [AvgOfYear Born],
Min([Year Born]) AS [MinOfYear Born], Max([Year Born]) AS [MaxOfYear Born]
FROM Authors
```

The single record contains four fields, each reporting one statistic about the records in the Authors table. The four bound labels on the form are each bound to one of the recordset fields.

Comments

The SQL statement used in the example for this How-To included this expression in its **SELECT** clause:

```
Count(*) as CountOfAuthor
```

Using the wildcard character * as the argument to the **Count** aggregate function indicates that you want the count of all the records in the table. You can achieve the same thing by using a field that you know to be non-**NULL** in every record (for example, the primary key of the table, which must by definition be non-**NULL**):

```
Count ([AuthorID]) as CountOfAuthor
```

However, it's better to use the wildcard character *, because the Jet database engine is optimized to perform **Count** queries with the wildcard. You get the same answer either way, but you get it faster with the wildcard.

COMPLEXITY
ADVANCED

3.9 How do I...
Create a recordset consisting of records with duplicate values?

Problem

I need to create a recordset that shows records with duplicate values. How can I do this with SQL?

Technique

Three features of SQL—the **GROUP BY** clause, the **HAVING** clause, and SQL **IN** subqueries—facilitate the identification of duplicate values in a table.

The GROUP BY **Clause**

SQL provides the **GROUP BY** clause, which combines records with identical values into a single record. If you include a SQL aggregate function (such as **COUNT**) in the **SELECT** statement, the **GROUP BY** clause applies that function to each group of records to create a summary value.

For example, to return a recordset with one record for each unique state/city pair from the Publishers table in BIBLIO.MDB, you can use this SQL statement:

```
SELECT State, City, COUNT(*) AS CountByCityAndState FROM Publishers
GROUP BY State, City
```

The HAVING **Clause**

The **HAVING** clause is similar to the **WHERE** clause, but you use **HAVING** with **GROUP BY**. The argument to **HAVING** specifies which grouped records created by **GROUP BY** should be included in the output recordset. For example, this SQL statement returns one record for each unique state/city pair from the Publishers table in BIBLIO.MDB, restricting the records to those in which the state is **CA**:

```
SELECT [State],[City] FROM [Publishers]
GROUP BY [State],[City]
HAVING [State] = 'CA'
```

You can use **HAVING** with the aggregate **COUNT** function (see the preceding How-To for information on aggregate functions) to restrict the output recordset to records in which the values grouped by the **GROUP BY** clause have a specified range of occurrences. This example selects only city/state pairs that occur more than once in the table:

```
SELECT [State],[City] FROM [Publishers]
GROUP BY [State],[City]
HAVING COUNT(*) > 1
```

The SELECT and GROUP BY clauses in this example create a recordset to which the HAVING clause applies the COUNT aggregate function. The HAVING COUNT(*) > 1 clause eliminates from the final output recordset record groups that occur only once.

You can use multiple criteria with the HAVING clause. This example selects only city/state pairs that occur more than once in the table where the state is CA:

```
SELECT [State],[City] FROM [Publishers]
GROUP BY [State],[City]
HAVING COUNT(*) > 1 AND [State] = 'CA'
```

SQL IN Subqueries

An IN subquery is a SELECT statement nested inside the WHERE clause of another SELECT statement. The subquery returns a set of records, each consisting of a single field. The WHERE clause then compares a field from the "main" SELECT statement to the field returned by the subquery. The resultant recordset consists of those records from the main recordset where the main field equals the subquery field.

Consider this simple SELECT query:

```
SELECT [City], [Company Name] FROM [Publishers]
ORDER BY [City]
```

This query creates a recordset consisting of one record for every record in the [Publishers] table, sorted by [City]. Now add a WHERE clause containing an IN subquery:

```
SELECT [City], [Company Name] FROM [Publishers]
WHERE [City] IN
        (SELECT [City] FROM [Publishers]
        GROUP BY [City]
        HAVING COUNT(*) > 1)
ORDER BY [City]
```

The subquery in the example is parenthesized and indented. (The parentheses are required; the indenting is not.) The subquery returns one record for every [City] value that occurs more than one time in the [Publishers] table. If a [City] value occurs only once, it is not included in the subquery output.

The WHERE clause of the main query compares the [City] field of every record in the table to the set of [City] values returned by the subquery. If there is a match, the record is included in the main query's output recordset. If there is no match, the record is excluded from the output recordset. Because the subquery [City] values include only those occurring more than once in the table, the WHERE clause includes in the output recordset only those records with a [City] value that occurs more than once.

If you need a recordset based on a single duplicated field, the last illustration is sufficient. If you need to compare multiple fields to find duplicate values, additional steps are required. For example, your [Publishers] table contains records in which the [City] field is duplicated but in which the [State] field differs, as in the following table:

```
CITY                STATE
Springfield         IL
Springfield         MA
Springfield         OH
```

(The BIBLIO.MDB database supplied with Visual Basic does not have any records in which this condition exists, but a real-life example might.)

Finding the true duplicates here requires additions to the subquery. The additions to the original subquery are shown here in bold:

```
(SELECT [City] FROM [Publishers] AS Tmp
GROUP BY [City], [State]
HAVING COUNT(*) > 1 AND [State] = Publishers.[State])
```

The addition of the State field to the GROUP BY clause creates a record for every unique combination of City and State; the three Springfields will now each appear in the recordset returned by the GROUP BY. The additional criterion, State = Publishers.State, in the HAVING clause compares the State field in each GROUP BY record output to the State field in the original Publishers table and selects only those in which the fields are equal; note that the table name on the right side of the equal sign is mandatory. Because of the additional criterion in the HAVING clause, it is necessary to assign the output of the subquery to a temporary variable—arbitrarily called Tmp—but any legal name that does not duplicate an existing field name will do.

You can use up to 10 criteria in a subquery. For additional criteria, simply append them to the GROUP BY clause with a comma and to the HAVING clause with the AND keyword.

Steps

Open and run the project SELECT9.VBP. The form shown in Figure 3.11 appears. The grid control on the form shows records from the Publishers table for which the city and state appear more than once in the table.

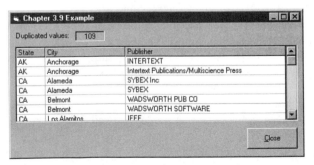

Figure 3.11. The duplicate SELECTer form on startup.

1. Create a new project called SELECT9.VBP. Use **Form1** to create the objects and properties listed in Table 3.13, and save the form as SELECT9.FRM.

Table 3.13. Objects and properties for the Duplicate SELECTer form.

OBJECT	PROPERTY	SETTING
Form	Name	Form1
	Caption	Chapter 3.9 Example
Label	Name	lblCount
	Alignment	2 - Center
	BorderStyle	1 - Fixed Single
Label	Name	lblDupValues
	Caption	Duplicated values:
Grid	Name	grdValues
	Cols	3
	FixedCols	0
	Scrollbars	2 - Vertical
CommandButton	Name	cmdClose
	Cancel	True
	Caption	&Close

2. Add the following code to the declarations section of **Form1**:

```
Option Explicit

Private Const BIBLIO_PATH = _
"D:\Program Files\Microsoft Visual Studio\VB6\Biblio.MDB"
```

3. Enter the following code as the **Load** event for **Form1**. For the **Form_Load** event, the routine first creates a **Database** object. Then it starts creating the SQL statement from the inside out by first creating the subquery in the **strSubQuery** string and then "wrapping" the rest of the query around it inside the **strSQL** string. After execution, if records are present, the **grdValues** grid is configured and populated with the contents of the [State], [City], and [Company Name] fields.

```
Private Sub Form_Load()
    Dim dbfBiblio As Database, recSelect As Recordset
    Dim strSQL As String, strSubQuery As String
    Dim intCount As Integer, intGridRow As Integer

    ' Get the database name and open the database.
```

continued on next page

continued from previous page

```
            Set dbfBiblio = _
        DBEngine.Workspaces(0).OpenDatabase(BIBLIO_PATH)

            ' Build the subquery, starting with its SELECT statement.
            strSubQuery = "SELECT City FROM Publishers AS Tmp " & _
                "GROUP BY City, State " & _
                "HAVING COUNT(*) > 1 AND State = Publishers.State "

            ' Build the SQL statement
            ' Start by designating the fields to be included in the
            ' recordset and the WHERE IN clause
            strSQL = "SELECT City, State, [Company Name]" & _
                "FROM Publishers " _
                "WHERE City IN (" & strSubQuery & ") " & _
                "ORDER BY State, City"

            ' Run the query.
            Set recSelect = dbfBiblio.OpenRecordset(strSQL, _
                dbOpenSnapshot)

            ' Make sure the query returned at least one record
            If recSelect.RecordCount > 0 Then

                ' Get a count of records in the recordset and display it
                ' on the form.
                recSelect.MoveLast
                intCount = recSelect.RecordCount
                lblCount.Caption = intCount

                ' Initialize the grid
                With grdValues
                    .Rows = intCount + 1
                    .ColWidth(0) = 700: .ColWidth(1) = 2000: _
                                .ColWidth(2) = 4000
                    .Row = 0: .Col = 0: .Text = "State"
                    .Col = 1: .Text = "City"
                    .Col = 2: .Text = "Publisher"
                End With

                'Populate the grid
                recSelect.MoveFirst
                For intGridRow = 1 To intCount
                    With grdValues
                        .Row = intGridRow
                        .Col = 0: .Text = recSelect![State]
                        .Col = 1: .Text = recSelect![City]
                        .Col = 2: .Text = recSelect![Company Name]
                    End With
                    recSelect.MoveNext
                Next intGridRow
            End If
        End Sub
```

4. Enter the following code as the `Click` event of `cmdClose`. This event ends the application.

```
Private Sub cmdClose_Click()
        End
End Sub
```

How It Works

The `Form_Load()` event subroutine creates a SQL statement, first by building the subquery and then by creating the main query with the inserted subquery. (Refer to the "Technique" section for an explanation of the syntax of the SQL statement.) The subroutine then executes the query and creates a `Recordset` object. If the recordset contains at least one record, the subroutine initializes the grid control and inserts each record into the grid.

Comments

If you insert the word `NOT` in front of the word `IN`, a `SELECT` statement containing an `IN` subquery returns a recordset consisting of records that do not meet the criteria of the subquery. Assume that you changed the query in the example by inserting the word `NOT`:

```
SELECT [City], [Company Name] FROM [Publishers]
WHERE [City] NOT IN
        (SELECT [City] FROM [Publishers] AS Tmp
         GROUP BY [City], [State]
         HAVING COUNT(*) > 1 AND [State] = Publishers.[State])
ORDER BY [City]
```

This query would produce a recordset consisting of records with a city/state combination that occur only once in the table.

COMPLEXITY

INTERMEDIATE

3.10 How do I...
Use Visual Basic functions within a SQL statement?

Problem

I need to create a recordset with special formatting based on the contents of a field, but I can't find any standard SQL function to use for the formatting.

Technique

One of the benefits of using the Jet database engine and Data Access Objects is the capability of embedding Visual Basic for Applications (VBA) functions in Access SQL for various tasks that SQL by itself could not accomplish easily.

Steps

Open and run the project SELECT10.VBP. The form shown in Figure 3.12 appears. The grid control on the form shows records from the Publishers table, before and after the execution of the LCase() function to convert the case from uppercase to lowercase.

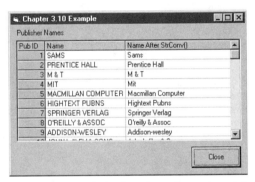

Figure 3.12. The Visual Basic code with SQL form, showing Publishers data.

1. Create a new project called SELECT10.VBP. Use **Form1** to create the objects and properties listed in Table 3.14, and save the form as SELECT10.FRM.

Table 3.14. Objects and properties for the Duplicate SELECTer form.

OBJECT	PROPERTY	SETTING
Form	Name	Form1
	Caption	Chapter 3.10 Example
Label	Name	lblPublishers
	Caption	Publisher Names
MSFlexGrid	Name	grdValues
	Cols	3
	FixedCols	1
	AllowUserResizing	1 - flexResizeColumns
	Scrollbars	2 - Vertical
	Width	5655

OBJECT	PROPERTY	SETTING
CommandButton	Name	cmdClose
	Cancel	True
	Caption	&Close

2. Add the following statements to the declarations section of **Form1**. Ensure that the **BIBLIO_PATH** constant is set to the location of BIBLIO.MDB on your workstation.

```
Option Explicit

Private Const BIBLIO_PATH = _
"D:\Program Files\Microsoft Visual Studio\VB6\Biblio.MDB"
```

3. Enter the following code as the **Load** event for **Form1**. As with the preceding How-To, the event starts by creating a **Database** object, opening BIBLIO.MDB for use. Then a SQL statement is created, using the VBA function **LCase** to convert the string to lowercase, as denoted by the second parameter in the command. (For more information on the **LCase** command, search for **LCase** in the Visual Basic Help Index.) Note that the constant for the second parameter, **vbProperCase**, was not used here—some constants might not be accessible by the SQL precompiler used by the DAO library.

```
Private Sub Form_Load()
    Dim dbfBiblio As Database, recSelect As Recordset
    Dim strSQL As String
    Dim intCount As Integer, intGridRow As Integer

    Set dbfBiblio = _
DBEngine.Workspaces(0).OpenDatabase(BIBLIO_PATH)

    ' Build the query, starting with its SELECT statement.
    ' Note the LCase() function; a VBA function, NOT a SQL
    ' function.
    strSQL = "SELECT Publishers.PubID, Publishers.Name, " & _
            "LCase([Publishers].[Name],3) AS CheckedName " & _
            "FROM Publishers;"

    ' Run the query to create the recordset.
    Set recSelect = _
        dbfBiblio.OpenRecordset(strSQL, dbOpenSnapshot)

    ' Make sure the query returned at least one record
    If recSelect.RecordCount > 0 Then

        'Get the record count & display it on the form
        recSelect.MoveLast
        intCount = recSelect.RecordCount
        lblPublishers.Caption = "Publisher Names (" & _
CStr(intCount) & "records)"
```

continued on next page

continued from previous page

```
'Initialize the grid
With grdValues
    .Rows = intCount + 1
    .ColWidth(0) = 700: .ColWidth(1) = 2000:
    .ColWidth(2) = 4000
    .Row = 0: .Col = 0: .Text = "Pub ID"
    .Col = 1: .Text = "Name"
    .Col = 2: .Text = "Name After LCase()"
End With

'Populate the grid
recSelect.MoveFirst
For intGridRow = 1 To intCount
    With grdValues
        .Row = intGridRow
        .Col = 0: .Text = recSelect![PubID]
        .Col = 1: .Text = recSelect![Name]
        .Col = 2: .Text = recSelect![CheckedName]
    End With
    recSelect.MoveNext
Next intGridRow
    End If
End Sub
```

4. Enter the following code as the `Click` event of `cmdClose`:

```
Private Sub cmdClose_Click()
    End
End Sub
```

How It Works

The `Form_Load()` event creates a SQL statement, showing both the raw data in the `[Name]` field and the same data after processing by the `LCase()` VBA function to "scrub" the raw data. The recordset data is placed directly into the grid with no further processing.

Comments

VBA functionality can expand DAO query power enormously, allowing for everything from math functions to string processing within the SQL. Rather than the tedious and time-consuming process of performing the same action by looping through a recordset and using the same VBA function to modify the data field by field, the ease of using a single SQL statement should strongly encourage you to experiment with VBA functions in Access SQL.

COMPLEXITY
INTERMEDIATE

3.11 How do I...
Make bulk updates to database records?

Problem

I need to make an identical change to a number of records that meet certain criteria. How can I accomplish this task with a single SQL statement?

Technique

In addition to **SELECT** queries, which create recordsets based on criteria you specify, SQL provides a group of action query statements. One type of action query is the **UPDATE** query, which makes specified changes to a set of records that meet designated criteria.

An **UPDATE** query contains the clauses shown in Table 3.15. The example shown in Table 3.15 increases the **[Price Each]** field by 3% for each record in the [Parts List] table that has a **[Part Number]** beginning with the string **"XYZ7"**.

Table 3.15. The *UPDATE* statement.

CLAUSE	PURPOSE	EXAMPLE
UPDATE	Names the table	UPDATE [Parts List]
SET	Designates the fields to be updated and their new values	SET [Price Each] = [Price Each] * 1.03
WHERE	Specifies the records to be updated	WHERE [Part Number] LIKE "XYZ7*"

You run a SQL action query statement using the **Execute** method of the **Database** object. Assuming that you have a **Database** object **db**, you would run the query shown in the table using this Visual Basic code (the entire statement would normally appear on one line):

```
db.Execute("UPDATE [Parts List] SET [Price Each] = " & _
    "[Price Each] * 1.03 WHERE [Part Number] LIKE 'XYZ7'")
```

Steps

The BIBLIO.MDB file distributed with Visual Basic contains outdated information about four publishers. These publishers were formerly located on College Ave. in Carmel, IN. They have moved to an address in Indianapolis. The

UPDATE.VBP project updates all four publishers' records to show their new address. It also provides the capability to restore the firms' original Carmel address.

Open the project UPDATE.VBP and run the project. Click the Update button and the form appears as shown in Figure 3.13. Click the Restore button, and the addresses change to show the Carmel address.

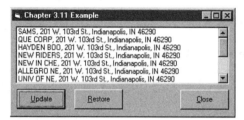

Figure 3.13. The SQL Update form after the update.

1. Create a new project called UPDATE.VBP. Use **Form1** to create the objects and properties listed in Table 3.16, and save the form as UPDATE.FRM.

Table 3.16. Objects and properties for the UPDATEr form.

OBJECT	PROPERTY	SETTING
Form	Name	Form1
	Caption	UPDATEr
CommandButton	Name	cmdClose
	Cancel	True
	Caption	&Close
CommandButton	Name	cmdRestore
	Caption	&Restore
CommandButton	Name	cmdUpdate
	Caption	&Update
ListBox	Name	lstData

2. Add the following statements to the declarations section of **Form1**:

```
Option Explicit

Private Const BIBLIO_PATH = _
"D:\Program Files\Microsoft Visual Studio\VB6\Biblio.MDB"
Private dbfBiblio As Database
```

3. Add the following code as the Click event of cmdUpdate.

```
Private Sub cmdUpdate_Click()
Dim strSQL As String

    On Error GoTo UpdateError
        'Build the UPDATE statement.
        strSQL = "UPDATE Publishers " & _
            "SET City = 'Indianapolis', " & _
                Address = '201 W. 103rd St.', " & _
            "Zip = '46290' " & _
            "WHERE ([City] = 'Carmel') AND " & _
                (Address LIKE '*11711*College*')"

        'Execute the update query.
        dbfBiblio.Execute strSQL

        ListRecords "Indianapolis"
    On Error GoTo 0
Exit Sub

UpdateError:
    MsgBox Err.Description, vbExclamation
Exit Sub

End Sub
```

This procedure builds a SQL **UPDATE** statement that changes the contents of the [City], [Address], and [Zip] fields for each record that meets the criteria. The criteria are the city being equal to "Carmel" and the address containing the strings "11711" and "College". The LIKE clause in the address is necessary because BIBLIO.MDB, as supplied, uses a different form of the same address for each of the four publishers at 11711 N. College Ave.

The procedure executes the SQL statement, using the **Execute** method of the **Database** object. It then calls the **ListRecords** subroutine to display the records.

4. Add the following code as the Click event of cmdRestore. The cmdRestore routine reverses the action of cmdUpdate, using the same methodology.

```
Private Sub cmdRestore_Click()
Dim strSQL As String

    On Error GoTo RestoreError
        'Build the UPDATE statement.
        strSQL = "UPDATE Publishers " & _
            "SET City = 'Carmel', " & _
                    "Address = '11711 N. College Ave.', " & _
            "Zip = '46032' " & _
            " WHERE ([City] = 'Indianapolis') AND " & _
                "(Address = '201 W. 103rd St.')"
```

continued on next page

continued from previous page

```
                    'Execute the update query.
                    dbfBiblio.Execute strSQL

                    ListRecords "Carmel"
                On Error GoTo 0
            Exit Sub

            RestoreError:
                MsgBox Error$, vbExclamation
            Exit Sub
            End Sub
```

5. Create the subroutine `ListRecords` by entering the following code.
`ListRecords` builds a SQL **SELECT** statement that selects records, based on
the city name passed as the parameter, and then lists these records in the
list box on the form.

```
Private Sub ListRecords(cityName As String)
    Dim recSelect As Recordset
    Dim strSQL As String, strAddress As String

    On Error GoTo ListError
        ' Set the correct street address based on the city name.
        strAddress = IIf(strCity = "Indianapolis", _
                    "201 W. 103rd St.", _
                    "11711 N. College Ave.")

        ' Create the recordset for the list box.
        strSQL = "SELECT [Company Name], [Address], [City], " & _
            "[State], [Zip] " & _
            "FROM Publishers " & _
            "WHERE [City] = '" & strCity & "'" & _
                "AND [Address] = '" & _
            strAddress & "'"

        'Construct the recordset.
        Set recSelect = _
                dbfBiblio.OpenRecordset(strSQL, dbOpenSnapshot)

        'Clear the list box
        lstData.Clear

        'Show each record in the list box.
        If recSelect.RecordCount > 0 Then
            recSelect.MoveFirst
            Do
                lstData.AddItem
                    Left$(recSelect![Company Name], 10) _
                    & ", " & recSelect![Address] & ", " & _
                            recSelect![City] _
                    & ", " & recSelect![State] & " " & _
                            recSelect![Zip]
                recSelect.MoveNext
            Loop While Not recSelect.EOF
        End If
```

```
        On Error GoTo 0
    Exit Sub

    ListError:
        MsgBox Err.Description, vbExclamation
    Exit Sub
    End Sub
```

6. Add the following code as the `Click` event of `cmdClose`:

```
    Private Sub cmdClose_Click()
        End
    End Sub
```

How It Works

Until the user clicks either the Update or the Restore button, the form just lies in wait. If the user clicks the Update button, the form executes a SQL statement, modifying any record the statement finds with specific [City] and [Address] field contents, changing the [City], [Address], and [Zip] fields. The Restore performs exactly the same action but reverses the actions taken by the Update button, searching for the newly altered records and restoring them to their previous values.

Comments

This method is usually the best way to make bulk updates to records in any database; it gets the database to do the work rather than the calling application, usually in a more efficient fashion. But, as with any powerful tool, this method can be misused. Ensure that your WHERE clause incorporates *only* those records to be changed. Have too "loose" a selection, and records might be mistakenly altered; this might happen much too quickly for the error to be stopped. Be cautious, and your caution will serve you well.

COMPLEXITY
INTERMEDIATE

3.12 How do I...
Create and delete tables?

Problem

I need to create a temporary table, use it for a while, and then get rid of it. How can I accomplish this using SQL?

Technique

SQL provides two statements that allow you to create and delete tables. CREATE TABLE creates a new table, using a name and field list that you specify. DROP TABLE deletes a named table.

To create a table with CREATE TABLE, you need to pass it two arguments: the name of the table to be created and a field list, with the field list enclosed in parentheses. The field list consists of a set of field descriptions separated by commas. Each field description has two parts: a field name and a data type. The field name and data type are separated by a space.

Execute the CREATE TABLE statement by passing it as the parameter of the Execute method of the Database object. The following Visual Basic statement creates a new table in the database represented by the Database object variable dbfTest. The new table is named My Parts and has two fields: [Part Name], which is a text field, and [Quantity], which is a long integer.

```
dbfTest.Execute("CREATE TABLE [My Parts] ([Part Name] TEXT, " & _
    "[Quantity] LONG)")
```

As with any table or field name, the brackets are required if the name contains a space, and they are optional if there is no space. The convention is to capitalize the data type, but this capitalization is not required.

The data type names used by the Jet database engine do not exactly match the names required by SQL. Table 3.17 shows the SQL data types and the corresponding Jet data type for each.

Table 3.17. SQL data types used by *CREATE TABLE* and their corresponding Jet database engine data types.

SQL DATA TYPE	EQUIVALENT JET DATA TYPE
BINARY	N/A—for queries on attached tables that define a BINARY data type
BIT	Yes/No
BYTE	Numeric—Byte
COUNTER	Counter
CURRENCY	Currency
DATETIME	Date/Time
SINGLE	Numeric—Single
DOUBLE	Numeric—Double
SHORT	Numeric—Integer
LONG	Numeric—Long
LONGTEXT	Memo
LONGBINARY	OLE objects
TEXT	Text

The DROP TABLE requires just one argument—the name of the table to be removed from the database. Like CREATE TABLE, the DROP TABLE statement is executed through the Execute method of the Database object. The following Visual Basic statement deletes the table My Parts from the database represented by dbfTest:

```
dbfTest.Execute("DROP TABLE [My Parts]")
```

Steps

The NEWTABLE.VBP project lets you create tables in BIBLIO.MDB and assign the table's fields using any data type. Open the project NEWTABLE.VBP and run the project. The form shown in Figure 3.14 appears.

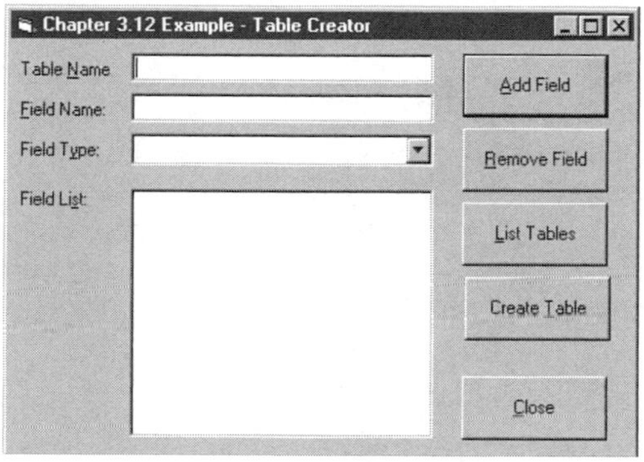

Figure 3.14. The SQL Create Table form at startup.

Click the List Tables button, and the form shown in Figure 3.15 appears. This form lists the tables currently in BIBLIO.MDB. Click Close to return to the Table Creator form.

In the Table Name text box, type any legal table name. In the Field Name text box, type a field name; then select a field type from the drop-down list. Click Add Field to create the field. Create several additional fields; for each field, type a field name, select a field type, and click Add Field. When you have several fields defined, the form will appear as shown in Figure 3.16. Click Create Table to add the table to BIBLIO.MDB. The table name and field names will disappear to prepare the Table Creator form to create another table. You can click List Tables to see your table BIBLIO.MDB.

After you've created several tables, click List Tables. Select one of the tables you created and click Delete. (The program will not let you delete a table with data in it, so you will not be able to delete any of the original BIBLIO.MDB tables.) The table disappears from the table list.

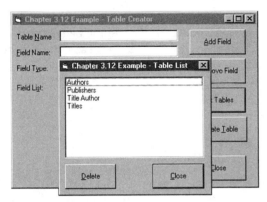

Figure 3.15. The Table List form, showing table names.

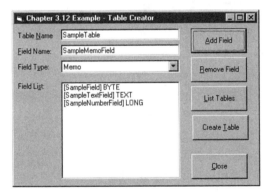

Figure 3.16. The SQL Create Table form, with new fields added.

1. Create a new project called NEWTABLE.VBP. Rename **Form1** to **frmMain**, create the objects and properties listed in Table 3.18, and save the form as NEWTABLE.FRM.

Table 3.18. Objects and properties for the Table Creator form.

OBJECT	PROPERTY	SETTING
Form	Name	frmMain
	Caption	Chapter 3.12 Example - Table Creator
CommandButton	Name	cmdListTables
	Caption	&List Tables
CommandButton	Name	cmdCreateTable

OBJECT	PROPERTY	SETTING
	Caption	Create &Table
CommandButton	Name	cmdRemoveField
	Caption	&Remove Field
CommandButton	Name	cmdAddField
	Caption	&Add Field
	Default	True
CommandButton	Name	cmdClose
	Cancel	True
	Caption	&Close
ComboBox	Name	cboFieldTypes
	Style	2 - Dropdown List
ListBox	Name	lstFields
TextBox	Name	txtFieldName
TextBox	Name	txtTableName
Label	Name	lblTableName
	Caption	&Table Name:
Label	Name	lblFieldName
	Caption	&Field Name:
Label	Name	lblFieldType
	Caption	Field T&ype:
Label	Name	lblFieldList
	Caption	Field Li&st:

2. Insert a new form into the project. Rename it `frmTableList`, create the objects and properties listed in Table 3.19, and save the form as TABLIST.FRM.

Table 3.19. Objects and properties for the Current Tables form.

OBJECT	PROPERTY	SETTING
Form	Name	frmTableList
	BorderStyle	3 - Fixed Dialog
	Caption	Chapter 3.12 Example - Table List
	MaxButton	False
	MinButton	False
CommandButton	Name	cmdDelete

continued on next page

continued from previous page

OBJECT	PROPERTY	SETTING
	Caption	&Delete
CommandButton	Name	cmdClose
	Caption	Close
ListBox	Name	lstTables
	Sorted	True

3. Add the following statements to the declarations section of **frmMain**:

```
Option Explicit

Private Const IllegalCharacters = "[].!'"
Private Const FIELDNAME = 1
Private Const TABLENAME = 2

Private Const BIBLIO_PATH = _
"D:\Program Files\Microsoft Visual Studio\VB6\Biblio.MDB"
```

4. Enter the following code for the **Form_Load** event for **frmMain**:

```
Private Sub Form_Load()
    'Fill the Field Type combo box.
    FillTypeList
End Sub
```

5. Create the **FillTypeList** subroutine in **frmMain** with the following code. This procedure fills the drop-down list with the available data types, using the Jet database engine names.

```
Sub FillTypeList()
'Fill the Field Type combo box with types of available fields
    With cboFieldTypes
        .AddItem "Counter"
        .AddItem "Currency"
        .AddItem "Date/Time"
        .AddItem "Memo"
        .AddItem "Number: Byte"
        .AddItem "Number: Integer"
        .AddItem "Number: Long"
        .AddItem "Number: Single"
        .AddItem "Number: Double"
        .AddItem "OLE Object"
        .AddItem "Text"
        .AddItem "Yes/No"
    End With
End Sub
```

6. Enter the following code as the **Click** event of **frmMain**'s **cmdListTables**. This subroutine displays the **List Tables** form modally.

```
Private Sub cmdListTables_Click()
    ' Display the Table List form modally.
    frmTableList.Show vbModal
End Sub
```

7. Enter the following code as the `Click` event of `frmMain`'s `cmdAddField`. The `cmdAddField` routine first calls the `LegalName` function to verify that the user has entered a legal field name and verifies that the user has selected a field type. It then translates the data type shown in the drop-down list from the Jet name to the SQL name. It formats the field name and data type and adds it to the field list. It then clears the field name and field type for entry of the next field.

```
Private Sub cmdAddField_Click()
Dim strFieldType As String

    'Check first if the Field Name text box contains a legal name
    If LegalName(FIELDNAME) Then
        'If it does, check if the Field Type has been selected.
        If cboFieldTypes.ListIndex > -1 Then
            'If both criteria are satisfied, store the SQL field
            'type in the strFieldType string.
            Select Case cboFieldTypes.Text
                Case "Counter"
                    strFieldType = "COUNTER"
                Case "Currency"
                    strFieldType = "CURRENCY"
                Case "Date/Time"
                    strFieldType = "DATETIME"
                Case "Memo"
                    strFieldType = "LONGTEXT"
                Case "Number: Byte"
                    strFieldType = "BYTE"
                Case "Number: Integer"
                    strFieldType = "SHORT"
                Case "Number: Long"
                    strFieldType = "LONG"
                Case "Number: Single"
                    strFieldType = "SINGLE"
                Case "Number: Double"
                    strFieldType = "DOUBLE"
                Case "OLE Object"
                    strFieldType = "LONGBINARY"
                Case "Text"
                    strFieldType = "TEXT"
                Case "Yes/No"
                    strFieldType = "BIT"
            End Select

            'Add the new field to the Field List list box.
            lstFields.AddItem "[" & txtFieldName & "] " & _
                            strFieldType
```

continued on next page

continued from previous page

```
                            'Reset the Field Name and Field Type controls.
                            txtFieldName = ""
                            cboFieldTypes.ListIndex = -1
                    Else
                        MsgBox "You must select a field type.", vbExclamation
                    End If
            End If
    End Sub
```

8. Create the **LegalName** function in **frmMain** by entering the following code. The function performs a number of checks to verify that the name entered by the user as a table name or field name is acceptable to the Jet engine. For each check, it generates a user-defined error if the name fails the test. The error-handling code displays a message that explains to the user what the problem is and then returns **False** to the calling routine. If the name passes all the tests, the error-handling code is never called, and the function returns **True**.

```
Function LegalName(intNameType As Integer) As Boolean
    Dim i As Integer
    Dim strObjectName As String
    Dim dbfBiblio As Database, tdfNewTable As TableDef

    On Error GoTo IllegalName
        'Depending on the type of name being checked, store either
        'the field or table name text box contents.
        If intNameType = FIELDNAME Then
            strObjectName = txtFieldName
        Else
            strObjectName = txtTableName
        End If

        'If blank, raise an error.
        If Len(strObjectName) = 0 Then Err.Raise 32767
        'If it has a leading space, raise an error.
        If Left$(strObjectName, 1) = " " Then Err.Raise 32766
        'If it contains any of the characters in the
        'IllegalCharacters constant, raise an error.
        For i = 1 To Len(IllegalCharacters)
            If InStr(strObjectName, Mid(IllegalCharacters,
                i, 1)) > 0 Then Err.Raise 32765
        Next i
        'If it contains any ANSI character from Chr$(0) to
        'Chr$(31), (you guessed it) raise an error.
        For i = 0 To 31
            If InStr(strObjectName, Chr(i)) > 0 _
                Then Err.Raise 32764
        Next i
```

```
            'Check if the field or table name already exists.  If so,
            'raise an error.
            If intNameType = FIELDNAME Then
                For i = 0 To lstFields.ListCount - 1
                    If strObjectName = lstFields.List(i) _
                        Then Err.Raise 32763
                Next i
            ElseIf intNameType = TABLENAME Then
                Set dbfBiblio = _
                    DBEngine.Workspaces(0).OpenDatabase(BIBLIO_PATH)
                For Each tdfNewTable In dbfBiblio.TableDefs
                    If tdfNewTable.Name = strObjectName _
                        Then Err.Raise 32762
                Next
            End If

            'If they've managed to get through all that validation,
            'the function should be True, to indicate success.
            LegalName = True
        On Error GoTo 0
    Exit Function

IllegalName:
    Dim strErrDesc As String, context As String

        'Note the use of an IIf statement to reduce code size.
        context = IIf(intNameType = FIELDNAME, "field name", _
                    "table name")

        'Build an error message based on the user-defined error that
        'occurred.
        Select Case Err.Number
            Case 32767
                strErrDesc = "You must enter a " & context & "."
            Case 32766
                strErrDesc = "The " & context & _
                            " cannot begin with a space."
            Case 32765
                strErrDesc = "The " & context & _
                    " contains the illegal character " & _
                    Mid(IllegalCharacters, i, 1) & "."
            Case 32764
                strErrDesc = "The " & context & _
                    " contains the control character " & _
                    "with the ANSI value" & Str$(i) & "."
            Case 32763
                strErrDesc = "The field name " & strObjectName & _
                    " already exists in the field name list."
            Case 32762
                strErrDesc = "The table name " & strObjectName & _
                    " already exists in the database " & _
                        BIBLIO_PATH & "."
            Case Else
```

continued on next page

continued from previous page

```
                        ' Visual Basic's default error message.
                    strErrDesc = Err.Description
            End Select

            MsgBox strErrDesc, vbExclamation

            'The function indicates False, or failure.
            LegalName = False
    Exit Function

    End Function
```

9. Enter the following code as the `Click` event of frmMain's cmdRemoveField. This procedure deletes the field selected by the user.

```
Private Sub cmdRemoveField_Click()
    ' If the user has selected a field, remove it from the list.
    ' Otherwise, just ignore the click.
    If lstFields.ListIndex > -1 Then lstFields.RemoveItem _
        lstFields.ListIndex
End Sub
```

10. Enter the following code as the `Click` event of frmMain's cmdCreateTable. This procedure calls **LegalName** to verify that the table name is acceptable and verifies that the user has defined at least one field. It creates the field list for the SQL statement by reading through the data in **lstFields** and building a comma-delimited string from the entries in that list box. It then builds the SQL statement and uses the **Execute** method of the **Database** object to create the table.

```
Private Sub cmdCreateTable_Click()
    Dim strSQL As String, strFieldList As String
    Dim i As Integer
    Dim dbfBiblio As Database

    On Error GoTo CreateTableError
        Screen.MousePointer = vbHourglass

        If LegalName(TABLENAME) Then
            If lstFields.ListCount > 0 Then
                strFieldList = " (" & lstFields.List(0)
                For i = 1 To lstFields.ListCount - 1
                    strFieldList = strFieldList & ", " & _
                                    lstFields.List(i)
                Next i
                strFieldList = strFieldList & ") "
                strSQL = "CREATE TABLE [" & txtTableName & "]" _
                        & strFieldList

                Set dbfBiblio = DBEngine.Workspaces(0). _
                        OpenDatabase(BIBLIO_PATH)
                dbfBiblio.Execute (strSQL)

                Screen.MousePointer = vbDefault
```

```
                    MsgBox "Table created successfully."

                    txtTableName = ""
                    lstFields.Clear
                Else
                    Screen.MousePointer = vbDefault
                    MsgBox "You must define at least one field.", _
                        vbExclamation
                End If
            End If
        On Error GoTo 0
    Exit Sub

    CreateTableError:
        Screen.MousePointer = vbDefault
        MsgBox Error$, vbExclamation
    Exit Sub
    End Sub
```

11. Enter the following code as the **Click** event of **frmMain**'s **cmdClose**. Unlike most of the **cmdClose_Click** events in previous How-To's, this one has a bit more to it. If the user has entered a partial table definition (as determined by a table name or one or more created fields), a message box appears, asking the user whether to abandon the current creation, and it requires a Yes or No answer. If the user answers Yes, the program ends. If there is no partial table definition, the program ends without showing the message box.

```
Private Sub cmdClose_Click()
    Dim strErrDesc As String

    ' If the user has entered a partial table definition, make
    ' sure that the user wants to abandon it. If so, end the
    ' program.
    If txtTableName <> "" Or lstFields.ListCount > 0 Then
        strErrDesc = "Do you want to abandon operations on " & _
                    "the current table?"
        If MsgBox(strErrDesc, vbQuestion + vbYesNo +
            vbDefaultButton2) = vbYes Then
            End
        End If
    Else
        ' No partial table definition, so just end the program
        End
    End If
End Sub
```

12. Switch to **frmTableList**. Enter the following code into the declarations section of **frmTableList**, modifying the path in the **Const** statement to point to your copy of BIBLIO.MDB.

```
Option Explicit

Private Const BIBLIO_PATH = _
"D:\Program Files\Microsoft Visual Studio\VB6\Biblio.MDB"
```

13. Enter the following code as **frmTableList**'s **Form_Load** event. This calls the **ListTables** subroutine, explained in the next step, to fill the **lstTables** list box with the database's tables.

```
Private Sub Form_Load()
    ' Fill the list box with the current non-system tables in
    ' BIBLIO.MDB.
    ListTables
End Sub
```

14. Create the **ListTables** subroutine in **frmTableList** by entering the following code. **ListTables** is called when the form loads and when the user deletes a table. It uses the **TableDefs** collection of the **Database** object to build a list of tables in the BIBLIO.MDB database. The **TableDefs** collection contains one record for each table in the database, including the (normally hidden) system tables. Because the **Name** property of all system table **TableDef** objects begins with the string "**MSys**", this procedure assumes that any table starting with that string is a system table and ignores it. The names of all other tables get added to the **lstTables** list box.

```
Private Sub ListTables()
Dim dbfBiblio As Database, tdfTableList As TableDef

    On Error GoTo ListError
        Screen.MousePointer = vbHourglass
        'Clear the list box, then open the database.
        lstTables.Clear
        Set dbfBiblio = _
            DBEngine.Workspaces(0).OpenDatabase(BIBLIO_PATH)
        ' Cycle through the table definitions in BIBLIO_PATH.
        ' If the table is a system table (name begins with MSys),
        ' ignore it. Otherwise, add it to the list.
        For Each tdfTableList In dbfBiblio.TableDefs
            If Left$(tdfTableList.Name, 4) <> "MSys" Then _
                lstTables.AddItem tdfTableList.Name
        Next

        Screen.MousePointer = vbDefault
    On Error GoTo 0
Exit Sub

ListError:
    Screen.MousePointer = vbDefault
    MsgBox Err.Description, vbExclamation
    Unload frmTableList
Exit Sub
End Sub
```

15. Enter the following code as the `Click` event frmTableList's `cmdDelete`. `DROP TABLE` deletes a table whether or not the table contains data. Because you do not want to delete any tables with data, this procedure checks to make sure that the table is empty and then deletes it.

```
Private Sub cmdDelete_Click()
Dim dbfBiblio As Database

    On Error GoTo DeleteError
        Screen.MousePointer = vbHourglass
        'If a table is selected, then continue
        If lstTables.ListIndex > -1 Then
            'Confirm that the table has no records
            If TableIsEmpty() Then
                ' Delete the selected table from BIBLIO_PATH.
                Set dbfBiblio = DBEngine.Workspaces(0). _
                    OpenDatabase(BIBLIO_PATH)
                dbfBiblio.Execute ("DROP TABLE [" & _
                                    lstTables.Text & "]")

                ' Display the modified list of tables.
                ListTables
                Screen.MousePointer = vbDefault
            Else
                'The table has records, so inform the user.
                Screen.MousePointer = vbDefault
                MsgBox lstTables.Text & " is not empty.", _
                        vbExclamation
            End If
        Else
            'No table has been chosen, so inform the user.
            Screen.MousePointer = vbDefault
            MsgBox "You have not selected a table to delete.", _
                    vbExclamation
        End If
    On Error GoTo 0
Exit Sub

DeleteError:
    Screen.MousePointer = vbDefault
    MsgBox Err.Description, vbExclamation
    Unload frmTableList
Exit Sub
End Sub
```

16. Create the `TableIsEmpty` function by entering the following code into `frmTableList`. This function returns `True` if the table currently selected in `lstTables` is empty.

```
Function TableIsEmpty() As Boolean
Dim dbfBiblio As Database, tdfTableList As TableDef
```

continued on next page

continued from previous page

```
                    On Error GoTo TableIsEmptyError
                        Set dbfBiblio =
                            DBEngine.Workspaces(0).OpenDatabase(BIBLIO_PATH)

                        ' Cycle through the table definitions in BIBLIO_PATH.
                        ' When the table currently selected in lstTables is found,
                        ' check to see whether it has records. If it does not,
                        ' return True; otherwise, return False.
                        For Each tdfTableList In dbfBiblio.TableDefs
                            If tdfTableList.Name = lstTables.Text Then
                                TableIsEmpty = IIf(tdfTableList.RecordCount = 0, _
                                    True, False)
                                Exit For
                            End If
                        Next
                    On Error GoTo 0
                Exit Function

                TableIsEmptyError:
                    MsgBox Err.Description, vbExclamation
                    Unload frmTableList
                Exit Function
                End Function
```

17. Enter the following code as the `Click` event of `frmTableList`'s `cmdClose`:

```
                Private Sub cmdClose_Click()
                    Unload frmTableList
                End Sub
```

How It Works

The `frmMain` form essentially builds a **CREATE TABLE** SQL statement by using the table name listed in the `lstTables` control, with the fields listed in the `lstFields` list box. This might seem greatly simplified, but it guides all the reasoning behind the code added in this How-To.

The main action occurs in the `cmdCreateTable_Click` event of `frmMain`. Here, based on the choices the user made regarding the name of the table and the name and type of the fields to be added, the **CREATE TABLE** SQL statement is concatenated and executed. Clicking the `cmdListTables` button displays a list of existing tables in the Access database in case the user wants to rewrite an existing empty table. (The `TableIsEmpty` function is used to ensure that valuable data is not overwritten; the program will destroy only an empty table.) The `cboFieldTypes` combo box allows the program to filter the various field types in a manner accessible to the user.

Comments

One of the key items to remember in this How-To is the destructive behavior of the **CREATE TABLE** statement, as mentioned in step 15. If a **CREATE TABLE** statement is issued defining a table with the same name as one that already exists in the Access database, it destroys the existing table. Although this behavior is not true across all database platforms, it's usually better to be safe than sorry and include a routine similar to the **TableIsEmpty** function in this How-To.

COMPLEXITY
INTERMEDIATE

3.13 How do I...
Append and delete records?

Problem

I have a table to which I'd like to add records that are built from records in other tables. I'd also like to delete records based on criteria I specify. How can I accomplish these tasks with SQL?

Technique

SQL provides two statements, the **INSERT INTO** and **DELETE** statements, that append records to a table and delete records from a table, respectively.

The INSERT INTO Statement

SQL's **INSERT INTO** statement is used to append records to an existing table. The **INSERT INTO** statement has three clauses, shown in Table 3.20.

Table 3.20. The syntax of the *INSERT INTO* statement.

CLAUSE	PURPOSE	EXAMPLE
INSERT INTO	Names the table and fields into which data are to be inserted	INSERT INTO [Publisher Titles] ([Name], [Title])
SELECT	Names the fields from which data are to be taken	SELECT Publishers.Name, Titles.Title
FROM	Names the table or other source of the data	FROM Publishers INNER JOIN Titles ON Publishers.PubID = Titles.PubID

The **INSERT INTO** clause takes two parameters, the table name ([Publisher Titles] in the example) and the field names into which data are to be inserted. The field names are enclosed in parentheses and delimited by commas.

The SELECT clause statement consists of a list of fields from which the data to be inserted into the fields named in the INSERT INTO clause will be drawn. There must be a one-to-one correspondence between the fields in the INSERT INTO clause and the fields in the SELECT clause. If you have more INSERT INTO fields than SELECT fields, or vice versa, an error will result. If the field names are from multiple tables—as in the example—and if the names are ambiguous (that is, both tables have fields with the same names), they must be qualified with the table names.

The FROM clause statement names the table or other source of the fields named in the SELECT clause. In the example, the FROM clause names not a single table but a pair of tables linked by an INNER JOIN. (See How-To 3.6 for details on INNER JOINs.)

As with other SQL action queries, you run the INSERT INTO clause by using it as the argument for the Execute method of the Database object. To execute the query shown in the table against a database object represented by the variable dbfTest, you would create the following Visual Basic statement (note the continuation character):

```
dbfTest.Execute("INSERT INTO [Publisher Titles] ([Name], " & _
    "[Title]) SELECT Publishers.Name, " & _
    "Titles.Title FROM Publishers INNER JOIN Titles ON " & _
    "Publishers.PubID = Titles.PubID")
```

The DELETE Statement

Use the SQL DELETE statement to delete records from a table, based on criteria you specify in the DELETE statement. The DELETE statement has the syntax shown in Table 3.21.

Table 3.21. The syntax of the *DELETE* statement.

CLAUSE	PURPOSE	EXAMPLE
DELETE FROM	Names the table from which records are to be deleted	DELETE FROM [Publisher Titles]
WHERE	Criteria that select records for deletion	WHERE [Publication Date]

Execute the DELETE statement by passing it as the parameter to the Execute method statement of the Database object. If you have a Database object variable named dbfTest, this Visual Basic statement executes the SQL shown in the table:

```
dbfTest.Execute("DELETE FROM [Publisher Titles] WHERE [Publication Date] <= 1990")
```

Steps

Open and run the project UPDATE.VBP. Click the Create Table button and then the Append Records button. These two actions create a table named [Publisher

Titles], fill it with records, and display the records in the form, as shown in Figure 3.17. Notice the titles from Addison-Wesley on your screen. (You might need to scroll down to see them.)

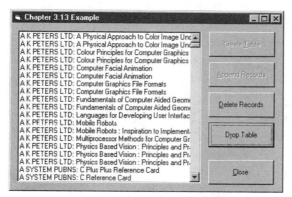

Figure 3.17. The SQL Insert Into form, showing appended records.

Click the Delete Records button. The Select Publisher form shown in Figure 3.18 appears. Select Addison-Wesley and click OK. The previous form reappears with the list refreshed to show the records currently in the [Publisher Titles] table. Notice that the Addison-Wesley titles are missing.

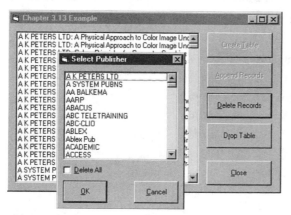

Figure 3.18. The Publisher List form, showing publisher names.

1. Create a new project called APPEND.VBP. Rename Form1 to frmMain, create the objects and properties listed in Table 3.22, and save the form as APPEND.FRM.

Table 3.22. Objects and properties for the Append and Delete form.

OBJECT	PROPERTY	SETTING
Form	Name	frmMain
	Caption	Chapter 3.13 - Example
ListBox	Name	lstData
	Sorted	True
CommandButton	Name	cmdDeleteRecords
	Caption	&Delete Records
CommandButton	Name	cmdClose
	Caption	&Close
CommandButton	Name	cmdDropTable
	Caption	D&rop Table
CommandButton	Name	cmdAppendRecords
	Caption	&Append Records
CommandButton	Name	cmdCreateTable
	Caption	Create &Table

2. Insert a new form into the project. Rename it to `frmSelectPublisher`, create the objects and properties listed in Table 3.23, and save the form as PublisherSelect.FRM.

Table 3.23. Objects and properties for the Select Publisher form.

OBJECT	PROPERTY	SETTING
Form	Name	frmSelectPublisher
	BorderStyle	3 - Fixed Dialog
	Caption	Chapter 3.13 - Publisher List
	MaxButton	False
	MinButton	False
CommandButton	Name	cmdOK
	Caption	&OK
	Default	True
CommandButton	Name	cmdCancel
	Caption	&Cancel
CheckBox	Name	chkDeleteAll
	Caption	&Delete All
ListBox	Name	lstPublishers
	Sorted	True

3. Add the following statements to the declarations section of `frmMain`:

```
Option Explicit

Private Const BIBLIO_PATH = _
"D:\Program Files\Microsoft Visual Studio\VB6\Biblio.MDB"

Private strPublisherToDelete As String
Private dbfBiblio As Database
```

4. Enter the following code as in the **Load** event of `frmMain`. The `Form_Load` code checks to see whether the [Publisher Titles] table exists in the database and, if it exists, whether it has any records. It then enables and disables the appropriate command buttons.

```
Private Sub Form_Load()
Dim tdfTable As TableDef
    Dim blnTableFound As Boolean

    On Error GoTo LoadError
        blnTableFound = False

        'Open the database.
        Set dbfBiblio = _
            DBEngine.Workspaces(0).OpenDatabase(BIBLIO_PATH)
        'Iterate through the TableDefs collection.  If the table
        '"Publisher Titles" is found, configure the
        'form's buttons appropriately.
        For Each tdfTable In dbfBiblio.TableDefs
            If tdfTable.Name = "Publisher Titles" Then
                blnTableFound = True
                cmdDropTable.Enabled = True
                cmdCreateTable.Enabled = False

                If tdfTable.RecordCount > 0 Then
                    cmdDeleteRecords.Enabled = True
                    cmdAppendRecords.Enabled = False
                    FillList
                Else
                    cmdDeleteRecords.Enabled = False
                    cmdAppendRecords.Enabled = True
                End If
                Exit For
            End If
        Next

        'If the table is not found, configure the form's buttons
        'appropriately.
        If blnTableFound = False Then
            cmdDropTable.Enabled = False
            cmdCreateTable.Enabled = True
            cmdAppendRecords.Enabled = False
```

continued on next page

continued from previous page

```
                            cmdDeleteRecords.Enabled = False
                  End If
              On Error GoTo 0
          Exit Sub

          LoadError:
              MsgBox Err.Description, vbExclamation
              Unload Me
          Exit Sub

          End Sub
```

5. Create the **FillList** subroutine in **frmMain** by entering the following code. The **FillList** routine fills the list box **lstData** with the records from the [Publisher Titles] table.

```
Sub FillList()
Dim recSelect As Recordset
    Dim strSQL As String

    On Error GoTo FillListError
        'Clear the list box.
        lstData.Clear
        'Get all the records from the Publisher Titles table.
        Set recSelect = dbfBiblio.OpenRecordset( _
            "SELECT * FROM " & _
            "[Publisher Titles]", _
            dbOpenSnapshot)

        'Put the records into the list box.
        If recSelect.RecordCount > 0 Then
            recSelect.MoveFirst
            Do Until recSelect.EOF
                lstData.AddItem recSelect![Name] & ": " & _
                                recSelect![Title]
                recSelect.MoveNext
            Loop
        End If
    On Error GoTo 0
    Exit Sub

FillListError:
    MsgBox Err.Description, vbExclamation
    Exit Sub
End Sub
```

6. Enter the following code as the **Click** event for **frmMain**'s **cmdCreateTable**. This code creates the [Publisher Titles] table. Refer to the preceding How-To for information on the **CREATE TABLE** statement.

```
Private Sub cmdCreateTable_Click()
    Dim strSQL As String

    On Error GoTo CreateTableError
        'Build the CREATE TABLE statement.
```

```
            strSQL = "CREATE TABLE [Publisher Titles] " & _
                "([Name] TEXT, [Title] TEXT)"
            'Execute the statement.  Since it's an action query,
            'you don't use the OpenRecordset command.  It would
            'fail, since an action query does not return a recordset.
            dbfBiblio.Execute (strSQL)

            'Configure the form's buttons appropriately.
            cmdCreateTable.Enabled = False
            cmdDropTable.Enabled = True
            cmdAppendRecords.Enabled = True
    On Error GoTo 0
Exit Sub

CreateTableError:
    MsgBox Err.Description, vbExclamation
Exit Sub
End Sub
```

7. Enter the following code as the **Click** event for **frmMain**'s **cmdDropTable**. This code deletes the [Publisher Titles] table. Refer to the preceding How-To for information on the **DROP TABLE** statement.

```
Private Sub cmdDropTable_Click()
Dim dbName As String

    On Error GoTo DropTableError
        'Build & execute the DROP TABLE statement.
        dbfBiblio.Execute ("DROP TABLE [Publisher Titles]")

        'Configure the form's buttons appropriately.
        cmdDropTable.Enabled = False
        cmdCreateTable.Enabled = True
        cmdAppendRecords.Enabled = False
        cmdDeleteRecords.Enabled = False

        'Clear the list box.
        lstData.Clear
    On Error GoTo 0
Exit Sub

DropTableError:
    MsgBox Err.Description, vbExclamation
Exit Sub
End Sub
```

8. Enter the following code as the **Click** event for **frmMain**'s **cmdAppendRecords**. This command builds the SQL statement that will append the records to the database and then executes the statement. The SQL statement is identical to that shown in Table 3.20.

```
Private Sub cmdAppendRecords_Click()
    Dim strSQL As String

    On Error GoTo AppendRecordsError
```

continued on next page

continued from previous page

```
            Screen.MousePointer = vbHourglass
            'Build the INSERT INTO statement
            strSQL = _
                "INSERT INTO [Publisher Titles] ( [Name], Title ) " & _
                "SELECT Publishers.Name, Titles.Title " & _
                "FROM Publishers INNER JOIN Titles " & _
                "ON Publishers.PubID = Titles.PubID"

            'Execute the statement.
            dbfBiblio.Execute (strSQL)

            'Fill the list box via the FillList subroutine.
            FillList

            'Configure the form's buttons appropriately.
            cmdDeleteRecords.Enabled = True
            cmdAppendRecords.Enabled = False

            Screen.MousePointer = vbDefault
        On Error GoTo 0
    Exit Sub

    AppendRecordsError:
        Screen.MousePointer = vbDefault
        MsgBox Err.Description, vbExclamation
    Exit Sub
    End Sub
```

9. Enter the following code as the `Click` event for `frmMain`'s
`cmdDeleteRecords`. This procedure deletes the designated records from
the database. It calls the `GetPublisher` function of `frmSelectPublisher`,
returning a value to be placed in `strPublisherToDelete`. Then it examines
the public variable `strPublisherToDelete`; if `strPublisherToDelete` is
an empty string, it indicates that the user wants to cancel the deletion, so
no records are deleted. If `strPublisherToDelete` is `"*"`, the user wants to
delete all the records. Otherwise, `frmSelectPublisher` contains the name
of the publisher whose titles the user wants to delete. The procedure builds
the appropriate `SQL DELETE` statement and then executes the statement.

```
Private Sub cmdDeleteRecords_Click()
    Dim strSQL As String

    On Error GoTo DeleteRecordsError

    'Use the GetPublisher function on frmSelectPublisher to return
    'a publisher to delete.
    strPublisherToDelete = frmSelectPublisher.GetPublisher
    'If one is selected, then delete it.
    If strPublisherToDelete <> "" Then
        'Build the DELETE statement.
        strSQL = "DELETE FROM [Publisher Titles]"
        'If the publisher to delete isn't the * wildcard, then
        'modify the SQL to choose the selected publisher(s).
```

```
                    If strPublisherToDelete <> "*" Then
                        strSQL = strSQL & _
                                " WHERE [Publisher Titles].[Name] = " & _
                            """" & strPublisherToDelete & """"
                    End If

                    'Execute the statement.
                    dbfBiblio.Execute (strSQL)

                    'Fill the list box.
                    FillList
                End If

                cmdAppendRecords.Enabled = (lstData.ListCount = 0)
                cmdDeleteRecords.Enabled - (lstData.ListCount > 0)
    Exit Sub

    DeleteRecordsError:
        MsgBox Err.Description, vbExclamation
    Exit Sub
    End Sub
```

10. Enter the following code as the `Click` event for `frmMain`'s `cmdClose`:

```
Private Sub cmdClose_Click()
    End
End Sub
```

11. Switch to `frmPublisherSelect` and enter the following code into the declarations section. Modify the path in the `Const` statement to point to your copy of BIBLIO.MDB.

```
Option Explicit

Private Const BIBLIO_PATH = _
        "D:\Program Files\Microsoft Visual Studio\VB6\Biblio.MDB"

Private strPublisherToDelete As String
```

12. Enter the following code as the `Load` event for `frmSelectPublisher`. On loading, the form builds a recordset of publisher names in the [Publisher Titles] table through a SQL `SELECT` statement with the `DISTINCT` keyword. (See How-To 3.2 for information on the `DISTINCT` keyword.) It uses that recordset to fill the `lstPublishers` list box.

```
Private Sub Form_Load()
    Dim dbfBiblio As Database, recSelect As Recordset
    Dim strSQL As String

    On Error GoTo LoadError
        Set dbfBiblio = _
            DBEngine.Workspaces(0).OpenDatabase(BIBLIO_PATH)
        strSQL = "SELECT DISTINCT [Name] FROM [Publisher Titles]"
        Set recSelect = dbfBiblio.OpenRecordset(strSQL)
```

continued on next page

continued from previous page

```
            If recSelect.RecordCount > 0 Then
                recSelect.MoveFirst
                Do Until recSelect.EOF
                    lstPublishers.AddItem recSelect![Name]
                    recSelect.MoveNext
                Loop
            End If
        On Error GoTo 0
    Exit Sub

    LoadError:
        MsgBox Err.Description, vbExclamation
        strPublisherToDelete = ""
        Me.Hide
    Exit Sub
    End Sub
```

13. Enter the following code as the **Click** event for **frmSelectPublisher**'s **cmdOK**. This procedure sets the public variable **strPublisherToDelete**. If the user has clicked the Delete All button, **strPublisherToDelete** is set to the string **"*"**. Otherwise, **strPublisherToDelete** is set to the name of the selected publisher.

```
Private Sub cmdOK_Click()
If chkDeleteAll Then
        strPublisherToDelete = "*"
        Me.Hide
    ElseIf lstPublishers.ListIndex > -1 Then
        strPublisherToDelete = lstPublishers.Text
        Me.Hide
    End If
End Sub
```

14. Enter the following code as the **DblClick** event for **frmSelectPublisher**'s **lstPublishers**. This allows the program to call the **cmdOK_Click** event, preventing duplication of code. A double-click of the Publishers list brings about exactly the same result as if the user had selected a publisher with a single left-click and then clicked the OK button.

```
Private Sub lstPublishers_DblClick()
    cmdOK_Click
End Sub
```

15. Enter the following code as the **Click** event for **frmSelectPublisher**'s **cmdCancel**. This code ensures that the **strPublisherToDelete** string is blank, preventing the calling form's code from inadvertently deleting a publisher. Note that the form is hidden (as opposed to unloaded) here. This form is called by the **GetPublisher** public function and is unloaded by that function.

```
Private Sub cmdCancel_Click()
    strPublisherToDelete = ""
    Me.Hide
End Sub
```

16. Enter the following code to create the **GetPublisher** method for **frmSelectPublisher**. This is a public function, allowing you to use this form like a dialog box, resulting in this function being sent back to the calling form. You will find that this method for using forms is preferable to the "one use" form in many situations, especially when a "generic" form is used for multiple purposes.

```
Public Function GetPublisher() As String
    Me.Show vbModal
    GetPublisher = strPublisherToDelete
    Unload Me
End Function
```

How It Works

When the user clicks the **cmdCreateTable** button, a **CREATE TABLE** statement is executed (for more information on the **CREATE TABLE** statement, see the preceding How-To) to create an empty table in BIBLIO.MDB. The **cmdAppendRecords** button, when clicked, fills that empty table by executing the **INSERT...INTO** statement, creating the information from a **SELECT** query run on two other tables in the database. When the table is fully populated, the list box **lstTitles** fills from the new table's data via the **FillList** subroutine. The **cmdDeleteRecords** button, which deletes the newly created records, first calls the **GetPublisher** public function on the **frmSelectPublisher** form. The form presents a dialog box with options to delete records from either a single publisher or all publishers in the table. Based on this selection, the **GetPublisher** function returns either a publisher's name or the asterisk wildcard character. Using this information, the **cmdDeleteRecords** button builds and executes a **DELETE** statement. Last, but not least, the **cmdDropTable** button simply executes a **DROP TABLE** statement on the new table.

Comments

One of the more interesting capabilities of Visual Basic is its capacity for public functions and subroutines on forms. This allows for a wide degree of flexibility in the way you can use forms, including your ability to use a form in a manner similar to that of, say, a common dialog, by calling a public function on the form. This functionality serves well in this How-To because it makes the selection process for deletion of a group of records much easier and cleaner in terms of design and user interface.

The **INSERT...INTO** and **DELETE** statements are useful for creating and emptying temporary tables. Temporary tables, although not always the most efficient way to go, do have their purposes, and these two new tools in your arsenal should go a long way toward their proper and efficient management.

COMPLEXITY
INTERMEDIATE

3.14 How do I...
Create a new table with data from existing tables?

Problem

I know I can use CREATE TABLE and INSERT INTO to create a table and add records to it. But in my application, I do this many times, and I'd like to accomplish it all with a single SQL operation. How can I do this?

Technique

The SELECT...INTO statement lets you create a new table with data from existing tables in a single operation. Table 3.24 shows its syntax. Similar to INSERT...INTO and DELETE statements, both covered in the preceding How-To, this tool provides an excellent way to work with temporary tables.

Table 3.24. The syntax of the *SELECT...INTO* statement.

CLAUSE	PURPOSE	EXAMPLE
SELECT	Names the fields in the existing table that will be re-created in the new table	SELECT Publishers.Name, Titles.Title
INTO	Names the new table	INTO [Publisher Titles]
FROM	Names the table (or other source) of the data	FROM Publishers INNER JOIN Titles ON Publishers.PubID = Titles.PubID

To run the SELECT...INTO query, use the Execute method of the Database object. The following Visual Basic statement (on one line) executes the query shown in the table on the database represented by the variable dbfTest:

```
dbfTest.Execute("SELECT Publishers.Name, " & _
    "Titles.Title INTO [Publisher Titles]" & _
    " FROM Publishers INNER JOIN Titles ON Publishers.PubID = Titles.PubID")
```

With the example presented previously, a new table, titled [Publisher Titles], is created in the database, constructed from information gleaned from two other tables, connected by an INNER JOIN. The difference between the SELECT...INTO command and the INSERT...INTO command is simple: the INSERT...INTO command creates new records and performs an INSERT on the existing recipient table, whereas the SELECT...INTO creates a new recipient table before performing an INSERT. The SELECT...INTO statement, because of this behavior, is the ideal method of creating a temporary table in one step. In the preceding How-To, you needed two steps—one to create the table and one to add the records. SELECT...INTO combines these two steps into one, making it simpler to use and simpler to debug if problems arise. Note that the behavior on some databases differs as to exactly what happens when a SELECT...INTO statement is executed, with the recipient table having the same name as an existing table in the database. In a Microsoft Access database, the SELECT...INTO command deletes the existing table first. Some databases, however, might trigger an error in performing this action. To examine this behavior, you should create a sample table with data, execute a SELECT...INTO statement with that sample table as recipient, and note the results.

Steps

Open and run the project MAKETABL.VBP. Click the Create Table button; the list box fills with the records added to the newly created table (see Figure 3.19). Click the Drop Table button to delete the table.

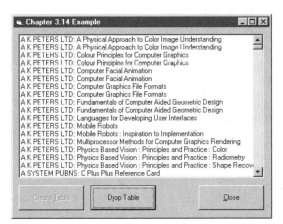

Figure 3.19. The SQL Select Into form, with new table and records.

1. Create a new project called MAKETABL.VBP. Use **Form1** to create the objects and properties listed in Table 3.25, and save the form as MAKETABL.FRM.

Table 3.25. Objects and properties for the Table Maker form.

OBJECT	PROPERTY	SETTING
Form	Name	Form1
	Caption	Chapter 3.14 Example
ListBox	Name	lstData
	Sorted	True
CommandButton	Name	cmdClose
	Caption	&Close
CommandButton	Name	cmdDropTable
	Caption	D&rop Table
CommandButton	Name	cmdCreateTable
	Caption	Create &Table

2. Add the following statements to the declarations section of **Form1**:

```
Option Explicit

Private Const BIBLIO_PATH = _
"D:\Program Files\Microsoft Visual Studio\VB6\Biblio.MDB"
Private dbfBiblio As Database
```

3. Enter the following code as the **Load** event for **Form1**. On loading, this procedure looks for the [Publisher Titles] table in the database. If it finds the table, it fills the list box with the table's data and enables the Drop Table button. If it does not find the table, it enables the Create Table button.

```
Private Sub Form_Load()
Dim tdfTable As TableDef
    Dim blnTableFound As Boolean

    On Error GoTo LoadError
        blnTableFound = False
        'Open the database
        Set dbfBiblio = _
            DBEngine.Workspaces(0).OpenDatabase(BIBLIO_PATH)

        'Check each table in the TableDefs collection;
        'if the name matches, then allow the user to drop the
        'table, and populate the list box.
        For Each tdfTable In dbfBiblio.TableDefs
            If tdfTable.Name = "Publisher Titles" Then
                blnTableFound = True
                cmdDropTable.Enabled = True
                cmdCreateTable.Enabled = False
                FillList
```

```
                    Exit For
                End If
            Next

            'If no table was found, allow the user to create the
            'table.
            If blnTableFound = False Then
                cmdDropTable.Enabled = False
                cmdCreateTable.Enabled = True
            End If
    On Error GoTo 0
Exit Sub

LoadError:
    MsgBox Err.Description, vbExclamation
    Unload Me
Exit Sub
End Sub
```

4. Create the **FillList** subroutine by entering the following code into
Form1. This subroutine fills the list box with the contents of the [Publisher
Titles] table.

```
Sub FillList()
Dim recSelect As Recordset
    Dim strSQL As String

    On Error GoTo FillListError
        'Clear the list box
        lstData.Clear

        'Get the [Publisher Titles] table in a recordset
        Set recSelect = dbfBiblio.OpenRecordset( _
            "SELECT * FROM " & _
            "[Publisher Titles]", dbOpenSnapshot)
        'If there are any records, fill the list box
        If recSelect.RecordCount > 0 Then
            recSelect.MoveFirst
            Do Until recSelect.EOF
                lstData.AddItem recSelect![Name] & ": " & _
                                recSelect![Title]
                recSelect.MoveNext
            Loop
        End If
    On Error GoTo 0
Exit Sub

FillListError:
    MsgBox Err.Description, vbExclamation
Exit Sub
End Sub
```

5. Enter the following code as the **Click** event for **cmdCreateTable**. This
procedure builds the **SELECT...INTO** SQL statement, building the

[Publisher Titles] table from the combination of the [Name] field from the [Publishers] table and the [Title] field from the [Titles] table, as described in the "Technique" section of this How-To. When built, it then executes the statement and calls the FillList subroutine to fill the list box on the form. Finally, this step enables the Delete Records button, because (you hope) you now have records to delete.

```
Private Sub cmdCreateTable_Click()
Dim strSQL As String

    On Error GoTo CreateTableError
        Screen.MousePointer = vbHourglass

        'Build the SELECT INTO statement.
        strSQL = "SELECT Publishers.Name, Titles.Title " & _
            "INTO [Publisher Titles] " & _
            "FROM Publishers INNER JOIN Titles " & _
            "ON Publishers.PubID = Titles.PubID"

        'Create the new table by executing the SQL statement.
        dbfBiblio.Execute (strSQL)

        'Fill the list box with records.
        FillList

        'Set the command buttons.
        cmdCreateTable.Enabled = False
        cmdDropTable.Enabled = True

        Screen.MousePointer = vbDefault
    On Error GoTo 0
Exit Sub

CreateTableError:
    Screen.MousePointer = vbDefault
    MsgBox Err.Description, vbExclamation
Exit Sub
End Sub
```

6. Enter the following code as the Click event for cmdDropTable. The routine executes a DROP TABLE statement against the newly created [Publisher Titles] table and reenables the Create Table button.

```
Private Sub cmdDropTable_Click()
On Error GoTo DropTableError
        'Execute the DROP TABLE statement
        dbfBiblio.Execute ("DROP TABLE [Publisher Titles]")

        'Set the command buttons
        cmdDropTable.Enabled = False
        cmdCreateTable.Enabled = True

        'Clear the list box.
        lstData.Clear
    On Error GoTo 0
```

```
    Exit Sub

DropTableError:
    MsgBox Err.Description, vbExclamation
Exit Sub
End.Sub
```

7. Enter the following code as the **Click** event for **cmdClose**:

```
Private Sub cmdClose_Click()
    End
End Sub
```

How It Works

When **Form1** loads, it first attempts to find the [Publisher Titles] table. If it finds the table, it loads the table's information into the list box by calling the **FillList** subroutine, disables the Create Table button, and then enables the Drop Table buttons. If it doesn't find the table, it enables the Create Table button and disables the Drop Table button.

If the Create Table button is enabled, when clicked, it constructs and executes a **SELECT...INTO** statement, creating the [Publisher Titles] table and pulling in information from both the [Publishers] and the [Titles] table to populate it in one step. When complete, it loads the data into the list box by using the **FillList** subroutine.

The Drop Table button, if enabled, issues a **DROP TABLE** statement when clicked, destroying your [Publisher Titles] table in one fell swoop.

Comments

When you use **SELECT...INTO** to create the table, the fields in the new table inherit only the data type and field size of the corresponding fields in the query's source table. No other field or table properties are picked up from the existing table.

COMPLEXITY
INTERMEDIATE

3.15 How do I...
Modify a table's structure?

Problem

I need to be able to add or drop columns from a table without having to use Access or go through the lengthy process of working with **TableDef** and **Field** objects. Can I do this with a simple SQL statement?

Technique

The ALTER TABLE statement lets you add or drop columns or indexes as needed, with a single SQL operation. The syntax is explained in Table 3.26, with a sample statement.

Table 3.26. The syntax of the *ALTER TABLE* statement.

CLAUSE	PURPOSE	EXAMPLE
ALTER TABLE	Selects the table to be altered	ALTER TABLE [Publisher Titles]
ADD COLUMN	Adds a column, defining its data type at the same time	ADD COLUMN [Notes] MEMO NOT NULL

The ALTER TABLE statement uses several other keywords, as listed in Table 3.27.

Table 3.27. Additional syntax for the *ALTER TABLE* statement.

CLAUSE	PURPOSE	EXAMPLE
DROP COLUMN	Removes a column	DROP COLUMN [Notes]
ADD CONSTRAINT	Adds an index to the table	ADD CONSTRAINT [Key1] [Notes]
DROP CONSTRAINT	Removes an index statement	DROP CONSTRAINT [Key1]

The Execute method is used on a Database object to perform an ALTER TABLE statement. The following example executes the queries shown in Table 3.26 on the database represented by the variable dbfTest:

```
dbfTest.Execute("ALTER TABLE [Publisher Titles] ADD COLUMN [Notes]
        MEMO NOT NULL")
```

Steps

Open and run the project ADDFIELD.VBP. Type a valid field name into the Field Name text box. Select a field type from the Field Type drop-down list and then click the Add Field button; the list box fills with the fields added to the newly created table (see Figure 3.20). Highlight one of the newly created fields and click the Remove Field button to delete the field. Note that this example is similar in appearance to the example in How-To 3.12.

1. Create a new project called ADDFIELD.VBP. Use Form1 to create the objects and properties listed in Table 3.28, and save the form as MAKETABL.FRM.

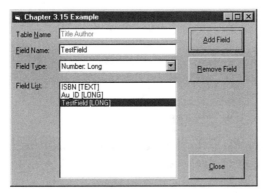

Figure 3.20. The SQL Alter Table form on startup.

Table 3.28. Objects and properties for the Table Maker form.

OBJECT	PROPERTY	SETTING
Form	Name	Form1
	Caption	Chapter 3.14 Example
ListBox	Name	lstFields
	Sorted	True
Label	Name	lblTableName
	Caption	Table &Name:
Label	Name	lblFieldName
	Caption	&Field Name:
Label	Name	lblFieldType
	Caption	Field T&ype:
Label	Name	lblFieldList
	Caption	Field Li&st:
TextBox	Name	txtTableName
	Enabled	False
TextBox	Name	txtFieldName
ComboBox	Name	cboFieldType
	Style	2 - Dropdown List
CommandButton	Name	cmdClose
	Caption	&Close
CommandButton	Name	cmdAddField
	Caption	&Add Field
CommandButton	Name	cmdRemoveField
	Caption	&Remove Field

2. Add the following statements to the declarations section of **Form1**:

```
Option Explicit

Private Const BIBLIO_PATH = _
"D:\Program Files\Microsoft Visual Studio\VB6\Biblio.MDB"

Private Const IllegalCharacters = "[].!'"
Private dbfBiblio As Database
```

3. Add the following statements to the **Load** event of **Form1**. The **FillTypeList** and **FillFieldList** routines, detailed next, are called to prepare the form for use.

```
Private Sub Form_Load()
    'Open the database
    Set dbfBiblio = _
        DBEngine.Workspaces(0).OpenDatabase(BIBLIO_PATH)
    'Set the txtTableName control to the table that will be
    'edited.
    txtTableName = "Title Author"
    'Fill the Field Type combo box
    FillTypeList
    'Fill the Field List list box
    FillFieldList
End Sub
```

4. Create the following subroutine in **Form1**. The **FillFieldList** subroutine will iterate through the **Fields** collection of the [Title Author] table, including the names and data types in the **lstFields** list box.

```
Sub FillFieldList()
    Dim tbfTemp As TableDef, fldTemp As Field
    Dim strFieldType As String

    'Iterate through the TableDefs collection of the database,
    'searching for the table name specified in the txtTableName
    'edit control.
    For Each tbfTemp In dbfBiblio.TableDefs
        'If we find the table, iterate through the Fields
        'collection, adding each field and its field type to the
        'Field List list box
        If tbfTemp.Name = txtTableName.Text Then
            For Each fldTemp In tbfTemp.Fields
                Select Case fldTemp.Type
                    Case dbBigInt
                        strFieldType = "BIGINT"
                    Case dbBinary
                        strFieldType = "BINARY"
                    Case dbBoolean
                        strFieldType = "BOOLEAN"
```

```
                    Case dbByte
                        strFieldType = "BYTE"
                    Case dbChar
                        strFieldType = "CHAR(" _
                                    & fldTemp.FieldSize & ")"
                    Case dbCurrency
                        strFieldType = "CURRENCY"
                    Case dbDate
                        strFieldType = "DATE"
                    Case dbDecimal
                        strFieldType = "DECIMAL"
                    Case dbDouble
                        strFieldType = "DOUBLE"
                    Case dbFloat
                        strFieldType = "FLOAT"
                    Case dbGUID
                        strFieldType = "GUID"
                    Case dbInteger
                        strFieldType = "INTEGER"
                    Case dbLong
                        strFieldType = "LONG"
                    Case dbLongBinary
                        strFieldType = "LONGBINARY"
                    Case dbMemo
                        strFieldType = "LONGTEXT"
                    Case dbNumeric
                        strFieldType = "NUMERIC"
                    Case dbSingle
                        strFieldType = "SINGLE"
                    Case dbText
                        strFieldType = "TEXT"
                    Case dbTime
                        strFieldType = "TIME"
                    Case dbTimeStamp
                        strFieldType = "TIMESTAMP"
                    Case dbVarBinary
                        strFieldType = "VARBINARY"
                End Select
                lstFields.AddItem fldTemp.Name & _
                            " [" & strFieldType & "]"
            Next
        Exit For
        End If
    Next
End Sub
```

5. Create the following subroutine in Form1. The FillTypeList subroutine adds the various data types to the cboFieldType drop-down combo box.

```
Sub FillTypeList()
    'Fill the Field Type combo box with types of available fields
    With cboFieldTypes
        .AddItem "Counter"
        .AddItem "Currency"
        .AddItem "Date/Time"
```

continued on next page

continued from previous page

```
                .AddItem "Memo"
                .AddItem "Number: Byte"
                .AddItem "Number: Integer"
                .AddItem "Number: Long"
                .AddItem "Number: Single"
                .AddItem "Number: Double"
                .AddItem "OLE Object"
                .AddItem "Text"
                .AddItem "Yes/No"
        End With
End Sub
```

6. Add the following code to the **Click** event of **cmdAddField**. The routine checks for a field name, ensures that the name is legal (no invalid characters, no leading spaces, and so on), determines its data type from the Field Type combo box, and finally builds the SQL needed to send the **ALTER TABLE** command to the database.

```
Private Sub cmdAddField_Click()
    Dim strFieldType As String, strSQL As String

    'Check first if the Field Name text box contains a legal name
    If LegalName(True) Then
        On Error GoTo BadAdd
            'If it does, check if the Field Type has been
            'selected.
            If cboFieldTypes.ListIndex > -1 Then
                'If both criteria are satisfied, store the SQL
                'field type in the strFieldType string.
                Select Case cboFieldTypes.Text
                    Case "Counter"
                        strFieldType = "COUNTER"
                    Case "Currency"
                        strFieldType = "CURRENCY"
                    Case "Date/Time"
                        strFieldType = "DATETIME"
                    Case "Memo"
                        strFieldType = "LONGTEXT"
                    Case "Number: Byte"
                        strFieldType = "BYTE"
                    Case "Number: Integer"
                        strFieldType = "SHORT"
                    Case "Number: Long"
                        strFieldType = "LONG"
                    Case "Number: Single"
                        strFieldType = "SINGLE"
                    Case "Number: Double"
                        strFieldType = "DOUBLE"
                    Case "OLE Object"
                        strFieldType = "LONGBINARY"
                    Case "Text (25 chars)"
                        strFieldType = "TEXT(25)"
                    Case "Yes/No"
                        strFieldType = "BIT"
```

```
                    End Select

                    'Crate the ALTER TABLE statement
                    strSQL = "ALTER TABLE [" & txtTableName.Text & _
                        "] ADD COLUMN " _
                        & "[" & txtFieldName & "] " & strFieldType
                    'Execute the SQL
                    dbfBiblio.Execute (strSQL)
                    'Add the new field to the Field List list box.
                    lstFields.AddItem txtFieldName & " [" & _
                                    strFieldType & "]"

                    'Reset the Field Name and Field Type controls.
                    txtFieldName = ""
                    cboFieldTypes.ListIndex = -1
                Else
                    MsgBox "You must select a field type.", _
                            vbExclamation
                End If
            On Error GoTo 0
        End If
    Exit Sub

    BadAdd:
        MsgBox Err.Description, vbExclamation
    End Sub
```

7. Create the `LegalName` function in `Form1` with the following code. This
function checks for a valid field name containing at least one character,
without trailing spaces, that doesn't contain an illegal character. If it passes
all that, it performs one more check, depending on the value of
`intAction`. If `intAction` is `True`, indicating that the field is to be added,
the function checks whether a field already exists. If `intAction` is `False`,
indicating that the field is to be deleted, it ensures that there is no data in
the field anywhere in the table.

```
Function LegalName(intAction As Boolean) As Boolean
    Dim i As Integer
    Dim recNameCheck As Recordset

    On Error GoTo IllegalName
        'If blank, raise an error.
        If Len(txtFieldName.Text) = 0 Then Err.Raise 32767
        'If it has a leading space, raise an error.
        If Left$(txtFieldName.Text, 1) = " " Then Err.Raise 32766
        'If it contains any of the characters in the
        'IllegalCharacters constant, raise an error
        For i = 1 To Len(IllegalCharacters)
            If InStr(txtFieldName.Text, Mid(IllegalCharacters, _
                i, 1)) _
                > 0 Then Err.Raise 32765
        Next i
```

continued on next page

continued from previous page

```
'If it contains any ANSI character from Chr$(0) to
'Chr$(31), (you guessed it) raise an error.
For i = 0 To 31
    If InStr(txtFieldName.Text, Chr(i)) > 0 _
        Then Err.Raise 32764
Next i

If intAction Then
    'It's an add field; ensure that the name doesn't
    'already exist. If so, raise an error.
    For i = 0 To lstFields.ListCount - 1
        If txtFieldName.Text = lstFields.List(i) _
            Then Err.Raise 32763
    Next i
Else
    'It's a drop field; ensure that the field being erased
    'contains no data. If so, raise an error
    Set recNameCheck = dbfBiblio.OpenRecordset( _
        "SELECT [" & _
        txtFieldName.Text & "] FROM [" _
                            & txtTableName.Text & _
        "] WHERE [" & txtFieldName.Text & "] IS NOT NULL")
    If recNameCheck.RecordCount Then Err.Raise 32762
End If

'If they've managed to get through all that validation,
'the function should be True, to indicate success.
LegalName = True
On Error GoTo 0
Exit Function

IllegalName:
Dim strErrDesc As String
'Build an error message based on the user-defined error that
'occurred.
Select Case Err.Number
    Case 32767
        strErrDesc = "You must enter a field name."
    Case 32766
        strErrDesc = _
            "The field name cannot begin with a space."
    Case 32765
        strErrDesc = _
            "The field name contains the illegal character " & _
            Mid(IllegalCharacters, i, 1) & "."
    Case 32764
        strErrDesc = _
            "The field name contains the control character " & _
            "with the ANSI value" & Str$(i) & "."
    Case 32763
        strErrDesc = "The field name " & txtFieldName.Text & _
```

```
                        " already exists in the field name list."
            Case 32762
               strErrDesc = "The field name " & txtFieldName.Text & _
                  " has data; it cannot be deleted."
            Case Else
               ' Visual Basic's default error message.
               strErrDesc = Err.Description
         End Select

         MsgBox strErrDesc, vbExclamation

         'The function indicates False, or failure.
         LegalName = False
   Exit Function

   End Function
```

8. Add the following code to the **Click** event of **cmdRemoveField**:

```
Private Sub cmdRemoveField_Click()
    Dim strSQL As String, strTemp As String

    ' If the user has selected a field, remove it from the list.
    ' Otherwise, just ignore the click.
    If lstFields.ListIndex > -1 Then
        'Call the lstFields_Click event, to ensure that
        'txtFieldName is still populated. The user might have
        'erased it after selecting a
        'field to delete.
        Call lstFields_Click
        If LegalName(False) Then
            'Build the ALTER TABLE statement
            strSQL = "ALTER TABLE [" & txtTableName.Text & _
                "] DROP COLUMN [" & _
                txtFieldName.Text & "]"
            'Execute the SQL
            dbfBiblio.Execute (strSQL)
            'Delete the field from the Field List
            lstFields.RemoveItem lstFields.ListIndex
        End If
    End If
End Sub
```

9. Add the following code to the **Click** event of **lstFields**. This code extracts the name of the field selected in **lstFields** and passes it to the **txtFieldName** text box.

```
Private Sub lstFields_Click()
    Dim strTemp As String

    'If a field has been selected, extract the field's name from
    'the list entry and display it in the txtFieldName control.
    If lstFields.ListIndex > -1 Then
        strTemp = lstFields.List(lstFields.ListIndex)
```

continued on next page

continued from previous page

```
                strTemp = Left(strTemp, InStr(strTemp, "[") - 2)
                txtFieldName.Text = strTemp
            End If
        End Sub
```

10. Add the following code to the **Click** event of **cmdClose**:

```
        Private Sub cmdClose_Click()
            End
        End Sub
```

How It Works

When you load **Form1**, it prepares for use by running the **FillTypeList** routine, which loads the **cboFieldTypes** combo box with the various field types allowed by Visual Basic, and the **FillFieldList** routine, which loads all the field information from a given table into the **lstFields** list box. The **Form_Load** event defaults the table name for this routine to the [Title Author] table.

Each time the user adds a field to the table, an **ALTER TABLE** statement is concatenated in the **cmdAddField_Click** routine. Several steps are performed to ensure that the entered field is valid and meets the criteria for the statement. The routine uses the **LegalName** function to determine whether the field name specified is legal for use—doesn't have any illegal characters, has at least one character, and doesn't start with a space (ASCII 32). After that step, the routine fetches the field's type from the **cboFieldTypes** combo box and translates the English-readable selection into a valid SQL data type. After the translation is complete, it builds and executes the **ALTER TABLE** statement, using the **ADD COLUMN** keywords to create the field. If run successfully, it adds the newly created field to the **lstFields** list box.

Removing a field, however, is much less involved. Given the selected field name from the **lstFields** list box, and after the **LegalName** function is called to ensure that the selected field contains no data, another **ALTER TABLE** statement is issued, this time utilizing the **DROP COLUMN** keywords to remove the field from the table. After execution is complete, the field is then removed from the **lstFields** list box.

Comments

The **ALTER TABLE** has different behaviors depending on the database platform. Microsoft SQL Server, for example, won't allow a field-level constraint (for example, restricting a field's data to a certain range of values) to be added to an already existing field. As with the **SELECT...INTO** statement (covered previously in How-To 3.14), the best way to ensure that you get a complete understanding of how the database reacts to the **ALTER TABLE** statement is to experiment and observe the results.

COMPLEXITY
ADVANCED

3.16 How do I...
Create a crosstab query?

Problem

I need to be able to supply a worksheet-style query showing cross-referenced information easily. How do I do this?

Technique

The new features of the Microsoft Jet (3.5 and above) engines include the capability to create *crosstab*, or cross-tabulated, queries. Think of a crosstab query as a spreadsheet, with the information provided by the query read by referencing the row and column of the spreadsheet. For example, using your old familiar friend BIBLIO.MDB, you need to get a count of all the titles published since 1975, year by year, listed by publisher. Normally, this job would take a couple of queries, but the crosstab query allows you to use some SQL "sleight of hand" in performing this action by adding a couple of new SQL keywords to your arsenal.

In the following sample query, notice the **TRANSFORM** and **PIVOT** keywords. These new additions allow Jet to construct a crosstab query.

```
TRANSFORM Count(Titles.Title) AS [TitlesCount]
    SELECT Publishers.Name FROM Publishers INNER JOIN Titles ON
    (Titles.PubID = Publishers.PubID) WHERE Titles.[Year Published]
    > 1975 GROUP BY Publishers.Name
PIVOT Titles.[Year Published]
```

Table 3.29 lists the **TRANSFORM** and **PIVOT** keywords, used to create a crosstab query.

Table 3.29. The syntax of the crosstab query.

CLAUSE	PURPOSE	EXAMPLE
TRANSFORM	Selects the data to be shown in the body of the query	`TRANSFORM Count(Titles.Title)` `AS [TitlesCount]`
SELECT	Chooses the row information for the query, in a crosstab query	`SELECT Publishers.Name FROM` `Publishers INNER JOIN Titles` `ON( Titles.PubID =` `Publishers.PubID) WHERE` `Titles.[Year Published] > 1975`
PIVOT	Selects the column information for the query	`PIVOT Titles.[Year Published]`

To better understand the results of this query, visualize the results as a spreadsheet. The SELECT creates the rows of the spreadsheet; in the preceding example, a row is created for each publisher with a title published after 1975. The PIVOT creates the columns of the spreadsheet—a column for each year a title was published after 1975. The TRANSFORM statement creates the information on the spreadsheet where each row and column intersect—in the preceding query, a count of titles.

Steps

Open and run the project CROSSTAB.VBP. When the form appears, a grid displays the count of all the titles published after 1975, listed by publisher, as shown in Figure 3.21.

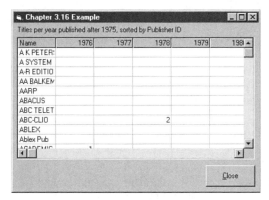

Figure 3.21. The SQL Transform form, displaying crosstab data.

1. Create a new project called CROSSTAB.VBP. Use **Form1** to create the objects and properties listed in Table 3.30, and save the form as CROSSTAB.FRM.

Table 3.30. Objects and properties for the Crosstab form.

OBJECT	PROPERTY	SETTING
Form	Name	Form1
	Caption	Chapter 3.16 Example
Data	Name	dtaData
MSFlexGrid	Name	grdCrossTab
	DataSourcw	dtaData

OBJECT	PROPERTY	SETTING
Label	Name	lblCrossTab
	Caption	Titles per year published
		after 1975, sorted by
		Publisher ID
CommandButton	Name	cmdClose
	Caption	&Close

2. Add the following statements to the declarations section of Form1.

```
Option Explicit

Private Const BIBLIO_PATH = _
"D:\Program Files\Microsoft Visual Studio\VB6\Biblio.MDB"
```

3. Add the following statements to the **Load** event of **Form1**. At this point, the event constructs the SQL statement used for the crosstab query (explained earlier in this How-To) and places it in the **RecordSource** property of the **dtaData** Data control. After it's added, the Data control is refreshed to execute the query and return the needed records, which will automatically display in the bound **MSFlexGrid** control, **grdCrossTab**.

```
Private Sub Form_Load()
    Dim strSQL As String

    'Construct the crosstab query statement.  Note the use of
    'several new SQL keywords, including TRANSFORM and PIVOT.
    'These two keywords are the building blocks of the crosstab
    'query.
    strSQL = "TRANSFORM Count(Titles.Title) AS [TitlesCount] " & _
        "SELECT Publishers.Name FROM Publishers "& _
                INNER JOIN Titles " & _
        "ON (Titles.PubID " & _
        "= Publishers.PubID) " & _
           WHERE Titles.[Year Published] > 1975 " & _
        "GROUP BY Publishers.Name " & _
        "PIVOT Titles.[Year Published]"

    'Set up the Data control
    With dtaData
        .DatabaseName = BIBLIO_PATH
        .RecordSource = strSQL
        .Refresh
    End With

End Sub
```

4. Add the following statements to the `Click` event of `cmdClose`:

```
Private Sub cmdClose_Click()
     End
End Sub
```

How It Works

When `Form1` loads, it constructs the sample crosstab query detailed earlier in the How-To. It then uses the `dtaData` Data control to execute it and retrieve the records for display in `grCrossTab`.

Comments

The crosstab query is a powerful tool for generating tabular data, especially aggregate or arithmetically derived information such as counts or statistical data, for a quick summary. Normally, without the `TRANSFORM` or `PIVOT` keywords, performing a query like the one you used would require two or three queries and possibly a temporary table, making it a complex task not only to execute but also to maintain. A crosstab query takes all that work and hands it to the database to perform, making the tedious job of cross-indexing information that much faster and easier.

DESIGNING AND IMPLEMENTING A DATABASE

4

DESIGNING AND IMPLEMENTING A DATABASE

How do I...

4.1 Create a new database?

4.2 Define tables and fields?

4.3 Define the primary key and other indexes?

4.4 Define relations between tables?

4.5 Use the Jet database engine to enforce business rules?

No amount of Visual Basic coding skill can overcome the problems of a poorly designed database. This chapter introduces some fundamental principles of relational database design. You'll see how you can use Visual Basic code to create databases and database objects, including tables, fields, indexes, and relationships. You'll also see how you can use the properties of these database objects to enforce business rules for your application.

4.1 Create a New Database

Creating a database with Data Access Object (DAO) code can be done with a single method. This How-To shows you how.

4.2 Define Tables and Fields

Every database design starts with tables and fields. This How-To examines time-tested principles of table design and demonstrates how you can use DAO code to create your database objects.

4.3 Define the Primary Key and Other Indexes

Indexes are the key to establishing relationships between tables and improving database application performance. This How-To introduces several types of indexes and shows you how to create indexes with Visual Basic code.

4.4 Define Relations Between Tables

This How-To shows you how to use Visual Basic to create the relations for your database.

4.5 Use the Jet Database Engine to Enforce Business Rules

There are two ways to enforce business rules in your database applications. You can write Visual Basic code to enforce your rules, or you can build the rules right into the database schema. This How-To shows you how to use the properties of the objects in your database to enforce business rules.

COMPLEXITY
BEGINNING

4.1 How do I...

Create a new database?

Problem

My application needs to create a database at a location chosen by the user. How can I do this with Visual Basic?

Technique

The `CreateDatabase` method of the `Workspace` object creates a database and returns a database object you can use in your application. The `CreateDatabase` method takes three arguments:

> ✔ name. The database name. VB appends `mdb` if you do not supply an extension. You can also use a UNC name in the form *server**share**path**file* if your network supports it.

✔ `locale`. The language used for the sort order. You can also use the `locale` argument to create a password-protected database by appending a password string to the locale constant. Locale constants are shown in Table 4.1.

✔ `option`. An optional constant or a combination of constants you can use to specify a database version or to encrypt the database. If you want to specify a version and encrypt the database, use the bitwise `Or` operator to combine the constants. `Option` constants are shown in Table 4.2.

Table 4.1. Locale constants for the *CreateDatabase* method.

CONSTANT	COLLATING ORDER
dbLangGeneral	Western European: English, German, French, Portuguese, Italian, and modern Spanish
dbLangArabic	Arabic
dbLangChineseSimplified	Simplified Chinese
dbLangChineseTraditional	Traditional Chinese
dbLangCyrillic	Russian
dbLangCzech	Czech
dbLangDutch	Dutch
dbLangGreek	Greek
dbLangHebrew	Hebrew
dbLangHungarian	Hungarian
dbLangIcelandic	Icelandic
dbLangJapanese	Japanese
dbLangKorean	Korean
dbLangNordic	Nordic languages (Microsoft Jet database engine version 1.0 only)
dbLangNorwDan	Norwegian and Danish
dbLangPolish	Polish
dbLangSlovenian	Slovenian
dbLangSpanish	Traditional Spanish
dbLangSwedFin	Swedish and Finnish
dbLangThai	Thai
dbLangTurkish	Turkish

Table 4.2. Options constants for the *CreateDatabase* method.

CONSTANT	DESCRIPTION
dbEncrypt	Creates an encrypted database
dbVersion10	Creates a database that uses the Microsoft Jet database engine version 1.0 file format
dbVersion11	Creates a database that uses the Microsoft Jet database engine version 1.1 file format
dbVersion20	Creates a database that uses the Microsoft Jet database engine version 2.0 file format
dbVersion30	(Default) Creates a database that uses the Microsoft Jet database engine version 3.0 file format (compatible with version 3.51)

Steps

Open and run HT401.VBP. Click the Create Database button. Choose a directory and filename using the common dialog, and click Save to create the database, as shown in Figure 4.1.

Figure 4.1. Creating a database.

1. Create a new Standard EXE project, and save it as HT401.VBP. Create the objects and properties listed in Table 4.3, and save the form as FCreateDB.frm.

Table 4.3. Objects and properties for the *Database Creator* form.

OBJECT	PROPERTY	SETTING
Form	Name	FCreateDB
	Caption	Create Database
CommonDialog	Name	dlgCreateDB
CommandButton	Name	cmdCreate
	Caption	Create Database

2. Add Option Explicit to the declarations section.

3. Create the GetDBName() function. This function sets up the Common Dialog control with the appropriate filters and flags and returns the file selected by the user as the return value of the function.

```
Private Function GetDBName() As String
' Get the desired name using the common dialog
On Error GoTo ProcError

    Dim strFileName As String

    ' set up the file save dialog file types
    dlgCreateDB.DefaultExt = "mdb"
    dlgCreateDB.DialogTitle = "Create Database"
    dlgCreateDB.Filter = "VB Databases (*.mdb)|*.mdb"
    dlgCreateDB.FilterIndex = 1
    ' set up flags
    dlgCreateDB.Flags = _
    cdlOFNHideReadOnly Or _
    cdlOFNOverwritePrompt Or _
    cdlOFNPathMustExist
    ' setting CancelError means the control will
    ' raise an error if the user clicks Cancel
    dlgCreateDB.CancelError = True
    ' show the SaveAs dialog
    dlgCreateDB.ShowSave
    ' get the selected name
    strFileName - dlgCreateDB.filename
    ' dialog prompted for overwrite,
    ' so kill file if it exists
    On Error Resume Next
    Kill strFileName

ProcExit:
    GetDBName = strFileName
    Exit Function

ProcError:
    strFileName = ""
    Resume ProcExit
End Function
```

4. Create the CreateDB() procedure. This procedure takes a filename as a parameter and creates a database using the **CreateDatabase** method of the Workspace object.

```
Private Sub CreateDB(strDBName As String)
' create the database

    Dim db As Database

    ' if desired, you can specify a version or encrypt
    ' the database as the optional third parameter to
    ' the CreateDatabase method
    Set db = DBEngine(0).CreateDatabase(strDBName, dbLangGeneral)
End Sub
```

5. Add the following code as the `cmdCreateDB_Click` event procedure. This procedure calls the `GetDBName` function to obtain a filename and passes it to `CreateDB` to create the database.

```
Private Sub cmdCreateDB_Click()
On Error GoTo ProcError

    Screen.MousePointer = vbHourglass

    Dim strDBName As String

    strDBName = GetDBName()

    If Len(strDBName) > 0 Then
        CreateDB strDBName
    End If

ProcExit:
    Screen.MousePointer = vbDefault
    Exit Sub

ProcError:
    MsgBox Err.Description
    Resume ProcExit
End Sub
```

How It Works

Two simple procedures—`GetDBName` and `CreateDB`—do all the work. The first obtains a filename from the user via the Common Dialog control, and the second creates the database using the filename provided.

THE SQL *CREATE DATABASE* **STATEMENT**

Some database engines provide a CREATE DATABASE statement as a command in their SQL dialects. Jet, however, does not. Although you can create tables, fields, indexes, relationships, and queries using Jet SQL, you must use the `CreateDatabase` method to create the actual .mdb file.

Comments

You might be able to avoid creating a database in code by using a model database. If you will be distributing an application that will always use the same database structure, you can create an empty version of the database and have the setup program install the empty model.

Although this approach will work in many cases, two common scenarios preclude the use of this technique:

1. If the database schema is not constant, a model will serve little or no purpose.

2. If the database must be secured at the installation point, you will need to have your code create the database using the account that will be the database owner. Although you can change the owner of database objects, you cannot change the owner of the database itself. See Chapter 11, "The Windows Registry and State Information," for additional information about working with secured databases.

COMPLEXITY
BEGINNING

4.2 How do I...
Define tables and fields?

Problem

I need a database that is flexible, accurate, and reliable. How do I design my table and column structure to ensure that this is what I get?

Technique

RECORDS AND ROWS—FIELDS AND COLUMNS

The terms *row* and *record* are interchangeable, as are the terms *column* and *field*. Referring to tables in terms of rows and columns is the generally accepted terminology for most literature on database design and for most database engines, except Jet. The Data Access Objects (DAO) object model and most of the Visual Basic documentation use the terms *record* and *field*. This kind of variation in terminology doesn't stop at the database design level. Most server databases, for example, describe the data returned by a query as a *result set*, whereas the Jet engine named its object a Recordset. Don't let the terminology confuse you. Whether you are dealing with records, rows, columns, or fields, the concepts are still the same.

Building a database structure is a process of examining the data that is useful and necessary for an application, and then breaking it down into a relatively simple row-and-column format. You should understand two points about tables and columns that are the essence of any database:

✔ Tables store data about an object.

An object, in this case, could be something tangible (such as a physical object) or intangible (such as an idea), but the primary consideration is that a table must contain data about only one thing.

✔ Columns contain the attributes of the object.

Just as a table contains data about a single type of object, each column should contain only one item of data about that object. If, for example, you're creating a table of addresses, there's no point in having a single column contain the city, state, and postal code when it is just as easy to create three columns and record each attribute separately.

The simplest model for any database is a flat table. The trouble with flat files is that they waste storage space and are problematic to maintain. Table 4.4 shows a flat table design that could be used to store information about students and classes at a school

Table 4.4. A flat table.

STUDENT	ADVISOR	COURSE1	DESCRIPTION1	INSTRUCTOR1	COURSE2	DESCRIPTION2	INSTRUCTOR2
B. Williams	H. Andrews	VB1	Intro to VB	C. MacDonald	DAO1	Intro to DAO	S. Garrett
L. Duncan	P. Lowell	DAO1	Intro to DAO	S. Garrett	SQL1	Jet SQL	K. Olson
H. Johnson	W. Smith	API1	API Basics	W. Smith	OOP1	VB Objects	T. Carter
F. Norris	J. Carter	VB1	Intro to VB	C. MacDonald	API1	API Basics	W. Smith

Several problems arise with this flat table:

✔ *Repeating groups.* The course ID, description, and instructor are repeated for each course. If a student wanted to take a third course, you would need to modify the table design. Although you could add columns for Course3, Course4, and so on, no matter how many columns you initially add, one day a student might need one more. Additionally, in most cases all the extra columns would be a waste of storage. What is required is a means of associating a student with any number of courses.

✔ *Inconsistent data.* If after entering the data, you discover that the SQL1 course should be titled "Transact-SQL" rather than "Jet SQL," you would need to examine two columns in each row to make all the necessary changes. You should be able to update this by changing only a single entry.

✔ *Delete anomalies*. If you want to remove S. Garrett's Intro to DAO course from the course list, you would need to delete two students, two advisors, and one additional instructor to do it. The data for each of these objects (students, advisors, instructors, and courses) should be independent of each other.

✔ *Insert anomalies*. Imagine that the department head wants to add a new course titled "Advanced Client/Server Programming" but has not yet created a schedule or even assigned an instructor. What do you enter in the other columns to record this information? You need to be able to add rows for each of the objects independently of the others.

The solution to these problems is a technique known in relational database parlance as *normalization*. *Normalization* is the process of taking a wide table with lots of columns but few rows and redesigning it as several narrow tables with fewer columns but more rows. A properly normalized design enables you to use storage space efficiently, eliminate redundant data, reduce or eliminate inconsistent data, and ease the data maintenance burden.

Several forms of normalization will be discussed shortly, but one cardinal rule absolutely must be followed:

YOU MUST BE ABLE TO RECONSTRUCT THE ORIGINAL FLAT VIEW OF THE DATA.

If you violate this rule, you will have defeated the purpose of normalizing the design.

NORMALIZATION IS *NOT* A PANACEA

Don't be misled into thinking that all database design woes can be cured with proper normalization. In fact, the opposite can be true. Taken to extremes, normalization can cause as many problems as it cures. Although you might be able to cure every type of data anomaly that could possibly occur, you will send performance on a downward spiral if your design requires more than two or three relational joins in a query to reconstruct a flat view of your data.

Consider this scenario:

You are designing a customer database. It's a well-known fact that in the United States, a postal zip code defines a specific city and state, and a nine-digit zip code defines a specific delivery point. You could, then, store only a zip code in the customer table and eliminate the city and state columns that would typically be required. However, every time the city and state needed to be retrieved, the database engine would have to perform an additional join. This might or might not be acceptable in your situation.

continued on next page

continued from previous page

Now take this scenario to an additional level of detail. It's also true that although millions of people live in the United States, there are a limited number of first and last names and only 26 possible middle initials. Theoretically, you could create a foreign key column in place of the normal last name column and do the same for the first name. This level of normalization, however, steps into the realm of the ridiculous. It is pointless complexity that adds no real benefit for data accuracy.

Forms of Normalization

Relational database theorists have divided normalization into several rules, called *normal forms*:

✔ *First normal form*. No repeating groups.

✔ *Second normal form*. No nonkey attributes depend on a portion of the primary key.

✔ *Third normal form*. No attributes depend on other nonkey attributes.

Additionally, for a database to be in second normal form, it must be in first normal form, and so on. Fourth and fifth normal forms also exist, but these are rarely applied. In fact, it might be practical at times to violate even the first three forms of normalization (see the sidebar "Normalization Is *Not* a Panacea").

First Normal Form

First normal form requires that a table does not contain repeating groups. A repeating group is a set of columns, such as the `CourseID`, `Description`, and `Instructor` columns in Table 4.4. Repeating groups are removed by creating a separate table from the columns that repeat.

NOTE

If you have a set of columns with names that end in numbers, such as the `CourseID1` and `CourseID2` columns in the example, it's a clear sign that you have encountered repeating groups. At this point, you need to think about removing the columns to a separate table.

Table 4.5 is a revised version of the sample table, with the repeating groups for the course moved to their own table. (Note that in this table and the following several tables, primary key columns have been put in bold type. The primary key concept is explained a little later in the chapter.)

Table 4.5. First normal form.

STUDENTS	STUDENTCOURSES
	SCStID
StID	SCCourseID
StName	SCCourseDesc
StAdvisorName	SCCourseInstrName

The repeating group has been eliminated by creating a second table. The student can now enroll in any number of courses (including no courses). Although the repeating group is gone, we can still reconstruct the original table by joining the two via the new SCStID column in the StudentCourses table. This column is a foreign key that matches the value of the StID column in the Students table.

TABLE AND COLUMN NAMING CONVENTIONS

A naming convention has been applied to these table and column names:

✔ Names are restricted to 30 characters and can contain only letters, numbers, and the underscore character. A letter must be the first character. The 30-character limit provides compatibility with Microsoft SQL Server. The other restrictions eliminate the need to use square brackets as delimiters around column names in SQL statements and VB code.

✔ Tables are named using the plural form of the objects they represent.

✔ Columns are named to represent the attribute they record.

✔ Each table is assigned a unique column name prefix. With the addition of a prefix to the column names, all columns within the name space of a database have a unique name. This eliminates the need to fully qualify the column with the table name in SQL statements.

Naming conventions have an annoying tendency to start religious wars among programmers, but nearly all programmers will—perhaps grudgingly—admit their usefulness. You can adopt this convention or any other convention that suits you or your company. What's important is not the particular convention you choose but that you choose one and follow it faithfully.

Second Normal Form

Second normal form requires that no nonkey attributes depend on a portion of the primary key. To understand this rule, you need to understand the concept of a primary key. A *primary key* is a column, or set of columns, in a table that uniquely identifies a single record. The primary key for a table is most often an arbitrary value, such as an autoincrement column (Jet refers to this as a counter), although the primary key can be any type of data.

NOTE

Proceed with caution if you decide to use anything other than an arbitrary value as the primary key for a table. Even seemingly reliable data such as a social security number can fail if used as a primary key. An arbitrary value provided by the database engine is guaranteed to be unique and independent of the data in the table.

Second normal form really applies only to tables in which the primary key is defined by two or more columns. The essence is that if certain columns can be identified by only part of the primary key, they must be in their own table. The StudentCourses table in Table 4.5 violates second normal form because the course information can be identified without using the SCStID column. Table 4.6 shows the same data reorganized so that it meets the requirements for second normal form.

Table 4.6. Second normal form.

STUDENTS	STUDENTCOURSES	COURSES
	SCStID	
StID	SCCourseID	CourseID
StName		CourseDesc
StAdvisorName		CourseInstrName

The partial dependence on the primary key has been eliminated by moving the course information to its own table. The relationship between students and courses has at last revealed itself to be a many-to-many relationship (see the following section,"Advanced Design Techniques"). Each student can take many courses, and each course can have many students. The StudentCourses table now contains only the two foreign keys to Students and Courses.

Third Normal Form

Third normal form requires that no attributes depend on other nonkey attributes. This means that all the columns in the table contain data about the entity that is defined by the primary key. The columns in the table must contain data about only one thing. Like second normal form, this is used to remove columns that belong in their own table.

Table 4.7 shows a revised version of these tables, with a few columns added to help illustrate third normal form.

Table 4.7. Detail columns added.

STUDENTS	STUDENTCOURSES	COURSES
	SCStID	
StID	SCCourseID	CourseID
StFirstName		CourseDesc
StLastName		CourseInstrName
StAddress		CourseInstrPhone
StCity		
StState		
StZIP		
StAdvisorName		
StAdvisorPhone		

To complete the normalization, we need to look for columns that are not dependent on the primary key of the table. In the Students table, we have two data items about the student's advisor: the name and phone number. The balance of the data pertains only to the student and so is appropriate in the Students table. The advisor information, however, is not dependent on the student. If the student leaves the school, the advisor and the advisor's phone number remain the same. The same logic applies to the instructor information in the Courses table. The data for the instructor is not dependent on the primary key CourseID because the instructor is unaffected if the course is dropped from the curriculum (unless school officials fire the instructor when they drop the course). Table 4.8 shows the revised schema in third normal form.

Table 4.8. Third normal form.

STUDENTS	ADVISORS	INSTRUCTORS	STUDENTCOURSES	COURSES
StID	AdvID	InstrID	SCStID	CourseID
			SCCourseID	
StAdvID	AdvFirst	InstrFirst		CourseInstrID
StFirst	AdvLast	InstrLast		CourseDesc
StLast	AdvPhone	InstrPhone		
StAddress				
StCity				
StState				
StZIP				

The database is now in third normal form:

✔ It is in first normal form because there are no repeating groups in any table.

✔ It is in second normal form because it is in first normal form and because there are no nonkey attributes that depend on a portion of the primary key in any table.

✔ It is in third normal form because it is in first and second normal form and because no attributes depend on other nonkey attributes in any table.

Advanced Design Techniques

Look again at Table 4.8. You can see two types of relationships between tables:

✔ *One-to-many.* A row in one table can have zero or more related rows in another table. The relationship between advisors and students, for example, is a one-to-many relationship. Any advisor can have no students, one student, or more than one student.

✔ *Many-to-many.* Rows in one table can have many related rows in a second table, and the second table can have many related rows in the first table. The relationship between students and courses is a many-to-many relationship. Each student can be enrolled in zero or more courses, and each course can have zero or more students enrolled.

A third possible type of relationship exists between tables: a one-to-one relationship. Table 4.8 reveals a possible use of a one-to-one relational design. Both the Advisors table and the Instructors table contain identical lists of columns. In a real-world database, each of these tables would contain additional columns specific to the role of advisor or instructor and would also contain additional information about the individual faculty member who has that role. If you examine Table 4.4, you will notice that faculty members can act in both roles—as advisors and instructors. Table 4.9 shows a more detailed view of the advisor and instructor data.

Table 4.9. Advisors and instructors.

ADVISORS	INSTRUCTORS
AdvID	InstrID
AdvFirst	InstrFirst
AdvLast	InstrLast
AdvPhone	InstrPhone
AdvGradeLevel	InstrSpecialty

For this example, it is assumed that advisors handle students by grade level (undergraduate or graduate) and that instructors have a specialty area that they teach. For example, in a computer science department, an instructor might specialize in teaching classes related to a particular language.

Much of the data in these two tables is shared. You could duplicate the columns in both tables, or you could further subdivide these tables, as shown in Table 4.10.

Table 4.10. The school faculty.

FACULTY	ADVISORS	INSTRUCTORS
FacID	**AdvFacID**	**InstrFacID**
FacFirst	AdvGradeLevel	InstrSpecialty
FacLast		
FacPhone		

The columns that are shared by both tables have been removed to the Faculty table. The Advisors and Instructors tables now contain only a foreign key to the faculty table and the columns that relate specifically to the role of advisor or instructor. The foreign key columns in this case also act as the primary key for these tables because there must be one (and only one) row in the Faculty table for any advisor or instructor. This is a one-to-one relationship. The Advisors and Instructors tables define extensions to the Faculty table for subsets of the data in that table.

Designing the tables so that they use the shared Faculty table allows for the reuse of the code required to manage that data and common querying of all members of the school staff.

The design of the database for the mythical school is nearly complete, but one set of data is still missing. All but the smallest of organizations generally employ a hierarchical management structure. If the school is a large university, it probably has several campuses, each of which have several colleges. Each college is probably further divided into several departments, and even those departments might be subdivided. The trouble with hierarchical organizations is that you often can't know in advance how many levels will exist within the hierarchy. A solution to this problem does exist, however. Table 4.11 expands the view of the faculty information.

Table 4.11. The school faculty.

FACULTY	DEPARTMENTS
FacID	**DeptID**
FacDeptID	DeptName
FacFirst	DeptParentDeptID
FacLast	
FacPhone	

A foreign key to the Departments table has been added to the Faculty table. This enables a faculty member to be assigned to a department. The Departments table has three columns: `DeptID`, the primary key; `DeptName`, the department name; and the key to establishing the hierarchical relationship, the `DeptParentDeptID` column. This column is a foreign key, but the key points back into the Departments table. This relationship might be easier to understand if you look at some sample data, as shown in Table 4.12.

Table 4.12. The Departments table.

DEPTID	DEPTNAME	DEPTPARENTDEPTID
1	Minnesota State University	Null
2	Institute of Technology	1
3	College of Liberal Arts	1
4	College of Medicine	1
5	Department of Internal Medicine	4
6	Oncology Department	5

Looking at the sample data, you can see that the College of Medicine is directly under the university, the Department of Internal Medicine is under the College of Medicine, and the Oncology Department is under the Department of Internal Medicine. This type of structure can be reassembled as a flat table using a self-join. In a self-join, a table is included twice in the same query.

> **NOTE**
>
> The TreeView control is an excellent choice as a tool for displaying hierarchical data.

Creating Tables and Columns with Visual Basic

A well-designed database schema is critical, but that's only half the work of creating a database. You still need to create the actual database objects. You can use two methods to create database objects in a Jet database:

✔ *SQL statements.* You can use SQL **CREATE TABLE** and **ALTER TABLE** statements to create tables. Using a SQL statement is fast and easy, but it limits the control you have over the database objects. Many of the properties available for tables and columns cannot be set using SQL alone. You can also use the SQL **DROP** statement to delete tables. Chapter 3, "Creating Queries with SQL," provides detailed instructions for using SQL statements to create database objects.

✔ *Data Access Objects.* The `TableDef` object and `TableDefs` collection are used to create tables, and the `Field` object and `Fields` collection are used to create columns. In this How-To, you use DAO code to create database objects. Using the `Delete` method of the `TableDefs` collection is also demonstrated.

Creating a table with DAO code is a three-step process:

1. Create the `TableDef` object by using the `CreateTableDef` method.

2. Create the `Field` objects by using the `CreateField` method, and add them to the `TableDef` object using the `Append` method.

3. Add the `TableDef` object to the collection by using the `Append` method.

Steps

Open and run project HT402.vbp. A sample database based on the tables shown in Table 4.8 and Table 4.10 has been created and saved as HT402.mdb. You can open the sample database and inspect it, or you can create a new database by using the File | New menu command. First, create the Students, Courses, and StudentCourses tables (as shown in Table 4.8) and then create the Faculty, Advisors, and Instructors tables (as shown in Table 4.10). To create the tables, select Table | Add. Figure 4.2 shows the Create TableDef form with the Students table in progress.

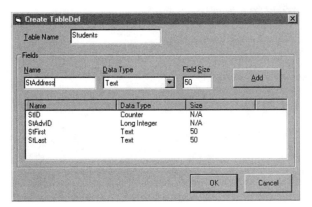

Figure 4.2. Creating the Students table.

NOTE

This example and the two examples that follow in How-To 4.3 and How-To 4.4 use the Microsoft Windows Common Dialog 6.0, the Microsoft Windows Common Controls 6.0, and the Microsoft DAO 3.51 Object Library components.

1. Create a new project called HT402.vbp. Add BMain.bas to the project. This standard module contains procedures to open an existing database and create a new database. These procedures are based in large part on the example presented in How-To 4.1.

2. Add frmMain.frm to the project. This is based on a form created by the VB Application Wizard. The wizard-generated code manages the split view for the tree and list panes of the main form. For simplicity, a considerable amount of the wizard-generated code was removed. The right pane supports only the report view, and all the toolbar buttons and menu controls were removed, along with their associated event procedures. Menu controls and associated code were then added for the File and Table menus. Table 4.13 shows the menu controls that were added for the example. In the declarations section, an object variable is declared for the CDBExplorer class:

```
Private mcdbExp As CDBExplorer
```

Table 4.13. Menu controls for *frmMain*.

NAME	CAPTION
mnuFile	&File
mnuFileOpen	&Open
mnuFileNew	&New
mnuFileBar1	-
mnuFileClose	&Close

NOTE

Because of space limitations, all the wizard-generated code that manages the split Explorer view for the left and right panes of the main form has not been included here.

3. The following code controls the File menu for the main form. The
`mnuFileOpen_Click` and `mnuFileNew_Click` event procedures call
routines in BMain.bas to open or create a database and then create and
initialize the `mcdbExp` object variable. When initialized using the
`ExploreDatabase` method, the `CDBExplorer` class accepts a database
name, a reference to a TreeView control, and a reference to a ListView
control as parameters. Code within the class then handles most of the
management of the tree and list panes of the form.

```
Private Sub mnuFileOpen_Click()
' open a database
On Error GoTo ProcError

  Dim strDBName As String

  Screen.MousePointer = vbHourglass

  strDBName = GetOpenDBName(dlgCommonDialog)
  If Len(strDBName) Then
    Set mcdbExp = Nothing
    Set mcdbExp = New CDBExplorer
    mcdbExp.ExploreDatabase strDBName, tvTreeView, lvListView
  End If

  ' no node is selected by default, so we
  ' select the root node here
  SelectRootNode

ProcExit:
  Screen.MousePointer = vbDefault
  Exit Sub

ProcError:
  MsgBox Err.Description
  Resume ProcExit

End Sub

Private Sub mnuFileNew_Click()
' create a new database
On Error GoTo ProcError

  Dim strDBName As String

  Screen.MousePointer = vbHourglass

  ' get the filename
  strDBName = GetNewDBName(dlgCommonDialog)
  ' kill it if it exists
  ' note that GetDBName prompts to confirm overwrite
  On Error Resume Next
  Kill strDBName
```

continued on next page

continued from previous page

```
                            ' create the database
                            CreateDB strDBName

                            ' explore it
                            Set mcdbExp = New CDBExplorer
                            mcdbExp.ExploreDatabase strDBName, tvTreeView, lvListView

                            SelectRootNode

                       ProcExit:
                          Screen.MousePointer = vbDefault
                          Exit Sub

                       ProcError:
                          MsgBox Err.Description
                          Resume ProcExit
                       End Sub

                       Private Sub mnuFileClose_Click()
                          'unload the form
                          Unload Me
                       End Sub
```

4. The following code passes the **Expand** and **NodeClick** events for the tree
pane on to the **CDBExplorer** class:

```
Private Sub tvTreeView_Expand(ByVal Node As ComctlLib.Node)
' Expand the node
On Error GoTo ProcError

   Screen.MousePointer = vbHourglass

   ' the class does the work
   mcdbExp.ExpandNode Node

ProcExit:
   Screen.MousePointer = vbDefault
   Exit Sub

ProcError:
   MsgBox "Error: " & Err.Number & vbCrLf & Err.Description
   Resume ProcExit
End Sub

Private Sub tvTreeView_NodeClick(ByVal Node As ComctlLib.Node)
' Display the properties of the selected node in the listview
On Error GoTo ProcError

   Screen.MousePointer = vbHourglass

   ' the class does the work
   mcdbExp.ListProperties Node
```

```
ProcExit:
  Screen.MousePointer = vbDefault
  Exit Sub

ProcError:
  MsgBox "Error: " & Err.Number & vbCrLf & Err.Description
  Resume ProcExit
End Sub
```

5. Add the CDBExplorer.cls class module to the project. Code in this class module does most of the work of mapping database objects to nodes in the tree pane of the form. This was developed as a class module to provide a degree of isolation between the database engine and the user interface in the form. The class presents a hierarchical view of a database, including tables, fields, indexes, queries, and relationships in a tree.

The class works by examining the **Expand** and **NodeClick** events of a TreeView control. When a node in the tree is expanded, the class populates that branch of the tree (empty dummy nodes are initially written to unexpanded nodes so that the node will be expandable on the form). After a node is selected by the user, the class determines what database object is associated with the node by examining the position of the node in the tree; then the class displays the properties of the associated object in the list pane. The property list works by iterating the **Properties** collection common to all DAO objects (except collections) and adding them as items in the ListView control. In this How-To, **mnuTableAdd** and **mnuTableDelete** call the **AddTable** and **DeleteTable** methods of the class. These methods add or remove a **TableDef** object and refresh the **TableDefs** branch of the tree on **frmMain**.

```
Public Sub AddTable()
  Load frmCreateTableDef

  Set frmCreateTableDef.Database = mdb

  frmCreateTableDef.Show vbModal

  ' refresh the tabledefs node
  ExpandNode mtvw.Nodes("TableDefs")
End Sub

Public Sub DeleteTable(strTableDefName As String)

  ' delete the TableDef
  mdb.TableDefs.Delete strTableDefName

  ' refresh the tree
  ExpandNode mtvw.Nodes("TableDefs")
End Sub
```

> **NOTE**
>
> Because of the length of the code in the CDBExplorer class, it was not possible to present all of it here. Source code comments in the class and the CDBExplorer.html file included in the project as a related file on the CD-ROM provide additional details about the class.

6. Add a new form to the project and save it as frmCreateTableDef.frm. Add the objects and properties shown in Table 4.14. Except for lblTableDefName, txtTableDefName, and the cmd command button array, all controls should be drawn within the fraFields frame.

Table 4.14. *frmCreateTableDef* objects and properties.

OBJECT	PROPERTY	VALUE
Form	Name	frmCreateTableDef
	Caption	Create TableDef
	BorderStyle	3-Fixed Dialog
Label	Name	lblTableDefName
	Caption	&Table Name
TextBox	Name	txtTableDefName
Frame	Name	fraFields
	Caption	Fields
Label	Name	lblFieldName
	Caption	&Name
TextBox	Name	txtFieldName
Label	Name	lblFieldType
	Caption	&Data Type
ComboBox	Name	cboFieldDataType
	Style	2-Dropdown List
Label	Name	lblFieldSize
	Caption	Field &Size
TextBox	Name	txtFieldSize
CommandButton	Name	cmdAdd
	Caption	&Add
ListView	Name	lvwFields
CommandButton	Name	cmd
	Index	0
	Caption	OK
	Default	True

OBJECT	PROPERTY	VALUE
CommandButton	Name	cmd
	Index	1
	Caption	Cancel
	Cancel	True

7. Add the following code to the declarations section. The database object is used to create the **TableDef** object. The two constants are indexes into the **cmd** CommandButton control array.

```
Option Explicit

' database object
Private mdb As Database

' command button array index constants
Private Const cmdOK = 0
Private Const cmdCancel = 1
```

8. Add the **Form_Load** event procedure. This procedure populates the field type list, sets up the list view headers, and disables the frame and OK button. The frame is enabled after a table name is provided. OK is enabled when a table name is provided and at least one field has been added to the field list.

```
Private Sub Form_Load()
' set up form
On Error GoTo ProcError

  Screen.MousePointer = vbHourglass

  ' set up fields controls
  cmdAdd.Enabled = False

  ' fill the data types combo
  With cboFieldDataType
    ' Note: not all field types are
    ' included here
    .Clear
    .AddItem "Boolean"
    .AddItem "Counter"
    .AddItem "Date/Time"
    .AddItem "Long Integer"
    .AddItem "Text"
    .AddItem "Memo"
  End With
  cboFieldDataType.Text = "Text"

  ' set up list view
  lvwFields.View = lvwReport
```

continued on next page

continued from previous page

```
            With lvwFields.ColumnHeaders
              .Add , "Name", "Name"
              .Item("Name").Width = 2000
              .Add , "Type", "Data Type"
              .Add , "Size", "Size"
            End With

            ' disable the entire fields frame
            fraFields.Enabled = False

            ' disable OK button
            cmd(cmdOK).Enabled = False

          ProcExit:
            Screen.MousePointer = vbDefault
            Exit Sub

          ProcError:
            MsgBox "Error: " & Err.Number & vbCrLf & Err.Description
            Resume ProcExit
          End Sub
```

9. Add the `cboFieldDataType_Click` procedure. This enables or disables the field size text box, depending on the type of field selected.

```
          Private Sub cboFieldDataType_Click()

            If cboFieldDataType.Text = "Text" Then
              lblFieldSize.Enabled = True
              txtFieldSize.Enabled = True
            Else
              txtFieldSize.Text = ""
              lblFieldSize.Enabled = False
              txtFieldSize.Enabled = False
            End If
          End Sub
```

10. Add the `cmdAdd_Click` event procedure. This procedure uses the data in the FieldName, DataType, and Size controls to add the field to the field list in the ListView control. It then enables the OK button and returns focus to the FieldName control.

```
          Private Sub cmdAdd_Click()
          ' add to the listview
          On Error GoTo ProcError

            Screen.MousePointer = vbHourglass

            Dim li As ListItem
            Dim strFieldName As String
            Dim strFieldDataType As String
```

```
    strFieldName = txtFieldName.Text
    strFieldDataType = cboFieldDataType.Text

    Set li = lvwFields.ListItems.Add _
      (, strFieldName, strFieldName)
    With li
      .SubItems(1) = strFieldDataType
      ' only add size if applicable
      If strFieldDataType = "Text" Then
        .SubItems(2) = txtFieldSize.Text
      Else
        .SubItems(2) = "N/A"
      End If
    End With

    ' prep for new entry
    txtFieldName.Text = ""
    txtFieldName.SetFocus

    ' enable the OK button
    cmd(cmdOK).Enabled = True

ProcExit:
  Screen.MousePointer = vbDefault
  Exit Sub

ProcError:
  MsgBox "Error: " & Err.Number & vbCrLf & Err.Description
  Resume ProcExit
End Sub
```

11. Add the `Change` event procedures for the `txtTableDefName` and `txtFieldName` controls. These enable or disable other controls on the form based on the current values.

```
Private Sub txtTableDefName_Change()
' Enable/disable controls

  cmd(cmdOK).Enabled = False
  fraFields.Enabled = False

  If Len(txtTableDefName) > 0 Then
    fraFields.Enabled = True
    If lvwFields.ListItems.Count > 0 Then
      cmd(cmdOK).Enabled = True
    End If
  End If
End Sub

Private Sub txtFieldName_Change()

  If Len(txtFieldName.Text) > 0 Then
    cmdAdd.Enabled = True
```

continued on next page

continued from previous page

```
      Else
        cmdAdd.Enabled = False
      End If
End Sub
```

12. Add the `cmd_Click` event procedure. This procedure adds the table if OK is chosen or unloads the form if Cancel is chosen.

```
Private Sub cmd_Click(Index As Integer)
On Error GoTo ProcError

  Screen.MousePointer = vbHourglass

  Select Case Index
    Case cmdOK
      ' add the table
      AddTable
    Case cmdCancel
      ' just unload the form
  End Select

  Unload Me

ProcExit:
  Screen.MousePointer = vbDefault
  Exit Sub

ProcError:
  MsgBox "Error: " & Err.Number & vbCrLf & Err.Description
  Resume ProcExit
End Sub
```

13. Create the `AddTable` procedure. `AddTable` creates the `TableDef` object, then extracts the field information from the ListView to create and add each `Field` object. After the fields have been added to the table, the table is added to the database using the `Append` method of the `TableDefs` collection.

```
Private Sub AddTable()
  Dim li As ListItem

  Dim td As TableDef
  Dim fld As Field
  Dim lngType As Long

  Dim strFieldName As String
  Dim strFieldDataType As String

  Set td = mdb.CreateTableDef(txtTableDefName.Text)

  ' add the fields
  For Each li In lvwFields.ListItems
```

```
     ' get the name
     strFieldName = li.Text
     ' get the data type
     strFieldDataType = li.SubItems(1)
     Select Case strFieldDataType
       Case "Boolean"
         lngType = dbBoolean
       Case "Counter"
         lngType = dbLong
       Case "Date/Time"
         lngType = dbDate
       Case "Long Integer"
         lngType = dbLong
       Case "Text"
         lngType = dbText
       Case "Memo"
         lngType = dbMemo
     End Select
     ' check field type
     If lngType = dbText Then
       ' text, create with size
       Set fld = td.CreateField _
         (strFieldName, dbText, CInt(li.SubItems(2)))
     Else
       ' other, create without size
       Set fld = td.CreateField(strFieldName, lngType)
       If strFieldDataType = "Counter" Then
         fld.Attributes = fld.Attributes Or dbAutoIncrField
       End If
     End If
     td.Fields.Append fld
     Set fld = Nothing
   Next  ' ListItem

   ' append the tabledef
   mdb.TableDefs.Append td
End Sub
```

14. Add the **Database** property. This is used by the **AddTable** procedure and must be set before the form is shown.

```
Public Property Set Database(db As DAO.Database)
  Set mdb = db
End Property
```

How It Works

The **AddTable** procedure in **frmCreateTableDef** is the critical procedure for this How-To. This routine creates the table using the name provided on the form, then iterates the items in the list to create and append the fields. When all the fields have been added, the table is appended to the database. The balance of the code on the form serves only to manage and coordinate the user interface.

Comments

Much of the code provided on the CD-ROM supports the main Explorer form and class module, but the code in `frmCreateTableDef` does all the work of creating a table and its fields. It is helpful, but not necessary, to fully understand the code in the class module and the wizard-generated code in the main form.

The sample application is not limited to creating the sample database described in this How-To. You can inspect or modify any Jet database using the project.

COMPLEXITY
BEGINNING

4.3 How do I...
Define the primary key and other indexes?

Problem

I know that a primary key is an important component in a proper relational database design and that indexes can significantly improve database performance. How do I choose fields to index and create the indexes for those fields?

Technique

Database indexes can be broadly grouped into two categories:

- ✔ *Constraints*. The primary key and other unique indexes place constraints on the data that can be entered into the columns bound to the indexes.

- ✔ *Performance indexes*. Some, perhaps most, indexes are added strictly for performance reasons. An index speeds access to data by enabling the database engine to more quickly retrieve rows from the tables. (Of course, the additional performance gain for the query operation occurs at the expense of modifying the index during the insert, update, and delete operations.)

Many developers consider indexes—particularly indexes that act as constraints—to be part of the database schema or overall table design. In reality, however, indexes serve only to enforce the constraints that must be applied to the data. The constraints, or rules, form the database design. Indexes serve as a tool to implement those constraints. It is possible (although not recommended) to create tables that do not have primary keys or unique indexes and still have a fully functional relational design, but it is much more efficient to have the database engine enforce rules at that level.

Establishing indexes on tables is a two-step process. First you must determine what columns need to be indexed and the type of indexes the columns require, and then you must create the indexes using the properties and methods provided by the database engine.

Constraints

In How-To 4.2, you learned about primary keys and relationships between tables, including one-to-many, many-to-many, and one-to-one relationships. Although you can create a table without a primary key, this technique is not recommended. In most situations, it is also recommended that an arbitrary value, such as a number provided by the database engine, be used as the primary key. For those tables that act as the junction table of a many-to-many relationship between tables, the combination of the two foreign key columns typically acts as the primary key. In a one-to-one relationship, the foreign key column alone is the primary key. Only one primary key can be defined for a table, although you can define additional unique indexes.

A primary key imposes some constraints on the data in the columns included in the index:

✔ Each entry in the index must be unique. For single-column indexes, every value in the column must be unique. In multiple-column indexes, each combination of values must be unique.

✔ Every column in the index must contain a value. You cannot have nulls in columns included in the primary key.

Indexing for Performance

In addition to imposing constraints on your data, indexes can be added strictly to improve performance. The database engine can optimize SELECT queries if it has useful indexes available. Determining what constitutes a useful index can be more of an art than a science, but the following guidelines are appropriate in most situations:

✔ Index foreign key columns. These are almost always excellent candidates for indexes.

✔ Index columns that are frequently used for restrictive criteria in the WHERE clause of SELECT queries.

✔ Index columns that are used for sorting in the ORDER BY clause of SELECT queries.

✔ If you frequently do multiple field sorts, create a multiple field index ordered using the same order used in the sort. Sorts are normally ascending but can be descending.

To obtain the best performance in your own applications, you should experiment with various indexing strategies and use profiling techniques to determine which indexes provide the greatest advantage.

WHEN NOT TO INDEX

Don't think that you can index every column to gain optimum performance. Although indexes accelerate data retrieval, they slow inserts, updates, and deletes because the database engine not only has to update the tables but also must update the indexes.

Additionally, the database engine might not find all indexes useful, especially on small tables. If you have tables with very few rows (such as lookup tables of coded values, tables of United States states, and the like), it is likely that the database engine can perform a table scan (read every row in the table) faster than it can find a row using an index.

Finally, some situations can force a table scan, in which case all indexes are ignored.

Defining Indexes

Indexes are created by using the `CreateIndex` method of the `TableDef` object in a three-step process:

1. Call `CreateIndex` to create an `Index` object.

2. Create the fields in the index by using the `CreateField` method, and then use the `Append` method to add them to the `Fields` collection of the index.

3. Use the `Append` method of the `Indexes` collection to add the index to the `TableDef` object.

NOTE

If you think this process looks remarkably similar to that of creating a table using DAO code, you're right—the processes are nearly identical.

Steps

Open and run HT403.vbp. You can create the indexes shown in Table 4.15 by choosing the Index|Add command and using the form shown in Figure 4.3.

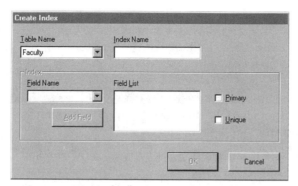

Figure 4.3. The Create Index form.

NOTE

The database file HT403.mdb contains the tables without the indexes. Also included is HT403A.mdb. This is the same file with all the indexes already created for you. You can examine this file with the Explorer form if you don't want to create all the indexes shown in Table 4.15.

Table 4.15. Indexes in HT403.mdb.

TABLE	INDEX	PROPERTIES	FIELDS
Advisors	apkAdvisors	Primary	AdvFacID
Courses	apkCourses	Primary	CourseID
	idxCourseIstrID		
	CourseInstrID		
Faculty	apkFaculty	Primary	FacID
	idxFacLast		FacLast
Instructors	apkInstructors	Primary	InstrFacID
StudentCourses	apkStudentCourses	Primary	SCStID
			SCCourseID
	idxSCStID		SCStID
	idxSCCourseID		SCCourseID
Students	apkStudents	Primary	StID
	idxStAdvID		StAdvID
	idxStLast		StLast
	idxStState		StState

The indexes shown in Table 4.15 are recommended based on the guidelines listed in this How-To. Each table has a primary key, all foreign key columns are indexed, and several additional columns are indexed as likely candidates for use as query selection or sort columns.

INDEX NAMES

The following naming convention was used to determine the index names shown in Table 4.15:

✔ Primary keys are named using the prefix *apk*, followed by the table name. This convention provides forward compatibility if the database is later upsized to a database server such as SQL Server or Oracle. With remote server tables, the Jet engine assumes that the first index in an alphabetical list is the primary key. The *apk* prefix places the primary key first in the list.

✔ Unique nonprimary indexes use the prefix *udx*, followed by the name of the indexed column or columns. (No unique, nonprimary indexes are present in Table 4.15.)

✔ Other indexes use the prefix *idx*, followed by the column name or names.

This project is an extended version of the project developed in How-To 4.2. Code was added to the main form and class module to launch `frmCreateIndex`, which handles the balance of the code to create indexes.

1. Create a new Standard EXE project, and save it as HT403.vbp. Add BMain.bas to the project. This module contains code used to open or create a new database and is based largely on the code developed in How-To 4.1.

2. Add `frmMain` to the project. This form is based on an Explorer-style form generated by the VB Application Wizard. The wizard form was modified for this project, as described in How-To 4.2. In addition to the modifications added for How-To 4.2, the menu controls in Table 4.16 were added to create the Index menu.

Table 4.16. The Index menu controls.

NAME	CAPTION
mnuIndex	&Index
mnuIndexAdd	&Add
mnuIndexDelete	&Delete

3. Three event procedures support the Index menu. The top-level menu
`mnuIndex_Click` event enables or disables the delete command based on
the currently selected object. The add command calls on the services of
the `CDBExplorer` class via the `mcdbExp` module-level object variable to
create a new index, and the delete command uses the same object to
delete an index.

```
Private Sub mnuIndex_Click()
On Error GoTo ProcError

  If mcdbExp Is Nothing Then
    ' no database open
    mnuIndexAdd.Enabled = False
    mnuIndexDelete.Enabled = False
  Else
    ' enable add
    mnuIndexAdd.Enabled = True
    ' only enable delete if an Index is selected
    If mcdbExp.NodeType(tvTreeView.SelectedItem) = _
      "Index" Then
      mnuIndexDelete.Enabled = True
    Else
      mnuIndexDelete.Enabled = False
    End If
  End If

ProcExit:
  Exit Sub

ProcError:
  MsgBox "Error: " & Err.Number & vbCrLf & Err.Description
  Resume ProcExit

End Sub

Private Sub mnuIndexAdd_Click()
On Error GoTo ProcError

  mcdbExp.AddIndex

ProcExit:
  Exit Sub

ProcError:
  MsgBox "Error: " & Err.Number & vbCrLf & Err.Description
  Resume ProcExit

End Sub

Private Sub mnuIndexDelete_Click()
' Note: mnuIndex_Click already determined
```

continued on next page

continued from previous page

```
                      ' that an index is selected in the tree
                      On Error GoTo ProcError

                        Dim strTableDefName As String
                        Dim strIndexName As String

                        ' get the index name
                        strIndexName = tvTreeView.SelectedItem.Text
                        ' get its parent table name
                        strTableDefName = tvTreeView.SelectedItem.Parent.Parent.Text

                        mcdbExp.DeleteIndex strTableDefName, strIndexName

                      ProcExit:
                        Exit Sub

                      ProcError:
                        MsgBox "Error: " & Err.Number & vbCrLf & Err.Description
                        Resume ProcExit
                      End Sub
```

4. Add the CDBExplorer.cls class module to the project. This is the same
class as that developed in How-To 4.2, with methods added to support
creating and deleting indexes. The class manages the population of the
items in the tree and list views of the Explorer-style main form. Additional
information about the class module can be found in CDBExplorer.html,
which is included as a related file in the project on the CD. The two
procedures added to this class to support the creation and deletion of
indexes are the **AddIndex** and **DeleteIndex** methods. **AddIndex** uses the
frmCreateIndex form to create the index, but it first attempts to determine
whether the current item in the tree is located within the branch of a table.
If so, it passes the table name to the index creation form, saving the user a
step in data entry. The **DeleteIndex** method accepts a table name and an
index name as parameters and constructs a call to the **Delete** method of
the **Indexes** collection of the appropriate **TableDef** object. Both
procedures also refresh the tree.

```
Public Sub AddIndex()
  Dim obj As Object

  Set obj = GetDAOObjectFromNode(mtvw.SelectedItem)

  Select Case TypeName(obj)
    Case "TableDef"
      ' initialize the form with a table name
      frmCreateIndex.Initialize mdb, obj.Name
    Case "Indexes"
```

```
            frmCreateIndex.Initialize _
              mdb, mtvw.SelectedItem.Parent.Text
          Case "Index"
            frmCreateIndex.Initialize mdb, _
              mtvw.SelectedItem.Parent.Parent.Text
          Case "Field"
            ' if it's a table field, get the table name
            ' the great-grandparent node tells the type
            If mtvw.SelectedItem.Parent.Parent.Parent.Text _
              = "TableDefs" Then
              ' get the name from the grandparent node
              frmCreateIndex.Initialize _
                mdb, _
                mtvw.SelectedItem.Parent.Parent.Text
            Else
              frmCreateIndex.Initialize mdb
            End If
          Case Else
            frmCreateIndex.Initialize mdb
        End Select

        frmCreateIndex.Show vbModal

        ' check cancel flag
        If Not frmCreateIndex.Cancelled Then
          ' expand the tabledef node
          ExpandNode _
            mtvw.Nodes(frmCreateIndex.TableDefName)
          ' now expand the index node for the tabledef
          ExpandNode _
            mtvw.Nodes(frmCreateIndex.TableDefName & "Indexes")
        End If
      End Sub

      Public Sub DeleteIndex( _
        strTableDefName As String, _
        strIndexName As String)

        ' delete the index from the indexes collection of the
        ' tabledef provided
        mdb.TableDefs(strTableDefName).Indexes.Delete strIndexName
        ' refresh the tree
        ExpandNode mtvw.Nodes(strTableDefName & "Indexes")
      End Sub
```

5. Add a new form to the project, create the objects and properties shown in Table 4.17, and save the form as frmCreateIndex.frm.

Table 4.17. Objects and properties of *frmCreateIndex*.

OBJECT	PROPERTY	VALUE
Form	Name	frmCreateIndex
	Caption	Create Index
	BorderStyle	3-Fixed Dialog
Label	Name	lblTableDefName
	Caption	&Table Name
ComboBox	Name	cboTableDefName
	Style	2-Dropdown List
Label	Name	lblIndexName
	Caption	&Index Name
TextBox	Name	txtIndexName
Frame	Name	fraIndex
	Caption	Index

Draw the following controls within the `fraIndex` frame:

Label	Name	lblFieldName
	Caption	&Field Name
ComboBox	Name	cboFieldName
	Style	2-Dropdown List
CommandButton	Name	cmdAddField
	Caption	&Add
Label	Name	lblFields
	Caption	Field &List
ListBox	Name	lstFields
CheckBox	Name	chkPrimary
	Caption	&Primary
CheckBox	Name	chkUnique
	Caption	&Unique

Draw the following two command buttons below the `fraIndex` frame at the lower-right corner of the form:

CommandButton	Name	cmd
	Index	0
	Caption	OK
	Default	True

OBJECT	PROPERTY	VALUE
CommandButton	Name	cmd
	Index	1
	Caption	Cancel
	Cancel	True

NOTE

Figure 4.3, which appears at the beginning of this section, shows the visual layout of the completed form.

6. Add the following code to the declarations section of the form. Several module-level variables are created. The database object **mdb** is used to create the index. The **mblnCancel** flag is used to mark that the user cancelled the addition of the index. Several flag variables are used to control when the OK button should be enabled or disabled—each of the flags must be true before OK can be enabled and the index created. The **mstrTableDefName** variable stores the name of the table in which the index was created so that when control returns to the class module and the main form, the proper collection can be refreshed. Finally, the two constants are the indexes into the **cmd** CommandButton control array.

```
Option Explicit

' database object
Private mdb As Database

' cancel flag
Private mblnCancel As Boolean

' flags for controlling the OK button
Private mblnHasTableDefName As Boolean
Private mblnHasIndexName As Boolean
Private mblnHasFields As Boolean

' tabledefname for property get
Private mstrTableDefName As String

' command button array constants
Private Const cmdOK = 0
Private Const cmdCancel = 1
```

7. Add the `Initialize` method. This procedure is used when the form is loaded, but before it is shown, to set up module-level variables and populate controls on the form.

```
Public Sub Initialize( _
  db As DAO.Database, _
  Optional strTableDefName As String = "")
  ' initialize the form
  ' NOTE: must be called before the form is shown

  Set mdb = db
  ' populate the table combo
  GetTables

  ' set an initial table name if provided
  If strTableDefName <> "" Then
    cboTableDefName.Text = strTableDefName
    ' fill the field list
    GetFields (strTableDefName)
  End If
End Sub
```

8. Add the public `TableDefName` and `Cancelled` properties. These are used after the form is dismissed and control returns to the main form and class to determine which, if any, branch of the tree should be refreshed.

```
Public Property Get TableDefName() As String
  TableDefName = mstrTableDefName
End Property
Public Property Get Cancelled() As Boolean
  Cancelled = mblnCancel
End Property
```

9. The `EnableOK` and `EnableIndex` procedures check several flags and enable or disable the OK button and the index frame, based on the current status of the form.

```
Private Sub EnableOK()
  If mblnHasTableDefName _
    And mblnHasIndexName And mblnHasFields Then
    cmd(cmdOK).Enabled = True
  Else
```

```
      cmd(cmdOK).Enabled = False
    End If
  End Sub

  Private Sub EnableIndex()
    If mblnHasTableDefName And mblnHasIndexName Then
      fraIndex.Enabled = True
    Else
      fraIndex.Enabled = False
    End If
  End Sub
```

10. Add the `GetTables` and `GetFields` procedures. These routines populate the table and field list combo boxes.

```
  Private Sub GetTables()
  ' fill the table list combo

    Dim td As TableDef

    With cboTableDefName
      ' clear what (if anything) is there
      .Clear
      For Each td In mdb.TableDefs
        ' check for system table
        If (td.Attributes And dbSystemObject) = 0 Then
          ' not a system table, add it
          .AddItem td.Name
        End If
      Next  ' TableDef
    End With
  End Sub

  Private Sub GetFields(strTableDefName As String)
  ' fill the field list combo

    Dim fld As Field

    With cboFieldName
      ' clear it
      .Clear
      For Each fld In mdb.TableDefs(strTableDefName).Fields
        ' add it
        .AddItem fld.Name
      Next  ' Field
    End With
  End Sub
```

11. Add the `Form_Load` event procedure. This routine performs some initial setup of the controls on the form.

```
Private Sub Form_Load()
' set up controls

  ' disabled until a name is set and
  ' at list one field is in the field list
  cmd(cmdOK).Enabled = False

  ' disabled until a field is chosen
  cmdAddField.Enabled = False

  ' disable the entire fraIndex frame
  ' until a table and index name are chosen
  fraIndex.Enabled = False
End Sub
```

12. The `Click` and `Change` event procedures for the table name, IndexName, FieldName, and CheckBox controls set module-level variables and enable or disable the index frame and OK button depending on the status of the data. Before the index frame is enabled, a table name and an index name must be provided. To create an index, at least one field must have been added.

```
Private Sub cboTableDefName_Click ()
' set up controls and status

  ' copy it to the module-level variable
  ' for later property get
  mstrTableDefName = cboTableDefName.Text
  ' text it and set flags
  If mstrTableDefName <> "" Then
    ' enable the Index frame
    mblnHasTableDefName = True
  Else
    mblnHasTableDefName = False
  End If

  EnableIndex
  EnableOK
End Sub

Private Sub txtIndexName_Change()
' set control and status flags

  If txtIndexName.Text <> "" Then
    mblnHasIndexName = True
  Else
    mblnHasIndexName = False
  End If
```

```
      EnableIndex
      EnableOK
End Sub

Private Sub cboFieldName_Click()
' enable/disable add field button

  If cboFieldName.Text <> "" Then
    ' enable the add field button
    cmdAddField.Enabled = True
  Else
    cmdAddField.Enabled = False
  End If
End Sub

Private Sub chkPrimary_Click()
' if it's primary, it must be unique
' set control status to indicate the
' user doesn't need to deal with the
' unique check box if primary is set

  If chkPrimary Then
    chkUnique = 1
    chkUnique.Enabled = False
  Else
    chkUnique.Enabled = True
  End If
End Sub
```

13. Create the `Click` event procedure for the `cmdAddField` button. This code adds the current field in the combo box to the list, removes it from the combo box, and returns the focus to the combo box.

```
Private Sub cmdAddField_Click()
' add to list and remove from combo

  lstFields.AddItem cboFieldName.Text
  cboFieldName.RemoveItem cboFieldName.ListIndex

  ' set status flag
  mblnHasFields = True

  EnableOK

  ' return to field name combo
  cboFieldName.SetFocus
End Sub
```

14. Add the `cmd_Click` event procedure. This procedure creates the index if the OK button is clicked, or it unloads the form (setting the Cancelled flag) if the Cancel button is clicked.

```
Private Sub cmd_Click(Index As Integer)
' add the index or unload the form
On Error GoTo ProcError

  Screen.MousePointer = vbHourglass

  Select Case Index
    Case cmdOK
      ' add the index
      CreateIndex
      ' set cancel flag
      mblnCancel = False
      Unload Me
    Case cmdCancel
      ' set cancel flag and unload
      mblnCancel = True
      Unload Me
  End Select

ProcExit:
  Screen.MousePointer = vbDefault
  Exit Sub

ProcError:
  MsgBox "Error: " & Err.Number & vbCrLf & Err.Description
  Resume ProcExit
End Sub
```

15. Add the `CreateIndex` procedure. This code creates the index object by reading the data entered on the form. The index is created by first calling the `CreateIndex` method, then looping through the fields in the list box, calling `CreateField` and `Append` for each. Finally, the `Append` method adds the index to the table.

```
Private Sub CreateIndex()
' create the index
' called only from cmd(cmdOK) click

  Dim td As TableDef
  Dim idx As Index
  Dim fld As Field
  Dim intListIndex As Integer

  ' get a reference to the tabledef and
  ' create the index
  Set td = mdb.TableDefs(cboTableDefName.Text)
  Set idx = td.CreateIndex(txtIndexName.Text)

  ' add the fields
  For intListIndex = 0 To lstFields.ListCount - 1
    lstFields.ListIndex = intListIndex
```

```
      Set fld = idx.CreateField(lstFields.Text)
      idx.Fields.Append fld
      Set fld = Nothing
   Next   ' item in list

   ' set primary or unique flags
   If chkPrimary = 1 Then
      idx.Primary = True
   ElseIf chkUnique = 1 Then
      idx.Unique = True
   End If

   ' append the index
   td.Indexes.Append idx
End Sub
```

How It Works

Although additional code was added to the main Explorer form to coordinate the user interface, the CreateIndex procedure in frmCreateIndex does all the work of creating the index objects in this example. The procedure extracts the data provided on the form to create an index, adds the fields from the list box, and then appends the index to the Indexes collection of the selected table.

The only information that must be provided to the form is supplied by the Initialize procedure as the db parameter. The optional strTableDefName parameter is a convenience added for the benefit of the users (so that they don't need to select the table name again if they have already chosen one on the Explorer form). Because the interaction between the forms takes place through a public interface, this form could be plugged into any database management application.

Comments

If you worked through this How-To and How-To 4.2, you probably discovered that the procedures for creating an index using DAO code are nearly identical to those for creating a table. As you will see in the next How-To, the procedure for creating a relation is also very similar.

ANOTHER WAY TO CREATE AN INDEX

You can use SQL statements rather than DAO code to create indexes for your tables. Constraints can be created using the CREATE TABLE statement or the ALTER TABLE...ADD CONSTRAINT statement. Indexes can also be created using the CREATE INDEX statement. SQL statements are simple to use and require only a single line of code to execute, but they do not expose all the available properties of an index. Chapter 2, "Accessing a Database with Data Access Objects," provides the details of using SQL statements to create and manage database objects.

4.4 How do I...
Define relations between tables?

Problem

I know that if I define relations for my database, the Jet engine will enforce referential integrity. How do I define relations with Visual Basic?

Technique

Like indexes, defined relationships are a tool you can use to enforce rules and improve application performance. How-To 4.2 described the different types of relationships between tables: one-to-one, one-to-many, and many-to-many. Building the database schema with related tables is only the first step. You also need to enforce those relationships. The best way to do that is to let the database engine do it for you by creating `Relation` objects.

Defining a `Relation` enforces three rules to maintain referential integrity between tables:

✔ No row on the many side of a relationship may reference a primary key value on the one side that does not exist.

✔ No row on the one side of a relationship can be deleted if related rows exist on the many side.

✔ The primary key values on the one side cannot be changed if related rows exist on the many side.

Creating the Relation

Creating a `Relation` object with DAO code is similar to creating a table or index. The creation is carried out in four steps:

1. Use the `CreateRelation` method to obtain a reference to a `Relation` object.

2. Assign the `Table` and `ForeignTable` properties.

3. Create and add each of the `Field` objects to the `Fields` collection of the `Relation` object. For each field, you must set the `Name` and `ForeignName` properties.

4. Add the `Relation` to the `Relations` collection of the database by using the `Append` method.

In addition to creating the relationship and adding the fields, you can specify some additional properties that affect how the database engine treats the relationship:

✔ *Cascading updates.* If cascading updates are specified, changes to the primary key values on the one side of a relationship are propagated through the related records on the many side.

✔ *Cascading deletes.* If cascading deletes are specified, deleting a record on the one side of a relationship will also delete all records on the many side.

BE CAREFUL WITH CASCADING UPDATES AND DELETES

The concept of specifying cascading updates and deletes seems powerful and convenient at first glance, but it can be dangerous if not used with caution. Consider the following scenario:

You have a lookup table of United States states that includes the state name and two-letter postal code. A unique index is defined on the postal code so that it can be used as the one side of a relationship. This table is then used to enforce that any value entered for a state as part of a set of address columns in another table is valid. This setup is good so far—the database engine will now validate any state postal code entered in the database. If, however, you created this relationship with cascading updates and deletes, you could inadvertently change every address in one state to another state with a single update, or delete every address in a state with a single delete. If you were to run the query DELETE FROM States;, you would delete every row in your database that has a state column!

This is a somewhat contrived and extreme example. But the point is that by using cascading updates and deletes, you hand off work to the database engine, and you might forget later that the database engine is doing the work for you. An alternative to this approach is to define the relationship without specifying cascading updates or deletes. When you try to perform an operation that violates referential integrity constraints, a trappable error will be raised. You can then examine that error and decide whether to cancel the change or manually perform the cascade by running additional update or delete queries. See Chapter 3, "Creating Queries with SQL," for additional information on building and executing update or delete queries.

In addition to specifying cascading updates and deletes, you can also indicate that the relationship is one-to-one or one-to-many. Don't let yourself be confused by the difference. One-to-one relationships are really just a special case of one-to-many relationships. Instead of allowing multiple rows on the many side, the database engine allows only one. Many-to-many relationships are defined using two one-to-many relationships.

Steps

Open and run project HT404.vbp. Open the database HT404.mdb. You can use the Relation|Add menu command to create the relationships shown in Table 4.18. Figure 4.4 shows the form used to create a relationship.

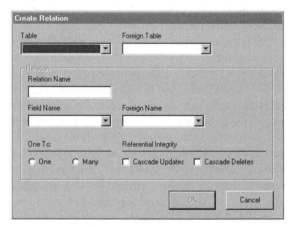

Figure 4.4. The Create Relation form.

> **NOTE**
>
> File HT404A.mdb is identical to HT404.mdb except that all the relations have already been created for you. If you do not want to create all the relationships shown in the table, you can open HT404A.mdb and inspect the objects using the Explorer form.

Table 4.18. Relations in HT404.mdb.

NAME	TABLE	FOREIGN TABLE	FIELD NAME	FOREIGN NAME	TYPE	CASCADE
fkAdvFacID	Faculty	Advisors	FacID	AdvFacID	1-1	Deletes
fkInstrFacID	Faculty	Instructors	FacID	InstrFacID	1-1	Deletes
fkCourse-InstrID	Instructors	Courses	InstrFacID	CourseInstrID	1-Many	N/A

NAME	TABLE	FOREIGN TABLE	FIELD NAME	FOREIGN NAME	TYPE	CASCADE
fkSCStID	Students	StudentCourses	StID	SCStID	1-Many	N/A
fkSCCourseID	Courses	StudentCourses	CourseID	SCCourseID	1-Many	N/A
fkStAdvID	Advisors	Students	AdvFacID	StAdvID	1-Many	N/A

1. Create a new Standard EXE project and save it as HT404.vbp. Add BMain.bas to the project. This module contains code derived from the example in How-To 4.1 used to open or create a database.

2. Add frmMain.frm to the project. This is the same form used for How-To 4.3. Add the menu controls shown in Table 4.19 for the Relation menu.

Table 4.19. The Relation menu controls.

NAME	CAPTION
mnuRelation	&Relation
mnuRelationAdd	&Add
mnuRelationDelete	&Delete

3. Three event procedures control the Relation menu. The top-level `mnuRelation_Click` event procedure determines which of the other menu controls should be enabled based on the currently selected object in the TreeView control on the form. The **Add** command uses the `mcdbExp` object to show the form used to create a relationship and update the TreeView control. The **Delete** command calls on the **DeleteRelation** method of the `mcdbExp` object to delete the currently selected relationship.

```
Private Sub mnuRelation_Click()
On Error GoTo ProcError

  If mcdbExp Is Nothing Then
    ' no database open
    mnuRelationAdd.Enabled = False
    mnuRelationDelete.Enabled = False
  Else
    ' enable add
    mnuRelationAdd.Enabled = True
    ' only enable delete if an Index is selected
    If mcdbExp.NodeType(tvTreeView.SelectedItem) = _
      "Relation" Then
      mnuRelationDelete.Enabled = True
    Else
      mnuRelationDelete.Enabled = False
```

continued on next page

continued from previous page

```
            End If
          End If

        ProcExit:
          Exit Sub

        ProcError:
          MsgBox "Error: " & Err.Number & vbCrLf & Err.Description
          Resume ProcExit
        End Sub

        Private Sub mnuRelationAdd_Click()
        On Error GoTo ProcError

          mcdbExp.AddRelation

        ProcExit:
          Exit Sub

        ProcError:
          MsgBox "Error: " & Err.Number & vbCrLf & Err.Description
          Resume ProcExit
        End Sub

        Private Sub mnuRelationDelete_Click()
        On Error GoTo ProcError

          Dim strRelationName As String

          ' get the name
          strRelationName = tvTreeView.SelectedItem.Text

          mcdbExp.DeleteRelation strRelationName

        ProcExit:
          Exit Sub

        ProcError:
          MsgBox "Error: " & Err.Number & vbCrLf & Err.Description
          Resume ProcExit
        End Sub
```

4. Add the class module CDBExplorer.cls to the project. This is the same class module used in How-To 4.3, but with code added to support creating and deleting relationships in the database. The **AddRelation** method loads, initializes, and shows **frmCreateRelation** and then refreshes the node in the Explorer form tree for relationships. The

DeleteRelation method takes the name of a Relation object as a parameter and deletes the Relation object from the Relations collection of the database.

```
Public Sub AddRelation()
' load the form to create a relation

  Load frmCreateRelation

  ' pass it the database reference
  Set frmCreateRelation.Database = mdb

  frmCreateRelation.Show vbModal

  ' refresh the tabledefs node
  ExpandNode mtvw.Nodes("Relations")
End Sub

Public Sub DeleteRelation(strRelationName As String)
' delete a relation

  ' delete it
  mdb.Relations.Delete strRelationName
  ' refresh the relations node
  ExpandNode mtvw.Nodes("Relations")
End Sub
```

5. Add a new form to the project, create the objects and properties shown in Table 4.20, and save the form as frmCreateRelation.frm.

Table 4.20. Objects and properties of *frmCreateRelation*.

OBJECT	PROPERTY	VALUE
Form	Name	frmCreateRelation
	Caption	Create Relation
	Border Style	3-Fixed Dialog
Label	Name	lblTableDefName
	Caption	Table
ComboBox	Name	cboTableDefName
	Style	2-Dropdown List
Label	Name	lblForeignTableDefName
	Caption	Foreign Table
ComboBox	Name	cboForeignTableDefName
	Style	2-Dropdown List

continued on next page

continued from previous page

OBJECT	PROPERTY	VALUE
Frame	Name	fraRelation
	Caption	Relation

Draw the following controls within the **fraRelation** frame:

OBJECT	PROPERTY	VALUE
Label	Name	lblRelationName
	Caption	Relation Name
TextBox	Name	txtRelationName
Label	Name	lblFieldName
	Caption	Field Name
ComboBox	Name	cboFieldName
	Style	2-Dropdown List
Label	Name	lblForeignName
	Caption	Foreign Name
ComboBox	Name	cboForeignName
	Style	2-Dropdown List
Label	Name	lblOneTo
	Caption	One To:
Line	Name	Line1
OptionButton	Name	optOneTo
	Caption	One
	Index	0
OptionButton	Name	optOneTo
	Caption	Many
	Index	1
Label	Name	lblReferentialIntegrity
	Caption	Referential Integrity
Line	Name	Line2
CheckBox	Name	chkRef
	Caption	Cascade Updates
	Index	0
CheckBox	Name	chkRef

OBJECT	PROPERTY	VALUE
	Caption	Cascade Deletes
	Index	1

Draw the following two command buttons at the bottom right of the form below the `fraRelation` frame:

CommandButton	Name	cmd
	Caption	OK
	Default	True
	Index	0
CommandButton	Name	cmd
	Caption	Cancel
	Cancel	True
	Index	1

Figure 4.4 shows the visual design of the form at runtime.

6. Add the following code to the declarations section of the form. Module-level variables are defined to store the database object, the table and foreign table names, and the field name and foreign name properties.

Three pairs of constants are also defined as indexes into the three control arrays on the form.

```
Option Explicit

' database
Private mdb As Database

' table
Private mstrTableDefName As String
' foreign table
Private mstrForeignTableDefName As String

' relation name
Private mstrRelationName As String
' field name
Private mstrFieldName As String
' foreign name
Private mstrForeignName As String

' control array constants
Private Const optOneToOne = 0
Private Const optOneToMany = 1

Private Const chkRefCascadeUpdates = 0
Private Const chkRefCascadeDeletes = 1

Private Const cmdOK = 0
Private Const cmdCancel = 1
```

7. Add the **Database** property procedure. This property is used to enable the **CDBExplorer** class to pass a database object to the form. After the database has been provided, the table and foreign table combo boxes are populated with lists of table names.

```
Public Property Set Database(db As DAO.Database)
' set database object and set up form

  ' assign the database object
  Set mdb = db

  ' populate the table combo boxes
  GetTables cboTableDefName
  GetTables cboForeignTableDefName
End Property
```

8. Add the **EnableOK** and **EnableRelation** procedures. These procedures examine the current state of the data on the form to determine whether the **fraRelation** frame and the OK button should be enabled or disabled.

```
Private Sub EnableOK()
' to create a relation, you need the following
' a table name
' a foreign table name
' a relation name
' a field name
' a foreign name for the field
' additionally, CreateRelation will fail if the
' field data types do not match correctly

  If mstrTableDefName = "" Or _
     mstrForeignTableDefName = "" Or _
     mstrRelationName = "" Or _
     mstrFieldName = "" Or _
     mstrForeignName = "" Then
    cmd(cmdOK).Enabled = False
  Else
    cmd(cmdOK).Enabled = True
  End If

End Sub

Private Sub EnableRelation()
' enable/disable the relation frame

  If _
     mstrTableDefName = "" Or _
     mstrForeignTableDefName = "" _
     Then
    fraRelation.Enabled = False
  Else
    fraRelation.Enabled = True
  End If
End Sub
```

9. Add the `GetTables` and `GetFields` procedures. These procedures
populate a combo box with a list of tables or fields by examining the
`TableDefs` collection of the database or the `Fields` collection of a table.

```
Private Sub GetTables(cbo As ComboBox)
' fill the table list combo

  Dim td As TableDef

  With cbo
    ' clear what (if anything) is there
    .Clear
    For Each td In mdb.TableDefs
      ' check for system table
      If (td.Attributes And dbSystemObject) = 0 Then
        ' not a system table, add it
        .AddItem td.Name
      End If
    Next  ' TableDef
  End With
End Sub

Private Sub GetFields(cbo As ComboBox, strTableDefName As String)
' fill the field list combo

  Dim fld As Field

  With cbo
    ' clear it
    .Clear
    For Each fld In mdb.TableDefs(strTableDefName).Fields
      ' add it
      .AddItem fld.Name
    Next  ' Field
  End With
End Sub
```

10. Add the `Form_Load` event procedure. The relation frame and OK button
are disabled by this procedure.

```
Private Sub Form_Load()
On Error GoTo ProcError

  ' disable the relations frame
  fraRelation.Enabled = False

  ' disable the OK button
  cmd(cmdOK).Enabled = False

ProcExit:
  Exit Sub
```

continued on next page

continued from previous page

```
ProcError:
  MsgBox "Error: " & Err.Number & vbCrLf & Err.Description
  Resume ProcExit
End Sub
```

11. Add the `Click` event procedures for the `cboTableDefName` and
`cboForeignTableDefName` ComboBox controls. These procedures store
the values of the combo boxes in the module-level variables and call the
`GetFields` procedure to populate the field lists. They then call both
`EnableOK` and `EnableRelation` to enable or disable both the relationship
frame container and the OK button.

```
Private Sub cboTableDefName_Click()
On Error GoTo ProcError

  Screen.MousePointer = vbHourglass

  mstrTableDefName = cboTableDefName.Text

  If mstrTableDefName <> "" Then
    GetFields cboFieldName, mstrTableDefName
  End If

  EnableOK
  EnableRelation

ProcExit:
  Screen.MousePointer = vbDefault
  Exit Sub

ProcError:
  MsgBox "Error: " & Err.Number & vbCrLf & Err.Description
  Resume ProcExit
End Sub

Private Sub cboForeignTableDefName_Click()
On Error GoTo ProcError

  Screen.MousePointer = vbHourglass

  mstrForeignTableDefName = cboForeignTableDefName.Text

  If mstrForeignTableDefName <> "" Then
    GetFields cboForeignName, mstrForeignTableDefName
  End If

  EnableOK
  EnableRelation
```

```
ProcExit:
  Screen.MousePointer = vbDefault
  Exit Sub

ProcError:
  MsgBox "Error: " & Err.Number & vbCrLf & Err.Description
  Resume ProcExit
End Sub
```

12. Add the `Click` events for the `cboFieldName` and `cboForeignName` controls. The current values in the combo boxes are passed to the module-level variables, and the `EnableOK` procedure is called to enable or disable the OK button.

```
Private Sub cboFieldName_Click()
On Error GoTo ProcError

  mstrFieldName = cboFieldName.Text

  EnableOK

ProcExit:
  Exit Sub

ProcError:
  MsgBox "Error: " & Err.Number & vbCrLf & Err.Description
  Resume ProcExit
End Sub

Private Sub cboForeignName_Click()
On Error GoTo ProcError

  mstrForeignName = cboForeignName.Text

  EnableOK

ProcExit:
  Exit Sub

ProcError:
  MsgBox "Error: " & Err.Number & vbCrLf & Err.Description
  Resume ProcExit
End Sub
```

13. Add the `txtRelation_Change` event. This procedure passes the contents of the text box to the module-level variable and calls the `EnableOK` procedure to enable or disable the OK button.

```
Private Sub txtRelationName_Change()
On Error GoTo ProcError

  mstrRelationName = txtRelationName

  EnableOK

ProcExit:
  Exit Sub

ProcError:
  MsgBox "Error: " & Err.Number & vbCrLf & Err.Description
  Resume ProcExit
End Sub
```

14. Add the `cmd_Click` procedure. This procedure either calls the
`CreateRelation` procedure and unloads the form, or it simply unloads
the form.

```
Private Sub cmd_Click(Index As Integer)
' create the relation or unload
On Error GoTo ProcError

  Screen.MousePointer = vbHourglass

  Select Case Index
    Case cmdOK
      ' create relation and unload
      CreateRelation
      Unload Me
    Case cmdCancel
      ' just unload
      Unload Me
  End Select

ProcExit:
  Screen.MousePointer = vbDefault
  Exit Sub

ProcError:
  MsgBox "Error: " & Err.Number & vbCrLf & Err.Description
  Resume ProcExit
End Sub
```

15. Add the `CreateRelation` procedure. This procedure uses the steps
described earlier in this How-To to create the `Relation` object based on
the values saved in the module-level variables. The procedure calls
`CreateRelation`, creates and appends a `Field` object to the `Fields`
collection, and finally uses the `Append` method to add the `Relation` to the
`Relations` collection.

```
Private Sub CreateRelation()
' create the relation
' called only from cmd(cmdOK) click event

  Dim rel As Relation
  Dim fld As Field
  Dim lngAttributes As Long

  ' set up attributes
  If optOneTo(optOneToOne) Then
    lngAttributes = dbRelationUnique
  End If
  If chkRef(chkRefCascadeUpdates) Then
    lngAttributes = lngAttributes Or dbRelationUpdateCascade
  End If
  If chkRef(chkRefCascadeDeletes) Then
    lngAttributes = lngAttributes Or dbRelationDeleteCascade
  End If
  ' create the relation
  Set rel = mdb.CreateRelation( _
      mstrRelationName, _
      mstrTableDefName, _
      mstrForeignTableDefName, _
      lngAttributes)
  Set fld = rel.CreateField(mstrFieldName)
  ' set the foreign name
  fld.ForeignName = mstrForeignName
  ' append the field to the relation
  rel.Fields.Append fld
  ' append the relation to the database
  mdb.Relations.Append rel
End Sub
```

How It Works

If you've worked through the previous examples in this chapter, the method and the code used to create relationships will look quite familiar. Again, a single procedure—in this case, the **CreateRelation** procedure in **frmCreateRelation**—does all the real work of creating the relationship. Based on values entered by the user, the procedure creates the **Relation** object. It then adds the desired field and assigns the **ForeignName** property, and finally it appends the field and the relation to their respective collections. The rest of the code in the form coordinates the user interface.

NOTE

This example does not implement the capability to create relationships with multiple fields. If you need to create such a relationship, just repeat the code that creates and appends the field for each field in the relationship.

Comments

The Jet database engine also enables you to use SQL statements to create relationships between tables by using a **CONSTRAINT** clause in a **CREATE TABLE** or **ALTER TABLE** statement. See Chapter 3, "Creating Queries with SQL," for details on using SQL statements to create relationships with SQL statements.

COMPLEXITY
BEGINNING

4.5 How do I...
Use the Jet database engine to enforce business rules?

Problem

I need to make sure that certain rules are followed when data is entered into my database. How do I get the database engine to enforce these rules for me?

Technique

Various rules can be applied against tables and columns in a database:

✔ Values for columns can be restricted to a specific list of values, or the value can be restricted by a formula. For example, a numeric column can be required to be greater than zero.

✔ Columns can require an entry.

✔ Values for one column can be dependent on the values for another column.

The collective term for these types of restrictions on data is *business rules*. You can enforce rules in your database in two ways:

✔ Write Visual Basic code to examine the data and apply the rules before inserts, updates, or deletes are completed.

✔ Build the rules into the design of the tables and columns and let the database engine enforce them for you.

Although in certain situations the rules will be too complex to be entered using the available properties for **TableDef** and **Field** objects, you should allow the database engine to enforce as many of your rules as it is capable of enforcing.

If you have worked through the examples in How-To 4.2 through 4.4, you have already been enforcing some simple rules in your database:

✔ When a column is defined, the data type restricts the data that can be entered in the column.

✔ Defining a primary key or unique index restricts the data in a column to unique entries.

✔ Defining a relationship between tables restricts the values in foreign key columns to the available values in the primary key from the table on the other side of the relationship.

In addition to these constraints on data, you can specify an additional property for tables and three additional properties for columns that further restrict the data that can be entered:

✔ The `Required` property for `Field` objects can be used to disallow `Null` values in the column. Setting this property to `True` means that a value is required.

✔ The `ValidationRule` property applies to both tables and columns and can be used to force the data to conform to an expression. The partner of the `ValidationRule` property is the `ValidationText` property. This property can be used to provide the text of the error message that is generated when the rule is violated.

✔ The `AllowZeroLength` property can be used to allow or disallow zero-length strings as valid entries for a column. The Jet engine treats zero-length strings and nulls separately. Developers can use the two to distinguish between values that are unknown (most often using `Null`) and values that are known to be nothing (using a zero-length string). For example, if a middle name column allows a zero-length string, a `Null` would indicate that the data was not available, whereas a zero-length string would indicate that the person has no middle name. Although this is a potentially useful tool, the subtle difference between these values will probably be lost on most users. Additionally, not all types of databases support this differentiation.

`Required` and `AllowZeroLength` are both Boolean properties. If the `Required` property is set to `True`, `Null` values will not be allowed. If the `AllowZeroLength` property is set to `True`, the column will allow a zero-length string as a valid value.

The `ValidationRule` property is a string and can be any valid Visual Basic expression. It cannot, however, contain a reference to a user-defined function, SQL aggregate functions, a query, or, in the case of a table, columns in another table.

The `ValidationText` property can be any string expression and is provided as the description of the trappable error that results when the rule is violated.

Steps

Open and run project HT405 .vbp. The form shown in Figure 4.5 appears. Choose File | Open and open database HT405.mdb. This is the school database developed and refined in How-To 4.2 through How-To 4.4. Click the Add Rules button to apply the rules shown in Table 4.21 to the database.

Figure 4.5. The Create Rules form.

Table 4.21. Business rules for HT405.mdb.

TABLE	FIELD	PROPERTY	VALUE
Advisors	AdvGradeLevel	Required	True
Advisors		ValidationRule	IN ('Freshman', 'Sophomore', 'Junior', 'Senior')
		ValidationText	Grade level must be Freshman, Sophomore, Junior, or Senior
Courses	CourseDesc	Required	True
Faculty	FacFirst	Required	True
	FacLast	Required	True
Students	StFirst	Required	True
Students	StLast	Required	True

In addition to the field-level rules in Table 4.21, the following rule applies to the Students table:

```
ValidationRule
  IIf(
    (
      (Not IsNull([StAddress])) Or
      (Not IsNull([StCity])) Or
      (Not IsNull([StState])) Or
      (Not IsNull([StZIP]))
    ),
    (
      IIf(
        (
```

```
      (Not IsNull([StAddress])) And
      (Not IsNull([StCity])) And
      (Not IsNull([StState])) And
      (Not IsNull([StZIP])
      )
   ), True, False)
), True)
```

ValidationText
    If provided, the address must be complete.

This rather cumbersome-looking expression enforces the rule that if any of the address columns (StAddress, StCity, StState, StZIP) contain data, they all must contain data. Because Jet restricts the ValidationRule property to a single expression, the nested IIf statements must be used. The outer IIf returns True if any of the columns contains data; the inner IIf returns True only if they all contain data.

A MISLEADING STATEMENT IN THE HELP FILE

The following statement appears in the Visual Basic help file topic for the ValidationRule property:

For an object not yet appended to the Fields collection, this property is read/write.

This would seem to imply that after the field has been created, the property can no longer be assigned. In fact, the ValidationRule and ValidationText properties for both tables and fields can be assigned after the objects have been created, and the Required property can be assigned after a field has been created—all as demonstrated in the sample application.

1. Create a new Standard EXE project and name it HT405.vbp.

2. Change the name of Form1 to frmMain, and create the objects and properties shown in Table 4.22.

Table 4.22. Objects and properties for *frmMain*.

OBJECT	PROPERTY	VALUE
Form	BorderStyle	3-Fixed Dialog
	Caption	Create Rules
CommonDialog	Name	dlg
CommandButton	Name	cmdAddRules
	Caption	Add Rules
Menu	Name	mnuFile
	Caption	&File

continued on next page

OBJECT	PROPERTY	VALUE
Menu	Name	mnuFileOpen
	Caption	&Open
	Shortcut	Ctrl-O
Menu	Name	mnuFileBar
	Caption	-
Menu	Name	mnuFileExit
	Caption	E&xit
	Shortcut	Ctrl-Q

3. Add the following code to the declarations section of the form:

```
Option Explicit

Private mdb As Database
```

4. Add the **cmdAddRules_Click** event procedure. This procedure calls the **AddRules** subroutine described here.

```
Private Sub cmdAddRules_Click()
On Error GoTo ProcError

   Screen.MousePointer = vbHourglass

   AddRules
   MsgBox "Rules Added"
   cmdAddRules.Enabled = False

ProcExit:
   Screen.MousePointer = vbDefault
   Exit Sub

ProcError:
   MsgBox "Error: " & Err.Number & vbCrLf & Err.Description
   Resume ProcExit
End Sub
```

5. Add the **mnuFileOpen_Click** procedure. This procedure calls the **GetOpenDBName** function show next, opens the database using the filename returned, and enables the **cmdAddRules** button.

```
Private Sub mnuFileOpen_Click()
On Error GoTo ProcError

   Dim strDBName As String

   Screen.MousePointer = vbHourglass

   ' use the common dialog to get the db name
   strDBName = GetOpenDBName(dlg)
```

```
      If Len(strDBName) Then
        Set mdb = DBEngine(0).OpenDatabase(strDBName)
        cmdAddRules.Enabled = True
      End If

ProcExit:
  Screen.MousePointer = vbDefault
  Exit Sub

ProcError:
  MsgBox "Error: " & Err.Number & vbCrLf & Err.Description
  Resume ProcExit
End Sub
```

6. Create the `mnuFileExit_Click` event. This procedure unloads the form, ending the application.

```
Private Sub mnuFileExit_Click()
On Error GoTo ProcError

  Screen.MousePointer = vbHourglass

  ' close the database and unload the form
  mdb.Close
  Unload Me

ProcExit:
  Screen.MousePointer = vbDefault
  Exit Sub

ProcError:
  MsgBox "Error: " & Err.Number & vbCrLf & Err.Description
  Resume ProcExit
End Sub
```

7. Create the `GetOpenDBName` function. This function sets up the Common Dialog control and returns the filename selected by the user as its return value.

```
Private Function GetOpenDBName(dlg As CommonDialog) As String
' Get the desired name using the common dialog
On Error GoTo ProcError

  Dim strFileName As String

  ' set up the file save dialog file types
  dlg.InitDir = App.Path
  dlg.DefaultExt = "mdb"
  dlg.DialogTitle = "Open Database"
  dlg.Filter = "VB Databases (*.mdb)|*.mdb"
  dlg.FilterIndex = 1
  ' set up flags
  dlg.Flags = _
    cdlOFNHideReadOnly Or _
```

continued on next page

continued from previous page

```
        cdlOFNFileMustExist Or _
        cdlOFNPathMustExist
    ' setting CancelError means the control will
    ' raise an error if the user clicks Cancel
    dlg.CancelError = True
    ' show the SaveAs dialog
    dlg.ShowOpen
    ' get the selected name
    strFileName = dlg.filename

ProcExit:
  GetOpenDBName = strFileName
  Exit Function

ProcError:
  strFileName = ""
  Resume ProcExit
End Function
```

8. Create the **AddRules** routine. This routine assigns the **Required**, **ValidationRule**, and **ValidationText** properties described previously. Each of the values is directly assigned to the property. The various **With...End With** blocks add some efficiency by eliminating extra object references.

```
Private Sub AddRules()

    Dim td As TableDef
    Dim fld As Field

    ' Advisors table
    ' AdvGradeLevel field
    Set fld = mdb.TableDefs("Advisors").Fields("AdvGradeLevel")
    With fld
        ' require entry
        .Required = True
        ' require a value in a list
        .ValidationRule = _
            "IN ('Freshman', 'Sophomore', 'Junior', 'Senior')"
.ValidationText = _
            "Grade level must be Freshman, " & _
            "Sophomore, Junior or Senior"
End With
    Set fld = Nothing
    ' Courses table
    ' CourseDesc field
    mdb.TableDefs("Courses").Fields("CourseDesc").Required = True
    ' Faculty table
    Set td = mdb.TableDefs("Faculty")
    With td
        ' FacFirst required
        .Fields("FacFirst").Required = True
        ' FacLast required
        .Fields("FacLast").Required = True
```

4.5

USE THE JET DATABASE ENGINE TO ENFORCE BUSINESS RULES 295

```
      End With
      Set td = Nothing
      ' Students table
      Set td = mdb.TableDefs("Students")
      With td
        ' first and last names are required
        .Fields("StFirst").Required = True
        .Fields("StLast").Required = True
        ' table rule - if any part of the
        ' address is provided, all of it
        ' must be provided
        ' the outer IIf evaluates if any field is not null
        ' the inner IIf evaluates if all fields are not null
        .ValidationRule = _
          "IIf(" & _
            "(" & _
              "(Not IsNull([StAddress])) Or " & _
              "(Not IsNull([StCity])) Or " & _
              "(Not IsNull([StState])) Or " & _
              "(Not IsNull([StZIP])) " & _
            "), " & _
            "(IIf(" & _
              "(" & _
                "(Not IsNull([StAddress])) And " & _
                "(Not IsNull([StCity])) And " & _
                "(Not IsNull([StState])) And " & _
                "(Not IsNull([StZIP])) " & _
              "), " & _
              "True, False)" & _
            "), " & _
            "True)"
        .ValidationText = _
            "If provided, the address must be complete."
      End With
      Set td = Nothing
    End Sub
```

How It Works

This How-To provides the final refinement to the database that has been developed throughout the chapter by adding some basic business-rule enforcement at the level of the database engine. The rules are established by obtaining references to the appropriate table and field objects and by setting the **ValidationRule**, **ValidationText**, and **Required** properties.

As you can see in the examples, it can be difficult to implement even relatively simple rules due to the limitations of these properties. Thus, you might need to supplement the properties provided by the database engine with additional validation code. Chapter 1, "Accessing a Database with Bound Controls," and Chapter 2, "Accessing a Database with Data Access Objects," provide additional information on using Visual Basic code to enforce rules on the data in your database.

Comments

Unless you specify otherwise, field validation rules are applied when the record is updated. If you want the rule to be applied as soon as the entry is applied to the field, set the `ValidateOnSet` property of the `Field` object to `True`.

CHAPTER 5

MICROSOFT ACCESS DATABASES

5

MICROSOFT ACCESS DATABASES

How do I...

5.1 Determine the number of records in a table and the table's creation and last-modified dates?

5.2 Attach a table from another database file?

5.3 Import a text file?

5.4 Save graphics in a database file?

5.5 Make sure that an operation involving multiple tables is not left partially completed?

5.6 Compact a database or repair a corrupted database?

5.7 Use parameter queries stored in Microsoft Access databases?

Although you have a choice of database formats, such as indexed sequential access method (ISAM) or Open Database Connectivity (ODBC) drivers, you will find it easiest to work with Visual Basic's "native" database format, Microsoft

Access. Because Visual Basic and Microsoft Access have been created to work in tandem, you have a rich feature set available to you. This chapter shows you how to use many of the unique features of Microsoft Access database files.

5.1 Determine the number of records in a table and the table's creation and last-modified dates

A Microsoft Access database contains information about each table in the database—including, among other items, when the table was created, when it was last modified, and the number of records it currently contains. This How-To consists of a tool for extracting and displaying that information.

5.2 Attach a table from another database file

In some cases, it is necessary or desirable to make the contents of a table available to more than one Microsoft Access database. A database can access a table from another database by attaching the table to itself. This How-To shows you how to attach Microsoft Access tables to Microsoft Access databases through Visual Basic.

5.3 Import a text file

The source of your application's data might be files consisting of delimited ASCII or ANSI text. This How-To shows how to use Visual Basic classes and collections to convert text files into records that you can add to Microsoft Access tables.

5.4 Save graphics in a database file

The capability to store graphics in a database can be very useful, but sometimes challenging. This How-To explains two methods of saving graphics, as well as providing an example of one of them.

5.5 Make sure that an operation involving multiple tables is not left partially completed

A well-designed relational database uses multiple tables that are related. A single "logical" add, delete, or update operation often requires making a change to more than one table. If an error occurs during a multitable operation, you generally want to abort the entire operation and return all the tables to the condition in which they existed at the start of the operation. This How-To shows how to use the transaction features of the Jet database engine to ensure the integrity of your tables.

5.6 Compact a database or repair a corrupted database

The Jet database engine has the capability to recover space after deletion of data, but it does not perform the operation automatically. The Jet engine also can repair certain types of database damage—but again, it will not make the attempt unless it is instructed to do so. This How-To shows how to use Visual Basic to initiate the Jet engine's database-compact and database-repair capabilities.

5.7 Use Parameter Queries Stored in Microsoft Access Databases

Microsoft Access queries can be designed to use replaceable parameters. A query with a replaceable parameter must be provided with a value for that parameter each time the query is run. This How-To shows how to use stored queries with replaceable parameters from Visual Basic.

COMPLEXITY
BEGINNING

5.1 How do I...
Determine the number of records in a table and the table's creation and last-modified dates?

Problem

I have an application that periodically adds records to a table. No other user or application ever modifies this table. To make sure that I don't perform the same update twice, I'd like to check the current record count and the date the last changes were made to the table's recordset. How can I do this from Visual Basic?

Technique

The `TableDefs` collection of the `Database` object consists of `TableDef` objects, each of which represents one table from the database. The properties of the `TableDef` object describe the table. Table 5.1 lists the properties of `TableDef` objects applicable to native Microsoft Access database tables.

Table 5.1. Properties of a *TableDef* object applicable to Microsoft Access tables.

PROPERTY	DESCRIPTION
Attributes	Characteristics of the table, including whether the table is an attached table
DateCreated	The date and time the table was created
LastUpdated	The date and time the table was most recently changed
Name	The name of the table
RecordCount	The number of records in the table
SourceTableName	The name of the base table, if the `TableDef` is for an attached table
Updatable	Specification of whether `SourceTableName`, `ValidationRule`, and
	`ValidationText` properties of the `TableDef` can be modified

continued on next page

continued from previous page

PROPERTY	DESCRIPTION
ValidationRule	An expression used to set the criteria for accepting a new record or a modification to an existing record
ValidationText	The message returned if a change fails to meet the ValidationRule criteria

Steps

The Table Status application displays four of the most useful properties for each user table in a database. Open and run TableData.VBP. You'll see a standard Windows File Open dialog box. Choose a Microsoft Access (*.MDB) file, and click OK. The form shown in Figure 5.1 appears with a list of the tables in the database shown in the list box. After you select a table, the table's creation date, last modification date, and current record count appear in the boxes on the form, similar to Figure 5.2.

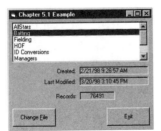

Figure 5.1. The table statistics form on startup.

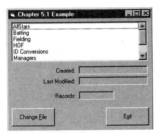

Figure 5.2. The table statistics form with the statistics from the Title Author table shown.

1. Create a new project called TableData.VBP. Create the objects and properties listed in Table 5.2, and save the form as TableData.FRM.

Table 5.2. Objects and properties for the Table Status form.

OBJECT	PROPERTY	SETTING
Form	Name	Form1
	Caption	"Chapter 5.1 Example"
CommandButton	Name	cmdChangeFile
	Caption	"Change &File"
CommandButton	Name	cmdExit
	Cancel	True
	Caption	"E&xit"
ListBox	Name	lstTables
	Sorted	True
CommonDialog	Name	cdlTableData
	CancelError	True
	DefaultExt	"MDB"
	DialogTitle	"Database File"
	FileName	"*.MDB"
	Filter	"*.MDB"
Label	Name	lblCreated
	Alignment	2 (Center)
	BorderStyle	1 (Fixed Single)
Label	Name	lblModified
	Alignment	2 (Center)
	BorderStyle	1 (Fixed Single)
Label	Name	lblRecords
	Alignment	2 (Center)
	BorderStyle	1 (Fixed Single)
Label	Name	lblTableData
	Index	0
	Caption	"Created:"
Label	Name	lblTableData
	Index	1
	Caption	"Last Modified:"
Label	Name	lblTableData
	Index	2
	Caption	"Records:"

2. Add the following code to the declarations section of **Form1**. The **Collection** object created by the declaration is used by several procedures within the form, so it is declared at form level to give all of the procedures access to it.

```
Option Explicit

Private colTableData As Collection
```

3. Add the following code to the **Form_Load** event of **Form1**. **Form_Load** calls the **GetDatabase** subroutine, which controls the rest of the application.

```
Private Sub Form_Load()
    GetDatabase
End Sub
```

4. Create the **GetDatabase** subroutine with the following code. This procedure gets a database selection from the user, retrieves information from its nonsystem table definitions into **clsTableStatus** objects, and puts the **clsTableData** objects into **colTableData**. (The **clsTableData** class is discussed later in this section.) It then lists the table names in the form's list box.

```
Private Sub GetDatabase()
    Dim dbfTableData As Database
    Dim tdfTables As TableDefs, tdfSelectedTable As TableDef
    Dim objTable As clsTableData
    Dim strDatabaseName As String

    On Error GoTo NoDatabaseError
        'Call the ShowOpen method of the CommonDialog control, so
        'the user can select a database.
        cdlTableData.ShowOpen
        On Error GoTo GetDatabaseError
            strDatabaseName = cdlTableData.filename
            Screen.MousePointer = vbHourglass
            'Open the chosen database
            Set dbfTableData = _
                DBEngine.Workspaces(0).OpenDatabase( _
                strDatabaseName, False, True)
            'Fetch the TableDefs collection & place in a local
            'variable.  This has the benefit of slightly faster
            'processing
            Set tdfTables = dbfTableData.TableDefs
            'Set up the collection class we're using, so new
            'instances of our clsTableData class can be stored in
            'it.
            Set colTableData = New Collection
            'For each TableDef in TableDefs, use the clsTableData
            'to get the needed info from the table, and place the
            'table's name and its index within the collection in
            'the list box.
```

```
                For Each tdfSelectedTable In tdfTables
                    If Left$(tdfSelectedTable.Name, 4) <> "MSys" Then
                        Set objTable = New clsTableData
                        objTable.ExtractStatusData tdfSelectedTable
                        colTableData.Add objTable
                        With lstTables
                            .AddItem objTable.Name
                            .ItemData(lstTables.NewIndex) = _
                                        colTableData.Count
                        End With
                    End If
                Next
                'Now that it's not needed, close the database.
                dbfTableData.Close
            On Error GoTo 0
            Screen.MousePointer = vbDefault
        On Error GoTo 0
    Exit Sub

    NoDatabaseError:
        'If the user didn't select a database, end the application.
        End

    GetDatabaseError:
        Screen.MousePointer = vbDefault
        MsgBox Err.Description, vbExclamation
        End
    End Sub
```

5. Add the following code to the **Click** event of **lstTables**. When the user clicks on a table name in the list box, this procedure extracts the properties from the selected **clsTableData** object and displays those properties in the boxes on the form.

```
Private Sub lstTables_Click()
    Dim objTable As clsTableData, intPosition As Integer

    'Get the ItemData from the list, the index of the selected
    'clsTableData stored in our collection.
    intPosition = lstTables.ItemData(lstTables.ListIndex)

    'Using this index, fetch our selected instance of
    'clsTableData.
    Set objTable = colTableData.Item(intPosition)

    'Read the properties of our class into the labels
    lblCreated = Format$(objTable.WhenCreated, "General Date")
    lblModified = Format$(objTable.WhenModified, "General Date")
    lblRecords = objTable.NumRecords
End Sub
```

6. Add the following code to the **Click** event of **cmdChangeFile**. This procedure first clears the data from the controls on the form and empties the **Collection** object. It then resets the common dialog default filename to *.MDB and calls **GetDatabase**.

```
Private Sub cmdChangeFile_Click()
    'Clear out the form, and flush the existing collection.
    lstTables.Clear
    lblCreated = "": lblModified = "": lblRecords = ""
    Set colTableData = Nothing

    'Reset our CommonDialog control, and get another database.
    cdlTableData.filename = "*.MDB"
    GetDatabase
End Sub
```

7. Add the following code to the **Click** event of **cmdExit**:

```
Private Sub cmdExit_Click()
    End
End Sub
```

8. Insert a new class module into the project and name it **clsTableData**; then add the following code to the declarations section of the class module. The four private variables represent the properties of the class. As private class-module-level variables, they are accessible to all routines within the class but accessible to outside procedures only through the methods defined for the class.

```
Option Explicit

'Module-level variables used to hold property values.  They are
'not accessible, or not "exposed," outside of the class directly.
'Property Get statements are used to "expose" this data to other
'objects that may request it.
Private mlngNumRecords As Long
Private mdatWhenModified As Date
Private mdatWhenCreated As Date
Private mstrName As String
```

9. Add the following code to **clsTableData** as the **ExtractStatusData** method. This public method sets the class properties to the values of the table definition object passed as an argument.

```
Public Sub ExtractStatusData(tblDef As TableDef)
    'This subroutine retrieves the property data from a given
    'TableDef.
    mstrName = tblDef.Name
    mdatWhenModified = tblDef.LastUpdated
    mdatWhenCreated = tblDef.DateCreated
    mlngNumRecords = tblDef.RecordCount
End Sub
```

10. Add the following four `Property Get` methods to `clsTableData`. Each of these methods returns the value of a property to the requesting procedure.

```
Property Get Name() As String
    Name = mstrName
End Property

Property Get NumRecords() As Long
    NumRecords = mlngNumRecords
End Property

Property Get WhenModified() As Date
    WhenModified = mdatWhenModified
End Property

Property Get WhenCreated() As Date
    WhenCreated = mdatWhenCreated
End Property
```

How It Works

When the application's only form loads, it calls the `GetDatabase` procedure, which uses the Windows common dialog to prompt the user to enter the name of the database to be examined. It then opens the database and the `TableDefs` collection of the database, cycling through the `TableDefs` collection and examining each `TableDef` object in the collection to see whether it represents a system table or a user-defined table. If it is a user-defined table, `GetDatabase` creates a new `clsTableData` object and points the variable `objTable` to the object. The `clsTableData` object extracts four properties from the `TableDef` object. These `TableDef` properties become the properties of the `clsTableData` object. `GetDatabase` then adds the `clsTableData` object to the `colTableData`. When all the `TableDef` objects in the `TableDefs` collection have been examined, `GetDatabase` closes the database. It then cycles through the `clsTableData` objects in the `colTableData` and adds the name of each table in the collection to the list box.

When the user clicks on a table name in the list box, the `Click` routine extracts the information about the chosen table from the `clsTableData` object in `colTableData` and displays the information on the form.

Comments

Each Microsoft Access database includes a set of system tables that maintain information about the objects in the database. These tables all have names beginning with "MSys." You can access some of these tables directly. The tables are not documented and, therefore, are subject to change in a new release of Access, so it's generally not a good idea to build an application that relies on direct access to the MSys tables. Fortunately, the `TableDefs` object described in this How-To gives you a documented way to get at much of the most useful information in these system tables, including status information on each table in the database.

COMPLEXITY
INTERMEDIATE

5.2 How do I...
Attach a table from another database file?

Question

My application has a Microsoft Access database file with several tables that it "owns." But it also needs to work with data in a table that resides in another Microsoft Access file, a table that my application must share with other applications. How can I use a table in a different Microsoft Access file?

Technique

A "database" in older PC database products (such as dBASE, FoxPro, and Paradox products) consists of multiple files—data files, index files, form files, report files, procedure files, and so on. Microsoft Access, on the other hand, uses a single file, into which it incorporates multiple objects—data objects (tables), queries, indexes, forms, reports, macros, and Access Basic code modules. The "database" is a single file.

In most situations, the Microsoft Access way is better. This method eases system administration and makes it less likely that a needed file will be inadvertently moved or deleted. But it's not an advantage when multiple applications each maintain separate databases—and, therefore, separate database files—and the applications also need to share some common data.

Microsoft Access provides the capability to share data between separate databases through the use of attached tables. Attaching a table creates a link between a database file and a table that physically resides in a different file. When you attach a table to a Microsoft Access database, you can treat that table very much like you treat the internal tables of the database—with a few restrictions.

The major restriction in working with attached tables is that you cannot use them with table-type recordsets—you can use only dynaset- or snapshot-type recordsets. Because you cannot work with attached table-type recordsets, you cannot use the Seek method to access data. The Seek method is usually the fastest way to randomly access data from a single table, so this might or might not be a significant restriction, depending on the needs of your application. (See the introduction to Chapter 3, "Creating Queries with SQL," for a discussion of the conditions under which the Seek method provides faster access than the use of SQL SELECT queries.)

Attaching Tables

Each Microsoft Access database file contains a set of table definitions. When you create a **Database** object and connect a database file to that object, the file's table definitions constitute the **TableDefs** collection of the **Database** object. If tables have been attached to the database, the **TableDefs** collection includes **TableDef** objects for each attached table; one of the properties of the **TableDef** object indicates that it is an attached table. For more detailed information on the steps needed to attach a table in a Microsoft Access database, be sure to closely follow step 5 in this How-To.

Steps

Open the project ATTACH.VBP and then run the project. The form shown in Figure 5.3 appears. Click Attach a Table and a standard File Open dialog box appears. Select a Microsoft Access database file to which you want to attach a table (the destination file), and then select the source file for the table (you must select different files). After you have selected both files, the form shown in Figure 5.4 appears with a list of the tables in the source file. Select a table from the list and click OK. A message appears indicating successful attachment, and then the form shown in Figure 5.3 reappears.

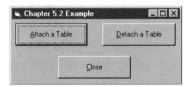

Figure 5.3. The attach and detach table example on startup.

Click Detach a Table and select the same file you used as the destination file when you attached a table. The form shown in Figure 5.4 appears again, this time listing the attached tables in the selected file. Select the table you just attached, and click OK.

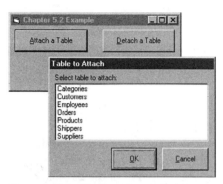

Figure 5.4. The project's Table
List form, showing table names.

1. Create a new project called ATTACH.VBP. Rename **Form1** to **frmAttach**
and use it to create the objects and properties listed in Table 5.3. Save the
form as frmAttach.FRM.

Table 5.3. Objects and properties for *frmAttach*.

OBJECT	PROPERTY	SETTING
Form	Name	frmAttach
	Caption	"Chapter 5.2 Example"
CommandButton	Name	cmdAttach
	Caption	"&Attach a Table"
CommandButton	Name	cmdDetach
	Caption	"&Detach a Table"
CommandButton	Name	cmdClose
	Caption	"&Close"
CommonDialog	Name	cdlFile

2. Add a new form to the project, and create the objects and properties
shown in Table 5.4.

Table 5.4. Objects and properties for *frmSelector*.

OBJECT	PROPERTY	SETTING
Form	Name	frmSelector
ListBox	Name	lstBox
Label	Name	lblList
	Caption	" "

OBJECT	PROPERTY	SETTING
CommandButton	Name	cmdOK
	Caption	"&OK"
	Default	True
CommandButton	Name	cmdCancel
	Cancel	True
	Caption	"&Cancel"

3. Add a new module to the project, name it **basAttach**, and add the following code. The **GetFileName** function, given a full path and filename string, extracts and returns just the name of the file. It does so in an inefficient but workable manner, by stepping backward through the string, checking each character until it finds a backslash. When the backslash is found, the function retrieves everything to the right of that backslash and returns it as the filename.

```
Public Function GetFileName(ByVal strFullPath As String) As String
    Dim I As Integer, strTemp As String

    If Len(strFullPath) Then
        For I = Len(strFullPath) To 1 Step -1
            If Mid(strFullPath, I) = "\" Then strTemp = _
            Right(strFullPath, Len(strFullPath) - I)
        Next
        If strTemp = "" Then strTemp = strFullPath
    End If

    GetFileName = strTemp
End Function
```

4. Add the following code to the declarations section of **frmAttach**. These constants will be used later for the **GetMDBFile** function.

```
Option Explicit

Const SOURCE_FILE = 1
Const DESTINATION_FILE = 2
Const DETACH_FILE = 3
```

5. Enter the following code in **frmAttach** as the **Click** event of **cmdAttach**. This routine gets the user's choices of the destination and source files for the table to be attached. It then gets the user's selection of the table to be attached. If a table is selected, it performs several steps—it creates a **TableDef** object with the name of the table to be attached, and provides a **Connect** string with the name of the source database and then providing the **SourceTableName** property. All three items are needed to attach an external table. After all these items have been provided, the `Attach` method is called to attach the new `TableDef` to our `Database` object.

```
Private Sub cmdAttach_Click()
    Static strSourceFile As String, strDestFile As String
    Dim strTableName As String
    Dim dbfAttach As Database, tdfAttach As TableDef

    strDestFile = GetMDBFile(DESTINATION_FILE)

    If Len(strDestFile) Then strSourceFile = _
        GetMDBFile(SOURCE_FILE)

    If Len(strSourceFile) Then
        'Call the custom method, Display, from frmSelector.  This
        'will return either "" or the name of a selected table.
        strTableName = frmSelector.Display(True, strSourceFile)
        On Error GoTo BadAttach
            If Len(strTableName) Then
                'If we have a table, let's attach it.
                Set dbfAttach = _
                    Workspaces(0).OpenDatabase(strDestFile)
                'Generate a TableDef object
                Set tdfAttach = _
                    dbfAttach.CreateTableDef(strTableName)
                'Provide the connection info
                tdfAttach.Connect = ";DATABASE=" & strSourceFile
                'Provide the table's name
                tdfAttach.SourceTableName = strTableName
                'Append it to the database's TableDefs collection
                dbfAttach.TableDefs.Append tdfAttach
                'And it's good!
                MsgBox "Table " & strTableName & _
                    " attached to " & _
                        GetFileName(strDestFile) & "."
            End If
        On Error GoTo 0
    End If
Exit Sub

BadAttach:
    MsgBox Err.Description, vbExclamation
End Sub
```

6. Enter the following code in `frmAttach` as the `Click` event of `cmdDetach`. This routine gets the user's choices of the file from which the table is to be detached, and then the user's selection of the table to be detached from the file. After these items have been retrieved, the routine finds the appropriate `TableDef` in our `Database` object and runs the `Delete` method to remove it from the database.

```
Private Sub cmdDetach_Click()
    Static strDetachFile As String
```

```
        Dim strTableName As String
        Dim dbfDetach As Database

        strDetachFile = GetMDBFile(DETACH_FILE)

        'Call frmSelector's Display method
        If Len(strDetachFile) Then strTableName = _
            frmSelector.Display(False, strDetachFile)

        On Error GoTo BadDetach
            If Len(strTableName) Then
                'If we have a table, then detach it.
                Set dbfDetach = _
                    Workspaces(0).OpenDatabase(strDetachFile)
                dbfDetach.TableDefs.Delete strTableName
                MsgBox "Table " & strTableName & " detached from " & _
                    GetFileName(strDetachFile) & "."
            End If
        On Error GoTo 0
    Exit Sub

BadDetach:
    MsgBox Err.Description, vbExclamation
End Sub
```

7. Enter the following code in **frmAttach** as the **GetMDBFile** subroutine. This subroutine is used for three related purposes: to get a source file for an attached table, to get a destination file for an attached table, and to get the file from which a table is to be attached. This subroutine uses the Windows File Open common dialog box for all three purposes. It sets the defaults for the common dialog box to facilitate the opening of an existing Microsoft Access (MDB) file. If the user selects a file, the routine returns the name and path of that file. If the user does not select a file (that is, the user clicks Cancel when the common dialog box appears), the function returns an empty string.

```
Private Function GetMDBFile(intPurpose As Integer) As String
    On Error GoTo GetMDBFileError
        Select Case intPurpose
            Case SOURCE_FILE
                cdlFile.DialogTitle = _
                        "Select Source File For Attach"
            Case DESTINATION_FILE
                cdlFile.DialogTitle = _
                        "Select Destination File For Attach"
            Case DETACH_FILE
                cdlFile.DialogTitle = _
                        "Select Source File For Detach"
        End Select

        With cdlFile
            .DefaultExt = "*.MDB"
```

continued on next page

continued from previous page

```
                .Filter = "Access Files *.MDB¦*.MDB¦All Files *.*¦*.*"
                'The user must select an existing file.
                .Flags = cdlOFN_FILEMUSTEXIST
                .CancelError = True
                .filename = "*.MDB"
                .ShowOpen
            End With

            GetMDBFile = cdlFile.filename
        On Error GoTo 0
    Exit Function

GetMDBFileError:
        Exit Function
End Function
```

8. Enter the following code in **frmAttach** as the **ExtractPath** function of **frmAttach**. This function extracts the pathname from a fully qualified filename (drive, path, and file) and returns the drive and path to the calling routine.

```
Private Function ExtractPath(fileName As String, fullPath As
String)
    ExtractPath = Left$(fullPath, _
Len(fullPath) - (Len(fileName) + 1))
End Function
```

9. Enter the following code in **frmAttach** as the **Click** event of **cmdClose**:

```
Private Sub cmdClose_Click()
    End
End Sub
```

10. That completes **frmAttach**. Now turn your attention to **frmSelector** and add the following line to its declarations section:

```
Option Explicit
```

11. Add the following new function to **frmSelector**. This function is used for two purposes: to list the tables that are candidates for attachment and to list the already-attached tables. The method that displays **frmSelector** determines the reason for which the form is being displayed by providing a Boolean variable. This method, **Display**, sets the form's captions appropriately and then calls **ListTables** to fill the list box. The arguments to **ListTables** specify the file and what kind of tables to list.

```
Private Function ListTables(blnAttach As Boolean, _
strFileSpec As String) _
As Integer
```

```
            Dim dbfTemp As Database, tdfTemp As TableDef
            Dim intTablesAdded As Integer

            lstBox.Clear

            On Error GoTo ListTablesError
                Screen.MousePointer = vbHourglass
                Set dbfTemp = _
                    DBEngine.Workspaces(0).OpenDatabase(strFileSpec)
                intTablesAdded = 0

                For Each tdfTemp In dbfTemp.TableDefs
                    If blnAttach Then
                        If Left$(tdfTemp.Name, 4) <> "MSys" And _
                            tdfTemp.Attributes <> dbAttachedTable And _
                            tdfTemp.Attributes <> dbAttachSavePWD And _
                            tdfTemp.Attributes <> dbAttachExclusive Then
                                lstBox.AddItem tdfTemp.Name
                                intTablesAdded = intTablesAdded + 1
                        End If
                    ElseIf tdfTemp.Attributes = dbAttachedTable Or _
                        tdfTemp.Attributes = dbAttachSavePWD Or _
                        tdfTemp.Attributes = dbAttachExclusive Then
                            lstBox.AddItem tdfTemp.Name
                            intTablesAdded = intTablesAdded + 1
                    End If
                Next

            Screen.MousePointer = vbDefault

            ListTables = intTablesAdded

        Exit Function

        ListTablesError:
            Screen.MousePointer = vbDefault
            MsgBox Err.Description, vbExclamation
            ListTables = 0
        Exit Function

        End Function
```

12. Enter the following code in **frmSelector** as the **Display** function. This is the public function that is called by **frmAttach** to provide a table name to attach or detach. The **blnAttach** Boolean determines the form's purpose when called: if set to **True**, it configures for attachment; otherwise, it configures for detachment. The **strFileSpec** is the name of the database that was provided in **frmAttach** via the **GetMDBFile** function.

```
Public Function Display(ByVal blnAttach As Boolean, _
  ByVal strFileSpec As String) As String

    With Me
        .Caption = "Table to " & IIf(blnAttach, "Attach", _
"Detach")
```

continued on next page

continued from previous page

```
                                  .lblList = "Select table to " & _
                                      IIf(blnAttach, "attach:", "detach:")
                            End With

                            If ListTables(blnAttach, strFileSpec) Then
                                Me.Show vbModal
                            Else
                                MsgBox "There are no attached tables in " & _
                                        GetFileName(strFileSpec) & "."
                            End If

                            If lstBox.ListIndex > -1 Then Display = lstBox.Text

                        End Function
```

13. Enter the following code in `frmSelector` as the `Click` event of `cmdOK`. If
the user has made a selection, the routine hides the form. Because the
form is opened modally, this allows the `Display` function to complete,
passing back the selected table name.

```
Private Sub cmdOK_Click()
    If lstBox.ListIndex > -1 Then
        frmSelector.Hide
    Else
        MsgBox "You have not yet made a selection.", vbExclamation
    End If
End Sub
```

14. Enter the following code in `frmSelector` as the `DblClick` event of `lstBox`.
If the user has made a selection, the routine updates the `Public` variable
`TableName` and hides the form.

```
Private Sub lstBox_DblClick()
    cmdOK_Click
End Sub
```

15. Enter the following code in `frmSelector` as the `Click` event of `cmdCancel`.
The user does not want to designate a table, so set the list box's `ListIndex`
to `-1` and then hide the form.

```
Private Sub cmdCancel_Click()
    lstBox.ListIndex = -1
    frmSelector.Hide
End Sub
```

How It Works

When the user clicks the Attach a Table button, the `Click` event uses the
Windows File Open common dialog box to get the destination and source files
for the attachment. It then calls the `Display` method of `frmSelector`, setting
`blnAttach` to `True` to indicate that `frmSelector` is to display those tables

eligible for attachment from the designated source file. When the user makes a selection in `frmSelector`, the subroutine creates a new `TableDef` object and appends it to the destination file's `TableDefs` collection.

When the user clicks Detach a Table, the `Click` event uses the Windows File Open common dialog box to get the file from which the table is to be detached. It then calls the `Display` method of `frmSelector` again, setting `blnAttach` to `False` to indicate that `frmSelector` is to display the attached tables in the designated file. When the user makes a selection in `frmSelector`, the subroutine removes the selected `TableDef` object from the designated file's `TableDefs` collection.

Comments

The capability to attach external tables opens a lot of possibilities for the Visual Basic database application developer. The DAO engine is capable of providing many services that would otherwise be inconvenient to duplicate with extensive ODBC-related code, with a familiar object hierarchy. Also, when you need to import and export data, the capability to attach tables comes in very handy, making a sometimes tedious process of reading from one database and writing to another a snap. At a client/server level, the flexibility granted by the capability to attach tables from several different external database platforms allows for an ease of data access, whether for mainframe databases, server databases, or even several locally accessed workstation databases, without having to program for each database platform.

COMPLEXITY
INTERMEDIATE

5.3 How do I...
Import a text file?

Problem

I periodically get downloads from a mainframe database (or other source) as delimited text files that I need to import into my database. If I could be sure that users had Microsoft Access installed, my program could use OLE to invoke the import capability of Access—but some users might not have a copy of Access. How can I use Visual Basic to import text files into a database file?

Technique

Visual Basic has a rich variety of features for working with text files. You can employ these capabilities to open the text file and read the text data. From that point, the problem resolves to using the delimiters in the text file to split the text into records and fields and storing the data in the appropriate database tables.

You need to be prepared to handle errors, both the normal data access errors and any errors that incorrect input text might cause.

Steps

This How-To uses text data from the text files VENDORS.DAT and INVOICES.DAT imported into a Microsoft Access database, ACCTSPAY.MDB. The text files use an end-of-line sequence (a carriage return followed by a line feed) as a record delimiter and a tab character as a field delimiter. The Vendors table in the ACCTPAY.MDB has the following fields, with [Vendor Number] as the primary key:

✔ Vendor Number

✔ Name

✔ Address

✔ FEIN (Federal Employer Identification Number, required for tax reporting purposes)

The Invoices table in the database has the following fields. The primary key is a composite of [Vendor Number] and [Invoice Number].

✔ Vendor Number

✔ Invoice Number

✔ Date

✔ Amount

The tables are related on the [Vendor Number] field; every record in the Invoices table must have a corresponding record in the Vendors table.

Open and run TextImport.VBP. You'll see the form shown in Figure 5.5. Click the Import Data button, and the application imports the contents of the text files VENDORS.DAT and INVOICES.DAT into the Vendors and Invoices tables of ACCTSPAY.MDB. Click List Vendors, and a list of the vendors imported appears in the list box at the top of the form. Select a vendor name; if any invoices for that vendor were imported, a list of the invoices appears in the grid control at the bottom of the form. With a vendor selected, click Vendor Details, and you'll see the vendor details form shown in Figure 5.6.

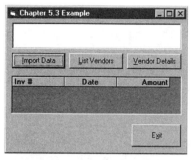

Figure 5.5. The program's
Text Import form on startup.

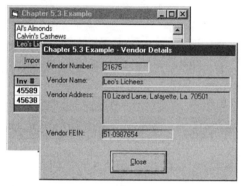

Figure 5.6. The program's Vendor
Details form, showing vendor information.

1. Create a new project called TextImport.VBP. Rename **Form1** to
frmVendorDetails, and then create the objects and properties listed in
Table 5.5. Save the form as Vendors.FRM.

Table 5.5. Objects and properties for the Vendor Details form.

OBJECT	PROPERTY	SETTING
Form	Name	frmVendorDetails
	Caption	"Chapter 5.3 Example - Vendor Details "
Label	Name	lblNumber
	BorderStyle	1 (Fixed Single)
	Caption	" "

continued on next page

continued from previous page

Label	Name	lblName
	BorderStyle	1 (Fixed Single)
	Caption	""
Label	Name	lblAddress
	BorderStyle	1 (Fixed Single)
	Caption	""
Label	Name	lblFEIN
	BorderStyle	1 (Fixed Single)
	Caption	""
Label	Name	lblVendor
	Index	0
	Caption	"Vendor Number:"
Label	Name	lblVendor
	Index	1
	Caption	"Vendor Name:"
Label	Name	lblVendor
	Index	2
	Caption	"Vendor Address:"
Label	Name	lblVendor
	Index	3
	Caption	"Vendor FEIN:"
CommandButton	Name	cmdClose
	Caption	"&Close"
	Default	True

2. Insert the following code into the **Click** event of **cmdClose** on
frmVendorDetails (this is the only code needed for this form):

```
Private Sub cmdClose_Click()
    Unload frmVendorDetails
End Sub
```

3. Insert a second form into the project. Change its name to **frmMain**, and
then create the objects and properties listed in Table 5.6. Save the form as
TextImp.FRM.

Table 5.6. Objects and properties for the main Text Import form.

OBJECT	PROPERTY	SETTING
Form	Name	frmMain
	Caption	"Chapter 5.3 Example"
ListBox	Name	lstVendors
	Sorted	True
MSFlexGrid	Name	grdInvoices
	Cols	4
	Scrollbars	2 - flexScrollBarVertical
CommandButton	Name	cmdImport
	Caption	"&Import Data"
CommandButton	Name	cmdListVendors
	Caption	"&List Vendors"
CommandButton	Name	cmdVendorDetails
	Caption	"&Vendor Details"
CommandButton	Name	cmdExit
	Cancel	True
	Caption	"Exit"

4. Insert the following code into the declarations section of **frmMain**. Edit the pathnames in the **Const** declarations to point to the locations of the indicated files on your system.

```
Option Explicit

'Change this constant to whatever path you have installed the
'CD contents into.

Const DATA_PATH = "D:\VB6DBHT"

Private VendorFile As String, InvoiceFile As String, DatabaseFile
As String
```

5. Add the following code to the **Load** event of **frmMain**. When the form loads, it calls the **InitializeGrid** subroutine to set up the grid and then deletes all existing data from the Vendors and Invoices tables in the database. You wouldn't ordinarily delete all the existing data before importing new data, but with this demonstration program, this step is necessary if you want to run it more than once using the same input files. Otherwise, you'll get primary key errors when you try to add new records that duplicate existing primary key values.

```
Private Sub Form_Load()
    Dim dbfTemp As Database

    'Assign fully qualified pathnames to the form level data file
    'variables.
    VendorFile = DATA_PATH & "\CHAPTER05\VENDORS.DAT"
    InvoiceFile = DATA_PATH & "\CHAPTER05\INVOICES.DAT"
    DatabaseFile = DATA_PATH & "\CHAPTER05\ACCTSPAY.MDB"

    ' Initialize the grid control.
    InitializeGrid

    ' Delete any existing data in the Vendors and Invoices tables.
    Set dbfTemp = _
        DBEngine.Workspaces(0).OpenDatabase(DatabaseFile)
    dbfTemp.Execute ("DELETE Vendors.* from Vendors")
    dbfTemp.Execute ("DELETE Invoices.* from Invoices")
End Sub
```

6. Create the following subroutine in **frmMain**. This code sets the grid column widths and alignments and inserts the column titles. Because the initial state of the grid (before a vendor is selected) shows no invoices, it is initialized with only the title row visible.

```
Private Sub InitializeGrid()

    With grdInvoices
        .ColWidth(0) = 0:
        .ColWidth(1) = 1300
        .ColWidth(2) = 1300
        .ColWidth(3) = 1300
        .ColAlignment(1) = flexAlignLeftCenter
        .ColAlignment(2) = flexAlignCenterCenter
        .ColAlignment(3) = flexAlignRightCenter
        .FixedAlignment(1) = flexAlignLeftCenter
        .FixedAlignment(2) = flexAlignCenterCenter
        .FixedAlignment(3) = flexAlignRightCenter
        .Row = 0
        .Col = 1: .Text = "Inv #"
        .Col = 2: .Text = "Date"
        .Col = 3: .Text = "Amount"
        .Rows = 1
    End With
End Sub
```

7. Add the following code to the **Click** event of **cmdImport**. This procedure imports vendor and invoice records from the text files named by the form-level variables **VendorFile** and **InvoiceFile**, respectively. As the procedure imports the file, it creates from each record an object of the class **clsVendor** or **clsInvoice**. (These classes are defined by vendor and invoice class modules, which are discussed later.) The **cmdImport_Click** subroutine then adds each **clsVendor** or **clsInvoice** object to a **Collection** object. One **Collection** object receives all the **clsVendor**

objects, and a second `Collection` object receives all `clsInvoice` objects. After both collections have been built, the subroutine appends the objects in each collection to the Vendors table or Invoices table, as is appropriate.

```
Private Sub cmdImport_Click()
    Dim dbfTemp As Database, tblVendors As Recordset, tblInvoices _
        As Recordset
    Dim objVendor As clsVendor, objInvoice As clsInvoice
    Dim colVendors As New Collection, colInvoices _
        As New Collection

    Dim strInputLine As String, strErrMsg As String
    Dim blnNeedRollback As Boolean
    Dim intFileHandle As Integer

    On Error GoTo ImportTextError
        Screen.MousePointer = vbHourglass

        'Get the vendor text file, and create an instance
        'of objVendor for each line found in the text file,
        'passing the line to the DelimitedString property
        'of the instance of objVendor.
        intFileHandle = FreeFile
        Open VendorFile For Input As intFileHandle
        Do Until EOF(intFileHandle)
            Line Input #intFileHandle, strInputLine
            Set objVendor = New clsVendor
            objVendor.DelimitedString = strInputLine
            colVendors.Add objVendor
        Loop
        Close intFileHandle

        'Same as above, but with the invoice text file.
        intFileHandle = FreeFile:
        Open InvoiceFile For Input As intFileHandle
        Do Until EOF(intFileHandle)
            Line Input #intFileHandle, strInputLine
            Set objInvoice = New clsInvoice
            objInvoice.DelimitedString = strInputLine
            colInvoices.Add objInvoice
        Loop
        Close intFileHandle

        'Prepare for addition
        Set dbfTemp = _
            DBEngine.Workspaces(0).OpenDatabase(DatabaseFile)
        Set tblVendors = _
            dbfTemp.OpenRecordset("Vendors", dbOpenTable)
        Set tblInvoices = _
            dbfTemp.OpenRecordset("Invoices", dbOpenTable)

        'This is where we start the transaction processing.  None
        'of the changes we make will be committed to the database
        'until the CommitTrans line, some lines below.
```

continued on next page

continued from previous page

```
            Workspaces(0).BeginTrans
            blnNeedRollback = True

            'Iterate through our collection of clsVendor objects,
            'calling the StoreNewItem method and passing our newly
            'opened table.
            If colVendors.Count Then
                For Each objVendor In colVendors
                    If objVendor.StoreNewItem(tblVendors) = False Then
                        strErrMsg = _
                      "An error occurred while importing vendor #" & _
                        CStr(objVendor.Number)
                        Err.Raise 32767
                    End If
                Next
            End If

            'Same as above, but for invoices. (Deja vu...?)
            If colInvoices.Count Then
                For Each objInvoice In colInvoices
                    If objInvoice.StoreNewItem(tblInvoices) = False
                        Or objInvoice.VendorNumber = 0 Then
                        strErrMsg = _
                        "An error occurred while importing invoice #" & _
                        objInvoice.InvoiceNumber
                        Err.Raise 32767
                    End If
                Next
            End If

            'Here's where the data is committed to the database.
            'Had an error occurred, we would never reach this point;
            'instead, the Rollback command in our error
            'trapping routine would have removed our changes.
            Workspaces(0).CommitTrans

            Screen.MousePointer = vbDefault
        On Error GoTo 0
    Exit Sub

ImportTextError:
    Screen.MousePointer = vbDefault
    If strErrMsg = "" Then strErrMsg = _
                    "The following error has occurred:" & vbCr _
        & Err.Description
    strErrMsg = strErrMsg & _
                " No records have been added to the database."
    MsgBox strErrMsg, vbExclamation
    'Here's the Rollback method; if the blnNeedRollback variable
    'is still set to True, we undo our uncommitted changes.
    If blnNeedRollback Then Workspaces(0).Rollback
Exit Sub

End Sub
```

The error handling in this subroutine requires comment. If the error is due to faulty input data, you want to give the user enough information to identify the specific record that caused the problem. For import data errors, therefore, the error message that will be displayed for the user is built into the body of the code. Error messages for errors encountered when importing vendors include the vendor number; error messages for errors encountered when importing invoices include both the vendor and the invoice numbers. Other types of errors, those not due to input data problems, have a standard error message built into the error-handling routine.

In this application, it's highly likely that you don't want to import some of the records—you want to import all of them or, if an error occurs, none of them. You accomplish this task by enclosing the code that actually appends the records to the database tables between **BeginTrans** and **CommitTrans** statements. This converts all the database modifications into a single atomic transaction. Any changes made within an atomic transaction (that is, changes made after **BeginTrans** and before **CommitTrans**) are not irrevocably committed to the database until **CommitTrans**. In this subroutine, if an error occurs between **BeginTrans** and **CommitTrans**, control is transferred to the error-handling routine, which executes a **Rollback** statement. The **Rollback** statement tells the Jet engine, "Back out all the changes made since the **BeginTrans** statement."

Rollback is executed only when the value of the Boolean variable **blnNeedRollback** is **True**. Initially, **blnNeedRollback** is **False** and is set to **True** at the beginning of the transaction in the statement immediately following **BeginTrans**. This provision is needed to ensure that **Rollback** doesn't get executed by an error that occurs before **BeginTrans**—because trying to execute a **Rollback** outside a transaction is itself an error.

8. Add the following code to the **Click** event of **cmdListVendors**. This procedure lists the vendors in the database and in the list box on the form. It uses the **ItemData** property of the list box to attach the vendor number to the vendor name. Other procedures in the application use **ItemData** to uniquely identify the vendor.

```
Private Sub cmdListVendors_Click()
    Dim dbfTemp As Database, tblVendors As Recordset

    On Error GoTo ListVendorsError
    Set dbfTemp = _
        DBEngine.Workspaces(0).OpenDatabase(DatabaseFile, _
            False, True)
    Set tblVendors = dbfTemp.OpenRecordset("Vendors", dbOpenTable)
    If tblVendors.RecordCount <> 0 Then
        tblVendors.MoveFirst
        Do Until tbl.EOF
```

continued on next page

continued from previous page

```
                                lstVendors.AddItem tblVendors!Name
                                lstVendors.ItemData(lstVendors.NewIndex) = _
                                        tblVendors![Vendor Number]
                                tblVendors.MoveNext
                    Loop
                End If
                tblVendors.Close

            Exit Sub

            ListVendorsError:
                lstVendors.Clear
                MsgBox Err.Description
            End Sub
```

9. Add the following code to the **Click** event of **lstVendors**. This procedure retrieves the vendor number from the selected item's **ItemData** value and passes that value to the **FillInvoiceList** routine, which fills the grid with invoices linked to this vendor.

```
Private Sub lstVendors_Click()
    FillInvoiceList lstVendors.ItemData(lstVendors.ListIndex)
End Sub
```

10. Create the **FillInvoiceList** subroutine by entering the following code into **frmMain**. This list box **Click** event calls **FillInvoiceList** when the user clicks on a vendor name. This subroutine fills the grid with information about the invoices for the selected vendor by creating a collection of all the invoice objects with vendor numbers that match the argument passed to the subroutine. It then cycles though the collection and adds each invoice to the grid.

```
Private Sub FillInvoiceList(intVendor As Integer)
    Dim dbfTemp As Database, recInvoices As Recordset
    Dim intRow As Integer, strSQL As String

    Dim colInvoices As New Collection, objInvoice As clsInvoice

    On Error GoTo FillInvoiceListError
        'Open the database & recordset used to fill the list box
        Set dbfTemp =
            DBEngine.Workspaces(0).OpenDatabase(DatabaseFile, _
                False, True)
        strSQL = "SELECT [Invoice Number] FROM Invoices " & _
            "WHERE [Vendor Number] = " & intVendor
        Set recInvoices = _
            dbfTemp.OpenRecordset(strSQL, dbOpenSnapshot)

        If recInvoices.RecordCount > 0 Then
            recInvoices.MoveFirst
            Do Until recInvoices.EOF
                Set objInvoice = New clsInvoice
                If objInvoice.Retrieve(dbfTemp, intVendor, _
                    recInvoices("Invoice Number")) _
```

```
                        Then colInvoices.Add objInvoice
                    recInvoices.MoveNext
                Loop

                grdInvoices.Rows = colInvoices.Count + 1

                For intRow = 1 To colInvoices.Count
                    Set objInvoice = colInvoices(intRow)
                    objInvoice.AddToGrid grdInvoices, intRow
                Next intRow
            Else
                grdInvoices.Rows = 1
            End If
        On Error GoTo 0
    Exit Sub

    FillInvoiceListError:
        grdInvoices.Rows = 1: lstVendors.ListIndex = -1
        MsgBox Err.Description, vbExclamation
    Exit Sub

    End Sub
```

11. Add the following code to the **Click** event of **cmdVendorDetails**. This procedure displays a form with information about the currently selected vendor in the list box.

```
Private Sub cmdVendorDetails_Click()
    Dim dbfTemp As Database
    Dim tblVendors As Recordset
    Dim intVendorNumber As Integer

    On Error GoTo VendorDetailsError
        If lstVendors.ListIndex > -1 Then
            intVendorNumber =
                lstVendors.ItemData(lstVendors.ListIndex)
            Set dbfTemp =
                DBEngine.Workspaces(0).OpenDatabase(DatabaseFile, _
                    False, True)
            Set tblVendors = dbfTemp.OpenRecordset("Vendors", _
                dbOpenTable)

            tblVendors.Index = "PrimaryKey"
            tblVendors.Seek "=", intVendorNumber

            With frmVendorDetails
                .lblNumber = tblVendors![Vendor Number]
                .lblName = IIf(IsNull(tblVendors!Name), "", _
                        tblVendors!Name)
                .lblAddress = IIf(IsNull(tblVendors!Address), "", _
                        tblVendors!Address)
                .lblFEIN = IIf(IsNull(tblVendors!FEIN), "", _
                        tblVendors!FEIN)
            End With

            tblVendors.Close
            frmVendorDetails.Show vbModal
```

continued on next page

continued from previous page

```
            Else
                Beep
                MsgBox "You haven't selected a vendor.", vbExclamation
            End If
        On Error GoTo 0
    Exit Sub

    VendorDetailsError:
        MsgBox Error(Err)
    Exit Sub

End Sub
```

12. Add the following code to the `Click` event of `cmdExit`:

```
Private Sub cmdExit_Click()
    End
End Sub
```

13. Insert a new class module into the project. Name the module `clsVendor`. Each object of the `clsVendor` class will represent one vendor record.

14. Insert the following code into the declarations section of `clsVendor`. The class has five properties, maintained in five private variables, each starting with the prefix **prop**. One property, `propDelimitedString`, is set to the "raw" vendor data as read from the text file. The other four properties each hold a value that corresponds to a field in the Vendors table. Because these are private variables, they are not directly accessible to routines outside the class module, but can be accessed only through methods of the class.

```
Option Explicit

Private mintNumber As Integer
Private mstrCompany As String
Private mstrAddress As String
Private mstrFEIN As String
Private mstrDelimitedString As String
```

15. Create the following `Property Let` method in `clsVendor`. This method is passed a delimited string representing one vendor record. It stores the passed argument as the `DelimitedString` property by assigning it to the private variable `mstrDelimitedString`. The `Property Let` `DelimitedString` method also parses the string into fields and stores the individual field values as the appropriate object properties.

```
Property Let DelimitedString(strInput As String)
    Dim strDelimiter As String, strTextNumber As String
    Dim intEnd As Integer, intField As Integer, intStart As _
        Integer
    Dim I As Integer
```

```
        strDelimiter = Chr$(9): mstrDelimitedString = strInput
        intStart = 1: intField = 1

    Do
        intEnd = InStr(intStart, strInput, strDelimiter)
        If intEnd = 0 Then intEnd = Len(strInput) + 1

        Select Case intField
            Case 1
                strTextNumber = ExtractField(intStart, intEnd)
                If IsNumeric(strTextNumber) Then
                    If strTextNumber >= 1 And _
                        strTextNumber <= 32767 Then
                        mintNumber = Val(strTextNumber)
                    Else
                        mintNumber = 0
                    End If
                Else
                    mintNumber = 0
                End If
            Case 2
                mstrCompany = ExtractField(intStart, intEnd)
            Case 3
                mstrAddress = ExtractField(intStart, intEnd)
            Case 4
                mstrFEIN = ExtractField(intStart, intEnd)
        End Select

        intStart = intEnd + 1: intField = intField + 1
    Loop While intEnd < Len(strInput) And intField <= 4
End Property
```

16. Create **ExtractField** as a private function in **clsVendor**. As a private function, it can be called only by other procedures within the class module. **ExtractField** returns a selection of text from the private variable **mstrDelimitedString**. The text to return is defined by the start and end positions received as arguments.

```
Private Function ExtractField(intStart As Integer, intEnd As
        Integer)
    ExtractField = Mid$(mstrDelimitedString, intStart, _
                    (intEnd - intStart))
End Function
```

17. Create the public method **StoreNewItem** in **clsVendor**. This method inserts the object into the database as a new record. It returns **True** if it successfully stores the object, it returns **False** otherwise. **StoreNewItem** calls a private function, **WriteItem**, to actually assign property values to fields. Splitting the code into two functions allows the **WriteItem** code to be shared with another routine that would update an existing record. (This demonstration program does not include such a routine, but an actual application might.)

```
Public Function StoreNewItem(rs As Recordset) As Boolean
    On Error GoTo StoreNewError
        rs.AddNew
        If WriteItem(rs) Then
            rs.Update
        Else
            GoTo StoreNewError
        End If

        StoreNewItem = True
    On Error GoTo 0
Exit Function

StoreNewError:
    StoreNewItem = False
    Exit Function
End Function
```

18. Create the private function `WriteItem` in `clsVendor` with the following code. It assigns the current property values to the Vendor table fields in the current record. `WriteData` returns `True` unless an error occurs.

```
Private Function WriteItem(recTemp As Recordset) As Boolean
    On Error GoTo WriteItemError
        recTemp("Vendor Number") = mintNumber
        recTemp("Name") = mstrCompany
        recTemp("Address") = mstrAddress
        recTemp("FEIN") = mstrFEIN
        WriteItem = True
    On Error GoTo 0
Exit Function

WriteItemError:
    WriteItem = False
    Exit Function
End Function
```

19. Create the following four `Property Get` methods in `clsVendor`. These methods allow outside routines to access the values of the record represented by the object.

```
Property Get Number() As Integer
    Number = mintNumber
End Property

Property Get Company() As String
    Company = mstrCompany
End Property

Property Get Address() As String
    Address = mstrAddress
End Property

Property Get FEIN() As String
    FEIN = mstrFEIN
End Property
```

20. Insert a new class module into the project. Name the module `clsInvoice`. Each object of the `clsInvoice` class will represent one invoice record.

21. Insert the following code into the declarations section of `clsInvoice`. Like `clsVendor`, `clsInvoice` has five properties maintained in five private variables, each starting with the prefix **prop**. One property, `mstrDelimitedString`, is set to the "raw" invoice data as read from the text file. The other four properties each contain a value that corresponds to a field in the Invoices table. Because these are all private variables, they are not directly accessible to routines outside the class module but can be accessed only through public methods of the class.

```
Option Explicit

Const FLD_VENNUMBER = 1
Const FLD_INVNUMBER = 2
Const FLD_DATE = 3
Const FLD_AMOUNT = 4

Private mintVendorNumber As Integer
Private mstrInvoiceNumber As String
Private mdatDate As Date
Private mcurAmount As Currency
Private mstrDelimitedString As String
```

22. Copy these four routines from the `clsVendor` class module and paste them into `clsInvoice`: Let `DelimitedString`, `ExtractField`, `StoreNewItem`, and `WriteItem`. (In the following steps, you will modify `Let Delimited String` and `WriteItem`. `ExtractField` and `StoreNewItem` require no modifications.)

23. In `clsInvoice`, modify the six program lines shown in bold in the following listing. (All the statements to be modified are in the `Select Case` structure.)

```
Property Let DelimitedString(strInput As String)
    Dim strDelimiter As String
    Dim intEnd As Integer, intField As Integer, intStart As _
        Integer
    Dim I As Integer
    Dim strTextNumber As String

    strDelimiter = Chr$(9): mstrDelimitedString = strInput
    intStart = 1: intField = 1

    Do
        intEnd = InStr(intStart, strInput, strDelimiter)
        If intEnd = 0 Then intEnd = Len(strInput) + 1
        Select Case intField
            Case 1
                strTextNumber = ExtractField(intStart, intEnd)
```

continued on next page

continued from previous page

```
                        If IsNumeric(strTextNumber) Then
                            If strTextNumber >= 1 And strTextNumber <= _
                                32767 Then
                                mintVendorNumber = Val(strTextNumber)
                            Else
                                mintVendorNumber = 0
                            End If
                        Else
                            mintVendorNumber = 0
                        End If
                    Case 2
                        mstrInvoiceNumber = ExtractField(intStart, intEnd)
                    Case 3
                        mdatDate = CDate(ExtractField(intStart, intEnd))
                    Case 4
                        mcurAmount = CCur(ExtractField(intStart, intEnd))
                End Select

                intStart = intEnd + 1: intField = intField + 1
        Loop While intEnd < Len(strInput) And intField <= 4
    End Property
```

24. Make the four modifications shown in bold to the `WriteItem` function of `clsInvoice`:

```
Private Function WriteItem(recTemp As Recordset) As Boolean
    On Error GoTo WriteItemError
        recTemp("Vendor Number") = mintVendorNumber
        recTemp("Invoice Number") = mstrInvoiceNumber
        recTemp("Date") = mdatDate
        recTemp("Amount") = mcurAmount
        WriteItem = True
    On Error GoTo 0
Exit Function

WriteItemError:
    WriteItem = False
Exit Function

End Function
```

25. Create the public `Retrieve` method in `clsInvoice`. This method retrieves the invoice with the primary key values named in the arguments from the Invoices table and assigns the field values to the object's properties. It returns `True` if a corresponding record is located and successfully read; it returns `False` otherwise.

```
Public Function Retrieve(dbfTemp As Database, VendorNumber As _
        Integer, _
InvoiceNumber As String) As Boolean
    Dim recTemp As Recordset

    On Error GoTo RetrieveError
        Set recTemp = dbfTemp.OpenRecordset("Invoices", _
            dbOpenTable, dbReadOnly)
```

```
                recTemp.Index = "PrimaryKey"
                recTemp.Seek "=", VendorNumber, InvoiceNumber
                DBEngine.Idle dbFreeLocks

                If Not recTemp.NoMatch Then
                    mintVendorNumber = VendorNumber
                    mstrInvoiceNumber = InvoiceNumber
                    mdatDate = recTemp("Date")
                    mcurAmount = recTemp("Amount")
                    Retrieve = True
                Else
                    Retrieve = False
                End If
        On Error GoTo 0
    Exit Function

    RetrieveError:
        Retrieve = False
    Exit Function

    End Function
```

26. Create the `AddToGrid` method in `clsInvoice`. This method receives a grid and grid row as its arguments and inserts the object's property values into the grid row.

```
Public Sub AddToGrid(grdTemp As MSFlexGrid, intGridRow As Integer)
    With grdTemp
        .Row = intGridRow
        .Col = 1: .Text = mstrInvoiceNumber
        .Col = 2: .Text = Format$(mdatDate, "Short Date")
        .Col = 3: .Text = Format$(mcurAmount, "Currency")
    End With
End Sub
```

27. Create the following four `Property Get` methods in `clsInvoice`. These public methods allow outside routines to access the values of the record represented by the object.

```
Property Get VendorNumber() As Integer
    VendorNumber = mintVendorNumber
End Property

Property Get InvoiceNumber() As String
    InvoiceNumber = mstrInvoiceNumber
End Property

Property Get InvoiceDate() As Date
    InvoiceDate = mdatDate
End Property

Property Get Amount() As Currency
    Amount = mcurAmount
End Property
```

How It Works

The `Form_Load` event of `frmMain` initializes the grid and deletes any existing values from the database tables. (As noted in the discussion for step 5, you probably would not delete the records in a real production application.) When the user clicks the Import Data button, the data is imported from the text files into objects of the `clsVendor` and `clsInvoice` classes, and these objects are collected into `Collection` classes. The contents of each `Collection` class are then written to the database tables.

The `cmdImport_Click` routine controls the import process and does the portion of the work that does not require knowledge of the structure of the database tables or the format of the individual records within the imported text strings. The processing that does require such knowledge is encapsulated into the objects by providing methods within the objects to perform the needed operations.

Each line in the vendor and invoice input files represents one record. The `cmdImport_Click` routine reads a line, creates a new `clsVendor` or `clsInvoice` object, and passes the record to the object through the object's `Property Let DelimitedString` method. `Property Let DelimitedString` parses the text string into individual fields and assigns the field values to the object's property variables. Later, `cmdImport_Click` cycles through each of the collection objects and causes each object to store itself into the database by invoking the object's `StoreNewItem` method.

When the user clicks the List Vendors button, `cmdListVendors_Click` retrieves the vendor list from the Vendors table and displays it in the list box. When the user then clicks on a vendor name, the list box `Click` routine passes the vendor number of the selected vendor to `frmMain`'s `FillInvoiceList` subroutine. `FillInvoiceList` creates a snapshot consisting of the invoice numbers of invoices for which the vendor numbers match the selected vendor. It then creates a `clsInvoice` object for each invoice, causes each object to retrieve itself from disk by invoking the object's `Retrieve` method, and adds the invoice object to a `Collection` object. When all the matching invoices have been retrieved, the list box `Click` subroutine cycles through the collection, causing each invoice object in the collection to display itself in a grid row.

Comments

A significant amount of code is duplicated, or duplicated with minor changes, between the two classes in this How-To. If Visual Basic were a full object-oriented programming language that supported class hierarchies with inheritance, this duplication would be unnecessary. The common code could be put into a parent object from which both `clsVendor` and `clsInvoice` would inherit. Each class would then add methods and override inherited methods as necessary to implement its unique needs.

Because Visual Basic doesn't have this feature, another approach would be to put the identical and nearly identical routines in code modules as `Public` procedures and let the class routines call them as needed. This option would certainly reduce code size, but it would also introduce two problems:

✔ Using `Public` procedures in code modules violates the object-oriented programmer's principle of encapsulation. Class methods have privileged access to the object's private data (that is, its properties). Converting class methods to `Public` procedures in a code module means that any data that the "methods" share can also be accessed by other routines in the same code module.

✔ The more a shared routine deviates from a common form, the harder it is to implement this option. In the example in this How-To, you have two record types, and each has four fields; so a four-option `Select Case` structure in the `Property Let DelimitedString` procedure fits both. What if you had 15 records, varying in size from 2 fields to 40? Yes, it could be done by passing parameters and lots of convoluted `If...Then` logic. No, you wouldn't want to write it, and you surely wouldn't want to maintain it.

The bottom line: If encapsulation and simple code are more important to you than the smallest possible code size, use the technique described in this How-To. If minimizing the amount of code is more important, consider using `Public` procedures in code modules.

COMPLEXITY
INTERMEDIATE

5.4 How do I...
Save graphics in a database file?

Problem

I have an application that tracks employee information for generating company ID cards, and I need to include a picture of the employee in the database. How can I do this from Visual Basic?

Technique

There are two basic techniques, each with its benefits and detriments, for saving graphical data in a Microsoft Access database. One method, the easier but more limiting of the two, is to use a `PictureBox` control as a data-bound control and link it to an `OLE Object` field in the Access database (the data type is represented by the constant `dbLongBinary`), allowing direct loading and saving of data to the database by use of the `LoadPicture` and `SavePicture` commands.

This technique makes it simple to import pictures in common formats, such as the Windows bitmap (.BMP) format, the Graphic Interchange Format (.GIF), or the JPEG (.JPG) format, used by many graphics-processing software packages. However, the data is saved as raw binary information and is difficult to use outside of your application without allowing for an import/export feature in your Visual Basic code.

The second technique, which is more versatile, but much more complex, is to use an OLE `Container` control as a data-bound control, linking it to an OLE `Object` field in a manner similar to that used by the `PictureBox` control discussed in the first technique. The data, however, is stored as an OLE object, available for export by any application that can employ OLE Automation techniques for importing the data. This technique has its own problems. The data is linked to a specific OLE class; your user might not be able to work with the data from another application if he does not have that specific OLE class registered by the external application. Also, it assumes that the external application, in most instances, will be used to edit the object; this adds overhead to your application that might not be needed.

The first technique tends to be more commonly employed, but the second technique is used enough to make it worthwhile to provide further information on the subject. The Microsoft Knowledge Base, an excellent tool for programming research, provides several articles on the subject. Table 5.7 provides the names and article IDs of several relevant Knowledge Base entries.

Table 5.7. Knowledge Base entries.

ARTICLE ID	NAME AND DESCRIPTION
Q147727	"How To View Photos from the NWIND.MDB Database in VB 4.0." Although the article is for VB 4.0, its code is still up-to-date. The code provides a complete but complex method of loading the stored graphics in NWIND.MDB, a database provided with Visual Basic, into a `PictureBox` control with some API prestidigitation. Very educational.
Q103115	"PRB: Invalid Picture Error When Trying To Bind Picture Control." If you have ever attempted to bind a `PictureBox` to an OLE `Object` database field and received this error, it's due to the fact that the control expects bitmap information, not an OLE object. The article explains in more detail.
Q153238	"HOW TO: Use GetChunk and AppendChunk Methods of RDO Object." This article describes how to interact with Binary Large Objects (BLOBs) with certain RDO data sources, such as Microsoft SQL Server.

Steps

Open and run PicLoad.VBP. You'll see a form appear, similar to the one displayed in Figure 5.7. Click the <u>L</u>oad Picture button, and a File Open common dialog appears. Select a bitmap file, and click the Open button. That bitmap now displays in the center of the form, and it is added to the database. Move forward, then back, with the data control and the graphic reappears, loaded from the database.

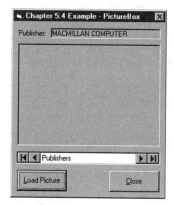

Figure 5.7. The saving graphics form at startup.

1. Create a new project called PicLoad.VBP. Create the objects and properties listed in Table 5.8, and save the form as PicLoad.FRM.

Table 5.8. Objects and properties for the Picture Load form.

OBJECT	PROPERTY	SETTING
Form	Name	Form1
	Caption	"Chapter 5.4 Example"
Data	Name	dtaData
	Caption	"Publishers"
	RecordSource	"Publishers"
Label	Name	lblPublishers
	Caption	"Publisher: "
Label	Name	lblPublisherName
	Caption	" "
	BorderStyle	1 - Fixed Single

continued on next page

continued from previous page

OBJECT	PROPERTY	SETTING
	DataSource	dtaData
	DataField	"Name"
PictureBox	Name	picPicture
	DataSource	dtaData
	DataField	"Logo"
CommandButton	Name	cmdLoad
	Caption	"&Load Picture"
CommandButton	Name	cmdClose
	Caption	"&Close"
	Cancel	True
CommonDialog	Name	cdlPicture
	Filter	"Bitmap files (*.bmp)¦*.bmp¦JPEG files (*.jpg, *.jpeg)¦*.jpg;*.jpeg¦GIF Files (*.gif)¦*.gif¦All Files (*.*)¦*.*"
	DefaultExt	"BMP"
	Flags	&H1000

2. Add the following code to the declarations section of **Form1**:

```
Option Explicit

Const BIBLIO_PATH = _
     "C:\Program Files\Microsoft Visual Studio\VB6\Biblio.MDB"
```

3. Add the following subroutine to **Form1**. The **CheckForLogoField** subroutine checks our beloved BIBLIO.MDB and adds a new field to the Publishers table, called **Logo**. Our graphics loading and saving will be done from and to that field when run.

```
Private Sub CheckForLogoField()
    Dim dbfTemp As Database, tdfTemp As TableDef, fldTemp As Field
    Dim blnLogoFieldExists As Boolean

    On Error GoTo BadCheck
        Set dbfTemp = Workspaces(0).OpenDatabase(BIBLIO_PATH)
        For Each tdfTemp In dbfTemp.TableDefs
            If tdfTemp.Name = "Publishers" Then
                For Each fldTemp In tdfTemp.Fields
                    If fldTemp.Name = "Logo" Then
                        blnLogoFieldExists = True
                        Exit For
                    End If
                Next
                Exit For
            End If
        Next
```

```
            If blnLogoFieldExists = False Then
                If tdfTemp.Updatable Then
                    Set fldTemp = New Field
                    With fldTemp
                        .Name = "Logo"
                        .Type = dbLongBinary
                    End With
                    tdfTemp.Fields.Append fldTemp
                Else
                    MsgBox "The database needs to be updated " & _
                            to Jet 3.0 format. " & _
                           "See How-To 5.7 for more information.", " & _
                            vbExclamation
                End If
            End If
        On Error GoTo 0
    Exit Sub

BadCheck:
    MsgBox Err.Description, vbExclamation
    End
End Sub
```

4. Add the following code to the Load event of Form1. The form will, when
loading, check the BIBLIO.MDB database for the existence of our graphics
field via the CheckForLogoField subroutine, constructed in the preceding
step.

```
Private Sub Form_Load()
    dtaData.DatabaseName = BIBLIO_PATH
    CheckForLogoField
End Sub
```

5. Add the following code to the Click event of cmdLoad. The Load Picture
button uses the CommonDialog control cdlPicture to enable the user to
select a graphics file to load into the database. When a file is selected, the
LoadPicture method is used to copy the information from the file to the
PictureBox control, picPicture. Because picPicture is data-bound, the
database field Logo now contains that graphics information. When the
data control is moved to a different record, that information is committed
to the database.

```
Private Sub cmdLoad_Click()
    On Error GoTo CancelLoad
        cdlPicture.ShowOpen
        On Error GoTo BadLoad
            picPicture = LoadPicture(cdlPicture.filename)
        On Error GoTo 0
    On Error GoTo 0
Exit Sub

CancelLoad:
    If Err.Number <> cdlCancel Then
```

continued on next page

continued from previous page

```
                MsgBox Err.Description, vbExclamation
        Else
            Exit Sub
        End If

    BadLoad:
        MsgBox Err.Description, vbExclamation
        Exit Sub
    End Sub
```

6. Add the following code to the **Click** event of **cmdClose**:

```
Private Sub cmdClose_Click()
    End
End Sub
```

How It Works

When **Form1** loads, it sets up the **dtaData** data control, using the **BIBLIO_PATH** constant to set the **DatabaseName** property and point it at BIBLIO.MDB. Then, using the **CheckForLogoField** routine, it confirms that the **[Logo]** field exists in the [Publishers] table; if the **[Logo]** field does not exist, it adds the field. Because the **PictureBox** control is bound to the data control, all aspects of displaying the data from the **[Logo]** field are handled as any other bound control, including field updates. The **cmdLoad** button allows new data to be added to the field using the **LoadPicture** method. Because the new data is added to the bound control, the loaded picture is saved to the database and is automatically displayed when the record is again shown.

Comments

The method previously detailed is quick to implement and makes ensuring security easy. The data stored in the **Logo** field is stored as raw binary data; as such, it's not recognized as an OLE object and is not easily edited. This is also the primary drawback to this method, making it less portable (not easily used by other applications). This method does conserve space, because the OLE object requires other information stored with it to describe what it is, how it can be processed, and so on. But for sheer flexibility, the OLE object approach is superior, and the articles mentioned in Table 5.8 should be reviewed. Be warned, however, that the information covered in those articles is advanced and should be reviewed only when you are confident in your understanding of the technique demonstrated in this How-To.

COMPLEXITY
INTERMEDIATE

5.5 How do I...
Make sure that an operation involving multiple tables is not left partially completed?

Question

I have an operation that requires that several tables be updated. Because of the nature of the operation, I want all the tables to be updated—or, if an error occurs, none of the tables to be updated. How can I ensure that only complete operations are applied to my database?

Technique

In database parlance, a *transaction* is a single logical operation that can involve multiple physical operations. Take, for example, a simple transaction in a banking environment, one in which money is withdrawn from a checking account and deposited to a savings account. If the money is withdrawn from the checking account but not applied to the savings account, the depositor will be unhappy. If the money is deposited to the savings account but never withdrawn from the checking account, the bank will be equally unhappy.

Various things might go wrong to cause the update to either account to fail. There might be a power failure or an error in the program. In a multiuser environment, the table representing one of the accounts might be locked by another user. Because it is important that both accounts be updated—or that neither account be updated—there needs to be some way to ensure that if any part of the transaction fails, the entire transaction is abandoned.

To tell Visual Basic and the Jet database engine to enforce transaction integrity, you enclose (or "wrap") all the program code implementing the transaction between two statements. The statement `BeginTrans` tells the database engine, "The transaction starts here. From here on, don't actually update the database. Make sure that it's possible to perform every operation I specify, but instead of actually changing the database, write the changes to a memory buffer." The statement `CommitTrans` tells the engine, "There have been no errors since the last `BeginTrans`, and this is the end of the transaction. Go ahead and write the changes to the database." The process of "making the changes permanent" is known as *committing* the transaction.

You can cancel the transaction in one of two ways. One method is to close the `Workspace` object without executing the `CommitTrans` statement—that automatically cancels the transaction. Another way, the preferred way, is to execute a **Rollback** statement. **Rollback** simply tells the database engine, "Cancel the transaction." Upon calling **Rollback**, the database is set back to the untouched state it was in before the transaction occurred.

The normal way to use these statements is to turn on error trapping before executing the **BeginTrans** statement. Wrap the operations that implement the transaction between a **BeginTrans...CommitTrans** pair. If an error occurs, execute the **Rollback** statement as part of your error routine.

Here's an example. Assume that **WithdrawFromChecking** is a subroutine that withdraws funds from a checking account, and that **DepositToSaving** deposits funds to a savings account. Both take two arguments: the account number and the amount.

```
Sub CheckingToSaving(strAccountNumber as String, curAmount as Currency)
    On Error Goto CheckingToSavingError
    BeginTrans
            WithdrawFromChecking strAccountNumber, curAmount
            DepositToSaving strAccountNumber, curAmount
    CommitTrans
    Exit Sub
CheckingToSavingError:
    Rollback
    MsgBox Err.Description, vbExclamation
    Exit Sub
End Sub
```

If an error occurs in either the **WithdrawFromChecking** or the **DepositToSaving** routine, the error trapping causes execution to branch to the **CheckingToSavingError** label. The code there executes the **Rollback** statement to terminate the transaction, displays an error message, and then exits from the subroutine. You can, of course, implement more sophisticated error handling, but the principle illustrated is the same—in the error routine, cancel the pending transaction with a **Rollback**.

Steps

Open and run the project TRANSACT.VBP. The form shown in Figure 5.8 appears. Enter the following record:

```
Author:        Heyman, Bill          [type this in as a new entry]
Title:         Visual Basic 6.0 Database How-To
Publisher:     Sams  [select from the list]
ISBN:          0-0000000-0-0          [not the actual ISBN!]
Year Published:                       1998
```

Click Save. The record is saved and the form is cleared, ready for another entry. Enter the same data again, this time choosing the author's name from the author list. Be sure to enter exactly the same ISBN. Click Save, and an error message should appear. The ISBN number is the primary key of the Titles table, and you cannot save two records with identical primary keys. Because this application uses the transaction protection features of the Jet engine and the error occurred within the transaction, no changes were made to the database.

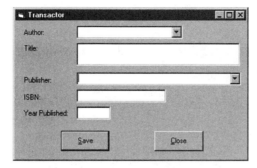

Figure 5.8. The Transactor form on startup.

1. Create a new project called Transact.VBP. Use **Form1** to create the objects and properties listed in Table 5.9, and save the form as TRANSACT.FRM.

Table 5.9. Objects and properties for the Transactor form.

OBJECT	PROPERTY	SETTING
Form	Name	Form1
	Caption	"Chapter 5.5 Example"
ComboBox	Name	cboAuthor
	Sorted	True
ComboBox	Name	cboPublisher
	Sorted	True
TextBox	Name	txtYearPublished
	Text	""
TextBox	Name	txtISBN
	Text	""
TextBox	Name	txtTitle
	Text	""
CommandButton	Name	cmdSave
	Caption	"&Save"
	Default	True
CommandButton	Name	cmdClose
	Cancel	True
	Caption	"&Close"

continued on next page

continued from previous page

OBJECT	PROPERTY	SETTING
Label	Name	lblTransact
	Index	0
	Caption	"Author:"
Label	Name	lblTransact
	Index	1
	Caption	"Title:"
Label	Name	lblTransact
	Index	2
	Caption	"Publisher:"
Label	Name	lblTransact
	Index	3
	Caption	"ISBN:"
Label	Name	lblTransact
	Index	4
	Caption	"Year Published:"

2. Add the following code to the declarations section of **Form1**:

```
Option Explicit

Const BIBLIO_PATH = "C:\Program Files\Microsoft Visual
Studio\VB6\Biblio.MDB"

Const AUTHOR_LIST = 1
Const PUBLISHER_LIST = 2
Private blnFormIsDirty As Boolean
Private blnRefillAuthorList As Boolean
Private blnRefillPublisherList As Boolean
```

3. Enter the following code as the **Load** event of **Form1**. The event makes use of the **FillList** subroutine, explained in the next step, to populate the Authors and Publishers combo boxes. It then sets the **blnFormIsDirty** variable to **False**, meaning that no data has yet been changed in the form.

```
Private Sub Form_Load()
    FillList AUTHOR_LIST: FillList PUBLISHER_LIST
    blnFormIsDirty = False
End Sub
```

4. Create the **FillList** subroutine in **Form1** with the following code. This subroutine, depending on the list type, retrieves a list of authors or publishers and loads them into their respective combo boxes.

```
Sub FillList(intListType As Integer)
    Dim cboTemp As ComboBox
    Dim dbfTemp As Database, recTemp As Recordset

    On Error GoTo FillListError

    Set dbfTemp = DBEngine.Workspaces(0).OpenDatabase(BIBLIO_PATH)

    Select Case intListType
        Case AUTHOR_LIST
            Set cboTemp = cboAuthor
            Set recTemp = dbfTemp.OpenRecordset( _
                "SELECT [Au_ID], " & _
                "[Author] FROM [Authors]")
        Case PUBLISHER_LIST
            Set cboTemp = cboPublisher
            Set recTemp = dbfTemp.OpenRecordset( _
                "SELECT [PubID], " & _
                "[Name] FROM [Publishers]")
    End Select

    cboTemp.Clear

    If recTemp.RecordCount Then
        recTemp.MoveFirst
        Do
            cboTemp.AddItem recTemp.Fields(1)
            cboTemp.ItemData(cboTemp.NewIndex) = recTemp.Fields(0)
            recTemp.MoveNext
        Loop Until recTemp.EOF
    End If
Exit Sub

FillListError:
    Dim strErrMsg As String

    strErrMsg = "Error while filling " & _
        IIf(intListType = AUTHOR_LIST, "Author", "Publisher") & _
                        " list."
    strErrMsg = strErrMsg & vbCr & Err.Number & " - " & _
            Err.Description

    MsgBox strErrMsg, vbCritical
    End
End Sub
```

5. Create the SaveRecord function in Form1 with the following code.
SaveRecord creates a transaction by wrapping a series of database-
updating statements between BeginTrans and CommitTrans statements. If
an error occurs anywhere within the transaction, the SaveError error-
handling routine is called. SaveError uses a Rollback statement to cancel
the transaction and then informs the user of the specific error.

```
Function SaveRecord() As Boolean
     Dim lngAuthorID As Long, lngPublisherID As Long
     Dim dbfTemp As Database, recTemp As Recordset

   On Error GoTo SaveError
       Workspaces(0).BeginTrans

       If cboAuthor.ListIndex = -1 Then
           If cboAuthor.Text = "" Then Error 32767
1000       lngAuthorID = CreateAuthor(cboAuthor.Text)
           blnRefillAuthorList = True
       Else
           lngAuthorID = cboAuthor.ItemData(cboAuthor.ListIndex)
       End If

       If cboPublisher.ListIndex = -1 Then
           If cboPublisher.Text = "" Then Error 32766
1050       lngPublisherID = CreatePublisher(cboPublisher.Text)
           blnRefillPublisherList = True
       Else
           lngPublisherID = _
               cboPublisher.ItemData(cboPublisher.ListIndex)
       End If

       If txtTitle <> "" And txtISBN <> "" Then
           Set dbfTemp = _
               DBEngine.Workspaces(0).OpenDatabase(BIBLIO_PATH)

1100       Set recTemp = dbfTemp.OpenRecordset( _
               "Titles", dbOpenTable)
           With recTemp
               .AddNew
               ![PubID] = lngPublisherID
               ![ISBN] = txtISBN
               ![Title] = txtTitle
               ![Year Published] = txtYearPublished
               .Update
           End With

1150       Set recTemp = dbfTemp.OpenRecordset( _
                       "Title Author", dbOpenTable)
           With recTemp
               .AddNew
               ![Au_ID] = lngAuthorID
               ![ISBN] = txtISBN
               .Update
           End With
       Else
           If txtTitle = "" Then Error 32765 Else Error 32764
       End If

       Workspaces(0).CommitTrans

   On Error GoTo SaveErrorNoRollback
       ClearForm
```

```
                blnFormIsDirty = False
                SaveRecord = True
            On Error GoTo 0
        Exit Function

    SaveError:
        Dim strErrMsg As String

        Workspaces(0).Rollback

        Select Case Err
            Case 32767
                strErrMsg = "You have not entered an author name"
            Case 32766
                strErrMsg = "You have not entered a publisher name"
            Case 32765
                strErrMsg = "You have not entered a title"
            Case 32764
                strErrMsg = "You have not entered an ISBN number"
            Case Else
                Select Case Erl
                    Case 1000
                        strErrMsg = "Error " & Err.Number & _
                                    " (" & Err.Description & _
                                "} encountered creating new Authors " & _
                                "record."
                    Case 1050
                        strErrMsg = "Error " & Err.Number & _
                                    " (" & Err.Description & _
                                "} encountered creating new Publishers " _
                                "& record."
                    Case 1100
                        strErrMsg = "Error " & Err.Number & _
                                    " (" & Err.Description & _
                                "} encountered creating new Titles " & _
                                "record."
                    Case 1150
                        strErrMsg = "Error " & Err.Number _
                                    & " (" & Err.Description & _
                                "} encountered creating new Title Author " _
                                "& record."
                    Case Else
                        strErrMsg = Err.Description
                End Select
        End Select
        MsgBox strErrMsg, vbExclamation

        SaveRecord = False
    Exit Function

    SaveErrorNoRollback:
        MsgBox Err.Description, vbExclamation
        Resume Next
    End Function
```

Errors are generated by Visual Basic (or the Jet engine) for various reasons. To enable the display of an informative error message, line numbers are used within the transaction, and the error-handling routine uses these line numbers to tell the user where the error occurred.

The function also employs user-generated errors—the `Error` statement followed by an error number in the 32000 range. User-handler errors are set when the application detects that the user has entered data the application "knows" is incorrect—for example, if the user has failed to enter an author. These user errors have the same effect as the Visual Basic-generated errors: They call the error handler, which cancels the transaction. The error handler uses the user error number to display an informative error message; this lets the user correct the error and try to save again.

After `CommitTrans` has been executed, a different error routine must be used, because the original error routine contains a `Rollback` statement. The `CommitTrans` closes the pending transaction, and trying to execute a `Rollback` when there is no pending transaction will cause an error.

6. Enter the following code in `Form1` as the `CreateAuthor` function. `CreateAuthor` creates a new record in the Authors table and returns the `Au_ID` assigned to the new author.

```
Function CreateAuthor(strAuthorName As String) As Long
    Dim dbfTemp As Database, recTemp As Recordset

    Set dbfTemp = DBEngine.Workspaces(0).OpenDatabase(BIBLIO_PATH)

    Set recTemp = dbfTemp.OpenRecordset("Authors", dbOpenTable)
    With recTemp
        .AddNew
        ![Author] = strAuthorName
        .Update
        .Bookmark = .LastModified
    End With

    CreateAuthor = recTemp![Au_ID]
End Function
```

7. Enter the following code in `Form1` as the `CreatePublisher` function. `CreatePublisher` creates a new record in the Publishers table and returns the `PubID` assigned to the new publisher.

```
Function CreatePublisher(strPublisherName As String) As Long
    Dim dbfTemp As Database, recTemp As Recordset
    Dim lngLastID As Long

    Set dbfTemp = DBEngine.Workspaces(0).OpenDatabase(BIBLIO_PATH)

    Set recTemp = dbfTemp.OpenRecordset("Publishers", dbOpenTable)
    With recTemp
```

```
            .Index = "PrimaryKey"
            .MoveLast
            lngLastID = ![PubID]
            .AddNew
            ![PubID] = lngLastID + 1
            ![Name] = strPublisherName
            .Update
        End With

        CreatePublisher = lngLastID + 1
    End Function
```

8. Enter the following code in **Form1** as the **ClearForm** subroutine. **ClearForm** clears the text and combo boxes on the form. If the previous record resulted in a new author or publisher being added, **ClearForm** refreshes the appropriate combo box to put the new author or publisher into the list.

```
Sub ClearForm()

    If blnRefillAuthorList Then
        FillList AUTHOR_LIST
        blnRefillAuthorList = False
    Else
        cboAuthor.ListIndex = -1
    End If

    If blnRefillPublisherList Then
        FillList PUBLISHER_LIST
        blnRefillPublisherList = False
    Else
        cboPublisher.ListIndex = -1
    End If

    ' Clear the text boxes.
    txtTitle = ""
    txtISBN = ""
    txtYearPublished = ""
End Sub
```

9. Enter the following code into **Form1** as the **Click** event of **cmdClose**. If the form has an unsaved record, the subroutine gives the user a chance to save the record or cancel the close event.

```
Private Sub cmdClose_Click()
    If blnFormIsDirty Then
        Select Case MsgBox("Do you want to save the current " & _
                record?", _
            vbQuestion + vbYesNoCancel)
            Case vbYes
                If SaveRecord() = False Then Exit Sub
            Case vbNo
                End
```

continued on next page

continued from previous page

```
                    Case vbCancel
                         Exit Sub
                End Select
        End If
        End
End Sub
```

10. Enter the following five subroutines into Form1 as the Change events for txtISBN, txtTitle, txtYearPublished, cboAuthor, and cboPublisher. Each of these event routines sets the blnFormIsDirty flag when the user types an entry into the control.

```
Private Sub txtISBN_Change()
    blnFormIsDirty = True
End Sub

Private Sub txtTitle_Change()
    blnFormIsDirty = True
End Sub

Private Sub txtYearPublished_Change()
    blnFormIsDirty = True
End Sub

Private Sub cboAuthor_Change()
    blnFormIsDirty = True
End Sub

Private Sub cboPublisher_Change()
    blnFormIsDirty = True
End Sub
```

11. Enter the following two subroutines into Form1. These subroutines set the blnFormIsDirty flag when the user changes the entry in one of the combo boxes by selecting an item from the list.

```
Private Sub cboAuthor_Click()
    If cboAuthor.ListIndex <> -1 Then blnFormIsDirty = True
End Sub

Private Sub cboPublisher_Click()
    If cboPublisher.ListIndex <> -1 Then blnFormIsDirty = True
End Sub
```

How It Works

When the user clicks Save, the cmdSave_Click event calls SaveRecord, which does most of the work. If the user has entered a new author or new publisher (instead of selecting an existing item from the author or publisher list), SaveRecord calls a function (CreateAuthor or CreatePublisher) to create the new record. It then saves the record. If an error occurs (either a Visual Basic error or a user-generated error), the error handler in `SaveRecord` rolls back the transaction.

Comment

The main use of transactions is to maintain integrity when you're updating more than one table as part of a single logical operation. You can also use `BeginTrans`, `CommitTrans`, and `Rollback` when you're performing multiple operations on a single table and you want to make sure that all the operations are performed as a unit.

Transactions can also speed up some database operations. Under normal conditions, every time you use the `Update` method, the Jet engine writes the changes to disk. Multiple small disk writes can significantly slow down an application. Executing a `BeginTrans` holds all the operations in memory until `CommitTrans` executes, which can noticeably improve execution time.

The transaction features described in this How-To work when you are using Microsoft Access database files and most of the other file types supported by the Jet engine. Some database types—Paradox is one example—do not support transactions. You can check whether the database supports transactions by reading the `Transactions` property of the database object:

```
Dim dbfTemp as Database
Dim blnSupportsTransactions as Boolean
...
blnSupportsTransactions = dbfTemp.Transactions
...
```

Using the transactions statements `BeginTrans`, `CommitTrans`, and `Rollback` with a database that does not support transactions does not generate an error—but you need to be aware that you won't get the transaction integrity protection these statements would normally provide.

COMPLEXITY
BEGINNING

5.6 How do I...
Compact a database or repair a corrupted database?

Question

I know that Microsoft Access provides the capability to make a database smaller by compacting it. Microsoft Access also enables me to repair a database that has been corrupted. How can I perform these operations from my Visual Basic program?

Technique

When you delete data (or database objects) from a Microsoft Access database file, the Jet engine does not automatically shrink the size of the file to recover the no-longer-needed space. If the user deletes a significant amount of data, the file size can grow very large, and include a lot of wasted space. You can use the `CompactDatabase` method of the `DBEngine` object to recover this space.

Occasionally, a database file becomes corrupted by a General Protection Fault, a power failure, a bug in the database engine, or some other cause. Most corrupted databases can be restored by the `RepairDatabase` method of the `DBEngine` object.

Steps

Open the project REPAIR.VBP and run it. The form shown in Figure 5.9 appears. Choose Compact a database and click OK. The application asks you to designate an existing database and to supply a new filename for the compacted version of the database. When you have done so, the application compacts the database and displays a message indicating completion.

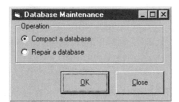

Figure 5.9. The Database Maintenance form on startup.

Choose Repair a database and click OK. The application asks you to designate a database to be repaired. When you have done so, the application repairs the database and displays a message indicating success.

1. Create a new project called Repair.VBP. Use `Form1` to create the objects and properties listed in Table 5.10, and save the form as Repair.FRM.

Table 5.10. Objects and properties for the Database Maintenance form.

OBJECT	PROPERTY	SETTING
Form	Name	Form1
	Caption	"Chapter 5.6 Example"
Frame	Name	grpOperation
	Caption	"Operation"
OptionButton	Name	optCompact

OBJECT	PROPERTY	SETTING
	Caption	"Compact a database"
OptionButton	Name	optRepair
	Caption	"Repair a database"
CommandButton	Name	cmdOK
	Caption	"OK"
	Default	True
CommandButton	Name	cmdClose
	Cancel	True
	Caption	"&Close"

2. Add the following code to the declarations section of **Form1**:

```
Option Explicit
```

3. Enter the following code into **Form1** as the **Click** event of **cmdOK**. The setting of optCompact determines whether the user wants to compact or repair the database. This procedure uses the Windows File Open common dialog box to get the name of the file to compact or repair. In the case of a compact operation, it then uses the File Save common dialog box to get the name of the output file. It then uses the DBEngine's **CompactDatabase** or **RepairDatabase** method to perform the operation.

```
Private Sub cmdOK_Click()
    Dim strInput As String, strOutput As String

    On Error GoTo OKError
        With cdlDatabase
            .DialogTitle = "Select File To " & _
                IIf(optCompact, "Compact", "Repair")
            .ShowOpen
        End With
        strInput = cdlDatabase.filename

        If optCompact Then
            With cdlDatabase
                .DialogTitle = "Repaired Filename"
                .filename = ""
                .ShowSave
            End With
            strOutput = cdlDatabase.filename
            Screen.MousePointer = vbHourglass
            DBEngine.CompactDatabase strInput, strOutput
            Screen.MousePointer = vbDefault
            MsgBox "Database " & strInput & _
                    " compacted to " & strOutput
        Else
            Screen.MousePointer = vbHourglass
```

continued on next page

continued from previous page

```
            DBEngine.RepairDatabase strInput
            Screen.MousePointer = vbDefault
            MsgBox "Repair of " & strInput & " successful."
        End If
    On Error GoTo 0
Exit Sub

OKError:
    Screen.MousePointer = vbDefault
    If Err <> 32755 Then MsgBox Err.Description
Exit Sub
End Sub
```

4. Enter the following into `Form1` as the `Click` event of `cmdClose`:

```
Private Sub cmdClose_Click()
    End
End Sub
```

How It Works

The `cmdOK` button supplies almost all the project's action. Depending on the selected option button, the `cmdOK_Click` event code first uses the `CommonDialog` control to retrieve the name of a valid Access database. After a name is returned, it issues either a `CompactDatabase` method or a `RepairDatabase` method, depending on the selected option button. If a `CompactDatabase` is required, the routine will again use the `CommonDialog` control to get the desired name for the compacted database. It has to do this because the `CompactDatabase` command cannot compact a database back into itself; instead, it rebuilds the database from the ground up, so to speak, into another Access database file. The `RepairDatabase` method, however, does not write to another database file and is instead called directly on the selected database.

Comments

It is strongly recommended that `CompactDatabase` be performed on Access databases regularly, because it reclaims wasted space and re-indexes tables to enable faster, more efficient use. `RepairDatabase`, on the other hand, should be used only when an Access database is indicated as corrupt. In Visual Basic, a trappable error is triggered when an Access database is corrupt, so automating this process is relatively easy. By setting up an `On Error` trap in your function and checking if `Err` is equal to 3049, you can make a call to the RepairDatabase method.

COMPLEXITY
INTERMEDIATE

5.7 How do I...
Use parameter queries stored in Microsoft Access databases?

Question

I'd like to use stored `QueryDef` objects to reduce the execution time for my program. But I need to change one or two values each time I run my SELECT query. How can I use stored queries with replaceable parameters from Visual Basic?

Technique

Microsoft Access provides the *parameter query* as a variation of the standard `SELECT` query. The definition of a parameter query specifies one or more *replaceable* parameters—values to be supplied each time the query executes. Each replaceable parameter is represented by a name, which is used much like a field name. The name can be any legal object name, provided that the name has not already been used as a field name in any of the tables in the query.

For example, you have a query that extracts information about customer accounts from several tables. Each time the query runs, it requires a value for the `[Customer Number]` field in the Customers table. If the name of the replaceable parameter was `CustNum`, the `WHERE` clause of the query would be this:

```
WHERE Customers.[Customer Number] = [CustNum]
```

When run from Microsoft Access, a parameter query pops up an input box for the user at runtime. The user types a value, and this value is used as the replaceable parameter. When you use a stored parameter query from Visual Basic, your code must provide the value for the replaceable parameter before you execute the query.

You provide the replaceable value through the `QueryDef` object. Each `QueryDef` object owns a `Parameters` collection, which consists of a set of `Parameter` objects, each with a name. When you assign a value to a `Parameter` object, the `QueryDef` object uses that as the replaceable value when you run the query.

Following is the full syntax for assigning a value to a `QueryDef` `Parameter` object (where `myQueryDef` is an object variable assigned to a `QueryDef` object and `CustNum` is the name of a `Parameter` object):

```
qdfTempQueryDef.Parameters("CustNum") = 141516
```

This can be abbreviated using the bang operator like so:

```
qdfTempQueryDef![CustNum] = 141516
```

The sequence for using a stored parameter query from your Visual Basic code, therefore, is this:

1. Declare the appropriate variables:

```
Dim dbfTemp as Database
Dim qdfTemp as QueryDef
Dim recTemp as Recordset
```

2. Set the **Database** and **QueryDef** variables to valid objects:

```
Set dbfTemp = DBEngine.Workspaces(0).OpenDatabase("ACCOUNTS.MDB")
Set qdfTemp = dbfTemp.OpenQueryDef("Customer Data")
```

3. Assign an appropriate value to each replaceable parameter of the **QueryDef** object. If the Customer Data QueryDef has two parameters, **CustNum** and **Start Date**, this would be your code:

```
qdfTemp![CustNum] = 124151
qdfTemp![Start Date] = #1/1/97#      ' the # signs delimit a date
```

4. Use the **OpenRecordset** method of the **QueryDef** object to create the recordset:

```
Set recTemp = qdfTemp.OpenRecordset()
```

Steps

Open and run the project ParameterQuery.VBP. The form shown in Figure 5.10 appears. Select a publisher and then click OK. Then the form shown in Figure 5.11 appears with the first record in BIBLIO.MDB belonging to that publisher. If the publisher has no titles in the database, the form is blank. Browse through the records by using the browse buttons. To select a different publisher, click the Publisher button.

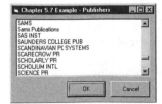

Figure 5.10. The project's Publisher Parameters form, showing publisher names.

Figure 5.11. The project's Publisher Titles form, showing publisher title information.

1. Create a new project called ParameterQuery.VBP. Rename **Form1** to **frmMain**. Then create the objects and properties listed in Table 5.11, and save the form as ParameterQuery.FRM.

Table 5.11. Objects and properties for the Query User form.

OBJECT	PROPERTY	SETTING
Form	Name	frmMain
	Caption	"Publisher Information"
Data	Name	dtaData
	Caption	"Publisher's Titles By Author"
TextBox	Name	txtPublisher
	DataSource	dtaData
	DataField	"Name"
TextBox	Name	txtYearPublished
	DataSource	dtaData
	DataField	"Year Published"
TextBox	Name	txtISBN
	DataSource	dtaData
	DataField	"ISBN"
TextBox	Name	txtTitle
	DataSource	dtaData
	DataField	"Title"
TextBox	Name	txtAuthor
	DataSource	dtaData
	DataField	"Author"

continued on next page

continued from previous page

OBJECT	PROPERTY	SETTING
Label	Name	lblQuery
	Index	0
	Caption	"Author:"
Label	Name	lblQuery
	Index	1
	Caption	"Title:"
Label	Name	lblQuery
	Index	2
	Caption	"ISBN:"
Label	Name	lblQuery
	Index	3
	Caption	"Published:"
Label	Name	lblQuery
	Index	4
	Caption	"by:"
CommandButton	Name	cmdPublisher
	Caption	"&Publisher"
CommandButton	Name	cmdClose
	Cancel	True
	Caption	"&Close"

2. Add a new form to the project. Name it `frmSelectPublisher`. Create the objects and properties listed in Table 5.12, and save the form as Publishers.FRM.

Table 5.12. Objects and properties for the Query User form.

OBJECT	PROPERTY	SETTING
Form	Name	frmSelectPublisher
	Caption	"Chapter 5.7 Example - Publishers"
ListBox	Name	lstPublishers
CommandButton	Name	cmdOK
	Caption	"&OK"
	Default	True
CommandButton	Name	cmdCancel
	Cancel	True
	Caption	"&Cancel"

3. Enter the following code into the declarations section of `frmMain`:

```
Option Explicit

'NOTE:  The constant does NOT include the database name this time.
Const BIBLIO_PATH = "C:\Program Files\Microsoft Visual Studio\VB6"
'Because the variable is public (exposed for use by other
'objects), the naming conventions for variables do not apply
'here - treat as a property.
Public SelectedPubID As Integer
```

4. Enter the following code into `frmMain` as its `Load` event. The `CheckDatabaseVersion` routine, called in this event, ensures that the BIBLIO.MDB database is Jet 3.0 compatible; if the database was created with an earlier version of Access, there could be some difficulties.

```
Private Sub Form_Load()
    'Older versions of BIBLIO.MDB must be converted to the Jet 3.0
    'format before a parameter query can be saved to it.
    CheckDatabaseVersion
    dtaData.DatabaseName = BIBLIO_PATH & "\Biblio.MDB"
    cmdPublisher_Click
End Sub
```

5. Enter the following code into `frmMain` as the `Click` event for `cmdPublisher`. If a publisher's ID has been selected, the `RunQuery` subroutine is called. If not, the form is still displayed, but with a different title and no data.

```
Private Sub cmdPublisher_Click()
    frmSelectPublisher.Show vbModal

    If SelectedPubID > 0 Then
        RunQuery
    Else
        frmMain.Caption = "Chapter 5.7 Example - No Titles"
    End If
End Sub
```

6. Enter the following code into `frmMain` as the `CheckDatabaseVersion` subroutine. This subroutine checks the version of the Access database to ensure that it's compatible with Jet 3.0. It does so by creating a `Database` object and then checking the `Version` property, which supplies a formatted string indicating the major and minor number of the database version. If less than 3.0, the program uses the `CompactDatabase` method to convert the database to Jet 3.0 format, backing it up in the process, just in case.

```
Private Sub CheckDatabaseVersion()
    Dim dbfTemp As Database, sngVersion As Single

    Set dbfTemp = Workspaces(0).OpenDatabase(BIBLIO_PATH & _
              "\Biblio.MDB")
    'If the database's Version property is less than 3.0, then it
    'needs to be converted before we can save a parameter query to
    'it from 32-bit Visual Basic.
    sngVersion = Val(dbfTemp.Version)
    dbfTemp.Close: DBEngine.Idle dbFreeLocks

    If Val(sngVersion) < 3 Then
        'First, we'll back up the old database
        FileCopy BIBLIO_PATH & "\Biblio.MDB", BIBLIO_PATH & _
              "\BiblioBackup.MDB"
        'Then, we'll use the CompactDatabase method to convert it
        'to the version 3.0 format
        CompactDatabase BIBLIO_PATH & "\Biblio.MDB", _
            BIBLIO_PATH & "\BiblioNew.MDB", , dbVersion30
        'Next, we'll delete the old database after we're sure the
        'new one exists.
        If Len(Dir("BiblioNew.MDB")) Then Kill BIBLIO_PATH & _
          "\Biblio.MDB"
        'Finally, we'll rename the new database to the old name,
        '"Biblio.MDB".
        If Len(Dir(BIBLIO_PATH)) = 0 Then
            Name BIBLIO_PATH & "\BiblioNew.MDB" As BIBLIO_PATH & _
                "\Biblio.MDB"
        End If
    End If
End Sub
```

7. Enter the following code into frmMain as the RunQuery subroutine. This subroutine searches for the query definition [Publisher's Titles By Author]. If it doesn't find what it's seeking, it creates the query and saves that query in BIBLIO.MDB. It next inserts the PubID code of the selected publisher into the Publisher parameter of the query definition. Then it runs the query and uses DisplayRecord to display the data.

```
Sub RunQuery()
    Dim dbfTemp As Database, recTemp As Recordset
    Dim qdfTemp As QueryDef
    Dim strSQL As String
    Dim blnFoundQuery As Boolean

    On Error GoTo QueryError
        Set dbfTemp = Workspaces(0).OpenDatabase(BIBLIO_PATH & _
            "\Biblio.MDB")
        For Each qdfTemp In dbfTemp.QueryDefs
            If qdfTemp.Name = "Publisher's Titles By Author" Then
                blnFoundQuery = True
                Exit For
```

```
                    End If
            Next

            If blnFoundQuery = False Then
                strSQL = "PARAMETERS pintPubID Long; " & _
                    "SELECT Authors.Author, Titles.Title, " & _
                        "Titles.ISBN, " & _
                    "Titles.[Year Published], Publishers.Name " & _
                    "FROM (Publishers INNER JOIN Titles ON "
                strSQL = strSQL & "Publishers.PubID = " _
                        "Titles.PubID) " & _
                        "INNER JOIN " & _
                    "(Authors INNER JOIN [Title Author] ON " & _
                    "Authors.Au_ID = [Title Author].Au_ID) ON " & _
                    "Titles.ISBN = [Title Author].ISBN WHERE " & _
                        "Publishers.PubID " & _
                    "= pintPubID ORDER by Authors.Author;"
                Set qdfTemp = dbfTemp.CreateQueryDef( _
                    "Publisher's Titles By " & _
                    "Author", strSQL)
            Else
                Set qdfTemp = dbfTemp.QueryDefs( _
                            "Publisher's Titles By Author")
            End If

            qdfTemp.Parameters![pintPubID] = SelectedPubID

            Set dtaData.Recordset = qdfTemp.OpenRecordset()
            If dtaData.Recordset.RecordCount > 0 Then
                frmMain.Caption = "Chapter 5.7 Example - " & _
                    Str$(dtaData.Recordset.RecordCount) & _
                    IIf(dtaData.Recordset.RecordCount = 1, _
                        " Title", " Titles")
            Else
                frmMain.Caption = frmMain.Caption = "Chapter 5.7 _
                                Example - No Titles"
            End If
        On Error GoTo 0
    Exit Sub

    QueryError:
        MsgBox Err.Description, vbExclamation
    Exit Sub
    End Sub
```

8. Enter the following code into **frmMain** as the **Click** event of **cmdClose**:

```
Private Sub cmdClose_Click()
    End
End Sub
```

9. Now that **frmMain** is complete, let's move on to **frmSelectPublisher**. Add the following code to its declarations section:

```
Option Explicit
```

10. Enter the following code as the Load event of frmSelectPublisher:

```
Private Sub Form_Load()
    Dim dbfTemp As Database, recTemp As Recordset
    Dim strSQL As String

    On Error GoTo LoadError
        Set dbfTemp = Workspaces(0).OpenDatabase(BIBLIO_PATH)
        strSQL = "SELECT [PubID], [Company Name] FROM " & _
                "[Publishers]"
        Set recTemp = dbfTemp.OpenRecordset(strSQL)

        If recTemp.RecordCount Then
            recTemp.MoveFirst
            Do Until recTemp.EOF
                If Not IsNull(recTemp![Company Name]) Then
                    lstPublishers.AddItem recTemp![Company Name]
                Else
                    lstPublishers.AddItem ""
                End If
                lstPublishers.ItemData(lstPublishers.NewIndex) = _
                            recTemp![PubID]
                recTemp.MoveNext
            Loop
        Else
            MsgBox "There are no publishers in the database.", _
                vbCritical
            End
        End If
    On Error GoTo 0
Exit Sub

LoadError:
    MsgBox Err.Description, vbCritical
    End
End Sub
```

11. Enter the following code into frmSelectPublisher as the Click event of cmdOK. This routine gets the PubID of the selected publisher from the list box ItemData property, puts that value into the public variable SelectedPubID, and then hides the form.

```
If lstPublishers.ListIndex > -1 Then
        frmMain.SelectedPubID = _
                lstPublishers.ItemData(lstPublishers.ListIndex)
        Me.Hide
    Else
        MsgBox "You have not selected a publisher", vbExclamation
    End If
End Sub
```

12. Enter the following code into frmSelectPublisher as the DblClick event of lstPublishers:

```
Private Sub lstPublishers_DblClick()
    cmdOK_Click
End Sub
```

13. Enter the following code into frmSelectPublisher as the Click event of cmdCancel. This routine puts the value **0** into the public variable SelectedPubID and then hides the form.

```
Private Sub cmdCancel_Click()
    frmMain.SelectedPubID = 0
    Hide
End Sub
```

How It Works

When frmMain loads, it immediately generates a Click event for cmdPublisher to display the Select Publisher form. When the user makes a selection from the publisher list and clicks OK, the PubID of the selected publisher is used to set the Public variable SelectedPubID. The value of SelectedPubID is then used as the parameter passed to the [Publisher's Titles by Author] query definition. After its parameter has been set, the QueryDef is used to create the recordset of title information.

Comments

The parameter query allows for the flexibility of dynamically built SQL statements, but with the optimized speed of static SQL. One of the other benefits to using a parameter query is the Requery method, which enables you to re-execute a parameter query with different values. Access will actually reuse the existing connection and be able to run the query faster. Also, the optimization engine built into Jet works best on static SQL (that is, SQL stored in the database, as opposed to the SQL statements stored in code), so you can get even more benefit from the use of a parameter query that is saved to a Microsoft Access database. For a similar example on the use of a parameter query, How-To 3.5 is another good reference, especially with the use of the Requery method.

CONNECTING TO AN ODBC SERVER

6

CONNECTING TO AN ODBC SERVER

How do I...

6.1 Use the ODBC Administrator to maintain data sources?

6.2 Use ODBC with the Visual Basic Data control?

6.3 Create an ODBC-accessible data source by using RegisterDatabase**?**

6.4 Prevent the login dialog box from being displayed when I open an ODBC database?

6.5 Determine what services an ODBC server provides?

6.6 Use ODBCDirect to connect to database servers?

The Open Database Connectivity (ODBC) standard has made accessing disparate database formats much easier than in older versions of Visual Basic. Starting with version 3.0, Visual Basic data access methods and properties include built-in support for ODBC data sources. This means you can use Visual Basic and ODBC together, either through the Jet database engine that comes with Visual Basic or through direct calls to the ODBC Application Programming Interface (API) or by using both together.

When using Visual Basic to completely handle the connection to the ODBC system, just make a few changes to the Visual Basic `OpenDatabase` method. This is the syntax of the statement:

```
Set database = workspace.OpenDatabase(dbname[, exclusive[, read-only[, _
    source]]])
```

The source argument is the main difference when you're using ODBC. In the How-To's throughout this chapter, you'll see how an ODBC connect string is used in the source to specify to which ODBC data source to connect. If you're not sure which data source you want to use, just make the source argument "ODBC" and Visual Basic will team up with ODBC and automatically present a list of the available data sources. Few things in Visual Basic are as straightforward as this.

You can perform many ODBC tasks—including running Structured Query Language (SQL) queries, retrieving results, looping through recordsets, and sending pass-through queries—in Visual Basic without getting any more involved in ODBC than making this change to the `OpenDatabase` method. Essentially, if Visual Basic has a data access method or property to do what you want, you can almost always use Visual Basic directly without knowing anything about ODBC beyond the existence of the data source you want to use.

ODBC can add a whole new dimension to your application's database access, going far beyond the functionality of Visual Basic's data access function. You can retrieve a wealth of information about a database and manipulate it to your heart's—or client's—content.

Through the How-To's in this chapter, you'll get the details of using straight Visual Basic to access the ODBC API, using the ODBC API directly and bypassing Visual Basic, and combining the two techniques to get the job done.

The guiding philosophy of this chapter is that if there is a way to do it in Visual Basic, that's the way it should be done—unless there is a good reason not to do it that way. The main reason for going straight to the ODBC API is when Visual Basic can't perform the particular task by itself. But there are a few other reasons you'll see along the way.

Using Visual Basic and ODBC Together

If you are going to do any serious work with ODBC, get a copy of *Microsoft ODBC 3.0 Programmer's Reference and SDK Guide*, published by Microsoft Press. The Software Development Kit (SDK) has all the detailed information you need and a list of all the ODBC functions. This section covers most of the details you'll need in order to use ODBC with Visual Basic.

The ODBC system has four components. Figure 6.1 shows the relationship of these four elements in a Visual Basic ODBC application.

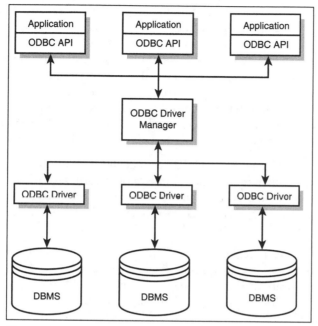

Figure 6.1. An overview of ODBC architecture.

✔ *Application:* This is your application program. Whether it makes calls through the Visual Basic data access methods and properties or makes direct calls to the ODBC API, the application sends SQL statements to ODBC and receives data as the results of those statements.

✔ *ODBC Driver Manager:* The ODBC Driver Manager is the layer of the ODBC system that sits between your application and the database driver. Some of the ODBC API calls are handled directly by the Driver Manager, but many are passed on to the driver. For some functions, the Driver Manager passes the call on to the driver if the function is implemented in the driver; if not, the Driver Manager handles the task itself.

✔ *Driver:* An ODBC driver is software, virtually always a dynamic link library (DLL), that handles the connection between the ODBC Driver Manager and the database server. A driver is usually written by the manufacturer of a database system, but many drivers are available from third parties.

✔ *Data source:* A data source is an installed database server that ODBC has associated with a particular ODBC driver and a specific database with its location on your local hard drive or network.

Following are a few other terms you'll encounter when reading about the ODBC system:

✔ *Connect string:* To make a connection to an ODBC data source, the ODBC system needs certain information. The first piece of information it always needs is the *data source name* (DSN). This is the descriptive name ODBC uses to keep track of installed databases, and it is used any time you are presented with a list of data sources. The connect string varies by database, driver, and network setup, but a typical string would be the data source name, user ID, password, and authorization string. The particular database server might have other required and optional items. In How-To 6.5, you'll learn exactly what connect string a database requires.

✔ *Translator:* When you've worked with ODBC for a while, you'll probably encounter the term *translator*. A translator translates data flowing through the ODBC system. A common use is to translate between different character sets, such as between ASCII and EBCDIC on IBM mainframes and minis.

✔ *ODBC input and output buffers:* ODBC requires the use of input and output buffers to hold data it passes back and forth between the database and your application. The good news is that in most cases in Visual Basic, you won't be calling any ODBC API functions directly that need to have a buffer allocated. More good news is that a `NULL` pointer to a buffer sometimes works. The really good news is that Visual Basic, through the Jet engine, manages all this for you most of the time.

ODBC Handles

Before making any direct calls to functions in the ODBC API, you must allocate memory and receive a handle from ODBC for the particular operation. All this means is that ODBC is setting aside a small chunk of memory, through its DLL, to hold information about some aspect of the ODBC system. The handle is essentially a pointer in the Windows environment. As usual, if you are using ODBC through Visual Basic methods only, without direct calls to the ODBC API, you don't need to know or worry about handles at all.

Three handles are necessary for calls to the different ODBC functions:

✔ *Environment handle* (`hEnv`): Your application needs to allocate and use one environment handle. The environment handle manages the overall connection between your application and ODBC.

✔ *Connection handle* (`hDbc`): For each connection you make to a database, you must allocate and use one connection handle. Your application can have virtually any number of connection handles at any given time, and many databases can even have multiple simultaneous handles to a single data source.

✔ *Statement handle* (hStmt): For each SQL statement you send to a database, you must allocate and use a statement handle. The statement handle is how ODBC keeps straight what statement you are referring to for information. You can also have multiple statement handles active at any given time.

All ODBC handles must be released before terminating your application. Otherwise, there is no guarantee that the allocated memory will be released at the end of the application, and that is just not good Windows program manners! Eventually, the program will "leak" enough memory to cause performance problems with Windows or even disrupt the operating system entirely.

The handles form a hierarchy. All connection handles in your application are associated with a single environment handle, and all statement handles are associated with one and only one connection handle. In general, all the lower-level handles in the hierarchy must be freed before the next handle in the hierarchy is freed. All the handles can be released and then reused.

ODBC API Conformance Levels

In response to the wide variety of database system capabilities available on every hardware and software platform, ODBC breaks its function list into three levels of conformance. A driver must support, at minimum, the Core-level conformance to be considered an ODBC driver. ODBC also specifies SQL grammar conformance levels, which are not directly related to the API conformance level, as listed here:

✔ *Core:* The Core level is the minimum API conformance level a driver and database must support. This level corresponds to the X/Open and SQL Access Group Call Level Interface specification of 1992.

✔ *Level 1:* Conformance Level 1 adds significant functionality to ODBC's capabilities. All drivers used with Visual Basic's data access object must be Level 1 compliant because Visual Basic assumes that certain services are available for it to use with the database. You can use a Core-level driver, however, if you limit the use of ODBC strictly to direct Level 1 ODBC API calls.

✔ *Level 2:* Conformance Level 2 is the highest conformance level. It adds another large jump in functionality.

It is important to understand that just because a driver calls itself, say, a Level 1 ODBC driver doesn't necessarily mean that it supports *all* the options of *every* function at that level. The amount of support is usually tied directly to the capabilities of the underlying database, its limitations, and how aggressively a driver manufacturer is in building capabilities into its driver.

WARNING

No independent body certifies drivers as meeting the requirements of an ODBC conformance level. The developer of each driver makes the conformance claim. Buyer beware!

The ODBC API: Visual Basic Declare Statements and ODBC Constants

Because ODBC is implemented in Windows as a DLL, you must include a Declare statement for any ODBC functions you call from a Visual Basic application. By requiring a Declare statement, Visual Basic knows what DLL file to load and the types of parameters each function uses so that it can perform type checking and flag any incorrect types you try to use in a function. The ODBCAPI.BAS file, on the CD-ROM that accompanies this book, contains these ODBC Declare statements and other ODBC constants and user-defined types, ready to be copied to your application.

Debugging ODBC Applications

Even if you don't have access to the ODBC SDK, ODBC provides one valuable tool for debugging applications: the *trace log* (sometimes called the *trace file*). This is a log of all calls made by your application and Visual Basic through the ODBC system. The log can be quite educational about how ODBC works, and it lets you see exactly what is being done.

Data Type Conversions Between ODBC and Visual Basic

The correspondence between ODBC and Visual Basic data types is not one-to-one. Fortunately, with Visual Basic's slightly expanded list of data types, the correspondence is a bit closer. Table 6.1 lists the available ODBC data types and the Visual Basic equivalents.

Table 6.1. Data type conversions between ODBC and Visual Basic.

ODBC DATA TYPE	GRAMMAR LEVEL	VISUAL BASIC DATA TYPE
SQL_BIT	Extended	Boolean
SQL_TINYINT	Extended	Byte
SQL_SMALLINT	Core	Integer
SQL_INTEGER	Core	Long
SQL_BIGINT	Extended	No equivalent
SQL_REAL	Core	Single
SQL_FLOAT, SQL_DOUBLE	Core	Double
SQL_TIMESTAMP, SQL_DATE	Extended	DateTime
SQL_TIME	Extended	Time
SQL_CHAR	Minimum	String

ODBC DATA TYPE	GRAMMAR LEVEL	VISUAL BASIC DATA TYPE
SQL_VARCHAR	Minimum	String
SQL_BINARY	Extended	Binary
SQL_VARBINARY	Extended	Binary
SQL_LONGVARBINARY	Extended	Binary
SQL_LONGVARCHAR	Minimum	String
SQL_DECIMAL	Core	Refer to Table 6.3.
SQL_NUMERIC	Core	Refer to Table 6.3.

As reflected in Table 6.2, special handling is required for the SQL_DECIMAL and SQL_NUMERIC data types. Both data types supply a scale and precision to determine what range of numbers the fields can handle. Using this scale and precision, you can make a good determination of variable scope for Visual Basic. In addition, there are two exceptions to this rule because SQL Server can employ a Currency field. ODBC interprets this with two different scope and precision combinations, as mentioned in Table 6.2.

Table 6.2. Numeric precision conversion between ODBC and Visual Basic.

SCALE	PRECISION	VISUAL BASIC DATA TYPE
0	1 to 4	Integer
0	5 to 9	Long
0	10 to 15	Double
0	16+	Text
1 to 3	1 to 15	Double
4	1 to 15	Double
4	16+	Text
4	10 or 19	Currency (SQL Server only)

ODBC data types correspond to the SQL grammar level that a driver and database support, similar to the conformance levels that ODBC's functions support. These are the SQL grammar conformance levels:

✔ *Minimum:* This is the minimum SQL grammar that a driver must support to be compliant with the ODBC standard. Only three data types are specified: SQL_CHAR, SQL_VARCHAR, and SQL_LONGVARCHAR. You won't be limited to these data types very often.

✔ *Core:* The Core SQL grammar expands the number of data types available to a far more workable number, and it includes many of the more common variable types.

✔ *Extended:* The Extended SQL grammar expands the list of variables to all the data types listed in Table 6.1. As with the Minimum level, you won't see a database that supports the full Extended level very often.

A database is not necessarily required to support all the data types at a given level, so an application should check to see what variables are available for a given data source by using the `SQLGetTypeInfo` function (an ODBC Conformance Level 1 function). See How-To 6.5 for a discussion of retrieving such information about an ODBC database.

ODBC Catalog Functions and Search Pattern Arguments

There are certain ODBC functions, called catalog functions, that return information about a data source's system tables or catalog. Most of the catalog functions are Conformance Level 2, so you probably won't encounter them when using Visual Basic and ODBC. Four of the functions, however, are Level 1: `SQLColumns`, `SQLSpecialColumns`, `SQLStatistics`, and `SQLTables`.

All the catalog functions allow you to specify a search pattern argument, which can contain the metacharacters underscore (_) and percent (%), as well as a driver-defined escape character. A *metacharacter* in this context is nothing more than a character that has a meaning other than just the character itself. Following is a detailed explanation of the search pattern characters:

✔ Use the underscore to represent any single character. This is equivalent to an MS-DOS question mark (?) when searching for files.

✔ Use the percent character to represent any sequence of zero or more characters. This is analogous to the asterisk (*) in MS-DOS.

✔ The driver-defined escape characters allow you to search for one of the two metacharacters as a literal character (that is, to search for a string with either an underscore or a percent character in the string).

✔ All other characters represent themselves.

For example, to search for all items with a *P*, use the search pattern argument `%P%`. To search for all table names having exactly four characters with a *B* in the second and last positions, use `_B_B`. Similarly, if the driver-defined escape character is a backslash, use `%\_\%` to find all strings of any length with an underscore in the second-to-last position and a percent in the last position of the string.

The driver-defined escape character can be found for any ODBC driver using the `SQLGetInfo` technique demonstrated in How-To 6.6.

Miscellaneous ODBC Topics

This section covers a few miscellaneous details that will make using ODBC and Visual Basic together a bit easier.

✔ Some ODBC databases support default drivers and data sources. A `[Default]` section in ODBCINST.INI (default driver) and/or ODBC.INI (default data source) is created during installation of the ODBC system or driver. In general, you won't want a default driver; you usually want to connect with one and only one specific data source and/or driver.

✔ If the driver uses a translator, it will be installed with the driver, and the usage should be transparent to you and your Visual Basic application.

✔ Get the *Microsoft ODBC 3.0 Programmer's Reference and SDK Guide*! If you are going to do any continuing work with ODBC at almost any level, buy the SDK. It has detailed references for all the functions, including various functions for installing ODBC drivers and systems. It also comes with some very useful debugging tools, including ODBC Test, which lets you interactively test various function calls, and ODBC Spy, which gives you a detailed record of which ODBC calls are being made. ODBC Spy also provides the capability to emulate either an application or a driver, letting you test applications without a driver. The SDK is highly recommended, and it is a must-have if you plan to develop your own drivers.

✔ In Windows NT and Windows 95, information on ODBC data sources, configuration, and tuning parameters is stored in the system registry, as is configuration information for Visual Basic. You should never need to modify that by hand, but if you do, at least now you know where to look.

✔ Any default installation of ODBC installs the ODBC Administrator. This is a handy utility you can use to set up drivers and data sources, as well as to get information about installed ODBC drivers. Everything you can do with the ODBC Administrator you can do in code with the ODBC API, but the utility simplifies some of the tasks.

Assumptions

This chapter assumes some things about what you are doing and the tools you are using:

✔ You are using ODBC version 2 or later. Many things changed between versions 1 and 2. You can take advantage of these changes even if you are working with a driver that supports only a previous version, as long as ODBC itself is the latest version.

✔ ODBC is installed on your development system. It would be quite difficult to develop ODBC applications with no access to ODBC.

✔ There are no heavy-duty data conversion issues. Most data conversions, if they go beyond those listed in Table 6.1 and 6.2, require some very specialized processing and will be very unusual. If you have such a situation, *definitely* get the ODBC SDK.

6.1 Use the ODBC Administrator to Maintain Data Sources

Under Windows 95 and Windows NT, ODBC data sources, explained in greater detail in this How-To, have become more complex entities, especially when it comes to issues such as security and network administration. This How-To explains how a simple Control Panel applet turns the administration of these data sources into a simple task.

6.2 Use ODBC with the Visual Basic Data Control

Using Visual Basic's Data control to access ODBC demonstrates the power of both Visual Basic and ODBC. Accessing databases through ODBC without using the ODBC API is a simple matter, whether that data is on your own hard disk in a format Visual Basic doesn't directly support or half a world away on your network. This How-To shows how easy it is to make the connection.

6.3 Create an ODBC-Accessible Data Source by Using `RegisterDatabase`

Even though ODBC might install the driver you need for your application, a data source name must exist before the database can be used by any application. The `RegisterDatabase` method provides a way to enter a new data source if one doesn't exist (or even if it does!) so that your application can use the database through ODBC.

6.4 Prevent the Login Dialog Box from Being Displayed When I Open an ODBC Database

As long as you have the correct and complete connect string to feed to ODBC, you should be able to connect with any database to which you have access. But how do you discover the exact connect string for each database? ODBC provides the functionality and Visual Basic makes it easy to use, as discussed in this How-To.

6.5 Determine What Services an ODBC Server Provides

Even though ODBC makes connecting with databases through a standard interface much easier, and provides some of the services itself, it still relies on database systems to do most of the work. Not all databases are created equal, with equal capabilities. You'll discover how you can find out what services a database provides, all within your applications.

6.6 Use ODBCDirect to Connect to Database Servers

ODBCDirect, like DAO (Data Access Objects) and RDO (Remote Data Objects), is a way to access databases. Unlike DAO and RDO, however, ODBCDirect is just a thin, but well-behaved, wrapper around the ODBC API. This How-To shows the first step in using this new technology by connecting to a data source and providing detailed information on the ODBCDirect `Connection` object.

COMPLEXITY
BEGINNING

6.1 How do I...
Use the ODBC Administrator to maintain data sources?

Problem

My Visual Basic program needs access to a Microsoft SQL Server database on another computer. How do I use the ODBC Administrator to connect to that database?

Technique

Visual Basic is a very powerful tool when it comes to quick database application development. At times, however, Visual Basic's native database tools are simply not enough, such as whenever a connection to SQL Server or Oracle databases is needed. ODBC makes the gap between Visual Basic and these databases easy to navigate by providing a way to bridge the two resources with an ODBC connection.

ODBC connections usually start with a data source, an alias used by ODBC to refer an ODBC driver to a specified database so that an ODBC connection can happen. Although you can create an ODBC data source with code, it's much easier to use the ODBC Administrator, a tool specifically designed to perform data source–related tasks.

Data sources under Windows 95 and Windows NT are divided into three major types, as explained in Table 6.3. These three types make a difference in your application; the user DSN, for example, won't work with another user logged in to the same machine. The system DSN assumes that all users on the same machine have security access, and the file DSN is used on a case-by-case basis.

Table 6.3. Data source name types.

TYPE	PURPOSE
System DSN	This DSN is usable by all users on a workstation, regardless of user security.
User DSN	The default, this DSN is usable only by certain users on a workstation (usually the user who created it).
File DSN	A "portable" data source, this DSN can be very useful with network-based applications. The DSN can be used by any user who has the correct ODBC driver(s) installed.

Steps

The ODBC Administrator is a Control Panel applet, so the first step is to locate the ODBC Administrator icon.

1. Double-click your Control Panel icon. You should see a window appear similar to the one shown in Figure 6.2. In that window, you should find an icon like the one highlighted in the figure.

Figure 6.2. The Control Panel, with ODBC Administrator highlighted.

2. Double-click the ODBC Administrator icon (usually titled "32bit ODBC") to start the Administrator applet. A dialog box similar to the one shown in Figure 6.3 should appear, displaying several property pages. The first three property pages deal with DSN entries, with each page representing a level of security. The User DSN property page provides ODBC access for a data source to a given user on a given workstation only; the System DSN allows ODBC access for a data source to a given workstation only, but to any user on that workstation. A File DSN entry is a file-based data source, usable by any and all who have the needed ODBC drivers installed, and it does not need to be local to a user or a workstation

Also, you'll notice three more property pages. The ODBC Drivers property page allows the display of all installed ODBC drivers, including the version and file information. The Tracing property page offers the capability of tracking all ODBC activity for a given data source and saving it to a log file for debugging purposes. And, last of all, the About property page gives version and file information on the core components that compose the ODBC environment.

3. For your needs, you are going to create a User DSN. Click the Add button to start the process of adding a new data source. The first dialog box that appears gives you the list of available ODBC drivers from which to choose. One thing you'll want to note is the helpful information on each dialog box and property page, summarizing its purpose.

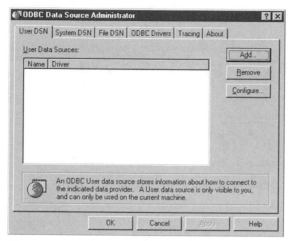

Figure 6.3. ODBC Data Source Administrator property pages.

4. Select the Microsoft Access Driver from the list of drivers and then click the Finish button. The next step is to provide the database-related information for the data source, and to that end a dialog box appears, similar to that displayed in Figure 6.4. The dialog box that appears is driver specific; that is, if you had selected a different ODBC driver, you would probably have gotten a dialog box with a completely different set of properties.

5. Type Biblio in the Data Source Name field. Then click the Select button in the Database frame and choose your copy of BIBLIO.MDB. Then click the OK button.

How It Works

Based on your selections, the ODBC Administrator adds entries to the Registry (or to a file, if you are creating a File DSN.) These Registry entries are vital to the ODBC drivers that require them; in many cases, the entries can determine not only the database that the driver will access but also how and by whom it will be accessed. The only other recommended method for adding ODBC information to the Registry is the RegisterDatabase method, which is covered later in this chapter. Avoid attempting to manually edit ODBC driver Registry entries without first researching the settings to ensure that you fully understand how they work.

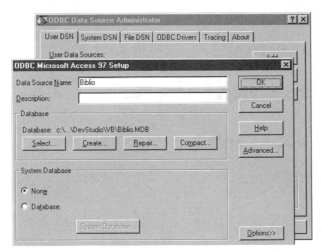

Figure 6.4. The ODBC Microsoft Access 97 Setup dialog box.

Comments

It is important to emphasize the fact that each ODBC driver's setup dialog box will be different; if you're creating data sources by hand and using only one driver, this isn't a difficult thing to support. If, however, you really want to ensure a wide degree of compatibility for your programs, you might want to use the method detailed in How-To 6.3 to create your data sources. This technique uses the `RegisterDatabase` method to create data sources, and it can support a wide variety of options (even running "silently," displaying nothing to the user, if all the information needed for the data source is supplied.)

COMPLEXITY
BEGINNING

6.2 How do I...
Use ODBC with the Visual Basic Data control?

Problem

I'm using the Visual Basic Data control to process and display data in my application. However, the data I need to access is on the network, in a format that Visual Basic doesn't directly support. How can I get the data and display it in a form? Can I use the Data control?

Technique

The steps necessary to bind the Visual Basic Data control and other bound controls are simple—not that much different from connecting to one of Visual Basic's native data formats using the Jet database engine. This How-To shows exactly what is necessary to set up the controls to make the connection.

Steps

Open the Person.VBP project file. Modify the project to use an existing ODBC data source, or use the database on the CD-ROM included with this book. Having your OBDC source point to that database might make this How-To easier to follow. Run the project. Use the Visual Basic Data control's navigation buttons at the bottom of the form, as shown in Figure 6.5, to move through the database, and then click Quit when you are finished.

Figure 6.5. Chapter 6.2 example.

1. Create a new project, name it Person.VBP, and add a new form with property settings as listed in Table 6.4. Save the form as PERSON.FRM.

```
Private Sub Form_Load()
    'Set up the form and connect to data source
    Dim dbfTemp As Database, recTemp As Recordset

    'Connect to the database
    'Change this to your data source
    dtaData.Connect = "ODBC;DSN=Personnel Database"

    'Set the Data control's RecordSource property
    'Change this to your table name
    dtaData.RecordSource = "SELECT * FROM Contacts"

    'Connect each of the text boxes with the appropriate fieldname
    txtContact.DataField = "Contact"
    txtName.DataField = "Name"
    txtAddress1.DataField = "Addr1"
    txtAddress2.DataField = "Addr2"
    txtCity.DataField = "City"
```

continued on next page

continued from previous page

```
            txtState.DataField = "State"
            txtZip.DataField = "Zip"
        End Sub
```

Table 6.4. Objects and properties for PERSON.FRM.

OBJECT	PROPERTY	SETTING
Form	Name	frmODBC
	Caption	Chapter 6.2 Example
	StartUpPosition	2 - CenterScreen
CommandButton	Name	cmdQuit
	Caption	&Quit
	Default	True
TextBox	Name	txtZip
	DataSource	dtaData
TextBox	Name	txtState
	DataSource	dtaData
TextBox	Name	txtCity
	DataSource	dtaData
TextBox	Name	txtAddress2
	DataSource	dtaData
TextBox	Name	txtAddress1
	DataSource	dtaData
TextBox	Name	txtName
	DataSource	dtaData
TextBox	Name	txtContact
	DataSource	dtaData
Data	Name	dtaData
	Align	2 - Align Bottom
	Caption	Personnel Database
	RecordSource	""
	DefaultType	1 - UseODBC
Label	Name	lblPerson
	Caption	Zip:
	Alignment	1 - Right Justify
	Index	5
Label	Name	lblPerson
	Alignment	1 - Right Justify
	Caption	State:
	Index	4

OBJECT	PROPERTY	SETTING
Label	Name	lblPerson
	Alignment	1 - Right Justify
	Index	3
	Caption	City:
Label	Name	lblPerson
	Alignment	1 - Right Justify
	Index	2
	Caption	Address:
Label	Name	lblPerson
	Alignment	1 - Right Justify
	Index	1
	Caption	Company:
Label	Name	lblPerson
	Alignment	1 'Right Justify
	Index	0
	Caption	Contact:

2. Add the following code to the declarations section of the form. To avoid naming problems, **Option Explicit** tells Visual Basic to make sure that you declare all variables and objects before using them.

```
Option Explicit
```

3. Add the following code to the form's **Load** event procedure. After centering the form, set the **Connect** and **RecordSource** properties of the Data control, as well as the **DataField** properties of the text boxes that will hold the fields of the database. This step links each needed field with the text boxes that hold each record's data.

Change the data source name in the **Connect** property statement indicated to an available name in ODBC—or leave the DSN part of the **Connect** string out, and ODBC will prompt you for the information it needs. Also, set the SQL statement to a table in that data source, and change the text boxes to actual fields in that table.

4. Add the following code to the **Click** event of the **cmdQuit** command button. This is the exit point that terminates the program.

```
Private Sub cmdQuit_Click()
    End
End Sub
```

How It Works

The preceding code is all that is required to use ODBC with Visual Basic's Data control. With the built-in navigation controls, you can move about the database.

Several important details are involved in setting up this procedure for use with ODBC. Note that in this How-To most of the setup and initialization is done in code, but you can easily set the properties of the Data control and bound text boxes when designing the form and then simply load the form. In this case, Visual Basic will make the connection for you and display the data directly, and you won't need any code in the form's **Load** event. To ensure that this happens smoothly, follow the steps outlined here:

1. Leave the Data control's **DatabaseName** property blank to use an ODBC data source. If you enter a database name here, Visual Basic attempts to open the database using its native data formats.

2. Set the **Connect** property of the Data control to the connect string that ODBC needs to connect to the database. This is the same connect string that other How-To's in this chapter use for defining a **QueryDef**, in **RegisterDatabase**, and in setting up other uses of ODBC directly. You can also simply set this property to **ODBC**, and ODBC will prompt the user at runtime for information it needs in order to make the connection.

3. Set the Data control's **RecordSource** property to a SQL statement or the name of a table you want to use to select the data from the database. Any SQL statement that creates a resultset can be used by Visual Basic to populate the bound text boxes.

4. Set each text box's **DataSource** to the name of the Data control—**dtaData** in this example. This is the normal Visual Basic way of binding a control to a Data control. Remember too that you can have as many Data controls on a form as you want, with different sets of controls bound to different bound controls and, therefore, to different databases.

5. Set the Data control's DefaultType to **1 - UseODBC**. If this property is not set, trying to access an ODBC database with the Data control will cause Visual Basic to hang.

6. Lastly, set each text box's **DataField** property to the particular field name in the resultset of data records. This might be the name of the field in the database itself, but it is actually the name of the field that is returned in the resultset. The two can be the same, but the SQL statement can rename the fields or even return calculated fields that don't exist in the database.

Comments

The method for ODBC access presented previously is usually the first, and simplest, method employed by programmers when delving into the ODBC library. You will find, however, that for more complex applications, your needs will quickly outstrip the capabilities of the Data control. For a quick application or basic database access, though, this is a great way to start.

COMPLEXITY
BEGINNING

6.3 How do I...
Create an ODBC-accessible data source by using RegisterDatabase?

Problem

ODBC provides a program, ODBC Administrator, to make manual changes to a data source, but how can I install a new ODBC data source name using code? I can't make the users of the application do it, and I can't expect them to have the information to give to ODBC. Does this mean that I have to make direct calls to the ODBC API?

Technique

The **RegisterDatabase** method of Visual Basic is a quick and easy way to register a new data source with ODBC. The method takes four arguments: **dbname**, **driver**, **silent**, and **attributes**, which are discussed more fully later in this section. After a data source name is created, it becomes available to any application using ODBC, whether it's a Visual Basic application or not.

Steps

Open the REGISTER.VBP file. The ODBC Data Sources form loads, shown in Figure 6.6, getting the list of currently installed drivers and data source names through direct calls to the ODBC system. Enter a name for the new data source, an optional description, and the driver that ODBC will use to connect with the database. Click the New Data Source command button to add it to the ODBC system. If any additional information is necessary to make a connection to the database, another dialog box appears, prompting for any missing items. (Figure 6.4 shows the dialog box for adding a Microsoft Access data source.) The list of data sources then updates to show a current list of installed data sources.

1. Create a new project named REGISTER.VBP. Add the form ODBCErrors.FRM and the code module ODBC API Declarations.BAS, using Visual Basic's File|Add menu command. The code module contains all the declarations needed for the ODBC API functions and the constants used in many of the functions, and the form makes it easier to examine ODBC errors.

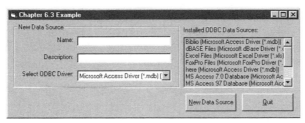

Figure 6.6. The project's ODBC Data Sources form, displaying the data source list.

2. Make sure that the Microsoft Common Controls components are available to this project. To add, select the Project|Components menu item. When the dialog box appears, look for a component titled Microsoft Windows Common Controls 6.0, and ensure that it is checked. Click OK. The ODBCErrors.FRM form uses the TreeView control to display ODBC errors in a hierarchical fashion.

3. Name the new project's default form `frmODBC` and save the file as REGISTER.FRM. Add the controls shown in Figure 6.6, setting the properties as given in Table 6.5.

Table 6.5. Objects and properties for REGISTER.FRM.

OBJECT	PROPERTY	SETTING
Form	Name	frmODBC
	Caption	ODBC Data Sources
CommandButton	Name	cmdCreateDSN
	Caption	&New Data Source
Frame	Name	fraRegister
	Caption	New Data Source
TextBox	Name	txtDSNdesc
TextBox	Name	txtDSNname
ComboBox	Name	lstODBCdrivers
	Sorted	True
	Style	2 - Dropdown List
Label	Name	lblRegister
	Alignment	1 'Right Justify
	Index	2
	Caption	Select ODBC Driver:

OBJECT	PROPERTY	SETTING
Label	Name	lblRegister
	Alignment	1 'Right Justify
	Index	1
	Caption	Description:
Label	Name	lblRegister
	Alignment	1 'Right Justify
	Index	0
	Caption	Name:
CommandButton	Name	cmdQuit
	Caption	&Quit
ListBox	Name	lstODBCdbs
	Sorted	True
	TabStop	0 'False
Label	Name	lblRegister
	Index	3
	Caption	Installed ODBC Data Sources:

4. Put the following code in the declarations section of frmODBC. Option Explicit tells Visual Basic to check the variables for you. The dynamic arrays hold the information about installed drivers and data sources retrieved from calls to the ODBC API.

```
Option Explicit

'Dynamic arrays to hold data
Dim strDBNames() As String
Dim strDBDescs() As String
Dim strDvrDescs() As String
Dim strDvrAttr() As String
```

5. Add the following code to the **Load** event of frmODBC. This code handles all the setup chores, including centering the form on the screen and allocating an ODBC environment handle. Each ODBC application that calls the API needs to have one, and only one, environmental handle. ODBC keeps track of what information goes where through the use of this handle, along with the connection and statement handles. The actual work of extracting the lists of data sources and drivers is handled in other procedures in this form, but called from here.

```
Private Sub Form_Load()
    'Allocate the ODBC environment handle
    If SQLAllocEnv(glng_hEnv) = SQL_SUCCESS Then
        'Load the current list of data sources to list box
        GetODBCdbs
```

continued on next page

continued from previous page

```
                'Get the list of installed drivers
                GetODBCdvrs
                lstODBCdrivers.ListIndex = 0
                frmODBC.Show
                txtDSNname.SetFocus
        End If
End Sub
```

6. Insert these procedures into **frmODBC**. The first procedure, **cmdCreateDSN_Click**, calls the procedure that validates data and actually creates the data source name in ODBC. The second procedure, **cmdQuit_Click**, creates an exit point in the application.

```
Private Sub cmdCreateDSN_Click()
    CreateNewDSN
End Sub

Private Sub cmdQuit_Click()
    End
End Sub
```

7. Add the following subroutine to **frmODBC**. Here is the first of two subroutines that extract the existing lists of data sources and drivers from ODBC. **GetODBCdbs** obtains the list of data source names and the descriptions of each, employing a function named **ODBCDSNList** in the ODBC API Declarations.BAS as a wrapper for the **SQLDataSources** API call. The **ODBCDSNList** function does all the work; the **Do While** loop extracts one data source name at a time with a call to **SQLDataSources**. If no error is returned from the function call, the data source name and its description are concatenated and added to the **lstODBCdbs** list box, showing all the data sources that are already installed. When the last data source has been returned to this function, the **SQLDataSources** function returns the **SQL_NO_DATA_FOUND** result, and the loop terminates. The function returns a variant array, if successful, or nothing, if unsuccessful.

```
Private Sub GetODBCdbs()
    Dim varTemp As Variant, I As Integer

    lstODBCdbs.Clear
    'Call the ODBCDSNList function in ODBC API Declarations.BAS.
    varTemp = ODBCDSNList(glng_hEnv, True)

    'If the ODBCDSNList function returns an array, populate
    'the list box.
    If IsArray(varTemp) Then
        For I = LBound(varTemp) To UBound(varTemp)
            lstODBCdbs.AddItem varTemp(I)
        Next
    End If
End Sub
```

8. The next function, GetODBCdvrs, gets a list of the drivers that ODBC has installed. Put the following code in frmODBC. This function operates very similarly to GetODBCdbs, calling a function named ODBCDriverList, which loops through calls to the ODBC SQLDrivers function, returning one driver name at a time, and returning the names and descriptions in a local variant array to be added to the cboODBCdrivers drop-down list.

```
Private Sub GetODBCdvrs()
    Dim varTemp As Variant, I As Integer

    cboODBCdrivers.Clear
    varTemp = ODBCDriverList(glng_hEnv, True)

    'If tho ODBCDriverList function returns an array,
    'populate the list box.  If not, let the user know.
    If IsArray(varTemp) Then
        For I = LBound(varTemp) To UBound(varTemp)
            cboODBCdrivers.AddItem varTemp(I)
        Next
    Else
        MsgBox "No ODBC drivers installed or available.", _
        vbExclamation
    End If
End Sub
```

9. Add the following code to frmODBC. The CreateNewDSN procedure sets up and calls RegisterDatabase so that the new data source name is recorded in the ODBC system. The procedure first checks to make sure that a name is entered in the txtDSNname text box so that a descriptive name will be in the list (the description is optional). If all is well, the procedure assembles the following set of variables to pass to RegisterDatabase:

✔ The new data source name

✔ The driver to be used to connect to the physical data

✔ Connection information

Before actually making the call to RegisterDatabase, the Visual Basic error handler is set to go to the CantRegister error-handling routine if there is any problem registering the data source. If there is an error, a MsgBox informs the user of what the trouble is and continues the procedure—giving the user the opportunity to rectify any problems and try again. If the error is anything other than error 3146, it is passed on to the default Visual Basic error-handling routines.

```
Sub CreateNewDSN()
    'Add a new data source name to the ODBC system
    Dim strDSNname As String, strDSNattr As String, strDSNdriver _
        As String
    Dim intResult As Integer, intSaveCursor As Integer
```

continued on next page

continued from previous page

```
            If txtDSNname = "" Then
                MsgBox "You must enter a name for the new data source."
                txtDSNname.SetFocus
            Else
                intSaveCursor = Screen.MousePointer
                Screen.MousePointer = vbHourglass

                'Format the arguments to RegisterDatabase
                strDSNname = txtDSNname.text
                strDSNattr = "Description=" & txtDSNdesc.text
                strDSNdriver = _
                    cboODBCdrivers.List(cboODBCdrivers.ListIndex)

                On Error GoTo CantRegister
                    'Trap any errors so we can respond to them
                    DBEngine.RegisterDatabase strDSNname, strDSNdriver, _
                    False, strDSNattr
                On Error GoTo 0

                'Now, rebuild the list of data source names
                GetODBCdbs

                Screen.MousePointer = intSaveCursor
            End If

            Exit Sub

        CantRegister:
            If Err.Number = 3146 Then
                'ODBC couldn't find the setup driver specified
                'for this database in ODBCINST.INI.
                MsgBox "Cannot find driver installation DLL.", vbCritical
                Resume Next
            Else
                MsgBox Err.Number, vbExclamation
            End If
        End Sub
```

10. Add this code in the Unload event of frmODBC. This code makes cleanup calls to ODBC functions, releasing the memory and handles allocated to make the calls to the ODBC API. The first call is to ODBCDisconnectDS, which releases and then frees the connection handle and memory. The second call, SQLFreeEnv, releases the ODBC environment handle and memory.

```
Private Sub Form_Unload(Cancel As Integer)
    Dim intResult As Integer

    'Clean up the ODBC connections that we allocated
    'and opened.
    intResult = ODBCDisconnectDS(glng_hEnv, glng_hDbc, glng_hStmt)
    intResult = SQLCFreeEnv(ghEnv)
End Sub
```

How It Works

By providing the RegisterDatabase method, Visual Basic takes care of many details involved in establishing a new data source in ODBC. This is the syntax for the method:

```
DBEngine.RegisterDatabase dbname, driver, silent, attributes
```

The first argument is *dbname*. The Visual Basic Help file describes *dbname* as "a string expression that is the name used in the OpenDatabase method that refers to a block of descriptive information about the data source." All true, of course, but *dbname* is just a descriptive name that you chose to call the data source. The name could reflect the origins of the data (such as being from an Oracle database) or the nature of the data (such as Corporate Marketing Research Data).

The *driver* argument is the name of the ODBC driver used to access the database. This is not the same as the name of the DLL file comprising the driver, but is instead a short, descriptive name that the author of the driver gave to it. SQL Server, Btrieve data, and Oracle are names of widely used drivers.

The third argument is *silent*. No, the argument isn't silent, but it is your opportunity to control whether ODBC prompts the user for more information when ODBC doesn't have enough information to make the requested connection. The options are True for no dialog boxes and False for ODBC to prompt for the missing information. If *silent* is set to True and ODBC can't make the connection because of a lack of information, your application will need to trap the error that will occur.

The fourth argument is *attributes*. Each database system you connect to has its own requirements for the information it needs in order to make a connection. For some items there is a default; for others there isn't. The more attributes you specify here, the fewer the user will need to specify. The *attributes* string is the string returned from the Connect property of the Data control or the Database, QueryDef, or TableDef objects after a connection is made. How-To 6.5 discusses this information in more detail and shows a way to easily obtain the exact information needed to connect with a particular database. In fact, this How-To and How-To 6.5 give you all the information you need to make an ODBC connection.

Essentially, all RegisterDatabase does is add information to the ODBC.INI file usually located in your \WINDOWS directory—with some validation routines thrown in by ODBC. It checks to make sure that you provide all the information needed to make a connection and that the database is out there someplace and is accessible.

One error that might be returned from ODBC when you use the RegisterDatabase method is The configuration DLL ([*file name*]) for the [*driver name*] could not be loaded. When you request that a new data source be established, ODBC looks in an ODBCINST.INI file, located in the same place as the ODBC.INI file, for the name of the DLL that contains the setup routines for that driver. Here are some sample lines for different drivers (there is additional information in each section for each driver):

```
[Microsoft Access Driver (*.mdb)]
Driver=C:\WINDOWS\SYSTEM\odbcjt16.dll
Setup=C:\WINDOWS\SYSTEM\odbcjt16.dll

[Microsoft Dbase Driver (*.dbf)]
Driver=C:\WINDOWS\SYSTEM\odbcjt16.dll
Setup=C:\WINDOWS\SYSTEM\oddbse16.dll

[SQL Server Driver]
Driver=C:\WINDOWS\SYSTEM\sqlsrvr.dll
Setup=C:\WINDOWS\SYSTEM\sqlsrvr.dll
```

As you can see, sometimes the setup driver is the same as the driver used for data access, but more commonly the two are different. If that driver is not available at the location specified, ODBC returns an error for the `RegisterDatabase` call.

Comments

One of the nice things about using ODBC is that it goes out of its way to give you the information you need in order to make the connections to databases. In this How-To, you have seen how ODBC prompts with its own dialog box if you don't give it enough information to make the connection. This is one area in which using Visual Basic to handle the conversation with ODBC doesn't hide any details from you. You'll see another example of using this ODBC feature to good advantage in How-To 6.5, in which the dialog box is used to construct connect strings that you can use directly in an application.

Perhaps, to state the obvious, it is necessary for the ODBC driver to be installed before `RegisterDatabase` is used. If this method only added entries to the .INI file, the driver wouldn't need to be installed before a data source was created using that driver. But because ODBC does some validation from Visual Basic in response to this method, the driver needs to be available along with the information stored in ODBC.INI and ODBCINST.INI by the driver setup program.

In response to the availability of `RegisterDatabase` in Visual Basic, it is logical to wonder whether there is an equivalent `UnRegisterDatabase` or `DeleteDatabase`. Alas, there is not. For that you would need to make a call to an ODBC Installer DLL function, `SQLConfigDataSource`, available since ODBC version 1.0. Some other interesting installation functions that were introduced with version 2.0 (`SQLCreateDataSource`, `SQLGetAvailableDrivers`, `SQLGetInstalledDrivers`, and `SQLManageDataSources`) give finer control over the ODBC setup. Driver manufacturers use these and other functions to install drivers and ODBC itself if necessary, but any application can use them. Information about these functions is available in the *Microsoft ODBC 3.0 Programmer's Reference and SDK Guide*.

Another Visual Basic property that is useful in connection with `RegisterDatabase` is the `Version` property. `Version` is a property of both the `Database` object and the `DBEngine` object. When returned from the `Database` object, `Version` identifies the data format version of the object, usually as a major and minor version number.vbp, such as 4.03. This gives you one more piece of information about the different components making up your applications.

COMPLEXITY
INTERMEDIATE

6.4 How do I...
Prevent the login dialog box from being displayed when I open an ODBC database?

Problem

I'm trying to use an ODBC driver to open a data source that is on the network, but the driver documentation is not very helpful regarding the information needed to make a connection. I need my application to make the connection (if it is at all possible) without requiring users to make decisions or respond to dialog boxes. How can I get the right connect string without wasting time by guessing? If the connection can't be made, why not?

Technique

As long as you are able to tell Visual Basic that you want to make some sort of connection through ODBC, all you need to do is make a call to Visual Basic's `OpenDatabase` method with certain default arguments. ODBC responds by prompting for information about what data source you want (from those data sources installed on the system). Then you can define a temporary `QueryDef`, make the connection, and examine the Visual Basic `Connect` property. The `Connect` property at that point contains the fully formed connect string required to make a connection to that data source. The string stored in the `Connect` property can be copied and used directly in future attempts to connect to the database.

Steps

Open and run the CONNECT.VBP Visual Basic project file. The Retrieve ODBC Connect String window opens, as shown in Figure 6.7. Click on the Connect to Data Source command button, and the ODBC SQL Data Sources window appears, prompting you to select an installed data source name. Visual Basic and ODBC obtain from that data source a list of available tables and put them in the

Tables Available list box on the main form. Either double-click on one of the tables or select one and click the Get Connect String command button. The application establishes a connection to that database table and returns the complete connect string, placing it in the Connect String text box, as shown in Figure 6.8. Click the Copy Connect String command button to put the string on the Windows clipboard, and then paste it into your application.

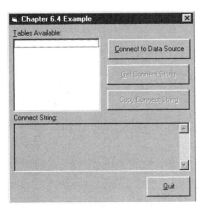

Figure 6.7. The project's main form on startup.

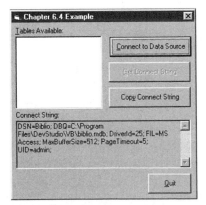

Figure 6.8. The project's main form, after ODBC connect string retrieval.

1. Create a new project named CONNECT.VBP. Add the form ODBCErrors.FRM and the code module ODBC API Declarations.BAS, using Visual Basic's File|Add menu command. The code module contains all the declarations needed for the ODBC API functions and the constants used in many of the functions.

2. Name the default form **frmODBC**, and save the file as CONNECT.FRM. Add the controls as shown in Figure 6.7, setting the properties as listed in Table 6.6.

Table 6.6. Objects and properties for CONNECT.FRM.

OBJECT	PROPERTY	SETTING
Form	Name	frmODBC
	Caption	Chapter 6.4 Example
CommandButton	Name	cmdCopyConnect
	Caption	Cop&y Connect String
	Enabled	0 - False
CommandButton	Name	cmdGetConnect
	Caption	&Get Connect String
	Enabled	0 - False
CommandButton	Name	cmdQuit
	Caption	&Quit
TextBox	Name	txtConnect
	MultiLine	True
	ScrollBars	2 - Vertical
	TabStop	False
CommandButton	Name	cmdConnect
	Caption	&Connect to Data Source
ListBox	Name	lstTables
	Sorted	True
Label	Name	lblConnect
	Index	0
	Caption	Connect String:
Label	Name	lblConnect
	Index	1
	Caption	&Tables Available:

3. Add the following code to the declarations section of **frmODBC**. To avoid naming problems, **Option Explicit** tells Visual Basic to make sure that you declare all variables and objects before using them.

```
Option Explicit

'Module level globals to hold connection info
Dim dbfTemp As Database, recTemp As Recordset
```

4. Add this code to the form's **Load** event. After the form is loaded, memory and a handle for the ODBC environment and connection are allocated. If either of these fails, there is no need to proceed, so the program is exited.

```
Private Sub Form_Load()
    'Log on to an ODBC data source
    'First, allocate ODBC memory and get handles
    Dim intResult As Integer

    'Allocate the ODBC environment handle
    If SQLAllocEnv(glng_hEnv) <> SQL_SUCCESS Then End

    intResult = SQLAllocConnect(glng_hEnv, glng_hDbc)
    If intResult <> SQL_SUCCESS Then
        intResult = frmODBCErrors.ODBCError("Dbc", glng_hEnv, & _
        glng_hDbc, 0, intResult, "Error allocating connection _
            handle.")
        End
    End If

    frmODBC.Show
End Sub
```

5. Add the following code to the **Click** event of **cmdConnect**. Before you can get connection data, you need to select a data source name for the connection information you want. For this procedure, let the built-in ODBC dialog boxes do the work. The line

```
Set dbfTemp = OpenDatabase("", False, False, "ODBC;")
```

tells Visual Basic to open a database but gives no information about which one, other than it is an ODBC database. ODBC responds by opening its Select Data Source dialog box for selection of a data source, as shown in Figure 6.9.

```
Private Sub cmdConnect_Click()
    'Connect to a data source and populate lstTables
    Dim I As Integer
    Dim strConnect As String
    Dim tbfTemp As TableDef

    Screen.MousePointer = vbHourglass
    lstTables.Clear

    On Error GoTo ErrHandler
        Set dbfTemp = OpenDatabase("", False, False, "ODBC;")
    On Error GoTo 0

    For Each tbfTemp In dbfTemp.TableDefs
        lstTables.AddItem tbfTemp.Name
    Next

    Screen.MousePointer = vbDefault
```

```
        If lstTables.ListCount Then
            cmdGetConnect.Enabled = True
        Else
            MsgBox "No tables are available. " & _
                "Please connect to another data source."
        End If

    Exit Sub

    ErrHandler:
        Screen.MousePointer = vbDefault
        Select Case Err.Number
            Case 3423
                'This data source can't be attached, (or the
                'user clicked Cancel, so use ODBC API
                APIConnect
            Case 3059
                'The user clicked on Cancel
                Exit Sub
            Case Else
                'The error is something else, so send it back to
                'the VB exception handler
                MsgBox Err.Number, vbExclamation
        End Select
End Sub
```

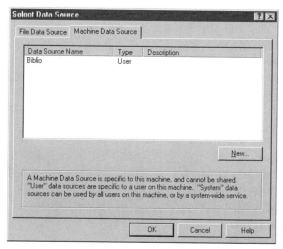

Figure 6.9. The Select Data Source selection
dialog box.

After the user selects a data source name, the procedure loops through
the TableDefs collection using a Visual Basic For Each...Next loop,
retrieves the table name of each table available in that data source, and
adds each table name to the lstTables list box. If a connection is made
and any tables are available, the cmdGetConnect command button is

Enabled for the next step, which is retrieving the connection information. The error-handling routine is important in this procedure and is discussed with the APIConnect procedure code.

6. Add the following code to the cmdGetConnect's Click event. This command button is enabled only when a connection is made and tables are available for selection. After you select a table name, a connection is made to that table by creating a dynaset. This makes the connection information available. The connection information is retrieved by copying the value of the dynaset's Connect property to the txtConnect text box, running it through the AddSpaces function as discussed in the following text. Finally, the cmdCopyConnect command button is enabled.

```
Screen.MousePointer = vbHourglass
    txtConnect.text = ""

    If Len(lstTables.text) Then
        Set recTemp = dbfTemp.OpenRecordset(lstTables.text)
        txtConnect.text = AddSpaces(dbfTemp.Connect)
    Else
        MsgBox "Please select a table first."
    End If

    cmdCopyConnect.Enabled = True
    Screen.MousePointer = vbDefault
End Sub
```

7. Add the following code to frmODBC. When you receive the raw connect string back from ODBC after making the connection to the database table, it is strung together with no spaces, unless a space happens to be in any of the strings enclosed in quotation marks. Sometimes the connect string can become lengthy, so use a text box with the MultiLine property set to True. Even with that, an unbroken string with no spaces can exceed any width you make the text box. So this function simply loops through the length of the string, replacing all the semicolon separators with a semicolon-space pair of characters. ODBC uses semicolons to separate the different phrases in a connect string.

```
Function AddSpaces (strC As String)
    Dim I As Integer
    Dim strNewStr As String, strNextChar As String
    Dim strNextChar As String

    For I = 1 To Len(strC)
        strNextChar = Mid$(strC, I, 1)
        If strNextChar = ";" Then
            strNewStr = strNewStr & strNextChar & " "
        Else
            strNewStr = strNewStr & strNextChar
        End If
    Next
    AddSpaces = strNewStr
End Function
```

8. Add the code for cmdCopyConnect's Click event as shown here. This is added as a convenience for the programmer. When you have connected to the data source and have received the connect string, just click the Copy Connect String command button, and the full string is copied to the Windows Clipboard, ready to paste into your application.

```
Private Sub cmdCopyConnect_Click()
    'Select the text in txtConnect
    With txtConnect
        .SetFocus: .SelStart = 0: .SelLength = _
        Len(txtConnect.text)
    End With

    ' Copy selected text to Clipboard.
    Clipboard.SetText Screen.ActiveControl.SelText
End Sub
```

9. Add the following code to the form's Unload event and the cmdQuit command button's event. The cmdQuit command button ends the program, triggering the form's Unload event. As usual for Visual Basic applications that make direct calls to the ODBC API, the code needs to clean up after itself, releasing the memory and handles needed for connection to ODBC.

```
Private Sub cmdQuit_Click()
    End
End Sub

Private Sub Form_Unload(Cancel As Integer)
    Dim intResult As Integer

    intResult = ODBCDisconnectDS(glng_hEnv, glng_hDbc, glng_hStmt)
    intResult = ODBCFreeEnv(glng_hEnv)
End Sub
```

10. Add the following code to the DblClick event procedure of the lstTables list box. This code simply adds the convenience of being able to double-click on a table in lstTables to retrieve the connect string, saving the work of also clicking the cmdGetConnect command button.

```
Private Sub lstTables_DblClick()
    cmdGetConnect_Click
End Sub
```

11. Add the following code to the code section of the form. Sometimes it is necessary to handle errors generated by Visual Basic but caused by the ODBC system. This is one example of such a situation.

There are two sorts of Visual Basic errors that need to be handled in the cmdConnect_Click procedure. The first sort of error is when, for any of a number of reasons, there is a problem making the connection to the data source (for example, the database is not available, the connection couldn't be made because of network traffic, and so on). One common error is the attempt to open an ODBC database that is one of the databases Visual Basic handles natively, such as an Access .MDB file or one of the ISAM databases.

This is where the **APIConnect** procedure comes in. Even though the error is generated by the Visual Basic error handler, there is some reason lurking in ODBC for why the connection can't be made, and a call to the ODBC **SQLError** function will usually (but not always) give more information about the problem. **SQLError** doesn't always have information to give, for whatever internal reason. Basically, **APIConnect** just calls **SQLError** from within the error procedure, gets whatever additional information it can obtain, disconnects the ODBC connection (but not the handle—you might need that again for another attempt to make a connection), and returns to *frmODBC*.

```
Sub APIConnect()
    'Can't connect through VB, so go direct
    Dim intResult As Integer
    Dim strConnectIn As String
    Dim strConnectOut As String * SQL_MAX_OPTION_STRING_LENGTH
    Dim intOutCount As Integer

    strConnectIn = ""

    intResult = SQLDriverConnect(glng_hDbc, Me.hWnd, _
        strConnectIn,
        Len(strConnectIn), strConnectOut, Len(strConnectOut), _
        intOutCount, SQL_DRIVER_PROMPT)
    If intResult <> SQL_SUCCESS Then
        intResult = frmODBCErrors.ODBCError("Dbc", glng_hEnv, _
                glng_hDbc, 0, _
            intResult, "Problem with call to SQLDriverConnect.")
        Exit Sub
    End If
    txtConnect.text = AddSpaces(strConnectOut)

    'Free the connection, but not the handle
    intResult = SQLDisconnect(glng_hDbc)
    If intResult <> SQL_SUCCESS Then
        intResult = frmODBCErrors.ODBCError("Dbc", glng_hEnv, _
            glng_hDbc, 0, _
            intResult, "Problem with call to SQLDriverConnect.")
    End If

    cmdCopyConnect.Enabled = True
End Sub
```

The other error that must be handled is one that occurs when the user clicks Cancel when ODBC's Select Data Source dialog box is shown. If this happens, the **Sub** procedure is exited and the user is returned to the main form.

How It Works

Three functions are available in the ODBC API for making a connection to a data source: `SQLConnect`, `SQLBrowseConnect`, and `SQLDriverConnect`. Table 6.7 explains these functions in more detail.

Table 6.7. ODBC functions for establishing data source connections.

FUNCTION	VERSION	CONFORMANCE	PRIMARY ARGUMENTS
SQLConnect	1.0	Core	hDbc, data source name, user ID, authorization string
SQLDriverConnect	1.0	1	hDbc, Windows handle (hwnd), connect string in, connect string out, completion option
SQLBrowseConnect	1.0	2	hDbc, connect string in, connect string out

SQLConnect

`SQLConnect` is the standard way of connecting to an ODBC data source. All the arguments must be complete and correct because if anything is wrong, ODBC generates an error. If everything is right, a connection is established. Valid return codes are `SQL_SUCCESS`, `SQL_SUCCESS_WITH_INFO`, `SQL_ERROR`, and `SQL_INVALID_HANDLE`. Because this function is in the Core conformance level, all ODBC drivers are guaranteed to support it (or as guaranteed as possible with drivers written by third-party developers attempting to adhere to a standard), so it is always available. The only flexibility that `SQLConnect` provides is when the specified data source name can't be found. In that case, the function looks for a default driver and loads that one if it is defined in ODBC.INI. If not, `SQL_ERROR` is returned, and you can obtain more information about the problem with a call to `SQLError`. This is the workhorse function of ODBC connections.

SQLDriverConnect

`SQLDriverConnect` offers a bit more flexibility for making ODBC connections. This function can handle data sources that require more information than the three arguments of `SQLConnect` (other than the connection handle `hDbc`, which all three functions require). `SQLDriverConnect` provides dialog boxes to prompt for any missing information needed for the connection, and it can handle connections not defined in the ODBC.INI file or registry. `SQLDriverConnect` provides three connection options:

✔ A connection string provided in the function call that contains all the data needed, including data source name, multiple user IDs, multiple passwords, and any other custom information required by the database.

✔ A connection string that provides only some of the data required to make the connection. The ODBC Driver Manager and the driver can prompt for any information that either of them needs in order to make the connection.

✔ A connection that is not defined in ODBC.INI or the registry. If any partial information is provided, the function uses it however it can.

When a connection is successfully made, the function returns SQL_SUCCESS and returns a completed connection string that can be used to make future connections to that database. It is a pretty safe bet that SQLDriverConnect is the function that Visual Basic uses when this How-To is employed to discover the connect string.

SQLDriverConnect can return SQL_SUCCESS, SQL_SUCCESS_WITH_INFO, SQL_NO_DATA_FOUND, SQL_ERROR, or SQL_INVALID_HANDLE. Valid choices for the completion option argument are SQL_DRIVER_PROMPT, SQL_DRIVER_COMPLETE, SQL_DRIVER_COMPLETE_REQUIRED, and SQL_DRIVER_NOPROMPT, as described here:

✔ SQL_DRIVER_PROMPT: This option displays dialog boxes (whether needed or not) to prompt for connection information. Any initial values included in the function call are used to fill in the appropriate controls in the dialog box.

✔ SQL_DRIVER_COMPLETE: If the connection information provided in the function call is sufficient to make the connection, ODBC goes ahead and makes the connection. If anything is missing, this option acts like SQL_DRIVER_PROMPT.

✔ SQL_DRIVER_COMPLETE_REQUIRED: This is the same as SQL_DRIVER_COMPLETE, except that any information not needed to make the connection is grayed out in the dialog box.

✔ SQL_DRIVER_NOPROMPT: If the information in the connect string is sufficient to make the connection, it goes ahead and makes the connection. If anything is missing, it makes no connection, and the function returns SQL_ERROR.

SQLBrowseConnect

The third function, SQLBrowseConnect, is perhaps the most interesting of the three functions. A call to this function initiates an interactive method of discovering what it takes to connect to a particular database. Each time SQLBrowseConnect is called, the function returns additional attributes that are needed to make a connection. An application making the call can parse out the resulting string containing missing attributes (which are marked as required or optional) and return successively more complete connect strings. Attributes that involve selection from a fixed list of items are returned as that full list so that an application can present a list box of choices to the user.

The bad news, for Visual Basic anyway, is that SQLBrowseConnect is a Conformance Level 2 function. Because Visual Basic is designed to require only Level 1 drivers, it doesn't have any functions that can directly use this function. But it is available to any application, including those written in Visual Basic, through direct calls to the ODBC API, if the driver supports Level 2 conformance.

Comments

As mentioned in the introduction to the chapter, you can't make an ODBC connection through an attached table to a database that Visual Basic natively supports, such as a Microsoft Access .MDB file or the ISAM databases Btrieve and dBASE. There normally isn't any reason to do so, although you can always do it by using the ODBC API directly.

COMPLEXITY
ADVANCED

6.5 How do I...
Determine what services an ODBC server provides?

Problem

I'd like to be able to connect with the different data sources scattered throughout our network. But all the various drivers have different capabilities, even though they are all accessible through ODBC. How can I find out through code which services are available for each server and keep the code as flexible and portable as possible?

Technique

This example develops a useful ODBC viewer that gathers in one place much of the information needed to evaluate the data sources and drivers available to a particular workstation. You can use the same techniques whether the data is located on a single computer with one hard disk or connected to a network with data of widely varying formats on different hardware.

Steps

Open and run the Visual Basic SERVICES.VBP project. Select an ODBC data source name from the Installed ODBC Data Sources list, and then click the Get Functions command button. After a moment, a list of the functions that can be used with the data source appears in the bottom half of the form, similar to the form shown later in Figure 6.11. Scroll through the list to see the functions available. Then, with the same data source highlighted, click the Get Properties command button. The Get Info window appears, as shown in Figure 6.10. Make the selections you want (from one to all the items in the list), and click the Get Info command button. The list of properties and their current values appears in the Biblio Properties window, as shown in Figure 6.11.

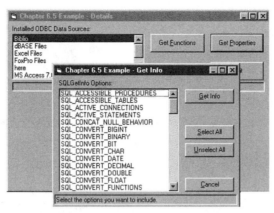

Figure 6.10. The project's Get Info form, showing the selected properties.

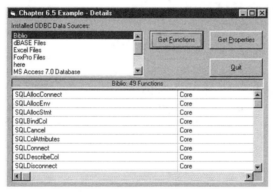

Figure 6.11. The project's Details form, showing the available functions.

1. Create a new project called SERVICES.VBP. Add the form ODBCErrors.FRM and the code module ODBC API Declarations.BAS using Visual Basic's File|Add menu command. The code module contains all the declarations necessary for the ODBC API functions and the constants used in many of the functions, and the form allows for an easy-to-read display of ODBC errors.

2. Add a new form, **frmODBC**, and save the file as SERVICES.FRM. Add the controls shown in Figure 6.11, setting the properties as given in Table 6.8. The area under the Properties label is the **MSFlexGrid** control, **grdResults**.

Table 6.8. Objects and properties for SERVICES.FRM.

OBJECT	PROPERTY	SETTING
Form	Name	frmODBC
	Caption	Chapter 6.5 Example - Details
CommandButton	Name	cmdProperties
	Caption	Get Properties
CommandButton	Name	cmdFunctions
	Caption	Get Functions
CommandButton	Name	cmdQuit
	Caption	Quit
ListBox	Name	lstODBCdbs
	Sorted	True
Label	Name	lblGrid
	Caption	Properties
	BorderStyle	1 - Fixed Single
Grid	Name	grdResults
	Visible	False
	Scrollbars	2 - flexScrollBarVertical
	Highlight	0 - flexHighlightNever
Label	Name	lblServices
	Caption	Installed ODBC Data Sources:

3. Put the following code in the declarations section of the form. This code declares the dynamic array that will be used to hold the names of the data sources and drivers available to ODBC. To avoid naming problems, `Option Explicit` tells Visual Basic to make sure you declare all variables and objects before using them.

```
Option Explicit

'Dynamic arrays to hold data
Dim strDBNames() As String
```

4. Add the following code to the form's **Load** event. First, the form is centered onscreen so that all the controls and information can be seen. Then, as with all applications that make direct calls to the ODBC API, the ODBC wrapper functions are called to allocate memory and assign a handle for the ODBC environment and for the database connection. This is followed by a call to the **GetODBCdbs Sub** procedure, which the following text explains.

```
Private Sub Form_Load()
    'Log on to an ODBC data source
    'First, allocate ODBC memory and get handles
    Dim intResult As Integer

    'Allocate the ODBC environment handle
    If ODBCAllocateEnv(glng_hEnv) = SQL_SUCCESS Then
        'Load the current list of data sources to list box
        GetODBCdbs
        'Show the form
        frmODBC.Show
    Else
        End
    End If
End Sub
```

5. Add the following routine to **frmODBC**. This procedure extracts the existing lists of data sources and drivers from ODBC. **GetODBCdbs** obtains the list of data source names and the descriptions of each. The **Do While** loop extracts one data source name at a time with a call to **SQLDataSources**. If no error is returned from the function call, the data source name is added to the **lstODBCdbs** list box, showing all the data sources that are already installed. When the last data source has been returned to this function, the **SQLDataSources** function returns the **SQL_NO_DATA_FOUND** result, and the loop terminates.

```
Private Sub GetODBCdbs()
    Dim varTemp As Variant, I As Integer

    lstODBCdbs.Clear
    varTemp = ODBCDSNList(glng_hEnv, False)

    If IsArray(varTemp) Then
        For I = LBound(varTemp) To UBound(varTemp)
            lstODBCdbs.AddItem varTemp(I)
        Next
    Else
        MsgBox "No ODBC data sources to load!", vbCritical
        End
    End If
End Sub
```

6. Add the following routine to **frmODBC**. This procedure first determines whether a data source name has been selected in the **lstODBCdbs** list box. If none has been selected, a message box lets the user know that and then exits the procedure.

Assuming that a data source is selected, a call is made to **ODBCConnectDS** to allocate connection memory and a handle, which is required for a later call to **SQLGetFunctions**. If a connection is made successfully, the call to **SQLGetFunctions** is made, which does the actual work of retrieving the function list. The list is put into the **FuncList** array, which has 100 elements. An element of this array is set to true (-1) or false

(**0**) if the referenced ODBC function is available with this data source. See the "How It Works" section for a discussion about how this array is used to identify available functions.

To set the number of rows in the **grdResults** grid, the number of array elements that are **True** must be counted. The first **For...Next** loop handles that, so that **j** is the number of true elements at the end of the loop. Then, after setting up the grid with the numbers of rows and columns to fit the data, the **intFuncList** array is looped through once again, to put the function names into each row of the grid.

```
Private Sub cmdFunctions_Click()
    Dim strDataSource As String
    Dim strUserName As String, strPassword As String
    Dim intResult As Integer, intErrResult As Integer
    ReDim intFuncList(100) As Integer
    Dim I As Integer, j As Integer

    'First, check to see if anything is selected
    'If not, notify user, then return to form.
    If lstODBCdbs.ListIndex >= 0 Then
        Screen.MousePointer = vbHourglass
        strDataSource = lstODBCdbs.List(lstODBCdbs.ListIndex)

        If SQLAllocStmt(glng_hDbc, glng_hStmt) Then _
            intResult = ODBCConnectDS(glng_hEnv, glng_hDbc, _
                glng_hStmt, strDataSource, strUserName, _
                strPassword)

        If intResult = SQL_SUCCESS Then _
            intResult = SQLGetFunctions(glng_hDbc, _
                SQL_API_ALL_FUNCTIONS, intFuncList(0))

        If intResult <> SQL_SUCCESS Then
            intErrResult = frmODBCErrors.ODBCError("Dbc", _
                glng_hEnv,
                glng_hDbc, 0, intResult, _
                "Error getting list of ODBC functions")
        Else
            'Run through the array and get the number of functions
            j = 0
            For I = 0 To 99
                If intFuncList(I) Then j = j + 1
            Next

            'Start by clearing the frmODBC grid
            With frmODBC.grdResults
                .Rows = j
                .Cols = 3
                .FixedCols = 1
                .FixedRows = 0
                .ColWidth(0) = 8
                .ColWidth(1) = 0.65 * frmODBC.grdResults.Width
                .ColWidth(2) = 0.35 * frmODBC.grdResults.Width
            End With
```

continued on next page

continued from previous page

```
                                  lblGrid.Caption = lstODBCdbs.text & ": " & _
                                              Trim(Val(j)) & _
                              " Functions"

                          'Populate the grid with the function names
                          j = 0
                          For I = 0 To 99
                              If intFuncList(I) <> 0 Then
                                  With frmODBC.grdResults
                                      .Row = j
                                      .Col = 0: .text = j
                                      .Col = 1: .text = ODBCFuncs(0, I)
                                      .Col = 2: .text = ODBCFuncs(1, I)
                                  End With
                                  j = j + 1
                              End If
                          Next

                          'Move to the top row
                          frmODBC.grdResults.Row = 0
                          frmODBC.grdResults.Col = 1

                          'free the data source connection
                          intResult = ODBCDisconnectDS(glng_hEnv, glng_hDbc, _
                                      SQL_NULL_HSTMT)

                          Screen.MousePointer = vbDefault
                          frmODBC.grdResults.Visible = True
                      End If
                  Else
                      MsgBox "Please select a data source name first.", _
                          vbCritical, "ODBC Functions"
                  End If
          End Sub
```

7. Put the following code in the `cmdProperties_Click` event subroutine. After the program checks to make sure that a data source is selected, it attempts to allocate a connection handle; then it loads the `frmGetInfo` form to continue obtaining information.

```
Private Sub cmdProperties_Click()
    Dim intResult As Integer
    If lstODBCdbs.ListIndex < 0 Then
        MsgBox "Please select a data source name first.", _
            vbCritical, "ODBC Properties"
    Else
        intResult = ODBCConnectDS(glng_hEnv, glng_hDbc, _
            glng_hStmt, lstODBCdbs.text, "", "")
        If intResult = SQL_SUCCESS Then Load frmGetInfo
    End If
End Sub
```

8. Enter the following two procedures to the code section of the form. The first procedure establishes a command button to quit the application. The

`Unload` event then cleans up and releases the memory and handles that were necessary for making calls to the ODBC API.

```
Private Sub cmdQuit_Click()
    End
End Sub

Private Sub Form_Unload(Cancel As Integer)
    Dim intResult As Integer

    intResult = ODBCDisconnectDS(glng_hEnv, glng_hDbc, glng_hStmt)
    intResult = ODBCFreeEnv(glng_hEnv)
End Sub
```

9. Add the following code to the code section of the form. This function provides a convenient way to convert some of the results of the properties to a more user-friendly and understandable form.

```
Private Function convCh(inChar As String, num As Variant)
    inChar = LTrim$(Left$(inChar, num))

    Select Case inChar
        Case "Y"
            convCh = "Yes"
        Case "N"
            convCh = "No"
        Case Else
            convCh = inChar
    End Select

End Function
```

10. Add a new form, `frmGetInfo`, and save the file as GETINFO.FRM. Add the controls shown in Figure 6.10, setting the properties as shown in Table 6.9.

Table 6.9. Objects and properties for GETINFO.FRM.

OBJECT	PROPERTY	SETTING
Form	Name	frmGetInfo
	Caption	Chapter 6.5 Example - Get Info
TextBox	Name	txtStatus
	Text	Select the options you want to include.
CommandButton	Name	cmdCancel
	Cancel	True
	Caption	Cancel
CommandButton	Name	cmdGetInfo
	Caption	Get Info

continued on next page

continued from previous page

OBJECT	PROPERTY	SETTING
CommandButton	Name	cmdSelection
	Caption	Unselect All
CommandButton	Name	cmdSelection
	Caption	Select All
ListBox	Name	lstGetInfoData
	MultiSelect	Extended
	Sorted	True
Label	Name	lblGetInfo

11. Add the following line of code to the declarations section of the GETINFO.FRM form. **Option Explicit** tells Visual Basic to make sure that you declare all variables and objects before using them, to avoid naming problems.

```
Option Explicit
```

12. Add the following code to the form's **Load** event. The main job of this procedure is to load the **lstGetInfoData** list box with all the available ODBC functions. All the function names are loaded into the **ODBCGetInfo** array in the **LoadGetInfo Sub** procedure in ODBC API Declarations.BAS. That array is an array of **GetInfo** types, defined in ODBC API as this:

```
Type GetInfo
    InfoType As String
    ReturnType As String
End Type
```

The array has **SQL_INFO_LAST** number of elements, as defined in ODBC API Declarations.BAS in the declarations section:

```
Private Sub Form_Load()
    'Load the list box with the ODBCGetInfo array
    Dim I As Integer
    For I = 0 To SQL_INFO_LAST
        If ODBCGetInfo(I).InfoType <> "" Then
            lstGetInfoData.AddItem ODBCGetInfo(I).InfoType
        End If
    Next
    frmGetInfo.Show
End Sub
```

13. Add the following code to the **cmdGetInfo**'s **Click** event procedure. Although this procedure looks foreboding, it is really doing only two main jobs: getting a count and a list of the **SQLGetInfo** options that have been selected in the list box and then looping through to get their current settings, populating the grid control on the **frmODBC** form with the results.

For more information on this procedure, review the "How It Works" section later in this How-To.

```vb
Private Sub cmdGetInfo_Click()
    Dim intSelCount As Integer        'count of selected items
    Dim I As Integer, j As Integer

    Dim ri As Integer
    Dim rs As String * 255
    Dim rb As Long, rl As Long

    Dim lngInfoValue As Long
    Dim lngInfoValueMax As Integer, intInfoValue As Integer, _
        intResult As Integer
    Dim intConnIndex As Integer
    Dim strTemp As String, strID As String, strErrMsg As String
    Dim strRowData() As String

    lngInfoValueMax = 255

    'Get the number of rows selected and the type of data
    intSelCount = 0
    For I = 0 To lstGetInfoData.ListCount - 1
        If lstGetInfoData.Selected(I) Then
            ReDim Preserve strRowData(intSelCount + 1)
            strRowData(intSelCount) = lstGetInfoData.List(I)
            intSelCount = intSelCount + 1
        End If
    Next

    If intSelCount = 0 Then
        MsgBox "No attributes were selected. Please select " & _
            "at least one and try again.", vbExclamation
        Exit Sub
    End If

    'Start by clearing the frmODBC grid
    With frmODBC.grdResults
        .Rows = intSelCount + 1: .Cols = 3
        .FixedCols = 1: .FixedRows = 1
        .ColWidth(0) = 8
        .ColWidth(1) = 0.45 * frmODBC.grdResults.Width
        .ColWidth(2) = 0.55 * frmODBC.grdResults.Width
        .Row = 0
        .Col = 1: .text = "Attribute Constant"
        .Col = 2: .text = "Value"
    End With
    frmODBC.lblGrid.Caption = frmODBC.lstODBCdbs.text & " " & _
            "Properties"

    For I = 0 To intSelCount - 1
        With frmODBC.grdResults
            .Row = I + 1
            .Col = 0: .text = I + 1
            .Col = 1: .text = strRowData(I)
            .Col = 2
```

continued on next page

continued from previous page

```
            End With

            'Get the index of ODBConn - have to do it this way
            'because there are gaps in the ODBC constants
            For j = LBound(ODBCGetInfo) To UBound(ODBCGetInfo)
                If strRowData(I) = ODBCGetInfo(j).InfoType Then Exit _
                    For
            Next

            'Format the data according the return type of
            'ODBCGetInfo
            Select Case Left$(ODBCGetInfo(j).ReturnType, 1)
                Case "S"     'String
                    intResult = SQLGetInfo(glng_hDbc, j, ByVal rs, _
                        Len(rs), intInfoValue)
                    If Len(Trim$(ODBCGetInfo(j).ReturnType)) > 1 Then
                        frmODBC.grdResults.text = _
                            SpecialStr(strRowData(I), _
                            Trim$(rs))
                    Else
                        frmODBC.grdResults.text = Trim$(rs)
                    End If
                Case "B"     '32-bit Bitmask
                    intResult = SQLGetInfo(glng_hDbc, j, rb, 255, _
                            intInfoValue)
                    frmODBC.grdResults.text = BitMask(rb)
                Case "I"     'Integer
                    intResult = SQLGetInfo(glng_hDbc, j, ri, 255, _
                            intInfoValue)
                    If Len(Trim$(ODBCGetInfo(j).ReturnType)) > 1 Then
                        frmODBC.grdResults.text = _
                            SpecialInt(strRowData(I), _
                            Trim$(ri))
                    Else
                        frmODBC.grdResults.text = ri
                    End If
                Case "L"     'Long
                    intResult = SQLGetInfo(glng_hDbc, j, rl, 255, _
                            intInfoValue)
                    If Len(Trim$(ODBCGetInfo(j).ReturnType)) > 1 Then
                        frmODBC.grdResults.text = _
                            SpecialLong(strRowData(I), _
                            Trim$(rl))
                    Else
                        frmODBC.grdResults.text = rl
                    End If
                Case Else
                    'Error in array
                    frmODBC.grdResults.text = "Error processing _
                        return value."
            End Select
            If intResult <> SQL_SUCCESS Then
                frmODBC.grdResults.text = "Error getting data."
            End If
        Next
```

```
        frmODBC.grdResults.Visible = True
        Unload Me
End Sub
```

14. Add the code for `SpecialStr` to the code section of the module. This is the first of the "special" processing functions that make the results of the call to `SQLGetInfo` more meaningful. Most of the `Select Case` options simply convert a "Y" or "N" to "Yes" or "No." Another processing function, `SQL_KEYWORDS`, returns a long list of keywords you can use. To keep things from getting too complex, this How-To just indicates that a list is available; you could easily put the list into a TextBox or List control to allow closer examination, or it could be used by the application.

The return value of the `SpecialStr` function is the string that is actually displayed in the grid.

```
Private Function SpecialStr(Opt As String, RetStr As String)
    'Do any special processing required for a SQLGetInfo string
    Select Case Opt
        Case "SQL_ODBC_SQL_OPT_IEF"
            SpecialStr = IIf(RetStr = "Y", "Yes", "No")
        Case "SQL_COLUMN_ALIAS"
            SpecialStr = IIf(RetStr = "Y", "Yes", "No")
        Case "SQL_KEYWORDS"
            SpecialStr = "List of keywords."        '&&&
        Case "SQL_ORDER_BY_COLUMNS_IN_SELECT"
            SpecialStr = IIf(RetStr = "Y", "Yes", "No")
        Case "SQL_MAX_ROW_SIZE_INCLUDES_LONG"
            SpecialStr = IIf(RetStr = "Y", "Yes", "No")
        Case "SQL_EXPRESSIONS_IN_ORDERBY"
            SpecialStr = IIf(RetStr = "Y", "Yes", "No")
        Case "SQL_MULT_RESULT_SETS"
            SpecialStr = IIf(RetStr = "Y", "Yes", "No")
        Case "SQL_OUTER_JOINS"
            Select Case RetStr
                Case "N"
                    SpecialStr = "No outer joins."
                Case "Y"
                    SpecialStr = "Yes, left-right segregation."
                Case "P"
                    SpecialStr = "Partial outer joins."
                Case "F"
                    SpecialStr = "Full outer joins."
                Case Else
                    SpecialStr = "Missing data."
            End Select
        Case "SQL_NEED_LONG_DATA_LEN"
            SpecialStr = IIf(RetStr = "Y", "Yes", "No")
        Case "SQL_LIKE_ESCAPE_CLAUSE"
            SpecialStr = IIf(RetStr = "Y", "Yes", "No")
        Case "SQL_ACCESSIBLE_PROCEDURES"
            SpecialStr = IIf(RetStr = "Y", "Yes", "No")
        Case "SQL_ACCESSIBLE_TABLES"
            SpecialStr = IIf(RetStr = "Y", "Yes", "No")
```

continued on next page

continued from previous page

```
            Case "SQL_DATA_SOURCE_READ_ONLY"
                SpecialStr = IIf(RetStr = "Y", "Yes", "No")
            Case "SQL_PROCEDURES"
                SpecialStr = IIf(RetStr = "Y", "Yes", "No")
            Case "SQL_ROW_UPDATES"
                SpecialStr = IIf(RetStr = "Y", "Yes", "No")
            Case Else
                SpecialStr = "Missing special processing."
        End Select
End Function
```

15. Add the code for the **SpecialInt** function to the code section of the form. This function handles special integer return values from **SQLGetInfo**. In all of these special cases, the return value is an index to a keyword defined in ODBCAPI.BAS. Simply use a **Select Case** nested within the overall **Select Case** structure to translate the value into a more meaningful string.

```
Private Function SpecialInt(Opt As String, RetInt As Integer)
    'Do any special processing required for a SQLGetInfo integer
    Select Case Opt
        Case "SQL_CORRELATION_NAME"
            Select Case RetInt
                Case SQL_CN_NONE
                    SpecialInt = "Not supported."
                Case SQL_CN_DIFFERENT
                    SpecialInt = "Supported but names vary."
                Case SQL_CN_ANY
                    SpecialInt = "Any valid user name."
                Case Else
                    SpecialInt = "Missing data."
            End Select
        Case "SQL_NON_NULLABLE_COLUMNS"
            Select Case RetInt
                Case SQL_NNC_NULL
                    SpecialInt = "All columns nullable."
                Case SQL_NNC_NON_NULL
                    SpecialInt = "May be non-nullable."
                Case Else
                    SpecialInt = "Missing data."
            End Select
        Case "SQL_FILE_USAGE"
            Select Case RetInt
                Case SQL_FILE_NOT_SUPPORTED
                    SpecialInt = "Not a single tier driver."
                Case SQL_FILE_TABLE
                    SpecialInt = "Treats data source as table."
                Case SQL_FILE_QUALIFIER
                    SpecialInt = "Treats data source as" _
                                    "qualifier."
                Case Else
                    SpecialInt = "Missing data."
            End Select
        Case "SQL_NULL_COLLATION"
```

```
            Select Case RetInt
                Case SQL_NC_END
                    SpecialInt = "NULLs sorted to end."
                Case SQL_NC_HIGH
                    SpecialInt = "NULLs sorted to high end."
                Case SQL_NC_LOW
                    SpecialInt = "NULLs sorted to low end."
                Case SQL_NC_START
                    SpecialInt = "NULLs sorted to start."
                Case Else
                    SpecialInt = "Missing data."
            End Select
    Case "SQL_GROUP_BY"
        Select Case RetInt
            Case SQL_GB_NOT_SUPPORTED
                SpecialInt = "Group By not supported."
            Case SQL_GB_GROUP_BY_EQUALS_SELECT
                SpecialInt = _
                    "All non-aggregated columns, no others."
            Case SQL_GB_GROUP_BY_CONTAINS_SELECT
                SpecialInt = _
                    "All non-aggregated columns, some others."
            Case SQL_GB_NO_RELATION
                SpecialInt = "Not related to select list."
            Case Else
                SpecialInt = "Missing data."
        End Select
    Case "SQL_IDENTIFIER_CASE"
        Select Case RetInt
            Case SQL_IC_UPPER
                SpecialInt = "Upper case."
            Case SQL_IC_LOWER
                SpecialInt = "Lower case."
            Case SQL_IC_SENSITIVE
                SpecialInt = "Case sensitive."
            Case SQL_IC_MIXED
                SpecialInt = "Mixed case."
            Case Else
                SpecialInt = "Missing data."
        End Select
    Case "SQL_QUOTED_IDENTIFIER_CASE"
        Select Case RetInt
            Case SQL_IC_UPPER
                SpecialInt = "Upper case."
            Case SQL_IC_LOWER
                SpecialInt = "Lower case."
            Case SQL_IC_SENSITIVE
                SpecialInt = "Case sensitive."
            Case SQL_IC_MIXED
                SpecialInt = "Mixed case."
            Case Else
                SpecialInt = "Missing data."
        End Select
    Case "SQL_ODBC_API_CONFORMANCE"
        Select Case RetInt
            Case SQL_OAC_NONE
```

continued on next page

continued from previous page

```
                            SpecialInt = "No conformance."
                    Case SQL_OAC_LEVEL1
                            SpecialInt = "Level 1 supported."
                    Case SQL_OAC_LEVEL2
                            SpecialInt = "Level 2 supported."
                    Case Else
                            SpecialInt = "Missing data."
                End Select
        Case "SQL_CURSOR_COMMIT_BEHAVIOR"
            Select Case RetInt
                    Case SQL_CB_DELETE
                            SpecialInt = "Close and delete statements."
                    Case SQL_CB_CLOSE
                            SpecialInt = "Close cursors."
                    Case SQL_CB_PRESERVE
                            SpecialInt = "Preserve cursors."
                    Case Else
                            SpecialInt = "Missing data."
                End Select
        Case "SQL_CURSOR_ROLLBACK_BEHAVIOR"
            Select Case RetInt
                    Case SQL_CB_DELETE
                            SpecialInt = "Close and delete statements."
                    Case SQL_CB_CLOSE
                            SpecialInt = "Close cursors."
                    Case SQL_CB_PRESERVE
                            SpecialInt = "Preserve cursors."
                    Case Else
                            SpecialInt = "Missing data."
                End Select
        Case "SQL_TXN_CAPABLE"
            Select Case RetInt
                    Case SQL_TC_NONE
                            SpecialInt = "Transactions not supported."
                    Case SQL_TC_DML
                            SpecialInt = _
                                "DML statements only, DDL cause error."
                    Case SQL_TC_DDL_COMMIT
                            SpecialInt = _
                                "DML statements, DDL commit transaction."
                    Case SQL_TC_DDL_IGNORE
                            SpecialInt = "DML statements, DDL ignored."
                    Case SQL_TC_ALL
                            SpecialInt = "Both DML and DDL statements."
                    Case Else
                            SpecialInt = "Missing data."
                End Select
        Case "SQL_QUALIFIER_LOCATION"
            Select Case RetInt
                    Case SQL_QL_START
                            SpecialInt = "Start of name."
                    Case SQL_QL_END
                            SpecialInt = "End of name."
                    Case Else
                            SpecialInt = "Missing data."
                End Select
        Case "SQL_CONCAT_NULL_BEHAVIOR"
```

```
                    Select Case RetInt
                        Case SQL_CB_NULL
                            SpecialInt = "Result is NULL valued."
                        Case SQL_CB_NON_NULL
                            SpecialInt = _
                                "Result is non-NULL concatenation."
                        Case Else
                            SpecialInt = "Missing data."
                    End Select
                Case Else
                    SpecialInt = "Missing special integer processing."
            End Select
    End Function
```

16. Add the code for the **BitMask** function to the code section of the form. One form of return value from the **SQLGetInfo** function is a 32-bit bitmask. A *bitmask* is a way of packing lots of information into a relatively compact variable because each of the 32 bits can be "on" or "off" (1 or **0**) to indicate the value of some option. This function simply converts the bitmask into a string of 32 1s and **0**s to show their content. You could expand this function (in a way similar to the nested **Select Case SpecialInt** function) to test for the various values of the different options, and you could present a list or otherwise use the information in your application.

In practical use in an application, you would be interested in checking for one or two characteristics contained in the bitmask and would check for that condition instead of just listing the contents of the bitmask.

```
Private Function BitMask(RetBit As Long)
    'Do processing required for a SQLGetInfo bit mask return
    Dim i As Long, bin As String
    Const maxpower = 30    ' Maximum number of binary digits
                           ' supported.
    bin = ""  'Build the desired binary number in this string,
              'bin.

    If RetBit > 2 ^ maxpower Then
        BitMask = "Error converting data."
        Exit Function
    End If

    ' Negative numbers have "1" in the 32nd left-most digit:
    If RetBit < 0 Then bin = bin + "1" Else bin = bin + "0"

    For i = maxpower To 0 Step -1
        If RetBit And (2 ^ i) Then    ' Use the logical "AND"
                                      ' operator.
            bin = bin + "1"
        Else
            bin = bin + "0"
        End If
    Next
    BitMask = bin ' The bin string contains the binary number.
End Function
```

17. Add the code for `SpecialLong` to the code section of the form. This is the last of the `Special` functions, and it is used with return type `Long`. The single case that must be handled here is for the `SQL_DEFAULT_TXN_ISOLATION` attribute, and it is handled similarly to the `SpecialInt` function. The same nested `Select Case` structure has been used to allow easy expansion of this function for future versions of ODBC and handle the error condition if an unexpected `Long` is sent to the function.

```
Private Function SpecialLong(Opt As String, RetInt As Integer)
    'Do any special processing required for a SQLGetInfo long
    Select Case Opt
        Case "SQL_DEFAULT_TXN_ISOLATION"
            Select Case RetInt
                Case SQL_TXN_READ_UNCOMMITTED
                    SpecialLong = _
                        "Dirty reads, nonrepeatable, phantoms."
                Case SQL_TXN_READ_COMMITTED
                    SpecialLong = _
                        "No dirty reads, but nonrepeatable " & _
                        "and phantoms."
                Case SQL_TXN_REPEATABLE_READ
                    SpecialLong = _
                        "No dirty or nonrepeatable reads." & _
                        "Phantoms okay."
                Case SQL_TXN_SERIALIZABLE
                    SpecialLong = "Serializable transactions."
                Case SQL_TXN_VERSIONING
                    SpecialLong = _
                        "Serializable transactions  with higher " & _
                        "concurrency."
                Case Else
                    SpecialLong = "Missing data."
            End Select

        Case Else
            SpecialLong = "Missing special Long processing."
    End Select
End Function
```

18. Add the code for the `cmdSelection` control array `Click` event. The Select All and Unselect All command buttons are provided for convenience in selecting items in the list. This procedure simply loops through the `lstGetInfoData` list box, selecting all items if the `Index` is 1 (Select All was clicked) and deselecting all items if the `Index` is 0 (Unselect All was clicked).

```
Private Sub cmdSelection_Click(Index As Integer)
    'Select all of the items in the list
    Dim I As Integer
    For I = 0 To lstGetInfoData.ListCount - 1
        lstGetInfoData.Selected(I) = (Index > -1)
    Next
End Sub
```

19. Add the code for the `cmdCancel` `Click` event. Even though `SQLGetInfo` uses an `hDbc` handle, the memory was allocated in the `frmODBC` form, so no special cleanup is necessary in this form. Therefore, no form `Unload` procedure is required.

```
Private Sub cmdCancel_Click()
    Unload Me
End Sub
```

How It Works

The `SQLGetInfo` function is a versatile way to get lots of information about an ODBC data source. In a typical application, you would check for a small number of properties, or if a particular function is implemented, instead of retrieving bulk results as in this How-To, you would use the techniques shown here.

Step 13 of this How-To performs and deciphers the `SQLGetInfo` through a procedure that appears daunting, but in fact is really doing only two main jobs: getting a count and a list of the `SQLGetInfo` options that have been selected in the list box and then looping through to get their current settings, populating the grid control on the `frmODBC` form with the results. Let's break this procedure down into more manageable chunks because this procedure is important for you to understand.

After the variables used in the procedure are declared, the `lstGetInfoData` list box is looped through to find out what selections have been made by the user. For each selection, the `RowData` dynamic array is expanded by one element, and the name of the option is added. That way, the array will be fully populated with the names of the options selected. The variable `selCount` keeps a running count of how many options have been selected.

After that process is complete, the options are checked to see whether any were selected. If not, the user is asked to make at least one selection and then try again. There is no reason to proceed if there is nothing to do.

Next, the code clears the `grdResults` grid control in the `frmODBC` form, setting it up with three columns and rows equal to `intSelCount` + 1. One additional row is necessary for column headings.

The real work of the procedure begins, looping through each of the options and actually making the call to the `SQLGetInfo` ODBC function. This function returns the current setting for the data source for a selected option. Two things make the code a bit more complex. First, an integer needs to be passed to `SQLGetInfo` representing an index into the attribute or option to be checked. To get that index, loop through the `ODBCGetInfo` array, comparing the `InfoType` member to the name in `strRowData`, until there is a match. Because the names in `strRowData` came from `ODBCInfo` in the first place, there will be a match somewhere.

The second complexity arises from the types of values returned from `SQLGetInfo`. Table 6.10 lists the possible return types.

Table 6.10. *SQLGetInfo* return types.

TYPE	INFOTYPE	DESCRIPTION
String	S	C type NULL-terminated string
Bitmask	B	32-bit, usually with multiple meanings
Integer	I	Standard Visual Basic 16-bit number
Long	L	Standard Visual Basic 32-bit number

The `InfoType` column refers to the `InfoType` member of the `GetInfo` structure defined in ODBCAPI.BAS. This is simply an arbitrarily chosen code for use in the `Select Case` in this procedure so that `SQLGetInfo` can be called with the right variable type to receive the results.

The `InfoType` member can be either one or two characters long. The second character, if present, means that some special processing is necessary to make the result meaningful when it is put in the grid on the `frmODBC` form.

The `Select Case` structure then puts the results directly into the `frmODBC` grid.

Some of the property values returned might not be available, in which case the `cmdGetInfo Click` event procedure places a value of `Error Getting Data` in the results grid. You might get this result for many reasons, but the primary reason exposes one of the quirks of the ODBC system. Although ODBC has some rather specific demarcations between conformance levels (drivers must be at a Conformance Level 1 to be usable with Visual Basic), there is no guarantee that a driver will implement all the functionality of a given function. `SQLGetInfo` is no exception to this rule, unfortunately.

One way to determine whether this is the case is to make a call to `SQLError` (or the `ODBCError` wrapper function) to obtain more information about the error. In any event, it is safe to assume in most cases that the particular attribute should not be used with the particular data source.

As noted in step 13 of this How-To, the syntax of the `SQLGetInfo` function is this:

```
SQLGetInfo(hDbc, fInfoType, rgbInfoValue, cbInfoValueMax, pcbInfoValue)
```

Table 6.11 shows the arguments to the function.

Table 6.11. Arguments for the *SQLGetInfo* ODBC function.

ARGUMENT	DESCRIPTION
hDbc	Connection handle
fInfoType	Type of information (in this How-To, from the ODBCGetInfo array)
rgbInfoValue	Variable of the proper type to store results
cbInfoValueMax	Maximum length of the *rgbInfoValue* buffer
pcbInfoValue	Total number of bytes available to return in *rgbInfoValue*

The syntax of **SQLGetFunctions** is this:

```
SQLGetFunctions(hDbc, fFunction, pfExists)
```

Table 6.12 shows the arguments to the function.

Table 6.12. Arguments for the *SQLGetFunctions* ODBC function.

ARGUMENT	DESCRIPTION
hDbc	Connection handle
fFunction	The particular function or, in this How-To, SQL_API_ALL_FUNCTIONS
pfExists	For SQL_API_ALL_FUNCTIONS, an array with 100 elements for output

If you look at the contents of the ODBCAPI.BAS file, you'll see two functions, **LoadGetInfo** and **ODBCLoadFuncs**, that load global arrays with information about the **SQLGetInfo** property options and the list of functions available in ODBC. These two arrays are used to provide selection lists for the program in this How-To and loop through to make the actual calls to **SQLGetInfo**. The **SQLGetInfo** function has many property options, too numerous to describe here—see the ODBC SDK for a more detailed description of the property options and in which ODBC version they first appeared.

What if a driver is written only to the Core conformance level? Well, in a way, that isn't a problem because you won't be using that driver with Visual Basic anyway: Visual Basic counts on Level 1 conformance to interact with ODBC. Running the program in this How-To will provide an ODBC error, and you are finished. You can still use the driver, but only by making direct calls to the ODBC API from Visual Basic. In that situation, you'll need to consult the driver's documentation to find out what it can and cannot do. As a practical matter, by far and away most drivers are at least Level 1 conformance, so this will rarely be a problem.

The nice thing about the **SQLGetFunctions** function is that, even though it is a conformance Level 1 function, it is implemented in the ODBC Driver Manager, which sits between all applications using ODBC and the ODBC driver. That way, if the driver doesn't implement **SQLGetFunctions**, the Driver Manager will still give a list. If the driver does implement the function, the Driver Manager passes the call to the driver.

Comments

Understanding the **SQLGetInfo** and **SQLGetFunctions** functions is an extremely important part of understanding the ODBC API. Before moving to another How-To, experiment with the use of these functions, especially between different ODBC drivers, to get a better understanding of how varied different drivers can be in terms of functionality.

COMPLEXITY
INTERMEDIATE

6.6 How do I...
Use ODBCDirect to connect to database servers?

Problem

My large application has been recently converted from DAO to ODBC, and the design specifications call for direct ODBC access. How can I get the power of ODBC with the ease of DAO programming in Visual Basic?

Technique

Well, here's good news. An extension of the DAO, called ODBCDirect, allows direct ODBC connection capability, with most of the flexibility of the DAO objects intact. ODBCDirect provides a **Connection** object, analogous to the DAO's **Database** object. It even has a **Database** property to simulate the **Database** object for your needs. The **Connection** object is the most important piece of the ODBCDirect object hierarchy, so that will be the focus of this example.

Steps

Open and run the ODBCDirect.VBP Visual Basic project file. Click the Open DSN button, and choose an ODBC data source. The form then opens a **Connection** object and displays the object's properties for the data source, similar to those shown in Figure 6.12.

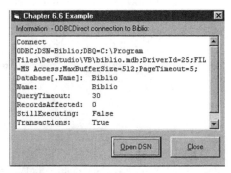

Figure 6.12. Chapter 6.6 example.

1. Create a new project, and save it as ODBCDirect.VBP.

2. Name the default form `Form1`, and save the file as TRANS.FRM. Add the controls shown in Figure 6.12, setting the properties as listed in Table 6.13.

Table 6.13. Objects and properties for the ODBCDirect form.

OBJECT	PROPERTY	SETTING
Form	Name	frmODBC
	Caption	Chapter 6.6 Example
TextBox	Name	txtProperties
	ScrollBars	2 - Vertical
	MultiLine	True
	Locked	True
	Font	Courier
	Font.Size	10
CommandButton	Name	cmdOpen
	Caption	&Open DSN
CommandButton	Name	cmdClose
	Caption	&Close
Label	Name	lblTables
	Caption	No information available

3. Add the following code to the declarations section of `Form1`:

```
Option Explicit
Dim conTemp As Connection
```

4. Add the following code to the form's `Load` event. The brevity of this routine doesn't explain its importance—the `DefaultType` property determines whether the DAO will construct a DAO or an ODBCDirect object. In this case, you are instructing the `DBEngine` that all objects created under it are ODBCDirect objects. If you planned to mix DAO and ODBCDirect access in the same application, you would perform this step at the workspace or database level, depending on your needs.

```
Private Sub Form_Load()
    'Notice the dbUseODBC parameter; this determines that DBEngine
    'will create an ODBCDirect workspace by default.
    DBEngine.DefaultType = dbUseODBC
End Sub
```

5. Add the following code to the `Click` event of `cmdOpen`. This routine first attempts to open an ODBCDirect `Connection` object by forcing the user to

select an ODBC driver from the ODBC Data Sources dialog box. After it is
selected, the **Connection** object is created and its properties concatenated
into the **txtProperties** text box for display.

```
Private Sub cmdOpen_Click()
    'Let's create a Connection object. This line will force
    'the ODBC driver to prompt the user.
    'The ODBCDirect Connection object is identical, in terms of
    'DAO object hierarchy, to the Database object.
    Set conTemp = Workspaces(0).OpenConnection("", , False, _
        "ODBC;")
    'If open, let's get the TableDefs from the Database
    'property of the Connection object.
    If IsObject(conTemp) Then
        'Since the Connection object does not support a
        'Properties collection, we must iterate through
        'each property manually.
        lblTables = "Information   - ODBCDirect connection to " & _
            conTemp.Name & ":"
        With conTemp
            txtProperties = "Connect            " & .Connect
            ' Property actually returns a Database object.
            txtProperties = txtProperties & vbCrLf & _
                "Database[.Name]: " & .Database.Name
            txtProperties = txtProperties & vbCrLf & _
                "Name:              " & .Name
            txtProperties = txtProperties & vbCrLf & _
                "QueryTimeout:      " & .QueryTimeout
            txtProperties = txtProperties & vbCrLf & _
                "RecordsAffected:  " & .RecordsAffected
            txtProperties = txtProperties & vbCrLf & _
                "StillExecuting:   " & .StillExecuting
            txtProperties = txtProperties & vbCrLf & _
                "Transactions:      " & .Transactions
            txtProperties = txtProperties & vbCrLf & _
                "Updatable:         " & .Updatable
        End With
    End If
End Sub
```

6. Add the following code to the **Click** event of **cmdClose**:

```
Private Sub cmdClose_Click()
    End
End Sub
```

How It Works

The **DBEngine** is initialized with the **dbUseODBC** flag, which tells DAO that all the
workspaces, connections, and so on will be generated via ODBCDirect, rather
than through the DAO. Note that it's not an either-or situation; the same
property exists on **Workspace** objects. A **Workspace** object can be created and
then flagged for use with ODBCDirect, so DAO and ODBCDirect workspaces
can exist together. This, by the way, proves very useful for projects involving

data conversion or for communication with server and mainframe databases. After the **DBEngine** is initialized and the user presses the Open DSN button, the **Connection** object is created. After successful creation, the form prints each property of the **Connection** object (laboriously—the **Connection** object supports neither the **Properties** nor **TableDefs** collection) to the text box for your perusal.

The lack of a **TableDefs** collection can make it difficult to maneuver around a database, but this can be surmounted by workarounds. For example, Microsoft SQL Server allows a user to query the **SysTables** table, which maintains a list of tables in the database. It might take some doing, but you can find workarounds for many database systems to supply this information.

Comments

One good use of ODBCDirect is in the scaling of an application—if you see the need to move your DAO-based workstation application into the client/server arena, you can do so with a minimum of recoding and still apply the flexibility of ODBC at the same time with the use of ODBCDirect.

SQL SERVER DATABASES AND REMOTE DATA OBJECTS

7

SQL SERVER DATABASES AND REMOTE DATA OBJECTS

How do I...

7.1 Browse a SQL Server database by using the RemoteData control?

7.2 Add and delete records in a SQL Server database by using the RemoteData control?

7.3 Connect to a SQL Server database by using Remote Data Objects?

7.4 Browse records in a SQL Server database by using Remote Data Objects?

7.5 Add, update, and delete records in a SQL Server database by using Remote Data Objects?

7.6 Execute a SQL Server stored procedure by using Remote Data Objects?

7.7 Execute a parameterized SQL Server stored procedure with Remote Data Objects?

7.8 Handle Remote Data Objects errors?

If you're building large, high-volume database applications for many users, working with a database server such as Oracle, Sybase, or Microsoft SQL Server is probably in your future. This chapter focuses on Microsoft SQL Server. Although the techniques can often be applied to other server databases, each database can have its own particular feature set and SQL dialect.

Unless you've been away on a trip to another planet for the past couple of years, you've undoubtedly noticed that various new technologies have been introduced for accessing server databases. Developers now have a choice of using the Data control, the RemoteData control (RDC), Data Access Objects (DAO), ODBC Direct Data Access Objects (still DAO), Remote Data Objects (RDO), the open database connectivity (ODBC) API, the VBSQL control and the native server API, or Microsoft's newest entries into remote server connectivity: OLEDB, and ADO. Each of these technologies can be a suitable candidate for any given task.

✔ *The Data Control*—This is the traditional entry point for new database developers and is often used for low-volume (and sometimes even high-volume) applications. However, the Data control is really best suited for access to desktop database engines like Jet. If you're scaling a database from Jet to SQL Server, the Data control will continue to work, but for optimum performance you should consider using another data access strategy.

✔ *The RemoteData Control*—The RemoteData control (RDC) is the companion to the Data control for remote server databases. Although convenient for many applications, it imposes some of the same restrictions and lack of control that come with the Data control.

✔ *Data Access Objects*—DAO is the first step beyond the Data control for most developers. It's a flexible and powerful object model for database application development. Using linked tables or SQL Passthrough, you can accomplish almost all server database tasks.

✔ *ODBC Direct*—With the latest release of DAO, Microsoft unbundled the Jet engine from the object model. ODBC Direct uses the DAO model but sends queries directly through to the database server using RDO (and via the RDO proxy by ODBC) bypassing Jet entirely. This enables you to use existing DAO code (with minor modifications) but gain the performance benefits of RDO. The limitations of DAO, however, still apply, meaning that many server database features will be unavailable or difficult to work with.

✔ *Remote Data Objects*—RDO is the remote server equivalent to DAO. It provides a similar (although not identical) object model but is optimized to work with intelligent server databases. Unlike DAO, which is bundled with the Jet engine, RDO does not contain a query engine; it expects all query processing to take place on the server. Because RDO is really just a thin object layer over the ODBC API, it exposes nearly all the capabilities of the database server with almost no impact on performance.

✔ *The ODBC API*—ODBC was designed to be a database-independent server programming interface. Cumbersome and complex to work with, it is the data access strategy for the hard-core programmer. Despite its difficulties, it might offer a minor performance advantage over RDO.

✔ *VBSQL*—Built on DBLib, the native programming interface to SQL Server, VBSQL is a time-tested and reliable data access strategy. However, although other technologies have continued to advance, VBSQL has not, and it has become an outdated technology. Many development shops are continuing to build new applications and update existing applications based on VBSQL despite its "lame duck" status—in part because it is still the only technology that provides access to all the features of SQL Server.

This is the new kid on the block:

✔ *OLEDB/ADO*—OLEDB is currently being touted as the new native interface to SQL Server. Originally targeted at Web based applications, OLEDB/ADO is expected to replace DAO and RDO.

That's a wide array of choices—at times you might feel as if you've joined the technology-of-the-month club—but for most applications, RDO is an excellent option. RDO is now in its second release and is a proven technology. It offers the simplicity of a DAO-like object model but performance equal to the ODBC API or VBSQL. For those techniques available only with the ODBC API, RDO also exposes the necessary handles so you can go directly to the API when you need it.

Along with all the new data access technologies comes a plethora of SQL Server specific and general concepts and buzzwords. Rather than dealing with database files, SQL Server gives you database devices, dump devices, databases, transaction logs, and so on. Instead of a simple user and group list for security, you have logins, users, and groups that can be set up using standard, integrated, or mixed security models. The list goes on to concepts like n-tier design, the use of transaction servers and object brokers, Web connectivity technologies, and more. All this goes far beyond the scope of this chapter, and many excellent books have been written that address some or all of these tools and technologies. Fortunately, SQL Server also comes with excellent documentation.

> **NOTE**
>
> Consider yourself lucky if you have a seasoned dba (database administrator) on staff to help handle the details of creating devices, databases, users, and so forth for you on the server. A good dba can save you days or weeks of work. If you don't have a veteran dba available, dive into the SQL Server documentation. There's a lot to cover, but you will learn it in time. Rome wasn't built in a day, and your client/server application won't be either.

This chapter assumes that you have already successfully installed Microsoft SQL Server 6.5, the pubs sample database, Visual Basic 6.0 Enterprise Edition, and the SQL Server client utilities. You will need to have the authority necessary to create a database on your server or access to a dba who can do it for you. You will also need to be able to execute SQL statements on the server using either SQL Enterprise Manager or ISQL/w. Consult the SQL Server documentation for more information on the installation and use of these utilities.

7.1 Browse a SQL Server Database by Using the RemoteData Control

This How-To introduces the most basic of operations on a database server: browsing the results of a query with the RemoteData control.

7.2 Add and Delete Records in a SQL Server Database by Using the RemoteData Control

In this How-To, you learn to use the RemoteData control to perform inserts and deletes on the remote SQL Server database.

7.3 Connect to a SQL Server Database by Using Remote Data Objects

Before you can do anything with remote server data, you must establish a connection to the server. This How-To shows you how to open an RDO Connection.

7.4 Browse Records in a SQL Server Database by Using Remote Data Objects

The RemoteData control, like the Data control, has its limitations. In this How-To, you learn to use Remote Data Objects to read SQL Server data.

7.5 Add, Update, and Delete Records in a SQL Server Database by Using Remote Data Objects

This How-To shows you how to insert, update, and delete records using RDO.

7.6 Execute a SQL Server Stored Procedure by Using Remote Data Objects

Most server databases rely heavily on stored procedures for database operations. This How-To teaches you to execute a simple, stored procedure that returns a result set.

7.7 Execute a Parameterized SQL Server Stored Procedure with Remote Data Objects

SQL Server stored procedures, like Visual Basic procedures, can have input and output parameters and return values. This How-To shows you how to execute a stored procedure with parameters.

7.8 Handle Remote Data Objects Errors

Despite your best efforts, things can go wrong on the remote database. In this How-To, you learn to trap and handle errors delivered to RDO by SQL Server.

COMPLEXITY
INTERMEDIATE

7.1 How do I...
Browse a SQL Server database by using the RemoteData control?

Problem

My data is on a SQL Server database. How do I access this data using the RemoteData control?

Technique

Accessing data from a SQL Server database need not be complex. With the RemoteData control (RDC), you can build a simple form based on SQL Server data in minutes. Building forms with the RDC is the ultimate in visual design— no code whatsoever is required.

Building a form with the RDC requires only a few simple steps:

1. Create an ODBC data source for your database.

2. Draw a RemoteData control on your form and set the `DataSourceName` and SQL properties.

3. Add controls to the form for the columns you need to display and set the `DataSource` and `DataField` properties.

That's all there is to it. The RDC handles everything else for you in conjunction with the ODBC drivers. Like the Data control, the RemoteData control handles updating the tables as well as providing navigation buttons for the rows in the query.

> **NOTE**
>
> This example and the rest of the examples in this chapter require that the pubs sample database be installed on your SQL Server and that an ODBC data source named pubs has been configured to connect to your server and the pubs sample database. See Chapter 6, "Connecting to an ODBC Server," for more information on configuring ODBC data sources.

Steps

Open and run project HT701.vbp. You can browse and update the rows returned by the query using the form shown in Figure 7.1.

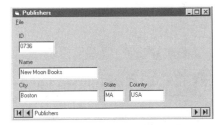

Figure 7.1. The Publishers form.

> **NOTE**
>
> Depending on the configuration of your SQL Server and network, you might or might not be prompted to provide a user name and password when connecting to the server. All of these examples were created using integrated security, which uses your network logon to validate your connection to the database server. SQL Server integrated security is available only if the server is a member of a Windows NT domain.

1. Create a new Standard EXE project, add the Microsoft RemoteData Control 6.0 to the toolbox, and save the project as HT701.vbp. Change the name of Form1 to FMain and create the objects and properties shown in Table 7.1.

Table 7.1. Objects and properties for *FMain*.

OBJECT	PROPERTY	VALUE
Form	Caption	Publishers
RemoteData Control	Name	rdc
	Caption	Publishers
	Align	2 - vbAlignBottom
	DataSourceName	pubs
	SQL	SELECT pub_id, pub_name,
		city, state, country
		FROM publishers
Label	Name	lbl
	Caption	ID
	Index	0
TextBox	Name	txtID
	DataSource	rdc
	DataField	pub_id
Label	Name	lbl
	Caption	Name
	Index	1
TextBox	Name	txtName
	DataSource	rdc
	DataField	pub_name
Label	Name	lbl
	Caption	City
	Index	2
TextBox	Name	txtCity
	DataSource	rdc
	DataField	city
Label	Name	lbl
	Caption	State
	Index	3
TextBox	Name	txtState
	DataSource	rdc
	DataField	state
Label	Name	lbl
	Caption	Country
	Index	4

continued on next page

continued from previous page

OBJECT	PROPERTY	VALUE
TextBox	Name	txtCountry
	DataSource	rdc
	DataField	country

2. Using the menu editor, create the menu shown in Table 7.2.

Table 7.2. Menu controls for *FMain*.

CAPTION	NAME
&File	mnuFile
----E&xit	mnuFileExit

3. Create the declarations section of the form:

```
Option Explicit
```

> **NOTE**
>
> You can and should set up Visual Basic to always use Option Explicit by checking the box marked Require Variable Declaration on the Editor tab of the Options dialog box.

4. Create the mnuFileExit_Click event procedure:

```
Private Sub mnuFileExit_Click()
    Unload Me
End Sub
```

How It Works

The RDC handles all the work for you in this application. When the application starts, the control opens a connection to the SQL Server, submits the query, and presents the results on the form. The navigation buttons provided by the control enable you to navigate among the rows returned by the query.

Comments

This simple application exemplifies the visual part of Visual Basic. The single line of executable code unloads the form and ends the program. Everything else required to enable live editing of data in the database is designed using visual tools.

COMPLEXITY
INTERMEDIATE

7.2 How do I...
Add and delete records in a SQL Server database by using the RemoteData control?

Problem

My users need to be able to add and delete rows in my SQL Server tables as well as view and update existing rows. How do I add and delete rows using the RemoteData control?

Technique

Writing just a small amount of code enables you to implement the ability to insert and delete rows with the RemoteData control. The RemoteData control's **Resultset** object provides the **AddNew** and **Delete** methods. You can implement both with just a few lines of code and a user interface mechanism to invoke the procedures.

Inserting a row is a two-step process:

1. Call the **AddNew** method of the RemoteData control's **Resultset** to set the row buffer to a blank new row.

2. Call the **Update** method of the **Resultset** to insert the row into the table.

Deleting a row requires only a single call to the **Delete** method of the **Resultset**; but after the delete has been performed, the current row will be undefined, so you need to add code to move to a valid row. This example uses the Microsoft Access convention of moving to the previous row, but you could just as easily move to the next row.

Steps

Open and run project HT702.vbp. This is the same as the project created for How-To 7.1, with code and controls added to support inserts and deletes. You can browse, update, insert, and delete rows in the Publishers table using the RemoteData control's navigation buttons and the commands on the Data menu, as shown in Figure 7.2.

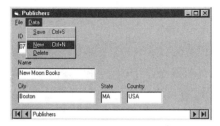

Figure 7.2. The Publishers form's New, Delete, and Save functions.

INSERTING AND DELETING ROWS IN THE PUBLISHERS TABLE.

The Publishers table in the sample database has a rather unusual rule for the pub_id column:

```
(pub_id = '1756' or (pub_id = '1622' or
(pub_id = '0877' or (pub_id = '0736' or (pub_id = '1389'))))) or
 (pub_id like '99[0-9][0-9]'))
```

This rule requires that the pub_id value be one of the five specific values shown (1756, 1622, 0877, 0736, or 1389) or that it be a four-digit number between 9900 and 9999. Don't be surprised if you see strange-looking rules like this appearing from time to time. This sort of thing is occasionally necessary to maintain compliance with legacy code, data, or both.

If you add rows to the table while working with the sample application, you need to make sure the pub_id column meets this rule. In a production application, you would probably want to add code to automatically generate a valid value for this column.

Additionally, there are other tables in the database that contain foreign key references to the Publishers table, so you might not be able to delete some of the existing rows. A complete application based on the pubs database would need to implement methods of dealing with these foreign key references. Alternately, you could write a delete trigger for the Publishers table that would delete any related rows in related tables.

1. Create a new Standard EXE project, add the Microsoft RemoteData Control 2.0 to the toolbox, and save the project as HT702.vbp.

2. FMain.frm is the same form developed for How-To 7.1. You can add the existing file from the previous How-To, or refer to Table 7.1 to add the RemoteData control, labels, text boxes, and refer to Table 7.2 to create the File menu controls.

3. Use the Menu Editor to add the menu controls for the Data menu as shown in Table 7.3.

Table 7.3. Specifications for the Data menu.

CAPTION	NAME	SHORTCUT KEY
&Data	mnuData	
----&Save	mnuDataSave	Ctrl+S
-----	mnuDataBar	
----&New	mnuDataNew	Ctrl+N
----&Delete	mnuDataDelete	

4. Add `Option Explicit` to the declarations section.

5. Create the `Form_Unload` event procedure. This procedure sets up an error handler and calls the `SaveRecord` procedure described in step 10.

```
Private Sub Form_Unload(Cancel As Integer)
On Error GoTo ProcError

    SaveRecord

ProcExit:
  Exit Sub

ProcError:
  MsgBox Err.Number & vbCrLf & Err.Description
  Resume ProcExit

End Sub
```

6. Create the `mnuFileExit_Click` event procedure. This code is identical to the code in How-To 7.1.

```
Private Sub mnuFileExit_Click()
On Error Resume Next

  Unload Me
  If Err.Number <> 0 Then
    MsgBox Err.Number & vbCrLf & Err.Description
  End If

End Sub
```

7. Add code for the Data menu controls. The `New`, `Delete`, and `Save` commands call the corresponding `AddRecord`, `DeleteRecord`, and `SaveRecord` procedures described in steps 8, 9, and 10.

```
Private Sub mnuDataNew_Click()
On Error GoTo ProcError
```

continued on next page

continued from previous page

```
        AddRecord

ProcExit:
  Exit Sub

ProcError:
  MsgBox Err.Number & vbCrLf & Err.Description
  Resume ProcExit

End Sub
Private Sub mnuDataDelete_Click()
On Error GoTo ProcError

  DeleteRecord

ProcExit:
  Exit Sub

ProcError:
  MsgBox Err.Number & vbCrLf & Err.Description
  Resume ProcExit

End Sub
Private Sub mnuDataSave_Click()
On Error GoTo ProcError

  SaveRecord

ProcExit:
  Exit Sub

ProcError:
  MsgBox Err.Number & vbCrLf & Err.Description
  Resume ProcExit

End Sub
```

8. Create the **AddRecord** procedure. This procedure calls the **AddNew** method of the RemoteData control's **Resultset** to create the new record. The new row is inserted into the table later by the **SaveRecord** procedure.

```
Private Sub AddRecord()

  ' add it
  rdc.Resultset.AddNew
  txtID.SetFocus

End Sub
```

9. Add the **DeleteRecord** procedure. This procedure uses the **Delete** method of the RemoteData control's **Resultset** to remove the row from the table, then repositions the row pointer to a valid row in the table. The code first moves to the previous row, then checks for the beginning of the **Resultset** and, if necessary, moves to the first row.

```
Private Sub DeleteRecord()

  ' delete the row
  rdc.Resultset.Delete
  ' back up one row
  rdc.Resultset.MovePrevious
  ' check for beginning of set
  If rdc.Resultset.BOF Then
    rdc.Resultset.MoveFirst
  End If

End Sub
```

10. The **SaveRecord** procedure uses the **EditMode** property of the RemoteData control's **Resultset** to determine how to save the current row using a **Select Case** block. If the row has not been changed, no action is necessary. If an existing row has been changed, the **UpdateRow** method is used to commit the changes. New rows are added to the table by calling the **Update** method of the **Resultset**.

```
Private Sub SaveRecord()

  Select Case rdc.Resultset.EditMode
    Case rdEditNone
      ' clean record, do nothing
    Case rdEditInProgress
      ' the control handles regular edits
      rdc.UpdateRow
    Case rdEditAdd
      ' use the Update method of the
      ' resultset
      rdc.Resultset.Update
  End Select

End Sub
```

How It Works

This is a basic bound control application. The only thing that differentiates the techniques from an application based on the Data control is the use of the RemoteData control and a few minor variations in the code syntax. The control handles most of the work of displaying and updating data, with a little help from a few lines of code.

Comments

The RemoteData control is a convenient, but limiting, method of working with remote server databases. In the following How-To's, you'll learn to use Remote Data Objects to connect to and manage data in SQL Server databases.

COMPLEXITY
BEGINNING

7.3 How do I...
Connect to a SQL Server database by using Remote Data Objects?

Problem

My application needs to connect to a SQL Server database without using the RemoteData control. How can I create a connection with Remote Data Objects?

Technique

If an ODBC data source has been configured, you can establish a connection to a SQL Server database with as little as a single line of code using the **OpenConnection** method of the **rdoEnvironment** object. By adding an extra line of code or two, you can also create a so-called "DSN-less" connection with no preconfigured ODBC data source name.

Using a preconfigured ODBC data source adds one additional required step in configuring the workstation but also enables you to share the connection among multiple applications. If you embed the connection information in the source code for the application, you eliminate one step in setting up the workstation.

The following example demonstrates both methods. Additionally, RDO 2.0 enables you to create an **rdoConnection** object without an explicit physical connection to a remote database. After you have assigned the necessary properties to the **rdoConnection** object, use the **EstablishConnection** method to open the connection.

Steps

Open project HT703.vbp. Before running this project using a DSN-less connection, you will need to change the values used in creating the connect string in the **OpenConnection** routine to reflect the correct user name (**UID=**), password (**PWD=**), and SQL Server machine name (**SERVER=**). If you check the box marked Use pubs DSN, the application will open a connection using an ODBC data source named pubs (which you should have already created using the 32-bit ODBC control panel applet). If the check box is cleared, a DSN-less connection will be created. The connection form is shown in Figure 7.3.

1. Create a new Standard EXE project, add a reference to Microsoft Remote Data Object 2.0, and save the project as HT703.vbp.

2. Change the name of **Form1** to **FMain** and add the objects and properties shown in Table 7.4.

Figure 7.3. The RDO Connect form.

Table 7.4. Objects and properties for *FMain*.

OBJECT	PROPERTY	VALUE
CheckBox	Name	chkUseDSN
	Caption	Use pubs DSN
CommandButton	Name	cmdConnect
	Caption	Connect

3. Add the following code to the declarations section. The module level variable **mcon** is used later by the **OpenConnection** routine.

```
Option Explicit

Private mcon As rdoConnection
```

4. Create the **cmdConnect_Click** event procedure. This routine sets up an error handler, calls **OpenConnection**, and displays a message indicating the success or failure of the connection.

```
Private Sub cmdConnect_Click()
On Error GoTo ProcError

  If OpenConnection() Then
    MsgBox "Connection Opened"
  Else
    MsgBox "Connection Failed"
  End If

ProcExit:
  Exit Sub

ProcError:
  MsgBox Err.Number & vbCrLf & Err.Description
  Resume ProcExit

End Sub
```

5. Create the **OpenConnection** function. This function uses the value of the check box to determine whether it should use the pubs DSN or create a DSN-less connection; it then calls the **OpenConnection** method of the default **rdoEnvironment** object to establish the connection to the remote server. The function returns true if the connection was successfully established.

```
Private Function OpenConnection() As Boolean
On Error GoTo ProcError

  Dim sConnect As String

  If chkUseDSN = vbChecked Then
    ' use pubs DSN
    Set mcon = rdoEnvironments(0).OpenConnection("pubs")
  Else
    ' use DSN-less connection
    sConnect = _
        "UID=sa;" & _
        "PWD=MyPassword;" & _
        "DATABASE=pubs;" & _
        "SERVER=MyServer;" & _
        "DRIVER={SQL SERVER};" & _
        "DSN='';"
    Set mcon = rdoEnvironments(0).OpenConnection( _
        "", rdDriverNoPrompt, False, sConnect, rdAsyncEnable)
  End If

  OpenConnection = True

ProcExit:
  Exit Function

ProcError:
  OpenConnection = False
  Resume ProcExit

End Function
```

How It Works

A single line of code is all that's required to connect to a remote server. The **OpenConnection** method (or alternately the **EstablishConnection** method) connects you to the SQL Server database. You can then use the connection to execute SQL statements and create other RDO objects.

Comments

If you're familiar with the DAO object model, the **rdoConnection** object is the rough equivalent of the **Database** object. Many of the properties and methods are similar. In fact, you'll find the entire Remote Data Objects hierarchy very similar to the Data Access Objects hierarchy. The similarities in the two models make it easier to not only learn to use RDO but also to convert existing code from DAO to RDO.

COMPLEXITY
INTERMEDIATE

7.4 How do I...
Browse records in a SQL Server database by using Remote Data Objects?

Problem

How can I use Remote Data Objects to browse rows in a SQL Server database?

Technique

Remote Data Objects (RDO) provide the `rdoResultset` object —similar to the DAO Recordset object—that you can use to capture and browse the results of a `SELECT` query. If you've programmed with DAO, you'll find the `rdoResultset` familiar. The various `Move` methods work the same as the methods of the Recordset, and you still use `AddNew`, `Edit`, and `Update` to make changes to the data in a row. Many of the properties are also the same as those of the DAO Recordset. In fact, much of the code written for `rdoResultsets` is so similar that you could change the declaration and the `Set` statement and use your existing DAO code.

Despite the code similarities, there are differences in the techniques used to access SQL Server data with `rdoResultsets`:

✔ The SQL statements used to retrieve data must be written in syntax that the remote server will understand. Unlike DAO, which uses the Jet database engine, RDO does not have its own query processor. All processing takes place on the remote server.

✔ There are no `Find` methods. You are expected to run a new query and select only the rows you need if the criteria for searching the data changes. You can also move through the resultset testing for the desired values on individual rows and columns.

✔ There's no equivalent to the table-type recordset and its associated methods, such as `Seek`.

✔ The types of `rdoResultsets` available are somewhat different from the types of Recordsets available. You can create a forward-only, keyset, dynamic, and static cursor.

✔ There are more locking strategies at your disposal. You can use read-only, pessimistic, optimistic based on row ID, optimistic based on row values, and batch updates.

✔ A single SQL Server query can return more than one set of results.

✔ You can't modify the structure of the database with RDO. SQL Enterprise manager provides visual tools for that purpose, and the Transact-SQL language also enables you to manipulate the database design.

A NOTE ON CURSORS

Don't be confused by all the new terminology. A *cursor* is essentially just a set of pointers to rows in a resultset that enables you to browse the results.

You create a resultset by using the `OpenResultset` method of an `rdoConnection`. You typically will provide a SQL statement to the method that specifies the rows to return. You can additionally specify the type of cursor, which by default is forward-only, and the type of locking which by default is read-only.

After you have created the resultset, you can browse the rows using the various navigation methods: `MoveFirst`, `MovePrevious`, `MoveNext`, `MoveLast`, and `Move`. Like the DAO Recordset, the `rdoResultset` object provides the BOF and EOF properties that you can use to test for the ends of the resultset.

NOTE

SQL Server queries can return more than one set of results. Use the `MoreResults` method to test for additional resultsets from the query.

Values for individual columns in the rows retrieved are obtained from the `rdoColumns` collection. This is the default collection for a resultset. You can use the same syntax styles for columns in a resultset that you use for fields in a DAO recordset:

✔ `rdoResultset.rdoColumns("column0")`

✔ `rdoResultset("column0")`

✔ `rdoResultset!column0`

Depending on the query, the type of cursor, and the type of locking, the data might be read-only or might be updatable.

Steps

Before you can use this example, you need to install the States table in the pubs sample database. Using SQL Enterprise Manager or I-SQL/W, load the States.sql script, select the pubs database, and run the script. The script creates and populates the States table with a list of the 50 states in the U.S. as well as the District of Columbia and Puerto Rico. After you have installed this table, you can run the sample application.

NOTE

You can run this script against any database where you need this table.

Open and run project HT704.vbp. You can use the form shown in Figure 7.4 to browse and update the rows in the sample table from the pubs database. This project makes a simple extension to the project used for How-To 7.2. The text box used for the **state** column in the Publishers table has been replaced with a combo box that contains a list of state postal codes, using a query and an rdoResultset object. This is a commonly implemented user interface convenience. Unless people work all day every day with a data entry application, few will remember the postal codes for all the states, so the combo box enables the user to pick a value from a list on the form.

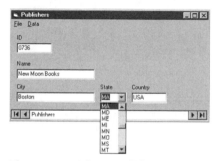

Figure 7.4. The modified Publishers form.

1. Create a new Standard EXE project, add a reference to Microsoft Remote Data Object 2.0, and save the project as HT704.vbp. Rename the default Form1 to FMain, save it as FMain.frm, and add the object and properties shown in Table 7.5. The menu controls for this example are identical to those in How-To 7.2.

Table 7.5. Objects and properties for *FMain*.

OBJECT	PROPERTY	VALUE
Form	Caption	Publishers
RemoteData Control	Name	rdc
	Caption	Publishers
	Align	2 - vbAlignBottom
	DataSourceName	pubs

continued on next page

continued from previous page

OBJECT	PROPERTY	VALUE
	SQL	SELECT pub_id, pub_name,
		city, state, country
		FROM publishers
Label	Name	lbl
	Caption	ID
	Index	0
TextBox	Name	txtID
	DataSource	rdc
	DataField	pub_id
Label	Name	lbl
	Caption	Name
	Index	1
TextBox	Name	txtName
	DataSource	rdc
	DataField	pub_name
Label	Name	lbl
	Caption	City
	Index	2
TextBox	Name	txtCity
	DataSource	rdc
	DataField	city
Label	Name	lbl
	Caption	State
	Index	3
ComboBox	Name	cboState
	DataSource	rdc
	DataField	state
Label	Name	lbl
	Caption	Country
	Index	4
TextBox	Name	txtCountry
	DataSource	rdc
	DataField	country

2. Add the following code to the declarations section. The `rdoConnection` object is used later to populate the state combo box.

```
Option Explicit

Private mcon As rdoConnection
```

3. Create the **Form_Load** event procedure. This procedure calls the
OpenConnection procedure to connect to the remote server and then calls
GetStates to populate the combo box.

```
Private Sub Form_Load()
On Error GoTo ProcError

   OpenConnection
   GetStates

ProcExit:
   Exit Sub

ProcError:
   MsgBox Err.Number & vbCrLf & Err.Description
   Resume ProcExit

End Sub
```

4. Add the following procedures to handle the click events for the menu
controls. These procedures are identical to those developed in How-To
7.2.

```
Private Sub mnuDataDelete_Click()
On Error GoTo ProcError

   DeleteRecord

ProcExit:
   Exit Sub

ProcError:
   MsgBox Err.Number & vbCrLf & Err.Description
   Resume ProcExit

End Sub
Private Sub mnuDataNew_Click()
On Error GoTo ProcError

   AddRecord

ProcExit:
   Exit Sub

ProcError:
   MsgBox Err.Number & vbCrLf & Err.Description
   Resume ProcExit

End Sub

Private Sub mnuDataSave_Click()
On Error GoTo ProcError
```

continued on next page

continued from previous page

```
      SaveRecord

ProcExit:
  Exit Sub

ProcError:
  MsgBox Err.Number & vbCrLf & Err.Description
  Resume ProcExit

End Sub
Private Sub mnuFileExit_Click()
On Error Resume Next

  Unload Me
  If Err.Number <> 0 Then
    MsgBox Err.Number & vbCrLf & Err.Description
  End If

End Sub
```

5. Create the AddRecord, NewRecord, and SaveRecord procedures. These procedures are also identical to those in How-To 7.2.

```
Private Sub AddRecord()

  rdc.Resultset.AddNew
  txtID.SetFocus

End Sub
Private Sub DeleteRecord()

  ' delete the row
  rdc.Resultset.Delete
  ' back up one row
  rdc.Resultset.MovePrevious
  ' check for beginning of set
  If rdc.Resultset.BOF Then
    rdc.Resultset.MoveFirst
  End If

End Sub
Private Sub SaveRecord()

  Select Case rdc.Resultset.EditMode
    Case rdEditNone
      ' clean record, do nothing
    Case rdEditInProgress
      ' the control handles regular edits
      rdc.UpdateRow
    Case rdEditAdd
      ' use the Update method of the
      ' resultset
      rdc.Resultset.Update
  End Select

End Sub
```

6. Create the OpenConnection procedure. This is based on How-To 7.3 and uses the pubs ODBC DSN to create the connection to the SQL Server.

```
Private Sub OpenConnection()

    Dim sConnect As String

    ' default using a configured DSN
    Set mcon = rdoEnvironments(0).OpenConnection("pubs")

End Sub
```

7. Create the GetStates subroutine. This code uses an rdoResultset to populate the cboState combo box. It creates a forward-only, read-only cursor based on the States table. Because only one pass through the results is required, a forward-only cursor is sufficient. The rdExecDirect option bypasses ODBC's normal step of creating a prepared statement and directly executes the query on the SQL Server.

```
Private Sub GetStates()
' populate the states combo box

    Dim sSQL As String
    Dim rsStates As rdoResultset

    sSQL = "SELECT StateCode FROM States"
    ' we only need one pass through this data,
    ' and will only need to do it once, so we
    ' use a read only, forward only cursor and
    ' the exec direct option
    Set rsStates = mcon.OpenResultset(sSQL, _
        rdOpenForwardOnly, rdConcurReadOnly, rdExecDirect)

    ' populate the combo box
    Do While Not rsStates.EOF
      cboState.AddItem rsStates!StateCode
      rsStates.MoveNext
    Loop

    ' clean up
    rsStates.Close

End Sub
```

How It Works

The primary object you will use in the Remote Data Objects hierarchy is the rdoResultset object. The rdoResultset object enables you to submit a SQL query (over an rdoConnection object) and process the results. Depending on the type of query, you might also be able to add, delete, and update the rows in the resultset.

In this example, the resultset in the GetStates procedure is used only to populate the combo box and avoid the use of a data bound ComboBox control.

Comments

Many of the objects in the Remote Data Objects hierarchy have events in addition to properties and methods. You can use these events by declaring the objects using the `WithEvents` keyword and write event procedures for these events. For example, the `rdoResultset` object provides the `RowStatusChanged` event that you can use to trigger code that should run if a row is updated or deleted.

COMPLEXITY
INTERMEDIATE

7.5 How do I...

Add, update, and delete records in a SQL Server database by using Remote Data Objects?

Problem

Bound controls use a database connection for each Data control; large applications based on bound controls would use too many connections. How can I create an unbound form based on SQL Server data using Remote Data Objects?

Technique

Building unbound applications with Remote Data Objects is no different from building unbound applications using any other data access approach, including Data Access Objects or standard Visual Basic file I/O techniques. Here are the steps:

1. Retrieve the data from the data source; in this example you will use an `rdoResultset` to manage the data.

2. Display the values in the controls on the form.

3. Update the tables in the database when the user moves to a new row, unloads the form, or explicitly requests that the data be saved.

If you've already read Chapter 2, "Accessing a Database with Data Access Objects," you will be familiar with these techniques. The only thing that has changed is the object model used to manage the data. In the previous How-To, you were introduced to using an `rdoResultset` to retrieve data from a SQL Server database. In this How-To, you will extend the use of the `rdoResultset` to inserting, updating, and deleting rows.

How-To 7.4 used a forward-only, read-only cursor—the default for `rdoResultset` objects created using the `OpenResultset` method of an `rdoConnection` object. Because you will now be making changes to the data as well as providing the capability to navigate both forward and backward through the rows, you will need a more flexible type of cursor. Using a keyset-type cursor enables you to add, update, or delete rows with minimal coding complexity and lower resource requirements than a dynamic cursor.

NOTE

If you did not install the States table in How-To 7.4, do so now by running the States.sql SQL script, using SQL Enterprise Manager or I-SQL/W. This script creates and populates a table of state names and postal codes for U.S. states.

Steps

Open and run project HT705.vbp. Use the form shown in Figure 7.5 to browse, add, update, or delete rows in the Publishers table. In this example, the RemoteData control has been replaced with Visual Basic code. Toolbar buttons created with a Toolbar control replace the navigation buttons provided by the RemoteData control. With the commands on the Data menu, you can create new rows, save changes to an existing row, or delete the current row.

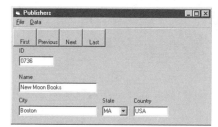

Figure 7.5. The unbound Publishers form.

1. Create a new Standard EXE project, add a reference to Microsoft Remote Data Object 2.0, and save the project as HT705.vbp. Rename **Form1** to **FMain**, save it as FMain.frm, and add the objects and properties shown in Table 7.6.

Table 7.6. Objects and properties for *FMain*.

OBJECT	PROPERTY	VALUE
Form	Caption	Publishers
Toolbar	Name	tb
Label	Name	lbl
	Caption	ID
	Index	0
TextBox	Name	txtID
Label	Name	lbl
	Caption	Name
	Index	1
TextBox	Name	txtName
Label	Name	lbl
	Caption	City
	Index	2
TextBox	Name	txtCity
Label	Name	lbl
	Caption	State
	Index	3
ComboBox	Name	cboState
Label	Name	lbl
	Caption	Country
	Index	4
TextBox	Name	txtCountry

2. Use the Menu Editor to create the menu controls shown in Table 7.7.

Table 7.7. Menu controls for *FMain*.

CAPTION	NAME	SHORTCUT KEY
&File	mnuFile	
----E&xit	mnuFileExit	
&Data	mnuData	
----&Save	mnuDataSave	Ctrl+S
-----	mnuDataBar	
----&New	mnuDataNew	Ctrl+N
----&Delete	mnuDataDelete	

3. Add the following code to the declarations section. The `rdoConnection` and `rdoResultset` objects are used by the form to manage the data in the sample database. The enumeration and the `mlRowState` variable are used to track the current state of the data on the form.

```
Option Explicit
' connection
Private mcon As rdoConnection
' resultset
Private mrsPublishers As rdoResultset
' record state
Private Enum RowState
  RowStateClean = 1
  RowStateDirty = 2
  RowStateNew = 3
End Enum
Private mlRowState As RowState
```

4. Create the `Form_Load` and `Form_Unload` event procedures. In the `Load` event, the form sets up the toolbar, opens the resultset for the Publishers table upon which the form is based, and populates the `cboState` combo box. In the `unload` event, the form saves any changes and closes and releases the object variables created in the declarations section. The `Initialize`, `GetStates`, and `SetupToolbar` procedures are described in steps 9, 11, and 20.

```
Private Sub Form_Load()
On Error GoTo ProcError

  SetupToolbar
  Initialize
  GetStates

ProcExit:
  Exit Sub

ProcError:
  MsgBox Err.Number & vbCrLf & Err.Description
  Resume ProcExit

End Sub
Private Sub Form_Unload(Cancel As Integer)
' save before exiting
On Error GoTo ProcError

  ' save the current row
  SaveRow
  ' close down resultset and connection
  Terminate

ProcExit:
  Exit Sub

ProcError:
```

continued on next page

continued from previous page

```
        MsgBox Err.Number & vbCrLf & Err.Description
        Resume ProcExit

End Sub
```

5. Create the **tb_ButtonClick** event procedure. This procedure calls procedures to navigate among the rows in the resultset.

```
Private Sub tb_ButtonClick(ByVal Button As ComctlLib.Button)
' toolbar handles navigation

  Select Case Button.Key
    Case "First"
      MoveFirst
    Case "Previous"
      MovePrevious
    Case "Next"
      MoveNext
    Case "Last"
      MoveLast
  End Select

End Sub
```

6. Add the following event procedures to track the edit state of the data on the form. Each procedure changes the module level **mlRowState** variable to **RowStateDirty** if the current value is **RowStateClean**. This enables later code to determine whether current changes should be sent to the SQL Server as an update or an insert.

```
Private Sub cboState_Click()
' mark row dirty

  If mlRowState = RowStateClean Then
    mlRowState = RowStateDirty
  End If

End Sub
Private Sub cboState_Change()
' mark row dirty

  If mlRowState = RowStateClean Then
    mlRowState = RowStateDirty
  End If

End Sub
Private Sub txtCity_Change()
' mark row dirty

  If mlRowState = RowStateClean Then
    mlRowState = RowStateDirty
  End If

End Sub
```

```
Private Sub txtCountry_Change()
' mark row dirty

  If mlRowState = RowStateClean Then
    mlRowState = RowStateDirty
  End If

End Sub
Private Sub txtID_Change()
' mark row dirty

  If mlRowState = RowStateClean Then
    mlRowState = RowStateDirty
  End If

End Sub
Private Sub txtName_Change()
' mark row dirty

  If mlRowState = RowStateClean Then
    mlRowState = RowStateDirty
  End If

End Sub
```

7. Create the `mnuFileExit_Click` event procedure. This procedure unloads the form, ending the application.

```
Private Sub mnuFileExit_Click()
On Error Resume Next

  Unload Me
  If Err.Number <> 0 Then
    MsgBox Err.Number & vbCrLf & Err.Description
  End If

End Sub
```

8. Add the following event procedures for the commands on the Data menu. Each menu command event procedure calls a corresponding subroutine in the form module to perform the requested operation. The **NewRow**, **SaveRow**, and **DeleteRow** procedures are described in steps 12, 13, and 14.

```
Private Sub mnuDataNew_Click()
On Error GoTo ProcError

  NewRow

ProcExit:
  Exit Sub

ProcError:
  MsgBox Err.Number & vbCrLf & Err.Description
  Resume ProcExit
```

continued on next page

continued from previous page

```
End Sub
Private Sub mnuDataSave_Click()
On Error GoTo ProcError

  SaveRow

ProcExit:
  Exit Sub

ProcError:
  MsgBox Err.Number & vbCrLf & Err.Description
  Resume ProcExit

End Sub
Private Sub mnuDataDelete_Click()
On Error GoTo ProcError

  DeleteRow

ProcExit:
  Exit Sub

ProcError:
  MsgBox Err.Number & vbCrLf & Err.Description
  Resume ProcExit

End Sub
```

9. Create the **Initialize** procedure. This subroutine is called from the **Form_Load** event procedure. It opens a connection to the SQL Server database, creates a resultset using the same query used in the previous RemoteData control examples, and then calls the **ColumnsToControls** procedure to display the first row in the resultset on the form. A keyset cursor with optimistic locking based on row values is used so that the resultset will be updatable.

```
Private Sub Initialize()
' connect and open the publishers resultset
  Dim sConnect As String
  Dim sSQL As String

  ' default using a configured DSN
  Set mcon = rdoEnvironments(0).OpenConnection( _
      "pubs")

  ' initialize the publishers resultset
  ' create the SQL statement
  sSQL = "SELECT pub_id, pub_name, city, state, country " & _
      "FROM publishers"
  ' use a keyset cursor
  Set mrsPublishers = _
      mcon.OpenResultset(sSQL, rdOpenKeyset, rdConcurValues)
```

```
    ' display the first row
    ColumnsToControls
    ' mark it clean
    mlRowState = RowStateClean

End Sub
```

10. The `Terminate` procedure, called from the `Form_Unload` event, performs a cleanup operation by closing the module level `rdoConnection` and `rdoResultset` objects:

```
Private Sub Terminate()
' clean up

    mrsPublishers.Close
    mcon.Close

End Sub
```

11. The `GetStates` procedure is the same code used in How-To 7.4:

```
Private Sub GetStates()
' populate the states combo box

    Dim sSQL As String
    Dim rsStates As rdoResultset

    sSQL = "SELECT StateCode FROM States ORDER BY StateCode"
    ' we only need one pass through this data,
    ' and will only need to do it once, so we
    ' use a read only, forward only cursor and
    ' the exec direct option
    Set rsStates = mcon.OpenResultset(sSQL, _
        rdOpenForwardOnly, rdConcurReadOnly, rdExecDirect)

    ' populate the combo box
    Do While Not rsStates.EOF
      cboState.AddItem rsStates!StateCode
      rsStates.MoveNext
    Loop

    ' clean up
    rsStates.Close

End Sub
```

12. Create the `NewRow` procedure. This code saves the current data, clears the controls, and sets the module level `mlRowState` state variable to `RowStateNew`, in preparation for the creation of a new row in the table.

```
Private Sub NewRow()
' create a new row

    ' save current data
    SaveRow
```

```
      ClearControls
      mlRowState = RowStateNew

End Sub
```

13. Create the `SaveRow` subroutine. The code uses either the `Edit` or `AddNew` method of the `rdoResultset` object to update an existing row or insert a new row, based on the value of the `mlRowState` module level state flag.

```
Private Sub SaveRow()
' save current data

  Select Case mlRowState
    Case RowStateDirty
      mrsPublishers.Edit
      ControlsToColumns
      mrsPublishers.Update
      mlRowState = RowStateClean
    Case RowStateNew
      mrsPublishers.AddNew
      ControlsToColumns
      mrsPublishers.Update
      mlRowState = RowStateClean
      mrsPublishers.Move 0
    Case Else
      ' nothing to do
  End Select

End Sub
```

14. The `DeleteRow` procedure uses the `Delete` method of the `mrsPublishers` `rdoResultset` object to delete the current row; the procedure then calls `MovePrevious` to back up to the previous row:

```
Private Sub DeleteRow()
' delete the current row

  mrsPublishers.Delete
  MovePrevious

End Sub
```

15. Create the `MoveFirst` and `MoveLast` subroutines. Each routine saves the current row, performs the appropriate move operation, displays the new row, and marks it as being clean.

```
Private Sub MoveFirst()
' goto first row

  SaveRow
  mrsPublishers.MoveFirst
  ColumnsToControls
  mlRowState = RowStateClean
```

```
End Sub
Private Sub MoveLast()
' goto last row

   SaveRow
   mrsPublishers.MoveLast
   ColumnsToControls
   mlRowState = RowStateClean

End Sub
```

16. Create the `MovePrevious` and `MoveNext` procedures. These are similar to the `MoveFirst` and `MoveLast` routines, but with code added to test for BOF and EOF conditions so that a valid row will always be displayed by the form.

```
Private Sub MovePrevious()
' goto previous row

   SaveRow
   mrsPublishers.MovePrevious
   If mrsPublishers.BOF Then
      mrsPublishers.MoveFirst
   End If
   ColumnsToControls
   mlRowState = RowStateClean

End Sub
Private Sub MoveNext()
' MoveNext w/ EOF handling

   SaveRow
   mrsPublishers.MoveNext
   If mrsPublishers.EOF Then
      mrsPublishers.MoveLast
   End If
   ColumnsToControls
   mlRowState = RowStateClean

End Sub
```

17. Create the `ColumnsToControls` routine. This procedure copies the values from the current row in the resultset to the controls on the form. In order to eliminate the possibility of writing `Null` values to the `Text` property of the text boxes, a zero-length string is appended to the value of the column.

```
Private Sub ColumnsToControls()
' load the current row in mrsPublishers to the controls

   txtID = mrsPublishers!pub_id & ""
   txtName = mrsPublishers!pub_name & ""
   txtCity = mrsPublishers!city & ""
   cboState = mrsPublishers!state & ""
```

```
    txtCountry = mrsPublishers!country & ""

End Sub
```

18. Create the `ControlsToColumns` procedure. This procedure compares the values on the form to the values in the columns and—if they have changed—copies the new values to the columns.

```
Private Sub ControlsToColumns()
' copy controls to current row

  Dim sID As String
  Dim sName As String
  Dim sCity As String
  Dim sState As String
  Dim sCountry As String

  ' get the values
  sID = txtID
  sName = txtName
  sCity = txtCity
  sState = cboState
  sCountry = txtCountry

  ' copy to columns only if changed
  With mrsPublishers
    If !pub_id <> sID Then
      !pub_id = sID
    End If
    If !pub_name <> sName Then
      !pub_name = sName
    End If
    If !city <> sCity Then
      !city = sCity
    End If
    If !state <> sState Then
      !state = sState
    End If
    If !country <> sCountry Then
      !country = sCountry
    End If
  End With

End Sub
```

19. The `ClearControls` subroutine writes zero-length strings to each of the controls and is called when creating a new row:

```
Private Sub ClearControls()
' clear existing values from controls

  txtID = ""
  txtName = ""
  txtCity = ""
  cboState = ""
```

```
        txtCountry = ""

End Sub
```

20. Enter the following code as the `SetupToolbar` subroutine. This procedure is called at startup and adds the four navigation buttons to the Toolbar control.

```
Private Sub SetupToolbar()
' setup toolbar buttons

  With tb.Buttons
    .Add , "First", "First"
    .Add , "Previous", "Previous"
    .Add , "Next", "Next"
    .Add , "Last", "Last"
  End With

End Sub
```

NOTE

In a production application, you should set up more pleasing buttons with appropriate images in an associated ImageList control.

How It Works

At startup, the form connects to the SQL Server, submits a query, and captures the results of the query in the `mrsPublishers` `rdoResultset` object. Code attached to the menu controls and toolbar buttons provides the capability for navigation, inserts, updates, and deletes using the methods of the `rdoResultset` object.

NOTE

You can easily implement an undo command by reloading the current row from the `rdoResultset` into the controls with a call to the `ColumnsToControls` procedure. A column-level undo command could be implemented by restoring only a single column value from the `rdoResultset` object.

Comments

In Chapter 2, "Accessing a Database with Data Access Objects," a more robust approach was implemented using a class module to encapsulate all the data access code. That approach would work equally well with this example. For the sake of simplicity, the more direct approach of placing the data access code directly in the form module was used. Although this code might be somewhat simpler to understand, over the lifetime of an application, it might prove more difficult to maintain because of the tight coupling of the data access code with the user interface code.

QUERYING THE DATABASE

The SQL statement used to provide the source of the data for this form is somewhat simplistic for a server database. Although the pubs sample database contains only a handful of rows, many tables will have hundreds, thousands, or even millions of rows of data. If you issue a SELECT query with no WHERE clause against such a large table in a production application, you will at best produce an application with terrible performance and will quite possibly be summoned to the office of your database administrator and be given a painful lesson in how to submit a proper query. Submitting queries that return only the data you need is always good advice for any database application but is even more critical if you are sending the query to a busy database server.

COMPLEXITY
INTERMEDIATE

7.6 How do I...
Execute a SQL Server stored procedure by using Remote Data Objects?

Problem

Many of the queries I need to run are returned as the results of stored procedures on the server. How can I execute a stored procedure and capture the resultset with Remote Data Objects?

Technique

A SQL Server stored procedure is a precompiled set of Transact-SQL statements that are executed using a single statement. Because the statements have been precompiled and the queries have already been optimized, SQL Server can often execute stored procedures much more efficiently than ad hoc SQL statements submitted for processing. Many large database applications are built almost entirely using stored procedures to retrieve and edit rows. Additionally, stored procedures can provide an added measure of security by allowing access to tables and columns that would otherwise be unavailable. A user only needs permission to execute a stored procedure, regardless of the permissions on the underlying tables and columns.

Stored procedures can range from simple SELECT queries that return results to complex Transact-SQL procedures that take input and output parameters and return values and multiple resultsets. Although the details of writing stored procedures on the server is beyond the scope of this chapter, it is not difficult to capture and use the results of stored procedures.

NOTE
Stored procedures always return read-only results.

Depending on the nature of the procedure, you might execute the procedure directly using the Execute method of an rdoConnection object, or you might capture results of a stored procedure by using an rdoQuery or rdoResultset object.

THE TROUBLE WITH STORED PROCEDURES
Transact-SQL, from a programming perspective, can be a difficult language to work with. SQL was designed to manage data and database objects, and the commands and system stored procedures are often cryptic. Debugging tools are limited, and in many cases you need to understand the inner workings of a procedure before you can use it. This can make it difficult to create procedures that act as "black boxes" with well-defined interfaces. However, the advantages in data processing efficiency offered by stored procedures often far outweigh these disadvantages, especially for heavily used, large database applications.

Steps

Use SQL Enterprise Manager or I-SQL/W to create the spStates stored procedure listed in step 2; then open and run project HT706.vbp. This example uses a form that is visually identical to the form shown in Figure 7.5 in the preceding How-To. Only two lines of code have been changed, but a minor change of this nature has the potential to provide a significant performance improvement in a production application.

1. Create a new Standard EXE project, add a reference to Microsoft Remote Data Object 2.0, and save the project as HT706.vbp. The single form for the application, FMain is identical to the FMain form used in HT705.vbp, with the exception of the change shown in step 3.

2. Using SQL Enterprise Manager or I-SQL/W, select the pubs database and execute the following SQL Script to create the **spStates** stored procedure:

```
CREATE PROCEDURE spStates AS
  SELECT StateCode FROM States ORDER BY StateCode
Go
GRANT EXECUTE ON spStates TO public
Go
```

NOTE

You will need to have already installed the States table using the States.sql script. The script shown above can be found in spStates.sql.

3. Replace the **GetStates** procedure with the following code. Two changes were made to the original procedure in HT705.vbp. The **sSQL** string variable and the assignment of the SQL statement were removed, and the name parameter of the **OpenResultset** method was replaced with the **spStates** stored procedure. The balance of the project is identical.

```
Private Sub GetStates()
' populate the states combo box

  Dim rsStates As rdoResultset

  ' we only need one pass through this data,
  ' and will only need to do it once, so we
  ' use a read only, forward only cursor and
  ' the exec direct option
  Set rsStates = mcon.OpenResultset("spStates", _
      rdOpenForwardOnly, rdConcurReadOnly, rdExecDirect)

  ' populate the combo box
  Do While Not rsStates.EOF
    cboState.AddItem rsStates!StateCode
    rsStates.MoveNext
  Loop

  ' clean up
  rsStates.Close

End Sub
```

How It Works

The original query was a **SELECT** statement submitted directly to the server for processing:

```
SELECT StateCode FROM States ORDER BY StateCode
```

This was replaced with a stored procedure that executes the same query. Because stored procedures have already been compiled and optimized, a few steps have been saved on the SQL Server each time this query has been submitted. Only a minor change is required for the GetStates procedure to take advantage of the stored procedure because the procedure was already designed to use a read-only resultset.

Comments

There might be no difference in the steps the SQL server takes to process the rows for this query. If you execute the original SQL statement directly in SQL Enterprise Manager and then execute the stored procedure (both with the Show Query Plan option turned on), you will see that the plan is identical for both queries. However, you are still saving the SQL Server the time required to compile and optimize the query.

For this type of data, you should design your application to run the query once (either at start time or the first time it is needed) and then cache the data locally for future use. On a table as stable as this one, you could consider permanently retaining a local copy and not querying the server at all. However, most database applications will need to run this type of query routinely. Often many small queries are run to populate lookup tables of coded values and other types of selection lists for combo boxes, list boxes, and so on. This type of data probably does not change often, but might not be stable enough to hardwire the values into the source code.

If you routinely submit a number of these queries in your application, a good solution might be to design a single stored procedure on the server that returns several or possibly all of these queries at once; then cache the results locally after the first execution. When you submit a query or stored procedure that returns multiple resultsets, you use the MoreResults method of the rdoResultset object to determine whether there are additional resultsets to process. You can also use the GetRows method to quickly and easily populate an array with the results of a query for temporary local storage.

COMPLEXITY
INTERMEDIATE

7.7 How do I...
Execute a parameterized SQL Server stored procedure with Remote Data Objects?

Problem

I need to capture the return value of a stored procedure that takes parameters. How can I do this with Remote Data Objects?

Technique

SQL Server stored procedures, like Visual Basic procedures, can take input and output parameters and can return values. To capture these values, you need to use a different technique from that used in How-To 7.6. The **rdoQuery** object provides the **rdoParameters** collection to manage the parameters of a stored procedure.

The question mark character is the placeholder for parameters in a SQL Server query. If a procedure takes parameters, you put question marks in the SQL statement where the parameters would be entered if you were submitting the query interactively. The following SQL statement would create a parameter query based on a **CustLast** column:

```
SELECT CustID, CustFirst, CustLast FROM Customers WHERE CustLast = ?
```

To supply this parameter when you execute the query, you need to create an **rdoQuery** object using the **CreateQuery** method:

```
' cn is a connection object defined elsewhere
' qry is an object variable declared as rdoQuery
' sSQL is a string variable
sSQL = "SELECT CustID, CustFirst, CustLast FROM Customers WHERE CustID = ?
Set qry = cn.CreateQuery("",sSQL)
```

This query will now have a single parameter in its **rdoParameters** collection. You can assign a value to the parameter and execute the query:

```
' the parameters collection is zero-based
qry(0) = 12
' rs is an rdoResultset object
Set rs = qry.Execute
```

Stored procedures can also take parameters, but to capture output parameters or return values, you need to use the OBDC call syntax. Here's the beginning of the **sp_addgroup** procedure from the master database:

```
create procedure sp_addgroup
@grpname varchar(30)
```

In addition to the **grpname** input parameter, **sp_addgroup** also returns a value indicating the success or failure of the procedure. With the ODBC call syntax, this query would be created as

```
{? = call sp_addgroup (?) }
```

The question mark at the beginning of the statement acts as a placeholder for the return value, and the question mark at the end acts as a placeholder for the **grpname** parameter. Normally, the ODBC driver can determine whether the parameters are input or output, but you can also supply the direction explicitly by using the **Direction** property of the **rdoParameter** object:

```
qry(0).Direction = rdDirectionInput
```

Along with input and output parameters, you can also use **rdParamReturnValue** to specify that a parameter is a stored procedure return value.

Steps

The sample project for this How-To is a SQL Server Change Password dialog box. Open and run project HT707.vbp to display the form shown in Figure 7.6. The dialog box uses the **sp_password** system stored procedure (in the master database) to change the password for the current user.

Figure 7.6. The Change Password dialog box.

1. Create a new Standard EXE project and save it as HT707.vbp. Change the name of **Form1** to **FMain** and save it as FMain.frm, and then create the objects and properties shown in Table 7.8.

Table 7.8. Objects and properties for *FMain*.

OBJECT	PROPERTY	VALUE
Form	Caption	Change Password
	Border Style	3 - Fixed Dialog
Label	Name	lbl
	Caption	Old Password
	Index	0
TextBox	Name	txtOld
Label	Name	lbl
	Caption	New Password
	Index	1
TextBox	Name	txtNew
Label	Name	lbl
	Caption	Confirm New Password
	Index	2
TextBox	Name	txtNewConfirm
CommandButton	Name	cmd
	Caption	OK
	Default	True
	Index	0
CommandButton	Name	cmd
	Caption	Cancel
	Cancel	True
	Index	1

2. Add **Option Explicit** to the declarations section of the form module, and then create the **cmd_Click** event procedure. This procedure calls the **ChangePassword** procedure if OK was clicked or unloads the form if Cancel was clicked.

```
Private Sub cmd_Click(Index As Integer)
On Error GoTo ProcError

   Select Case cmd(Index).Caption
     Case "OK"
        ChangePassword
     Case "Cancel"
        Unload Me
```

```
    End Select

ProcExit:
    Exit Sub

ProcError:
    MsgBox Err.Number & vbCrLf & Err.Description
    Resume ProcExit

End Sub
```

3. Add the following code as the **ChangePassword** function. This procedure uses the values entered in the text boxes to supply the parameters for the **sp_password** system stored procedure. The procedure first verifies that the user entered the same value in the New Password and Confirm New Password text boxes; it then opens a connection to the SQL Server.

4. The pubs DSN is used to open the connection, but any valid connection to the server will work because the procedure name is fully qualified in the master database. After the connection has been established, the procedure creates an **rdoQuery** object, sets the direction of the parameters, and assigns the values of the two input parameters. Finally, the query is executed using the **Execute** method of the **rdoQuery** object, and the return value is captured using the **rdoParameters** collection. The **sp_password** returns **0** if the password was successfully changed, and this value is tested to display an appropriate message based on the return value of the stored procedure.

```
Private Sub ChangePassword()
' change the current user's password
' using the sp_password system stored procedure

    Dim con As rdoConnection
    Dim sSQL As String
    Dim qry As rdoQuery

    Dim sOld As String
    Dim sNew As String
    Dim sNewConfirm As String

    sOld = txtOld
    sNew = txtNew
    sNewConfirm = txtNewConfirm

    If sNew <> sNewConfirm Then
        ' mismatch, inform, clear values and exit
        MsgBox "New passwords do not match."
        txtNew = ""
        txtNewConfirm = ""
        txtNew.SetFocus
        Exit Sub
```

continued on next page

continued from previous page

```
                End If

                Set con = _
                    rdoEnvironments(0).OpenConnection _
                    ("pubs")

                ' use the ODBC call syntax to capture the return value
                ' this is needed to know if the change succeeded
                sSQL = "{? = call master.dbo.sp_password (?,?) }"
                ' create the query object
                Set qry = con.CreateQuery("", sSQL)

                ' set direction for param 0
                qry(0).Direction = rdParamReturnValue
                qry(1).Direction = rdParamInput
                qry(2).Direction = rdParamInput

                ' this is equivalent to using
                ' qry.rdoParameters(1)
                qry(1) = sOld
                qry(2) = sNew

                ' run it
                qry.Execute

                ' sp_password returns 0 if successful
                ' the return parameters is always #0
                If qry(0) = 0 Then
                  MsgBox "Password changed."
                  Unload Me
                Else
                  MsgBox "Unable to change password."
                End If

            End Sub
```

How It Works

Only the ODBC call syntax can be used if you need to capture the output or return parameters from a stored procedure. By using this syntax in the SQL statement, you can create an **rdoQuery** object with an **rdoParameters** collection and use the parameters to supply input values and capture output and return values.

This procedure could also be run by directly providing the old and new password as part of the SQL statement and run using the **Execute** method of an **rdoConnection** object, but you would not be able to determine whether the procedure succeeded or failed because the return value would be unavailable.

Comments

This simple Change Password dialog box could easily be plugged into any SQL Server database application by changing the code used to open the connection to the server or by supplying a valid connection using a public property of the form.

COMPLEXITY
INTERMEDIATE

7.8 How do I...
Handle Remote Data Objects errors?

Problem

I know that there will be runtime errors generated in my application and that I must trap and handle these errors to make the application robust and reliable. How do I handle errors generated by Remote Data Objects?

Technique

As with any Visual Basic application, you must trap and handle the errors that are generated at runtime, or the Visual Basic runtime DLL will invoke its own default error handler—which simply displays a message and terminates your application. Error-handling techniques for Remote Data Objects applications are similar to the techniques used for handling any other Visual Basic runtime errors, with one subtle but important variation: More than one error can be generated by a single statement in Remote Data Objects.

To enable you to deal with this possibility, Remote Data Objects provides the `rdoErrors` collection. This is a collection of `rdoError` objects you can examine the same way you examine the Visual Basic **Err** object. You can check the **Number**, **Source**, and **Description** properties. An `rdoError` object also provides the **SQLRetCode** and **SQLState** properties for you to examine.

Each of these properties might or might not provide useful information. SQL Server error messages can often be cryptic at best, and although a Visual Basic runtime error is generated, you get only the first error in the `rdoErrors` collection. You will normally need to iterate the `rdoErrors` collection to find the true nature of the problem because the first error is often a generic message such as **Command has been aborted.**—a true but generally useless piece of information for debugging without having the underlying cause of the problem.

The other significant difference in handling errors generated by Remote Data Objects is that you need to be prepared to deal with a much wider array of possible problems, ranging from typical Visual Basic errors like **Invalid Use of Null** (a common error in database applications) to the sudden death of the SQL Server at the other end of the connection. Along with the normal array of possible data manipulation problems (invalid foreign key values, data missing from required columns, and so on), most large SQL Server databases will have a wide variety of often complex business rules that are enforced. If rules are enforced using SQL Server triggers or stored procedures, the error numbers and messages generated will be dependent on the developer that created the Transact-SQL code. If that developer was conscientious in developing the Transact-SQL code, you will receive descriptive and informative messages. If you are developing your own Transact-SQL code, provide as much information as you reasonably can and use a sensible convention for generating error numbers.

NOTE

You generate errors in Transact-SQL by using the RAISERROR statement.

Although there are standard techniques for trapping and examining errors, the means you use to handle the errors is entirely up to you and dependent on the context of the error. If a rule or some type of constraint is violated, you might be able to provide a message to the user with information about the problem and possible solutions. For more severe errors, such as a lost connection to the database server over the network, you might have little choice but to gracefully terminate the application, informing the user of the problem in the process. There are several avenues available for you to deal with possible problems:

✔ *Prevent the errors before they happen.* By using combo boxes, lists, and other user interface mechanisms that provide fixed lists of values for the user to select, you can prevent the entry of data that will violate database rules. If a column requires that a value be a member of a particular list of valid values, you should design the application so that only that list is available to the user.

✔ *Make explicit tests for known probable errors before submitting data to the server.* By handling the problem in advance of the generation of a runtime error, you gain more direct control over the problem and reduce the overhead on the server—which will need to process only validated data.

✔ *Iterate the* rdoErrors *collection with a* **For...Each** *loop to gather as much information as possible about the errors you do encounter.* To whatever degree is possible, do this while debugging the application and take steps to prevent the problems if you can.

✔ *As always, set up error handlers in* **Sub Main** *and all event procedures.* Because these procedures are by definition at the top of the Visual Basic call tree, errors in them cannot be raised and will be fatal to your application. If your application must be shut down due to a severe error, close it down gracefully with your own code rather than letting Visual Basic's default runtime error handling terminate the application for you. You might even be able to save edits in progress locally and submit them to the server later when the problem has been cleared up.

YOUR RESPONSIBILITIES AS A DATABASE APPLICATION DEVELOPER

As the developer of a database application, you have two responsibilities that can sometimes be at odds with each other. You need to provide an easy-to-use, high-performance application for the user. Users are mainly concerned with getting their work done and don't care much about the intricacies of SQL Server rules, foreign key constraints, and other problems. At the same time, you need to make sure that only valid data is stored in the database because the data can be worse than useless if it is not reliable.

Most database developers tend to err on the side of caution where data validation is concerned, often at the expense of end user productivity. How strictly you need to enforce your rules depends on the nature of the application. If you are working with a financial application where precision is paramount, you might need to be more severe in your enforcement of business rules. However, it is often the case that developers enforce rules that can potentially be ignored—at least temporarily—for the sake of the productivity of the end user.

Only you can determine how strict you need to be, but you should try to make an effort to sterilize the data only if it's truly necessary. In most cases, it's wishful thinking to believe that you can build an application where no bad data can be entered, so attempts to do so only hurt user productivity. If you are faced with a decision about data validation and rule enforcement, make the decision in the context of the overall goal of the application rather than looking only at the details of table or column level rules.

Steps

There is no specific project that demonstrates handling errors from Remote Data Objects. You are probably already well versed with basic Visual Basic error handling techniques, so rather than provide a contrived example, the following steps examine some of the problems you might encounter in the existing examples from How-To 7.2 and How-To 7.7. If you need a review of the essentials of Visual Basic error handling, see How-To 2.8, which covers the basic techniques of runtime error handling.

In How-To 7.2, a bound control application was developed that enables you to browse, update, insert, and delete rows in the Publishers table of the pubs sample database. There are two known problems involved in working with the

Publishers table that were described in the chapter. First, a rather strange check constraint is enforced on the **pub_id** column, and second, there are foreign keys in other tables that reference the **pub_id** column. Inserts, updates, and deletes can all generate violations of these rules, and the basic error handlers provided in the existing example do not provide any information about the true nature of the problem.

1. Open and run HT702.vbp. The first publisher displayed should be New Moon Books. Change the existing ID value from **0736** to **0737** and attempt to move to the next row using the navigation buttons provided by the RemoteData control. The message shown in Figure 7.7 will be displayed. Following this message will be another, shown in Figure 7.8.

Figure 7.7. The Command has been aborted message.

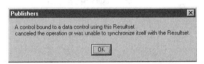

Figure 7.8. The operation canceled message.

2. Insert the following code as the **rdc_Error** event procedure. This procedure iterates the **rdoErrors** collection with a **For...Each** loop and builds a message using all the available errors. The message generated reveals the true nature of the problem: The column level check constraint on the **pub_id** column has been violated.

```
Private Sub rdc_Error( _
  ByVal Number As Long, _
  Description As String, _
  ByVal Scode As Long, _
  ByVal Source As String, _
  ByVal HelpFile As String, _
  ByVal HelpContext As Long, _
  CancelDisplay As Boolean)

Dim sMsg As String
  Dim rerr As rdoError

  For Each rerr In rdoErrors
    sMsg = _
```

```
      rerr.Number & ": " & rerr.Description & vbCrLf
  Next
  MsgBox sMsg

End Sub
```

3. In the `mnuDataSave_Click` event, replace the simple `MsgBox` statement in the error handler with the following code. This is the same approach used in the `rdc_Error` event procedure to find out what the real problem is with the error. The original message `Command has been aborted`—although true—is useless without the additional information provided by the `rdoErrors` collection.

```
Dim rerr As rdoError
Dim sMsg As String
For Each rerr In rdoErrors
  sMsg = rerr.Number & ": " & rerr.Description & vbCrLf
Next
MsgBox sMsg
```

4. Run the project again, but this time attempt to delete New Moon Books. The now familiar `Command has been aborted` message appears. Again the message is correct but useless. Replace the `MsgBox` statement in the error handler with the same code used in the two previous steps. If you run the project and again attempt the delete, the `rdoErrors` collection will now reveal that the underlying problem is the violation of a foreign key constraint. With this information available, you can deal with the problem by either cancelling the delete and informing the user or by deleting the associated rows in the foreign table.

5. Sometimes, despite your best efforts, the messages you receive from SQL Server just aren't going to provide any useful information. In How-To 7.7, you created a form that calls the system stored procedure `sp_password`. In SQL Enterprise Manager or I-SQL/w, you can run this stored procedure (which resides in the master database) from any database on the server and change your password. That's how system stored procedures are supposed to work and why they're called system stored procedures—they apply to the entire SQL Server. Based on this information, replace the line of code in the `ChangePassword` subroutine with the following line. At first glance you might expect this to work, but it doesn't. The rather bizarre error message shown in Figure 7.9 is displayed instead of a notification that the password was changed.

```
sSQL = "{? = call sp_password (?,?) }"
```

Figure 7.9. A not-so-helpful error message.

6. The trouble is that a fully qualified name for the procedure in the form database.owner.object is required. Unfortunately, the **rdoErrors** collection does not provide any further information. If you place a breakpoint in the procedure or set the Break on all Errors option in Visual Basic, you can examine the **rdoErrors** collection in the immediate window. The only error available is the one displayed, and it certainly doesn't indicate the true nature of the problem. A search of the Microsoft Technical Support Knowledge Base on the Microsoft Web site using the keywords **rdoquery error** returned (among others) the following article. This article indicates that you need to provide the full path to the stored procedure if you use the technique shown in How-To 7.7 (as well as an alternative method).

```
HOWTO: Call SQL Server System Stored Procedures from RDO

Last reviewed: April 18, 1997
Article ID: Q166211 The information in this article applies to:

·Microsoft Visual Basic Enterprise Edition for Windows, version
5.0
```

How It Works

Standard Visual Basic error-handling techniques, in conjunction with the **rdoErrors** collection, enable you to trap and examine runtime errors returned by Remote Data Objects. Armed with the information provided by the `rdoErrors` collection, you can build applications that trap and handle runtime errors effectively.

Comments

The information provided by the `rdoErrors` collection is often helpful, but not always—as demonstrated in the steps above. In order to be productive as a programmer, you'll need to be able to query the resources available in the help files, the Knowledge Base, and other sources to find the solutions to your problems. Finally, don't underestimate the power of your own intuition in solving problems and working out bugs in your application. As you gain experience in programming with Visual Basic and Remote Data Objects, you will eventually learn to anticipate problems and can often solve them with a simple educated guess.

CHAPTER 8
USING ACTIVEX DATA OBJECTS

8

USING ACTIVEX DATA OBJECTS

How Do I...

8.1 Browse a SQL Server database with the ADO Data control?

8.2 Create and delete records in a SQL Server database using the ADO Data control?

8.3 Retrieve results from a SQL Server using ActiveX Data Objects?

8.4 Alter data using ActiveX Data Objects?

8.5 Perform a transaction using ActiveX Data Objects?

8.6 Execute a SQL Server stored procedure using ActiveX Data Objects?

8.7 Execute a parameterized SQL Server stored procedure with ActiveX Data Objects?

8.8 Create and modify SQL Server objects with ActiveX Data Objects?

8.9 Execute batch updates with ActiveX Data Objects?

8.10 Make remote updates to data with ActiveX Data Objects?

8.11 Build a middle-tier business object using ActiveX Data Objects?

8.12 Incorporate a business object into Microsoft Transaction Server?

8.13 Handle ActiveX Data Objects errors?

Universal Data Access, OLE DB, ActiveX Data Objects…what do they all mean? Recently developers have been hit with another new wave of technology terms. Microsoft has once again pushed forward the frontier of data access.

Universal Data Access, referred to as UDA from here forward, is Microsoft's term for the idea that a developer should be able to use one data access method for any data source he is querying. ODBC was a great step forward. For the first time, no matter what relational database the application needed to talk to, you only needed to learn one API. The problem with ODBC is that it was aimed directly at relational databases and other sources of data did not fit its model very well. Instead of trying to tack functionality on to ODBC so that it could handle other data sources as well as it did relational databases, Microsoft decided to do things right and start from scratch. They built OLE DB without having to make any compromises to the existing architecture.

OLE DB is a COM-based interface between data providers and client applications. Data providers can be anything from relation databases to spread sheets to file systems. Like RDO was to the ODBC API, Microsoft knew it needed to create an easy-to-use object layer on top of OLE DB; thus ActiveX Data Objects were born.

ADO is the interface into OLE DB so that VB can reap the benefits of UDA. Got that? This chapter covers ADO from its simplest form, using the ADO Data control, to more complex forms, such as building three-tier applications using Microsoft Transaction Server.

This chapter makes a few assumptions:

✔ You need access to a SQL Server with the sample database pubs installed on it.

✔ A few of the samples require an ODBC datasource—pubs—set up to connect to that server and database. One of the first data providers Microsoft released was a data provider that sat on top of ODBC. Any database accessible to ODBC is accessible to ADO.

✔ For How-To 8.12, you will need Microsoft Transaction Server. It is available from Microsoft as part of the NT Server Option Pack.

CONNECTING TO OTHER DATABASES

All the How-Tos in this chapter use a Microsoft SQL Server, but ADO is not constrained to one database vender or even just databases. The "Provider" parameter of the connection string indicates which OLE DB data provider should be used. ADO 2.0 ships with several data providers including Jet, Oracle, and Microsoft Directory Services. Connecting to a different data provider is as easy as changing the connection string. For example, a typical connection string for an Access database would be "Provider=Microsoft.Jet.OLEDB.3.51;Data Source=mydb.mdb".

8.1 Browse a SQL Server Database with the ADO Data Control

This How-To shows the quickest and simplest way to get up and running using ADO, the ADO Data control.

8.2 Create and Delete Records in a SQL Server Database Using the ADO Data Control

With a little extra code you can insert and delete records using the ADO Data control. This How-To shows you how.

8.3 Retrieve Results from a SQL Server Using ActiveX Data Objects

Retrieve data without the use of the ADO Data control in this How-To.

8.4 Alter Data Using ActiveX Data Objects

This How-To shows you how to update, insert, and delete records using ADO.

8.5 Perform a Transaction Using ActiveX Data Objects

Most business applications require them; this How-To shows you how to perform a transaction in ADO.

8.6 Execute a SQL Server Stored Procedure Using ActiveX Data Objects

You can increase the performance of your ADO applications by using stored procedures. In this How-To you learn how to use SQL Server stored procedures with ADO.

8.7 Execute a Parameterized SQL Server Stored Procedure with ActiveX Data Objects

Some stored procedures have return values and output parameters. This How-To shows you what you need to know to handle parameterized stored procedures.

8.8 Create and Modify SQL Server Objects with ActiveX Data Objects

The ADO object model does not let you modify SQL Server objects. This How-To shows you how to get around it.

8.9 Execute Batch Updates with ActiveX Data Objects

Saving many changes at once can increase performance. This How-To shows you how.

8.10 Make Remote Updates to Data with ActiveX Data Objects

In this How-To you will learn how to best update a `Recordset` using ADO when connections and bandwidth are limited.

8.11 Build a Middle-Tier Business Object Using ActiveX Data Objects

Move up to three-tier development in this How-To, where you learn how to build a middle-tier business object using ADO.

8.12 Incorporate a Business Object into Microsoft Transaction Server

When scalability becomes a problem, MTS is your answer. This How-To shows you how to take a middle-tier business component and tune it for Microsoft Transaction Server.

8.13 Handle ActiveX Data Objects Errors

This How-To shows you what to do when things do go wrong.

COMPLEXITY
BEGINNING

8.1 How do I...
Browse a SQL Server database with the ADO Data control?

Problem

My data is on SQL Server database. What is an easy way to get to get the data using ADO?

Technique

Like the Visual Basic Data control and the `RemoteData` control, the ADO Data control gives you a "no code" solution for data access. The difference lies in the data access method. The Visual Basic Data control uses the Jet Engine, the RemoteData control uses RDO, and the ADO Data control uses Microsoft's newest data access methodology, ActiveX Data Objects.

The technique to use the ADO Data control is very similar to its predecessors:

1. Draw an ADO Data control on your form and set the `ConnectionString` and `RecordSource` properties.

2. Add controls to the form to display the columns in the record source and set their `DataSource` and `DataField` properties.

In just a couple of steps, and no lines of code, an application with the ability to browse and edit the database is born. All the data access is handled by the ADO Data control.

Steps

Load and run ADODC.vbp. Figure 8.1 shows the ADODC application in action. Change the `ConnectionString` property of the ADO Data Control on frmMain to match your user and password, and then run the application. You can use the application to browse and edit the Authors table in the pubs database.

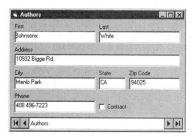

Figure 8.1. The Authors form using an ADO Data control.

1. Create a new Standard EXE project, and change the Project Name to ADODC in the Project Properties dialog box. Rename the default form frmMain.

2. Using Project | Components, add the Microsoft ADO Data Control 6.0 to the project. Add an ADO Data Control to frmMain along with the other controls listed in Table 8.1. Arrange the controls to match Figure 8.1 and set all the properties according to Table 8.1. Change the `ConnectionString` property of the ADO Data Control to match your user and password.

Table 8.1. Objects and properties for frmMain.

OBJECT	PROPERTY	VALUE
Form	Caption	Authors
ADO Data control	Name	adodc
	Caption	Authors
	Align	2 - vbAlignBottom
	ConnectionString	DSN=pubs;User Id=sa;Password=password
	RecordSource	authors
TextBox	Name	txtFirstName
	Text	" "
	DataSource	adodc
	DataField	au_fname
TextBox	Name	txtLastName
	Text	" "
	DataSource	adodc
	DataField	au_lname
TextBox	Name	txtAddress
	Text	" "
	DataSource	adodc
	DataField	address
TextBox	Name	txtCity
	Text	" "
	DataSource	adodc
	DataField	city
TextBox	Name	txtState
	Text	" "
	DataSource	adodc
	DataField	state
TextBox	Name	txtZip
	Text	" "
	DataSource	adodc
	DataField	zip
TextBox	Name	txtPhone
	Text	" "
	DataSource	adodc
	DataField	phone
CheckBox control	Name	chkContract
	Caption	Contract

OBJECT	PROPERTY	VALUE
	DataSource	adodc
	DataField	contract
Label	Name	lblFirstName
	Caption	First
Label	Name	lblLastName
	Caption	Last
Label	Name	lblAddress
	Caption	Address
Label	Name	lblCity
	Caption	City
Label	Name	lblState
	Caption	State
Label	Name	lblZip
	Caption	Zip Code
Label	Name	lblPhone
	Caption	Phone

How It Works

The ADO Data control does all the work in this application. Use the navigation buttons to move through the records and use the bound controls to edit and view the data.

Comments

This application is drag-and-drop programming at its best. With no code, a fully function application enables the user to edit and view a Recordset using ADO.

COMPLEXITY
INTERMEDIATE

8.2 How do I...
Create and delete records in a SQL Server database using the ADO Data control?

Problem

Viewing and editing existing records is nice, but my users need to do more. How do I create and delete records using the ADO Data control?

Technique

Creating an application to view and edit existing records is really easy and it requires no code at all. Unfortunately, the user's requirements are seldom that simple. The next obvious step is to grant the user the ability to add and delete records.

To add a record using the ADO Data control:

1. Use the `AddNew` method of the ADO Data control's `Recordset` property to create a new blank row in the row buffer.

2. Use the `Update` method of the ADO Data control's `Recordset` property to save the new row to the database.

The Recordset's `Delete` method is used to delete a record. However, the `Delete` method will not refresh the window with a valid record. You must move the ADO Data control to a new valid row. This How-To uses the convention of moving to the previous row when deleting.

Steps

Open ADODC2.vbp and change the `ConnectionString` property of the ADO Data Control on frmMain to match your user and password, then run. This is almost the same application from the first How-To. The changes are listed in the steps below.

1. Starting with the finished product of How-To 8.1, add the controls and menu items specified in Table 8.2. Use Figure 8.2 to help place the new controls.

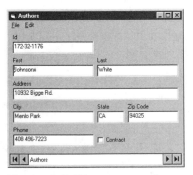

Figure 8.2. The new and improved Authors form.

Table 8.2. New objects and properties for frmMain.

OBJECT	PROPERTY	VALUE
TextBox	Name	txtId
	Text	" "

OBJECT	PROPERTY	VALUE
	DataSource	adodc
	DataField	au_id
Label	Name lblId	
	Caption Id	
Menu item	Name	mnuFile
	Caption	&File
Menu item	Name mnuNew	
	Caption &New	
	Indent	1
Menu item	Name	mnuSave
	Caption &Save	
	Indent	1
	Enabled	False
Menu item	Name	mnuExit
	Caption E&xit	
	Indent	1
Menu item	Name	mnuEdit
	Caption	&Edit
Menu item	Name mnuDelete	
	Caption &Delete	
	Indent	1

2. Add Option Explicit to the declarations section of the form if it is not already there.

3. Add the following code to the form. This sub checks to see if a new record has been added; if it has been added, the sub attempts to save the new record and disable the Save menu selection.

```
Private Sub Save()
    'if we need to save then save it
    If adodc.Recordset.EditMode = adEditAdd Then
        On Error GoTo SaveFailure:
        adodc.Recordset.Update
        On Error GoTo 0
        'don't need to save so disable that menu
        mnuSave.Enabled = False
    End If

SaveDone:
    Exit Sub
SaveFailure:
    MsgBox Err.Number & vbCrLf & Err.Description
    Resume SaveDone
End Sub
```

4. Adding the code adds the new empty row to the row buffer.

```
Private Sub mnuNew_Click()
    adodc.Recordset.AddNew
    'so we can save that new record
    mnuSave.Enabled = True
End Sub
```

5. Create the mnuSave_Click event procedure. It just calls the **Save** sub.

```
Private Sub mnuSave_Click()
    Save
End Sub
```

6. If the user tries to exit after adding a new row, check to see if she wants to save it in the mnuExit_Click event procedure.

```
Private Sub mnuExit_Click()
    If adodc.Recordset.EditMode = adEditAdd Then
        If MsgBox("Do you want to save?", vbYesNo) = vbYes Then
            Save
        End If
    End If
    Unload Me
End Sub
```

7. Finally, add the code to delete a row.

```
Private Sub mnuDelete_Click()
    On Error GoTo DeleteFailure:
    adodc.Recordset.Delete
    'current row is now invalid so move back one
    adodc.Recordset.MovePrevious
    'if we are before the beginning go to the first
    If adodc.Recordset.BOF Then
        adodc.Recordset.MoveFirst
    End If
DeleteDone:
    Exit Sub
DeleteFailure:
    MsgBox Err.Number & vbCrLf & Err.Description
    Resume DeleteDone
End Sub
```

How It Works

Like the previous How-To, this one relies on the ADO Data control to do much of the work. You can use the **AddNew**, **Update**, and **Delete** methods of the **Recordset** object to supplement the ADO Data control's basic functionality to build a simple data manipulation application.

Comments

The ADO Data control is nice for quick and easy applications, but this How-To shows that you quickly have to move up to manipulating ADO programmatically to get any advanced features. The rest of this chapter's How–To's focus on using ADO's objects directly without the ADO Data control.

COMPLEXITY
BEGINNING

8.3 How do I...
Retrieve results from a SQL Server using ActiveX Data Objects?

Problem

I want to get at my data without using a bound control. How do I retrieve results from SQL Server using ActiveX Data Objects?

Technique

The ADO `Connection` and `Recordset` objects provide direct access to data in ADO. If you have programmed in either DAO or RDO, the ADO objects will seem strangely familiar. Most DAO and RDO objects have counterparts in ADO, but one with significant difference.

The biggest difference between ADO and its predecessors is the flat nature of the ADO object model. RDO also has an `rdoRecordset` object, which is the child of an `rdoConnection`, which is the child of an `rdoEnvironment`, which is the child of the `rdoEngine`. RDO and DAO are very hierarchical; to get to a recordset, you must also have all the parent objects. ADO does not require the overhead of the hierarchy. To retrieve results from a data source, all you need is a connection and a recordset.

The steps to get data from SQL Server are listed below:

1. Create and open a connection.

2. Create and open a recordset with the connection as a parameter.

3. Close the recordset.

4. Close the connection.

Steps

Open the ListAuthors.vbp project. Before running the project you will have to change the username (User Id=), password (Password=), and server name (Location=) parameters of the connection string. The connection is opened in the `Form_Load` event of frmAuthors. The Authors form, shown in Figure 8.3, shows a list of authors and their addresses.

Figure 8.3. The Authors form shows a list of authors.

A NOTE ON CONNECTION STRINGS

It is often hard to remember the exact syntax for connection strings, but the ADO Data control has an excellent wizard for building and testing connection strings. Simply add the ADO Data control to your project, right-click on the control and select ADODC properties, then click the Build button next to the Use Connection String option. When you're finished creating and testing the connection string, cut and paste it from the text box and remove the ADO Data control from your project.

1. Create a new Standard EXE project, add a reference to Microsoft ActiveX Data Objects 2.0 Library, and add the Microsoft Windows Common Controls 6.0 component. Change the Project Name to ListAuthors and the Name of the default form to frmAuthors, and save the project.

2. Add the object and set the properties according to Table 8.3.

Table 8.3. New objects and properties for frmAuthors.

OBJECT	PROPERTY	VALUE
Form	Caption	Authors
ListView	Name	listAuthors
	View	3 - lvwReport
	LabelEdit	1 - lvwManual

3. Add the columns listed in Table 8.4 to the `ListView` control using the Column Headers property page.

Table 8.4. Column Headers for listAuthors.

COLUMN	WIDTH
Name	2000
Address	2000
City	1440
State	500
Zip	700

4. Add the following procedure. The `Form_Load` event/property opens the `Connection` object, opens the `Recordset` object, and fills the `ListView` control with the names and address from the Authors table. Remember to change the connection string for the `Connection` object's `Open` method.

```
Private Sub Form_Load()
    Dim cn As Connection
    Dim rs As Recordset
    Dim NewItem As ListItem

    'open the connection
    Set cn = New Connection
    cn.Open "Provider=SQLOLEDB.1;User ID=sa;Password=password;" _
        + "Location=WINEMILLER;Database=pubs"
    'could have also just specified an ODBC DSN like below
    'cn.Open "DSN=pubs"

    'now open the recordset
    Set rs = New Recordset
    rs.Open "authors", cn, adOpenForwardOnly, adLockReadOnly
    Do Until rs.EOF
        Set NewItem = listAuthors.ListItems.Add(, rs("au_id"), _
            rs("au_lname") & ", " & rs("au_fname"))
        NewItem.SubItems(1) = rs("address")
        NewItem.SubItems(2) = rs("city")
        NewItem.SubItems(3) = rs("state")
        NewItem.SubItems(4) = rs("zip")
        rs.MoveNext
    Loop
    'close and clean up
    rs.Close
    cn.Close
    Set rs = Nothing
    Set cn = Nothing
End Sub
```

How It Works

The code in `Form_Load` is typical for an ADO data retrieval operation.

1. Instance the `Connection` object.

2. Call the `Connection` object's `Open` method.

3. Instance the `Recordset` object.

4. Call the `Recordset` object's `Open` method, using the `Connection` object as a parameter.

5. Move through the `Recordset` until the `EOF` method returns a True.

6. Call the `Recordset` object's `Close` method.

7. Call the `Connection` object's `Close` method.

8. Set the `Recordset` and `Connection` objects to Nothing.

Opening connections is an expensive operation, so in most applications it is far better to keep a connection as a module or global level variable. The rules change when Microsoft Transaction Server is added to the pot; How-To 8.12 explains why you should open and close a connection in each call when using Microsoft Transaction Server.

Comments

In most applications you will probably want to keep a `Connection` object at the global or module level. This will save you from creating the object each time an operation is performed.

COMPLEXITY
INTERMEDIATE

8.4 How do I...
Alter data using ActiveX Data Objects?

Problem

Now that I know how to get to my data using ADO, I want to change it. How do I alter data using ActiveX Data Objects?

Technique

ADO provides two basic means for altering data: the Connection object's `Execute` method and the `Recordset` object. Using the `Execute` method, you can use SQL queries and commands such as UPDATE, INSERT, and DELETE. The

Recordset object exposes corresponding methods with its **Update**, **AddNew**, and **Delete** methods.

How-To 8.3 uses a forward-only, read-only cursor because it only needs to display data. This How-To uses keyset cursors with optimistic locking. This type of cursor allows updates and deletes to the recordset.

Steps

Open the ListAuthors2.vbp. As with How-To 8.3, you will need to update the connection string used to open the connection in the **Form_Load** before you can run it. This project is typical of many applications where you select from a list of objects and the objects' properties are displayed in a separate part of the window. There you can delete, edit, and add new records.

1. Create a new Standard EXE, and change the Project Name to ListAuthors2. Change the default form name to frmAuthors and save the project.

2. Add a reference to the Microsoft ActiveX Data Objects 2.0 Library and add the Microsoft Windows Common Controls 6.0.

3. Using Table 8.5, add the required objects to the form and set their properties. Use Figure 8.4 as a guide to lay out the position of the controls.

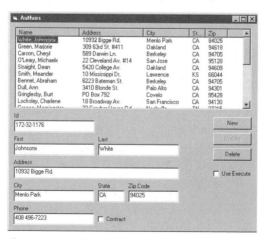

Figure 8.4. The Authors form.

Table 8.5. Objects and properties for frmAuthors.

OBJECT	PROPERTY	VALUE
Form	Caption	Authors
CommandButton	Name	cmdNew
	Caption	New
CommandButton	Name	cmdDelete
	Caption	Delete
CommandButton	Name	cmdUpdate
	Caption	Update
CheckBox	Name	chkExecute
	Caption	Use Execute
ListView	Name	listAuthors
	View	3 - lvwReport
	LabelEdit	1 - lvwManual
TextBox	Name	txtId
	Text	""
TextBox	Name	txtFirstName
	Text	""
TextBox	Name	txtLastName
	Text	""
TextBox	Name	txtAddress
	Text	""
TextBox	Name	txtCity
	Text	""
TextBox	Name	txtState
	Text	""
TextBox	Name	txtZip
	Text	""
TextBox	Name	txtPhone
	Text	""
CheckBox	Name	chkContract
	Caption	Contract
Label	Name	lblId
	Caption	Id
Label	Name	lblFirstName
	Caption	First

OBJECT	PROPERTY	VALUE
Label	Name	lblLastName
	Caption	Last
Label	Name	lblAddress
	Caption	Address
Label	Name	lblCity
	Caption	City
Label	Name	lblState
	Caption	State
Label	Name	lblZip
	Caption	Zip Code
Label	Name	lblPhone
	Caption	Phone

4. Add the columns listed in Table 8.6 to the ListView control using the Column Headers property page.

Table 8.6. Column headers for listAuthors.

COLUMN	WIDTH
Name	2000
Address	2000
City	1440
State	500
Zip	700

5. Add following code to the declarations section of frmAuthors.

```
Option Explicit

Private mConn As Connection
'has something changed
Private mbNeedSave As Boolean
'are we working with a new record
Private mbNewRecord As Boolean
'keep track of the current record
Private msCurrentRecord As String
```

6. The Form_Load event looks much like the one from How-To 8.3. This version does not close the connection because it will be used later. Add a Form_Load event with the following code. Remember to change the con-nection string to match your setup.

```
Private Sub Form_Load()
    Dim rs As Recordset
    Dim NewItem As ListItem

    'open the connection
    Set mConn = New Connection
    mConn.Open "Provider=SQLOLEDB.1;User ID=sa;Password=password" _
        + "Location=WINEMILLER;Database=pubs"

    'could have also just specified an ODBC DSN like below
    'mConnOpen "DSN=pubs"

    'now open the recordset
    Set rs = New Recordset
    rs.Open "authors", mConn, adOpenForwardOnly, adLockReadOnly
    Do Until rs.EOF
        Set NewItem = listAuthors.ListItems.Add(, rs("au_id"), _
            rs("au_lname") & ", " & rs("au_fname"))
        NewItem.SubItems(1) = rs("address")
        NewItem.SubItems(2) = rs("city")
        NewItem.SubItems(3) = rs("state")
        NewItem.SubItems(4) = rs("zip")
        rs.MoveNext
    Loop
    'close and clean up
    rs.Close
    Set rs = Nothing

    'set the first item
    listAuthors_ItemClick listAuthors.ListItems(1)
End Sub
```

7. Now add the **Form_Unload** event. This event closes the mConn and sets the object to Nothing.

```
Private Sub Form_Unload(Cancel As Integer)
    mConn.Close
    Set mConn = Nothing
End Sub
```

8. When the data fields change, the **mbNeedSave** flag is set and the cmdUpdate button is enabled. Add the following code to capture when a change happens.

```
Private Sub RecordChanged()
    mbNeedSave = True
    cmdUpdate.Enabled = True
End Sub

Private Sub chkContract_Click()
    RecordChanged
End Sub
Private Sub txtAddress_Change()
    RecordChanged
```

```
End Sub

Private Sub txtCity_Change()
    RecordChanged
End Sub

Private Sub txtFirstName_Change()
    RecordChanged
End Sub

Private Sub txtId_Change()
    RecordChanged
End Sub

Private Sub txtLastName_Change()
    RecordChanged
End Sub

Private Sub txtPhone_Change()
    RecordChanged
End Sub

Private Sub txtState_Change()
    RecordChanged
End Sub

Private Sub txtZip_Change()
    RecordChanged
End Sub
```

9. The New button clears the data and sets the mbNewRecord flag. Add the cmdNew_Click event.

```
Private Sub cmdNew_Click()
    'clear screen
    txtId.Text = ""
    txtFirstName.Text = ""
    txtLastName.Text = ""
    txtAddress.Text = ""
    txtCity.Text = ""
    txtState.Text = ""
    txtZip.Text = ""
    txtPhone.Text = ""
    chkContract.Value = vbChecked
    'set flags
    mbNewRecord = True
    mbNeedSave = True
    'nothing to delete
    cmdDelete.Enabled = False
    'no record selected
    Set listAuthors.SelectedItem = Nothing
    'start the user off in the right place
    txtId.SetFocus
End Sub
```

10. Add the code to handle the update. The **Update** function does most of the hard work in the application. Based on the value of the chkExecute checkbox, it either uses the **Connection** object's **Execute** method, or the **Recordset** object's **AddNew** and **Update** methods.

```
Private Sub cmdUpdate_Click()
    UpdateRecord
End Sub

Private Function UpdateRecord() As Boolean
    Dim sCmd As String
    Dim rs As Recordset

    If mbNewRecord Then
        'try to insert
        If chkExecute.Value = vbChecked Then
            'use the execute method of the connection
            sCmd = "insert into authors " _
                "(au_id,au_fname,au_lname,address" _
                + ",city,state,zip,phone,contract)"
            sCmd = sCmd + " values ("
            sCmd = sCmd + "'" + txtId.Text + "'"
            sCmd = sCmd + ",'" + txtFirstName.Text + "'"
            sCmd = sCmd + ",'" + txtLastName.Text + "'"
            sCmd = sCmd + ",'" + txtAddress.Text + "'"
            sCmd = sCmd + ",'" + txtCity.Text + "'"
            sCmd = sCmd + ",'" + txtState.Text + "'"
            sCmd = sCmd + ",'" + txtZip.Text + "'"
            sCmd = sCmd + ",'" + txtPhone.Text + "'"
            sCmd = sCmd + "," & IIf(chkContract.Value = vbChecked _
                1, 0)
            sCmd = sCmd + ")"
            On Error GoTo UpdateFailed:
            mConn.Execute sCmd
            On Error GoTo 0
        Else
            'use a Recordset Object to add it

            Set rs = New Recordset
            On Error GoTo UpdateFailed
            rs.Open "select * from authors where au_id = '"
                + txtId.Text + "'", mConn, adOpenKeyset, _
                adLockOptimistic
            rs.AddNew
            rs!au_id = txtId.Text
            rs!au_fname = txtFirstName.Text
            rs!au_lname = txtLastName.Text
            rs!address = txtAddress.Text
            rs!city = txtCity.Text
            rs!State = txtState.Text
            rs!zip = txtZip.Text
            rs!phone = txtPhone.Text
            rs!contract = (chkContract.Value = vbChecked)
            rs.Update
            On Error GoTo 0
```

```
            rs.Close
            Set rs = Nothing


        End If
        'no longer dealing with a new record
        mbNewRecord = False

        'add the new item to the list
        Dim NewItem As ListItem

        Set NewItem = listAuthors.ListItems.Add(, txtId.Text, _
            txtLastName.Text & ", " & txtFirstName.Text)
        NewItem.SubItems(1) = txtAddress.Text
        NewItem.SubItems(2) = txtCity.Text
        NewItem.SubItems(3) = txtState.Text
        NewItem.SubItems(4) = txtZip.Text

        Set listAuthors.SelectedItem = NewItem
    Else
        'try to update
        If chkExecute.Value = vbChecked Then
            'use the execute method of the connection
            sCmd = "update authors"
            sCmd = sCmd + " set "
            sCmd = sCmd + "au_id = '" + txtId.Text + "'"
            sCmd = sCmd + ",au_fname = '"
            sCmd = sCmd + txtFirstName.Text + "'"
            sCmd = sCmd + ",au_lname = '" + txtLastName.Text + "'"
            sCmd = sCmd + ",address = '" + txtAddress.Text + "'"
            sCmd = sCmd + ",city = '" + txtCity.Text + "'"
            sCmd = sCmd + ",state = '" + txtState.Text + "'"
            sCmd = sCmd + ",zip = '" + txtZip.Text + "'"
            sCmd = sCmd + ",phone = '" + txtPhone.Text + "'"
            sCmd = sCmd + ",contract = " & _
                IIf(chkContract.Value = vbChecked, 1, 0)
            sCmd = sCmd + " where au_id = '" "'"
            sCmd = sCmd + msCurrentRecord + "'"
            On Error GoTo UpdateFailed:
            mConn.Execute sCmd
            On Error GoTo 0
        Else
            'use a Recordset Object to make the changes

            Set rs = New Recordset
            On Error GoTo UpdateFailed
            rs.Open "select * from authors where au_id = '" _
                + msCurrentRecord + "'", mConn, adOpenKeyset _
                , adLockOptimistic

            'only update the primary key if it's changed
            'ADO acts like it's been updated even if the new
            'value is the same as the old so only set if it's
            'really changed
            If rs("au_id") <> txtId.Text Then
```

continued on next page

continued from previous page

```
                            rs!au_id = txtId.Text
                    End If
                    rs!au_fname = txtFirstName.Text
                    rs!au_lname = txtLastName.Text
                    rs!address = txtAddress.Text
                    rs!city = txtCity.Text
                    rs!State = txtState.Text
                    rs!zip = txtZip.Text
                    rs!phone = txtPhone.Text
                    rs!contract = (chkContract.Value = vbChecked)
                    rs.Update
                    On Error GoTo 0

                    rs.Close
                    Set rs = Nothing
                End If

                'update the item in the list
                Dim OldItem As ListItem
                Set OldItem = listAuthors.ListItems.Item(msCurrentRecord)
                OldItem.Key = txtId.Text
                OldItem.Text = txtLastName.Text & ", " & txtFirstName.Text
                OldItem.SubItems(1) = txtAddress.Text
                OldItem.SubItems(2) = txtCity.Text
                OldItem.SubItems(3) = txtState.Text
                OldItem.SubItems(4) = txtZip.Text
            End If
            'no longer need save
            mbNeedSave = False
            cmdUpdate.Enabled = False
            cmdDelete.Enabled = True
            UpdateRecord = True
    UpdateComplete:
            Exit Function
    UpdateFailed:
            ShowADOError
            GoTo UpdateComplete
    End Function
```

11. Create the **cmdDelete_Click** event. Like the **Update** function used previously, the **cmdDelete_Click** event uses the **Execute** or **Delete** methods based on the value of the chkExecute checkbox.

```
Private Sub cmdDelete_Click()
    If chkExecute.Value = vbChecked Then
        Dim sCmd As String
        sCmd = "delete from authors where au_id = '" _
            + msCurrentRecord + "'"
        On Error GoTo DeleteFailed
        mConn.Execute sCmd
        On Error GoTo 0
    Else
        Dim rs As Recordset
```

```
                            'now open the recordset
                            Set rs = New Recordset
                            On Error GoTo DeleteFailed
                            rs.Open "select * from authors where au_id = '" _
                                + msCurrentRecord + "'", mConn, adOpenKeyset _
                                adLockOptimistic
                            Do Until rs.EOF
                                rs.Delete
                                rs.MoveNext
                            Loop
                            On Error GoTo 0
                        End If
                        'remove the item from the list
                        listAuthors.ListItems.Remove msCurrentRecord
                        mbNeedSave = False
                        cmdUpdate.Enabled = False
                        listAuthors_ItemClick listAuthors.SelectedItem
                    DeleteComplete:
                        Exit Sub
                    DeleteFailed:
                        ShowADOError
                        GoTo DeleteComplete
                    End Sub
```

12. As an item is selected in the listAuthors control, the listAuthors_ItemClick event checks to see if the current record needs to be saved, and then it refreshes the detail controls.

```
Private Sub listAuthors_ItemClick(ByVal Item As
ComctlLib.ListItem)
    Dim rs As Recordset
    Set rs = New Recordset
    If mbNeedSave Then
        If Not UpdateRecord() Then
            Set listAuthors.SelectedItem = _
                listAuthors.ListItems.Item(msCurrentRecord)
            Exit Sub
        End If
    End If

    'now open the recordset
    Set rs = New Recordset
    rs.Open "select * from authors where au_id = '" + Item.Key + _
        "'" _
        , mConn, adOpenForwardOnly, adLockReadOnly
    Do Until rs.EOF
        'update the listview in case it's changed
        Item.Text = rs("au_lname") & ", " & rs("au_fname")
        Item.SubItems(1) = rs("address")
        Item.SubItems(2) = rs("city")
        Item.SubItems(3) = rs("state")
        Item.SubItems(4) = rs("zip")
        'fill the edit controls
        txtId.Text = rs("au_id")
```

continued on next page

continued from previous page

```
                    txtFirstName.Text = rs("au_fname")
                    txtLastName.Text = rs("au_lname")
                    txtAddress.Text = rs("address")
                    txtCity.Text = rs("city")
                    txtState.Text = rs("state")
                    txtZip.Text = rs("zip")
                    txtPhone.Text = rs("phone")
                    chkContract.Value = IIf(rs("contract"), vbChecked _
                        vbUnchecked)

                    rs.MoveNext
        Loop

        rs.Close
        Set rs = Nothing
        mbNeedSave = False
        cmdUpdate.Enabled = False
        cmdDelete.Enabled = True
        msCurrentRecord = txtId.Text

    End Sub
```

13. Finally, add the sub that displays the errors reported by ADO.

```
Private Sub ShowADOError()
    'spin through the errors collection and
    'display the constructed error message
    Dim ADOError As Error
    Dim sError As String
    For Each ADOError In mConn.Errors
        sError = sError + ADOError.Number & " - " & _
            ADOError.Description _
            + vbCrLf
    Next ADOError
    MsgBox sError
End Sub
```

How It Works

The ListAuthors2 project shows two ways of altering data using ADO. Based on the Use Execute option, it uses the **Execute** method to send SQL statements, or it uses the **AddNew**, **Delete**, and **Update** methods of the **Recordset** object.

Comments

The changes to the database in How-To 8.4 were very simple; insert a record, delete a record, and update a record. Often, multiple changes must occur at the same time, and if one fails, none of the remaining changes should commit. How-To 8.5 shows you how to wrap up your changes into a transaction where all the changes succeed or fail together.

Many operations in ADO can be performed multiple ways. In most cases the performance difference is negligible, unless the operation is performed in a loop. Generally, deciding which method to use is a matter of preference and a matter of which method can get the job done in the easiest manner possible for the developer. However, many companies today are moving to three-tier applications. In a three-tier application, an application developer manipulates the database through objects instead of executing SQL statements. Using the object model to perform data manipulation might help you get acclimated to using objects instead of SQL.

COMPLEXITY
INTERMEDIATE

8.5 How do I...
Perform a transaction using ActiveX Data Objects?

Problem

Now I know how to make changes to data, but several things must change together. If one fails, they should all fail. How do I perform a transaction using ActiveX Data Objects?

Technique

A transaction ensures that all changes within the transaction either succeed or fail together. The classic example of an application that requires transactions is a financial application in which money can be transferred from one account to another. Without transactions, if the debit is successful, but the credit is not, the customer has lost money. If the debit fails and the credit is successful, the institution loses money. Neither one is good if the company wants to stay in business for a long time.

In ADO, the `BeginTrans`, `CommitTrans`, and `RollbackTrans` methods of the `Connection` object provide the means to do transactions. The steps to perform a transaction are outlined below:

1. Call `BeginTrans`.

2. Make all changes on the same connection where the `BeginTrans` was called. Check each change to make sure it is successful.

3. If all changes were successful, call `CommitTrans`. If any change failed, call `RollbackTrans`.

Steps

Open the Transaction.vbp. You will need to update the connection string in the **Form_Load** event. Change the username (User Id=), password (Password=), and server name (Location=) parameters. Figure 8.5 shows the Transfer Funds application. Two lists are displayed; select accounts in the To and From lists, enter an amount, and press the Transfer button to move money from one account to another.

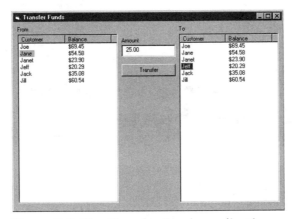

Figure 8.5. The Transfer Funds application.

1. Use SQL Enterprise Manager or ISQL/w to run the Accounts.sql script in your pubs database. This script creates a new table, Accounts, and test data for this How-To.

2. Create a new Standard EXE. Change the Project Name to Transaction and rename the default form frmMain.

3. Add a reference to the Microsoft ActiveX Data Objects 2.0 Library. Add the Microsoft Windows Common Controls 6.0 and the Microsoft Masked Edit Control 6.0.

4. Use Table 8.7 to add the objects and set the properties for frmMain.

Table 8.7. Objects and properties for frmMain.

OBJECT	PROPERTY	VALUE
Form	Caption	Transfer Funds
ListView	Name	listFrom
	View	3 - lvwReport
	LabelEdit	1 - lvwManual

OBJECT	PROPERTY	VALUE
ListView	Name	listTo
	View	3 - lvwReport
	LabelEdit	1 - lvwManual
Label	Name	lblAmount
	Caption	Amount
MaskEdBox	Name	maskedAmount
	Mask	####.##
CommandButton	Name	cmdTransfer
	Caption	Transfer

5. For each of the ListViews, add a column for Customer and Balance using the Column Headers tab of the ListView properties dialog box.

6. Add the following code to the Declarations section of frmMain.

```
Option Explicit
Private mConn As Connection
```

7. The Form_Load and Form_Unload events open and close the connection. Change the connection string of the Open method to connect to your server.

```
Private Sub Form_Load()
    'open the connection
    Set mConn = New Connection
    mConn.Open "Provider=SQLOLEDB.1;User ID=sa;Password=password" _
        + ";Location=WINEMILLER;Database=pubs"

    RefreshLists
End Sub

Private Sub Form_Unload(Cancel As Integer)
    mConn.Close
    Set mConn = Nothing
End Sub
```

8. Add the RefreshLists procedure. This procedure fills the two ListView controls with the list of account holders and their balances.

```
Private Sub RefreshLists()
    'refresh the lists with account holders and balances
    Dim NewItem As ListItem
    Dim rs As Recordset

    Set rs = New Recordset
    listFrom.ListItems.Clear
    listTo.ListItems.Clear
```

continued on next page

continued from previous page

```
        rs.Open "Accounts", mConn, adOpenForwardOnly, adLockReadOnly
        Do Until rs.EOF
            Set NewItem = listFrom.ListItems.Add(, "k" &
rs("AccountId") _
                    , rs("Name"))
            NewItem.SubItems(1) = Format(rs("Balance"), "$0.00")
            Set NewItem = listTo.ListItems.Add(, "k" _
                & rs("AccountId"), rs("Name"))
            NewItem.SubItems(1) = Format(rs("Balance"), "$0.00")
            rs.MoveNext
        Loop
        rs.Close
        Set rs = Nothing
    End Sub
```

9. Finally, add the `cmdTransfer_Click` event.

```
Private Sub cmdTransfer_Click()
    Dim lRowsAffected As Long
    Dim sError As String
    Dim sCmd As String
    Dim rs As Recordset

    If vbYes = MsgBox("Transfer " _
        & Format(Val(maskedAmount.Text), "$0.00") _
        & " from " & listFrom.SelectedItem.Text _
        & " to " & listTo.SelectedItem.Text & ".", vbYesNo) Then

        mConn.BeginTrans
        On Error GoTo TransferFailure
        'use the Connection's execute method
        sCmd = "update Accounts"
        sCmd = sCmd + " set Balance = Balance - "
        sCmd = sCmd + maskedAmount.Text
        'only do the update if the from account has enough money
        sCmd = sCmd + " where balance >= " & maskedAmount.Text
        sCmd = sCmd + " and AccountId = " _
            & Right(listFrom.SelectedItem.Key _
            , Len(listFrom.SelectedItem.Key) - 1)

        mConn.Execute sCmd, lRowsAffected
        If lRowsAffected = 0 Then
            sError = "Insufficient funds."
            GoTo TransferFailure
        End If

        'or use the Recordset's methods
        Set rs = New Recordset
        rs.Open "select * from Accounts where AccountId = " _
            & Right(listTo.SelectedItem.Key _
            , Len(listTo.SelectedItem.Key) - 1), mConn, _
            adOpenDynamic
                , adLockPessimistic
```

```
                    rs!Balance = rs("Balance") + Val(maskedAmount.Text)
                    rs.Update

                    'ok so far, commit it
                    mConn.CommitTrans
                    rs.Close
            End If

    TransferDone:
        On Error GoTo 0
        Set rs = Nothing
        RefreshLists
        Exit Sub
    TransferFailure:
        'something bad happened so rollback the transaction
        mConn.RollbackTrans
        Dim ADOError As Error

        For Each ADOError In mConn.Errors
            sError = sError & ADOError.Number & " - " & _
                ADOError.Description + vbCrLf
        Next ADOError
        MsgBox sError
    End Sub
```

How It Works

The beginning of the cmdTransfer_Click event calls the BeginTrans method. If
an error occurs or the originating account has insufficient funds, the transaction
is rolled back. Two methods of data manipulation are used during the
transaction: the Connection object's Execute method and the Recordset object's
Update method. There are no restrictions on mixing and matching data
manipulation methods during a transaction, as long as they are all done on the
same connection. If all the updates are successful, the transaction is committed
and the display is refreshed.

Comments

Transactions are an indispensable tool for the database application developer.
However when you begin to use transactions, you add a new level of complexity
to your application. One of the biggest problems with transactions is that they
easily lead to deadlocks.

A deadlock occurs when two connections try to make changes to resources
the other holds. There are a couple of strategies you can use to reduce the
chance of a deadlock.

1. Reduce the time of the transaction. Move all string manipulation and other
processing outside of the transaction. In this How-To, reduce the chances
of a deadlock by moving the code that assembles the UPDATE so that it is
before the BeginTrans.

2. Do transactions in the same order if possible. If all transactions start by changing the Orders table and then the Inventory table, there will never be a situation in which one transaction holds the Orders table, but wants the Inventory table, and another transaction holds the Inventory table, but wants the Orders table.

COMPLEXITY
INTERMEDIATE

8.6 How do I...
Execute a SQL Server stored procedure using ActiveX Data Objects?

Problem

My company uses stored procedures to increase performance and to encapsulate objects in the database. How do I execute a SQL Server?

Technique

Stored Procedures in ADO are very straight forward—if there are no parameters. Simply change the **Options** parameter of the **Recordset** object's **Open** method to **adCmdStoredProc**. This tells ADO the Source argument is a stored procedure. If you leave off the **Options** parameter, ADO will still work correctly, but it will have to do a little extra processing to figure out with what it is dealing. For the best performance, always use the **Options** parameter to tell ADO what type of command it is performing.

This How-To also introduces a new technique for creating a **Recordset**. As with most things in ADO, there are a couple of ways to tackle the problem of creating a **Recordset**. The **Connection** object's **Execute** method returns a **Recordset** if one is generated by the **CommandText** parameter. The **Recordset** returned from the **Execute** method is the same as a manually created **Recordset** that was specified as forward-only and read-only.

Steps

Open the StoredProcedure.vbp. Change the connection string in the **Form_Load** event of frmMain and run the application. The Stored Procedures application shown in Figure 8.6 displays two possible lists, based on which option is selected. If Title Author is selected, the book titles become the parents in the TreeView; otherwise, the authors are the parents.

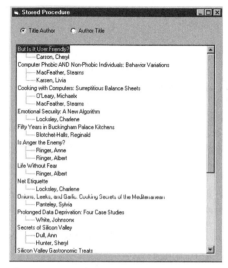

Figure 8.6. The Stored Procedures application.

1. Use SQL Enterprise Manager or ISQL/w to run the Stored Procedures.sql script in your pubs database. This script creates two new stored procedures in the pubs database: GetAuthorTitleList and GetTitleAuthorList.

2. Create a new Standard EXE. Change the Project Name to StoredProcedure and rename the default form to frmMain.

3. Add a reference to the Microsoft ActiveX Data Objects 2.0 Library and add the Microsoft Windows Common Controls 6.0.

4. Use Table 8.8 to add the objects and set the properties for frmMain.

Table 8.8. Objects and properties for frmMain.

OBJECT	PROPERTY	VALUE
Form	Caption	Stored Procedure
TreeView	Name	treeResults
OptionButton	Name	optTitleAuthor
	Caption	Title Author
OptionButton	Name	optAuthorTitle
	Caption	Author Title

5. Like the other How-To's in this chapter, the declarations section, the Form_Load event, and the Form_Unload event handle the Connection object.

```
Option Explicit
Private mConn As Connection

Private Sub Form_Load()
    'open the connection
    Set mConn = New Connection
    mConn.Open "Provider=SQLOLEDB.1;User ID=sa;Password=password"
        + ";Location=WINEMILLER;Database=pubs"

    RefreshList
End Sub

Private Sub Form_Unload(Cancel As Integer)
    mConn.Close
    Set mConn = Nothing
End Sub
```

6. Now add the code to call RefreshList when the OptionButtons change.

```
Private Sub optAuthorTitle_Click()
    RefreshList
End Sub

Private Sub optTitleAuthor_Click()
    RefreshList
End Sub
```

7. Finally add the RefreshList procedure.

```
Private Sub RefreshList()

    Dim rs As Recordset
    Dim NewNode As Node

    treeResults.Nodes.Clear

    If optTitleAuthor.Value = True Then
        'sort by titles
        Dim sLastTitle As String

        'use the Execute method to generate the Recordset
        'works the same as adOpenForwardOnly, adLockReadOnly
        Set rs = mConn.Execute("GetTitleAuthorList", , _
            adCmdStoredProc)
        Do Until rs.EOF
            If sLastTitle <> rs("title") Then
                'need a new parent
                sLastTitle = rs("title")
                Set NewNode = treeResults.Nodes.Add(, , _
                    rs("title") , rs("title"))
                NewNode.Expanded = True
            End If
            'add the child
            treeResults.Nodes.Add sLastTitle, tvwChild _
```

```
                        , sLastTitle + rs("au_lname") & ", " & _
                        rs("au_fname") _
                        , rs("au_lname") & ", " & rs("au_fname")
                    rs.MoveNext
                Loop
        Else
            'sort by authors
            Dim sLastAuthor As String
            Set rs = New Recordset

            rs.Open "GetAuthorTitleList", mConn, adOpenForwardOnly _
                , adLockReadOnly, adCmdStoredProc

            Do Until rs.EOF
                If sLastAuthor <> rs("au_lname") & ", " & _
                    rs("au_fname") Then
                    'need a new parent
                    sLastAuthor = rs("au_lname") & ", " & _
                        rs("au_fname")
                    Set NewNode = treeResults.Nodes.Add(, , _
                        sLastAuthor , sLastAuthor)
                    NewNode.Expanded = True
                End If
                'add the child
                treeResults.Nodes.Add sLastAuthor, tvwChild, _
                    sLastAuthor + rs("title"), rs("title")
                rs.MoveNext
            Loop
        End If
End Sub
```

How It Works

The RefreshList procedure opens a Recordset from a stored procedure almost exactly like a normal SELECT. The only difference is the adCmdStoredProc parameter. This parameter tells ADO the Source parameter is a stored procedure and tells ADO to do what it needs to do for stored procedures. Additionally RefreshList shows an alternative way to create a Recordset by using the Execute method.

Comments

Of course this is the simple case. In most applications, stored procedures without any parameters are few and far between. How-To 8.7 addresses the problem of dealing with stored procedures with input and output parameters.

COMPLEXITY
INTERMEDIATE

8.7 How do I...
Execute a parameterized SQL Server stored procedure with ActiveX Data Objects?

Problem

Some of the stored procedures I use have parameters and return values. How do I execute a parameterized SQL Server Stored Procedure with ActiveX Data Objects?

Technique

Parameterized, SQL Server-stored procedures are enabled through the use of ADO's `Command` and `Parameter` objects. The steps for executing a parameterized SQL Server stored procedure are outlined in the following numbered list:

1. Create a `Command` object and set its `ActiveConnection`, `CommandText`, and `CommandType` properties.

2. For each input parameter, output parameter, or return value, use the `Command` object's `CreateParameter` method to create and populate a `Parameter` object.

3. Append the new `Parameter` objects to the `Command` object's `Parameters` collection.

4. Call the `Command` object's `Execute` method. If you are expecting a `Recordset` object from the stored procedure, the `Execute` method returns a `Recordset` object.

5. After this, the `Recordset` is completely fetched out or closed. The return value and output parameters are available.

A NOTE ON STORED PROCEDURES AND ADO

Keep in mind that `Command` and `Parameter` objects do not need to be used for stored procedures with no output parameters or return values. You can open a `Recordset` with the adCmdText Option parameter and build the stored procedure call yourself in Transact SQL. This saves the overhead of creating `Command` and `Parameter` objects.

Steps

Open the ParameterStoredProcedure.vbp, change the connection string in the
Form_Load event, and run. The Royalty List application, shown in Figure 8.7,
displays a list of royalties. Selecting a royalty displays the list of authors and
titles to which that royalty was paid.

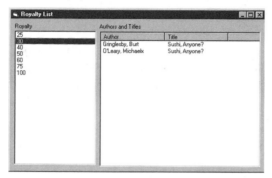

Figure 8.7. The Royalty List application.

1. Use SQL Enterprise Manager or ISQL/w to run the
AuthorTitleByRoyalty.sql script in your pubs database. This script creates
a new stored procedure in the pubs database, **AuthorTitleByRoyalty**.

2. Create a new Standard EXE. Change the Project Name to
ParameterStoredProcedure and rename the default form to frmMain.

3. Add a reference to the Microsoft ActiveX Data Objects 2.0 Library and add
the Microsoft Windows Common Controls 6.0.

4. Use Table 8.9 to add the objects and set the properties for frmMain.

Table 8.9. Objects and properties for frmMain.

OBJECT	PROPERTY	VALUE
Form	Caption	Royalty List
ListBox	Name	lstRoyalty
Label	Name	lblRoyalty
	Caption	Royalty
Label	Name	lblWorks
	Caption	Authors and Titles
ListView	Name	listWorks
	View	3 - lvwReport
	LabelEdit	1 - lvwManual

5. Add the columns listed in Table 8.10 to the `ListView` control using the Column Headers property page.

Table 8.10. Column Headers for listWorks.

COLUMN	WIDTH
Name	2000
Title	2000

6. Add the Declarations section, `Form_Load` event, and `Form_Unload` event to handle the `Connection` object. Remember to change the connection string in the `Form_Load` event for your server, user, and password.

```
Option Explicit
Private mConn As Connection

Private Sub Form_Load()
    'open the connection
    Set mConn = New Connection
    mConn.Open "Provider=SQLOLEDB.1;User ID=sa;Password=password" _
        + ";Location=WINEMILLER;Database=pubs"
    FillRoyalty
End Sub

Private Sub Form_Unload(Cancel As Integer)
    mConn.Close
    Set mConn = Nothing
End Sub
```

7. Add the `FillRoyalty` procedure. This procedure fills the ListBox control with all the possible royalty values.

```
Private Sub FillRoyalty()
    'fill the list with the royalty values
    Dim rs As Recordset
    lstRoyalty.Clear
    Set rs = mConn.Execute("select distinct royaltyper from" _
        "titleauthor" , , adCmdText)
    Do Until rs.EOF
        lstRoyalty.AddItem rs("royaltyper")
        rs.MoveNext
    Loop

    rs.Close
    Set rs = Nothing
End Sub
```

8. Finally add the `lstRoyalty_Click` event to display the list of authors and titles.

```
Private Sub lstRoyalty_Click()
    'display a list of authors and titles at the selected royalty
```

```
        'level
        Dim rs As Recordset
        Dim cmd As Command
        Dim param As adodb.Parameter
        Dim NewItem As ListItem

        Set cmd = New Command
        cmd.ActiveConnection = mConn
        cmd.CommandText = "AuthorTitleByRoyalty"
        cmd.CommandType = adCmdStoredProc

        'now build the parameter list

        'The stored procedure returns a true or false if there were
        'results
        Set param = cmd.CreateParameter("Return", adBoolean _
            , adParamReturnValue, , 0)
        cmd.Parameters.Append param

        'The input parameter
        Set param = cmd.CreateParameter("percentage", adInteger _
            , adParamInput, , Val(lstRoyalty.Text))
        cmd.Parameters.Append param

        'The output parameter, the number of rows as reported by
        '@@ROWCOUNT
        Set param = cmd.CreateParameter("numrows", adInteger, _
            adParamOutput)
        cmd.Parameters.Append param

        'clear the list
        listWorks.ListItems.Clear

        'cmd execute generates the Recordset for us then it's
        'business as usual
        Set rs = cmd.Execute
        Do Until rs.EOF
            Set ListItem = listWorks.ListItems.Add(, , _
                rs("au_lname") & ", " & rs("au_fname"))
            ListItem.SubItems(1) = rs("title")
            rs.MoveNext
        Loop

        rs.Close
        Set rs = Nothing
        Set NewItem = Nothing
        'use the return value and output parameter to display a
        'message
        If cmd("Return") = True Then
            MsgBox "This stored procedure returned " _
                & cmd("numrows") _
                & " rows as reported by @@ROWCOUNT"
        Else
            MsgBox "No rows were found."
        End If
End Sub
```

How It Works

The AuthorTitleByRoyalty stored procedure takes one input parameter and sends back one output parameter and a return value. After setting up the Command object, the lstRoyalty_Click event specifies all the parameters of the stored procedure. When the Recordset is completely fetched and closed, the return value and output parameter are available through the Command object. Those values are then used to display a message to the user.

Comments

Stored procedures can greatly enhance the performance of most SQL Server operations in addition to providing you with a way to encapsulate and hide data. SQL server checks the syntax and precompiles stored procedures so those steps are eliminated when the stored procedure is called instead of straight Transact SQL. For operations that take minutes or more to return, the overhead for syntax checking and compiling is relatively small, but on smaller operations that return quickly and are called often the savings are substantial.

COMPLEXITY
INTERMEDIATE

8.8 How do I...
Create and modify SQL Server objects with ActiveX Data Objects?

Problem

I need to do data definition through ADO. How do I create and modify SQL Server objects with ActiveX Data Objects?

Technique

Unlike DAO, ADO does not have any way through the object model to modify SQL Server objects. There is no Tables collection to which you can add; however, that does not prevent you from sending Transact SQL using the Connection object's Execute method and adCmdText in the Options Parameter.

Using Transact SQL, you can create, alter, and drop tables, devices, stored procedures, or anything you can do with SQL Enterprise manager. Appendix A has a full summary of SQL syntax including all the commands necessary to create and modify tables.

Steps

Open and run the AlterObjects.vbp. Remember to change the connection string in the **Form_Load** event. Figure 8.8 shows the Alter Objects application. The three buttons create, alter, and drop a sample table in the pubs database.

Figure 8.8. The Alter Objects application.

1. Create a new Standard EXE. Change the Project Name to AlterObjects, rename the default form to frmMain, and add a reference to the Microsoft ActiveX Data Objects 2.0.

2. Use Table 8.11 to add the objects and set the properties for frmMain.

Table 8.11. Objects and properties for frmMain.

OBJECT	PROPERTY	VALUE
Form	Caption	Alter Objects
CommandButton	Name	cmdCreate
	Caption	Create
CommandButton	Name	cmdAlter
	Caption	Alter
CommandButton	Name	cmdDrop
	Caption	Drop

3. Add the Declarations section, the **Form_Load** event, and the **Form_Unload** event to handle the **Connection** object.

```
Option Explicit
Private mConn As Connection

Private Sub Form_Load()
    'open the connection
    Set mConn = New Connection
    mConn.Open "Provider=SQLOLEDB.1;User ID=sa;Password=password"
        + ";Location=WINEMILLER;Database=pubs"
End Sub

Private Sub Form_Unload(Cancel As Integer)
    mConn.Close
    Set mConn = Nothing
End Sub
```

4. Finally, add the code behind the buttons.

```
Private Sub cmdAlter_Click()
    'alter the sample table
    Dim sCmd As String
    sCmd = "alter table HowToSample808 add MoreStuff CHAR(40) "
    sCmd = sCmd + "NULL"
    mConn.Execute sCmd, , adCmdText
End Sub

Private Sub cmdCreate_Click()
    'create the sample table
    Dim sCmd As String
    sCmd = "create table HowToSample808 (SampleId INTEGER NOT "
    sCmd = sCmd + "NULL"
    sCmd = sCmd + ", Stuff CHAR(40) NOT NULL)"
    mConn.Execute sCmd, , adCmdText
End Sub

Private Sub cmdDrop_Click()
    'drop the sample table
    Dim sCmd As String
    sCmd = "drop table HowToSample808"
    mConn.Execute sCmd, , adCmdText
End Sub
```

How It Works

Each of the CommandButton **Click** events assemble the Transact SQL commands for the database modifications and send them using the **Connection** object's **Execute** method. By using adCmdText for the **Options** parameter, any command the server understands can be sent to the server for processing.

Comments

Using the **Execute** method to do this opens a whole new realm of possibilities. Sometimes object models can be restrictive, as the designer does not foresee every use that might come about. Microsoft has left the door open so you can talk directly to the database, and you can use any command the database understands.

This power does not come without risks. Many companies might not want application developers with direct access to the database. Fortunately, SQL Server does have strong support for security, and most applications will not log in as the system administrator as this How-To does.

COMPLEXITY
INTERMEDIATE

8.9 How do I...
Execute batch updates with ActiveX Data Objects?

Problem

I want to make many changes to a recordset and apply all the changes at once. How do I execute batch updates with ActiveX Data Objects?

Technique

The `Recordset` object's `UpdateBatch` method applies multiple changes at once. There are three steps to performing a batch update with ADO:

1. Open a recordset with the `LockType` parameter set to adLockBatchOptimistic.

2. Move through the recordset making all the changes required.

3. Call the `Recordset` object's `UpdateBatch` method.

Steps

Load the BatchUpdate.vbp, change the connection string in the `Form_Load` event to match your setup, and run the application. The Authors application, displayed in Figure 8.9, shows a list of authors and their addresses. Double-clicking on an author presents the Edit Author dialog box, shown in Figure 8.10. After all changes are complete, click the Apply Changes button to perform the batch update.

Last	First	Address	City	St...	Zip
White	Johnsonx	10932 Bigge Rd.	Menlo Park	CA	9402
Green	Marjorie	309 63rd St. #411	Oakland	CA	9461
Carson	Cheryl	589 Darwin Ln.	Berkeley	CA	9470
O'Leary	Michaelx	22 Cleveland Av. #14	San Jose	CA	9512
Straight	Dean	5420 College Av.	Oakland	CA	9460
Smith	Meander	10 Mississippi Dr.	Lawrence	KS	6604
Bennet	Abraham	6223 Bateman St.	Berkeley	CA	9470
Dull	Ann	3410 Blonde St.	Palo Alto	CA	9430
Gringlesby	Burt	PO Box 792	Covelo	CA	9542
Locksley	Charlene	18 Broadway Av.	San Francisco	CA	9413
Greene	Morningstar	22 Graybar House Rd.	Nashville	TN	3721
Blotchet-Halls	Reginald	55 Hillsdale Bl.	Corvallis	OR	9733
Yokomoto	Akiko	3 Silver Ct.	Walnut Creek	CA	9455
del Castillo	Innes	2286 Cram Pl. #86	Ann Arbor	MI	4810
DeFrance	Michel	3 Balding Pl.	Gary	IN	4640
Stringer	Dirk	5420 Telegraph Av.	Oakland	CA	9460

Apply Changes

Figure 8.9. The Authors application enables batch updates.

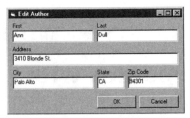

Figure 8.10. You can change names and address information using the Edit Authors dialog box.

1. Create a new Standard EXE. Change the Project Name to BatchUpdate, rename the default form to frmMain, and add a reference to the Microsoft ActiveX Data Objects 2.0.

2. Using the Components dialog box, add Microsoft Windows Common Controls 6.0.

3. Use Table 8.12 to add the objects and set the properties for frmMain.

Table 8.12. Objects and properties for frmMain.

OBJECT	PROPERTY	VALUE
Form	Caption	Authors
ListView	Name	listAuthors
	View	3 - lvwReport
	LabelEdit	1 - lvwManual
CommandButton	Name	cmdApply
	Caption	Apply Changes

4. Use Table 8.13 to add the columns for listAuthors.

Table 8.13. Column Headers for listAuthors.

COLUMN	WIDTH
Last	1440
First	1440
Address	2000
City	1440
State	500
Zip	700

5. In the Declarations section of frmMain, set Option Explicit and add the declaration for mConn.

```
Option Explicit
Private mConn As Connection
```

6. In the Form_Load event, the connection is opened and the ListView control is filled with the author table data. Remember to change the connection string on mConn's Open method to match your configuration.

```
Private Sub Form_Load()
    Dim rs As Recordset
    Dim NewItem As ListItem

    'open the connection
    Set mConn = New Connection
    mConn.Open "Provider=SQLOLEDB.1;User ID=sa;Password=password"
        + ";Location=WINEMILLER;Database=pubs"

    'fill the list
    Set rs = mConn.Execute("authors", , adCmdTable)
    Do Until rs.EOF
        Set NewItem = listAuthors.ListItems.Add(, rs("au_id") _
            , rs("au_lname"))
        NewItem.SubItems(1) = rs("au_fname")
        NewItem.SubItems(2) = rs("address")
        NewItem.SubItems(3) = rs("city")
        NewItem.SubItems(4) = rs("state")
        NewItem.SubItems(5) = rs("zip")
        rs.MoveNext
    Loop
    rs.Close
    Set rs = Nothing
End Sub
```

7. The Form_Unload event closes the connection and unloads the frmDetails.

```
Private Sub Form_Unload(Cancel As Integer)
    Unload frmDetails
    Set frmDetails = Nothing
    mConn.Close
    Set mConn = Nothing
End Sub
```

8. In the listAuthors_DblClick event, show the Edit Authors dialog box with all the author information. If the user clicks OK, update listAuthors.

```
Private Sub listAuthors_DblClick()
    'fill the detail screen
    frmDetails.txtLastName.Text = listAuthors.SelectedItem.Text
    frmDetails.txtFirstName.Text =
```

continued on next page

continued from previous page

```
listAuthors.SelectedItem.SubItems(1)
    frmDetails.txtAddress.Text =
listAuthors.SelectedItem.SubItems(2)
    frmDetails.txtCity.Text = listAuthors.SelectedItem.SubItems(3)
    frmDetails.txtState.Text =
listAuthors.SelectedItem.SubItems(4)
    frmDetails.txtZip.Text = listAuthors.SelectedItem.SubItems(5)

    frmDetails.OK = False
    frmDetails.Show vbModal

    If frmDetails.OK = True Then
        'user hit OK, update the list
        listAuthors.SelectedItem.Text =
frmDetails.txtLastName.Text
        listAuthors.SelectedItem.SubItems(1) =
frmDetails.txtFirstName.Text
        listAuthors.SelectedItem.SubItems(2) =
frmDetails.txtAddress.Text
        listAuthors.SelectedItem.SubItems(3) =
frmDetails.txtCity.Text
        listAuthors.SelectedItem.SubItems(4) =
frmDetails.txtState.Text
        listAuthors.SelectedItem.SubItems(5) =
frmDetails.txtZip.Text
    End If
End Sub
```

9. Add the code to apply the changes.

```
Private Sub cmdApply_Click()
    Dim rs As Recordset

    Set rs = New Recordset

    'to do a batch update be sure to open with
adLockBatchOptimistic
    rs.Open "authors", mConn, adOpenKeyset, _
        adLockBatchOptimistic _
        , adCmdTable
    Do Until rs.EOF
        rs("au_lname") = listAuthors.ListItems((rs("au_id"))).Text
        rs("au_fname") =
listAuthors.ListItems((rs("au_id"))).SubItems(1)
        rs("address") =
listAuthors.ListItems((rs("au_id"))).SubItems(2)
        rs("city") =
listAuthors.ListItems((rs("au_id"))).SubItems(3)
        rs("state") =
listAuthors.ListItems((rs("au_id"))).SubItems(4)
        rs("zip") =
listAuthors.ListItems((rs("au_id"))).SubItems(5)
        rs.MoveNext
    Loop
    'update batch commits all the changes
```

```
        rs.UpdateBatch

        rs.Close
        Set rs = Nothing
End Sub
```

10. Add a new form and name it frmDetails. Use Table 8.14 to add the objects and set properties for frmDetails.

Table 8.14. Objects and properties for frmDetails.

OBJECT	PROPERTY	VALUE
Form	Caption	Edit Authors
TextBox	Name	txtFirstName
	Text	" "
TextBox	Name	txtLastName
	Text	" "
TextBox	Name	txtAddress
	Text	" "
TextBox	Name	txtCity
	Text	" "
TextBox	Name	txtState
	Text	" "
TextBox	Name	txtZip
	Text	" "
Label	Name	lblFirstName
	Caption	First
Label	Name	lblLastName
	Caption	Last
Label	Name	lblAddress
	Caption	Address
Label	Name	lblCity
	Caption	City
Label	Name	lblState
	Caption	State
Label	Name	lblZip
	Caption	Zip Code
CommandButton	Name	cmdOK
	Caption	OK
CommandButton	Name	cmdCancel
	Caption	Cancel

11. Finally, add the code for frmDetails.

```
Option Explicit
Public OK As Boolean

Private Sub cmdCancel_Click()
    Hide
End Sub

Private Sub cmdOK_Click()
    OK = True
    Hide
End Sub
```

How It Works

The Edit Details dialog box enables the user to change the names and addresses of the authors, but does not change the database. All changes are collected till the Apply Changes button is pressed. The `Recordset` object is opened again, this time with adLockBatchOptimistic in the `LockType` parameter. Next, the application makes all the changes and calls the `UpdateBatch` method to apply all the changes.

Comments

Batch updates are often a way to squeeze more performance from a database operation. There is inherent overhead each time an update is performed. By using a batch update, that overhead cost is paid only once instead of at each separate update.

COMPLEXITY
INTERMEDIATE

8.10 How do I...
Make remote updates to data with ActiveX Data Objects?

Problem

My application will be running over the Web, where server connections and bandwidth are expensive. I want to minimize the server connections and bandwidth requirements. How do I make remote updates to data with ActiveX Data Objects?

Technique

ADO was designed with the Web in mind, and by using client side cursors, RDS enables an application to retrieve data, modify the data, and update the server using only one round trip. There are several steps required to enable this:

1. Open the connection using a remote provider. The connection string below uses the MS Remote provider to open an ODBC datasource.

```
Dim conn As Connection
Set conn = New Connection
conn.Open "Provider=MS Remote;Remote
Server=http://www.myserver.com" _
    + ";Remote Provider=MSDASQL;DSN=pubs"
```

A NOTE ON HTTP ADDRESSES

The Remote Server parameter in the `ConnectionString` expects an http address for the server. On a local network the http address is simply `http://myserver`.

2. Set the `Recordset` object's `CursorLocation` property to adUseClient.

3. Open the `Recordset` using adOpenStatic for the `CursorType` parameter and adLockBatchOptimistic for the `LockType` parameter.

4. After all the changes are collected, create a new `Connection` object using the same `ConnectionString` property that is used in the first `Connection`.

5. Create a new `Recordset` object. Open it using the original `Recordset` as the `Source` parameter and the new `Connection` object as the `ActiveConnection` parameter.

6. Call the second `Recordset` object's `UpdateBatch` method.

Steps

Open the ADODC.vbp, change the connection string in the `Form_Load` event to match your server, user, and password. The form, shown in Figure 8.11, is visually the same as the form in How-To 8.1, except this form uses a client-side cursor.

This How-To is a modification of How-To 8.1. If you have completed How-To 8.1, you can start from where it left off, or you can use the completed How-To 8.1 project from the CD.

1. Clear the `ConnectionString` and `RecordSource` properties of the ADO Data control.

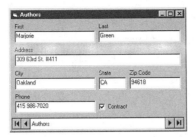

Figure 8.11. The New Authors application uses a client-side cursor.

2. Add the following code to frmMain to load the RecordSet in Form_Load event and update it in the Form_Unload event.

```
Private Sub Form_Load()
    Dim conn As Connection
    Dim rs As Recordset

    'open the connection
    Set conn = New Connection
    conn.Open "Provider=MS Remote" _
        + ";Remote Server=http://winemiller" _
        + ";Remote Provider=MSDASQL;DSN=pubs"

    'fill the list
    Set rs = New Recordset
    rs.CursorLocation = adUseClient
    rs.Open "authors", conn, adOpenStatic _
        , adLockBatchOptimistic, adCmdTable

    Set adodc.Recordset = rs
End Sub

Private Sub Form_Unload(Cancel As Integer)
    Dim rs As Recordset
    Dim conn As Connection

    'open the connection
    Set conn = New Connection
    Set rs = New Recordset

    On Error GoTo UpdateFailure
    conn.Open "Provider=MS Remote; _
        + "Remote Server=http://winemiller" _
        + ";Remote Provider=MSDASQL;DSN=pubs"

    rs.Open adodc.Recordset, conn
    rs.UpdateBatch
    On Error GoTo 0
UpdateDone:
    Exit Sub
```

```
UpdateFailure:
    ShowADOError conn
    GoTo UpdateDone
End Sub
```

3. Add the `ShowADOError` procedure to display any errors that occur during the update.

```
Private Sub ShowADOError(pConn As Connection)
    'spin through the errors collection and
    'display the constructed error message
    Dim ADOError As Error
    Dim sError As String
    For Each ADOError In pConn.Errors
        sError = sError & ADOError.Number & " - "
        sError = ADOError.Description + vbCrLf
    Next ADOError
    MsgBox sError
End Sub
```

How It Works

First, in the `Form_Load` event, a client-side recordset is opened and assigned to the ADO Data control's `Recordset` property. The user can make changes to all the records, moving back and forth through the entire recordset. When the form unloads, another `Recordset` object is created with the changes from the first. The `UpdateBatch` method commits the changes to the database.

Comments

Remote updates work great for single user applications, but open the window for concurrency problems if there is more than one user. If multiple users are running applications that perform remote updates, the second user (and any subsequent users) will get an error if he tries to update a record that has been changed since he first opened the recordset.

COMPLEXITY
ADVANCED

8.11 How do I...
Build a middle-tier business object using ActiveX Data Objects?

Problem

Our company has decided to move our applications to a three-tier architecture. How do I build a middle-tier business object using ActiveX Data Objects?

Technique

Remote updates work well where the application is small and concurrency is not a big issue; however, as applications and number of users grow, a new paradigm for application development becomes attractive. Three-tier applications typically move the data access and business rules from the client back to the server. This enables thin clients, sometimes just a browser, and easy deployment when it comes time to make changes.

Any data access method can be used to build middle-tier components, but ADO in particular is a good choice because of its ability to query almost anything and its light footprint.

When designing middle-tier objects there are several questions that must be answered:

✔ What objects will be exposed? Some companies choose to build an object for each physical database table, whereas others expose logical objects where several physical database tables are combined into one logical entity.

✔ What functions should those objects perform? Deletes, updates, and inserts are the first functions that come to mind, but that might not be appropriate in all circumstances. Imagine a medical application where a delete is not allowed, but a strikeout is.

✔ Is there a standard to which you should adhere? Many companies have guidelines about the type of interface a middle-tier component should have. If you are just starting your migration to three-tier, this might be where you should start. Defining this standard up-front will save time in the long run as other developers begin to use and build the middle-tier components.

✔ Do you plan to use Microsoft Transaction Server? Transaction Server is not necessary to deploy three-tier applications, but provides many benefits to applications that use it. The middle-tier component in this How-To is written with Transaction Server in mind, but does not require MTS. You will see why some of the unusual techniques used in this sample make sense in the next How-To.

Steps

Open the ThreeTier.vbg project group. Change the connection string in the **Class_Initialize** event of cAuthor to match your user, server, and password. Run the application. The UITier application, shown in Figure 8.12, is very similar to some of the other How-To's in this chapter. But, there is one important difference: there is no data access code in the application. All the data access is done through the MiddleTier.dll.

Figure 8.12. The UITier application uses a middle-tier component for data access.

1. Create a new ActiveX DLL. Change the project name to MiddleTier. Rename the default class from Class1 to cAuthor.

2. Add a reference to Microsoft ActiveX Data Objects 2.0 Library.

3. Add the following code for the Declarations section, the `Class_Initialize` event, and the `Class_Terminate` events. Remember to change the `ConnectionString` parameter on mConn's `Open` method to your configuration.

```
Option Explicit
Private mConn As Connection

Private Sub Class_Initialize()
    Set mConn = New Connection
    mConn.Open "Provider=SQLOLEDB.1;User ID=sa;Password=password" _
        + ";Location=WINEMILLER;Database=pubs"
End Sub

Private Sub Class_Terminate()
    mConn.Close
    Set mConn = Nothing
End Sub
```

4. Add the method to handle retrieving a list.

```
Public Function GetList(Optional psWhere As String) As Object
    'return a recordset to the client as object so she doesn't
    'even need to have a reference to ADO to use this object
    Dim sCmd As String
    Dim rs As Recordset

    sCmd = "select * from authors"
    'if she wanted a restricted list give it to her
```

continued on next page

continued from previous page

```
        If Len(psWhere) > 0 Then
            sCmd = sCmd + " where " + psWhere
        End If

        Set rs = New Recordset
        rs.CursorLocation = adUseClient
        rs.Open sCmd, mConn, adOpenForwardOnly, adLockReadOnly _
            , adCmdText

        Set GetList = rs
    End Function
```

5. Add the `DeleteAuthor` method. Given the author's ID, it constructs a delete statement and executes the delete. Notice that the `DeleteAuthor` method does not return a True or False indicating success or failure. Instead, if there is a problem, it raises an error. The reason for this is explained in How-To 8.13.

```
Public Sub DeleteAuthor(psau_id As String)
    'build delete string
    Dim sCmd As String
    sCmd = "delete authors"
    sCmd = sCmd + " where au_id = '" + psau_id + "'"
    'use execute to do the delete
    On Error GoTo DeleteError:
    mConn.Execute sCmd

    Exit Sub
DeleteError:
    Err.Raise vbObjectError, , "Error deleting"
End Sub
```

6. The `UpdateAuthor` method is next. Like the `DeleteAuthor` method, it also indicates failure through a raised error instead of a return value. By now you may have noticed something unusual about this class: there are no properties except the connection; everything is passed as a parameter! Each time an application calls a method or sets a property, one round trip must be made across the network, and that is assuming early binding. When a DLL is in process on the same machine, that hit is seldom noticeable, but in an environment where your middle-tier is running on a server that might not even be in the same country, the performance hit is definitely noticeable. This is perhaps the most important lesson to learn when building middle-tier components: They are not objects for holding data, rather they are objects for doing work.

```
Public Sub UpdateAuthor(psau_id As String, psau_lname As String _
    , psau_fname As String, psphone As String _
    , psaddress As String _
    , pscity As String, psstate As String, pszip As String _
    , pbcontract As Boolean)
    'build udpate string
```

```
      Dim sCmd As String
      sCmd = "update authors "
      sCmd = sCmd + " set"
      sCmd = sCmd + " au_lname = '" + psau_lname + "'"
      sCmd = sCmd + ",au_fname = '" + psau_fname + "'"
      sCmd = sCmd + ",phone = '" + psphone + "'"
      sCmd = sCmd + ",address = '" + psaddress + "'"
      sCmd = sCmd + ",city = '" + pscity + "'"
      sCmd = sCmd + ",state = '" + psstate + "'"
      sCmd = sCmd + ",zip = '" + pszip + "'"
      sCmd = sCmd + ",contract = " & IIf(pbcontract, 1, 0)
      sCmd = sCmd + " where au_id = '" + psau_id + "'"
      'use execute to do the update
      On Error GoTo UpdateError
      mConn.Execute sCmd

      Exit Sub
  UpdateError:
      Err.Raise vbObjectError, , "Error updating"
  End Sub
```

7. Finally, add the method to insert a new author.

```
  Public Sub NewAuthor(psau_id As String, psau_lname As String _
      , psau_fname As String, psphone As String _
      , psaddress As String _
      , pscity As String, psstate As String, pszip As String _
      , pbcontract As Boolean)
      'build insest string
      Dim sCmd As String
      sCmd = "insert authors (au_id, au_lname, au_fname , "
      sCmd = sCmd + "phone , address"
      sCmd = sCmd + ", city, state, zip, contract)"
      sCmd = sCmd + " values "
      sCmd = sCmd + "('" + psau_id + "'"
      sCmd = sCmd + ",'" + psau_lname + "'"
      sCmd = sCmd + ",'" + psau_fname + "'"
      sCmd = sCmd + ",'" + psphone + "'"
      sCmd = sCmd + ",'" + psaddress + "'"
      sCmd = sCmd + ",'" + pscity + "'"
      sCmd = sCmd + ",'" + psstate + "'"
      sCmd = sCmd + ",'" + pszip + "'"
      sCmd = sCmd + "," & IIf(pbcontract, 1, 0)
      sCmd = sCmd + ")"
      'use execute to do the insert
      On Error GoTo InsertError
      mConn.Execute sCmd

      Exit Sub
  InsertError:
      Err.Raise vbObjectError, , "Error inserting"
  End Sub
```

8. Now it is time to create the user interface level of the application. Using File | Add Project, add a new Standard EXE to the project group. Change the project name to UITier, change the default form name to frmMain, and save. When you are prompted to save the project group file, save it as ThreeTier.vbg.

9. Using the Project | References menu item, add references to Microsoft ActiveX Data Objects Recordset 2.0 Library and the `MiddleTier` project.

10. Using Table 8.15, add the objects for frmMain.

Table 8.15. Objects and properties for frmMain.

OBJECT	PROPERTY	VALUE
Form	Caption	Authors
ListView	Name	listAuthors
	View	3 - lvwReport
	LabelEdit	1 - lvwManual
CommandButton	Name	cmdNew
	Caption	New
CommandButton	Name	cmdDelete
	Caption	Delete
CommandButton	Name	cmdEdit
	Caption	Edit
CommandButton	Name	cmdExit
	Caption	Exit

11. Table 8.16 lists the columns and widths for the listAuthors `ListView` control.

Table 8.16. Column Headers for listAuthors.

COLUMN	WIDTH
Last	1000
First	1000
Address	2000
City	1440
State	500
Zip	700
Phone	1440
Contract	700

12. Add the Declarations section, the `Form_Load` event, and the `Form_Unload` event. This code takes care of creating and destroying the `mAuthors` object and filling the `ListView` control.

```
Option Explicit
Private mAuthors As cAuthor

Private Sub Form_Load()
    'fill the list with all the authors
    Dim rs As Recordset
    Dim NewItem As ListItem

    Set mAuthors = New cAuthor

    Set rs = mAuthors.GetList()
    Do Until rs.EOF
        Set NewItem = listAuthors.ListItems.Add(, rs("au_id"), _
            rs("au_lname"))
        NewItem.SubItems(1) = rs("au_fname")
        NewItem.SubItems(2) = rs("address")
        NewItem.SubItems(3) = rs("city")
        NewItem.SubItems(4) = rs("state")
        NewItem.SubItems(5) = rs("zip")
        NewItem.SubItems(6) = rs("phone")
        NewItem.SubItems(7) = rs("contract")
        rs.MoveNext
    Loop
End Sub

Private Sub Form_Unload(Cancel As Integer)
    Set mAuthors = Nothing
    Unload frmDetails
    Set frmDetails = Nothing
End Sub
```

13. Now, add the following code for the **cmdDelete_Click** event. The application tells the middle-tier component to delete the selected author. If it is successful, then it updates the list; otherwise it displays the trapped error.

```
Private Sub cmdDelete_Click()
    'delete the current author
    On Error GoTo DeleteError
    mAuthors.DeleteAuthor listAuthors.SelectedItem.Key
    listAuthors.ListItems.Remove listAuthors.SelectedItem.Key

    Exit Sub
DeleteError:
    MsgBox Err.Number + " - " + Err.Description
    Exit Sub
End Sub
```

14. The **cmdEdit_Click** event displays the Edit Authors dialog box, and if the user clicks OK, the event attempts to update the selected author's record through the middle-tier component. Like the **cmdDelete_Click** event, if the update is successful, the UI is updated; otherwise the trapped error is displayed.

```vb
Private Sub cmdEdit_Click()
    With frmDetails

        'fill the detail screen
        .txtId.Text = listAuthors.SelectedItem.Key
        .txtId.Locked = True
        .txtId.BackColor = vbButtonFace
        .txtLastName.Text = listAuthors.SelectedItem.Text
        .txtFirstName.Text = listAuthors.SelectedItem.SubItems(1)
        .txtAddress.Text = listAuthors.SelectedItem.SubItems(2)
        .txtCity.Text = listAuthors.SelectedItem.SubItems(3)
        .txtState.Text = listAuthors.SelectedItem.SubItems(4)
        .txtZip.Text = listAuthors.SelectedItem.SubItems(5)
        .txtPhone.Text = listAuthors.SelectedItem.SubItems(6)
        .chkContract.Value = _
            IIf(listAuthors.SelectedItem.SubItems(7) = "True" _
            , vbChecked, vbUnchecked)

        'show the edit dialog
        .OK = False
        .Caption = "Edit Author"
        .Show vbModal

        If .OK = True Then
            'user hit OK, update the database
            On Error GoTo EditError
            mAuthors.UpdateAuthor .txtId.Text, .txtLastName.Text _
                , .txtFirstName.Text, .txtPhone.Text, _
                .txtAddress.Text _
                , .txtCity.Text, .txtState.Text, .txtZip.Text _
                , .chkContract.Value = vbChecked
            On Error GoTo 0

            'update successfull change ui
            listAuthors.SelectedItem.Text = .txtLastName.Text
            listAuthors.SelectedItem.SubItems(1) = _
                .txtFirstName.Text
            listAuthors.SelectedItem.SubItems(2) = _
                .txtAddress.Text
            listAuthors.SelectedItem.SubItems(3) = .txtCity.Text
            listAuthors.SelectedItem.SubItems(4) = .txtState.Text
            listAuthors.SelectedItem.SubItems(5) = .txtZip.Text
            listAuthors.SelectedItem.SubItems(6) = .txtPhone.Text
            listAuthors.SelectedItem.SubItems(7) = _
                (.chkContract.Value = vbChecked)

        End If

    End With 'frmDetails
    Exit Sub
EditError:
    MsgBox Err.Number + " - " + Err.Description
    Exit Sub
End Sub
```

15. Add the `cmdNew_Click` event. It looks very similar to the `cmdEdit_Click` event, except that the `txtId` field is not locked when creating a new record.

```vb
Private Sub cmdNew_Click()
    With frmDetails

        'fill the detail screen
        .txtId.Text = ""
        .txtId.Locked = False
        .txtId.BackColor = vbWindowBackground
        .txtLastName.Text = ""
        .txtFirstName.Text = ""
        .txtAddress.Text = ""
        .txtCity.Text = ""
        .txtState.Text = ""
        .txtZip.Text = ""
        .txtPhone.Text = ""
        .chkContract.Value = vbUnchecked

        'show new dialog
        .OK = False
        .Caption = "New Author"
        .Show vbModal

        If .OK = True Then
            'user hit OK, update the database

            On Error GoTo NewError
            mAuthors.NewAuthor .txtId.Text, .txtLastName.Text _
                , .txtFirstName.Text, .txtPhone.Text, _
                .txtAddress.Text _
                , .txtCity.Text, .txtState.Text, .txtZip.Text _
                , .chkContract.Value = vbChecked
            On Error GoTo 0

            'update successfull change ui
            Dim NewItem As ListItem

            Set NewItem = listAuthors.ListItems.Add( _
                .txtId.Text _
                , .txtLastName.Text)
            NewItem.SubItems(1) = .txtFirstName.Text
            NewItem.SubItems(2) = .txtAddress.Text
            NewItem.SubItems(3) = .txtCity.Text
            NewItem.SubItems(4) = .txtState.Text
            NewItem.SubItems(5) = .txtZip.Text
            NewItem.SubItems(6) = .txtPhone.Text
            NewItem.SubItems(7) = (.chkContract.Value = vbChecked)

        End If

    End With 'frmDetails
    Exit Sub
NewError:
    MsgBox Err.Number + " - " + Err.Description
    Exit Sub

End Sub
```

16. Round out frmMain by adding a couple of miscellaneous procedures to activate the `cmdEdit_Click` event when the `listAuthors` control is double-clicked and unload the form when `cmdExit` is clicked.

```
Private Sub listAuthors_DblClick()
    cmdEdit_Click
End Sub

Private Sub cmdExit_Click()
    Unload Me
End Sub
```

17. Next add a new form to the project. Change its name to frmDetails. Use Table 8.17 and Figure 8.13 to add the objects for frmDetails.

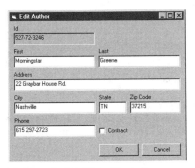

Figure 8.13. The Details dialog box is used to edit and create authors.

Table 8.17. Objects and properties for frmDetails.

OBJECT	PROPERTY	VALUE
TextBox	Name	txtId
	Text	""
TextBox	Name	txtFirstName
	Text	""
TextBox	Name	txtLastName
	Text	""
TextBox	Name	txtAddress
	Text	""
TextBox	Name	txtCity
	Text	""
TextBox	Name	txtState
	Text	""

OBJECT	PROPERTY	VALUE
TextBox	Name	txtZip
	Text	" "
TextBox	Name	txtPhone
	Text	" "
CheckBox	Name	chkContract
	Caption	Contract
Label	Name	lblId
	Caption	Id
Label	Name	lblFirstName
	Caption	First
Label	Name	lblLastName
	Caption	Last
Label	Name	lblAddress
	Caption	Address
Label	Name	lblCity
	Caption	City
Label	Name	lblState
	Caption	State
Label	Name	lblZip
	Caption	Zip Code
Label	Name	lblPhone
	Caption	Phone

18. Finally, add the following code to frmDetails so that the application can tell if the user clicked the OK button.

```
Option Explicit
Public OK As Boolean

Private Sub cmdCancel_Click()
    Hide
End Sub

Private Sub cmdOK_Click()
    OK = True
    Hide
End Sub
```

How It Works

The UITier application collects and displays data, but passes off all the work to the MiddleTier.dll. The UITier application could be replaced with DHTML, and no changes would be needed for the data access. Likewise, the underlying table structure could change, business rules could be added and deleted, and the UITier application would not have to change.

Comments

This How-To created a middle-tier component that would do its job of hiding the underlying data access and any business rules from the application, but scalability would be questionable. For each object created there would be a new database connection, and for each application using the object, there would be a separate instance of the object. The next logical step for any three-tier application is to try and reap the benefits of using Microsoft Transaction Server.

COMPLEXITY
ADVANCED

8.12 How do I...
Incorporate a business object into Microsoft Transaction Server?

Problem

I have a three-tier application in which I am experiencing scalability problems. How do I incorporate a business object into Microsoft Transaction Server?

Technique

MTS can greatly enhance the scalability of middle-tier components. There are two benefits to using MTS that most impact middle-tier components: object reuse and connection pools.

If MTS knows that an object has completed all the work that needs to be done and it is stateless, MTS will reuse that object. So, many applications using the cAuthor class from How-To 8.11 could all be using the same instance of that class. This saves time on the creation and destruction of objects, and it saves memory because only a few objects need to be instantiated instead of one for each client.

WHAT DO YOU MEAN BY STATELESS?

An object is said to be *stateless* if there are no properties that must stay the same between calls. If the cAuthor class from How-To 8.11 kept the author's name and other properties from one call to the next, it would be *statefull*. MTS could not reuse that object for different clients because each client would need the instance of cAuthor with their values intact.

The second benefit is the *connection pools*. MTS keeps a pool of database connections open. When an MTS object needs a new connection, MTS gives the object one of the connections that is already open. Many objects share the same connection without knowledge of this fact.

There are only a couple of things that an object needs to do to enjoy these benefits:

✔ Tell MTS when the object is complete and if it was successful. Keep MTS informed, and MTS can reuse the object in addition to providing transactions. MTS provides an ObjectContext; use the `SetAbort` or `SetComplete` methods of the ObjectContext to indicate that object is complete but unsuccessful, or complete and successful.

✔ Open a new connection on each call instead of holding them open. This enables MTS to grant connections and share them between objects.

Steps

This How-To uses the complete How-To 8.11 project and modifies it to take advantage of MTS. If you have completed How-To 8.11, you can use your finished project as a starting point, or you can copy the completed How-To 8.11 project from the CD and start from there.

1. Open the MiddleTier.vbp and a reference to Microsoft Transaction Server Type Library.

2. Change the `NewAuthor` procedure to tell MTS when it is done and to open the connection each time it's called. The changes are listed below in bold.

```
Public Sub NewAuthor(psau_id As String, psau_lname As String _
    , psau_fname As String, psphone As String _
    , psaddress As String _
    , pscity As String, psstate As String, pszip As String _
    , pbcontract As Boolean)
    Dim Conn As Connection

    Set Conn = New Connection
    Conn.Open "Provider=SQLOLEDB.1;User ID=sa;Password=password" _
        + ";Location=WINEMILLER;Database=pubs"

    'build insest string
    Dim sCmd As String
    sCmd = "insert authors (au_id, au_lname, au_fname , "
    sCmd = sCmd + "phone , address"
    sCmd = sCmd + ", city, state, zip, contract)"
    sCmd = sCmd + " values "
    sCmd = sCmd + "('" + psau_id + "'"
    sCmd = sCmd + ",'" + psau_lname + "'"
    sCmd = sCmd + ",'" + psau_fname + "'"
    sCmd = sCmd + ",'" + psphone + "'"
    sCmd = sCmd + ",'" + psaddress + "'"
```

continued on next page

continued from previous page

```
            sCmd = sCmd + ",'" + pscity + "'"
            sCmd = sCmd + ",'" + psstate + "'"
            sCmd = sCmd + ",'" + pszip + "'"
            sCmd = sCmd + "," & IIf(pbcontract, 1, 0)
            sCmd = sCmd + ")"
            'use execute to do the insert
            On Error GoTo InsertError
            Conn.Execute sCmd

            GetObjectContext().SetComplete
            Exit Sub
    InsertError:
            GetObjectContext().SetAbort
            Err.Raise vbObjectError, , "Error inserting"
    End Sub
```

3. Next, change the `UpdateAuthor` procedure the same way. Again, all the changes are listed in bold.

```
    Public Sub UpdateAuthor(psau_id As String, psau_lname As String _
        , psau_fname As String, psphone As String _
        , psaddress As String _
        , pscity As String, psstate As String, pszip As String _
        , pbcontract As Boolean)
        Dim Conn As Connection

        Set Conn = New Connection
        Conn.Open "Provider=SQLOLEDB.1;User ID=sa;Password=password" _
            + ";Location=WINEMILLER;Database=pubs"

        'build udpate string
        Dim sCmd As String
        sCmd = "update authors "
        sCmd = sCmd + " set"
        sCmd = sCmd + " au_lname = '" + psau_lname + "'"
        sCmd = sCmd + ",au_fname = '" + psau_fname + "'"
        sCmd = sCmd + ",phone = '" + psphone + "'"
        sCmd = sCmd + ",address = '" + psaddress + "'"
        sCmd = sCmd + ",city = '" + pscity + "'"
        sCmd = sCmd + ",state = '" + psstate + "'"
        sCmd = sCmd + ",zip = '" + pszip + "'"
        sCmd = sCmd + ",contract = " & IIf(pbcontract, 1, 0)
        sCmd = sCmd + " where au_id = '" + psau_id + "'"
        'use execute to do the update
        On Error GoTo UpdateError
        Conn.Execute sCmd

        GetObjectContext().SetComplete
        Exit Sub
    UpdateError:
        GetObjectContext().SetAbort
        Err.Raise vbObjectError, , "Error updating"
    End Sub
```

4. Now change the `DeleteAuthor` method.

```
Public Sub DeleteAuthor(psau_id As String)
    Dim Conn As Connection

    Set Conn = New Connection
    Conn.Open "Provider=SQLOLEDB.1;User ID=sa;Password=password" _
        + ";Location=WINEMILLER;Database=pubs"

    'build delete string
    Dim sCmd As String
    sCmd = "delete authors"
    sCmd = sCmd + " where au_id = '" + psau_id + "'"
    'use execute to do the delete
    On Error GoTo DeleteError:
    Conn.Execute sCmd

    GetObjectContext().SetComplete
    Exit Sub
DeleteError:
    GetObjectContext().SetAbort
    Err.Raise vbObjectError, , "Error deleting"
End Sub
```

5. Change the `GetList` method to include the new code.

```
Public Function GetList(Optional psWhere As String) As Object
    Dim Conn As Connection

    Set Conn = New Connection
    Conn.Open "Provider=SQLOLEDB.1;User ID=sa;Password=password" _
        + ";Location=WINEMILLER;Database=pubs"

    'return a record set to the client as object so he doesn't
    'even need to have a reference to ADO to use this object
    Dim sCmd As String
    Dim rs As Recordset

    sCmd = "select * from authors"
    'if they wanted a restricted list give it to them
    If Len(psWhere) > 0 Then
        sCmd = sCmd + " where " + psWhere
    End If

    Set rs = New Recordset
    rs.CursorLocation = adUseClient

    On Error GoTo GetListError:
    rs.Open sCmd, Conn, adOpenForwardOnly, adLockReadOnly, _
        adCmdText

    Set GetList = rs
```

continued on next page

continued from previous page

```
        GetObjectContext().SetComplete
        Exit Function
GetListError:
        GetObjectContext().SetAbort
        Err.Raise vbObjectError, , "Error getting list"
End Function
```

6. Finally, remove the `mConn` variable from the Declarations section and delete the `Class_Initialize` and `Class_Terminate` events. Compile the new DLL and fix any errors.

7. Using Microsoft Management Console, create a new MTS package and add the MiddleTier.dll to the package so that your package and objects appear like Figure 8.14.

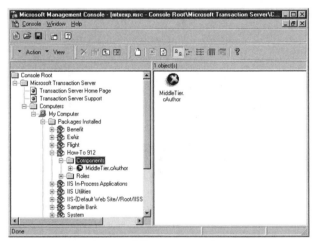

Figure 8.14. The MiddleTier.cAuthors component configured in MTS.

8. If you are running MTS on a separate machine, use dcomcnfg.exe to tell the local machine to create the MiddleTier.cAuthor component on the MTS server. Load the UITier.vbp project and run it. Without any changes to the user interface tier, the application now runs under MTS.

How It Works

Like How-To 8.11, the UI does very little work, and the MiddleTier.dll does the data access. However, now the middle-tier is optimized for MTS. By using the `SetAbort` and `SetComplete` methods of the ObjectContext, MTS knows when the object is completed and stateless so it can be reused. MTS can also hand out connections as needed because the middle-tier opens a connection for each call. MTS can immediately reuse those connections after the call is complete.

Comments

The MiddleTier.dll is now a highly scalable middle-tier component. Because this particular application would probably spend only a little time within the middle-tier's code, compared to the user's time typing and browsing, hundreds of clients could be serviced using probably only a small number of actual objects.

The only thing lacking in the cAuthor class is some really nice error reporting; "Error getting list" does not really help much. How-To 8.13 shows you how to handle ADO errors.

COMPLEXITY
INTERMEDIATE

8.13 How do I...
Handle ActiveX Data Objects errors?

Problem

To make my application more robust and easier to debug, I need to deal with and report to the user ADO errors. How do I handle ActiveX Data Objects errors?

Technique

ADO reports errors through the Connection object's Errors collection. The values from the last Error object in the Error's collection will also be repeated in Visual Basic's Err object. Typical error handling looks something like the code below. Before calling on an ADO object's methods or properties, use On Error Goto. Depending on the level of the application, you can then either raise an error or display a message to the user. This code below comes from a middle-tier component and raises an error for the UI tier to display.

```
'open the connection
On Error GoTo InitializeError
mConn.Open "Provider=SQLOLEDB.1;User ID=sa;Password=password;" _
    + "Location=WINEMILLER;Database=pubs"


Exit Sub
InitializeError:
Err.Raise aeInitializeError, , FormatError(mConn _
    , "An error occurred while making the database connection.")
```

Steps

This How-To uses the complete How-To 8.11 project and modifies it to better deal with and report ADO errors. If you have completed How-To 8.11, you can use your finished project as a starting point, or you can copy the completed How-To 8.11 project from the CD and start from there.

1. Open the MiddleTier.vbp and add the following code to the cAuthor class.

```
Private Function FormatError(pConn
 As Connection, psAdditionalMessage _
    As String) As String

'start it with any message passed in
    Dim Error As Error
    Dim sTemp As String
    If Len(psAdditionalMessage) > 0 Then
        sTemp = psAdditionalMessage + vbCrLf
    End If

    'spin through the errors collection and add in all those
    'errors
    For Each Error In pConn.Errors
        sTemp = sTemp + Error.Source + " reported " _
            & Error.Number _
            & " - " + Error.Description + vbCrLf
    Next Error
    FormatError = sTemp
End Function
```

2. Add the following enumeration to the Declarations section of **cAuthor**. By providing meaningful error codes, a UI tier developer could decide how critical the error is.

```
Public Enum cAuthorErrors
    aeInsertError = (vbObjectError + 1)
    aeUpdateError = (vbObjectError + 2)
    aeDeleteError = (vbObjectError + 3)
    aeFillError = (vbObjectError + 4)
    aeInitializeError = (vbObjectError + 5)
End Enum
```

3. Add error handling to the **Class_Initialize** procedure. Changes are highlighted in bold.

```
Private Sub Class_Initialize()
    Set mConn = New Connection
    'open the connection
    On Error GoTo InitializeError
    mConn.Open "Provider=SQLOLEDB.1;User ID=sa;Password=password" _
        + ";Location=WINEMILLER;Database=pubs"

    Exit Sub
InitializeError:
```

```
Err.Raise aeInitializeError, , FormatError(mConn _
    , "An error occurred while making the database _
        connection.")
End Sub
```

4. Make similar changes to the `GetList`, `UpdateAuthor`, `DeleteAuthor`, and `NewAuthor` procedures. Again changes are highlighted in bold. In addition, each function also has a chance to introduce an error. Those are also highlighted in bold. You can use those errors to see the results of the error handling.

```
Public Sub NewAuthor(psau_id As String, psau_lname As String _
    , psau_fname As String, psphone As String _
    , psaddress As String _
    , pscity As String, psstate As String, pszip As String _
    , pbcontract As Boolean)
    'build insest string
    Dim sCmd As String
    sCmd = "insert sauthors (au_id, au_lname, au_fname , "
    sCmd = sCmd + "phone , address"
    sCmd = sCmd + ", city, state, zip, contract)"
    sCmd = sCmd + " values "
    sCmd = sCmd + "('" + psau_id + "'"
    sCmd = sCmd + ",'" + psau_lname + "'"
    sCmd = sCmd + ",'" + psau_fname + "'"
    sCmd = sCmd + ",'" + psphone + "'"
    sCmd = sCmd + ",'" + psaddress + "'"
    sCmd = sCmd + ",'" + pscity + "'"
    sCmd = sCmd + ",'" + psstate + "'"
    sCmd = sCmd + ",'" + pszip + "'"
    sCmd = sCmd + "," & IIf(pbcontract, 1, 0)
    sCmd = sCmd + ")"
    'use execute to do the insert
    On Error GoTo InsertError
    mConn.Execute sCmd

    Exit Sub
InsertError:
    Err.Raise aeInsertError, , FormatError(mConn _
        , "An error occured while inserting the author.")
End Sub

Public Sub UpdateAuthor(psau_id As String, psau_lname As String _
    , psau_fname As String, psphone As String _
    , psaddress As String _
    , pscity As String, psstate As String, pszip As String _
    , pbcontract As Boolean)
    'build udpate string
    Dim sCmd As String
    sCmd = "udpate authors "
    sCmd = sCmd + " set"
    sCmd = sCmd + " au_lname = '" + psau_lname + "'"
    sCmd = sCmd + ",au_fname = '" + psau_fname + "'"
    sCmd = sCmd + ",phone = '" + psphone + "'"
```

continued on next page

continued from previous page

```
        sCmd = sCmd + ",address = '" + psaddress + "'"
        sCmd = sCmd + ",city = '" + pscity + "'"
        sCmd = sCmd + ",state = '" + psstate + "'"
        sCmd = sCmd + ",zip = '" + pszip + "'"
        sCmd = sCmd + ",contract = " & IIf(pbcontract, 1, 0)
        sCmd = sCmd + " where au_id = '" + psau_id + "'"
        'use execute to do the update
        On Error GoTo UpdateError
        mConn.Execute sCmd

        Exit Sub
UpdateError:
        Err.Raise aeUpdateError, , FormatError(mConn _
            , "An error occured while updating the author.")
End Sub

Public Sub DeleteAuthor(psau_id As String)
        'build delete string
        Dim sCmd As String
        sCmd = "delete authorsx"
        sCmd = sCmd + " where au_id = '" + psau_id + "'"
        'use execute to do the delete
        On Error GoTo DeleteError:
        mConn.Execute sCmd

        Exit Sub
DeleteError:
        Err.Raise aeDeleteError, , FormatError(mConn _
            , "An error occured while deleting the author.")
End Sub

Public Function GetList(Optional psWhere As String) As Object
        'return a record set to the client as object so they don't
        'even need to have a reference to ADO to use this object
        Dim sCmd As String
        Dim rs As Recordset

        sCmd = "zselect * from authors"
        'if they wanted a restricted list give it to them
        If Len(psWhere) > 0 Then
            sCmd = sCmd + " where " + psWhere
        End If

        Set rs = New Recordset
        rs.CursorLocation = adUseClient
        On Error GoTo GetListError
        rs.Open sCmd, mConn, adOpenForwardOnly, adLockReadOnly, _
            adCmdText

        Set GetList = rs
        Exit Function
GetListError:
        Err.Raise aeFillError, , FormatError(mConn _
            , "An error occured while getting the list of authors.")
End Function
```

How It Works

The On Error Goto statements trap the ADO errors. Each procedure then uses the FormatError function to raise another error that a top-level component can display to the user. Figure 8.15 shows a sample of the error message generated by FormatError.

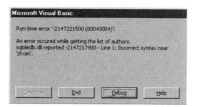

Figure 8.15. The formatted error message generated by FormatError.

Comments

Consistent and thorough error handling is a must for creating robust applications and components. Often, error handling is the last thing that is added to an application. By taking the time up front to develop a consistent and required approach to error handling, it will become second nature and save you time in the long run as your code starts to debug itself instead of being debugged by your customers.

CHAPTER 9
MICROSOFT DATA REPORT

9

MICROSOFT DATA REPORT

How do I...

9.1 **Create a report using Microsoft Data Report Designer?**

9.2 **Add Calculated Fields to a Microsoft Data Report?**

9.3 **Select if the Microsoft Data Report will be displayed, printed, or exported using Visual Basic code?**

9.4 **Display a report based on criteria I choose using a Microsoft Data Report?**

9.5 **Determine which records will be printed using Crystal Reports?**

9.6 **Create subtotals and other calculated fields using Crystal Reports?**

9.7 **Control the order in which records will be printed using Crystal Reports?**

9.8 **Print labels using Crystal Reports?**

9.9 **Create and print form letters with Crystal Reports?**

9.10 Print field data without extra spaces between the fields with Crystal Reports?

9.11 Prevent blank lines from being printed when a field contains no data using Crystal Reports?

9.12 Create cross-tab reports with Crystal Reports?

9.13 Generate reports using user-entered variables with Crystal Reports?

With Visual Basic 6 there are two methods for developing reports. Reports can be created within the Visual Basic development environment by using Microsoft Data Reports, or by using the version of Crystal Reports included with Visual Basic by accessing Crystal Reports' .RPT file via the Crystal's ActiveX control. (Of course, you also can use another version of Crystal Reports or another third-party reporting program; however, Data Reports and Crystal Reports 4.6.1 both come with Visual Basic 6.)

Microsoft Data Reports

With the new Microsoft Data Reports, a developer can add a report directly to a Visual Basic project. The report can be designed, saved, and compiled with a project just as a form or class would be. This feature integrates well with the Visual Basic IDE, and you can create reports natively and intuitively as you would create any other form.

There are two major differences between creating reports with Microsoft Data Reports and creating other forms within the project:

✔ The Data Report dimension is based on the printed page, whereas a form is based on twips.

✔ The Data Report does not use the intrinsic controls or ActiveX controls that regular Visual Basic forms use; they have their own report intrinsic controls.

With Microsoft Data Reports, a report can be displayed to the screen in the form of a Print Preview window. From this window the user can print the report to a printer or export the report to a file (including HTML). The report can be printed to a printer or exported to a file without any user intervention by using Visual Basic code.

Crystal Reports

Crystal Reports is still included with Visual Basic 6. It includes the Crystal Reports Designer, ActiveX control, and necessary runtimes. Visual Basic 6 is backward-compatible with projects created with Crystal Reports with earlier versions of Visual Basic.

Any Crystal Reports report must be created using the report designer. Although certain report elements can be changed at runtime through the Crystal Reports OLE custom control, the control does not have the ability to create a report from scratch.

Running and Configuring Crystal Reports Designer

The Crystal Reports Designer works as a separate process from Visual Basic and keeps the report definition in a report definition file with a .rpt file extension. You should try to save your report definition files in your Visual Basic project directory to make project management and program distribution easier.

If you installed Visual Basic with the defaults, you'll find a Crystal Reports icon in the Microsoft Visual Basic 6.0 program group. You can also start Crystal Reports by selecting Add-Ins|Report Designer from the Visual Basic main menu.

All the How-To's in this chapter assume that your Crystal Reports Designer program is set up the way ours is. Select File|Options from the Crystal Reports main menu. On the Layout tab, check the Show Field Names option. On the New Report tab (see Figure 9.1), check the Use Report Gallery for new reports option. You can also enter a report directory as the default location for report definition files.

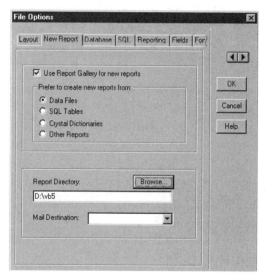

Figure 9.1. The Crystal Reports Designer File Options dialog box.

Printing Reports

You have two printing approaches with Crystal Reports:

✔ *Using the Crystal Reports report designer.* This program must be used to design all reports, and it can print them as well. This means you don't need to run a Visual Basic application to print reports on data maintained by your application. The program, however, can't be distributed to users of your application.

✔ *Using Crystal Reports OLE custom control (OCX).* This OCX is included in the package and can be dropped into a Visual Basic form to control report printing. The control gives your application access to most of the more useful features of the Crystal Reports program. With this control, you can have the report displayed in a Print Preview window, printed directly to a printer, or exported to a file.

Which Report Engine Should I Use?

With both Microsoft Data Reports and Crystal Reports included with Visual Basic 6, you have alternatives not previously available with Visual Basic. The tool you use will depend on your particular situation and personal preferences. You need to consider the reporting engines' different approaches to designing reports and how Visual Basic interfaces with the respective reporting engines.

When to Use Microsoft Data Reports

Data Reports integrates very well into the Visual Basic environment. The reports are generated directly in the Visual Basic IDE. There are no separate report files, and the report definitions are stored in an ActiveX designer form with the Visual Basic project. This means when a project is compiled, the report definition is compiled within the executable file (EXE). The report retrieves the data to be used from a Data Connection within a Data Environment. This enables the report to retrieve data from this powerful new feature in Visual Basic 6.

Microsoft Data Reports integrates well with Visual Basic by using the new powerful Data Environment and enabling the programmer to create reports with similar methods in which forms are created. Data Reports is great for basic reports; however, it does not have the options or advanced report features of the mature Crystal Reports and is not backward compatible with Crystal Report .RPT files.

When to Use Crystal Reports

Crystal Reports takes a totally different approach to creating reports to use with Visual Basic. A separate application creates the report definitions, and these reports are stored in a separate .RPT file that must be distributed with the EXE file. Also, additional DLLs and an OCX control must be included for the Visual Basic application to use a Crystal Reports report. The distribution requirements are therefore much heavier than those for Microsoft Data Reports. Furthermore, a Crystal Reports report uses ODBC to connect to a data source, not to the new powerful Data Environment.

Crystal Reports is much more mature that Microsoft Data Reports. Many applications have already been written using Crystal Reports as their reporting engine. Also, Crystal Reports has a wider feature set than Data Reports. It can generate cross-tab reports and sub reports, and it has much more powerful formula and many number crunching features. Crystal Reports also has an upgrade path that provides new features and more power.

Crystal is a mature and proven product. It might be heavier than Data Reports, but it offers a richer feature set and has upgrade options for scalability.

CRYSTAL REPORTS UPGRADE OPTIONS

Crystal Reports Professional 6

This version of Crystal Reports Includes an updated feature set to Crystal 4.6.1, which is included with Visual Basic. An updated report designer and an ISAPI module is included, which allows reports to be placed on a IIS Web server. Java, ActiveX, and pure HTML viewers can be used to display a report on the Web server. This version of Crystal Reports enables you to export a report in various formats including HTML, MS-Excel, MS-Word, and Lotus 1-2-3.

Crystal Info

Crystal Info is a server-based solution that enables multiple users to view, schedule, and manipulate shared reports. It can be used as a central storage for reports, for multiple users to view. It can be used to schedule when complex and time consuming reports will be run so data can be viewed without having to run the report each time. What SQL Server is to Microsoft Access, Crystal Info is to Crystal Reports.

Crystal Report Designer

This is an ActiveX designer that works in the same vein as Microsoft Data Reports. It gives you 100% functionality of Crystal Reports 6 with the Visual Basic IDE. Take the way Microsoft Data Reports integrates into Visual Basic and add the power of Crystal Reports 6. WOW! Prior to the release of Visual Basic 6, the only version of this tool available was for Visual Basic 5, but keep an eye on the Seagate Software Web site (www.seagatesoftware.com) for a Visual Basic 6 version.

Sample Databases in the How-To's

The How-To's in this chapter use the Microsoft Access .MDB file BIBLIO.MDB that was shipped with Visual Basic. If you selected the default program locations when you installed Visual Basic, the Visual Basic files are located in the \Program Files\Visual Basic directory. If these files are not located in the default directories, you'll need to tell Crystal where to find them.

Table 9.1 lists the tables in the BIBLIO.MDB database. You might want to add one index (duplicates are OK) on the Au_ID field in the Title Author table to speed reporting. Use either Microsoft Access or the VisData sample application that is included with Visual Basic to add the index.

Table 9.1. Tables from BIBLIO.MDB.

TABLE NAME	DESCRIPTION
Authors	Book author names
Publishers	Names, phones, and other information about each publisher
Title Author	Records linking the Author and Titles tables
Titles	Books published by each company

You can find the next set of tables, shown in Table 9.2, in the file CRYSTAL.MDB, which is included on the CD-ROM. These files make up a basic order-entry system.

Table 9.2. Tables from CRYSTAL.MDB.

TABLE NAME	DESCRIPTION
Company	Company name and information
Header	Order invoice header
Detail	Order detail records

The last database is Mailing List, in the file MAIL.MDB. Create this new table using the fields shown in Table 9.3. It is easiest if you place the file in the same directory as the .RPT file that uses it.

Table 9.3. Mailing List table in MAIL.MDB.

FIELD NAME	DATA TYPE	SIZE
Contact	Text	30
Addr1	Text	40
City	Text	30
State	Text	20
Zip	Text	10
Week Day	Text	10

Enter some sample data in the Mailing List table. Table 9.4 lists a few sample lines of the table in MAIL.MDB on the CD-ROM enclosed with this book. Enter various Contact names and Week Days. Include a number of records from each

City, State, and Zip. There are more than 600 records in the MAIL.MDB on the CD-ROM.

Table 9.4. Sample data in Mailing List table in MAIL.MDB.

CONTACT	ADDR1	CITY	STATE	ZIP	WEEK DAY
Resident	4 Goodyear Street	Boulder	Colorado	80302-0302	Monday
Occupant	2291 Arapahoe	Irvine	California	92711-2002	Monday
Resident	8 Hazelnut	Irvine	California	92711-3810	Monday
Occupant	2 Orion	Aliso Viejo	California	92656-4200	Sunday
Medical Practitioner	1 Jenner	Tacoma	Washington	98402-8402	Thursday
Medical Practitioner	Civic Center	Anaheim	California	92805-2805	Tuesday
Occupant	2 Park Plaza	Irvine	California	92714-2714	Thursday

9.1 Create a report using Microsoft Data Report Designer

Using the Data Report Designer, you will lay out a report and place report intrinsic controls on the form to create a simple Data Report. This How-To will get your feet wet with the new Data Report Designer and how it relates to the Visual Basic IDE.

9.2 Add Calculated Fields to a Microsoft Data Report

Using the rptFunction report control you will add calculations to a Data Report. You will become familiar with various functions the control can offer when creating reports.

9.3 Select if the Microsoft Data Report will be displayed, printed, or export using Visual Basic code

Using Microsoft Data Report and some Visual Basic coding, this How-To will demonstrate how to display a report to the screen, print the report directly to the printer, or export the report to a file. The format of a file when exported can be text or HTML. The ability of exporting a report to HTML opens up multiple possibilities to Web enable your application.

9.4 Have a Report Displayed Based on Criteria I Choose Using a Microsoft Data Report

Have a Data Report display data based on a parameter passed to a SQL-based query contained in a **Data Environment** object.

9.5 Determine Which Records Will Be Printed Using Crystal Reports

Using the `Crystal Reports` custom control, you can specify at runtime the records to be printed by sending a Crystal Reports formula to the print engine. In this How-To, you'll create a report using three tables linked together and a simple Visual Basic program to show how you can control the records printed at runtime.

9.6 Create Subtotals and Other Calculated Fields Using Crystal Reports

Crystal Reports has a rich variety of built-in capabilities for creating very complex reports. This How-To describes how to create a bulk mail report based on an address file, sorting, grouping, and performing calculations needed for completion of a mailing's paperwork. You certainly can't get too much more complex than a system created over 200 years by the federal bureaucracy!

9.7 Control the Order in Which Records Will Be Printed Using Crystal Reports

Although the Crystal Reports design program provides a very flexible report design and creation environment, you can change the record sort order from a Visual Basic application, giving you essentially unlimited flexibility to print different reports, as you'll see in this How-To. You'll also see how to change the group sort order, giving you another level of flexibility using database reports.

9.8 Print Labels Using Crystal Reports

Crystal Reports makes it easy to produce almost any type of label using a database. In this How-To, you'll create mailing labels complete with attractive graphics and a return address.

9.9 Create and Print Form Letters with Crystal Reports

By using formulas and the flexible formatting in Crystal Reports, you can use your data to produce form letters. But how do you print different page headers and footers? And how do you customize the text for each recipient in your mailing list? This How-To gives you all the information you need to use Crystal Reports for form letters.

9.10 Print Field Data Without Extra Spaces Between the Fields with Crystal Reports

Although it is not as complete a set of tools as Visual Basic, Crystal Reports does have a number of useful string manipulation and conversion functions and operators. In this How-To, you'll design a customer directory showing names, addresses, and the page number as a single formula field, giving the report a more natural and finished look.

9.11 Prevent Blank Lines from Being Printed when a Field Contains No Data Using Crystal Reports

Crystal Reports provides two options that conserve space when reports are printed: the Suppress Blank Lines property for report sections and Print on Multiple Lines property for text boxes. Both options are put to good use in this How-To, creating a report from frequently incomplete data.

9.12 Create Cross-Tab Reports with Crystal Reports

Using Crystal Reports to produce cross-tab reports is very easy when you use the Cross-Tab layout window. In fact, the hardest part of creating the report is developing a clear picture of how to analyze the data, but Crystal Reports makes it easy to try different options until the report gives the information needed. This How-To demonstrates how to create a summary of customers by city and day of the week that they receive service.

9.13 Generate Reports Using User-Entered Variables with Crystal Reports

Many of the design elements of a Crystal report can be changed on-the-fly in a Visual Basic application. Although there aren't enough control properties to completely change an existing report or create a new report, there are enough changeable properties available that a Visual Basic application can create entirely different reports using the same data. This How-To creates a Visual Basic application and a Crystal report that allows records to be printed in different orders while filtering the records and customizing the report heading and page numbering.

COMPLEXITY
BEGINNING

9.1 How Do I...
Create a report using Microsoft Data Report Designer?

Problem

I need to create a report using data from a database that can be displayed to the user, easily printed or exported to HTML.

Technique

Using Visual Basic and the included Data Report Designer, a report can be created to represent the data as desired. Using the BIBLIO.MDB database included with Visual Basic, you will create a report that displays a list of authors.

The preview window used to display the report will enable the user to print and export the report directly from the preview.

Steps

Start Visual Basic, load then run the AuthorsDR.vbp project. Figure 9.2 displays how the report will look. The report can be printed by clicking the printer icon, or can be exported to text or HTML by clicking the book icon.

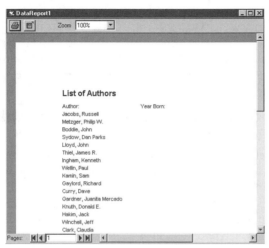

Figure 9.2. AuthorsDR form shown at runtime.

1. Start Visual Basic and select a new Standard EXE project. Select Add Data Environment from the Project menu. The window in Figure 9.3 will appear. Right click on the Connection1 item in the Data View window. Select the Properties item from the popup menu. The following screen is used to set the database and connection type. This How-To will use the BIBLIO.MDB database; therefore, select the Microsoft Jet 3.51 OLE DB Provider, then click on the Next button. Enter or select the location of the BIBLIO.MDB database; it should be in the same folder as Visual Basic. Click on the Test button to verify the connection. This handy option enables you to verify the database connection without having to write test codes. Run the project. Click the OK button.

2. Right-click on the Commands folder in the Data Environment window. Select the Add Command item from the popup menu. An item called Command1 will appear under the Commands folder. Right click on it and select the Properties item from the popup menu. The Properties dialog box that appears is used to select a table or query. Click the on Connection drop-down list and select Connection1. From the Database drop down select the Table object. From the Object drop-down list, select the Authors Table. The dialog should look like Figure 9.4 after the items have been chosen.

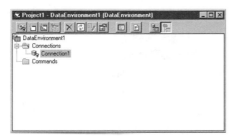

Figure 9.3. The Data View Window.

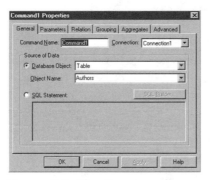

Figure 9.4. The Command1 Properties dialog box.

3. From the Visual Basic main menu, select the Add Data Report item from the Project menu. Set the properties of the Data Report as in Table 9.5. Then, right-click on the report and select Retrieve Structure from the popup menu. Retrieve Structure will make the sections of the report match the database connection layout.

Table 9.5. Properties for drBasic.dsr AuthorsDR.

OBJECT	PROPERTY	SETTING
DataReport	Name	drBasic
	DataMember	Command1
	DataSource	DataEnviroment1

4. The fields to be displayed can be added in two ways. The first method is to draw the fields on the report, then assign the proper **DataMember** and **DataField** properties to them. The second method is to open the Data

Environment window, and drag and drop the fields directly on the report.
After a field is dropped onto the detail section of the report, the field and
its caption are displayed on the report. Arrange the items as shown in
Figure 9.5.

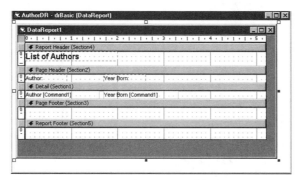

Figure 9.5. Arranged report objects.

5. Set the properties of the objects on the report form as in Table 9.6.

Table 9.6. Objects on drBasic.dsr.

OBJECT	PROPERTY	SETTING
RptCaption	Name	lbTitle
	Font	Arial
	Size	12
	Caption	"List of Authors"
RptCaption	Name	lbAuthorTitle
	Font	Arial
	Caption	Author:
RptCaption	Name	lbYearTitle
	Font	Arial
	Caption	"Year Born:"
RptText	Name	txtAuthor
	Font	Arial
	DataField	Author
	DataMember	Command1
RptText	Name	txtYearBorn
	Font	Arial
	DataField	"Year Born"
	DataMember	Command1
	DataSource	DataEnviroment1

6. Remove the form called Form1 that was automatically created when you started Visual Basic. Set the Startup Object to the report form. Run the project.

How It Works

First, a Data Environment must be defined. This is the gateway through which the report retrieves its data. Then, the report is assigned to a Data Connection. The structure of the Data Connection is mirrored by the report. Dragging and dropping the fields into the report creates the report layout. By running the Visual Basic project the report and data is displayed. At run-time the user can easily print or export the report.

Comments

Creating a Data report consists of three basic steps. First, a data connection must be created. This is the object the report will use to retrieve the data. With Visual Basic 6 the new Data Environment is very powerful and flexible as it enables the Data Reports to retrieve data from various data types. You are not limited to just Access MDB files, but can get data from any ODBC DataSource or use the built in functionality to connect directly to an Microsoft SQL server or an Oracle database.

The second step is to assign the report to a Data Connector created in the Data Environment and use the "Retrieve Structure" option so the report section matches the data connection.

The third step is to add the report controls to the report. These controls will display the data the report retrieves. These controls can range from displaying the names of the fields to calculated items that summarize data in the report.

COMPLEXITY
BEGINNING

9.2 How Do I...
Add Calculated Fields to my
Microsoft Data Report?

Problem

I have a report that generates a list of items. I need to have the report count the number of items in the list.

Technique

Using the Data Report designer included with Visual Basic 6, you can create reports that can do various calculations based on the data in the report.

This How-To will demonstrate how to make a group based on the Authors field and add a calculated field that will display the number of books each author has written. This How-To will be a base demonstration how to add calculated fields to a Data Report.

Steps

Open and run DataProject.vbp, which displays the Figure 9.7. This displays each author's list of book and a count of the number of books per author. By using the toolbar at the top of the report you can print or export the report.

1. Start Visual Basic and select a new Data Project. This will add the Data Environment and Data Report to the project. Remove the form that was added to the project and set the Data Report as the Startup object.

2. From the Project menu select the Add Data Environment. Double-click on the DataEnvironment1 object that was added to the Project window. Right-click on the Connection folder and select the Add Connection item from the popup menu. Right-click on the **Connection1** object and select the Properties item from the popup menu. Select the Microsoft Jet 3.51 OLE DB provider. The next dialog box that appears is used to find the BIBLIO.MDB file on your computer. Click the OK button. Right-click on the Command folder and select the Add Command item from the popup menu. Command1 will be added under the Commands folder. Right click on Command1 and select the Properties from the popup menu. Using the Data Object dropdown select the Tables item. Using the Object Name dropdown select the Titles item.

Steps 1 and 2 were to set up the Data Environment. Please refer to the chapters in this book for a more detail on the Data Environment.

3. Under the Grouping tab, check the Group Command Object checkbox. This will enable the items in the tab. Click on the Author field and click the ">" button. This will cause the Data Environment to group the data by Author. Click the OK button.

4. Set the DataMember and DataSource of the Data Report. Right-click on the bottom of the report and select the Retrieve Structure item from the popup menu. This will arrange the sections of the Data Report to match the data used.

5. Place the controls on the data report form as in Figure 9.6. Set the properties of the controls as in Table 9.7.

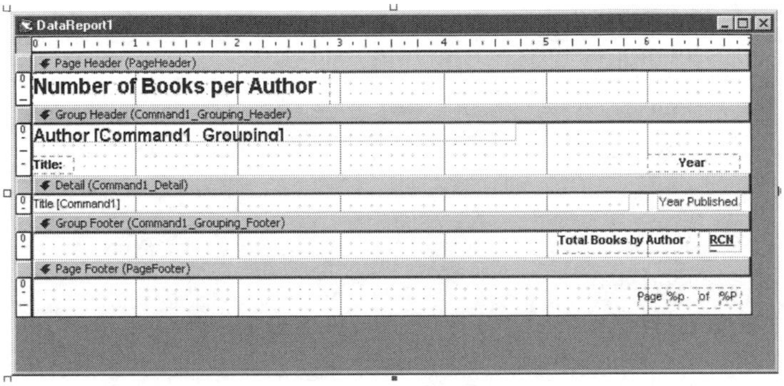

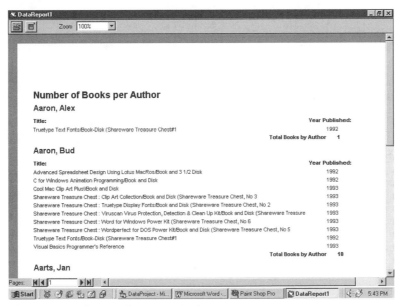

Figure 9.6. Objects arranged on the report.

Figure 9.7. The project at runtime.

Table 9.7. Objects and properties for drBasic.dsr.

OBJECT	PROPERTY	SETTING
DataReport	Name	DataReport1
	DataMember	Command1_Grouping
RptLabel	Name	lbTitle
	Font	Arial

continued on next page

continued from previous page

OBJECT	PROPERTY	SETTING
	FontSize	14.25
	Caption	"Number of Books per Author"
RptText	Name	"txtAuthor"
	Font	Arial
	FontSize	12
	DataField	Author
	DataMember	Command1_Grouping
RptLabel	Name	Label2
	Caption	Title:
RptLabel	Name	Label3of
	Caption	"Year Published:"
RptText	Name	txtTitle
	DataField	Title
	DataMember	Command1
RptText	Name	txtYearPublished
	DataField	"Year Published"
	DataMember	Command1
RptFunction	Name	Function1
	DataField	Title
	DataMember	Command1
	FunctionType	4 - rptFunRCnt
RptLabel	Name	lbTotalBooks
	Caption	"Total Books by Author"
RptLabel	Name	Label1
	Caption	"%p"
RptLabel	Name	lbPageTitle
	Caption	Page
RptLabel	Name	lbof
	Caption	of
RptLabel	Name	Label4
	Caption	"%P"

6. Run the project. It might take a few minutes to retrieve the data from the database. The result should be displayed as in Figure 9.7.

How It Works.

The report retrieves the data from the Data Environment. The Data Environment queries the database and groups the data by author. The rptFunction control that has been placed in the Group footer displays the total number of books per author. The rptFunction control can do various functions as in Table 9.8.

Table 9.8. rptFunction control functions description.

FUNCTION	SETTING	DESCRIPTION
Sum	0 - rptFuncSum	Adds the values of the field
Average	1 - rptFuncAve	Averages the values of the field
Minimum	2 - rptFuncMin	Displays the minimum value of the field
Maximum	3 - rptFuncMax	Displays the maximum value of the field
Row Count	4 - rptFuncRCnt	Displays the number of rows in a section
Value Count	5 - rptFuncVCnt	Displays the number of rows containing non-null values
Standard Deviation	6 - rptFuncSDEV	Displays the standard deviation
Standard Error	7 - rptFuncSERR	Displays the standard error

The rptFunction can be used to do various calculations based on the type of data in the field. By placing the `rptFunction` control in either a group or report footer, you can perform calculations on fields contained in the report.

Comments

Grouping is a very powerful function when generating reports. Grouping enables the report to list similar items together in the report.

For Example, the books were not added sequentially in the database, so when retrieving a list of authors and their books from the database all the authors are mixed up in the list. Grouping allows report to present all the books for one author then another. Another example is when creating a report to list the books per publisher. The grouping would be done on publishers not authors.

COMPLEXITY

INTERMEDIATE

9.3 How Do I...
Select whether the Microsoft Data Report will be displayed, printed, or exported using Visual Basic code?

Problem

I need to create an application that enables the user to choose the output method for the report. I would like the user to be able to choose whether the report is previewed to the screen, printed to the printer, or exported to a file.

Technique

The data report has various methods defined to output a report. By using these methods, the programmer can determine the output method for the report. This How-To will demonstrate the ways in which the application can enable the user to choose the output method for the report.

The `PrintReport` method will be used to print the report directly to the Printer. This method can be set to print directly to the printer without any user intervention, or the method can be used to display a dialog box to enable the user to select the print range and the number of copies to be printed.

The `ExportReport` method will be used to generate a file of the report data. This method can be set to generate the file without any user intervention or a dialog can be displayed so the user can select the file type and the page range.

The `Show` method will be used to display a print preview window of the report. This method is the same used to display any other Visual Basic form.

Steps

Open and run the OutputType.vbp project. This project enables the user to display, print, or export the report. When printing or exporting a report, the user can select the page range to be used. This is useful in large reports.

1. Start Visual Basic and choose a new Data Project. Have the Data Environment point to the BIBLO.MDB database.

2. Lay out the form as in Figure 9.8 and set the properties of the objects as in Table 9.9.

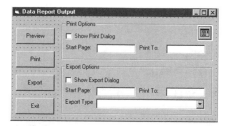

Figure 9.8. Arrangement of form frmOutPut.frm.

Table 9.9. rptFunction control functions description.

OBJECT	PROPERTY	SETTING
Form	Name	frmOutPut
	Caption	"Data Report Output"
Frame	Name	frExport
	Caption	"Export Options"
CheckBox	Name	chkExport
	Caption	"Show Export Dialog"
TextBox	Name	txtStartPageEx
TextBox	Name	txtPrintToEx
ComboBox	Name	cbExportType
Label	Name	lbExportType
	Caption	"Export Type"
Label	Name	lbStartPageEx
	Caption	"Start Page:"
Label	Name	lbPrintToEx
	Caption	"Print To:"
CommonDialog	Name	CD
Frame	Name	frPrint
	Caption	"Print Options"
TextBox	Name	txtPrintTo
TextBox	Name	txtStartPage
CheckBox	Name	chkShowDialog
	Caption	"Show Print Dialog"
Label	Name	lbPrintTo
	Caption	"Print To:"

continued on next page

continued from previous page

OBJECT	PROPERTY	SETTING
Label	Name	lbStart
	Caption	"Start Page:"
CommandButton	Name	cmdExit
	Caption	Exit
CommandButton	Name	cmdExport
	Caption	Export
CommandButton	Name	cmdPrint
	Caption	"Print"
CommandButton	Name	cmdPreview
	Caption	Preview

3. Add the following code in the **Load** event of the Form:

```
Private Sub Form_Load()
    cbExportType.AddItem "1 - HTML"
    cbExportType.AddItem "2 - Text"
    cbExportType.AddItem "3 - Unicode HTML"
    cbExportType.AddItem "4 - Unicode Text"
    cbExportType.ListIndex = 0
End Sub
```

This procedure will add the export types to the list box so the user can choose the format in which the report will be exported.

4. Add the following code to the **Click** event of the **cmdPreview** button:

```
Private Sub cmdPreview_Click()
    DataReport1.StartUpPosition = 0
    DataReport1.WindowState = 2
    DataReport1.Show
End Sub
```

This procedure will maximize the size of the report windows to the full screen, then display the report.

5. Add the following code to the Click event of the cmdPrint button:

```
Private Sub cmdPrint_Click()
    Dim fReturn As Long

    If txtStartPage.Text <> "" Or txtPrintTo.Text <> "" Then
        If IsNumeric(txtStartPage.Text) = False Or _
IsNumeric(txtPrintTo.Text) = False Then
            MsgBox "The start or end pages to print is invalid.", _
64
            Exit Sub
        End If
    End If
```

```
        If txtStartPage.Text = "" And txtPrintTo.Text = "" Then
            fReturn = DataReport1.PrintReport(chkShowDialog.Value * _
    -1, rptRangeAllPages)
        Else
            fReturn = DataReport1.PrintReport(chkShowDialog.Value * _
    -1, _
            txtStartPage.Text, txtPrintTo.Text)
        End If
        If fReturn = 2 Then
            MsgBox "Print Job Sent to Printer."
        Else
            MsgBox "Print Job Cancelled"
        End If
    End Sub
```

This procedure prints the report to the printer. There are three variables that can be passed to the **PrintReport** method. The first value is a Boolean value that determines if the Print dialog box is displayed. The second determines if all the pages are to be printed. If the second value is not set to **rptRangeAllPages**, then a third value can be used to determine the range of pages that will be printed.

6. Add the following code to the click event of the cmdExport button:

```
Private Sub cmdExport_Click()

    Dim Overwrite As Boolean

    If txtStartPageEx.Text <> "" Or txtPrintToEx.Text <> "" Then
        If IsNumeric(txtStartPageEx.Text) = False Or
IsNumeric(txtPrintToEx.Text) = False Then _
            MsgBox "The start or end pages to print is invalid.", _
64
            Exit Sub
        End If
    End If

    CD.ShowSave
    If CD.FileName <> "" Then
        If Dir(CD.FileName) <> "" Then
            Ans% = MsgBox("Do you want to overwrite this file ?", _
vbQuestion Or vbYesNo)
            If Ans% = 6 Then
                Overwrite = True
            Else
                Overwrite = False
            End If
        Else
            Overwrite = False
        End If

        If txtStartPageEx.Text = "" And txtPrintToEx.Text = "" _
Then
            DataReport1.ExportReport
```

continued on next page

continued from previous page

```
DataReport1.ExportFormats(CLng(Left$(cbExportType.List _
(cbExportType.ListIndex), 1))).Key, CD.FileName, Overwrite, _
chkExport.Value * -1, rptRangeAllPages
        Else
            DataReport1.ExportReport DataReport1.ExportFormats _
(CLng(Left$(cbExportType.List(cbExportType.ListIndex) _
, 1))).Key, CD.FileName, Overwrite, chkExport.Value * -1, _
txtStartPageEx.Text, txtPrintToEx.Text
        End If
    End If

End Sub
```

The **ExportReport** method is used to export a report to a file. There are two primary file types, HTML and text. Unicode versions of both types can also be exported. The **ExportReport** method has four (five if all pages are not selected) variables which can be passed to the method. The first is the format type in which the report will be exported. If this value is left blank, a dialog box will appear, asking the user which format is preferred. There are various ways to pass the export type using code. This example uses the **ExportFormats** collection of the report. These are predefined types as outlined in Table 9.10. The second value is the filename of the report to be written. In this example, the filename is set from the Common dialog box. The third variable determines if a file should be overwritten. The fourth variable determines if the Export dialog box should be displayed. The next two variables are identical to those used in **PrintReport** method and determine the page range to be exported.

Table 9.10. Export file types.

EXPORT TYPE	CONSTANT	DESCRIPTION
HTML	rptKeyHTML	Export in HTML Format
HTML Unicode	rptKeyUnicodeHTML_UTF8	Export in HTML Unicode Format
Text	rptKeyText	Export in Text Format
Text Unicode	rptKeyUnicodeText	Export in Text Unicode Format

Note that if the overwrite variable is set to **False** and if an attempt is made to overwrite a file, the Export dialog box will appear.

7. Add the following code to the Click event of the cmdExit button:

```
Private Sub cmdExit_Click()
    End
End Sub
```

Clicking this button will cause the application to end.

8. Lay out the report as in Figure 9.9. Set the properties as in Table 9.11.

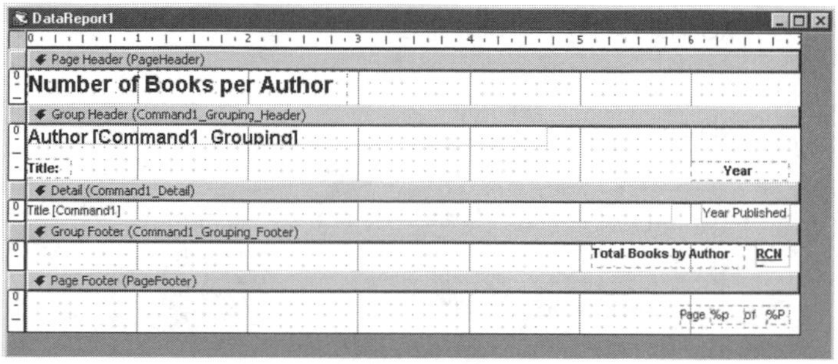

Figure 9.9. The arrangement of the report
DataReport1.dsr.

Table 9.11. Object and Properties for DataReport1.

OBJECT	PROPERTY	SETTING
DataReport	Name	DataReport1
DataMember		Command1_Grouping
rptLabel	Name	lbTitle
Font	Arial	
FontSize	14.25	
	Caption	"Number of Books per Author"
RptTextbox	Name	txtAuthor
	Font	Arial
FontSize		12
DataField		Author
DataMember		Command1_Grouping
RptLabel	Name	Label2
	Caption	Title:
RptLabel	Name	Label3
	Caption	"Year Published:"
RptTextbox	Name	txtTitle
DataField	Title	
DataMember	Command1	
RptTextbox	Name	txtYearPublished
DataField		"Year Published"
DataMember	Command1	
RptFunction	Name	Function1
DataField	Title	

continued on next page

continued from previous page

OBJECT	PROPERTY	SETTING
FunctionType		4 - rptFuncCnt
DataMember	Command1	
RptLabel	Name	lbTotalBooks
	Caption	"Total Books by Author"
RptLabel	Name	Label1
	Caption	"%p"
RptLabel	Name	lbPageTitle
	Caption	Page
RptLabel	Name	lbof
	Caption	of
Rptlabel	Name	Label4
Caption		"%P"

9. Run the project. Try the various combinations of report output.

How It Works

The **Show** method works as it does with a Visual Basic form. It has the report display to the screen. Before displaying the report to the screen settings like **StartupPosition** and **WindowState** can be set. The same properties used to display Visual Basic forms can be used to tailor the placement and position of the report on the screen when it is displayed.

The **PrintReport** is used to print the report directly to the printer. Setting the **ShowVariable** of the **PrintReport** determines if the report will be automatically routed to the printer or if a dialog box will appear to ask the user the page range and number of copies to be printed. Setting the range determines the pages that will be printed. If a value for the range is not set, all the pages will be printed.

The **ExportReport** method is a very powerful function. It can be used to export reports as text, HTML, or a user-defined HTML format. This method has six variables to set to control the way the report will be exported to a file.

ExportReport(ExportFormat, filename, Overwrite, ShowDialog, Range, PageFrom, PageTo**)**

The **ExportFormat** variable (**ExportFormats** collection item) is used to set the type of file that will be exported. This variable is a member of the **ExportFormats** collection. The **ExportFormats** is a collection that stores the type of report formats that can be exported. The **ListBox** was populated with the default items of the **ExportFormats** collection. The first character of each item in the **ListBox** is the index of that export type in the **ExportFormats** collection. The **Left$** function is used to grab the number from the item displayed in the **ListBox**.

The filename variable (a String value) is used to set the name of the file that will be generated. If a full path (such as C:\data\mynewfile.html) is not defined, the current working folder will be used.

The overwrite variable (a Boolean value) is set to determine if a file already exists as defined by the filename variable should be overwritten. If this value is set to False and a file does exist, then the Export dialog box will appear as if the `ShowDialog` variable was set to True.

The ShowDialog variable (a Boolean value) determines is the Export File dialog box is shown. If this value is True then the filename variable does not need to be set.

The Range variable(s) (a Long value) is set to determine the range of pages that will be exported.

Comments

By using Visual Basic code, a programmer can create an application that generates reports with or without any user intervention. This How-To could be a primer to create an application that prints large reports at night or generates HTML pages to be displayed on the Web.

COMPLEXITY
INTERMEDIATE

9.4 How Do I...
Have Visual Basic generate a Microsoft Data Report based on criteria I choose?

Problem

How do I pass parameters to the query in which my report is based?

Technique

Using Visual Basic and the Microsoft Data Reports, build an application that passes a variable as a parameter to a query contained in a Data Environment. The database used will be the BIBLIO.MDB. The recordset will be based on an SQL statement entered into the connection.

Steps

Open and run DataProject.vbp, which displays the screen in Figure 9.13. From this screen the report can be printed to a printer or exported to a file.

Adding and configuring the Data Environment in this How-To is similar to adding one in How-To 9.2. In this How-To, the Data Connection uses a SQL statement instead of retrieving data directly from a table in the BIBLIO database.

1. Start Visual Basic and select a new Data Project. This will add a Form, Report, and Data Environment automatically to your project.

2. Double-click the DataEnvironment1 item in the Project Explorer window. This causes the Data View window to appear. Right-click on the Connection1 connection and select the Properties item from the popup menu. The dialog box in Figure 9.10 will appear. Select Microsoft Jet 3.51 OLE DB Provider. Click on the Next button and select the BIBLIO.MDB database, then click the OK button. The BIBLIO.MDB database should be in the same folder as Visual Basic.

3. Right-click on the Command folder in the Data View window and select the Add Command item from the popup menu. You will see Command1 appear under the Commands folder. Right click on the Command1 command and select Properties from the popup menu. Click the SQL Statement radio button and enter the SQL statement found in Figure 9.10 and as shown below.

```
SELECT Author, `Year Born` FROM Authors WHERE (`Year Born` = ?)
```

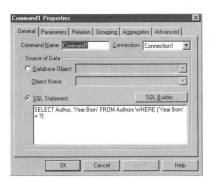

Figure 9.10. Data View window displaying SQL Statement.

4. Click on the Parameters tab and set the values of the parameter as in Figure 9.11. Then click on the OK button.

The variable will be assigned to this parameter, and the report will be generated based on the selected criteria.

5. Lay out the form as shown in Figure 9.12. Set the properties of the objects on the form as in Table 9.12.

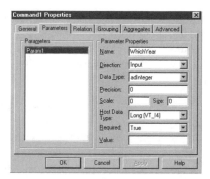

Figure 9.11. The Parameter Tab.

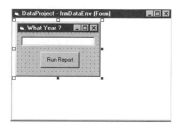

Figure 9.12. Form
frmDataEnv.frm.

Table 9.12. Objects and Properties of the frmDataEnv.frm Form.

OBJECT	PROPERTY	SETTING
Form	Name	frmDataEnv
	Caption	"What Year ?"
CommandButton	Name	cmdRunReport
Caption	"Run Report"	
TextBox	Name	txtYear

6. Add the following code in the Click event of the cmdRunReport button.

```
Private Sub cmdRunReport_Click()
    If IsNumeric(txtYear.Text) = True Then
        DataEnvironment1.Command1 txtYear.Text
        DataReport1.Show
    Else
        MsgBox "Please enter a valid year, YYYY", 64
    End If
End Sub
```

This code passes the variable from the text box to the parameter contained in Data Environment. This means the end of messy parsing and building SQL statement in code. The Data Environment is built and the parameters are defined, which makes passing variables to SQL statements as simple as using methods.

How It Works

By having the database connection based on a SQL statement with a parameter, the Visual Basic application can easily pass a value to the parameter to be used to query the database. No longer is there a need to create SQL in Visual Basic code on the fly for passing to a recordset. A database connection can be created, and a value can be passed cleanly to it, on which the recordset can be based.

Comments

A major difference between the Data Report designer and Crystal Reports is the way parameters are passed to the report engine.

Using the Data Reports, all the record selection is done by the Data Connection of the Data Environment. The report requests the data from the Data Connection, and it in turn does all the work of retrieving the proper data; the Data Report does not worry about that at all.

Crystal Reports does this in a completely different manner (as seen in How-To 9.5).

To set the criteria for Crystal Reports formula, follow these steps:

1. A formula must be defined when creating the report with the Crystal Reports' designer.

2. A Crystal Reports formula (a string) is set to the Selection Formula property of Crystal OLE control.

COMPLEXITY
BEGINNING

9.5 How do I...
Determine which records will be printed using Crystal Reports?

Problem

The recordset I need to print changes each time a report is run. How can I let the application user specify at runtime which records to print?

Technique

Many of the parameters used to print a Crystal report through a Visual Basic application can be set using the Crystal Reports custom control. In this How-To, you'll create a simple report of authors and the computer books they've written. Because our BIBLIO.MDB file contains several of the authors' birth years, you can write a Visual Basic program that enables users to set a range of birth years to be printed, set a minimum or a maximum birth year, or set no limits at all, printing all the authors.

Steps

Load and run the Visual Basic application Authors.vbp. The form shown in Figure 9.13 appears. Enter a starting or an ending year, or both, and click the Run Report button to print the report to a preview window. The BIBLIO.MDB contains more than 16,000 authors, so job this might take a little while.

Figure 9.13. The Author Birth Range selection form.

Start by creating a simple report that can be modified through Visual Basic during printing. Start the Crystal Reports program.

1. Click the New Report toolbar button or select File|New from the main menu. The New Report Gallery appears, as shown in Figure 9.14. Click the "Standard" option button.

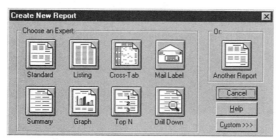

Figure 9.14. The New Report Gallery.

2. When the Create Report Expert appears, click the Data File button, and use the common dialog to select the location of your Biblio.MDB file.

3. Click the Next button to proceed to tab 2: Links. Notice that Crystal has automatically created a set of table *Smart Links* based on fields with the same names in different tables (see Figure 9.15).

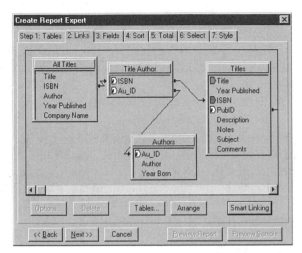

Figure 9.15. Automatic table links defined by Crystal Reports.

4. Click the Next button to proceed to tab 3: Fields. Add the fields listed in Table 9.13 to your report by double-clicking on the field name or selecting the field name and clicking Add.

Table 9.13. Computer author report tables and fields.

TABLE	FIELD
Authors	Author
Authors	Year Born
Titles	Title
Titles	Year Published

5. On tab 4: Sort, add the `Authors.Author` field as a grouping field, and specify ascending order.

6. On tab 5: Total, remove `Authors.Year Born` and `Titles.Year Published` from the Total Fields box. Add the `Titles.Title` field and specify `count` as the function in the pull-down list, as shown in Figure 9.16. Remove the checkmark next to Add Grand Totals.

7. Ignore tab 6: Select, and proceed to tab 7: Style. Enter the text `A Time for Computer Authors` as the report title.

8. Click Preview Sample to view the results. Enter **First 500** for the number of records to view. Experiment with the Report Zoom button (three different-sized squares), page navigation (upper-right), and scrollbars.

Hint: Crystal's button hints float in the status bar on the *bottom right* of the screen.

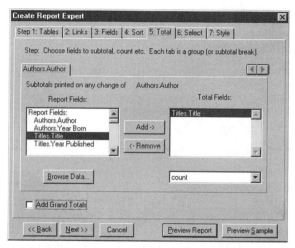

Figure 9.16. Author report total fields.

9. Click on the Design tab to return to design mode. Your report design should look like Figure 9.17. Move the **Year Born** data field from the Details band to the Group #1 Header band. Delete the **Author** field from the Details band.

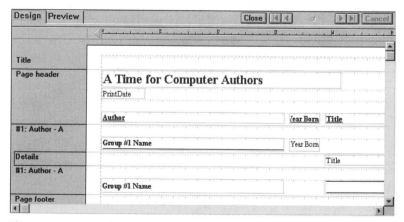

Figure 9.17. Author report design view.

10. Modify the number formats for **Year Born** and **Year Published** by right-clicking each field and choosing Change Formats. The dialog box shown in Figure 9.18 appears. Uncheck the Thousands Separator box.

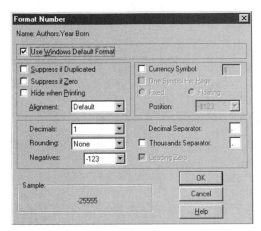

Figure 9.18. The Crystal Format
Number dialog box.

11. Save the report as Authors.rpt for use from the Author Birth Range form.

12. Create a new Standard EXE Visual Basic project in your work area. Save the default form as Authors.frm and the project as Authors.vbp.

13. From the Project Components menu, select Crystal Report Control and Microsoft Common Dialog Control 6.0, and click OK.

14. Place controls on the form as shown previously in Figure 9.13, setting the properties as shown in Table 9.14. Note that the common dialog and Crystal Report controls are invisible at runtime, so place them anywhere that is convenient.

Table 9.14. Objects and properties for Authors.frm.

OBJECT	PROPERTY	SETTING
Form	Name	frmAuthors
	Caption	"Author Birth Range"
TextBox	Name	txtEnd
TextBox	Name	txtStart
CommandButton	Name	cmdQuit
	Caption	"Quit"
CommandButton	Name	cmdReport
	Caption	"Run Report"
CommonDialog	Name	cdOpenReport
CrystalReport	Name	crptAuthors

OBJECT	PROPERTY	SETTING
Label	Name	Label2
	Caption	"End Year:"
Label	Name	Label1
	Caption	"Start Year:"

15. Select the Crystal Report control. Invoke the custom property pages for the control by clicking the Custom property in the property box and then the ellipsis button (…). The Property Pages dialog box shown in Figure 9.19 appears.

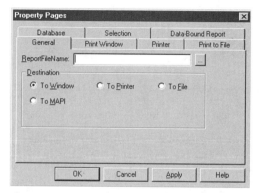

Figure 9.19. Crystal Report control property pages.

16. Be sure that the Crystal Report General properties are set as shown in Table 9.15. The ReportFileName text box is left blank because that value will be set using the common dialog control.

Table 9.15. Custom properties.

PROPERTY	SETTING
ReportFileName	" "
Destination	To Window

17. Add the following code to the form's Load event procedure. This code simply moves the form to the lower-right portion of the screen, out of the way of the report window when it appears.

```
Private Sub Form_Load()
    'Move the form to the lower-right of screen
    Me.Move Screen.Width - 1.1 * Me.Width, _
        Screen.Height - 1.25 * Me.Height
End Sub
```

18. Insert the following code in the `Click` event procedure of the `cmdReport` command button. This code performs two main functions: validating the data that has been entered in the two text boxes and setting the properties of the Crystal Report control.

Validation is performed for simple errors in the start and end years—checking that the start year is before or equal to the end year and that the years are in a reasonable range for computer book authors (being conservative: 1850 to the present!).

```
Private Sub cmdReport_Click()
    Dim strSelectCritera As String
    Dim strDbName As String
    Static strSaveDir As String

    'Check for errors in the input year boxes
    If (Val(txtStart.Text) > Val(txtEnd.Text)) And _
Val(txtEnd.Text) Then
        MsgBox "Start year must be before End year."
        Exit Sub
    End If
    If Val(txtStart.Text) And Val(txtStart.Text) < 1850 And _
        Val(txtStart.Text) > Year(Now) Then
        MsgBox "Please enter a start year in the range 1850 to " & _
Year(Now)
        Exit Sub
    End If
    If Val(txtEnd.Text) And Val(txtEnd.Text) < 1850 And _
        Val(txtEnd.Text) > Year(Now) Then
        MsgBox "Please enter an ending year in the range 1850 to " _
& Year(Now)
        Exit Sub
    End If

    'Get the file to print using Common Dialog
    cdOpenReport.InitDir = strSaveDir
    cdOpenReport.ShowOpen

    'Let's be nice and "remember" the directory for the next use
    strSaveDir = cdOpenReport.filename

    If Len(cdOpenReport.filename) Then
        'Adding the data to the control
        crptAuthors.Destination = 0 'To Window
        crptAuthors.ReportFileName = cdOpenReport.filename
        If Len(txtStart.Text) And Len(txtEnd.Text) Then
            'Year range entered
            strSelectCritera = "{Authors.Year Born} in " & _
                txtStart.Text & " to " & txtEnd.Text
        ElseIf Len(txtStart.Text) And Len(txtEnd.Text) = 0 Then
            'Only starting year selected
            strSelectCritera = "{Authors.Year Born} >= " & _
                txtStart.Text
        ElseIf Len(txtStart.Text) = 0 And Len(txtEnd.Text) Then
            strSelectCritera = "{Authors.Year Born} <= " & _
                txtEnd.Text
```

```
        Else
            'Both boxes are emtpy; don't limit range
            strSelectCritera = ""
        End If
        crptAuthors.SelectionFormula = strSelectCritera

        ' Get the Biblio.mdb database location
        strDbName = strBiblioDb()
        ' Assign the data file location for the report
        crptAuthors.DataFiles(0) = strDbName
'Run the report
        crptAuthors.Action = 1
    Else
        'User pressed Cancel in Common Dialog
        MsgBox "No report file selected."
    End If
End Sub
```

After activating a common dialog Open File window to get the name of the report to use (select AUTHORS.RPT), the program sets several properties of the Crystal Report control: `Destination`, `ReportFileName`, and `SelectionFormula`. Remember that you set a few properties in the control as well. The program checks to see that a combination of start and end were selected (all records will print if nothing was entered) and creates the selection string used to set the `SelectionFormula` property. Finally, the report is printed by setting the Crystal Report control's `Action` property to 1.

19. Add the following code to the `Click` event of the `cmdQuit` command button, to provide an exit point from the program:

```
Private Sub cmdQuit_Click()
    Unload Me
End Sub
```

How It Works

All the actions of the Crystal Reports control are controlled by the way various properties are set. A number of properties can specify exactly how the report is printed, as listed in Table 9.15 at the end of the chapter. There are additional properties, but those listed in the table are the most useful in controlling the print behavior of the report.

Setting the `Action` property of the control to 1 causes the report to print. The Crystal Reports control uses this property as a pseudo-control method. It is very important to note that printing the report does not tie up the program at the point where the `Action` property is set to 1. In most cases, after the report writer has begun, the Visual Basic program continues executing, so you can't perform any actions that are dependent on the completion of the report. On the other hand, your program can continue executing and performing other tasks while the report prints.

Crystal Reports Formula Formats

For the control properties that require formulas, such as `SelectionFormula` and `GroupSelectionFormula`, the formulas specified must be in the Crystal Reports format, which is quite different from the format of a Visual Basic statement. The formula itself is used to set the property as a Visual Basic string, so any literal strings needed in the formula must be enclosed in single quotation marks. In the case of the `Sub` procedure, `cmdReport_Click,` in this How-To, this formula is used when both a starting year and an ending year are specified:

```
"{Authors.Year Born} in " & txtStart.Text & " to " & txtEnd.Text
```

If the start year is 1940 and the end year is 1950, the actual formula sent to Crystal Reports is this:

```
"{Authors.Year Born} in 1940 to 1950"
```

The following example shows how a string in the Visual Basic variable `stateName` would be coded:

```
"{Market.State} = '" & stateName & "'"
```

Note the inclusion of the single quotation marks, because the string literal must be enclosed by single quotation marks. If California is the contents of the `stateName` variable, Crystal Reports receives this statement as this:

```
"{Market.State} = 'California'"
```

It is very important to avoid extraneous spaces in the string sent to the report. If the preceding Visual Basic string were instead set to

```
"{Market.State} = ' " & stateName & " '"
```

the following formula would be sent to the report:

```
"{Market.State} = ' California '"
```

As a result, only records with a leading space before "California" would print in the report, because of the extra space at the beginning of the criteria string.

More information about Crystal Reports formula formats can be found in the documentation for Crystal Reports.

Comments

Crystal Reports selects records differently than Microsoft Data Reports. With Crystal Reports, a String is created and assigned to the SelectionFormula properties of the Crystal Reports OLE control. If you are creating a formula to pass to the SelectionFormula property, all the error-checking must be done by the programmer. If the string is not valid, then Crystal Reports will generate a runtime error but will not tell you what part of the string is incorrect.

COMPLEXITY
ADVANCED

9.6 How do I...
Create subtotals and other calculated fields using Crystal Reports?

Problem

How do I make Crystal Reports calculate subtotals and make other calculations that I need? All of my data is in an Access .MDB file, but several of the fields I need aren't data fields at all, but are calculated from the fields in the file.

Technique

Crystal Reports supports a rich set of calculation tools and functions that enable you to make almost any type of calculation on database field data. It usually takes some work to get everything working properly, but when you are finished, you will have a powerful tool that can be used repeatedly.

In this How-To, you'll use those tools to create a bulk mail report, which can be used as the basis for completing the post office paperwork for bulk mailings. Getting the figures needed for the postage calculation involves sorting the zip codes, counting them in various groups, and checking to see which groups meet the minimum quantity requirements for the lowest postage rates.

Bulk Mailing Basics

This chapter won't be a primer on bulk mailing (the rules change constantly anyway), but here are a few basics so that the report created in this How-To will be clearer. The premise of the bulk mailing system is that if you are willing to do some of the work for the post office, you should get a break on postage. The breaks are attractive enough that a whole mailing industry has arisen around preparing mailings to qualify for those breaks.

This How-To uses a subset of all the different bulk mail categories. The categories you'll design into the report are five-digit presort, three-digit presort, state presort, and first class (the "catch-all" category). When you sort bulk mail, follow these steps:

1. Sort all the mailing pieces into groups that have 10 or more pieces going to the same first five digits of the zip code. Bundle those by the five-digit zip code, count them, and multiply the total by .191, the lowest postage cost of the categories used here. This gives you the total cost of that category of mail.

2. From the remaining pieces of mail (those that don't have at least 10 pieces per five-digit zip code), sort and extract the pieces that have at least 10 pieces going to the same first three digits of the zip code. Bundle those groups, multiply the postage by .191, and set them aside.

3. Again from the remaining pieces, select and sort all the pieces that have at least 10 pieces going to the same state. Bundle, calculate the postage using .238 per piece, and set the pieces aside.

4. Finally, gather all the remaining pieces and place first-class stamps on them. They can go with the mailing, but you aren't saving any money on them.

Before you start planning to pay your bills using bulk mail, you must have several hundred pieces mailed at the same time, and the same item must be mailed to every address. You can't even include a note in that letter, unless you include the same note to all the other people.

There is actually another category after the state level for multi-state pieces, but each additional layer complicates things at an increasing rate. So, to avoid having an entire book about a single Crystal report for bulk mailing, this How-To is limited to these categories.

Steps

The steps in this How-To show in detail how to create a bulk mail report that calculates postage and sorting order. On completion, the report, which will look as shown in Figure 9.20, will show two windows: one showing the report header and the other showing the report footer.

To open and run a report in Crystal Reports, select File|Open from the Crystal main menu, and select the BULKMAIL.RPT report. To print the report, click the Print button on the toolbar, or select File|Print from the main menu. To preview the report onscreen, click the Print Preview button on the toolbar, or select File|Print Preview from the Crystal Reports main menu. The general design details are shown in the various tables throughout this How-To. You'll go through the individual steps needed to create the bulk mail report. Figure 9.21 shows the main report elements in the Crystal Reports design window.

1. This How-To uses the MAIL.MDB database described in the introduction to this chapter. Start Crystal Reports, and start a new report by clicking the New Report toolbar button or selecting File|New from the main menu. Click on Standard when the Create New Report Gallery appears.

2. Click on Data File when the Create Report Expert appears. Use the dialog box to find the MAIL.MDB Access database file. Click Done to close the dialog box.

3. From the Fields tab, add the `Contact`, `City`, `State`, and `Zip` fields from the `MailingList` table.

4. On the Style tab, enter **Bulk Mail Calculation Report** as the title.

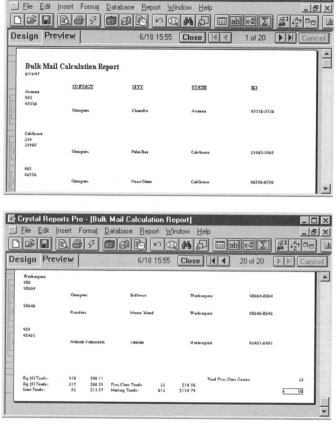

Figure 9.20. Print preview of bulk mail report.

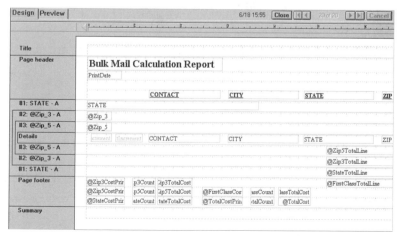

Figure 9.21. Crystal Reports design window for bulk mail reports.

5. Insert a formula field by either clicking the Insert Formula toolbar button or selecting Insert formula Field from the main menu. Name the formula **@Zip5Increment**. Be sure to leave off the @ when typing the name. Enter the following code in the Edit Formula window:

```
WhilePrintingRecords;
NumberVar Zip5Count;
Zip5Count := Zip5Count + 1;
```

The Edit Formula window should look like Figure 9.22 when you have entered the **@Zip5Increment** formula text. Click the Check button to have Crystal Reports evaluate the formula and check for errors. Click Accept when you're finished. After the Edit Formula window closes, your cursor is dragging a dotted box around the design window. Move your cursor to the Page Footer section of the screen, and click your left mouse button. This click "drops" the new field onto the report page. Don't worry about the exact location because we will hide the field later.

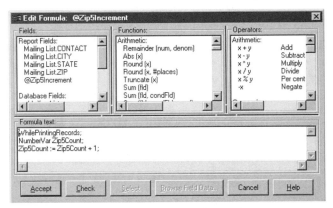

Figure 9.22. The `Zip5Increment` **formula entry.**

6. In the same way, enter the **@TotalCountIncrement** formula:

```
WhilePrintingRecords;
NumberVar Zip5Count;
Zip5Count := Zip5Count + 1;
```

7. Format the newly added fields by right-clicking each one and choosing Change Format from the popup menu. Check the Hide when printing box. (Notice the other format choices available, and try to keep the formatting options in mind when you develop your reports.)

8. Shorten each of the fields and headers by approximately one-half inch, and move all the fields to the right side of the page. Click on the Contact header, and then Ctrl-click on the contact field. Click over one of the black "ears" on the one Contact header, and shorten the field. You can also select multiple fields by choosing Edit|Select Fields from the main menu or by clicking the Select Fields toolbar button. After you make all the detail fields smaller, place them toward the right side of the detail line to leave room for section headers on the left side of the page.

9. Add a section to the report to group information by state. Select Insert|Group Section from the Crystal Reports main menu. From the first list box, select `Mailing List.STATE`. Note that the outermost group sections must be entered first, because subsequent sections will be inserted within the preceding innermost section. Make sure that the sorting field is set to ascending order, which is the default. Click OK to create the report section.

10. Insert the `STATE` field in the #1 State group by using Insert|Database Field from the main menu or the Insert Database Field toolbar button.

11. Insert the formula `@StatePrint`, which prints the total number of state addresses if they number at least 10. Place the field to the far right in the #1 State group footer band.

```
WhilePrintingRecords;
NumberVar StateCount;
NumberVar StateTotalCount;
NumberVar StateCost;
NumberVar StateUnitCost;
NumberVar FirstClassCount;
NumberVar FirstClassCost;

if StateCount >= 10 then
    StateCost := StateCost + (StateCount * StateUnitCost)
else
    FirstClassCount := FirstClassCount + StateCount;

if StateCount >= 10 then
    StateTotalCount := StateTotalCount + StateCount;

if StateCount >= 10 then
    StateCount;
```

12. Insert `@StateTotalLine`, which prints a text prompt for the total number of state addresses. Place the field just to the left of the `StatePrint` formula field.

```
WhilePrintingRecords;
NumberVar StateCount;

if StateCount >= 10 then
    "Total Count for " + {Mailing List.STATE} + ": "
else
    ""
```

13. Insert the formula `@StateReset`, which resets the `State` count to zero. The field will be hidden, so place the field anywhere in the #1 State group header band, make it a small width, and hide it by changing its format. It is usually convenient to place hidden fields to the far right. This formula is placed in the header area to ensure that the StateCount variable is reset to zero at the beginning of every state. The WhilePrintingRecords statement ensures that the Crystal Reports will calculate this formula during printing and not before reading records.

```
WhilePrintingRecords;
NumberVar StateCount;
StateCount := 0;
```

14. Format the @StateReset field to hide it while printing. Format the @StatePrint field to have zero decimal places. Check the Suppress if Zero box. The Format Number dialog box should look like Figure 9.23.

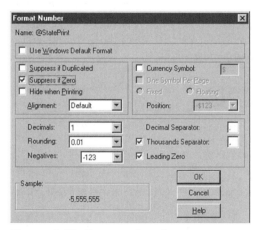

Figure 9.23. Formatting for zero decimal places.

15. Insert the formula field @Zip_3, which takes the first three digits of the zip code. For the moment, place the field on the report somewhere that is convenient. You'll move it in a moment, after creating the next group section.

```
{Mailing List.ZIP}[1 to 3]
```

16. Add the three-digit Zip group section. Select Insert|Group Section from the Crystal Reports main menu. From the first list box, select the formula @Zip_3. Make sure that the sorting field is set to ascending order, which is the default.

17. Move the @Zip_3 formula field to the far left of the #2 @Zip_3 group header band.

18. Insert the formula @Zip3Print, which prints the total number of three-digit zip code addresses if there are at least 10. Place the field to the far right of the #2 @Zip_3 group footer band.

```
WhilePrintingRecords;
NumberVar Zip3Count;
NumberVar Zip3TotalCount;
NumberVar Zip3Cost;
NumberVar Zip3UnitCost;
NumberVar StateCount;
if Zip3Count >= 10 then
    Zip3Cost := Zip3Cost + (Zip3Count * Zip3UnitCost)
else
    StateCount := StateCount + Zip3Count;
if Zip3Count >= 10 then
    Zip3TotalCount := Zip3TotalCount + Zip3Count;
if Zip3Count >= 10 then
    Zip3Count;
```

19. Insert the formula @Zip3TotalLine, which prints the text for the total number of three-digit zip addresses.

```
WhilePrintingRecords;
NumberVar Zip3Count;
if Zip3Count >= 10 then
    "Total Count for " + {Mailing LIst.ZIP}[1 to 3] + ": "
else
    " "
```

20. Insert the formula field @Zip3Reset, which resets the three-digit Zip count to zero. The field will be hidden, so place the field anywhere in the #2 @Zip_3 group section header band, and make it a minimum width. Placing hidden fields out of the way to the far right is usually most convenient.

```
WhilePrintingRecords;
NumberVar Zip3Count;
Zip3Count := 0;
```

21. Format the @Zip3Reset field to hide it while printing. Format the @Zip3Print field to have zero decimal places and to suppress if zero.

22. Insert the formula field @Zip_5, which takes the first five digits of the zip code. For the moment, place the field somewhere that is convenient on the report. You'll move it in a moment, after creating the next group section.

```
{Mailing List.ZIP}[1 to 5]
```

23. Now add the five-digit Zip group section. Select Insert|Group Section from the Crystal Reports main menu. From the first list box, select the formula @Zip_5. Make sure that the sorting field is set to ascending order, which is the default.

24. Move the @Zip_5 formula field to the far left of the #3 @Zip_5 group section header band.

25. Insert the formula @Zip5Print, which prints the total number of five-digit zip code addresses if there are at least 10. Place the field to the far right of the #3 @Zip_5 group section footer band.

```
WhilePrintingRecords;
NumberVar Zip5Count;
NumberVar Zip5TotalCount;
NumberVar Zip3Count;
NumberVar Zip5Cost;
NumberVar Zip5UnitCost;
if Zip5Count >= 10 then
    Zip5Cost := Zip5Cost + (Zip5Count * Zip5UnitCost)
else
    Zip3Count := Zip3Count + Zip5Count;
if Zip5Count >= 10 then
    Zip5TotalCount := Zip5TotalCount + Zip5Count;
if Zip5Count >= 10 then
    Zip5Count;
```

26. Insert the formula @Zip5TotalLine, which prints the text for the total number of five-digit zip addresses.

```
WhilePrintingRecords;
NumberVar Zip5Count;
if Zip5Count >= 10 then
    "Total Zip (5) Count for " + {Mailing LIst.ZIP}[1 to 5] + ": "
else
    " "
```

27. Insert the formula field @Zip5Reset, which resets the five-digit Zip count to zero. The field will be hidden, so place the field anywhere in the #3 @Zip_5 group section header band, and make it a minimum width. Placing hidden fields to the far right is usually convenient.

```
WhilePrintingRecords;
NumberVar Zip5Count;
Zip5Count := 0;
```

28. Format the @Zip5Reset field to hide it while printing. Format the @Zip5Print field to have zero decimal places and to suppress printing if zero.

29. Set the sorting order of the fields in the report by selecting Report Sort Records from the Crystal Reports main menu. The three group sections should already appear in the right Sort Fields list, because by default the order of group sections in the report are sorted by the group field. Add the zip code field by selecting that field in the Report Fields list on the left, and either double-click on that field or click the Add button. Make sure that the order setting is set to ascending, which is the default. The Record sort Order window should now appear as shown in Figure 9.24.

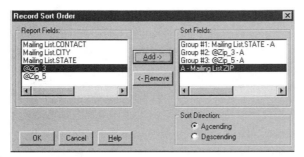

Figure 9.24. Setting the record sort order.

30. Insert the formula field `@TotalCountReset`, which sets the total count to zero at the beginning of the report. The field will be hidden, so place the field anywhere in the page header band, and make it a small width. Placing hidden fields to the far right is usually convenient. For convenience, this field also sets the postage amounts for the different classes of mail.

```
WhilePrintingRecords;
NumberVar Zip5UnitCost;
NumberVar Zip3UnitCost;
NumberVar StateUnitCost;
NumberVar FirstClassUnitCost;
Zip5UnitCost := .191;
Zip3UnitCost := .191;
StateUnitCost := .250;
FirstClassUnitCost := .320;
```

31. Next, add the fields to the page footer. This is where you'll place the various counts and total postage for the different classes of mail. Start by adding the `@FirstClassPrint` formula field, which is the total count of the "miscellaneous" category of mail. Place the field in the top line of the page footer section, as far right as possible.

```
WhilePrintingRecords;
NumberVar FirstClassCount;
NumberVar FirstClassCost;
NumberVar FirstClassUnitCost;
FirstClassCost := FirstClassCount * FirstClassUnitCost;
FirstClassCount;
```

32. Add the `@FirstClassTotalLine`, which is the heading for the total count of the "miscellaneous" category of mail. Place the field in the top line of the page footer section, just to the left of the `@FirstClassPrint` field.

```
WhilePrintingRecords;
NumberVar FirstClassCount;
"Total First Class Count: ";
```

33. Now add the various running and final total formula fields. Add the @Zip3CostPrint formula field, which is the total count label of the three-digit zip category of mail. Place the field in the top line of the page footer section, at the far left.

```
WhilePrintingRecords;
"Zip (3) Totals:"
```

34. Add the @Zip3Count formula field. This is the running count of the number of pieces of mail that qualify for three-digit zip bulk rates. Add the field just to the right of the @Zip3CostPrint field. Format the field to have zero decimal places.

```
WhilePrintingRecords;
NumberVar Zip3TotalCount;
Zip3TotalCount;
```

35. Add the @Zip3TotalCost formula field. This field prints the running cost of the three-digit zip mail. Add the field just to the right of the @Zip3Count field. The cost of each category is calculated as you go, so all you need to do here is print the total. Format the field to have a currency symbol by checking the Currency Symbol checkbox in the Format Number dialog box, shown previously in Figure 9.23.

```
WhilePrintingRecords;
NumberVar Zip3Cost;
Zip3Cost;
```

36. Add the @Zip5CostPrint formula field, which is the total count label of the five-digit zip category of mail. Place the field in the second line of the page footer section, to the far left.

```
WhilePrintingRecords;
NumberVar Zip5Cost;
"Zip (5) Totals:";
```

37. Add the @Zip5Count formula field. This is the running count of the number of pieces of mail that qualify for five-digit zip bulk rates. Add the field just to the right of the @Zip5CostPrint field. Format the field to have zero decimal places.

```
WhilePrintingRecords;
NumberVar Zip5TotalCount;
Zip5TotalCount;
```

38. Add the @Zip5TotalCost formula field. This field prints the running cost of the five-digit zip mail. Add the field just to the right of the @Zip5Count field. The cost of each category is calculated as the mail is processed, so only the total is printed here. Format the field to have a currency symbol by checking the Currency Symbol checkbox in the Format Number dialog box.

```
WhilePrintingRecords;
NumberVar Zip5Cost;
Zip5Cost;
```

39. Add the @StateCostPrint formula field, which is the total count label of the state category of mail. Place the field in the third line of the page footer section, to the far left.

```
WhilePrintingRecords;
"State Totals:";
```

40. Add the @StateCount formula field. This is the running count of the number of pieces of mail that qualify for state bulk rates. Add the field just to the right of the @StateCostPrint field. Format the field to have zero decimal places.

```
WhilePrintingRecords;
NumberVar StateTotalCount;
StateTotalCount;
```

41. Add the @StateTotalCost formula field. This field prints the running cost of the state mail. Add the field just to the right of the @StateCount field. The cost of each category is calculated as the mail is processed, so only the total is printed here. Format the field to have a currency symbol by checking the Currency Symbol checkbox in the Format Number dialog box.

```
WhilePrintingRecords;
NumberVar StateCost;
StateCost;
```

42. Add the @FirstClassCostPrint formula field, which is the total count label of the "miscellaneous" category of mail that is charged full fare. Place the field in the second line of the page footer section, to the right of the five-digit zip information.

```
WhilePrintingRecords;
"First Class Totals:";
```

43. Add the @FirstClassCount formula field. This is the running count of the number of pieces of mail that don't qualify for bulk rates. Add the field just to the right of the @FirstClassCostPrint field.

```
WhilePrintingRecords;
NumberVar FirstClassCount;
FirstClassCount;
```

44. Add the @FirstClassTotalCost formula field. This field prints the running cost of the first-class mail. Add the field just to the right of the @FirstClassCount field. The cost of each category is calculated as the mail is processed, so only the total is printed here.

```
WhilePrintingRecords;
NumberVar FirstClassCost;
FirstClassCost;
```

45. Add @TotalCostPrint formula field, which is the total count label of all the categories of mail. Place the field in the third line of the page footer section, below the first-class mail information.

```
WhilePrintingRecords;
"Mailing Totals:";
```

46. Add the @TotalCount formula field. This is the running count of the number of pieces of all the mail. Add the field just to the right of the @TotalCostPrint field.

```
WhilePrintingRecords;
NumberVar TotalCount;
TotalCount;
```

47. Add the @TotalCost formula field. This field prints the running cost of all the mail. Add the field just to the right of the @TotalCount field. The cost of each category is calculated as the mail is processed, so only the total is printed here.

```
WhilePrintingRecords;
NumberVar Zip5Cost;
NumberVar Zip3Cost;
NumberVar StateCost;
NumberVar FirstClassCost;
NumberVar TotalCost;
TotalCost := Zip5Cost + Zip3Cost + StateCost + FirstClassCost;
TotalCost;
```

48. When you are finished inserting the various fields and group sections, the design should look something like Figure 9.25. This screen shows the design window with the main menu File Options Show Field Names option checked and all the hidden fields unhidden so that they appear more clearly.

49. Select File|Print Preview to preview the report, or click on the Print Preview button in the toolbar. To print the report, select File|Print Printer in the main menu, or click on the Print toolbar button.

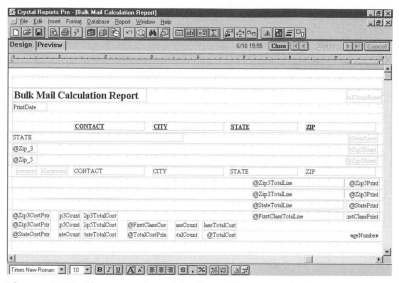

Figure 9.25. The completed bulk mail report design.

How It Works

Crystal Reports gives you all the tools you need to create complex reports. The bulk mail report created in this How-To approaches the upper limit of complexity of a typical database report.

By using formulas in Crystal Reports, you can create customized fields to present data in almost any form, including a wide variety of database formats to which you can connect with the Open Database Connectivity (ODBC) standard. See Chapter 6, "Connecting to an ODBC Server," for a discussion about ODBC.

Many formulas start with the `WhilePrintingRecords` function. Although it is probably overkill in some cases, this function forces the formula to be evaluated while records are being printed. This is the normal order of evaluation:

✔ If no database or group field is included in the formula, the formula is evaluated before the program reads database records.

✔ If a database is included in the formula, the formula is evaluated while the program reads database records.

✔ If a group field, page # field, subtotal, and so on is included in the formula, the formula is evaluated after database records are read and while the data from the records are being printed in the report.

Including `WhilePrintingRecords` ensures that formulas are evaluated as the report is being printed. Other functions, `BeforeReadingRecords` and `WhileReadingRecords`, can be used to perform formula evaluations at different times. For example, you might want to record the system time at the beginning of a report for use throughout. `WhileReadingRecords` lets the Crystal Reports formula check to make sure that you haven't included elements in the formula that need to be evaluated while printing, such as group calculations or report elements like a page number.

One important note must be made about the placement of the `@FirstClassCount` and `@FirstClassTotalCost` fields. The `@FirstClassTotalCost` field must be placed on a lower line than the `@FirstClassCount` field; otherwise, the total cost will be incorrect. Crystal Reports generally performs its calculations in a row order, so placing `@FirstClassTotalCost` on the same line to the left of `@FirstClassCount` calculates the cost before the final count is updated.

Subtotals and Other Group Calculations

Crystal Reports provides the capability to "band" the report, which means to group similar records for grouping, sorting, and calculating. Virtually any field or portion of a field can be used to group data at various levels. In this How-To, you grouped by state, five-digit zip code, and three-digit zip code. In the latter two groups, you used the first five or three digits of the zip code, using the following Crystal Reports substring array notation:

```
{database.field}[1 to 5]
```

Crystal Reports sorts records at various levels, providing options for sorting the different groups you designate, the groups themselves, and the records within the groups. This capability made it simple to put the records in the right sort order for the bulk mail groupings and to put them into the right groups. Formulas then determined whether the post office's requirement for a minimum number of mail pieces was met.

Crystal Reports provides a set of grand total functions that make it easy to provide subtotals and counts of data, as well as statistical analysis, at any group level. That way, complex formulas aren't needed in many cases. Everything in this How-To was done without any outside database processing.

Comments

Crystal formulas provide tremendous flexibility to meet your reporting needs, but they can become cumbersome, as they did in this How-To. It might make more sense to write complex reports through the use of intermediate database tables. Create the table with complex formulas in code and SQL, and then write a Crystal report to display the summarized information. The use of a private class module to build the reporting table helps make code maintenance easier.

9.7 How do I...
Control the order in which records will be printed using Crystal Reports?

Problem

I want to be able to print the same Crystal report in different sort orders, but this task is a pain—and it is time-consuming to leave my Visual Basic application to make a change to the report in the Crystal Reports design program. How can I set a report's sort order from my application?

Technique

Many of the parameters used to print a report through a Visual Basic application can be easily set using the Crystal Reports custom control. In this How-To, you'll create a list of computer book publishers. Through a Visual Basic program, you'll change the sort order of the report at runtime.

Steps

Load and run the Visual Basic application PUBLISH.VBP. Click one of the Report buttons to view the report in a preview window in zip, name, or city sort order. See Figure 9.26.

Figure 9.26. The Print Publishers' Names selection window.

Start by creating a simple report that can be modified through Visual Basic during printing. Start the Crystal Reports program.

1. Click on the New Report toolbar button, or select File|New from the main menu. The New Report Gallery appears. Click the Listing option button.

2. When the Create Report Expert appears, click the Data File button, and use the common dialog to select the location of your Biblio.MDB file.

3. On the Fields tab, add the fields listed in Table 9.15 to your report by either double-clicking on the field name or selecting the field name and clicking Add.

Table 9.15. Computer author report tables and fields.

TABLE	FIELD
Publishers	State
Publishers	Zip
Publishers	Telephone
Publishers	City
Publishers	Name

4. On the Style tab, enter the text **Computer Book Publishers** as the report title.

5. Preview the report.

6. Now add the State group section. Inserting this section keeps the records grouped by state, so the individual records are sorted by zip, name, or city within each state. Select Insert|Group Section from the Crystal Reports main menu. From the first list box, select **Publishers.State**. Make sure that the sorting option is set to ascending order, which is the default. You won't enter any other fields in this group section.

7. This is the report you'll use. Remember to save the file, calling it PUBLISH.RPT.

8. Start Visual Basic and create a new Standard EXE project in your work area. Save the default form as PUBLISH.FRM, and save the project as PUBLISH.VBP. Select Project Components from the Visual Basic main menu, and make sure that the Crystal Reports control is selected. Add the READINI.BAS file to the project to find your copy of the BIBLIO.MDB file.

9. Place controls on the form as shown in Figure 9.26, and set the properties as shown in Table 9.16. Note that the Crystal Reports control is invisible at runtime, so place it anywhere on the form that is convenient. Note also that the three report command buttons make up a control array.

Table 9.16. Objects and properties for. PUBLISH.FRM.

OBJECT	PROPERTY	SETTING
Form	Name	frmPublishers
	Caption	"Print Publishers' Names"
CommandButton	Name	cmdQuit
	Caption	"Quit"

OBJECT	PROPERTY	SETTING
CommandButton	Name	cmdReport
	Caption	"Report by Zip"
	Index	0
CommandButton	Name	cmdReport
	Caption	"Report by City"
	Index	1
CommandButton	Name	cmdReport
	Caption	"Report by Name"
	Index	2
CrystalReport	Name	crptPublishers
	ReportFileName	"D:\Waite\Chapter.11\How-to.113\Publish.rpt"
	Destination	0 'To Window

10. Add the following code to the **Click** event of the **cmdReport** command-button control array. This procedure sets the **ReportFileName** to **"PUBLISH.RPT"** in the application's path, sets the **SortFields** property of the Crystal Reports custom control to the sort order desired, and assigns the Crystal Reports print preview window title. Then it sets the **Action** property to 1 to print the report.

```
Private Sub cmdReport_Click(Index As Integer)

    Dim strDbName As String

    ' Get the Biblio.mdb database location
    strDbName = strBiblioDb()
    ' Assign the data file location for the report
    crptPublishers.DataFiles(0) = strDbName
    ' Assign the report file name
    crptPublishers.ReportFileName = App.Path & "\Publish.rpt"
    'Set up the Report control
    Select Case Index
        Case 0    'Print by Zip
            crptPublishers.SortFields(0) = "+{Publishers.Zip}"
            crptPublishers.WindowTitle = "Publishers by Zip Code"
        Case 1    'Print by City
            crptPublishers.SortFields(0) = "+{Publishers.City}"
            crptPublishers.WindowTitle = "Publishers by City"
        Case 2    'Print by Name
            crptPublishers.SortFields(0) = "+{Publishers.Name}"
            crptPublishers.WindowTitle = "Publishers by Company
Name"
    End Select
    crptPublishers.Action = 1
End Sub
```

11. Add the following code to the **Click** event of the **cmdQuit** command button, to provide an exit point from the program:

```
Private Sub cmdQuit_Click()
    Unload Me
End Sub
```

12. Add the following code to the form's **Load** event procedure. This code simply moves the form to the lower-right portion of the screen, out of the way of the report window when it appears.

```
Private Sub Form_Load()
    'Move the form to the lower right of screen
    Me.Move Screen.Width - 1.1 * Me.Width, _
        Screen.Height - 1.25 * Me.Height
End Sub
```

How It Works

This is all it takes to create a report in Crystal Reports and an application in Visual Basic that controls the sort order of the report. Entering a state group section causes the overall sort order of the report to always be by state. Then the individual publisher records are sorted within each state. Leaving out the group section would cause all records to be sorted by zip, city, or name, without regard to state.

This How-To used the properties of the Crystal Reports custom control. You had to change only a single property, **SortFields**, to set the sort order. **SortFields** is an array, so you can enter as many sort fields as you want. In fact, the following groups of Visual Basic code would also keep all the records sorted by state and then by the secondary sort order:

```
CrystalReport1.SortFields(0) = "+{Publishers.State}"
CrystalReport1.SortFields(1) = "+{Publishers.Zip}"

CrystalReport1.SortFields(0) = "+{Publishers.State}"
CrystalReport1.SortFields(1) = "+{Publishers.City}"

CrystalReport1.SortFields(0) = "+{Publishers.State}"
CrystalReport1.SortFields(1) = "+{Publishers.Name}"
```

The plus sign at the beginning of each field name means to sort the records in ascending order. Use a minus sign to sort in descending order. The use of ascending and descending sort orders for different fields can be mixed and matched in a single report as much as you like.

Crystal Reports also has the capability to sort the group sections in any order you like. This can be set either in the report itself or again through the Crystal Reports custom control using the **GroupSortFields** property in the same way as the **SortFields** property is used. So, for example, in this report you could have specified to sort the state groups in descending order, starting with Washington and progressing to Alaska at the end of the report.

Comments

This How-To has illustrated one of the most frequent changes required for a report—changing the sort order. Consider using this feature carefully on very large, frequently used reports if the underlying database does not provide a convenient index. The Crystal Reports engine is pretty good at using database indices to retrieve data in the order it is needed, but a poorly sorted report can take forever to run.

COMPLEXITY
BEGINNING

9.8 How do I...
Print labels using Crystal Reports?

Problem

I need to produce mailing labels for our marketing program. How can I use Visual Basic to automatically print the labels we need so that they are ready for use on our mailings?

Technique

This How-To uses Crystal Reports' Mailing Labels design window. Crystal Reports ships with various standard Avery label formats, so there is a pretty good chance that the exact label you need is one of the Avery formats. Even if it isn't, it is quite easy and straightforward to modify one of the formats or create your own label.

This How-To can be combined with How-To 9.6, which creates a bulk mailing report, to print labels already sorted for bulk mailing, with the postage already calculated.

Steps

The steps in this How-To show in detail how to create a shipping label. To open and run a report in Crystal Reports, select File|Open from the Crystal main menu, and select the SHIPLBL.RPT report file, as shown in Figure 9.27. To print the report, click the Print button on the toolbar, or select File|Print from the main menu. To preview the report on-screen, click the Print Preview button on the toolbar, or select File|Print Preview from the Crystal Reports main menu.

1. This How-To uses the MAIL.MDB database described in the introduction to this chapter. Start Crystal Reports, and start a new report by clicking the New Report toolbar button or selecting File|New from the main menu. Click on Mail Label when the Create New Report Gallery appears.

Figure 9.27. Crystal Reports design view for SHIPLBL.RPT.

2. Click on Data File when the Create Report Expert appears. Use the dialog box to find the MAIL.MDB Access database file. Click Done to close the dialog box.

3. From the Fields tab, add the `Contact` and `ADDR1` fields to the report.

4. Now, instead of placing the `City`, `State`, and `Zip` fields separately, you'll use a Crystal Reports formula so that all three fields appear on the same line without extra spaces. Start by clicking the Formula button on the Fields tab. Name the formula `CityStateZip`, click OK, and enter this formula:

```
TrimRight({Mailing LIst.CITY}) + ", " + TrimRight({Mailing
LIst.STATE}) _
    + " " + {Mailing LIst.ZIP}
```

The Crystal Reports `TrimRight` function removes extra spaces from text fields. Click Check to make sure that the formula is correct, and then click Accept to define the formula. Click the Add button to include `@CityStateZip` with the printed fields in the right-hand window.

5. On the Label tab, Select an Avery Shipping/Address label (Avery 5164). This label is 4 inches wide by 3.33 inches high, so there are two columns of three labels. That leaves room for both a snazzy return address and the addressee information.

Select the Avery 5164 label by scrolling down through the Choose Mailing Label Type list box. Click on that entry, and you are finished designing the label layout. The Label tab of the Create Report Expert dialog box should then look like the one shown in Figure 9.28. You can also select the print sequence, either across or down first, by making a selection in the Printing Direction box. Leave the default set at Across then Down. Click OK to insert this format into the report.

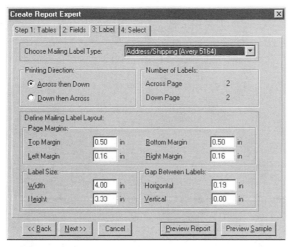

Figure 9.28. The Create Report Expert dialog box.

6. Click Preview Report to see the basic report. After reviewing the labels, switch to design view by clicking the Design tab.

7. Select the three fields on the report by Ctrl-clicking on each field in turn. Right-click and use the Change Font dialog box to increase the font size to 12 points. You can also change font attributes by using the font toolbar at the bottom of the Crystal Reports designer window. Drag the three fields down the label to just below the middle on the left side.

8. Add a graphic element in the upper-left corner. Select Insert|Picture from the main menu, or click the Insert Picture button on the toolbar. When the Choose Graphic File box appears, select a graphics file from any of the supported formats: Windows bitmap (BMP), CompuServe (GIF), PC Paintbrush (PCX), TIFF (TIF), or TARGA (TGA). EARTH.GIF, courtesy of NASA and the Galileo spacecraft program, is included on the CD-ROM that accompanies this book.

After you select the file, click OK and the image appears on the Crystal Reports design screen. Position it so that the upper-left corner of the image is at or near the upper-left corner of the label, inside the left vertical and top horizontal gray lines. Choose Format|Picture from the main menu, and format the picture 2 inches wide and 1.5 inches tall, as shown in Figure 9.29. You'll need to play with the aspect ratio (the ratio of height to width) to get it to look right. Because of different screen and printer aspect ratios, what looks right on the screen might not look right on your printer.

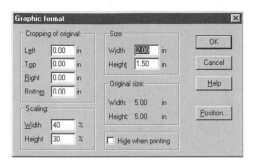

Figure 9.29. The Graphic format
dialog box.

9. Enter three text fields, and enter the text `Global Research Network`, `One Uranus Place`, and `Houston, Texas 04107`. Place these text fields in the upper-right quarter of the label next to the picture. Format the fields for a 12-point bold italic font.

10. Insert a horizontal dividing line to split the two address areas of the label, by either selecting Insert Line from the main menu or clicking on the Insert Line button on the toolbar. Place the point of the line drawing tool directly on the label's left border, with the gray vertical line near the left edge of the label. Click and hold down the left mouse button as you drag the tool to the right edge of the label. Release the mouse button. If you need to, adjust the position or length of the line just as you would with any other field. Format the line to your preferred thickness.

11. Some versions of Crystal Reports enlarge the label size on the design window when you increase the font size on a line of the report. This causes you to end up with only one or two rows of labels on the page, rather than three rows. To restore the proper label size, scroll down to the bottom of the label. Notice that the bottom section border (the line that extends into the gray area to the left of the design area) is one-half to one-fourth of an inch below the rectangle of the label. Drag the bottom section edge as far up as it will go, adjacent to the dashed gray line. In other words, the bottom edge of the label, the bottom edge of the section, and the dashed line should all be very close to one another.

12. Remember to save the file, calling it SHIPLBL.RPT.

How It Works

When you run this report, Crystal uses the label format specifications to repeat different records across and down the page. The selected graphic is automatically included on each label.

Comments

Designing labels with Crystal Reports is essentially the same as designing any other report. Crystal Reports has support for most of the labels you'll need. If none of the formats is exactly right, pick something close and change the sizes and format to fit your needs.

COMPLEXITY
BEGINNING

9.9   How do I...
Create and print form letters using Crystal Reports?

Problem

Now that I can print my mailing labels, how can I print the form letters that will go into the mailing envelopes? How can I use my database with text to prepare form letter reports?

Technique

By using a couple of formatting tricks with Crystal Reports, you can use the report writer to generate almost any type of database report you need. This How-To shows how you can use Crystal Reports to replace your word processor's mail merge, and how to use formulas and field formatting to present your data in the most attractive format.

Steps

The steps in this How-To show in detail how to create a multi-page form letter. To open and run a report in Crystal Reports, select File|Open from the Crystal main menu, and select the FORMLTR.RPT report file, as shown in Figure 9.30. To print the report, click the Print button on the toolbar, or select File|Print from the main menu. To preview the report on-screen, click the Print Preview button on the toolbar, or select File|Print Preview from the Crystal Reports main menu.

1. This How-To uses the MAIL.MDB database described in the introduction to this chapter. Start Crystal Reports, and begin a new report by clicking the New Report toolbar button or selecting File|New from the main menu. Click the Custom button when the Create New Report Gallery appears.

2. Click on Data File in the lower-right corner after the Create Report Expert expands. Use the dialog box to find the MAIL.MDB Access database file. Click Done to close the dialog box. A screen similar to that shown in Figure 9.31 appears.

Figure 9.30. Crystal Reports design view for FORMLTR.RPT.

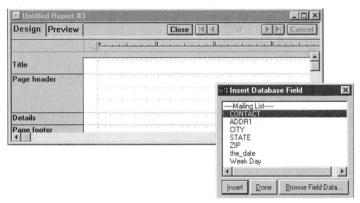

Figure 9.31. Crystal Reports blank report design view.

3. As you design the report, be sure to save your work periodically by selecting File|Save (or File|Save As, the first time) from the Crystal Reports main menu.

4. Because you don't want extra column headings for a form letter, Select File|Options from the main menu. On the Layout tab, uncheck the Insert Detail Field Titles option.

5. Start by inserting the date for the letter. Select Insert|Special Field|Print Date Field. Locate the field in the detail section, to the far left.

6. Expand the size of the detail section by dragging the bottom gray line of the section down as far as it will go. Alternatively, place the text cursor on the last line of the detail section and press Enter as many times as needed to expand the section.

7. In the Insert Database Field window, double-click on the Contact field; then enter it in the detail line, or drag it from the Insert Database Field window. Place the field on the second line after the **Date** field.

8. Repeat the last step for the **Addr1** field, placing it on the line after the **Contact** field.

9. Now, instead of placing the **City**, **State**, and **Zip** fields separately, you'll use a Crystal Reports formula so that all three fields appear on the same line without extraneous spaces. Start by clicking the Done button on the Insert Database Field window to get it out of the way. Select Insert|Formula Field from the Crystal Reports main menu, and enter the name **CityStateZip** in the Formula name text box. Click OK, and enter this formula:

```
TrimRight({Mailing LIst.CITY}) + ", " + TrimRight({Mailing _
LIst.STATE})
    + " " + {Mailing LIst.ZIP}
```

The Crystal Reports **TrimRight** function removes extra spaces from text fields. Click Check to make sure that the formula is correct; then click Accept to place the formula field on the report, on the line under the **Addr1** field.

10. You'll use another formula field for the salutation. Select Insert|Formula Field from the Crystal Reports main menu, and enter the name **Salutation** in the Formula name text box. Click OK, and enter this formula:

```
"Dear " + TrimRight({Mailing LIst.CONTACT}) + ","
```

The Contact file in the Mailing List table has generic names, such as Medical Practitioner and Occupant. You can easily modify this formula to accommodate a Salutation field, an actual name, or the ever-so-personal "Dear Sir or Madam."

11. Set the margins for the letter. Select File|Page Margins from the main menu, and enter 1.00 inch for the top and bottom margins, and 1.25 inches for the side margins. Click OK to return to the report and set the margins.

12. Now you'll enter the body of the letter. In this How-To, you'll enter the text in separate text fields for each paragraph so that you can enter fields in certain paragraphs to customize each letter. You can also enter all the text in a single text field if you don't need to customize the text, or even in a single formula field. The latter method tends to get a bit unwieldy and reduces your formatting options.

Crystal Reports has a rather serious flaw that turns what should be a single step into two steps. If you simply type each paragraph's text into the Edit Text Field window and enter the field into the report, Crystal Reports makes the field as wide as needed to fit the text. When you're using entire paragraphs, the field becomes several times the width of the report. When a Crystal Reports field extends beyond the right margin, there is no way to make the field narrower because Crystal Reports prevents you from grabbing the right edge of the field. On top of that, there is no field formatting option for field width. So you'll need to enter a text field with a single space in it and place that field on the report. You should then edit the text of the field, entering the text you actually want. Then you can size the field to the full width of the report.

Start by expanding the detail section, if necessary. Select Insert|Text Field from the main menu, or click the Insert Text button on the toolbar. Enter one or two spaces, and click OK to place the field on the report. Place the field on the second line after the salutation, at the left margin. Format the field's font for 12-point type.

13. Go back into the field to edit the text by right-clicking on the field and then selecting Edit Text Field from the popup menu, or by selecting Edit|Text Field from the main menu. Enter the following text in the Edit Text Field window. When you're finished typing, click the Accept button to insert the field on the report, and stretch the field to the full width of the report.

```
Welcome to the Slick Willy Sales Course!  I congratulate you on
your decision to take the course, because with hard work and study
the experience should greatly increase your sales skills.  I can
speak from experience—after I took the course five years ago, my
sales success went up dramatically.
```

The field remains one line long in the report design window. When you format the following fields, you'll set an option that tells Crystal Reports to expand the field vertically to show all the text.

14. Repeating the procedure in the preceding two steps, enter each of the following paragraphs in a separate text field. You'll need to enter a lot of text so that the letter is two pages long to illustrate how to format different page headers.

I am the Group Leader assigned to keep in contact with you throughout the course. I'll call you regularly to find out how you are doing, whether you need any help, answer any questions you might have, and help you get the most out of the course. I'd be happy to meet with you to discuss the course, too—sometimes face to face is the only way to work out issues. This applies not only to the class material but also to particular sales calls or prospects you might like to discuss.

Feel free to call on any of the other Group Leaders. Call on whatever resources you feel will best help you become a better salesperson.

Please come to class with the homework prepared, for two reasons. First, doing the work is the only way to learn the material. The class will be a waste of your time if you don't learn anything! Second, we will use the assignments in class the following week.

The reading assignments are important too, not just for the lessons they contain, but because you'll occasionally be called upon to give summaries of the readings.

And finally, read through the next week's lesson in the workbook, so you'll have an idea of what to expect in class and can be prepared to discuss the lessons.

The single most important way to learn the material and use it successfully is to use it during the following week. Plan ahead and incorporate it into your sales calls. Think about how to make it work for you. In fact, not everything will work for you directly, but you can almost always adapt a concept to your advantage.

Charley and all of the Group Leaders arrive at the classroom by 5:30 P.M. the night of each class, so come early if you'd like to discuss any of the material in person. Also, as I previously mentioned, any of us can meet with you during the week.

15. Now, enter a customized paragraph. Select Insert|Formula Field from the main menu, or click the Insert Formula Field button on the toolbar. Name the field CustomParagraph, and enter this formula:

```
WhilePrintingRecords;
StringVar para;
if {Mailing LIst.CONTACT} = "Medical Practioner" then
    para := "Since you live in the city of " +
    TrimRight({Mailing LIst.CITY}) +
    ", you can take advantage of our convenient MedShuttle. "
else
    if {Mailing LIst.CONTACT} = "Occupant" then
        para := "In the city of " + TrimRight({Mailing LIst.CITY}) _
        + ", there is an excellent rail system, " +
        "with a stop within walking distance of the meeting room."
    else
        para := " Please arrange your own transportation from "
        + TrimRight({Mailing List.CITY}) + ". ";

para := para +
"Please call us at 800-555-1212 if you need more information about
getting here."
```

16. Enter the final two text fields. The Sincerely yours...Group Leader lines can be in a single text field, using carriage returns at the end of each line.

```
We want you to be successful in the class and in your selling
future. Let us know if there is any way we can help you achieve
that success.

Sincerely yours,



Bill Morehours
Group Leader
```

17. Format these detail section fields as shown in Table 9.17. The most important setting is Print on Multiple Lines for all the paragraph fields so that the text fields will expand vertically to accommodate all the text in the paragraph.

Table 9.17. The detail section fields and formatting.

REPORT ELEMENT	VALUES
Detail Section	New Page After
PrintDate	Date, Default Alignment, 1 March, 1999
Mailing List.CONTACT	String, Default Alignment
Mailing List.ADDR1	String, Default Alignment
@CityStateZip	String, Default Alignment
@Salutation	String, Default Alignment
Paragraph text fields	String, Default Alignment, MultipleLines, 12 pt Font
@CustomParagraph	String, Default Alignment, MultipleLines, 12 pt Font

18. Now, enter the fields for the page header. You have two sets of fields: one for the first page of the letter with your company name and address, and another for the second page header showing the addressee, date, and page. Use a Boolean variable `FirstPage` to keep track of whether this is the first page of the letter.

Select Insert|Formula Field from the main menu, or click the Insert Formula Field button on the toolbar. Name the formula `Masthead1`, and enter the following formula. Place the field on the top line of the page header, at the left margin.

```
WhilePrintingRecords;
BooleanVar FirstPage;
if FirstPage then
    FirstPage := False
else
    FirstPage := True;
if FirstPage then
    "Slick Willy Sales and Aerobics Training";
```

19. Select Insert|Formula Field from the main menu, or click the Insert Formula Field button on the toolbar. Name the formula `Masthead2`, and enter the following formula. Place the field against the right margin on the second line of the page header.

```
WhilePrintingRecords;
BooleanVar FirstPage;
if FirstPage = True then
    "One Pennsylvania Avenue, Nashville, Tennessee 80104";
```

20. Select Insert|Formula Field from the main menu, or click the Insert Formula Field button on the toolbar. Name the formula `Masthead3`, and enter the following formula. Place the field against the right margin on the third line of the page header.

```
WhilePrintingRecords;
BooleanVar FirstPage;
if FirstPage = True then
    "(800) 555-9875";
```

21. Now, enter the second set of page header fields, for the second page of the letter. Select Insert|Formula Field from the main menu, or click the Insert Formula Field button on the toolbar. Name the formula `PageHead`, and enter the following formula. Place the field against the left margin on the second line of the page header, under @`Masthead1`.

```
WhilePrintingRecords;
BooleanVar FirstPage;
if FirstPage = False then
    {Mailing LIst.CONTACT};
```

22. Select Insert|Formula Field from the main menu, or click the Insert
Formula Field button on the toolbar. Name the formula `PageHeadDate`,
and enter the following formula. Place the field against the left margin on
the third line of the page header.

```
WhilePrintingRecords;
BooleanVar FirstPage;
if FirstPage = False then
    Today;
```

23. Select Insert|Formula Field from the main menu, or click the Insert
Formula Field button on the toolbar. Name the formula `PageHeadPage`,
and enter the following formula. Place the field against the left margin on
the third line of the page header.

```
WhilePrintingRecords;
BooleanVar FirstPage;
if FirstPage = False then
    "Page 2";
```

24. Expand the size of the page header section to be one line longer than the
bottom-most field so that both pages will have a blank line between the
page header and the start of the text (detail section).

25. Format the page header section fields as shown in Table 9.18.

Table 9.18. The page header section fields and formatting.

REPORT ELEMENT	VALUES
Header Section	Visible, New Page Before, Keep Together
@Masthead1	String, Default Alignment, 16pt Font, Bold Italic
@PageHead	String, Default Alignment
@Masthead2	String, Right Alignment, 10pt Font, Italic
@PageHeadDate	Date, Default Alignment, 1 March, 1999
@Masthead3	String, Right Alignment, 10pt Font, Italic
@PageHeadPage	String, Default Alignment

26. Run the report, making sure that the different page headers print on the
correct page.

How It Works

This How-To used a Crystal Reports Boolean variable to keep track of which
page was printing. Although Crystal Reports can print different headers and
footers on the first page of the report, it treats *all* subsequent pages as "nonfirst

page." In situations like this form letter, in which each record prints one or more full pages, keep track of where you are by using formulas.

As mentioned in the preceding set of steps, the text for the letter can be put into fields, it can come from the database in memo fields, or it can all be put into one large text field. It really depends on a few factors:

✔ If every letter will be the same, with only one or two small customizations, use the technique in this How-To, in which a text field is used for each paragraph. This technique gives you the best combination of formatting flexibility and also allows the customization.

✔ If all the text of the letters is the same, you could use one large text field to hold it all. This means all the text must be formatted the same, and you must use trial and error to get the page headers and footers to work right. Also, Crystal Reports has a problem with General Protection Faults and some video drivers, particularly when editing text fields that have some trailing space configurations.

✔ If the text in each letter changes substantially, and if much of the text is in the table you use for the report, you can use database fields in combination with text fields and formulas to control (to a low level of detail) how each letter is formatted and what information it contains.

Other than keeping track of which header to print, this form letter report is created in the same way as the other reports in this chapter. Crystal Reports formulas provide you with a great deal of flexibility in presenting database records in the most useful format.

Comments

Using Crystal Reports to print form letters probably isn't the best way to perform the task. Today's word processors make the job easy. Generally, they can use data in a wide variety of formats and provide far more formatting flexibility. But as this How-To shows, Crystal Reports has its own wide variety of flexible tools to perform many printing jobs on its own. Who was it who said, "If the only tool you have is a screwdriver, the whole world looks like a screw"?

COMPLEXITY
BEGINNING

9.10 How do I...
Print field data without extra spaces between the fields using Crystal Reports?

Problem

When I create a report, I always need to put individual fields on the report for each database field. My database splits a client's name into "Mr.," "John," and "Jones," and I'd like that name to appear as "Mr. John Jones." How can I do this in Crystal Reports?

Technique

This How-To creates a customer directory list using the string functions of Crystal Reports and operators to make the report fields appear as one field, even though the information is in several different fields. After the report is created, the functions and operators that Crystal Reports provides to manipulate strings in your database will be discussed.

Steps

The steps in this How-To show in detail how to create a customer directory in Crystal Reports. Select File|Open from the Crystal main menu, and select the CUSTDIR.RPT report file, as shown in Figure 9.32. To print the report, click the Print button on the toolbar, or select File|Print from the main menu. To preview the report on-screen, click the Print Preview button on the toolbar, or select File|Print Preview from the Crystal Reports main menu.

1. This How-To uses the CRYSTAL.MDB database described in the introduction to this chapter. Start Crystal Reports, and begin a new report by clicking the New Report toolbar button or selecting File|New from the main menu. Click the Custom button when the Create New Report Gallery appears.

2. Make sure that Detail field names are automatically inserted into the page header. Select File|Options from the main menu. On the Layout tab, check the Insert Detail Field Titles option.

3. Click on Data File in the lower-right corner after the Create Report Expert expands. Use the dialog box to find the CRYSTAL.MDB Access database file. Click Done to close the dialog box.

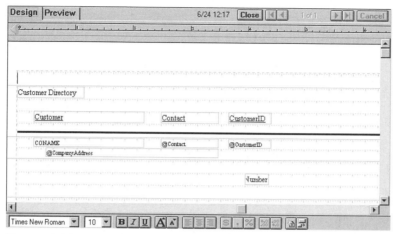

Figure 9.32. Crystal Reports design view for CUSTDIR.RPT.

4. Start by adjusting the margins for the report. Select File|Page Margins from the Crystal Reports main menu. Set the top margin to 0.5 inch and the other three margins to 1.0 inch.

5. Double-click on the CoName field and enter it in the detail line, or drag it from the Insert Database Field window. Place the field about one fourth of an inch from the left margin in the detail section.

6. Now, create an @Contact field, using the FormAddress, ContactFN, and ContactLN fields. Select Insert|Formula Field from the Crystal Reports main menu, or click the Insert Formula Field button on the toolbar. Name the field Contact, and enter this formula. Place the field to the right of the CoName field.

```
WhilePrintingRecords;
StringVar BuiltStr;

if Length({COMPANY.FORMADDRES}) > 0 then
    BuiltStr := TrimRight({COMPANY.FORMADDRES}) + " ";
BuiltStr := BuiltStr + TrimRight({COMPANY.CONTACTFN}) + " "
+ TrimRight({COMPANY.CONTACTLN});
```

7. Select Insert|Formula Field from the Crystal Reports main menu, or click the Insert Formula Field button on the toolbar. Name the field CustomerID, and enter this formula. Place the field to the right of the @Contact formula field.

```
TrimRight({COMPANY.CUSTNUM})
```

8. Enlarge the height of the detail section by one line by dragging the lower-section line down with the mouse. To expand the section using the keyboard, place the text cursor at the beginning of the last line of the section and press Enter once.

9. Select Insert|Formula Field from the Crystal Reports main menu, or click the Insert Formula Field button on the toolbar. Name the field `CompanyAddress`, and enter this formula. Place the field on the second line of the detail section, about one-half inch to the right of the left margin. Delete the field title Crystal Reports automatically generated from the Page Header section.

```
WhilePrintingRecords;
TrimRight({COMPANY.ADDRESS}) + ", " +
TrimRight({COMPANY.CITY}) + ", " +
TrimRight({COMPANY.STATE}) + " " +
{COMPANY.ZIP_POSTAL}
```

10. Format these detail section fields as shown in Table 9.19.

Table 9.19. The detail section fields and formatting.

REPORT ELEMENT	VALUES
Detail Section	Visible
@CustomerID	String, Centered Alignment
COMPANY.CONAME	String, Default Alignment
@Contact	String, Default Alignment
@CompanyAddress	String, Default Alignment, Multiple Lines

11. Insert a report heading in the page header. Select Insert|Text Field from the Crystal Reports main menu, and enter `Customer Directory`. Place the field at the upper-left corner of the report area. Wait to adjust the width of the field until you change the font size.

12. As you entered fields in the detail section, Crystal Reports should have inserted corresponding column titles in the page header section. Adjust those text fields so that they are more or less above the appropriate field. You'll need to adjust them later when everything else is finished so that they are aesthetically pleasing.

13. Expand the size of the page header by dragging the lower edge down one line of text. Select Insert|Line from the Crystal Reports main menu, or click the Insert Line button on the toolbar. Place the tip of the drawing tool at the left margin, just a bit lower than the bottom edge of the line of column headings. Drag the tool across the width of the report, and release the mouse button at the right margin. Click the line with the right mouse button, and select Change Format from the popup menu, or select Format|Line from the main menu. On the Width line, select the third box from the right, for a line width of 2.50 points. Click OK to close the Line Format window.

14. Add a page number in the page footer section. Select Insert|Special Field|Page Number.

15. Format the page header and footer section fields, as shown in Table 9.20.

Table 9.20. The page header and footer section fields and formatting.

REPORT ELEMENT	VALUES
Header Section	Visible, New Page Before, Keep Together
Text Field	Customer Directory
	String, Centered Alignment, 14pt Font, Bold Italic
Text Field	Contact
	String, Left Alignment
Text Field	Customer
	String, Left Alignment
Text Field	Customer ID
	String, Centered Alignment
Line	2.50pt Width
Footer Section	Visible, New Page After, Keep Together, Print at Page, Bottom
@PageNo	String, Right Alignment

16. This finishes the Customer Directory report. Remember to save the file, calling it CUSTDIR.RPT.

How It Works

Crystal Reports has several functions and operators for converting other data types to strings and manipulating strings to appear the way you want. Table 9.21 lists the primary functions that Crystal Reports provides for this purpose, and Table 9.22 lists the operators that are most useful.

Table 9.21. Useful Crystal Reports functions for manipulating strings.

FUNCTION	DESCRIPTION
Length(x)	Indicates the number of characters in the string, including leading and trailing spaces
LowerCase (x)	Converts all alphabetical characters in the string to lowercase
NumericText(fieldname)	Indicates whether all characters are numeric
ReplicateString(x, n)	Prints string x, n times
ToNumber (x)	Converts the string to a number
ToText (x)	Converts a number to a text string, with two decimal places
ToText (x, # places)	Converts a number to a text string, with # decimal places
TrimLeft (x)	Removes leading spaces from the string
TrimRight (x)	Removes trailing spaces from the string
UpperCase (x)	Converts all alphabetical characters in the string to uppercase

Table 9.22. Useful Crystal Reports operators for manipulating strings.

FUNCTION	DESCRIPTION
+	Concatenation
[ ]	Subscript
In	In string

Crystal Reports likes an array of characters, so you can use array notation to extract characters from a string, as shown in the following examples. Using a field called `Address`:

```
{Company.Address} = "1245 East Elm Lane"
```

Use the substring operator in the following lines to show different extractions:

```
{Company.Address}[1 to 5] equals "1245 "
{Company.Address}[6 to 200] equals "East Elm Lane"
{Company.Address}[3 to Len(TrimRight({Company.Address}))
    equals "45 East Elm Lane"
```

Here are a couple of final notes about strings in Crystal Reports:

✔ When you trim and concatenate strings, remember to add spaces where you need them. For example, you needed to include a space within the quotation marks when you concatenated the `FormAddress`, `ContactFN`, and `ContactLN` fields. Otherwise, there would have been no space between the names.

✔ In some databases, such as Paradox, it isn't necessary to use the `TrimRight` function to eliminate trailing spaces. Paradox includes a null character at the end of the string, effectively making the length of the string the number of characters without trailing spaces. It doesn't hurt to include the `TrimRight` function, because the format could change in the future or you might need to adapt the report to be used with another database.

Comments

Although Crystal provides many options for manipulating strings, consider carefully the best way to accomplish your goal, especially if the database server is able to perform your task. The use of SQL enables you to perform many string operations in the database and simplifies Crystal operations. In some cases, printing directly from Visual Basic might be the best solution.

COMPLEXITY
INTERMEDIATE

9.11 How do I...
Prevent blank lines from being printed when a field contains no data using Crystal Reports?

Problem

We use some tables that have many fields that only occasionally have data in them. How can I set up a report so that a line prints only when it has data, and still allow memo fields with lots of data to print in their entirety?

Technique

This How-To uses two of the space saving features of Crystal Reports—the Suppress Blank Lines option and Print on Multiple Lines option for text boxes. The Suppress Blank Lines option applies to an entire section, setting the report to print only lines that contain data. That means you can conserve paper and save trees that would otherwise be needed to print much longer reports containing many blank fields.

The Print on Multiple Lines option lets you place a text box on the report as a single line so that the box doesn't need to be made large enough to show the longest possible string, wasting space on the report. This option tells Crystal Reports to go ahead and expand the field vertically to fit the text if the text requires two or more lines. Otherwise, only the portion of the string that fits in the first line of the field will print on the report.

Even when using these two options, you still need to design reports intelligently. It would be easy to have a line with several fields, any of which could be blank or contain data. The line would print if *any* of the fields has data, so you need to try to put only a single field on each line or to group fields together that are likely to be blank at the same time.

This How-To uses the Publishers, Publishers Comments, and Titles tables in the BIBLIO.MDB file. Each table has several fields that are often blank mixed in with long memo fields.

Steps

The steps in this How-To show in detail how to create a fairly complex report from multiple tables and allow for missing information. To open and run a report in Crystal Reports, select File|Open from the Crystal main menu, and select the TITLES.RPT report file, as shown in Figure 9.33. To print the report, click the Print button on the toolbar, or select File|Print from the main menu. To preview the report onscreen, click the Print Preview button on the toolbar, or select File|Print Preview from the Crystal Reports main menu.

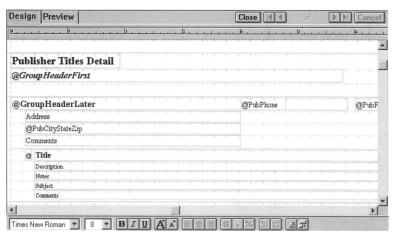

Figure 9.33. Crystal Reports design view for the publisher titles report.

1. This How-To uses the BIBLIO.MDB database described in the introduction to this chapter. Start Crystal Reports, and begin a new report by clicking the New Report toolbar button or selecting File|New from the main menu. Click the Custom button when the Create New Report Gallery appears.

2. Make sure that Detail field names are not automatically inserted into the page header section. Select File|Options from the main menu. On the Layout tab, uncheck the Insert Detail Field Titles option.

3. Click on Data File in the lower-right corner after the Create Report Expert expands. Use the dialog box to locate the BIBLIO.MDB Access database file installed with Visual Basic.

4. Start by adjusting the margins for the report. Select File|Page Margins from the Crystal Reports main menu. Set the top margin to 0.5 inch and the other three margins to 1.0 inch.

5. Add an asterisk at the beginning of the Details line to make the individual titles (Detail section) stand out more clearly to the reader of the report. Enter this as a formula field, because it is conceivable that a record in the table would not have a title but would still have other relevant information. Select Insert|Formula Field from the main menu, or click the Insert Formula Field button on the toolbar. Enter the formula name **Bullet**, and insert the following formula. Place the field about one-fourth of an inch from the left margin, and make its width just wide enough for the asterisk.

```
if Not IsNull({Titles.Title}) then
    "*"
```

6. Double-click on the `Titles.Title` field and enter it in the detail line, or drag it from the Insert Database Field window. Place the field just to the right of the Bullet field. Don't adjust the width until after the font size is set.

7. Expand the size of the detail section by dragging the lower boundary down as far as it will go. Because Crystal Reports limits the amount by which you can expand a section's size, you might need to expand the section again as you add fields.

8. Double-click on the Description field and enter it in the detail line, or drag it from the Insert Database Field window. Place the field on the line below the `Title` field, about one-fourth of an inch to the right of the Title. Drag the right border to the right margin so that the field takes up the remaining width of the report.

9. In the same way, add the `Notes`, `Subject`, and `Comments` fields to the report, adding each below the preceding field. Align the `Notes` and `Subject` fields with the `Description` field, and place the `Comments` field about one-fourth of an inch to the right. Expand all the fields so that the right edge of each field is at the right margin of the report.

10. Format these detail section fields as shown in Table 9.23. Remember to expand the `Title` field to the right margin after changing the font to bold. Also, if there are any blank lines at the bottom of the detail section, drag the lower detail section border up to the bottom of the `Comments` field. A very quick way to format for multiple lines is to double-click the field for which you want to format a string.

Table 9.23. The detail section fields and formatting.

REPORT ELEMENT	VALUES
Detail Section	Visible, Suppress Blank Lines
@Bullet	String, Default Alignment
Titles.Title	String, Default Alignment, Font 10pt Bold, Multiple Lines
Titles.Description	String, Default Alignment, Multiple Lines
Titles.Notes	String, Default Alignment, Multiple Lines
Titles.Subject	String, Default Alignment, Multiple Lines
Titles.Comments	Memo, Default Alignment, Multiple Lines

11. Now add the Company Name group section. Select Insert|Group Section from the Crystal Reports main menu. From the first list box, select `Publishers.Company Name`. Leave the sorting option set to ascending order, which is the default, and click OK to proceed.

12. The first field you'll enter in this group section is the publisher's company name. There is a problem, however, with simply adding the field to the report. Some of the publishers have a long list of books that span more than one page, whereas others have none. It would be nice to be able to reprint the company name at the beginning of the next page if that company's list of books continues from one page to the next. So you'll enter the company name as a formula, testing to see whether this is a continuation. Select Insert|Formula Field from the Crystal Reports main menu, or click the Insert Formula Field button on the toolbar. Name the formula `GroupHeaderLater`, and enter the following formula. The formula first checks to see whether the preceding company name was null, in which case the name is printed. Otherwise, the new company name is checked to see whether it is the same as the preceding name. If it isn't, you'll start a list for a new company, and print the name. If this is a continuation list, you'll print the name in a formula field that can be put in the page header.

```
If PreviousIsNull({Publishers.Company Name}) then
    {Publishers.Company Name}
else
     if Previous ({Publishers.Company Name})  {Publishers.Company
Name} then
        {Publishers.Company Name}
    else
        " "
```

13. Next, enter the publisher's phone number. There might not be a phone number in the file, and you want to label the number as the phone (and later the fax number as the fax); therefore, you should enter a formula field. That way, you won't have the word "Phone:" sitting in the report with nothing else there. Select Insert|Formula Field from the Crystal Reports main menu, or click the Insert Formula Field button on the toolbar. Name the formula `PubPhone`, and enter the following formula. Place the field to the right of the `@GroupHeadLater` field.

```
WhilePrintingRecords;
if Length({Publishers.Telephone}) > 0 then
    "Phone: " + {Publishers.Telephone}
```

14. Do the same thing for the fax number. Select Insert|Formula Field from the Crystal Reports main menu, or click the Insert Formula Field button on the toolbar. Name the formula **PubFax**, and enter the following formula. Place the field to the right of the **@PubPhone** field.

```
WhilePrintingRecords;
if Length({Publishers.Fax}) > 0 then
    "Fax: " + {Publishers.Fax}
```

15. Double-click on the **Address** field in the Insert Database Field window and enter it in the group section, or drag it from the Insert Database Field window. Place the field on the line below the **@GroupHeaderLater** field, about one-fourth of an inch to the right of that field. Drag the right border to make the width of the field the same as the **@GroupHeaderLater** field.

16. The city, state, and zip code should appear on one line, so enter them as a formula field. Select Insert|Formula Field from the Crystal Reports main menu, or click the Insert Formula Field button on the toolbar. Name the formula **PubCityStateZip**, and enter the following formula. Place the field on the line after the **Address** field in the group section header.

```
WhilePrintingRecords;
TrimRight({Publishers.City}) + ", " +
TrimRight({Publishers.State}) +
" " + {Publishers.Zip}
```

17. Double-click on the **Publisher.Comments** field in the Insert Database Field window and enter it in the group section, or drag it from the Insert Database Field window. Place the field on the line below the **@PubAddress** field, and align the left edge with that field. Drag the right edge of the field to the report's right margin.

18. Now, enter the fields in the group footer that show the number of titles the publisher has on the list. Select Insert|Text Field from the main menu, or click the Insert Text Field button on the toolbar. Enter **Title(s)** in the field, and place the field in the first group section footer line, at the far right margin. Adjust the size of the field so that it is only wide enough to show the text.

19. To insert a summary field, you must first highlight the field you want to count. Click on the **Title** field in the detail section, and then select Insert|Summary from the main menu so that the Insert Summary window appears. Select **Count** from the first list box, and leave the second list box to the default group section #1 sorting and grouping. The window should look like the one shown in Figure 9.34 just before you click OK to enter the field. Place this field so that it reaches from the left margin to the left edge of the Title(s) text box.

20. Format these group section fields as shown in Table 9.24.

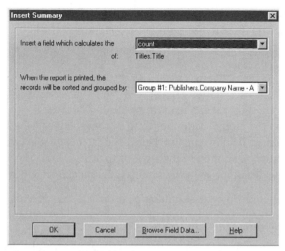

Figure 9.34. The Insert Summary window.

Table 9.24. The detail section fields and formatting.

REPORT ELEMENT	VALUES
Group header #1:	Suppress Blank Lines, Keep Section Together
@PubFax	String, Default Alignment
@PubPhone	String, Default Alignment
@GroupHeaderLater	String, Default Alignment, 12pt Font, Bold Italic, Multiple Lines
Publishers.Address	String, Default Alignment
@PubCityStateZip	String, Default Alignment
Comments	Default Alignment, Multiple Lines
Title(s)	String, Default Alignment
Group footer #1:	Suppress Blank Lines
Count of Titles.Title	Numeric, Default Alignment, Leading Minus, 0 Decimal Places, Rounding: None, Thousands Symbol: ',', Decimal Symbol: '.'

21. Now move to the page header and footer. Select Insert|Text Field from the main menu, or click the Insert Text Field button on the toolbar. Enter the text `Publisher Titles Detail`, and place the field at the upper-left corner of the page header section. Wait to widen the field until you change the font so that Crystal Reports doesn't make the field so wide that you can't adjust the right edge.

22. Now, enter a group header to print the publisher's company name if the list of titles continues from the preceding page. Select Insert|Formula Field from the main menu, or click the Insert Formula Field button on the toolbar. Name the formula `@GroupHeaderFirst`, and enter the following formula. Place the field on the third line of the page header, but don't adjust its width yet.

```
if Previous({Publishers.Company Name}) = {Publishers.Company Name} _
then
    {Publishers.Company Name} + " continued"
else
    " "
```

23. Now, enter a page number field in the page footer section. Select Insert|Formula Field from the main menu, or click the Insert Formula Field button on the toolbar. Name the formula `@PageNo`, and enter the following formula. Place the field on the third line of the page footer at the far-right edge of the line.

```
"Page " + ToText(PageNumber, 0)
```

24. Format these page header and footer fields as shown in Table 9.25.

Table 9.25. The page header and footer fields and formatting.

REPORT ELEMENT	VALUES
Text Field	Publisher Titles Detail, 14 pt Font, Bold
@GroupHeaderFirst	String, Default Alignment, 12pt Font, Bold Italic
@PageNo	String, Right Alignment

How It Works

When you run this report, you should see blank lines only where they were intentionally left in the report. Leave margins at the top and bottom of the page because some white space makes a report more easily read and understood.

Two interesting features were used to create this report. The first is the Suppress Blank Lines section formatting option. Using this option means that all you have to do is make sure that no extraneous text appears on a line that otherwise would be blank so that the line is not printed at all. The phone and fax fields were put into formulas rather than separate text fields to make some of the text fields the full (or nearly full) width of the report. This way, if any field is blank, the entire line won't print. If two or more fields could be blank on the same line, all the fields would have to be blank for the line not to print, resulting in a checkerboard effect if some fields contain data and others do not.

The other interesting feature used in this report was a summary field. Crystal Reports automatically calculates the maximum, minimum, count, and distinct count on any fields indicated. This How-To used a summary field to keep count of how many titles each publisher had on the list.

Comments

Most of this How-To has focused on making a report "pretty." Although programming style is tremendously important to how well a system works, good appearances will be remembered by anyone who sees your creations.

COMPLEXITY
INTERMEDIATE

9.12 How do I...
Create cross-tab reports with Crystal Reports?

Problem

I use a table that needs to be summarized weekly in a cross-tab style report. It is almost impossible to produce the report in Visual Basic before printing it. Can I use Crystal Reports to produce a cross-tab report from my tables?

Technique

Crystal Reports can analyze data as well as print it. One method is a cross-tab report, which summarizes two or more dimensions of data in tables. In this How-To you will create a marketing analysis report that produces a breakdown of customers by city and by the day of the week they were serviced, giving totals by weekday and by city.

Steps

The steps in this How-To show in detail how to create a cross-tab report. To open and run a report in Crystal Reports, select File|Open from the Crystal main menu, and select the MAILANAL.RPT report file, shown in Figure 9.35. To print the report, click the Print button on the toolbar, or select File|Print from the main menu. To preview the report onscreen, click the Print Preview button on the toolbar, or select File|Print Preview from the Crystal Reports main menu.

1. This How-To uses the MAIL.MDB database described in the introduction to this chapter. Start Crystal Reports, and start a new report by clicking the New Report toolbar button or selecting File|New from the main menu. Click on Cross-Tab when the Create New Report Gallery appears.

2. Click on Data File when the Create Report Expert appears. Use the dialog box to find the MAIL.MDB Access database file. Click Done to close the dialog box.

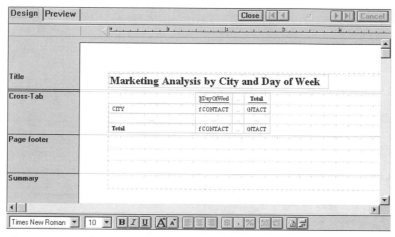

Figure 9.35. The Crystal Reports design window for marketing analysis report.

3. From the Fields tab, add the `Contact`, `City`, `State`, and `Zip` fields from the MailingList table.

4. On the Style tab, enter `Bulk Mail Calculation Report` as the title.

5. After you select the database file to use for the report, the CrossTab window appears, as shown in Figure 9.36. The layout of this window makes it easy to visualize the final report. You will need to enter the field or formula used for the rows and columns, and then enter a field or formula for the data that is contained in the body of the report. Crystal Reports will then handle all the calculations to produce the report.

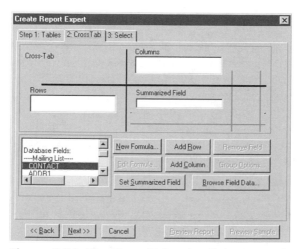

Figure 9.36. The Cross Tab tab of the Crystal Reports Create Report Expert.

6. Start by double-clicking on the Mailing List table name in the Fields list box so that the fields in the table appear. Drag the `Mailing List.CITY` field to the Rows cross-tab list. This tells Crystal Reports that a list of cities contained in the file will compose the rows of the report.

7. You will want to use the days of the week for the report columns. But first consider the space you have. There will be a column for each day of the week, plus one for the list of city names and another for the total for each city, so there will be nine columns altogether. If you don't abbreviate the days of the week, the data won't fit on a report, or part of the names will get cut off. Unfortunately, Crystal Reports can't print text vertically, so you should use a formula field to print only the first three characters of the day's name.

Click the New Formula button, and enter `DayOfWeek` as the formula name. Enter the following formula, which tells Crystal Reports to use a substring consisting of the first three characters of the name. Drag the new formula to the Columns cross-tab list.

```
{Mailing List.Week Day}[1 to 3]
```

8. The last step is to tell Crystal Reports what information will make up the body of the table. You just want to count contacts, so drag the `Contact` field to the `Summarized` field. (The default function for the summarized field is `Count`, so you won't need to make a change. You'll see in a moment how to change that.) That's all there is to designing the cross-tab layout, so click Preview Report to see the results so far.

9. All that is left to do is to reposition and resize the cross-tab fields so that the font can be read, and to enter a report title and page number. Start by setting the four margins of the report to 0.5 inch by selecting File|Page Margins from the main menu.

10. Next, move the cross-tab grid to the left so that there will be enough room on the page for all nine columns in the report. Use the mouse to drag the vertical line on the left side of the `DayOfWeek` column to the left until it is about 1 to 1.5 inches from the left margin, leaving enough room for the city names to print. The space to the right of the `Total` column will contain the day-of-the-week columns. Narrow the `Week Day` column to about three-fourths of an inch and the `Total` column to about one-half of an inch. You'll need to set the spacings by trial and error when all the report elements have been entered into the report.

11. To enter a report heading, select Insert|Text Field from the main menu, or click the Insert Text Field button on the toolbar. Enter `Marketing Analysis by City and Day of Week`, and place the field in the upper-left position in the page header. Change the font size to 14 point by using the list of font sizes in the font toolbar, and click the B in the toolbar to make the font bold.

12. Enter a page number field on the page footer. First, show the Page Footer section by right-clicking in the gray left margin of the design window and selecting Show/Hide Sections from the menu. Show the Page Footer section. Then, select Insert|Formula Field from the main menu, or click the Insert Formula Field button on the toolbar. Name the formula `PageNo`, and enter the following formula. Place the field in the lower-left portion of the page footer, against the left margin.

```
"Page " + ToText(PageNumber, 0)
```

13. If you want to make changes to the cross-tab design of the report, use the right mouse button to click in the gray area to the left of the page edge in the Cross-Tab detail section, and select Cross-Tab Layout from the popup menu. Then make any changes you want in the same Cross-Tab layout window you used to create the report. To use a summarization function other than `Count`, highlight the grid cell at the intersection of the City row and Week Day column, and select Edit|Summary Field from the main menu. Figure 9.37 shows the options available. The options for any given report depend on the type of field data selected for the `Summarization` field in the Cross-Tab layout window.

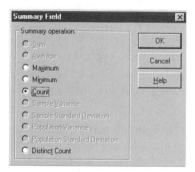

Figure 9.37. Cross-tab summarization function selections.

How It Works

Creating a cross-tab report in Crystal Reports is an almost trivial task after you understand how to present data using this type of report. The table used in this How-To consists of names, addresses, dates, and week days. By using a cross-tab report, you transform this data into a breakdown of clients by week, day, and geographic location. In fact, the hardest part of producing the report is to size and position the report elements so that all the fields show their data and everything fits on the page.

Creating the report is easy, partially because the same record selection, sorting, and formatting options are available with cross-tab reports as with other report formats used in this chapter.

Comments

One rather serious flaw of Crystal Reports is that any fields or columns that are off the right side of the report page do not print and cannot be reached in the report design window. You can change the page orientation to landscape by using File|Printer Setup, but even that orientation is not wide enough for some reports.

COMPLEXITY
INTERMEDIATE

9.13 How do I...
Generate reports using user-entered variables?

Problem

Each time I print a report, I need to change elements of the report, such as the record sort order, the heading, and the name of the person running the report. How can I run a report through a Visual Basic application and change selected elements of the report?

Technique

This How-To takes advantage of three of the properties that the Crystal Reports custom control provides to modify the conditions under which a report is printed at runtime in a Visual Basic application. It is simply a matter of setting the properties of the control.

Steps

Load and run the Visual Basic application MAILLIST.VBP. From the Print Sorted Mailing List window (see Figure 9.38), select a report type to print (City, State, or Zip) and either enter a particular value to use in selecting records or leave the field blank to include all records. Select a page number format to be used, and then click the Print Report button to preview the report.

1. Start by creating a simple report that you can modify when printing through Visual Basic (see Figure 9.39). Start Crystal Reports, and start a new report by clicking the New Report toolbar button or selecting File | New from the main menu. Click on Standard when the Create New Report Gallery appears.

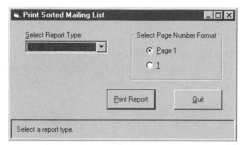

Figure 9.38. The Print Sorted Mailing List window (*frmMailList*).

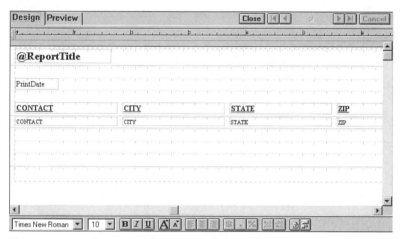

Figure 9.39. The Crystal Reports design window for a mailing list report.

2. Click on Data File when the Create Report Expert appears. Use the dialog box to find the MAIL.MDB Access database file. Click Done to close the dialog box.

3. From the Fields tab, add the Contact, City, State, Zip, and Week Day fields from the Mailing List table.

4. Preview the report and save the report file, calling it MAILLIST.RPT.

5. Because you want to be able to change the report heading from the Visual Basic application, enter the heading as a formula with a default value. That way, if the application doesn't change the title, something relatively meaningful will print. Select Insert | Text Field from the Crystal Reports main menu, or click the Insert Text Field button on the toolbar. Name the formula field `ReportTitle`, and enter this formula:

```
'Mailing List'
```

Format the title to be 14-point font, bold by using the font tool at the bottom of the Crystal Reports design window.

6. Insert the page number formula field `@PageFooter` by selecting Insert | Formula Filed from the main menu or clicking the Insert Formula Field button on the toolbar. Enter this formula:

```
"Page " + ToText(PageNumber,0)
```

7. That's all there is to the report. Note that you didn't set up any sorting at all, nor any group sections. Next, you'll see how to make changes through a Visual Basic application. Remember to save the report file, calling it MAILLIST.RPT.

8. Start Visual Basic and create a new project in your work area. Save the default form as MAILLIST.FRM, and save the project as MAILLIST.VBP. Select Project | Components from the Visual Basic main menu, and make sure that the Crystal Reports control is selected.

9. Place the controls on the form as shown in Figure 9.38, and set the properties as shown in Table 9.26. Note that the Crystal Reports control is invisible at runtime, so place it anywhere that is convenient. Note also that the three page-number-format option buttons make up a control array. The label control `lblInstruction` and text box `txtValue` have their `Visible` property set to `False`; place them in the open area below the Report Type list box. Note that you are "hard coding" the name of the report to use in the properties of the Crystal Reports control; change its location to wherever the report is located on your drive.

Table 9.26. Objects and properties for MAILLIST.FRM.

OBJECT	PROPERTY	SETTING
Form	Name	frmMailList
	Caption	"Print Sorted Mailing List"
CommandButton	Name	cmdQuit
	Caption	"&Quit"
CommandButton	Name	cmdReport
	Caption	"&Print Report"
	Default	-1 'True
TextBox	Name	txtValue
	Visible	0 'False
Frame	Name	Frame1
	Caption	"Select Page Number Format"
OptionButton	Name	optPageNoType
	Caption	"page &one"

OBJECT	PROPERTY	SETTING
OptionButton	Name	optPageNoType
	Caption	"&1"
OptionButton	Name	optPageNoType
	Caption	"&Page 1"
	Value	-1 'True
PictureBox	Name	Picture1
	Align	2 'Align Bottom
Label	Name	lblStatus
ComboBox	Name	lstReportType
	Style	2 'Dropdown List
Label	Name	Label1
	Caption	"&Select Report Type:"
Label	Name	lblInstruction
	AutoSize	-1 'True
	Visible	0 'False
CrystalReport	Name	CrystalReport1
	ReportFileName	"C:\VB\REPORT\MAILLIST.RPT"
		(Your local path)
	Destination	0 'To Print Preview Window
	SelectionFormula	" "
	GroupSelectionFormula	" "
	Connect	" "
	UserName	" "

10. Enter the following code in the **Load** event procedure of the form. This procedure initializes the **lstReportType** list box to the types of reports available and sets the default page format as "Page 1."

```
Private Sub Form_Load()
    'Load the lstReportType list box
    lstReportType.Clear
    lstReportType.AddItem "City"
    lstReportType.AddItem "State"
    lstReportType.AddItem "Zip"

    lblStatus.Caption = "Select a report type."

    'Set the report file name
    CrystalReport1.ReportFileName = App.Path & "\MAILLIST.RPT"
    'Set the initial value of the page format
    optPageNoType_Click (0)
End Sub
```

11. Add the following code to the **lstReportType Click** event procedure. When a particular report type is selected, the text of the **lblInstruction** label is set to prompt for the appropriate value, and it and the **txtValue** text box are made visible. If the text of the **lstReportType** field is empty, the **Visible** property of the two controls is set to **False**.

```
Private Sub lstReportType_Click()
    If Len(lstReportType.Text) Then
        Select Case lstReportType.Text
            Case "City"
                lblInstruction.Caption = "&Enter the City name:"
                lblStatus.Caption = _
                "Enter a city name or blank for all."
            Case "State"
                lblInstruction.Caption = "&Enter the State name:"
                lblStatus.Caption = _
                "Enter a state name or blank for all."
            Case "Zip"
                lblInstruction.Caption = "&Enter the Zip Code:"
                lblStatus.Caption = _
                "Enter a zip code or blank for all."
        End Select

        txtValue.Text = ""

        lblInstruction.Visible = True
        txtValue.Visible = True

        txtValue.SetFocus

    Else
        lblInstruction.Visible = False
        txtValue.Text = ""
        txtValue.Visible = False
    End If

End Sub
```

12. Add the following code to the **Click** event procedure of the **optPageNoType** option button control array. Recall that you entered the page number in the report footer as a formula field **@PageFooter**. You also set the default formula to print a page number in the form "page one." Any time the report is printed through the Crystal Reports program, the page number appears in the same form. This Visual Basic program simply sets the **@PageFooter** formula to whatever formula you want. In this case, one of the three formats shown in the option button group, "Page 1," "1," or "page one."

```
Private Sub optPageNoType_Click(Index As Integer)
    'Set the page number format
    Select Case Index
        Case 0
            CrystalReport1.Formulas(1) = "PageFooter= 'Page ' + _
                ToText(PageNumber, 0)"
```

```
        Case 1
                CrystalReport1.Formulas(1) = "PageFooter= _
ToText(PageNumber, 0)"
End Select

End Sub
```

13. Add the following code to the **Click** event procedure of the **cmdReport** command button. Now that the relevant properties of the report have been set, it is time to actually print it. In contrast to previous How-To's, a different technique for setting the properties is demonstrated here. They are all set at once at print time, instead of as they are changed on the form (with the exception of the page number format). Use whichever technique works best in the context of your application.

Three different types of reports can be printed using this program:

✔ For one city or all cities sorted by city and zip.

✔ For one state or all states sorted by state, city, and zip.

✔ For one zip code or all zip codes sorted by zip.

Any of the initial digits of a zip code can be entered to obtain a zip code list; the program selects all the zip codes that begin with those starting characters.

For each selected report type, this procedure first sets the **SelectionFormula**, which filters the records for the particular city, state, or zip code. If no value was entered, the records for all of that particular group are filtered. Then the formulas you built into the report are reset as appropriate. In the case of a city report, for example, the report title formula **@ReportTitle** is set to **"Mailing list for City of <city name>"** or **"Full City Mailing"** if no city name was entered. Finally, the **SortFields** array of fields for sorting are set. In each case, three elements of the array are set, clearing any elements that are not used for the particular report. If you didn't clear unused array elements, they would remain set for the next report unless explicitly overwritten.

```
Private Sub cmdReport_Click()
    Dim ZipDigits As String

    lblStatus.Caption = "Setting report options. Please wait..."
    DoEvents

    Select Case lstReportType.Text
      Case "City"
          'Set the filter and title for the report
          If Len(txtValue) Then
              CrystalReport1.SelectionFormula = _
"{Mailing LIst.CITY}= '" _
```

continued on next page

continued from previous page

```
                              & txtValue & "'"
                CrystalReport1.Formulas(0) = _
                    "ReportTitle= 'Mailing List for City of " & _
    txtValue & "'"
            Else
                CrystalReport1.SelectionFormula = ""
                CrystalReport1.Formulas(0) = _
                    "ReportTitle= 'Full City Mailing List'"
            End If

            'Set the sort order and clear second element
            CrystalReport1.SortFields(0) = "+{Mailing LIst.CITY}"
            CrystalReport1.SortFields(1) = "+{Mailing LIst.ZIP}"
            CrystalReport1.SortFields(2) = ""

        Case "State"
            'Set the filter and title for the report
            If Len(txtValue) Then
                CrystalReport1.SelectionFormula = _
                    "{Mailing LIst.STATE}= '" & txtValue & "'"
                CrystalReport1.Formulas(0) = _
                    "ReportTitle= 'Mailing List for State of " & _
    txtValue & "'"
            Else
                CrystalReport1.SelectionFormula = _
                    "{Mailing LIst.STATE}= {Mailing LIst.STATE}"
                CrystalReport1.Formulas(0) = _
                    "ReportTitle= 'Full State Mailing List'"
            End If

            'Set the sort order
            CrystalReport1.SortFields(0) = "+{Mailing LIst.STATE}"
            CrystalReport1.SortFields(1) = "+{Mailing LIst.CITY}"
            CrystalReport1.SortFields(2) = "+{Mailing LIst.ZIP}"
        Case "Zip"
            'Set the filter and title for the report
            If Len(txtValue) Then
                ZipDigits = Trim(Str(Len(txtValue)))
                CrystalReport1.SelectionFormula = _
                    "{Mailing LIst.ZIP}[1 to " _
                    & ZipDigits & "]= '" & txtValue & "'"
                CrystalReport1.Formulas(0) = _
                    "ReportTitle= 'Mailing List for Zip Code " & _
    txtValue & "'"
            Else
                CrystalReport1.SelectionFormula = _
                    "{Mailing LIst.ZIP}= {Mailing LIst.ZIP}"
                CrystalReport1.Formulas(0) = _
                    "ReportTitle= 'Full Zip Code Mailing List'"
            End If

            'Set the sort order
            CrystalReport1.SortFields(0) = "+{Mailing LIst.ZIP}"
            CrystalReport1.SortFields(1) = ""
            CrystalReport1.SortFields(2) = ""
    End Select
```

```
'Print the report
lblStatus.Caption = "Printing the report. Please wait..."
DoEvents
CrystalReport1.Action = 1

lblStatus.Caption = "Enter new selections and print or quit."
DoEvents

End Sub
```

14. Add the following code to the `Click` event of the `cmdQuit` command button to provide an exit point from the program:

```
Private Sub cmdQuit_Click()
    End
End Sub
```

How It Works

This How-To takes advantage of properties of the Crystal Reports custom control to modify the design of the report at runtime. These changes stay in effect only for the lifetime of the Crystal Reports custom control in the form, and they are not saved in the report file itself. This means that if the form with the control is unloaded, the options revert to the settings in the report until you explicitly set them again. This "stickiness" trait of the control makes it critical to set any unused formulas or fields to a null string if they aren't required for the current operation.

If you specified any particular sorting order in the report design, setting the particular formula or field through your application would replace that formula for this report. So if a report has five formula fields and you change only two, the other three fields remain as they were set in the report.

Three formula and field properties of the custom control were used in this How-To:

✔ **SelectionFormula**: There is one selection formula in each report. But because it is a Crystal Reports formula, it can be as complex as you care to make it. In this How-To, the `City`, `State`, and `Zip` fields of the report are set to the particular values entered; if no values are entered, they are set to empty strings so that all records print.

✔ **Formulas**: Any formula contained in the report file can be changed at runtime through the Crystal Reports control. In this How-To, the `@ReportTitle` and `@PageFooter` formulas were changed.

✔ **SortFields**: This property resets the record sort order of the report. A similar `GroupSortFields` property wasn't used in this program, but it can be used to reset the sorting order of any groups in the report. Both of these properties are implemented as arrays so that fields entered into the array are sorted in the order of the 0th element, 1st element, and so on.

It is important to remember that the format of any formulas set in Visual Basic must be in the Crystal Reports format of formulas, not Visual Basic's statement format. This requires placing the entire formula in "double" quotation marks and placing any literals used in the formula in "single" quotation marks. This is the reason for the convoluted form of this setting for the `Formulas(0)` property:

```
"ReportTitle= 'Mailing List for City of " & txtValue & "'"
```

Comments

This How-To has shown the power of Crystal Reports to improve your development by setting different OCX control properties. The creative combination of multiple control properties can help you deliver high-quality results to your customers.

CHAPTER 10

SECURITY AND MULTIUSER ACCESS

10

SECURITY AND MULTIUSER ACCESS

How do I...

10.1 Open a database so that others can't access it while the user is working with it?

10.2 Open a table so that others can't access it while the user is working with it?

10.3 Work with locked records?

10.4 Work with secured Microsoft Access database files?

10.5 Assign permissions for database objects?

10.6 Change ownership of database objects?

10.7 Change or delete database passwords?

10.8 Use a single password for data access for all users?

10.9 Add new users to a system database?

10.10 Define new groups in a system database?

10.11 Add users to groups and delete users from groups?

10.12 Track user activity in a database?

10.13 Create and use an encrypted database?

When multiple users have access to a database, two issues become overwhelmingly important:

✔ Ensuring that users accessing the database simultaneously do not inadvertently interfere with each other's operations.

✔ Ensuring that only authorized users have access to the data.

This chapter presents techniques for handling both of these issues. The first 3 How-To's deal with the issue of simultaneous multiuser access, and the remaining 10 How-To's show you how to use Visual Basic to implement security with the Jet database engine.

10.1 Open a Database So That Others Can't Access It While the User Is Working with It

When your application runs in a multiuser environment, the application and the Jet database engine need to work together to control access to common data. This How-To shows how to implement the most exclusive method of access to multiuser resources, locking an entire database.

10.2 Open a Table So That Others Can't Access It While the User Is Working with It

Most of the time, locking an entire database results in limited functionality of the client software that needs to access that database. In this How-To, you will learn how to gain exclusive read and write access to individual tables.

10.3 Work with Locked Records

If you decide not to lock an entire database or table for exclusive use, the Jet engine takes over and locks clusters of records one at a time as users access them. This How-To shows how to work with the Jet engine to implement record locking in your application.

10.4 Work with Secured Microsoft Access Database Files

Microsoft Access database files have a sophisticated set of security features that can be turned on simply by using password protection for the Admin account. You can implement the security features at two levels: the individual database file and the workgroup. The workgroup is defined by a system database. This How-To shows you how to work with secured Microsoft Access databases.

10.5 Assign Permissions for Database Objects

Each table and query in a Microsoft Access database file has associated with it a set of permissions for each user in the workgroup. This How-To shows you how to read and change permissions for users.

10.6 Change Ownership of Database Objects

The user who creates a table or query in a Microsoft Access database becomes its owner. With the appropriate permissions, you can change the owner of a table or query. This How-To shows you the technique to accomplish this task.

10.7 Change or Delete Database Passwords

The system administrator occasionally needs the ability to change a user's password and sometimes remove it all together. This How-To shows how to accomplish this job through Visual Basic.

10.8 Use a Single Password for Data Access for All Users

You know that you can set individual passwords for each user in a workgroup, but what if you simply want to put a password on the database itself? This How-To shows you how to do just that.

10.9 Add New Users to a System Database

A system database includes an entry for each user in the workgroup. This How-To shows you how to create new users and add them to that workgroup.

10.10 Define New Groups in a System Database

Just as you might need to add new users, you also might need to add new groups to a system database. This How-To shows you how to add new groups to a system database using Visual Basic.

10.11 Add Users to Groups and Delete Users from Groups

This How-To shows you how to add and remove any user in the system database to and from any group.

10.12 Track User Activity in a Database

It is nice to know which users did what to your database. Sometimes it would be useful if they had to sign what they did. The How-To will show you how to create an audit trail with any particular recordset to keep track of user activity in an Access database.

10.13 Create and Use an Encrypted Database

This How-To will show you how to create and convert encrypted databases so that others cannot access them with a product other than Access or Visual Basic.

COMPLEXITY
BEGINNING

10.1 How do I...

Open a database so that others can't access it while the user is working with it?

Problem

I have a database that I need to access from my application. It is important that no other user access the database while my application is running, even if he or she is using the same project that I am using. How can I ensure that only one instance of my program can access the database at a time?

Technique

Using the Microsoft Jet engine, shared data access is the default data mode. In this mode, the Jet engine takes care of page locking of the database. To open the database exclusively, you must explicitly state that this is your intention by passing a true value as the second parameter of the `OpenDatabase` method.

Steps

The Exclusive project is designed to illustrate the two distinct data modes used when opening a database, exclusive and shared. Open the Exclusive.vbp project and compile it to an EXE file. Invoke this executable twice to create two instances of the application. You should see the USER form opened twice, as shown in Figure 10.1. To open the database exclusively, click the Open Exclusive command button, or to open the database using the shared data mode, click the Open Shared command button. Notice the combinations permitted when opening the database with the two instances of the Exclusive project. You can open the database exclusively only if no other user has the database open at all, and you can open the database shared only if no other user has the database opened exclusively. To close the database, click the Close Database command button.

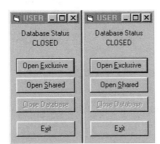

Figure 10.1. Two instances of the Exclusive project.

1. Create a new project and call it Exclusive.vbp. Change the properties of the default form, `Form1`, to those listed in Table 10.1, and save it as frmExclusive.frm.

Table 10.1. Objects and properties for the Exclusive project.

OBJECT	PROPERTY	SETTING
Form	Name	frmExclusive
	Caption	USER
Command button	Name	cmdOpenExclusive
	Caption	Open &Exclusive
Command button	Name	cmdOpenShared
	Caption	Open &Shared
Command button	Name	cmdCloseDatabase
	Caption	&Close Database
Command button	Name	cmdExit
	Caption	E&xit
	Cancel	-1 'True
	Default	-1 'True
Label	Name	lblDBStatusLabel
	Caption	Database Status
Label	Name	lblDBStatus
	Caption	" "

2. Enter the following form-level variable and constant declarations to be used throughout the project:

```
Option Explicit

' this is the database object variable used throughout this
' project
Private db As Database

' these are private constants used to indicate the desired state
' of the database when opened
Private Const OPEN_EXCLUSIVE = True
Private Const OPEN_SHARED = False
```

3. Now enter the code to initialize the frmExclusive form to display the database as closed by calling the cmdCloseDatabase_Click event.

```
Private Sub Form_Initialize()

    ' when the form is initialized, ensure that the proper states
    ' of the command buttons and labels are set by calling the
    ' Close Database command button's click event
    cmdCloseDatabase_Click

End Sub
```

4. Code both the `cmdOpenExclusive_Click` and the `cmdOpenShared_Click` events with a call to the `OpenDB` procedure, passing the appropriate form-level constant to indicate the data mode desired by the user.

```
Private Sub cmdOpenExclusive_Click()

    ' call the OpenDB procedure of this project, passing the
    ' OPEN_EXCLUSIVE constant (this constant holds the value of
    ' TRUE)
    OpenDB OPEN_EXCLUSIVE

End Sub

Private Sub cmdOpenShared_Click()

    ' call the OpenDB procedure of this project, passing the
    ' OPEN_SHARED constant (this constant holds the value of
    ' FALSE)
    OpenDB OPEN_SHARED

End Sub
```

5. When closing the database, set the **db** object variable to nothing, and set the command button **Enabled** properties to the correct state, allowing the user only to open the database, because it is now closed. Here is the code for the Close Database command button:

```
Private Sub cmdCloseDatabase_Click()

    ' set the database object variable to nothing, which is
    ' the equivalent of closing the database
    Set db = Nothing

    ' change the label that displays the database status to closed
    lblDBStatus = "CLOSED"

    ' only allow the user to open the database and not close it
    cmdOpenExclusive.Enabled = True
    cmdOpenShared.Enabled = True
    cmdCloseDatabase.Enabled = False

End Sub
```

6. Enter the code for the Exit command button. This code first calls the Close Database click event of the command button to set the database object to nothing, unloading the project afterward to terminate the project.

```
Private Sub cmdExit_Click()

    ' call the close database command button click event to ensure
    ' that the database is closed before we terminate the project
    cmdCloseDatabase_Click

    ' end the application by calling Unload
```

```
        Unload Me

    End Sub
```

7. Next, enter the code for the OpenDB procedure used to open the database for either exclusive or shared mode. If the user decides to open the database exclusively, the OPEN_EXCLUSIVE constant is passed to this procedure and onto the OpenDatabase method of the database object. This constant holds the value of True and opens the database exclusively. The other choice, OPEN_SHARED, passes a value of False to the OpenDatabase method.

```
Private Sub OpenDB(bDataMode As Boolean)

' if any error is encountered, call the code specified by the
' ERR_OpenDB label
On Error GoTo ERR_OpenDB:

    Dim sDBName As String

    ' on slower machines, this may take a moment; therefore,
    ' we will change the mouse pointer to an hourglass to indicate
    ' that the project is still working
    Screen.MousePointer = vbHourglass

    ' retrieve the database name and path from the ReadINI module
    sDBName = DBPath

    ' open the database using the desired data mode specified by
    ' the user if bDataMode = OPEN_EXCLUSIVE then the value of
    ' bDataMode is TRUE, telling the OpenDatabase method to open
    ' the database exclusively; otherwise, OPEN_SHARED = FALSE,
    ' opening the database in a shared mode
    Set db = dbengine.Workspaces(0).OpenDatabase(sDBName,
bDataMode)

    ' if we are at this point, then the database was opened
    ' succesfully, now display the appropriate label depending on
    ' the data mode selected
    Select Case bDataMode

        Case OPEN_EXCLUSIVE:
            lblDBStatus = "OPEN: EXCLUSIVE"

        Case OPEN_SHARED:
            lblDBStatus = "OPEN: SHARED"

    End Select
```

continued on next page

continued from previous page

```
                         ' only allow the user to close that database, and do not allow
                         ' opening of the database again
                         cmdOpenExclusive.Enabled = False
                         cmdOpenShared.Enabled = False
                         cmdCloseDatabase.Enabled = True

                         ' set the mouse pointer to the default icon
                         Screen.MousePointer = vbDefault

                 Exit Sub

                 ERR_OpenDB:

                         ' set the mouse pointer to the default icon
                         Screen.MousePointer = vbDefault

                         ' call the DatabaseError procedure, passing the Err object,
                         ' which describes the error that has just occurred
                         DatabaseError Err

                 End Sub
```

8. To finish this project, enter the code for responding to errors opening the database. This code is as follows:

```
Private Sub DatabaseError(oErr As ErrObject)

        Dim sMessage As String

        ' these are the constant values used to represent the two
        ' errors that we are going to trap in this code
        Const DB_OPEN = 3356     ' database already open in shared mode
        Const DB_IN_USE = 3045   ' database already open exclusively

        With oErr

                ' select the appropriate code depending upon the error
                ' number
                Select Case .Number

                        ' attempted to open the database exclusively, but it
                        ' is already open in shared mode
                        Case DB_OPEN:
                            sMessage = _
                            "You cannot open the database exclusively " _
                            & "because it is already opened by another user."

                        ' attempted to open the database either exclusively or
                        ' shared, but it is opened exclusively by another user
```

```
            Case DB_IN_USE:
                sMessage = _
                    "You cannot open the database because it is " _
                            & "opened exclusively by another user."

            ' unexpected error: display the error number and
            ' description for the user
            Case Else
                sMessage = "Error #" & .Number & ": " &
                            .Description

        End Select

    End With

    ' display the message for the user
    MsgBox sMessage, vbExclamation, "DATABASE ERROR"

    ' ensure that the database is closed because of the error, and
    ' properly set all the command button enabled properties as
    ' well as the status label
    cmdCloseDatabase_Click

End Sub
```

How It Works

When you open an Access database exclusively in one instance of the Exclusive project, assuming that the database is not opened by any other project, the Jet engine indicates that no other application can open the database by putting codes in the LDB file named after your database. In the case of this project, you use the ORDERS.MDB database. The file named ORDERS.LDB indicates how the database is opened and by whom.

Comments

This project uses an all-or-nothing concept when locking the data from other users. Either the data can be accessed by others or it cannot. Sometimes this is too general of a technique to use when developing a multiuser application. In How-To 10.2, you will use table locking to allow more flexible manageability of your database.

COMPLEXITY
BEGINNING

10.2 How do I...
Open a table so that others can't access it while the user is working with it?

Problem

My application accesses shared data through the Jet engine. The default record-locking scheme that Jet uses works great for many instances. I need advanced record locking on particular tables so that others cannot access the entire table when my application does. How do I open a table with exclusive access?

Technique

By default, the recordset that you add will have shared rights to other users unless you explicitly request otherwise. You can indicate what kind of permissions you will grant other users when accessing that table.

The syntax for the `OpenRecordset` method is

```
Set rs = db.OpenRecordset(TableName, dbOpenTable, Options)
```

where `rs` is your recordset object variable, `db` is your database object variable, and *TableName* is the name of a valid table in the `db` object. The second parameter, `dbOpenTable`, is the type of recordset to be used. This parameter can be replaced with `dbOpenDynaset`, `dbOpenSnapshot`, `dbOpenDynamic`, or `dbOpenForwardOnly`. Table 10.2 lists the valid options.

Table 10.2. Options for the *OpenRecordset* method.

OPTION	DESCRIPTION
dbDenyRead	Denies read permissions to other users
dbDenyWrite	Denies write permissions to other users

By using the `dbDenyRead` and `dbDenyWrite` options, you can open a table exclusively or with partial sharing rights to other users.

Steps

Open and compile the TableLocker.vbp project. Create two instances of the TableLocker project by double-clicking its icon twice from Windows Explorer. Move one form down to reveal the other (they start up in the same position). You should see the forms shown in Figure 10.2.

Figure 10.2. Two instances of the
TableLocker project.

You can set the permissions assigned to opening the table by using the two
check boxes on the form and then pressing the Open Table command button.
You can add records and then close the table by pressing the appropriate
command buttons.

Experiment with opening the table with the two instances of the project. If
you open the table with exclusive rights (deny read access) with one instance
and then attempt to open it with the other in any way, you will be unsuccessful.
When this happens, the application asks whether you want to open the table
with Read Only access. If this is possible, the table will open but deny you the
right to add records.

1. Create a new project and save it as TableLocker.vbp. Edit **Form1** to include
the objects and properties listed in Table 10.3, and save it as
frmTableLocker.vbp.

Table 10.3. Objects and properties for the Exclusive project.

OBJECT	PROPERTY	SETTING
Form	Name	frmTableLocker
	Caption	USER
Frame	Name	fraTableSharing
Check box	Name	chkDenyRead
	Caption	Deny others Read Access to Table
Check box	Name	chkDenyWrite
	Caption	Deny others Write Access to Table
Command button	Name	cmdOpenTable
	Caption	&Open Table

continued on next page

continued from previous page

OBJECT	PROPERTY	SETTING
Command button	Name	cmdAddRecord
	Caption	&Add Record
Command button	Name	cmdCloseTable
	Caption	&Close Table
Command button	Name	cmdExit
	Caption	E&xit

2. Enter the following declarations for the form-level database and recordset object variables:

```
Option Explicit

' form-level object variables used to access the database and
' recordset objects used throughout this project
Private db As Database
Private rs As Recordset
```

3. Now enter the code to initialize the form to indicate that the table is closed:

```
Private Sub Form_Initialize()

    ' initialize the form controls to show that the table is
    ' closed upon startup of project
    cmdCloseTable_Click

End Sub
```

4. Open the database in the **Form_Load** event as shown next. The **DBPath** function is from the ReadINI module included with the distribution CD-ROM to indicate where the **ORDERS** database is located on your machine.

```
Private Sub Form_Load()

    Dim sDBName As String

    ' obtain the name and path of the table to be used in this
    ' project from the ReadINI module
    sDBName = DBPath

    ' open the database
    ' by not specifying an exclusive mode, the database is opened
    ' in shared mode
    Set db = DBEngine.Workspaces(0).OpenDatabase(sDBName)

End Sub
```

5. By placing the following code in the `Form_Unload` event, you can ensure
that it runs even if the user does not terminate the application by using the
Exit command button:

```
Private Sub Form_Unload(Cancel As Integer)

    ' close the database and recordset objects by setting them to
    ' nothing
    Set db = Nothing
    Set rs = Nothing

End Sub
```

6. Now enter the `cmdOpenTable_Click` event code as shown next. This event
opens the table using the check box values of the `frmTableLocker` form to
determine the permissions assigned to the opening of the table. If an error
occurs, the application calls the `TableError` routine to gracefully handle it
and might try opening the table again.

```
Private Sub cmdOpenTable_Click()

' if an error occurs, call the ERR_cmdOpenTable_Click code located
' at the end of this procedure
On Error GoTo ERR_cmdOpenTable_Click:

    ' local variable used to store permissions
    Dim nAccessValue As Integer

    ' set the mouse pointer to an hourglass because on some
    ' machines, this could take a few seconds
    Screen.MousePointer = vbHourglass

    ' default the permissions to nothing (all access okay)
    nAccessValue = 0

    ' apply the proper permissions that were restricted by the
    ' user
    If (chkDenyRead) Then nAccessValue = nAccessValue + dbDenyRead
    If (chkDenyWrite) Then nAccessValue = nAccessValue + _
        dbDenyWrite

    ' open the table using the permission variable
    Set rs = db.OpenRecordset("Customers", dbOpenTable, _
    nAccessValue)

    ' set the index to the PrimaryKey used later in GetPrimaryKey
    rs.Index = "PrimaryKey"

    ' release any locks that may be on the table, and process any
    ' data that is waiting to be completed
    DBEngine.Idle dbRefreshCache

    ' allow the correct status of the enabled property of the
```

continued on next page

continued from previous page

```
    ' frmTableLocker controls
    cmdOpenTable.Enabled = False
    chkDenyRead.Enabled = False
    chkDenyWrite.Enabled = False
    cmdAddRecord.Enabled = True
    cmdCloseTable.Enabled = True

    ' set the mousepointer back to its default because we are now
    ' finished
    Screen.MousePointer = vbDefault

Exit Sub

ERR_cmdOpenTable_Click:

    ' an error has occurred; therefore, change the mouse pointer
    ' back to an hourglass
    Screen.MousePointer = vbDefault

    ' call the TableError function, passing the error object
    ' describing the error that has occurred
    ' if a value of True is returned, we are going to try opening
    ' the table again with read-only access
    If (TableError(Err)) Then
        chkDenyRead = False
        chkDenyWrite = False
        nAccessValue = dbReadOnly
        Resume
    End If

End Sub
```

7. When the user clicks the Add Record command button, a dummy record is added to the table using a unique primary key that is obtained by calling the **GetUniqueKey** function. Again, if there is an error, the **TableError** routine is called to handle it. The code for the **cmdAddRecord_Click** event is as follows:

```
Private Sub cmdAddRecord_Click()

' if an error occurs, call the ERR_cmdAddRecord code located at
' the end of this procedure
On Error GoTo ERR_cmdAddRecord:

    Dim lPrimaryKey As Long
    Dim sMessage As String

    ' used to populate fields in Customer table
    ' this is necessary because most of the fields belong to
```

```
    ' indexes, making them required fields
    Const DUMMY_INFO = "<>"

    ' retrieve a unique key from the GetPrimaryKey routine
    lPrimaryKey = GetPrimaryKey

    With rs

        ' add a new record
        .AddNew

        ' fill in the required fields
        .Fields("Customer Number") = lPrimaryKey
        .Fields("Customer Name") = DUMMY_INFO
        .Fields("Street Address") = DUMMY_INFO
        .Fields("City") = DUMMY_INFO
        .Fields("State") = DUMMY_INFO
        .Fields("Zip Code") = DUMMY_INFO

        ' make saves (if an error will occur, it will be here)
        .Update

    End With

    ' if we got this far, add new record was successfull
    sMessage = "Record added successfully!"
    MsgBox sMessage, vbInformation, "ADD RECORD"

Exit Sub

ERR_cmdAddRecord:

    ' an error has occurred; call the TableError function and pass
    ' the Err object describing the error
    TableError Err

End Sub
```

8. Enter the following **cmdCloseTable_Click** event code. This code sets the
recordset object variable to nothing (the equivalent of closing the
recordset) and sets the **Enabled** property of the controls on the form to
their appropriate state.

```
Private Sub cmdCloseTable_Click()

    ' set the rs object variable to nothing, closing the recordset
    Set rs = Nothing

    ' properly display the controls on the frmTableLocker form
    chkDenyRead.Enabled = True
    chkDenyWrite.Enabled = True
    cmdOpenTable.Enabled = True
    cmdAddRecord.Enabled = False
    cmdCloseTable.Enabled = False

End Sub
```

9. Enter the `cmdExit_Click` code shown next to end the project. The `Unload Me` code will invoke the `Form_Unload` event where the database and recordset object variables will be set to nothing.

```
Private Sub cmdExit_Click()

    ' using Unload Me will call Form_Unload where the form-level
    ' database and recordset object variables will be set to
    ' nothing
    Unload Me

End Sub
```

10. The `GetPrimaryKey` function returns a unique key based on the `Customer Name` field of the Customers table you are accessing:

```
Private Function GetPrimaryKey()

    ' return a unique primary key based on the Customer Number
    ' field
    With rs

        ' if there are records in the table already, find the last
        ' one and add one to the Customer Number as a unique
        ' Primary Key; otherwise, there are no records in the
        ' table so return 1 for the first new record to be added
        If (Not (.EOF And .BOF)) Then

            .MoveLast

            GetPrimaryKey = .Fields("Customer Number") + 1

        Else

            GetPrimaryKey = 1

        End If

    End With

End Function
```

11. The `TableError` function contains the code that handles all the input and output errors that occur within this application. If users cannot open the table with the permissions that were requested, they are asked whether they want to try again with read-only access. Enter the code for the `TableError` function:

```
Private Function TableError(oErr As ErrObject) As Boolean

    Dim sMessage As String
```

```
Dim nResponse As Integer

' these are the constant values used to represent the four
' errors that we are going to trap in this code

Const TB_OPEN = 3262     ' database already open in shared mode
Const TB_IN_USE = 3261   ' database already open exclusively
Const TB_READ_ONLY = 3027    ' can't save, read only
Const TB_LOCKED = 3186       ' table is locked, cannot update

' default the return value of the function to false, which
' will indicate that we do not want to try again
TableError = False

With oErr

    ' select the appropriate code depending upon the error
    ' number
    Select Case .Number

        ' the table couldn't be opened using the permissions
        ' requested; ask the user if they would like to open it
        ' in read-only mode
        Case TB_OPEN, TB_IN_USE:

            sMessage = "There was an error opening the table. " _
                    & "Would you like to try read only mode?"

            nResponse = MsgBox(sMessage, vbYesNo + vbQuestion, _
            "ERROR")

                If (nResponse = vbYes) Then TableError = True

                Exit Function

        ' the table is read only and you cannot add a new
        ' record
        Case TB_READ_ONLY:

            sMessage = "You cannot add a record because the " _
                    & "database is currently opened with read " _
                    & "only status."

        ' the table is locked and you cannot add a new record
        Case TB_LOCKED:

            sMessage = "You cannot add a record because the " _
```

continued on next page

continued from previous page

```
                                        & "database is currently locked by
                                        & "another user."

                        ' unexpected error: display the error number and
                        ' description for the user
                        Case Else

                            sMessage = "Error #" & .Number & ": " & _
                            .Description

                End Select

            End With

            ' display the message for the user
            MsgBox sMessage, vbExclamation, "TABLE ERROR"

            ' ensure that the database is closed because of the error, and
            ' properly set all the command button enabled properties, as
            ' well as the status label
            cmdCloseTable_Click

        End Function
```

How It Works

This project uses the **dbDenyRead** and **dbDenyWrite** options when opening the Customer table to deny rights to other users when they attempt to open the table. If another user attempts to open the table that is already opened with **dbDenyRead**, it is considered opened exclusively. If the table is already opened with the **dbDenyWrite** option, the user can only open the table with a **dbReadOnly** option, not allowing new records or editing of ones that already exist.

Comments

There is another parameter you can specify when you open a table; this is called the **LockEdits** parameter. Table 10.4 describes the options you can use for the **LockEdits** parameter.

Table 10.4. The *LockEdits* parameter.

OPTION	DESCRIPTION
dbPessimistic	Page is locked at Edit method.
dbOptimistic	Page is locked at Update method.

dbPessimistic is the default value for this fourth parameter of the OpenRecordset method and indicates that the page is to be locked as soon as the Edit method is encountered. The dbOptimistic option works a little differently—it waits until the Update method is called to lock the page. The main reason for using the dbOptimistic option is to allow less time for the page to be locked. How-To 10.3 demonstrates these options.

COMPLEXITY
INTERMEDIATE

10.3 How do I...
Work with locked records?

Problem

My application is being designed to allow multiple users to access the same data. It is inevitable that sooner or later two users will attempt to edit the same data. How do I write proper record-locking code to guard my application from situations like this and to ensure database integrity?

Technique

As touched on in How To 10.2, you can set the way in which a record is locked by accessing the LockEdits property of the recordset. In doing this, you can set the value of this property to either pessimistic or optimistic. The default value for LockEdits is True, which corresponds to pessimistic. By setting this property to False, you obtain optimistic record locking.

Pessimistic record locking locks the record during the time indicated by the call to the Edit method and the call to the Update method of a recordset. Optimistic record locking locks the record during the call to the Update method.

With the potential danger of database corruption with multiuser access, you can expect to encounter numerous trappable runtime errors with record locking. The errors are listed here:

✔ Error 3167: Record is deleted.

✔ Error 3197: Record has changed; operation halted.

✔ Error 3260: Record currently locked by another user, cannot update.

It has become an acceptable programming technique to trap these errors and respond to them at such times. It is common to expect some or all of these errors when running a multiuser application, as you will see in this project.

Steps

Open the `RecordLocker` project and compile it. Open two instances of the project and run them simultaneously. You should see the forms shown in Figure 10.3. With one instance, open a record for editing. With the other instance, select pessimistic record locking and edit the record. You will receive an error because the application is attempting to lock the record from the time the `Edit` method is called. Try changing the record locking to optimistic and edit the record. You will be able to get to this point; however, if you now click the Update button, you will receive an error. This is because optimistic record locking attempts to lock the record when the `Update` method is called.

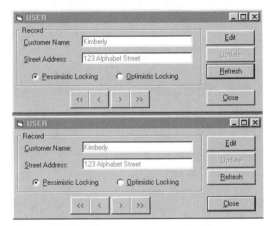

Figure 10.3. Two instances of the RecordLocker project.

The user can navigate the recordset by using the four buttons below the option buttons. The user can also refresh the current record by clicking the Refresh button. This step is useful to ensure that you have the most up-to-date information for the current record in case another user has already changed it.

1. Create a new project and call it RecordLocker.vbp. Create the objects and change the properties as listed in Table 10.5. Save the form as frmRecordlocker.frm. Note that the `cmdMove` command buttons are a control array.

Table 10.5. Objects and properties for the Exclusive project.

OBJECT	PROPERTY	SETTING
Form	Name	frmRecordLocker
	Caption	USER

OBJECT	PROPERTY	SETTING
Frame	Name	fraRecord
Text box	Name	txtCustomerName
Text box	Name	txtStreetAddress
Option button	Name	optPessimisticLocking
	Caption	Pessimistic Record Locking
Option button	Name	optOptimisticLocking
	Caption	Optimistic Record Locking
Command button	Name	cmdEdit
	Caption	&Edit
Command button	Name	cmdUpdate
	Caption	&Update
Command button	Name	cmdRefresh
	Caption	&Refresh
Command button	Name	cmdClose
	Caption	&Close
Command button	Name	cmdMove
	Caption	<<
	Index	0
Command button	Name	cmdMove
	Caption	<
	Index	1
Command button	Name	cmdMove
	Caption	>
	Index	2
Command button	Name	cmdMove
	Caption	>>
	Index	3
Label	Name	lblCustomerName
	Caption	&Customer Name
Label	Name	lblStreetAddress
	Caption	&Street Address

2. Enter the following form-level variables in the declarations section of your project. The first two variables are used to hold the database and recordset objects. The **m_bEditMode** variable is used to indicate whether the project is in edit mode. The last two declarations are constant values used to determine whether the **LockEdits** property of the recordset is set to pessimistic or optimistic.

```
Option Explicit

' form-level object variables that hold the database and recordset
' objects used throughout this project
Private db As Database
Private rs As Recordset

' form-level boolean variable used to indicate when the current
' record is in edit mode
Private m_bEditMode As Boolean

' form-level constant declarations used to indicate pessimistic or
' optimistic record locking
Private Const PESSIMISTIC = True
Private Const OPTIMISTIC = False
```

3. Now enter the code to open the database and recordset in the **Form_Load** event. This code also determines whether the recordset is empty (ending the application if so) and, if not, displays the first record.

```
Private Sub Form_Load()

    Dim sDBName As String

    ' get the path and name of the database used in this project
    ' from the ReadINI module
    sDBName = DBPath

    ' open the database and recordset
    Set db = DBEngine.Workspaces(0).OpenDatabase(sDBName)
    Set rs = db.OpenRecordset("Customers", dbOpenDynaset)

    With rs

        ' if the recordset is empty, then inform the user and end
        If (.EOF And .BOF) Then

            MsgBox "Table Empty!", vbExclamation, "ERROR"
            Unload Me

        Else

            ' move to the first record and display it
            .MoveFirst
            DisplayRecord

        End If

    End With

    ' set the optPessimisticLocking value to true (this will
    ' automatically call the optPessimisticLocking_Click event
    optPessimisticLocking = True

End Sub
```

4. The `Form_Unload` event is called when the application is terminated. By setting the form-level object variables **db** and **rs** to nothing, you achieve the same status as you would closing them with the **Close** method.

```
Private Sub Form_Unload(Cancel As Integer)

    ' set the form-level object variables for the database and
    ' recordset to nothing (this is the same as closing each
    ' object)
    Set db = Nothing
    Set rs = Nothing

End Sub
```

5. Enter the `cmdEdit_Click` code shown next. This event first checks to see whether the record is in edit mode and updates the record if it is. After this, the recordset is placed in edit mode via the **Edit** method. If an error is going to occur, it will be here. If the user has selected pessimistic locking and the record is currently open, an error will occur. If no error is encountered, the text boxes are enabled to allow editing, and the form-level Boolean flag, **m_bEditMode**, is set to **True** to indicate that edit mode is on.

```
Private Sub cmdEdit_Click()

' if there is an error, goto the code labeled by ERR_cmdEdit_Click
On Error GoTo ERR_cmdEdit_Click:

    ' if the current record is in edit mode, call UpdateRecord
    If (m_bEditMode) Then UpdateRecord

    ' set the record to edit mode
    rs.Edit

    ' indicate that the record is in edit mode through the
    ' m_m_bEditMode form-level boolean variable
    m_bEditMode = True

    ' disable the edit command button and enable the update
    ' command button and text box controls
    cmdEdit.Enabled = False
    cmdUpdate.Enabled = True
    txtCustomerName.Enabled = True
    txtStreetAddress.Enabled = True

Exit Sub

ERR_cmdEdit_Click:

    ' an error has occurred, call the RecordError routine with the
    ' error object that describes the error and a string
    ' indicating the method attempted at the time of the error
```

continued on next page

continued from previous page

```
        RecordError Err, "edit"

End Sub
```

6. The code for the **cmdUpdate_Click** event is easy. Simply call the **UpdateRecord** routine as shown here:

```
Private Sub cmdUpdate_Click()

    ' update the current record in the database
    UpdateRecord

End Sub
```

7. Now enter the code for the **cmdRefresh_Click** event as shown next. This code again updates the record if it is in edit mode; then it performs a requery of the recordset and displays the current record.

```
Private Sub cmdRefresh_Click()

    ' if the current record is in edit mode, call UpdateRecord
    If (m_bEditMode) Then UpdateRecord

    ' requery dynaset and move the record pointer
    With rs
        .Requery
        .MoveNext
        .MovePrevious
    End With

    ' redisplay the current record
    DisplayRecord

End Sub
```

8. Enter the code for the **cmdClose_Click** event as shown here. This ends the application, and the **Form_Unload** event is automatically called.

```
Private Sub cmdClose_Click()

    ' end the application, this will call the Form_Unload event
    Unload Me

End Sub
```

9. Now enter the code for both option buttons on the **frmRecordLocker** form as shown next. Each event checks to see whether the record is in edit mode and performs an update if it is. Next, the **LockEdits** property of the recordset is set to the locking method of choice.

```
Private Sub optPessimisticLocking_Click()

    ' if the current record is in edit mode, call UpdateRecord
    If (m_bEditMode) Then UpdateRecord

    ' set the LockEdits property of the recordset to Pessimistic
    ' record locking
    rs.LockEdits = PESSIMISTIC

End Sub

Private Sub optOptimisticLocking_Click()

    ' if the current record is in edit mode, call UpdateRecord
    If (m_bEditMode) Then UpdateRecord

    ' set the LockEdits property of the recordset to Optimistic
    ' record locking
    rs.LockEdits = OPTIMISTIC

End Sub
```

10. Now enter the code for the **cmdMove_Click** event. This event occurs when the user presses any of the four command buttons belonging to the control array **cmdMove**. By comparing the **Index** variable passed as an argument to this event with the constants defined, the correct recordset navigation is applied and the new record is displayed.

```
Private Sub cmdMove_Click(Index As Integer)

    ' local constant values used to indicate which command button
    ' was pressed
    ' each constant corresponds to the index of each command
    ' button
    Const MOVE_FIRST = 0
    Const MOVE_PREVIOUS = 1
    Const MOVE_NEXT = 2
    Const MOVE_LAST = 3

    ' if the current record is in edit mode, call UpdateRecord
    If (m_bEditMode) Then UpdateRecord

    With rs

        Select Case Index

            ' move to the first record
            Case MOVE_FIRST:
                .MoveFirst

            ' move to the previous record; if the record pointer
            ' is before the first record, then move to the first
            ' record
```

continued on next page

continued from previous page

```
                    Case MOVE_PREVIOUS:
                        .MovePrevious
                        If (.BOF) Then .MoveFirst

                    ' move to the next record; if the record pointer is
                    ' beyond the last record, then move to the last record
                    Case MOVE_NEXT:
                        .MoveNext
                        If (.EOF) Then .MoveLast

                    ' move to the last record
                    Case MOVE_LAST:
                        .MoveLast

                End Select

            End With

            ' display the current record after moving to a new one
            DisplayRecord

    End Sub
```

11. The following code displays the record. Enter this in the General section of your project. If a new record is displayed, it cannot be in edit mode; therefore, you set the **m_bEditMode** variable to **False** and disable the Update command button while enabling the Edit command button.

```
Private Sub DisplayRecord()

    ' disable the customer name and fill it with the current
    ' record's corresponding field value
    With txtCustomerName
        .Text = rs.Fields("Customer Name")
        .Enabled = False
    End With

    ' disable the street address and fill it with the current
    ' record's corresponding field value
    With txtStreetAddress
        .Text = rs.Fields("Street Address")
        .Enabled = False
    End With

    ' enable the edit and disable the update command buttons
    cmdEdit.Enabled = True
    cmdUpdate.Enabled = False

    ' currently not in edit mode
    m_bEditMode = False

End Sub
```

12. Enter the UpdateRecord code now. This procedure updates the recordset with the values shown on the form. If the recordset LockEdits property was set to optimistic and the record is currently opened by another user at this time, the Update method causes an error. Trap the error and call the RecordError procedure as shown toward the end of this procedure.

```
Private Sub UpdateRecord()

' if there is an error, goto the code labeled by ERR_UpdateRecord
On Error GoTo ERR_UpdateRecord:

    ' set the new values of the record fields to those displayed
    ' on the form and update the record (this is where an error
    ' can occur)
    With rs
        .Fields("Customer Name") = txtCustomerName
        .Fields("Street Address") = txtStreetAddress
        .Update
    End With

    ' display the updated record
    DisplayRecord

Exit Sub

ERR_UpdateRecord:

    ' an error has occurred, call the RecordError routine with the
    ' error object that describes the error and a string
    ' indicating the method attempted at the time of the error
    RecordError Err, "update"

End Sub
```

13. Finally, enter the RecordError code, which displays the proper error message for the user based on the error object that was passed to it as a parameter:

```
Private Sub RecordError(oErr As ErrObject, sAction As String)

    Dim sMessage As String

    ' error constant used to indicate that the current record is
    ' locked and cannot be updated or edited
    Const RECORD_LOCKED = 3260

    With Err

        Select Case .Number

            ' the record cannot be edited
```

continued on next page

continued from previous page

```
            Case RECORD_LOCKED:
                sMessage = "Cannot " & sAction & " at this time " _
                            & "because the record is currently locked " _
                            & "by another user."

            ' an unexpected error has occurred
            Case Else:
                sMessage = "ERROR #" & .Number & ": " & _
                            .Description

        End Select

    End With

    ' display the error message created above
    MsgBox sMessage, vbExclamation, "ERROR"

End Sub
```

How It Works

This How-To uses the LockEdits property of the recordset object to determine how a particular record is locked. If the user selects pessimistic locking, the default setting for the Jet engine, the record becomes locked immediately upon calling the Edit method of the recordset. This lock remains on until the Update method of the recordset is called.

On the other hand, if the user has selected optimistic record locking for the LockEdits property, the record is locked only when the Update method is called. The advantage to this alternative is that the record is not locked for a potentially long period as with pessimistic locking; however, the data in the record can change during the time between the calls to the Edit and Update methods. If this is the case, a trappable runtime error occurs.

This project allows navigation of the recordset with four command buttons that emulate the Data control VCR navigation buttons. When the user clicks a navigation button, the record pointer is repositioned to the first, previous, next, or last record. If the record pointer goes before the first record or after the last, the application traps the potential error and repositions the record pointer to the first or last record.

Comments

The preceding three How-To projects deal with constantly checking error codes to determine the state of a database, table, or record. It is very important to always be a courteous programmer. This means properly coding your applications so that they will prevent error messages from occurring not only in your own project but also in other developers' applications.

Table 10.6 lists the most common error messages you might encounter when dealing with locking databases.

Table 10.6. Common database-locking error messages.

ERROR NUMBER	IS GENERATED WHEN...
3167	You use `Edit`, and the record has been deleted since the last time you read it.
3186	You use `Update` on a new or edited record, and the record's page is locked by another user.
3197	You use `Edit` or `Update`, and the record has changed since the last time you read it.
3027	You try to write to a table you have opened as read only.
3260	You use `Addnew`, `Edit`, or `Update`, and the record's page is locked by another user.
3261	You try to open a table that another user has opened with `dbDenyRead` or `dbDenyWrite`.
3262	You try to open a table with `dbDenyRead` or `dbDenyWrite`, and another user has the table open.
3356	You try to open a database already opened exclusively by another user, or you try to open exclusively a database that another user already has opened.

These error messages can be detected at various points in a project and should be trapped whenever possible.

COMPLEXITY
INTERMEDIATE

10.4 How do I...
Work with secured Microsoft Access database files?

Problem

I need to create a secure Microsoft Access database file and have my Visual Basic program manipulate it. How can I do this?

Technique

Microsoft Access databases support a wide variety of security features. The Jet engine can control which users and applications can access databases, tables, or fields. Security features are managed through the use of a system database. By convention, the database is usually named SYSTEM.MDW.

Every Microsoft Access user is assigned to a workgroup, and a copy of SYSTEM.MDW is established for each workgroup. An entry for each user in the Windows Registry points to the correct copy of SYSTEM.MDW for the user's assigned workgroup. This file is specified with the key `HKEY_LOCAL_MACHINE\SOFTWARE\Microsoft\Office\8.0\Access\Jet\3.5\Engines`. In this How-To, you learn the techniques for accessing the objects in a secured Microsoft Access database.

Permissions

Each Microsoft Access database file includes a set of permissions that give users certain specified rights to the database and to the objects within the database. For the database itself, two permissions can be granted: the right to open the database (`Open Database`) and the right to open the database exclusively (`Open Exclusive`).

Although Microsoft Access security covers all database object types, the only data objects that can be accessed from Visual Basic are tables and queries. Table 10.7 lists the seven permissions that can be granted for table and query objects. Granting any of these permissions except Read Design implies granting others as well. Table 10.7 also shows these implied permissions.

Table 10.7. Permissions for Microsoft Access tables and queries.

PERMISSION	IMPLIES THESE ADDITIONAL PERMISSIONS
Read Design	(none)
Modify Design	Read Design, Read Data, Update Data, Delete Data
Administer	All other permissions
Read Data	Read Design
Update Data	Read Data, Read Design
Insert Data	Read Data, Read Design
Delete Data	Read Data, Read Design

Groups and Users

Everyone who accesses a Microsoft Access database is a user and is identified by a username. Users can also be assigned to groups. Every group has a group name. User and group information for a specified workgroup is stored in the system database (usually SYSTEM.MDW) file. You can use Microsoft Access (or Visual Basic) to create users and groups and to assign users to groups.

You grant permissions by users or by groups. Users inherit the rights of their group, unless you specify otherwise. Assume, for example, that you have a group named Payroll Department. You assign the entire group only Read Data permission to the Pay Rates table (and Read Design permission, which is implied by Read Data). For two users within the group, Tom and Betty, you also assign Update Data, Insert Data, and Delete Data permissions. For one user in the group, Pat, you revoke Read Data permission. The specific permission assignments you have made for users Tom, Betty, and Pat override the group permissions for these users.

Secured and Unsecured Systems

All the preceding information is transparent—and relatively unimportant—as long as you are working with an unsecured system. When the Workgroup Administrator application creates a new system database—and thereby creates a new workgroup—the system is by default an unsecured system. All users are assigned empty strings ("") as passwords. Users do not log in when they start Access, and your Visual Basic program does not need to provide a username or password because all users are logged in automatically with the default name Admin and the password "".

This all changes as soon as the Admin user's password changes, because a password-protected Admin account makes the system into a secured system. Each time a user starts Microsoft Access in a secured system, he or she must provide a username, and that name must be registered in the workgroup's copy of the system database. If the system database contains a password other than "" for the user, the password must be provided at login. In like manner, before your Visual Basic program can access a database in a secured system, it must provide a valid username and a password (if the user is assigned a password).

Security ID Numbers

Every user and group has a Security ID (SID)—a binary string created by the Jet engine and stored in the system database where the user or group is defined. With several important exceptions, the Jet database engine builds a user or group SID based on two pieces of information:

✔ The user's name.

✔ The user's personal identifier (PID)—an alphanumeric string between 4 and 20 characters that must be provided when a new user is added to the system database. (See How-To 10.9 for information on how to add users to the system database.)

The SID, therefore, uniquely identifies a user or group.

Security IDs and Object Permissions

Object permissions are defined by assignment to an SID. You can think of a permission as a keyhole through which access to an object can be obtained and the SID as a unique key that fits the keyhole (see Figure 10.4). Each object has a set of keyholes, one matching the SID "key" for each user or group that has a specific permission. When you assign permission for an object (a process covered in How-To 10.5), you in effect "drill another keyhole" into the object and encode it with the SID of a specific user or group.

Ensuring a Secure Database

It is altogether too easy to think you have "secured" a Microsoft Access database yet actually have a security system with gaping holes. The holes can exist because the predefined default users and groups are exceptions to the way SIDs are built. Default users' and groups' SIDs are built as shown in Table 10.8.

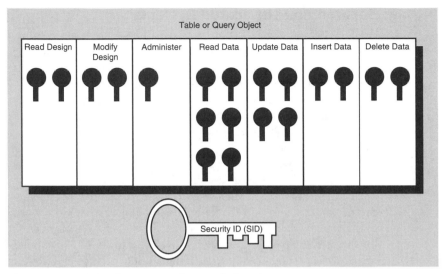

Figure 10.4. Security IDs and permissions.

Table 10.8. Security ID sources for default users and groups.

USER OR GROUP	SID SOURCE
Admin user	Hard-coded and identical in every system database
Guest user	Hard-coded and identical in every system database
Users group	Hard-coded and identical in every system database
Guests group	Hard-coded and identical in every system database
Admins group	Built by the Jet engine from three pieces of data: a username, a company name, and an ID number

The information in Table 10.8 has extremely important implications for database security. The Admin user's SID is hard-coded and identical in every system database; that means that objects created by the Admin user can be accessed by the Admin user in any system database. All someone needs to do to gain access to an object created by an Admin user from any system database is to create a new system database and log in as Admin. Admin is the default user; in an unsecured system, all users are Admin. Therefore, if you create an object in an unsecured system, that object belongs to Admin and cannot be secured.

One solution (recommended by Microsoft in the Microsoft Access documentation) is to delete the Admin user from the system database. This is permissible as long as the Admins group contains at least one other user.

Unlike the Admin user SID, the Admins group SID is unique to each system database. Note in Table 10.8 that the Admins group SID requires an ID number. If the system database was created by the Microsoft Access setup program, the ID number component of the Admins group SID is taken from the setup disks, and each set of setup disks is uniquely encoded. If the system database is created through the Microsoft Access Workgroup Administrator, the ID number component is computed based on an identifier entered by the person who creates the system database with the Workgroup Administrator.

This scheme prevents someone who is a member of an Admins group in one system database from automatically getting Admins group permissions when accessing database files through other system databases; because the Admins group SIDs are different, the permissions are different (recall the concept of unique keyholes and keys from Figure 10.4). But it also means that all users who are currently members of the Admins group of the system database in use when the database was originally created will always have the ability to change permissions on all objects in the database—and this ability cannot be removed by anyone. Therefore, when you create a database you intend to secure, you should be cognizant of who is defined to the system database as part of the Admins group.

Another implication of Table 10.8 is that permissions assigned to the Guests or Users group through one system database will be available to members of the Guests or Users group in any system database. Therefore, assign the Guests or Users groups only the permissions you are willing to give to anyone. If you need to assign permissions to a group of users and you want to restrict who can access the permissions, create a new group (see How-To 10.10 for details on how to create a group and assign users to it).

Accessing a Secured System Through Visual Basic

Before your application can access a secured Microsoft Access system, it needs to provide the Jet engine with several pieces of information:

✔ The application must specify which system database file the application wants to use. This is normally a file named SYSTEM.MDW.

✔ The application must provide a username that is listed in that system database file.

✔ If that username has a password, the application must provide the password.

After the Jet engine knows where to look for usernames and passwords, you provide a username and password. You can do this by straightforward assignment to DBEngine properties:

```
DBEngine.DefaultUser = "Annette"
DBEngine.DefaultPassword = "mouseketeer"
```

The username is not case-sensitive, but the password *is* case-sensitive. If the password is recorded in the system database as Mouseketeer and you supply mouseketeer, the login attempt will fail.

Workspaces and Sessions

The Jet engine implements most database security features through the `Workspace` object and its `Groups` and `Users` collection. A `Workspace` object is a member of the `Workspaces` collection of the `Database` object.

When you set the `IniPath`, `DefaultUser`, and `DefaultPassword` properties of the `DBEngine` object, you are actually setting the `UserName` and `Password` for the default workspace. The default workspace can be accessed by its name, `DBEngine.Workspaces("#Default Workspace#")`, in which the # symbols are part of the name, or as `DBEngine.Workspaces(0)`.

A `Workspace` object defines a session for a user. *Session* and *workspace* are close to being synonyms. Within a session, you can open multiple databases. Transactions occur within sessions.

For the default workspace, a session begins when you set the `DefaultUser` and `DefaultPassword` properties for the `DBEngine` object. After you have successfully initialized the default session, your program can create additional password-protected sessions.

To open a new session, you create a new `Workspace` object by using the `CreateWorkspace` method of the `DBEngine` object. The `CreateWorkspace` method takes three required arguments: `Name` (the name of the workspace), `UserName`, and `Password`. You can append the `Workspace` object to the `DBEngine` object's `Workspaces` collection—although you do not need to add the `Workspace` object to the collection to use the object. This code fragment initializes the default workspace and then creates a new `Workspace` object named `My Space` for the user `Lucy`, whose password is `diamonds`. It then opens a database within the new workspace.

```
Dim wkSpace as Workspace
Dim db as Database

DBEngine.IniPath = "D:\MYAPP\THEINI.INI"
DBEngine.DefaultUser = "Mary"
DBEngine.DefaultPassword = "contrary"
Set wkSpace = DBEngine.CreateWorkspace("My Space", "Lucy", "diamonds")
Set db = wkSpace.OpenDatabase("BIBLIO.MDB")
```

Note that you must be logged into the `DBEngine` object via the `DefaultUser` and `DefaultPassword` objects before you can create additional workspaces.

Steps

Open the Secure project (Secure.vbp) and make sure that the path in the GetWorkgroupDatabase function points to your SYSTEM.MDW file. Then run the Secure project. You will first see a dialog box indicating the system database name to be used in the application. The next dialog box is that of a typical logon screen, as shown in Figure 10.5. Here you can enter different usernames and passwords to access the database.

Figure 10.5. The Secure project.

1. Create a new project and name it Secure.vbp. Add the objects and edit the properties as shown in Table 10.9; then save the form as frmSecure.frm.

Table 10.9. Objects and properties for the Secure project.

OBJECT	PROPERTY	SETTING
Form	Name	frmSecure
	Caption	Secure
Text box	Name	txtUserName
Text box	Name	txtPassword
Command button	Name	cmdOK
	Caption	&OK
	Default	True
Command button	Name	cmdCancel
	Caption	&Cancel
	Cancel	True
Label	Name	lblUserName
	Caption	&User Name
Label	Name	lblPassword
	Caption	&Password.

2. There are no form-level variables to declare in this project, so go directly to entering the **Form_Load** code as shown next. This code sets the **DBEngine** properties with the default user and password to access the SYSTEM.MDW file.

```
Private Sub Form_Load()

' if there is an error, goto the code labeled by ERR_Form_Load
On Error GoTo ERR_Form_Load:

    ' local variables used to hold the user name and password
    Dim sUser As String
    Dim sPassword As String
```

continued on next page

continued from previous page

```
        With DBEngine

            ' set the system database INI path (registry key)
            DBEngine.IniPath = GetINIPath

            ' set system database file
            .SystemDB = GetWorkgroupDatabase

            ' set default user information
            sUser = "Admin"
            sPassword = "myturn"

            ' assign default user information
            .DefaultUser = sUser
            .DefaultPassword = sPassword

            ' display current system database
            MsgBox "The system database is " & .SystemDB,
    vbInformation

        End With

    Exit Sub


    ERR_Form_Load:

        ' display the error information and then end the application
        With Err
            MsgBox "ERROR #" & .Number & ": " & .Description,
    vbExclamation, _
                    "ERROR"
        End With

        Unload Me

    End Sub.
```

3. Now enter the code for **cmdOK_Click**. This event creates a new **Workspace** object with the supplied information from the **frmSecure** form, and if it is successful, it opens a recordset obtaining some information.

```
Private Sub cmdOK_Click()

' if an error occurs, then goto the code labeled by
' ERR_cmdOK_Click
On Error GoTo ERR_cmdOK_Click:

    ' local object variables used to hold the database, recordset,
    ' and workspace
    Dim db As Database
    Dim rs As Recordset
    Dim ws As Workspace

    ' local variable used to store database path and name
```

```
        Dim sDBName As String

        ' local variables used to store the username and password
        Dim sUserName As String
        Dim sPassword As String

        ' if there is no username, inform the user and exit the
        ' procedure if there is a username, assign the name and
        ' password
        If (txtUserName = "") Then

            MsgBox "You must enter a username.", vbExclamation, _
                    "ERROR"

            txtUserName.SetFocus
            Exit Sub

        Else

            sUserName = txtUserName
            sPassword = txtPassword

        End If

        ' create a new workspace for the user
        Set ws = DBEngine.CreateWorkspace _
                    ("NewWorkspace", sUserName, sPassword)

        ' obtain the database name and path from ReadINI and then open
        ' the database
        sDBName = DBPath
        Set db = ws.OpenDatabase(sDBName)

        ' ensure that we have connected by creating a recordset of
        ' some data
        Set rs = db.OpenRecordset("SELECT * FROM Customers")

        ' inform the user that we are successful
        MsgBox "User " & txtUserName & " connected successfully!", _
                vbInformation, "SUCCESS"

    Exit Sub

    ERR_cmdOK_Click:

        ' display the error information and then end the application
        ' With Err
            MsgBox "ERROR #" & .Number & ": " & .Description,
    vbExclamation, _
                    "ERROR"
        End With

    End Sub.
```

4. Now add the trivial code to end the project in the cmdCancel_Click event:

```
Private Sub cmdCancel_Click()

    ' end the application
    Unload Me

End Sub
```

How It Works

When the application starts, `frmSecure` is loaded. The `Load` event connects to the system database designated in the Windows Registry and, if it is successful, displays a message showing the name of that database. When the user clicks the OK button, the click event creates a new `Workspace` object, opens ORDERS.MDB, and opens a recordset based on a table in ORDERS.MDB. If these steps are successful, the username and password are valid and the user has Read Data privileges to the table.

Comments

In previous versions of Visual Basic, the Jet engine looked in INI files for the name of the system database file. With Visual Basic 6.0 and the Jet 3.51 engine, the system database file is located in the Windows Registry. Probably the most likely spot to find this file would be in your Windows system directory.

COMPLEXITY
ADVANCED

10.5 How do I...
Assign permissions for database objects?

Problem

I need to write an application for the system administrators where I work, to allow them to change the permissions of users for Access databases. These administrators don't necessarily have Access available to them. How do I provide this capability through my own Visual Basic application?

Technique

Permissions for a database are stored in a system table in the database. If you have Administer access to the database, you can change these permissions through Access or Visual Basic.

Each Microsoft Access `Database` object owns a `Containers` collection where the following are true:

✔ Each `Container` object in the `Containers` collection collects information about a specific type of object.

✔ The `Container` object named `Tables` contains information about all the `Table` and `Query` objects in the database.

✔ Each `Container` object owns a `Documents` collection.

✔ Each `Document` object in a `Documents` collection holds information about one instance of the object type represented by the container.

✔ Each `Document` object in the `Tables` container represents one `Table` or `Query` object.

✔ Each `Document` has a `UserName` property and a `Permissions` property.

✔ At any given time, the `Permissions` property value is a long integer that represents the permissions that the user named by the `UserName` property has to the table or query represented by the `Document` object.

The values of the `Permissions` object for each combination of permissions for users other than the Admin user are shown in Table 10.10. (The values for the Admin user, Administer, and Modify Design permissions vary, depending on whether the object represented by the document is a table or a query.) Each permission named in the Permission or Permissions column includes not only the named permission but also all implied permissions. For example, the value of permissions property is `20` when Read Data and its implied property Read Design are `True`; the value is `116` when Update Data and Delete Data and all the implied properties of both are `True`.

Table 10.10. Permissions property values for users other than Admin.

PERMISSION OR PERMISSIONS	VALUE OF PERMISSIONS PROPERTY
No permissions	0
Read Design	4
Read Data	20
Insert Data	52
Update Data	84
Update Data and Insert Data	116
Delete Data	148
Insert Data and Delete Data	180
Update Data and Delete Data	212
Update Data, Insert Data, and Delete Data	244
Modify Design	65756
Modify Design and Insert Data	65788
Administer	852478

You can determine the permissions a user has for a table or a query by setting the `UserName` property of the `Document` object to the user's name and then reading the `Permissions` property. If you have Administer permission for the table or query, you can set permissions for other users by setting the `UserName` property and then assigning a value to the `Permissions` property.

Steps

Open the Permitter project and make sure that the `GetWorkgroupDatabase` function returns the proper fully qualified path for the SYSTEM.MDW file. When this is done, run the application. You should see the form shown in Figure 10.6. Select a combination of a single user and a table or query from the two list boxes on the Permitter form. You can change various properties set for each combination and save them by clicking the Save button. Notice the permission code above the check boxes. It changes according to the combinations of permissions granted to the user for the given table or query.

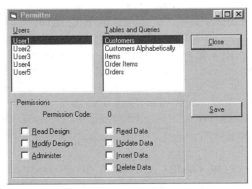

Figure 10.6. The Permitter project.

1. Create a new project and name it Permitter.vbp. Add and edit the objects and properties as listed in Table 10.11, and save the form as frmPermitter.frm. Note that all the check boxes are part of a control array.

Table 10.11. Objects and properties for the Permitter project.

OBJECT	PROPERTY	SETTING
Form	Name	frmPermitter
	Caption	Permitter
List box	Name	lstUsers
List box	Name	lstTablesAndQueries
Command button	Name	cmdSave
	Caption	&Save

OBJECT	PROPERTY	SETTING
Command button	Name	cmdClose
	Caption	&Close
	Cancel	-1 'True
	Default	-1 'True
Frame	Name	fraPermissions
	Caption	Permissions
Check box	Name	chkPermission
	Caption	&Read Design
	Index	0
Check box	Name	chkPermission
	Caption	&Modify Design
	Index	1
Check box	Name	chkPermission
	Caption	&Administer
	Index	2
Check box	Name	chkPermission
	Caption	R&ead Data
	Index	3
Check box	Name	chkPermission
	Caption	&Update Data
	Index	4
Check box	Name	chkPermission
	Caption	&Insert Data
	Index	5
Check box	Name	chkPermission
	Caption	&Delete Data
	Index	6
Label	Name	lblPermissionCode
	Caption	Permission Code:
Label	Name	lblPermissions
	Caption	0
Label	Name	lblUsers
	Caption	&Users
Label	Name	lblTablesAndQueries
	Caption	&Tables and Queries

2. First enter the following form-level declarations in the declarations section of the project. The database object variable will serve as the home of the database object referred to throughout the project. The constant declarations with the **PER_** prefix correspond to the seven check boxes on the **frmPermitter** form. The last set of declarations, those preceded by the **DB_** characters, are used to indicate the different values associated with the permissions.

```
Option Explicit

' form-level object variable used to store database object
Private db As Database

' form-level constant declarations which correspond to check boxes
' on the frmPermitter form
Const PER_READ_DESIGN = 0
Const PER_MODIFY_DESIGN = 1
Const PER_ADMINISTER = 2
Const PER_READ_DATA = 3
Const PER_UPDATE_DATA = 4
Const PER_INSERT_DATA = 5
Const PER_DELETE_DATA = 6

' form-level constant declarations which indicate various
' permissions
Const DB_NOPERMISSIONS = 0
Const DB_READDESIGN = 4
Const DB_READDATA = 20
Const DB_INSERTDATA = 52
Const DB_UPDATEDATA = 84
Const DB_UPDATEINSERTDATA = 116
Const DB_DELETEDATA = 148
Const DB_INSERTDELETEDATA = 180
Const DB_UPDATEDELETEDATA = 212
Const DB_UPDATEINSERTDELETEDATA = 244
Const DB_MODIFYDESIGN = 65756
Const DB_MODIFYDESIGN_INSERTDATA = 65788
Const DB_READSEC = 131072
Const DB_ADMINISTER = 852478
```

3. Enter the **Form_Load** event as shown next. This code sets the default user and password of the **DBEngine** object. You might have to change the values of these two variables to your system administrator's name and password. The database is then open, and the two list boxes on the form are populated. If there are no current users for the database, the application is terminated.

```
Private Sub Form_Load()

' if there is an error, then goto the code section labeled by
' ERR_Form_Load
On Error GoTo ERR_Form_Load:

    Dim sUserName As String
```

```vb
        Dim sPassword As String
        Dim sDBName As String

        ' assign default username and password
        sUserName = "Admin"
        sPassword = ""

        With DBEngine

            ' set system database path and name
            .SystemDB = GetWorkgroupDatabase

            ' set default user name and password
            .DefaultUser = sUserName
            .DefaultPassword = sPassword

            ' get path and name of database from ReadINI module
            sDBName = DBPath

            ' open database
            Set db = .Workspaces(0).OpenDatabase(sDBName)

        End With

        ' populate the two list boxes with the available users,
        ' tables, and queries from database
        FillUserList
        FillTableAndQueriesList

        ' if there are no valid users, inform the user and exit the
        ' application
        If (lstUsers.ListCount < 1) Then

            MsgBox "There are no users!", vbExclamation, "USERS"
            cmdClose_Click

        Else

            ' initialize the list boxes to point to the first item in
            ' each list box
            lstUsers.ListIndex = 0
            lstTablesAndQueries.ListIndex = 0

        End If

Exit Sub

ERR_Form_Load:

    ' display error for the user
    With Err
        MsgBox "ERROR #" & .Number & ": " & .Description, _
        vbExclamation, _
                "ERROR"
    End With

End Sub
```

4. Enter the following `Form_Unload` code now. This code ensures that the database object is released by setting it to nothing when the application is terminated.

```
Private Sub Form_Unload(Cancel As Integer)

    ' close the database
    Set db = Nothing

End Sub
```

5. Now enter both the `lstUsers` and the `lstTablesAndQueries Click` event code. Each event relies on the other's list box having a selected item. If there is a selected item in the corresponding list box, the `ReadPermissions` procedure is called to gather the permission information for the user and table/query combination, checking off the appropriate check boxes on the form.

```
Private Sub lstUsers_Click()

    ' if the TablesAndQueries list box is set to one of the items,
    ' call the ReadPermissions procedure, and if there was an
    ' error, unselect all check boxes
    If (lstTablesAndQueries.ListIndex >= 0) Then
        If (Not ReadPermissions()) Then

            lstUsers.ListIndex = -1
            UnCheckAll

        End If
    End If

End Sub

Private Sub lstTablesAndQueries_Click()

    ' if the Users list box is set to one of the items, call the
    ' ReadPermissions procedure, and if there was an error,
    ' unselect all check boxes
    If (lstUsers.ListIndex >= 0) Then
        If (Not ReadPermissions()) Then

            lstTablesAndQueries.ListIndex = -1
            UnCheckAll

        End If
    End If

End Sub
```

6. The chkPermission_Click event handles all seven check boxes found on the frmPermitter form. This code ensures that the correct combinations of check boxes are set. Enter the following code:

```
Private Sub chkPermission_Click(Index As Integer)

    Dim nCount As Integer


    With chkPermission(Index)

        ' set the appropriate check box values dependent upon the
        ' others
        Select Case Index

            Case PER_READ_DESIGN:
                If (.Value = vbUnchecked) Then
                    For nCount = 0 To 6
                        chkPermission(nCount).Value = vbUnchecked
                    Next nCount
                End If

            Case PER_MODIFY_DESIGN:
                If (.Value = vbChecked) Then
                    chkPermission(PER_READ_DESIGN).Value = _
                        vbChecked
                    chkPermission(PER_READ_DATA).Value = vbChecked
                    chkPermission(PER_UPDATE_DATA).Value = _
                        vbChecked
                    chkPermission(PER_INSERT_DATA).Value = _
                        vbChecked
                Else
                    chkPermission(PER_ADMINISTER).Value = _
                        vbUnchecked
                End If

            Case PER_ADMINISTER:
                If (.Value = vbChecked) Then
                    For nCount = 0 To 6
                        chkPermission(nCount).Value = vbChecked
                    Next nCount
                End If

            Case PER_READ_DATA:
                If (.Value = vbChecked) Then
                    chkPermission(PER_READ_DESIGN).Value = _
                        vbChecked
                Else
                    chkPermission(PER_MODIFY_DESIGN).Value = _
                        vbUnchecked
                    chkPermission(PER_UPDATE_DATA).Value = _
                        vbUnchecked
                    chkPermission(PER_DELETE_DATA).Value = _
                        vbUnchecked
```

continued on next page

continued from previous page

```
                              chkPermission(PER_INSERT_DATA).Value = _
                                  vbUnchecked
                              chkPermission(PER_ADMINISTER).Value = _
                                  vbUnchecked
                      End If

              Case PER_UPDATE_DATA:
                  If (.Value = vbChecked) Then
                      chkPermission(PER_READ_DESIGN).Value = _
                          vbChecked
                      chkPermission(PER_READ_DATA).Value = vbChecked
                  Else
                      chkPermission(PER_ADMINISTER).Value = _
                          vbUnchecked
                      chkPermission(PER_MODIFY_DESIGN).Value = _
                          vbUnchecked
                  End If

              Case PER_INSERT_DATA:
                  If (.Value = vbChecked) Then
                      chkPermission(PER_READ_DESIGN).Value = _
                          vbChecked
                      chkPermission(PER_READ_DATA).Value = vbChecked
                  Else
                      chkPermission(PER_ADMINISTER).Value = _
                          vbUnchecked
                  End If

              Case PER_DELETE_DATA:
                  If (.Value = vbChecked) Then
                      chkPermission(PER_READ_DESIGN).Value = _
                          vbChecked
                      chkPermission(PER_READ_DATA).Value = vbChecked
                  Else
                      chkPermission(PER_ADMINISTER).Value = _
                          vbUnchecked
                      chkPermission(PER_MODIFY_DESIGN).Value = _
                          vbUnchecked
                  End If

          End Select

      End With

  End Sub
```

7. Enter the `cmdSave_Click` event code now. This code calculates the Permission Code value from the check boxes on the form and saves it to the **Permissions** property of the appropriate **Document** object.

```
Private Sub cmdSave_Click()

' if there is an error, goto the code labeled by ERR_cmdSave_Click
On Error GoTo ERR_cmdSave_Click:
```

```
Dim oDocument As Document
Dim lPermissionCode As Long

' set the document object variable to the proper selected
' table or query from the list box
Set oDocument = _

db.Containers("Tables").Documents(lstTablesAndQueries.Text)

' create the proper permission code dependent upon the
' selected check boxes of frmPermitter

If chkPermission(PER_ADMINISTER) = vbChecked Then

    lPermissionCode = DB_ADMINISTER

ElseIf chkPermission(PER_MODIFY_DESIGN) = vbChecked Then
    If chkPermission(PER_INSERT_DATA) = vbChecked Then

        lPermissionCode = DB_MODIFYDESIGN_INSERTDATA

    Else

        lPermissionCode = DB_MODIFYDESIGN

    End If
ElseIf chkPermission(PER_UPDATE_DATA) = vbChecked Then
    If chkPermission(PER_INSERT_DATA) = vbChecked Then
        If chkPermission(PER_DELETE_DATA) = vbChecked Then

            lPermissionCode = DB_UPDATEINSERTDELETEDATA

        Else

            lPermissionCode = DB_UPDATEINSERTDATA

        End If
    Else

        lPermissionCode = DB_UPDATEDATA

    End If
ElseIf chkPermission(PER_INSERT_DATA) = vbChecked Then
    If chkPermission(PER_DELETE_DATA) = vbChecked Then

        lPermissionCode = DB_INSERTDELETEDATA

    Else

        lPermissionCode = DB_INSERTDATA

    End If
ElseIf chkPermission(PER_DELETE_DATA) = vbChecked Then
```

continued on next page

continued from previous page

```
                lPermissionCode = DB_DELETEDATA

          ElseIf chkPermission(PER_READ_DATA) = vbChecked Then

                lPermissionCode = DB_READDATA

          ElseIf chkPermission(PER_READ_DESIGN) = vbChecked Then

                lPermissionCode = DB_READDESIGN

          Else

                lPermissionCode = DB_NOPERMISSIONS

          End If

          With oDocument

                ' save the permission code to the document object for the
                ' proper user
                .UserName = lstUsers.Text

                If (UCase$(.UserName) = "ADMIN") Then _
                        lPermissionCode = lPermissionCode + DB_READSEC

                .Permissions = lPermissionCode
                lblPermissions.Caption = .Permissions

          End With

      Exit Sub

      ERR_cmdSave_Click:

          ' display the error for the user
          With Err
              MsgBox "ERROR #" & .Number & ": " & .Description, _
                      vbExclamation, "ERROR"
          End With

      End Sub
```

8. Enter the `cmdClose_Click` event code given next. This simply ends the application.

```
Private Sub cmdClose_Click()

    ' close the application
    Unload Me

End Sub
```

9. The UnCheckAll procedure, as shown here, is called from throughout the application to clear all the check boxes on the form:

```
Private Sub UnCheckAll()

    Dim nCount As Integer

    ' set all the permission check boxes to unchecked
    For nCount = 0 To 6
        chkPermission(nCount).Value = vbUnchecked
    Next nCount

End Sub
```

10. Now enter both the FillUserList and the FillTableAndQueriesList procedures as shown next. The FillUserList procedure populates the lstUsers list box with the information found in the Users collection of the new workspace, and the FillTableAndQueriesList procedure populates the lstTablesAndQueries list box with the tables and queries found in the Documents collection of the Tables container.

```
Private Sub FillUserList()

    Dim oUser As User

    ' populate the user list boxes with all users except CREATOR,
    ' ENGINE, and ADMIN (these shouldn't be changed)
    For Each oUser In DBEngine.Workspaces(0).Users

        With oUser

            If (UCase$(.Name) <> "CREATOR") _
            And (UCase$(.Name) <> "ENGINE") _
            And (UCase$(.Name) <> "ADMIN") Then

                lstUsers.AddItem .Name

            End If

        End With

    Next

End Sub

Private Sub FillTableAndQueriesList()

    Dim oDocument As Document

    ' populate the TableAndQueries list boxes with all the
    ' available tables and queries except the system ones
    For Each oDocument In db.Containers("Tables").Documents
```

continued on next page

continued from previous page

```
            With oDocument
                If (Left$(.Name, 4) <> "MSys") Then _
                        lstTablesAndQueries.AddItem .Name
            End With

        Next

    End Sub
```

11. The `ReadPermissions` function returns a Boolean value: `True` for success and `False` for failure. This code breaks down the `Permissions` property of the appropriate `Document` object and checks off the corresponding check boxes of the `frmPermitter` form.

```
Function ReadPermissions() As Boolean

' if there is an error, then goto the code labeled by
ERR_ReadPermissions
On Error GoTo ERR_ReadPermissions:

    Dim nCount As Integer
    Dim lPermissionCode As Long
    Dim oDocument As Document

    ' set the document object to the appropriately selected table
    ' or query
    Set oDocument = _

db.Containers("Tables").Documents(lstTablesAndQueries.Text)

    ' set the user name and get the current permissions for that
    ' user
    With oDocument
        .UserName = lstUsers.Text
        lblPermissions.Caption = .Permissions
        lPermissionCode = .Permissions
    End With

    ' set all check boxes to unchecked
    UnCheckAll

    ' set the appropriate check boxes for the current permission
    ' for the user selected
    Select Case lPermissionCode

        Case DB_READDESIGN
            chkPermission(PER_READ_DESIGN).Value = vbChecked

        Case DB_READDATA
            chkPermission(PER_READ_DATA).Value = vbChecked
            chkPermission(PER_READ_DESIGN).Value = vbChecked

        Case DB_INSERTDATA
            chkPermission(PER_INSERT_DATA).Value = vbChecked
```

```
            chkPermission(PER_READ_DESIGN).Value = vbChecked
            chkPermission(PER_READ_DATA).Value = vbChecked

        Case DB_UPDATEDATA
            chkPermission(PER_UPDATE_DATA).Value = vbChecked
            chkPermission(PER_READ_DESIGN).Value = vbChecked
            chkPermission(PER_READ_DATA).Value = vbChecked

        Case DB_UPDATEINSERTDATA
            chkPermission(PER_UPDATE_DATA).Value = vbChecked
            chkPermission(PER_INSERT_DATA).Value = vbChecked
            chkPermission(PER_READ_DESIGN).Value = vbChecked
            chkPermission(PER_READ_DATA).Value = vbChecked

        Case DB_DELETEDATA
            chkPermission(PER_DELETE_DATA).Value = vbChecked
            chkPermission(PER_READ_DESIGN).Value = vbChecked
            chkPermission(PER_READ_DATA).Value = vbChecked

        Case DB_INSERTDELETEDATA
            chkPermission(PER_DELETE_DATA).Value = vbChecked
            chkPermission(PER_READ_DESIGN).Value = vbChecked
            chkPermission(PER_READ_DATA).Value = vbChecked
            chkPermission(PER_INSERT_DATA).Value = vbChecked

        Case DB_UPDATEDELETEDATA
            chkPermission(PER_UPDATE_DATA).Value = vbChecked
            chkPermission(PER_READ_DESIGN).Value = vbChecked
            chkPermission(PER_READ_DATA).Value = vbChecked
            chkPermission(PER_DELETE_DATA).Value = vbChecked

        Case DB_UPDATEINSERTDELETEDATA
            chkPermission(PER_UPDATE_DATA).Value = vbChecked
            chkPermission(PER_READ_DESIGN).Value = vbChecked
            chkPermission(PER_READ_DATA).Value = vbChecked
            chkPermission(PER_DELETE_DATA).Value = vbChecked
            chkPermission(PER_INSERT_DATA).Value = vbChecked

        Case DB_MODIFYDESIGN
            chkPermission(PER_MODIFY_DESIGN).Value = vbChecked
            chkPermission(PER_READ_DESIGN).Value = vbChecked
            chkPermission(PER_READ_DATA).Value = vbChecked
            chkPermission(PER_UPDATE_DATA).Value = vbChecked
            chkPermission(PER_DELETE_DATA).Value = vbChecked

        Case DB_MODIFYDESIGN_INSERTDATA
            chkPermission(PER_MODIFY_DESIGN).Value = vbChecked
            chkPermission(PER_READ_DESIGN).Value = vbChecked
            chkPermission(PER_READ_DATA).Value = vbChecked
            chkPermission(PER_UPDATE_DATA).Value = vbChecked
            chkPermission(PER_INSERT_DATA).Value = vbChecked
            chkPermission(PER_DELETE_DATA).Value = vbChecked

        Case DB_ADMINISTER
            For nCount = 0 To 6
```

continued on next page

continued from previous page

```
                    chkPermission(nCount).Value = vbChecked
            Next nCount

    End Select

    ' indicate success
    ReadPermissions = True

Exit Function

ERR_ReadPermissions:

    ' display the error for the user
    With Err
        MsgBox "ERROR #" & .Number& & ": " & .Description, _
        vbExclamation, "ERROR"
    End With

    ' indicate failure
    ReadPermissions = False

End Function
```

How It Works

When the form loads, the program connects to the system database, opens the ORDERS database, and populates the two list boxes according to the available information from these two databases. When the user selects both a valid user and a table or query from the list boxes, the **ReadPermissions** function is called to display the options available for the combination through seven check boxes on the form. The user can change these permissions and then save them by clicking the Save button. The application then calculates a new value for the **Permissions** property of the appropriate user/document combination and saves it to the system database.

Comments

The Permissions help screen identifies built-in constants for representing values of the **Permissions** property. If you look up these constants in the Object Browser, you can see their values. Using these built-in variables is tricky, however, because it is not always clear which implied properties each is including. The values in Table 10.10 were obtained experimentally, by changing the permissions in Microsoft Access and reading the resulting value of the **Permissions** property through Visual Basic.

COMPLEXITY
INTERMEDIATE

10.6 How do I...
Change ownership of database objects?

Problem

How can I give system administrators the ability to change the ownership of various tables and queries through my Visual Basic application?

Technique

Every data object in Microsoft Access has an owner. The default owner is the creator of that object. The owner has specific permissions that others do not necessarily have. These permissions include the right to grant full privileges to himself or others.

The name of the owner of a table or query resides in the **Owner** property of the appropriate **Document** object that represents the data object. A user with Administer permission can change the owner of any data object by changing the name of the **Owner** property.

Steps

Open the project OWNERSHIP.VBP and make sure that the **GetWorkgroupDatabase** function is returning the proper fully qualified path to your SYSTEM.MDW file. When this is done, run the application. If the username and password variables, located in the **Form_Load** event, are correct, you should see the form shown in Figure 10.7. When a user clicks on a table or query in the list box, the owner of that data object is selected from the other list box. By selecting a different user from the list and clicking the Save Owner button, you can change ownership of the data object.

1. Create a new project and call it OWNERSHIP.VBP. Use **Form1** to create the objects and edit the properties as listed in Table 10.12. Save the form as frmOwnership.frm.

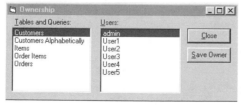

Figure 10.7. The Ownership project.

Table 10.12. Objects and properties for the Ownership project.

OBJECT	PROPERTY	SETTING
Form	Name	frmOwnership
	Caption	Ownership
List box	Name	lstUsers
List box	Name	lstTablesAndQueries
Command button	Name	cmdSave
	Caption	&Save
Command button	Name	cmdClose
	Caption	&Close
	Cancel	-1 'True
	Default	-1 'True
Label	Name	lblUsers
	Caption	&Users:
Label	Name	lblTablesAndQueries
	Caption	&Tables And Queries

2. Begin by entering the following code into the declarations section of the project:

```
Option Explicit

' form-level object variable used to hold the database object
Private db As Database
```

3. Now enter the **Form_Load** event code as listed next. Change the **sUserName** and **sPassword** variables to hold the values of your administrator's username and password.

```
Private Sub Form_Load()

' if there is an error, then goto the code section labeled by
ERR_Form_Load
On Error GoTo ERR_Form_Load:

    Dim sUserName As String
    Dim sPassword As String
    Dim sDBName As String

    ' assign default user name and password
    sUserName = "Admin"
    sPassword = ""

    With DBEngine

        ' set system database path and name
        .SystemDB = GetWorkgroupDatabase
```

```
                    ' set default user name and password
                    .DefaultUser = sUserName
                    .DefaultPassword = sPassword

                    ' get path and name of database from ReadINI module
                    sDBName = DBPath

                    ' open database
                    Set db = .Workspaces(0).OpenDatabase(sDBName)

            End With

            ' populate the two list boxes with the available users,
            ' tables, and queries from database
            FillUserList
            FillTableAndQueriesList

            ' if there are no valid users, inform the user and exit the
            ' application
            If (lstUsers.ListCount < 1) Then

                MsgBox "There are no users!", vbExclamation, "USERS"
                cmdClose_Click

            Else

                ' initialize the list boxes to point to the first item in
                ' each list box
                lstUsers.ListIndex = 0
                lstTablesAndQueries.ListIndex = 0

            End If

    Exit Sub

    ERR_Form_Load:

        ' display error for the user
        With Err
            MsgBox "ERROR #" & .Number & ": " & .Description,
    vbExclamation, _
                    "ERROR"
        End With

    End Sub
```

4. Enter the Form_Unload code to ensure that the database object variable is closed and released before the application terminates:

```
Private Sub Form_Unload(Cancel As Integer)

    ' close the database
    Set db = Nothing

End Sub
```

5. Now enter the code for both the `FillTableAndQueriesList` and the `FillUserList` procedures. These two routines are very similar to those found in the preceding How-To. The `FillTableAndQueriesList` procedure populates the `lstTablesAndQueries` list box with the names of the data objects in the `Tables` container. The `FillUserList` routine populates the `lstUsers` list box with the users found in the `Users` collection of the current `Workspace` object.

```
Private Sub FillTableAndQueriesList()

    Dim oDocument As Document

    ' populate the TableAndQueries list boxes with all the
    ' available tables and queries except the system ones
    For Each oDocument In db.Containers("Tables").Documents

        With oDocument
            If (Left$(.Name, 4) <> "MSys") Then _
                    lstTablesAndQueries.AddItem .Name
        End With

    Next

End Sub

Private Sub FillUserList()

    Dim oUser As User

    ' populate the user list boxes with all users except CREATOR
    ' and ENGINE (these shouldn't be changed)
    For Each oUser In DBEngine.Workspaces(0).Users

        With oUser

            If (UCase$(.Name) <> "CREATOR") _
            And (UCase$(.Name) <> "ENGINE") Then

                lstUsers.AddItem .Name

            End If

        End With

    Next

End Sub
```

6. Now enter the `lstTablesAndQueries_Click` event code as listed here. This code finds the owner of the selected data object from the Users list by comparing it to the `Owner` property of the selected `Document` object.

```
Private Sub lstTablesAndQueries_Click()

    Dim nCount As Integer
    Dim sCurOwner As String

    With lstUsers

        ' loop through each user until the owner of the selected
        ' table or query is found
        For nCount = 0 To .ListCount - 1

        sCurOwner = _

db.Containers("Tables").Documents(lstTablesAndQueries.Text).Owner

            If (.List(nCount) = sCurOwner) Then .ListIndex =
nCount

        Next nCount
    End With

End Sub
```

7. The cmdSave_Click event code simply changes the value of the Owner property of the Documents object to that of the selected user from the lstUsers list box:

```
Private Sub cmdSave_Click()

' if there is an error, goto the code labeled by ERR_cmdSave_Click
On Error GoTo ERR_cmdSave_Click:

    ' assign the new owner to the select table or query
    db.Containers("Tables").Documents(lstTablesAndQueries.Text).Owner = _
        lstUsers.Text

Exit Sub

ERR_cmdSave_Click:

    ' display error for the user
    With Err
        MsgBox "ERROR #" & .Number & ": " & .Description, _
            vbExclamation, "ERROR"
    End With

End Sub
```

8. Finally, enter the following code for the cmdClose_Click event to terminate the application:

```
Private Sub cmdClose_Click()

    ' end the application
    Unload Me

End Sub
```

How It Works

When the program starts, the system database is accessed using the default user and password properties. With this database, the `lstTablesAndQueries` list box is populated with the available data objects. The Users list box is populated with all the users available in the given workgroup. When the user selects a data object from the list, the `Owner` property of that data object is used to find the user who is the owner of it. With a click of the Save button on the `frmOwnership` form, the `Owner` property is changed to the currently selected user in the `lstUsers` list box.

Comments

You have added extensive error-handling code to the preceding few How-To's. This is because of the complexity involved, and the precision necessary, when accessing the system database. A lot of the code will vary from machine to machine and user to user, depending on usernames and passwords.

If you are working on a single PC that is not part of a network, there is a very good chance that you will have only one or two users listed in the `lstUsers` list box. To add more users to your system, jump to How-To 10.9 to see a project that enables you to add more users.

COMPLEXITY
BEGINNING

10.7 How do I...
Change or delete database passwords?

Problem

How do I give the system administrators at my site the ability to change users' passwords for Access databases from my Visual Basic applications?

Technique

Each user's password is stored in the `Password` property of the corresponding `User` object. The current user's password is stored in the `Password` property of the current `Workspace` object.

The **Password** property cannot be read through Visual Basic, and it cannot be directly set. To change the password, you must use the **NewPassword** method for a given user. The **NewPassword** method has two arguments—the first being the current password and the second being the new password. Ordinary users cannot change their password without knowing the current one.

Users with Administer power can change other users' passwords as well as their own without the need to know the current password. Instead, an empty string is passed to the **NewPassword** method in place of the current password.

Steps

Open and run the PASSWORDS.VBP project. A list of available users appears on the form, as shown in Figure 10.8. You can change the password of a given user by clicking the Change Password button, or you can delete the password for a user by clicking the Delete Password button.

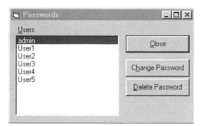

Figure 10.8. The Passwords project.

1. Create a new project and save it as PASSWORDS.VBP. Use **Form1** to add the objects and edit the properties as listed in Table 10.13. Save the form as frmPasswords.frm.

Table 10.13. Objects and properties for the Passwords project.

OBJECT	PROPERTY	SETTING
Form	Name	frmPasswords
	Caption	Passwords
List box	Name	lstUsers
Command button	Name	cmdChangePassword
	Caption	C&hange Password
Command button	Name	cmdDeletePassword
	Caption	&Delete Password
Command button	Name	cmdClose
	Caption	&Close

continued on next page

continued from previous page

OBJECT	PROPERTY	SETTING
	Cancel	-1 'True
	Default	-1 'True
Label	Name	lblUsers
	Caption	&Users

2. Begin by entering the Form_Load event code to access the system database and the call to FillUserList, which populates the lstUsers list box. If there are no users in the list, the application terminates.

```
Private Sub Form_Load()

' if there is an error, then goto the code section labeled by
' ERR_Form_Load
On Error GoTo ERR_Form_Load:

    Dim sUserName As String
    Dim sPassword As String

    ' assign default user name and password
    sUserName = "Admin"
    sPassword = ""

    With DBEngine

        ' set system database path and name
        .SystemDB = GetWorkgroupDatabase

        ' set default user name and password
        .DefaultUser = sUserName
        .DefaultPassword = sPassword

    End With

    ' populate the users list box with the available users
    FillUserList

    ' if there are no valid users, inform the user and exit the
    ' application
    If (lstUsers.ListCount < 1) Then

        MsgBox "There are no users!", vbExclamation, "USERS"
        cmdClose_Click

    Else

        ' initialize the list boxes to point to the first item in
        ' users list
        lstUsers.ListIndex = 0

    End If
```

```
Exit Sub

ERR_Form_Load:

    ' display error for the user
    With Err
        MsgBox "ERROR #" & .Number & ": " & .Description, _
                vbExclamation, "ERROR"
    End With

    ' end the application
    cmdClose_Click

End Sub
```

3. Enter the code for the `Click` event of the `cmdChangePassword` command button as shown next. This code asks for the old password, the new password, and a confirmation of the new password; then it calls the `ChangePassword` routine to change the password. Users logged in as Admin do not have to specify anything for the old password because they have the power to change the current password without any knowledge of it.

```
Private Sub cmdChangePassword_Click()

    ' local variables used to store passwords
    Dim sOldPassword As String
    Dim sNewPassword As String
    Dim sConPassword As String

    ' ask for old password
    sOldPassword = InputBox( _
                    "Please enter the old password for user '" _
                            & lstUsers.Text & "'.", _
                            "CHANGE PASSWORD")

    ' ask for new password
    sNewPassword = InputBox( _
                    "Please enter the new password for user '" _
                            & lstUsers.Text & "'.", _
                            "CHANGE PASSWORD")

    ' confirm new password
    sConPassword = InputBox("Please confirm new password for user '" _
                            & lstUsers.Text & "'.", _
                            "CHANGE PASSWORD")

    ' if new password is not equivalent to the confirmed password,
    ' notify the user and end the task; otherwise, change the
    ' password
    If (sNewPassword <> sConPassword) Then
```

continued on next page

continued from previous page

```
                    MsgBox "New password does not match confirmed password.", _
                           vbExclamation, "ERROR"

            Else

                ChangePassword sOldPassword, sNewPassword

            End If

    End Sub
```

4. Now enter the code to delete a password located in the `Click` event of the `cmdDeletePassword` command button. This event asks for the old password and calls the `ChangePassword` routine with an empty string as a new password to delete the current password. Again, if the user is logged on as Admin, as in this example, it is unnecessary to enter an old password.

```
Private Sub cmdDeletePassword_Click()

    ' local variable used to store old password
    Dim sOldPassword As String

    ' ask for old password
    sOldPassword = InputBox(_
"Please enter the old password for user '" _
                            & lstUsers.Text & "'.", _
                                     "DELETE PASSWORD")

    ' change the password
    ChangePassword sOldPassword, ""

End Sub
```

5. Enter the code for the `cmdClose_Click` event to terminate the application:

```
Private Sub cmdClose_Click()

    ' end the application
    Unload Me

End Sub
```

6. The `FillUserList` routine is listed next. This procedure adds all the current users of the workgroup to the `lstUsers` list box except for `CREATOR` and `ENGINE`. These should not be changed; therefore, they are not available for access by the user.

```
Private Sub FillUserList()

    Dim oUser As User
```

```
    ' populate the user list boxes with all users except CREATOR
    ' and ENGINE (these shouldn't be changed)
    For Each oUser In DBEngine.Workspaces(0).Users

        With oUser

            If (UCase$(.Name) <> "CREATOR") _
            And (UCase$(.Name) <> "ENGINE") Then

                lstUsers.AddItem .Name

            End If

        End With

    Next

End Sub
```

7. Finally, enter the **ChangePassword** routine listed here. This procedure
takes two arguments. The first is the old password, and the second is the
new password. If there are no errors, the password is changed using the
NewPassword method.

```
Private Sub ChangePassword(sOldPassword As String, _
                    sNewPassword As String)

    ' if there is an error, then goto the code labeled by
    ' ERR_ChangePassword
    On Error GoTo ERR_ChangePassword:

        ' constant used to define application-defined error
        Const ERR_PASSWORD_TOO_LONG = 32000

        ' if the new password is too long, raise application-defined
        ' error
        If (Len(sNewPassword) > 14) Then Error ERR_PASSWORD_TOO_LONG

        ' change password, given the old and new passwords
        DBEngine.Workspaces(0).Users(lstUsers.Text).NewPassword _
                sOldPassword, sNewPassword

        ' if we got this far, we must be successful; notify the user
        MsgBox "Password successfully changed for user '" _
                & lstUsers.Text & "'", vbInformation, "SUCCESS"

    Exit Sub

    ERR_ChangePassword:

        ' local variable used to hold error message
        Dim sMessage As String
```

continued on next page

continued from previous page

```
            With Err

                Select Case .Number

                    ' application-defined error, password too long
                    Case ERR_PASSWORD_TOO_LONG:
                        sMessage = _
                            "The password must be 14 characters or less."

                    ' unexpected error, create error message with number
                    ' and description
                    Case Else:
                        sMessage = "ERROR #" & .Number & ": " & _
                                    .Description

                End Select

            End With


            ' display error for the user
            MsgBox sMessage, vbExclamation, "ERROR"

        End Sub
```

How It Works

After the program accesses the system database in the `Form_Load` event, the list box on the form is populated with the available users in the workgroup. When a user selects a username from the list and clicks the Change Password button, old and new passwords are sent to the `ChangePassword` procedure, where a call to the `NewPassword` method changes the password. When the user clicks the Delete Password button, an empty string is passed to the `ChangePassword` procedure to set the new password to nothing, therefore deleting it.

 COMPLEXITY
BEGINNING

10.8 How do I...
Use a single password for data access for all users?

Problem

I want to secure my Access database, but I do not think it is necessary for each user to have his or her own password. Instead, I want to create a password that I can change for the entire database, regardless of the user. How do I create a single password for an entire Access database with Visual Basic?

Technique

The same concept shown in How-To 10.7 applies here. The `NewPassword` method is used to change the password for a given Access database.

The `NewPassword` not only applies to the `User` object, but it also is available with the `Database` object. When you specify a password for a database, you must connect to that database in the future with a string indicating the valid password.

This string is passed as an argument to the `OpenDatabase` method, as shown in this example:

```
Set db = _
  DBEngine.Workspaces(0).OpenDatabase(DBName, True, False, ";pwd=PASSWORD")
```

Here, `db` is a database object, *DBName* is a valid path and name of an Access database, and *PASSWORD* is the password for the given database.

Steps

Open and run the DatabasePassword.vbp project. You should see the form as shown in Figure 10.9. When a user clicks the Open Database button, she is prompted with an input box asking for the password for the database. If there is no password, the user simply presses Enter. After the database is open, the user can change the password by clicking the Change Password button. Just as with changing a user's password, the project prompts for the old password as well as the new and a confirmation of the new password. If all is successful, the password is changed.

Figure 10.9. The DatabasePassword project.

1. Create a new project and save it as DatabasePassword.vbp. Add the objects and edit the properties of **Form1** as shown in Table 10.14. Afterward, save the form as frmDatabasePassword.frm.

Table 10.14. Objects and properties for the DatabasePassword project.

OBJECT	PROPERTY	SETTING
Form	Name	frmDatabasePassword
	Caption	Database Password
Command button	Name	cmdOpenDatabase
	Caption	&Open Database
Command button	Name	cmdChangePassword
	Caption	Change &Password
Command button	Name	cmdCloseDatabase
	Caption	&Close Database
Command button	Name	cmdExit
	Caption	&Exit
	Cancel	-1 'True
	Default	-1 'True

2. Enter the following code in the declarations section of your project. The **db** object variable is used to store the database object, and the **NO_ERROR** constant declaration is used throughout the project to indicate success.

```
Option Explicit

' form-level object variable declaration used to hold database
' object
Private db As Database

' form-level constant declaration used to indicate success
Private Const NO_ERROR = 0
```

3. Now enter the familiar **Form_Load** event as shown next. This event, like the others in the previous How-To sections, establishes a link with the system database using a default user and password. These variables might need to be altered by the user to her own Administer values.

```
Private Sub Form_Load()

' if there is an error, then goto the code section labeled by
' ERR_Form_Load
On Error GoTo ERR_Form_Load:

    Dim sUserName As String
    Dim sPassword As String

    ' assign default user name and password
    sUserName = "Admin"
    sPassword = ""

    With DBEngine
```

```
                         ' set system database path and name
                         .SystemDB = GetWorkgroupDatabase

                         ' set default user name and password
                         .DefaultUser = sUserName
                         .DefaultPassword = sPassword

                     End With

                     ' initialize database to closed state to disable various
                     ' buttons
                     cmdCloseDatabase_Click

                 Exit Sub

                 ERR_Form_Load:

                     ' display error for the user
                     With Err
                         MsgBox "ERROR #" & .Number & ": " & .Description, _
                                 vbExclamation, _
                                 "ERROR"
                     End With

                     ' end the application
                     cmdExit_Click

                 End Sub
```

4. Add the code that ensures that the database is closed in the **Form_Unload** event as shown here:

```
Private Sub Form_Unload(Cancel As Integer)

    ' ensure that the database is closed upon shutdown of
    ' application
    cmdCloseDatabase_Click

End Sub
```

5. Now enter the code for the **cmdOpenDatabase_Click** event of the Open Database command button. This code prompts the user for the current database password, creates a password string, and passes it to the **OpenDatabase** method. If all is successful, the user is notified that the database is opened, and the Change Password and Close Database buttons are enabled.

```
Private Sub cmdOpenDatabase_Click()

' if there is an error, goto the code labeled by
' ERR_cmdOpenDatabase_Click
On Error GoTo ERR_cmdOpenDatabase_Click:
```

continued on next page

continued from previous page

```
        Dim sPassword As String
        Dim sDBName As String

        ' local constant declaration of application-defined error
        Const ERR_NOT_VALID_PASSWORD = 3031

        ' ask user for the password of the database
        sPassword = InputBox("Please enter database password.", _
                        "OPEN DATABASE")

        ' create connection string
        sPassword = ";pwd=" & sPassword

        ' retrieve database name and path from the ReadINI module
        sDBName = DBPath

        ' attempt to open the database
        Set db = DBEngine.Workspaces(0).OpenDatabase _
                (sDBName, True, False, sPassword)

ERR_cmdOpenDatabase_Click:

        Dim sMessage As String

        With Err

            ' determine error
            Select Case .Number

                ' there is no error, inform the user of success and
                ' enable the use of the change password and close
                ' database command buttons
                Case NO_ERROR:
                    sMessage = "Database opened successfully."

                    cmdOpenDatabase.Enabled = False
                    cmdChangePassword.Enabled = True
                    cmdCloseDatabase.Enabled = True

                ' password is incorrect
                Case ERR_NOT_VALID_PASSWORD:
                    sMessage = "Invalid password."

                ' unexpected error, inform the user
                Case Else:
                    sMessage = "ERROR #" & .Number & ": " & _
                            .Description

            End Select

            ' display the error for the user
            MsgBox sMessage, _
                    IIf(.Number = NO_ERROR, vbInformation, _
                            vbExclamation), _
                    IIf(.Number = NO_ERROR, "SUCCESS", "ERROR")
```

```
      End With

   End Sub
```

6. The `cmdChangePassword_Click` event prompts the user for the old password, the new, and a confirmation, and successfully changes the password by calling the `NewPassword` method of the **Database** object. Enter the following code:

```
Private Sub cmdChangePassword_Click()

' if there is an error,
' goto the code labeled by ERR_cmdChangePassword_Click
On Error GoTo ERR_cmdChangePassword_Click:

    ' local variables used to store passwords
    Dim sOldPassword As String
    Dim sNewPassword As String
    Dim sConPassword As String

    ' private constant declarations for application-defined errors
    Const ERR_PASSWORDS_DIFFER = 32000
    Const ERR_PASSWORD_TOO_LONG = 32001

    ' ask for old password
    sOldPassword = InputBox("Please enter the old password for " _
                        & "the database.", "CHANGE PASSWORD")

    ' ask for new password
    sNewPassword = InputBox("Please enter the new password for " _
                        & "the database.", "CHANGE PASSWORD")

    If (Len(sNewPassword) > 14) Then Error ERR_PASSWORD_TOO_LONG

    ' confirm new password
    sConPassword = InputBox("Please confirm new password for " _
                        & "the database.", "CHANGE PASSWORD")

    ' if new password is not equivalent to the confirmed password,
    ' notify the user and end the task; otherwise, change the
    ' password
    If (sNewPassword <> sConPassword) Then Error _
      ERR_PASSWORDS_DIFFER

    ' change the password
    db.NewPassword sOldPassword, sNewPassword

ERR_cmdChangePassword_Click:

    Dim sMessage As String

    With Err

        ' select appropriate error
```

continued on next page

continued from previous page

```
Select Case .Number

    ' no error has occurred, inform the user of success
    Case NO_ERROR:
        sMessage = "Password changed successfully."

    ' new and confirmed passwords are different
    Case ERR_PASSWORDS_DIFFER:
        sMessage = "The confirmed password does not " _
                & "match the new password."

    ' password is longer than 14 characters
    Case ERR_PASSWORD_TOO_LONG:
        sMessage = _
            "The password must be 14 characters or less."

    ' unexpected error, inform the user
    Case Else:
        sMessage = "ERROR #" & .Number & ": " & _
                    .Description

End Select

' display the error for the user
MsgBox sMessage, _
        IIf(.Number = NO_ERROR, vbInformation, _
                    vbExclamation), _
        IIf(.Number = NO_ERROR, "SUCCESS", "ERROR")

End With

End Sub
```

7. The `Click` event of the Close Database command button is listed next. This procedure simply releases the database object by setting it equal to nothing and disables the Change Password and Close Database buttons, as well as enables the Open Database button. The final event, `cmdExit_Click`, ends the application. Enter these procedures now:

```
Private Sub cmdCloseDatabase_Click()

    ' close the database
    Set db = Nothing

    ' only allow the user to open the database
    cmdOpenDatabase.Enabled = True
    cmdChangePassword.Enabled = False
    cmdCloseDatabase.Enabled = False

End Sub

Private Sub cmdExit_Click()

    ' end the application
```

```
        Unload Me

    End Sub
```

How It Works

When the `DatabasePassword` project is initialized, the system database is addressed with the default username and password. When the user opens the database, he is prompted for the current password. This password is used to create a string that is passed to the `OpenDatabase` method to open the database object.

When the user elects to change the current database password, he is asked to supply the old and new passwords, as well as a confirmation of the new password. With a call to the `NewDatabase` method of the database object, the password is changed.

You should note that the password cannot be changed when a database is opened in shared mode. As in this How-To, you must open the database exclusively (by specifying `True` as the second argument to the `OpenDatabase` method) to change the password.

Comments

Every How-To in this chapter uses the same database, the ORDERS.MDB database file. When you are through with this How-To, be sure to change the database password back to a `NULL` string so that the other How-To projects can successfully access the database!

COMPLEXITY
BEGINNING

10.9 How do I...
Add new users to a system database?

Problem

I need to give system administrators at my user sites the ability to add new users to the system database. How do I accomplish this task through Visual Basic?

Technique

The `Workspace` object has a collection called `Users`. Each user defined in the system database has a corresponding `User` object within the `Users` collection. To add a new user, you must first create a new `User` object. The new `User` object must be supplied a name, a PID, and, optionally, a password.

The PID is a case-sensitive alphanumeric string between 4 and 20 characters in length. The Jet engine uses this PID in combination with the username to build a security ID for a user.

After the User object is created, it is appended to the Users collection of the current Workspace object via the Append method.

Steps

Open and run the AddUser.vbp project. You should see the form shown in Figure 10.10. To add a user, click the Add User button and supply a username and password; the PID string is calculated from the username. If the user is successfully added, you will see a message box indicating so, and the list box on the form will be updated to include the new user.

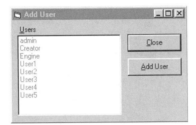

Figure 10.10. The AddUser project.

1. Create a new project and call it AddUser.vbp. Using Form1, add the objects and edit the properties as shown in Table 10.15, saving the form as frmAddUser.frm.

Table 10.15. Objects and properties for the AddUser project.

OBJECT	PROPERTY	SETTING
Form	Name	frmAddUser
	Caption	Add User
List box	Name	lstUsers
Command button	Name	cmdAddUser
	Caption	&Add User
Command button	Name	cmdClose
	Caption	&Close
	Cancel	-1 'True
	Default	-1 'True
Label	Name	lblUsers
	Caption	&Users

2. There are no form-level declarations in this project, so go ahead and enter the `Form_Load` event code as shown next. This code accesses the system database using the default username, Admin, and an empty string password. After this is done, the `FillUserList` procedure is called to show all the available users in the system database.

```
Private Sub Form_Load()

' if there is an error, then goto the code section labeled by
' ERR_Form_Load
On Error GoTo ERR_Form_Load:

    Dim sUserName As String
    Dim sPassword As String

    ' assign default user name and password
    sUserName = "Admin"
    sPassword = ""

    With DBEngine

        ' set system database path and name
        .SystemDB = GetWorkgroupDatabase

        ' set default user name and password
        .DefaultUser = sUserName
        .DefaultPassword = sPassword

    End With

    ' populate the users list box with the available users
    FillUserList

Exit Sub

ERR_Form_Load:

    ' display error for the user
    With Err
        MsgBox "ERROR #" & .Number & ": " & .Description, _
                vbExclamation, _
                "ERROR"
    End With

    ' end the application
    cmdClose_Click

End Sub
```

3. Now enter the code for the `Click` event of the `cmdAddUser` command button. This event asks the user for both a username and a password. After error-checking the input values, the procedure calls the `GetNewPID` procedure to receive a personal identifier. This event then creates a new

User object with this information and appends it to the Users collection
of the current Workspace object.

```
Private Sub cmdAddUser_Click()

' if there is an error, then goto code labeled by
' ERR_cmdAddUser_Click
On Error GoTo ERR_cmdAddUser_Click:

    ' local variables used to store passwords
    Dim sNewUserName As String
    Dim sNewPassword As String
    Dim sConPassword As String

    ' local variables used for the new user
    Dim sPID As String
    Dim oNewUser As User

    ' constant declarations for application-defined error messages
    Const ERR_NO_USER_NAME = 32000
    Const ERR_PASSWORD_TOO_LONG = 32001
    Const ERR_PASSWORDS_NOT_EQUAL = 32002

    ' enter a new username
    sNewUserName = InputBox("Please enter a new username.", _
"ADD USER")

    ' trim excess white spaces from the username
    sNewUserName = Trim$(sNewUserName)

    ' if no username is entered, notify the user and abandon task
    If (sNewUserName = "") Then Error ERR_NO_USER_NAME

    ' ask for new password
    sNewPassword = InputBox( _
                    "Please enter the new password for user '" _
                        & sNewUserName & "'.", "ADD USER")

    ' if the password is too long, notify the user and end the
    ' task
    If (Len(sNewPassword) > 14) Then Error ERR_PASSWORD_TOO_LONG

    ' confirm new password
    sConPassword = InputBox("Please confirm new password for user '" _
                        & sNewUserName & "'.", "ADD USER")

    ' if new password is not equivalent to the confirmed password,
    ' notify the user and end the task
    If (sNewPassword <> sConPassword) Then Error _
        ERR_PASSWORDS_NOT_EQUAL

    'get a PID for the new user
    sPID = GetNewPID(sNewUserName)

    With DBEngine
```

```vb
                        ' create a new user object from username, pid, and
                        ' password
                        Set oNewUser = .Workspaces(0).CreateUser(sNewUserName, _
                                                                 sPID, _
                                                                 sNewPassword)

                        ' append the new users to the workspace
                        .Workspaces(0).Users.Append oNewUser

                End With

                ' repopulate list box with new users
                FillUserList

                ' notify the user of success
                MsgBox "User '" & sNewUserName & "' added successfully.", _
                        vbInformation, "ADD USER"

        Exit Sub

        ERR_cmdAddUser_Click:

                ' variable used for error message
                Dim sMessage As String

                With Err

                        ' create an error message for given error code
                        Select Case .Number

                                Case ERR_NO_USER_NAME:
                                        sMessage = "You did not enter a user name."

                                Case ERR_PASSWORD_TOO_LONG:
                                        sMessage = _
                                                "The password must be 14 characters or less"

                                Case ERR_PASSWORDS_NOT_EQUAL:
                                        sMessage = "The confirmed password is not " _
                                                        & "equivalent to the new password."

                                ' unexpected error, create an error message from the
                                ' error number and description
                                Case Else:
                                        sMessage = "ERROR #" & .Number & ": " & _
                                                        .Description

                        End Select

                End With

                ' display the error message for the user
                MsgBox sMessage, vbExclamation, "ERROR"

        End Sub
```

4. Enter the following code to terminate the application:

```
Private Sub cmdClose_Click()

    ' end the application
    Unload Me

End Sub
```

5. Now enter the **FillUserList** procedure, which populates the **lstUsers** list box with all the users listed in the system database:

```
Private Sub FillUserList()

    Dim oUser As User

    With lstUsers

        ' clear current list of users
        .Clear

        ' populate the user list boxes with all users
        For Each oUser In DBEngine.Workspaces(0).Users
            .AddItem oUser.Name
        Next

    End With

End Sub
```

6. Finally, enter the **GetNewPID** function, which creates a new PID string for the specified username, ensuring that it is at least 4 but no more than 20 characters:

```
Private Function GetNewPID(sUserName As String) As String

    Dim sPID As String

    ' create new PID
    sPID = sUserName

    If (Len(sPID) > 20) Then

        ' if the PID is greater than 20 characters, shorten it
        sPID = Left$(sPID, 20)

    Else

        ' if the PID is less than 4 characters, add some
        ' underscores
        While (Len(sPID) < 4)
            sPID = sPID & "_"
        Wend

    End If
```

```
            ' return newly created PID value
            GetNewPID = sPID

        End Function
```

How It Works

When the **AddUser** project starts, the code reads the system database to populate the list box on the form with the available users. When the user decides to add a new user by clicking the Add User button, he must enter both a new username and a password. The username is used to create a PID string. The name, PID, and password are then used to create a new **User** object, which is appended to the existing **Users** collection.

Comments

To remove a user from the system database, simply use the **Delete** method of the **Workspace** object's **Users** collection to delete the desired user, as shown here:

```
DBEngine.Workspaces(0).Users("USERNAME").Delete
```

Here, *USERNAME* is a name of a user currently in the **Users** collection of the current workspace.

COMPLEXITY
BEGINNING

10.10 How do I...
Define new groups in a system database?

Problem

How do I give system administrators the ability to define new groups in the system database through Visual Basic?

Technique

The techniques used in this How-To directly correspond to those used in How-To 10.9. To add a new group to the **Groups** collection of the current **Workspace** object, you must first create a new **Group** object from a group name and a PID.

In previous versions of Microsoft Jet, the identifier used for a group was called a GID (group identifier). Now, to make things uniform, it is called a PID (personal identifier), as it is for a user.

The PID is used in the same manner for a group as for a user. It is used in conjunction with the group name to build an SID for the group. After you create the group with its name and PID, you can append it to the **Groups** collection of the current **Workspace** object.

Steps

Open and run the AddGroup.vbp project. You should see the form shown in Figure 10.11. To add a group, click the Add Group button and supply the application with a name for the new group. If all is successful, you will see a verification message box and the new group in the list of groups on the form.

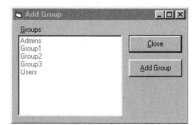

Figure 10.11. The AddGroup project.

1. Create a new project and save it as AddGroup.vbp. Use **Form1** to create the objects and edit the properties as listed in Table 10.16. Save this form as frmAddGroup.frm.

Table 10.16. Objects and properties for the AddGroup project.

OBJECT	PROPERTY	SETTING
Form	Name	frmAddGroup
	Caption	Add Group
List box	Name	lstGroups
Command button	Name	cmdAddGroup
	Caption	&Add Group
Command button	Name	cmdClose
	Caption	&Close
	Cancel	-1 'True
	Default	-1 'True
Label	Name	lblGroups
	Caption	&Groups

2. Enter the Form_Load event code shown next. This code accesses the system database with the default username and password assigned to the sUserName and sPassword variables, respectively. Then call the FillGroupList to populate the list box on the frmAddGroup form.

```
Private Sub Form_Load()

' if there is an error, then goto the code section labeled by
' ERR_Form_Load
On Error GoTo ERR_Form_Load:

    Dim sUserName As String
    Dim sPassword As String

    ' assign default username and password
    sUserName = "Admin"
    sPassword = ""

    With DBEngine

        ' set system database path and name
        .SystemDB = GetWorkgroupDatabase

        ' set default user name and password
        .DefaultUser = sUserName
        .DefaultPassword = sPassword

    End With

    ' populate the group list box with the available groups
    FillGroupList

Exit Sub

ERR_Form_Load:

    ' display error for the user
    With Err
        MsgBox "ERROR #" & .Number & ": " & .Description, _
               vbExclamation, _
               "ERROR"
    End With

    ' end the application
    cmdClose_Click

End Sub
```

3. Now enter the code for the Click event of the cmdAddGroup command button. This code asks the user for a new group name and calls GetNewPID to create a personal identifier for the new group. With this information, a new Group object is created and appended to the Groups collection of the current workspace.

```
Private Sub cmdAddGroup_Click()

' if there is an error, then goto code labeled by
' ERR_cmdAddGroup_Click
On Error GoTo ERR_cmdAddGroup_Click:

    ' local variables used to store new group name
    Dim sNewGroupName As String

    ' local variables used for the new group
    Dim sPID As String
    Dim oNewGroup As Group

    ' constant declaration for application-defined error message
    Const ERR_NO_GROUP_NAME = 32000

    ' enter a new group name
    sNewGroupName = InputBox("Please enter a new group name.", _
                    "ADD GROUP")

    ' trim excess white spaces from the group name
    sNewGroupName = Trim$(sNewGroupName)

    ' if no group name is entered, notify the user and abandon
    ' task
    If (sNewGroupName = "") Then Error ERR_NO_GROUP_NAME

    'get a PID for the new group
    sPID = GetNewPID(sNewGroupName)

    With DBEngine

        ' create a new group object from group name, PID, and
        ' password
        Set oNewGroup = .Workspaces(0).CreateGroup( _
                        sNewGroupName, sPID)

        ' append the new groups to the workspace
        .Workspaces(0).Groups.Append oNewGroup

    End With

    ' repopulate list box with new groups
    FillGroupList

    ' notify the user of success
    MsgBox "Group '" & sNewGroupName & "' added successfully.", _
           vbInformation, "ADD GROUP"

Exit Sub

ERR_cmdAddGroup_Click:

    ' variable used for error message
    Dim sMessage As String

    With Err
```

```
            ' create an error message for given error code
            Select Case .Number

                Case ERR_NO_GROUP_NAME:
                    sMessage = "You did not enter a group name."

                ' unexpected error, create an error message from the
                ' error number and description
                Case Else:
                    sMessage = "ERROR #" & .Number & ": " & _
                                .Description

            End Select

        End With

        ' display the error message for the user
        MsgBox sMessage, vbExclamation, "ERROR"
        Stop
        Resume
    End Sub
```

4. Enter the code for the `cmdClose_Click` event, which terminates the application:

```
Private Sub cmdClose_Click()

    ' end the application
    Unload Me

End Sub
```

5. Now enter the `FillGroupList` procedure, which populates the `lstGroups` list box with the groups found in the system database:

```
Private Sub FillGroupList()

    Dim oGroup As Group

    With lstGroups

        ' clear current list of groups
        .Clear

        ' populate the group list boxes with all groups
        For Each oGroup In DBEngine.Workspaces(0).Groups
            .AddItem oGroup.Name
        Next

    End With

End Sub
```

6. To complete the project, enter the `GetNewPID` function, which accepts the new `GroupName` as an argument used to create the PID that is returned. The PID will be between 4 and 20 characters in length.

```
Private Function GetNewPID(sGroupName As String) As String

    Dim sPID As String

    ' create new PID
    sPID = sGroupName

    If (Len(sPID) > 20) Then

        ' if the PID is greater than 20 characters, shorten it
        sPID = Left$(sPID, 20)

    Else

        ' if the PID is less than 4 characters, add some
        ' underscores
        While (Len(sPID) < 4)
            sPID = sPID & "_"
        Wend

    End If

    ' return newly created PID value
    GetNewPID = sPID

End Function
```

How It Works

This application begins by accessing the system database and populating the list box with the groups listed within it. When a user decides to add a new group by clicking the Add Group button, he is asked to supply a new group name. A PID is then created from this group name, and with both of these variables, a new `Group` object is created. This object is then appended to the `Groups` collection of the current workspace using the `Append` method. Finally, the list box is repopulated with the inclusion of the new group.

Comments

To remove a group from a system database, simply use the `Delete` method of the `Workspace` object's `Groups` collection to delete the desired group, as shown here:

```
DBEngine.Workspaces(0).Groups("GROUPNAME").Delete
```

Here, *GROUPNAME* is a valid name of a group that belongs to the `Groups` collection of the current `Workspace` object.

COMPLEXITY
BEGINNING

10.11 How do I...
Add users to groups and delete users from groups?

Problem

How do I give system administrators at my user sites the ability to add and remove users from different groups by using Visual Basic?

Technique

The Group object owns a collection called Users. Each user who belongs to the group is represented by a User object within the Users collection. If a User object exists in a system database, you can add that user to a group by first using the CreateUser method of the Group object to create a temporary User object, supplying the username of a user who is defined within the current system database.

After this job is done, you append the temporary User object to the Users collection of an existing Group object.

Steps

Open and run the AddUsersToGroups.vbp project. You should see the form shown in Figure 10.12. You can select the group you want to work with from the combo box at the top of the form. A list box on the left lists all the available users in the system database, and the list box on the right shows the users who are currently part of the selected group.

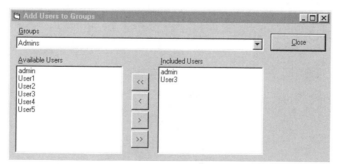

Figure 10.12. The AddUsersToGroups project.

To move a user into the currently selected group, select a user from the list of available users and click the > button to move that user to the list of included users. To remove a user from a group, select the user from the list of included users and click the < button. To add all users to a group, click the >> button, and to remove all users from a group, click the << button. Changes are immediate, so be careful!

To delete a user from a group, use the **Delete** method of the **Group** object's **Users** collection.

1. Create a new project and name it AddUsersToGroups.vbp. Add and edit the objects and properties as shown in Table 10.17, and save the form as frmAddUsersToGroups.frm. Notice that the four **cmdMove** command buttons are part of a control array.

Table 10.17. Objects and properties for the AddUsersToGroups project.

OBJECT	PROPERTY	SETTING
Form	Name	frmAddUsersToGroups
	Caption	Add Users to Groups
Combo box	Name	cboGroups
	Style	2 'Dropdown List
List box	Name	lstAvailableUsers
	Sorted	-1 'True
List box	Name	lstIncludedUsers
	Sorted	-1 'True
Command button	Name	cmdMove
	Caption	<<
	Index	0
Command button	Name	cmdMove
	Caption	<
	Index	1
Command button	Name	cmdMove
	Caption	>
	Index	2
Command button	Name	cmdMove
	Caption	>>
	Index	3
Command button	Name	cmdClose
	Caption	&Close
	Cancel	-1 'True
	Default	-1 'True

OBJECT	PROPERTY	SETTING
Label	Name	lblGroups
	Caption	&Groups
Label	Name	lblAvailableUsers
	Caption	&Available Users
Label	Name	lblIncludedUsers
	Caption	&Included Users

2. Enter the code for the Form_Load event as shown here. This code initializes the DBEngine with the default username and passwords defined in the sUserName and sPassword variables. The event then calls the FillAvailableUserList and FillGroupCombo procedures to populate the form with the available users and groups from the system database.

```
Private Sub Form_Load()

' if there is an error, then goto the code section labeled by
' ERR_Form_Load
On Error GoTo ERR_Form_Load:

    Dim sUserName As String
    Dim sPassword As String

    ' assign default username and password
    sUserName = "Admin"
    sPassword = ""

    With DBEngine

        ' set system database path and name
        .SystemDB = GetWorkgroupDatabase

        ' set default user name and password
        .DefaultUser = sUserName
        .DefaultPassword = sPassword

    End With

    ' populate the users list box with the available users
    FillAvailableUserList

    ' if there are no valid users, inform the user and exit the
    ' application
    If (lstAvailableUsers.ListCount < 1) Then

        MsgBox "There are no users!", vbExclamation, "USERS"
        cmdClose_Click

    Else
```

continued on next page

continued from previous page

```
                            ' populate the group combo box and select the first group
                            ' automatically
                            FillGroupCombo
                            cboGroups.ListIndex = 0

                    End If

            Exit Sub

            ERR_Form_Load:

                    ' display error for the user
                    With Err
                        MsgBox "ERROR #" & .Number & ": " & .Description, _
                        vbExclamation, _
                                    "ERROR"
                    End With

                    ' end the application
                    cmdClose_Click

            End Sub
```

3. Now enter the code that repopulates the **lstIncludedUsers** list box when the user selects a new group from the **cboGroups** combo box:

```
Private Sub cboGroups_Click()

        ' fill the included users text boxes for the selected group
        FillIncludedUsers

End Sub
```

4. Enter the code for the **Click** event of the **cmdMove** command buttons now. This event handles all four of the move buttons between the two list boxes on **frmAddUsersToGroups**. Using the locally declared constants to indicate the different buttons, users are either removed or added to the current group by a call to either **RemoveUserFromGroup** or **AddUserToGroup**.

```
Private Sub cmdMove_Click(Index As Integer)

        Dim nCount As Integer

        ' constant declarations that correspond to the four move
        ' buttons on the frmAddUsersToGroups form
        Const MOVE_REMOVE_ALL = 0
        Const MOVE_REMOVE = 1
        Const MOVE_ADD = 2
        Const MOVE_ALL = 3
```

```
Select Case Index

    ' remove all included users from list
    Case MOVE_REMOVE_ALL:
        With lstIncludedUsers
            For nCount = 0 To .ListCount - 1
                RemoveUserFromGroup .List(nCount)
            Next nCount
        End With

    ' if a user is selected, remove it
    Case MOVE_REMOVE:
        With lstIncludedUsers
            If (.ListIndex < 0) Then Exit Sub
            RemoveUserFromGroup .Text
        End With

    ' if a user is selected, add it
    Case MOVE_ADD:
        With lstAvailableUsers
            If (.ListIndex < 0) Then Exit Sub
            AddUserToGroup .Text
        End With

    ' add all users from available users list box
    Case MOVE_ALL:
        With lstAvailableUsers
            For nCount = 0 To .ListCount - 1
                AddUserToGroup .List(nCount)
            Next nCount
        End With

End Select

' repopulated the included user list box
FillIncludedUsers

End Sub
```

5. Enter the code to terminate the application in the **cmdClose_Click** event:

```
Private Sub cmdClose_Click()

    ' end the application
    Unload Me

End Sub
```

6. Now enter the **FillGroupCombo**, **FillAvailableUserList**, and
FillIncludedUsers procedures, which all use the system database to
populate their corresponding controls with groups available, users
available, or users in selected group:

```
Private Sub FillGroupCombo()

    Dim oGroup As Group

    ' populate the group combo box with all available groups
    For Each oGroup In DBEngine.Workspaces(0).Groups
        cboGroups.AddItem oGroup.Name
    Next

End Sub

Private Sub FillAvailableUserList()

    Dim oUser As User

    ' populate the user list boxes with all users except CREATOR
    ' and ENGINE
    For Each oUser In DBEngine.Workspaces(0).Users
        With oUser
            If (UCase$(.Name) <> "CREATOR") _
            And (UCase$(.Name) <> "ENGINE") Then

                lstAvailableUsers.AddItem .Name

            End If
        End With
    Next

End Sub

Private Sub FillIncludedUsers()

    Dim oUser As User

    With lstIncludedUsers

        ' clear the included users list box
        .Clear

        ' add all the included users for the given group
        For Each oUser In _

DBEngine.Workspaces(0).Groups(cboGroups.Text).Users

            .AddItem oUser.Name

        Next

    End With

End Sub
```

7. Next enter the code to add a new user to a group. This procedure creates a new **User** object with the name of the selected user and then appends the object to the **Users** collection of the selected group.

```
Private Sub AddUserToGroup(sUserName As String)

' if there is an error, goto code labeled by ERR_AddUserToGroup
On Error GoTo ERR_AddUserToGroup:

    Dim oUser As User

    ' constant declaration for error when user is already in group
    Const ERR_USER_IN_GROUP = 3032

    With DBEngine.Workspaces(0).Groups(cboGroups.Text)

        ' create a user and add him to the group
        Set oUser = .CreateUser(sUserName)
        .Users.Append oUser

    End With

Exit Sub

ERR_AddUserToGroup:

    With Err
        Select Case .Number

            ' if user is in group already, continue execution
            Case ERR_USER_IN_GROUP:
                Resume Next

            ' unexpected error, notify user
            Case Else
                MsgBox "ERROR #" & .Number & ": " & .Description, _
                        vbExclamation, "ERROR"

        End Select
    End With

End Sub
```

8. Finally, enter the code to remove a user from a group. The procedure **RemoveUserFromGroup**, shown next, uses the **Delete** method of the **Users** collection to remove the specified user from the **Group** object.

```
Private Sub RemoveUserFromGroup(sUserName As String)

    ' remove user from group
    DBEngine.Workspaces(0).Groups( _
            cboGroups.Text).Users.Delete sUserName

End Sub
```

How It Works

When the application begins, it accesses the system database with default values for username and password. This database is used to populate the combo box of `frmAddUsersToGroups` with all the available groups and the Available Users list box with all the users listed in the database.

When a user selects a group, the `Users` collection of that `Group` object is used to populate the Included Users list box. To move users in to the specified group, a new `User` object is created and appended to the `Users` collection. To remove users from the group, the `Remove` method of the `Users` collection is used with the specified user.

COMPLEXITY
BEGINNING

10.12 How do I...
Track user activity in a database?

Problem

I want to somehow keep a log to track which users created or edited records in my Access database. How do I track user activity in a database using Visual Basic?

Technique

By creating two fields in a recordset, you can track both the user who modified a record and the date and time a record was modified. The first field, used to track the user, is populated with the current username taken from the `UserName` property of the current `Workspace` object.

The second field, the date and time a user modified a record, is populated with the function `Now`, which returns the current date and time.

Steps

Open and run the project Tracker.vbp. After entering a valid username and password, you should see the form shown in Figure 10.13. A ListView control shows the records of the Customers table in the ORDERS.MDB database. The Order Number, User Name, and Last Modified information is displayed.

By clicking the Add Record button, you can add a dummy record to the recordset that becomes populated in the ListView control. The username specified at the start of the application is used to populate the `User Name` field of the recordset, and the current date and time is entered into the `Last Modified` field.

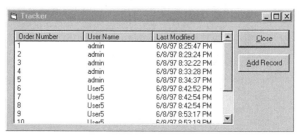

Figure 10.13. The Tracker project.

1. Create a new project and name it Tracker.vbp. Go to the Project |
Components menu selection and choose Microsoft Windows Common
Controls 6.0 from the list to include the ListView control in your project.

2. Use Form1 in your project to add and edit the objects and properties as
shown in Table 10.18. Use the (Custom) property in the property window
of the ListView control to add the three ColumnHeaders listed in Table
10.18. Save the form as frmTracker.frm.

Table 10.18. Objects and properties for the Tracker project.

OBJECT	PROPERTY	SETTING
Form	Name	frmTracker
	Caption	Tracker
ListView	Name	lstCustomers
	View	3 'Report View
	HideColumnHeaders	0 'False
ColumnHeader	Text	Order Number
ColumnHeader	Text	User Name
	SubItemIndex	1
ColumnHeader	Text	Last Modified
	SubItemIndex	2
Command button	Name	cmdAddRecord
	Caption	&Add Record
Command button	Name	cmdClose
	Caption	&Close
	Cancel	-1 'True
	Default	-1 'True

3. Now enter the form-level object variables in the declarations section of
your project. These variables are used to hold both the database and the
recordset objects used throughout the Tracker project.

```
Option Explicit

' form-level object variables used to store database and recordset
' objects
Private db As Database
Private rs As Recordset
```

4. Enter the **Form_Load** event code as shown next. This code asks the user to enter both a valid username and a password from those in the system database to open the Orders database and call the **PopulateListView** procedure.

```
Private Sub Form_Load()

' if there is an error, goto the code labeled by ERR_Form_Load
On Error GoTo ERR_Form_Load:

    ' local constant declaration for invalid user name or password
    ' error
    Const ERR_INVALID_INFORMATION = 3029

    Dim sUserName As String
    Dim sPassword As String
    Dim sDBName As String

    ' get username
    sUserName = InputBox("Enter user name.", "LOGON")

    ' get user password
    sPassword = InputBox("Enter password.", "LOGON")

    With DBEngine

        ' set system database path and name
        .SystemDB = GetWorkgroupDatabase

        ' set default passwords
        .DefaultUser = sUserName
        .DefaultPassword = sPassword

        ' retrieve database path and name from ReadINI module
        sDBName = DBPath

        ' open database with given user and password
        Set db = .Workspaces(0).OpenDatabase(sDBName)

    End With

    ' populate the list view control
    PopulateListView

Exit Sub

ERR_Form_Load:

    Dim sMessage As String
```

```
        With Err

            Select Case .Number

                ' invalid user or password
                Case ERR_INVALID_INFORMATION:
                    sMessage = "Invalid user name or password."

                ' unexpected error, notify the user
                Case Else
                    sMessage = "ERROR #" & .Number & ": " & _
                            .Description

            End Select

        End With

        ' display the message for the user
        MsgBox sMessage, vbExclamation, "ERROR"

        ' end the application
        cmdClose_Click

End Sub
```

5. Enter the code to close and release the database and recordset object variables in the **Form Unload** event:

```
Private Sub Form_Unload(Cancel As Integer)

    ' close the recordset and database
    Set rs = Nothing
    Set db = Nothing

End Sub
```

6. Now enter the **cmdAddRecord_Click** event code to add a new record. Notice the two fields, **User Last Modified** and **DateTime Last Modified**. These are populated with the **UserName** property of the current workspace and the **Now** method to successfully create an auditing trail that you will use to track which user created a given record.

```
Private Sub cmdAddRecord_Click()

' if an error occurs, call the ERR_cmdAddRecord code located at
' the end of this procedure
On Error GoTo ERR_cmdAddRecord:

    Dim sMessage As String
    Dim lPrimaryKey As Long

    ' used to populate fields in Customer table
```

continued on next page

continued from previous page

```
                    ' this is necessary because most of the fields belong to
                    ' indexes making them required fields
                    Const DUMMY_INFO = "<>"

                    ' retrieve a unique key from the GetPrimaryKey routine
                    lPrimaryKey = GetPrimaryKey

                    With rs

                        ' add a new record
                        .AddNew

                        ' fill in the required fields
                        .Fields("Customer Number") = lPrimaryKey
                        .Fields("Customer Name") = DUMMY_INFO
                        .Fields("Street Address") = DUMMY_INFO
                        .Fields("City") = DUMMY_INFO
                        .Fields("State") = DUMMY_INFO
                        .Fields("Zip Code") = DUMMY_INFO

                        ' set the username, date, and time of new record to track
                        ' users
                        .Fields("User Last Modified") = _
                                DBEngine.Workspaces(0).UserName
                        .Fields("DateTime Last Modified") = Now

                        ' make saves (if an error will occur, it will be here)
                        .Update

                    End With

                    PopulateListView

                    ' if we got this far, add new record was successfull
                    sMessage = "Record added successfully!"
                    MsgBox sMessage, vbInformation, "ADD RECORD"

                Exit Sub

                ERR_cmdAddRecord:

                    ' display error for user
                    With Err
                        MsgBox "ERROR #" & .Number & ": " & .Description, _
                        vbExclamation, _
                                "ERROR"
                    End With

                End Sub
```

7. Enter the code to terminate the application on pressing the **cmdClose** command button:

```
Private Sub cmdClose_Click()

    ' end the application
    Unload Me

End Sub
```

8. Now enter the **GetPrimaryKey** function, which uses the **Customer Number** field of the last record in the ORDERS.MDB database to create a new unique key:

```
Private Function GetPrimaryKey()

    ' return a unique primary key based on the Customer Number
    ' field
    With rs

        ' if there are records in the table already, find the last
        ' one and add one to the Customer Number as a unique
        ' Primary Key; otherwise there are no records in the
        ' table, so return 1 for the first new record to be added
        If (Not (.EOF And .BOF)) Then

            .MoveLast

            GetPrimaryKey = .Fields("Customer Number") + 1

        Else

            GetPrimaryKey = 1

        End If

    End With

End Function
```

9. Finally, enter the code for the **PopulateListView** procedure, which repopulates the ListView control with the entire Customer table, showing which user added which Order Number, along with the date and time the record was added:

```
Private Sub PopulateListView()

    Dim oItem As ListItem

    ' show headers of list view and clear the contents of the
    ' ListItems collection
    With lstCustomers
        .HideColumnHeaders = False
```

continued on next page

continued from previous page

```
                .ListItems.Clear
        End With

        ' repopulate the recordset
        Set rs = db.OpenRecordset("Customers", dbOpenTable)

        With rs

            ' order the records by the primary key
            .Index = "PrimaryKey"

            ' add all records to the list view
            While (Not rs.EOF)

                Set oItem = lstCustomers.ListItems.Add(, , _
                            .Fields("Customer Number"))

                oItem.SubItems(1) = "" & .Fields("User Last Modified")
                oItem.SubItems(2) = "" & .Fields( _
                                    "DateTime Last Modified")

                .MoveNext

            Wend

        End With

    End Sub
```

How It Works

When the application begins, it asks the user to enter a username and password, which are checked against the system database when the `OpenDatabase` method is used to access ORDERS.MDB. If the user correctly entered a valid username and corresponding password, the ListView control of the Tracker project is populated with the contents of the Customer table showing the `Order Number`, `User Last Modified`, and `DateTime Last Modified` fields to form an auditing trail of the modification to the recordset.

When the user chooses to add a record by clicking the Add Record button, a new record is created using a newly created primary key. In addition, the current date and time as well as the current username (taken from the `UserName` property of the current `Workspace` object) are used.

Comments

When you set the `DefaultUser` and `DefaultPassword` properties of the `DBEngine` object, you are logging in to the system database with that user. You should note that after you set these properties, you cannot change them during the life of your application. You must terminate the program and restart it to log on as a new user.

COMPLEXITY
BEGINNING

10.13 How do I...
Create and use an encrypted database?

Problem

I want to prohibit other users from viewing my Access database files from various word processors and spy applications. How can I encrypt my database using Visual Basic?

Technique

To encrypt an Access database, you must either specify encryption upon creation of the database or compact the database into a newly encrypted file. To decrypt an Access database, you must decrypt it to a newly created file using `CompactDatabase`.

Steps

Open and run the Encryptor.vbp project. You should see the form shown in Figure 10.14. To create a newly encrypted database, click the Create a New Encrypted Database button. You then are asked to specify a database path and name through a common dialog form.

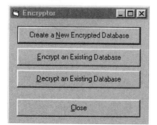

Figure 10.14. The Encryptor project.

To encrypt an existing database, click the Encrypt an Existing Database button, and specify the database to encrypt and a database path and name of the file to encrypt to. Conversely, to decrypt a database, click the Decrypt an Existing Database button, and enter the database to decrypt along with the database to decrypt to. Do not enter a current database name to encrypt or decrypt to; rather, enter a name of a database that does not exist.

1. Create a new project and call it Encryptor.vbp. Go to the Project |
Components menu selection and choose Microsoft Common Dialog
Control 6.0 from the list to include the File Open Common Dialog control
in your project.

2. Add the objects and edit the properties as shown in Table 10.19. Save the
form as frmEncryptor.frm.

Table 10.19. Objects and properties for the Encryptor project.

OBJECT	PROPERTY	SETTING
Form	Name	frmEncryptor
	Caption	Encryptor
Common Dialog	Name	cdlFile
	Filter	MS Access Databases (*.mdb)
Command button	Name	cmdCreateDatabase
	Caption	Create a &New Encrypted Database
Command button	Name	cmdEncryptDatabase
	Caption	&Encrypt an Existing Database
Command button	Name	cmdDecryptDatabase
	Caption	&Decrypt an Existing Database
Command button	Name	cmdClose
	Caption	&Close
	Cancel	-1 'True
	Default	-1 'True

3. Now enter the following constant declarations in the declarations section
of your project. These are used to indicate application-defined errors later
in the project.

```
Option Explicit

' form-level constant declarations of application-defined errors
Private Const NO_ERROR = 0
Private Const ERR_DATABASE_EXISTS = 3204
```

4. Enter the code for the `Form_Load` event as shown here. Not only does this
code log on to the system database as the other How-To projects did, but
it also initializes the Common Dialog control used in this project.

```
Private Sub Form_Load()

' if there is an error, goto the code labeled by ERR_Form_Load
On Error GoTo ERR_Form_Load:

    Dim sUserName As String
    Dim sPassword As String
```

```
        sUserName = "admin"
        sPassword = ""

    With DBEngine

        ' set system database path and name
        .SystemDB = GetWorkgroupDatabase

        ' set default passwords
        .DefaultUser = sUserName
        .DefaultPassword = sPassword

    End With

    With cdlFile

        ' set various properties of the common dialog control
        .Flags = cdlOFNExplorer
        .DefaultExt = "mdb"

    End With

Exit Sub

ERR_Form_Load:

    ' display the error message for the user
    With Err
        MsgBox "ERROR #" & .Number & ": " & .Description, _
        vbExclamation, _
                "ERROR"
    End With

    ' end the application
    cmdClose_Click

End Sub
```

5. Now enter the code for the **Click** event of the **cmdCreateDatabase** command button. This code uses the Common Dialog control to ask the user the name of the database to create. When given this name, the event creates an empty encrypted database.

```
Private Sub cmdCreateDatabase_Click()

' if there is an error, goto the code labeled by
' ERR_cmdCreateDatabase_Click
On Error GoTo ERR_cmdCreateDatabase_Click:

    Dim db As Database
    Dim sNewDatabase As String

    With cdlFile

        ' get the name of the database to encrypt or decrypt to
```

continued on next page

continued from previous page

```
            .filename = ""
            .DialogTitle = "DATABASE TO CREATE"
            .Action = 1
            sNewDatabase = .filename

            ' if the name was not given, abandon task
            If (sNewDatabase = "") Then Exit Sub

        End With

        ' create the encrypted database
        Set db = DBEngine(0).CreateDatabase(sNewDatabase, _
                    dbLangGeneral, dbEncrypt)

        ' close the database
        Set db = Nothing

    ERR_cmdCreateDatabase_Click:

        Dim sMessage As String

        With Err

            ' determine error
            Select Case .Number

                ' there is no error, inform the user of success
                Case NO_ERROR:
                    sMessage = "Database created successfully. "

                ' the database already exists
                Case ERR_DATABASE_EXISTS:
                    sMessage = "You must choose a database that does " _
                            & "not already exist."

                ' unexpected error, inform the user
                Case Else:
                    sMessage = "ERROR #" & .Number & ": " & _
                    .Description

            End Select

            ' display the error for the user
            MsgBox sMessage, _
                    IIf(.Number = NO_ERROR, vbInformation, _
                    vbExclamation), _
                    IIf(.Number = NO_ERROR, "SUCCESS", "ERROR")

        End With

    End Sub
```

6. Enter the code for the cmdEncryptDatabase_Click and the cmdDecryptDatabase_Click events as shown next. These procedures both call the Encryptor routine to either encrypt or decrypt a database, depending on the argument passed to the routine.

```
Private Sub cmdEncryptDatabase_Click()

    ' call procedure to encrypt database
    Encryptor dbEncrypt

End Sub

Private Sub cmdDecryptDatabase_Click()

    ' call procedure to decrypt database
    Encryptor dbDecrypt

End Sub
```

7. Enter the cmdClose_Click event code to terminate the application:

```
Private Sub cmdClose_Click()

    ' terminate the application
    Unload Me

End Sub
```

8. Finally, enter the following Encryptor procedure, which takes an Integer argument that will be passed to the CompactDatabase method. This argument will be either dbEncrypt or dbDecrypt, depending on which button the user presses.

```
Private Sub Encryptor(nAction As Integer)

' if there is an error, goto the code labeled by ERR_Encryptor
On Error GoTo ERR_Encryptor:

    Dim sCurDatabase As String
    Dim sNewDatabase As String

    Dim sActionString As String

    ' create string depending upon action decided by user
    If (nAction = dbEncrypt) Then
        sActionString = "ENCRYPT"
    Else
        sActionString = "DECRYPT"
    End If

    With cdlFile

        ' get the name of the database to encrypt or decrypt
        .filename = ""
```

continued on next page

continued from previous page

```
                        .DialogTitle = "DATABASE TO " & sActionString
                        .Action = 1
                        sCurDatabase = .filename

                        ' if the name was not given, abandon task
                        If (sCurDatabase = "") Then Exit Sub

                        ' get the name of the database to encrypt or decrypt to
                        .filename = ""
                        .DialogTitle = "DATABASE TO " & sActionString & " TO"
                        .Action = 1
                        sNewDatabase = .filename

                        ' if the name was not given, abandon task
                        If (sNewDatabase = "") Then Exit Sub

            End With

            ' encrypt the database
            DBEngine.CompactDatabase sCurDatabase, sNewDatabase, , nAction

    ERR_Encryptor:

        Dim sMessage As String

        With Err

            ' determine error
            Select Case .Number

                ' there is no error, inform the user of success
                Case NO_ERROR:
                    sMessage = "Database successfully " _
                            & LCase$(sActionString) & "ed to file '" _
                            & sNewDatabase & "'."

                ' the database already exists
                Case ERR_DATABASE_EXISTS:
                    sMessage = "You must choose a database that does " _
                            & "not already exist."

                ' unexpected error, inform the user
                Case Else:
                    sMessage = "ERROR #" & .Number & ": " & _
                            .Description

            End Select

            ' display the error for the user
            MsgBox sMessage, _
                    IIf(.Number = NO_ERROR, vbInformation, _
                            vbExclamation), _
                    IIf(.Number = NO_ERROR, "SUCCESS", "ERROR")

        End With

    End Sub
```

How It Works

At the start of this application, the user is logged on to the system database using the default values for both the username and the password. When the user decides to create a new database, the `dbEncrypt` option is included in the `CreateDatabase` method to indicate that encryption is to be used on the database.

If the user decides to either encrypt or decrypt an existing database, he must actually create a new database from the existing one by using the `CompactDatabase` method with an option of `dbEncrypt` or `dbDecrypt`. The database to be created from the `CompactDatabase` method cannot already exist.

Comments

In this How-To, you started off accessing the system database in the `Form_Load` event given the default Admin username and password, although the project did not necessarily need to access the system database.

Encryption is not really going to help you much unless you also add a password, which you did not do in this application. Encryption stops others from viewing an Access database with anything but Access itself and Visual Basic. Because both these tools are readily available, do not count on encryption as your only source of security. The framework is here for system database security, and this is why you included its access in the `Form_Load` event.

CHAPTER 11

THE WINDOWS REGISTRY AND STATE INFORMATION

11

THE WINDOWS REGISTRY AND STATE INFORMATION

How do I...

11.1 Enter and retrieve Windows Registry entries from Visual Basic?

11.2 Put data access-related information into an application's section of the Registry?

11.3 Determine which database and report-related files need to be distributed with my applications?

11.4 Tune the Jet database engine through Windows Registry entries?

11.5 Tune the ODBC engine using Windows Registry entries?

The Windows Registry is a remarkable component of Windows 95. It is used to store information about every application installed on your machine and replaces the original INI files of Windows 3.x. The information that is held in the Registry ranges from file paths to encrypted registration keys for ActiveX controls.

You can view the contents of the Windows Registry by locating the RegEdit application in your Windows directory. After launching this application, you can view the contents of any key stored in the Registry. You can also edit, create, or delete folders and keys within these folders; however, you should take extreme caution in doing so, because these values are of great importance. Make sure you know and realize what you are doing with the information in the Windows Registry before you decide to change anything.

REGISTRY SAFEGUARDS

Always have at least one workable version of the Registry backed up before making any type of adjustment to it.

If you have made changes to the Registry but not restarted Windows since the change, you can restore the Registry to its state at the last successful Windows startup. Shut down Windows by choosing Restart in MS-DOS mode. Then when you see the MS-DOS prompt, type

```
scanreq /restore
```

If you are having a problem restarting Windows after Registry changes, you can reboot from an emergency boot floppy disk, and type the preceding command from the MS-DOS prompt.

In this chapter, we will dive into the Windows Registry and see how we can get it to work for us. We will accomplish this by using it to save state information for our application and our data access. We will also look into changing specific information that is inherent on every user's machine to tune and maximize performance in our applications.

11.1 Enter and Retrieve Windows Registry Entries from Visual Basic

When you exit most applications and then restart them later, you will notice that the screens appear to be just as you left them earlier. This technique of storing an application's state information is discussed in this How-To.

11.2 Put Data Access-Related Information into an Application's Section of the Registry

Sometimes it is important to use data access specifications that most other applications do not use. It is important, however, to maintain the reliability of the original specifications in the Window Registry. This How-To presents a project used to store state information for data access in the Windows Registry and to temporarily change the settings for data access.

11.3 Determine Which Database and Report-Related Files Need to Be Distributed with My Applications

Many times when creating a set of distribution disks for your application, you forget to include specific files relating to databases or reports. This How-To explains which files are necessary for each of these components.

11.4 Tune the Jet Database Engine Through Windows Registry Entries

If you are the down-and-dirty type when it comes to tweaking your machine for optimum performance, this How-To is for you. Here we show you how to fine-tune each of the keys relating to the Jet database engine tick.

11.5 Tune the ODBC Engine Using Windows Registry Entries

As well as fine-tuning the Jet database engine through the Windows Registry, you can also tune the ODBC engine. In this How-To, we will explain just how to do this.

COMPLEXITY
BEGINNING

11.1 How do I...
Enter and retrieve Windows Registry entries from Visual Basic?

Problem

My applications need to store specific state information. For example, I would like to store the position and size of the windows used in my projects so that the next time a user loads the program, it appears to continue where he left off. How do I store state information for my applications using Visual Basic?

Technique

Back in the days of Windows 3.x, applications used INI files to store state information for their programs. Apparently, this led to numerous INI files spread throughout user's drives. With the introduction of Windows 95, we now have what is called the Windows Registry.

The Windows Registry acts as a Grand Central Station for **INI** files. Not only is application state information stored in the Registry, but registrations for OCXs also reside here. By using the same statements that we used to access INI files for Windows 3.x applications, we can work with the Windows Registry. There are four in all:

✔ GetSetting—Used to retrieve a single key's setting.

✔ GetAllSettings—Used to retrieve all keys and their corresponding settings for a given section in the Registry.

✔ `SaveSetting`—Used to save a setting for a particular key.

✔ `DeleteSetting`—Used to delete a key for a given section.

Visual Basic has set a special section set aside for state information of user's applications. This section is labeled by the key HKEY_CURRENT_USER\ Software\VB and VBA Program Settings. By using the four statements previously listed, we can create, read, and alter settings in the VB and VBA Program Settings area of the Windows Registry to effectively record our application's state information.

Steps

Load and run `RegistryEditor.vbp`. You will see the form shown in Figure 11.1. The Application Name and Section text boxes are set to the default values used for this application. Change these values to see different section keys. After you select a key, you can edit it and click the Save Setting command button to save the setting. End the application by clicking the Close button.

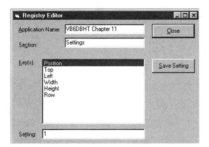

Figure 11.1. The Registry Editor project.

1. Create a new project and name it `RegistryEditor.vbp`. Add the objects listed in Table 11.1 and edit their properties as shown. Save the form as `frmRegistryEditor.frm`.

Table 11.1. Objects and properties for the Registry Editor project.

OBJECT	PROPERTY	SETTING
Form	Name	frmRegistryEditor
	Caption	"Registry Editor"
Text box	Name	txtApplicationName
	Caption	"VB6DBHT Chapter 11"
Text box	Name	txtSection
	Caption	"Settings"

OBJECT	PROPERTY	SETTING
Text box	Name	txtSetting
	Caption	" "
List box	Name	lstKeys
Command button	Name	cmdClose
	Caption	"&Close"
	Cancel	-1 'True
	Default	-1 'True
Command button	Name	cmdSave
	Caption	"&Save Setting"
Label	Name	lblApplicationName
	Caption	"&Application Name:"
Label	Name	lblSection
	Caption	"Se&ction:"
Label	Name	lblKeys
	Caption	"&Key(s):"
Label	Name	lblSetting
	Caption	"Se&tting:"

2. Enter the declaration for the form-level variant variable used to store keys and settings from the Windows Registry:

```
Option Explicit

' form-level variable used to store keys and settings for
' desired application and section
Private m_vSettings As Variant
```

3. When the application begins, automatically populate the screen with the default information by calling the **RepopulateKeys** routine that we will enter later:

```
Private Sub Form_Load()

    ' initialize the application by populating the key list box
    RepopulateKeys

End Sub
```

4. Now enter the code for the **lstKeys_Click** event shown here. When the user changes the key to be displayed, the application will load the new corresponding setting and display it in the setting text box.

```
Private Sub lstKeys_Click()

    ' error message of choice when error has occurred
    ' obtaining setting
    Const ERRMSG_INVALID_SETTING = "<ERROR>"

    ' set the txtSetting text box to the value of the key in
    ' the Registry
    txtSetting = GetSetting(txtApplicationName, _
                            txtSection, _
                            lstKeys.Text, _
                            ERRMSG_INVALID_SETTING)

    ' if there was an error in the retrieval process, disable
    ' editing of the key's setting
    If (txtSetting <> ERRMSG_INVALID_SETTING) Then
        lstKeys.Enabled = True
        txtSetting.Enabled = True
        cmdSave.Enabled = True
    End If

End Sub
```

5. When the user changes the name of the application or the section to find keys for, we want to repopulate the list box displaying them. This is done with a call to the RepopulateKeys routine in the txtApplicationName_Change and txtSection_Change events, as shown here:

```
Private Sub txtApplicationName_Change()

    ' repopulate the key list box when the application name
    ' has changed
    RepopulateKeys

End Sub

Private Sub txtSection_Change()

    ' repopulate the key list box when the section name
    ' has changed
    RepopulateKeys

End Sub
```

6. Enter the following code to end the application:

```
Private Sub cmdClose_Click()

    ' end the application
    Unload Me

End Sub
```

7. Now enter the code for the `cmdSave_Click` event, which uses the `SaveSetting` statement to save the information on the form to the Windows Registry:

```
Private Sub cmdSave_Click()

    ' save the selected key information from the desired
    ' information on the form
    SaveSetting txtApplicationName, _
                txtSection, _
                lstKeys.Text, _
                txtSetting

End Sub
```

8. Finally, enter the following code for the `RepopulateKeys` routine. When this code is called, the application attempts to populate the list box with all the available keys for the given application and section name. If this information does not correspond to a section in the Registry, an error occurs. The `RepopulateKeys` routine traps this error and gracefully exits the procedure, leaving the key list box empty and disabling any controls used to edit key settings.

```
Private Sub RepopulateKeys()

' if there is an error, goto the code labeled by
ERR_RepopulateKeys
On Error GoTo ERR_RepopulateKeys:

    Dim nCount As Integer

    ' errors that are expected to be encountered
    Const ERR_INVALID_PROC_CALL = 5
    Const ERR_TYPE_MISMATCH = 13


    With lstKeys

        ' clear the listbox and setting text box
        .Clear
        txtSetting = ""

        ' disable editing functions
        lstKeys.Enabled = False
        txtSetting.Enabled = False
        cmdSave.Enabled = False

        ' retrieve available keys for given application name
        ' and section this will cause an ERR_INVALID_PROC_CALL
        ' error if one of the text box controls are empty
        m_vSettings = GetAllSettings(txtApplicationName, _
            txtSection)
```

continued on next page

continued from previous page

```
                    ' add each setting to the key list box
                    ' this will cause an ERR_TYPE_MISMATCH error if there
                    ' are no keys for the selected application and section
                    ' names
                    For nCount = 0 To UBound(m_vSettings, 1)
                        .AddItem m_vSettings(nCount, 0)
                    Next nCount

                    ' select the first item in the list box
                    .ListIndex = 0

                End With

        Exit Sub

        ERR_RepopulateKeys:

            With Err

                Select Case .Number

                        ' if the error is expected, do nothing but end the
                        ' procedure
                        Case ERR_INVALID_PROC_CALL, ERR_TYPE_MISMATCH:

                        ' unexpected error, display for the user
                        Case Else:
                            MsgBox "ERROR #" * .Number & ": " & _
                                    .Description, _
                                    vbExclamation, "ERROR"

                End Select

            End With

        End Sub
```

How It Works

When this project is run, the list box control of the form is populated with the keys available for the given application and section names using the **GetAllSettings** statement. If the section does not exist in the Windows Registry, an error occurs, and the application is ended gracefully. If there are keys, the list box is populated and the controls that are related to editing the key's setting are enabled.

After you decide to change the setting for a given key selected from the list box, you click the Save Setting button. The code that is in the **cmdSave_Click** event uses the **SaveSetting** statement to save the current key's value.

Choosing a new key from the list box control causes the code to execute the **GetSetting** statement, which retrieves an individual setting for a specified application name, section, and key.

Comments

In this project, we saved all the key's settings as strings in the Windows Registry. This is because the **txtSetting** text box's **Text** property returns a string value. If you were to use this project to save the information for your application's position and size, you would have to change the string value returned to a **Long** value.

This problem can be avoided by using a variable with a **Long** data type in the **SaveSetting** statement. Visual Basic creates a new key with the data type of the specified setting.

COMPLEXITY
BEGINNING

11.2 How do I...
Put data access-related informa-tion into an application's section of the Registry?

Problem

My application calls for DAO settings that are not considered standard. I can manually edit the Registry key settings to the values that my application requires; however, other programs will be affected by my changes. How do I temporarily change the DAO settings every time a user runs my projects?

Technique

By using the techniques discussed in How-To 11.1, we know that we can save state information for our application. Visual Basic does not care what kind of information this is; therefore, we can just as easily store DAO setting information as we can the application's position and height.

To temporarily change the DAO settings for the Jet engine, we can use the **SetOption** method of the DBEngine. Using this command we can change the values of parameters that Jet uses to access data. These changes are made until we change them again or the DBEngine is actually closed.

In all, there are 11 parameters we can use to alter the Jet and DAO's behavior. These parameters and their associated key—in the Jet\3.5\Engines\Jet 3.5\ section of the Windows Registry—are listed in Table 11.2.

Table 11.2. Objects and properties for the Set Options project.

KEY	PARAMETER ENUMERATION CONSTANT
PageTimeout	dbPageTimeout
SharedAsyncDelay	dbSharedAsyncDelay
ExclusiveAsyncDelay	dbExclusiveAsyncDelay
LockRetry	dbLockRetry
UserCommitSync	dbUserCommitSync
ImplicitCommitSync	dbImplicitCommitSync
MaxBufferSize	dbMaxBufferSize
MaxLocksPerFile	dbMaxLocksPerFile
LockDelay	dbLockDelay
RecycleLVs	dbRecycleLVs
FlushTransactionTimeout	dbFlushTransactionTimeout

Steps

Open and run SetOptions.vbp. You will see the form shown in Figure 11.2. By selecting the key from the combo box, you will see the associated setting for the key in the Setting text box. Changing the key's setting and clicking the Save Setting button will not only save the value of the setting, but also temporarily change the parameter for the DBEngine object. If you delete the key by clicking the Delete Key button, you will remove the key from the section for our state information in the Registry. The next time you go to view the key, you will see the default setting of the key.

Figure 11.2. The Set Options project.

1. Create a new project and name it SetOptions.vbp. Add the controls and edit their properties as shown in Table 11.3 for the default form, Form1. Save the form as frmSetOptions.frm.

Table 11.3. Objects and properties for the Set Options project.

OBJECT	PROPERTY	SETTING
Form	Name	frmSetOptions
	Caption	"Set Options"
Combo box	Name	cboKeys
	Style	2 'Dropdown List
Text box	Name	txtSetting
	Caption	" "
Command button	Name	cmdClose
	Caption	"&Close"
	Cancel	-1 'True
	Default	-1 'True
Command button	Name	cmdSave
	Caption	"&Save Setting"
Command button	Name	cmdDelete
	Caption	"&Delete Key"
Label	Name	lblKey
	Caption	"&Key:"
Label	Name	lblSetting
	Caption	"Se&tting:"

2. Now enter the following code in the declarations section of the project. The form-level **Long** variable is used to store the currently selected key from the combo box on the form. The other two declarations are constants and are used to represent the default application and section names used for this project.

```
Option Explicit

' form-level variable used to store the selected parameter from
' the list in the keys combo box
Private m_lSelectedParameter As Long

' form-level constant declarations used throughout the
' application to name the application and section when
' using the Get and Save settings methods
Private Const APPLICATION_TITLE = "VB6DBHT Chapter 11"
Private Const SECTION_NAME = "Jet 3.5"
```

3. Now enter the **Form_Load** event code as shown next. This code calls the **LoadJetRegistryInformation** routine, which we will code in a separate module later, to retrieve all the keys for the specified application and section of the Windows Registry. The event then adds all the available parameters to the combo box control and selects the first one.

```
Private Sub Form_Load()

    ' load all Jet Registry settings from application section
    ' of the Windows Registry
    LoadJetRegistryInformation APPLICATION_TITLE, SECTION_NAME

    With cboKeys

        ' add all the available parameters for the SetOption
        ' method

        .AddItem "dbPageTimeout"
        .AddItem "dbSharedAsyncDelay"
        .AddItem "dbExclusiveAsyncDelay"
        .AddItem "dbLockRetry"
        .AddItem "dbUserCommitSync"
        .AddItem "dbImplicitCommitSync"
        .AddItem "dbMaxBufferSize"
        .AddItem "dbMaxLocksPerFile"
        .AddItem "dbLockDelay"
        .AddItem "dbRecycleLVs"
        .AddItem "dbFlushTransactionTimeout"

        ' select the first item in the combo box control
        .ListIndex = 0

    End With

End Sub
```

4. Now enter the code for the **cboKeys_Click** event, which is called every time the user selects a new key from the combo box. This event retrieves the current setting for the chosen key from the application's section of the Windows Registry. If there is no specified entry for the key in this section, the **lDefaultSetting** is used instead.

```
Private Sub cboKeys_Click()

    Dim lDefaultSetting As Variant

    With cboKeys

        ' get a long value from the text version of the key
        m_lSelectedParameter = GetParameterFromKey(.Text)

        ' obtain the default setting for the key
        lDefaultSetting = GetDefaultKeySetting(.Text)

        ' display the current setting from the application's
        ' Registry settings if there is one; otherwise,
        ' display the default
        txtSetting = GetSetting(APPLICATION_TITLE, _
                                SECTION_NAME, _
                                .Text, _
                                lDefaultSetting)
```

```
      End With

   End Sub
```

5. Enter the following code to end the application:

```
Private Sub cmdClose_Click()

    ' end the application
    Unload Me

End Sub
```

6. The following code is used to save the current key and setting combination to the application's section of the Registry. This is done with the **SaveSetting** statement. In addition to the Registry entry, the **SetOption** method of the **DBEngine** object is called to temporarily change the setting of the desired parameter to the new value. If the user entered an incorrect data type for the key, an error is generated and the user is notified.

```
Private Sub cmdSave_Click()

' if there is an error, goto the code labeled by ERR_
' cmdSave_Click
On Error GoTo ERR_cmdSave_Click:

    ' constant declarations for expected errors
    Const ERR_TYPE_MISMATCH = 13
    Const ERR_RESERVED_ERROR = 3000

    ' attempt to set the DBEngine option for the given key
    ' an error will occur here if an incorrect setting data
    ' type is entered by the user
    DBEngine.SetOption m_lSelectedParameter, _
            GetValueFromSetting(txtSetting)

    ' if the SetOption method was successful, save the
    ' new setting value in the application Registry section
    SaveSetting APPLICATION_TITLE, SECTION_NAME, _
            cboKeys.Text, txtSetting

    ' inform the user of the success
    MsgBox "Change has been made.", vbInformation, "Set Option"

Exit Sub

ERR_cmdSave_Click:

    Dim sMessage As String

    With Err
```

continued on next page

continued from previous page

```
            Select Case .Number

                ' wrong data type entered for key setting
                Case ERR_TYPE_MISMATCH, ERR_RESERVED_ERROR:
                    sMessage = "Value is of incorrect format."

                ' unexpected error, create a message from the error
                Case Else:
                    sMessage = "ERROR #" & .Number & ": " & _
                            .Description

            End Select

        End With

        ' inform the user of the error
        MsgBox sMessage, vbExclamation, "ERROR"

        ' repopulate the setting text box with the current or
        ' default key setting and set focus to the text box

        cboKeys_Click
        txtSetting.SetFocus

    End Sub
```

7. The following code simply deletes the key from the application's section in the Windows Registry and notifies the user of the success:

```
Private Sub cmdDelete_Click()

    ' remove the setting from the application section of the
    ' Windows Registry
    DeleteSetting APPLICATION_TITLE, SECTION_NAME, cboKeys.Text

    ' refresh the setting text box with the default value
    cboKeys_Click

    ' inform the user of the success
    MsgBox "Key has been deleted.", vbInformation, "Delete Key"

End Sub
```

8. The second half of this project begins with adding a new module. This can be done by choosing Project|Add Module from the Visual Basic menu. Rename the module `RegistryInformation` and save it as `RegistryInformation.bas`. The remaining code for this project should be entered in this module.

9. In the `RegistryInformation` module, enter the first routine to be used, which is the `LoadJetRegistryInformation` as shown here. This routine loads all the settings and keys for the given application and section names. For each key specified in the corresponding section of the Registry, the `SetOption` method of the `DBEngine` object is called to temporarily change the value of the given parameter for the life of this application. If there are no settings for the given application and section names, an error is trapped and the routine exits gracefully.

```
Public Sub LoadJetRegistryInformation( _
        sApplicationName As String, _
        sSectionName As String)

' if there is an error, goto the code labeled by
' ERR_LoadJetRegistryInformation
On Error GoTo ERR_LoadJetRegistryInformation:

    Dim vSettings As Variant
    Dim nCount As Integer

    ' constant declaration for expected error
    Const ERR_TYPE_MISMATCH = 13

    ' obtain all the settings from the Registry section for
    ' the given application
    vSettings = GetAllSettings(sApplicationName, sSectionName)

    ' set all the options that were specified in the Jet 3.5
    ' section for the current application
    For nCount = 0 To UBound(vSettings, 1)

        DBEngine.SetOption GetParameterFromKey _
                (vSettings(nCount, 0)), _
                GetValueFromSetting( _
                vSettings(nCount, 1))

    Next nCount

Exit Sub

ERR_LoadJetRegistryInformation:

    With Err

        Select Case .Number

            ' there was no settings specified in the Registry
            ' for the given application, just continue without
            ' displaying an error message
            Case ERR_TYPE_MISMATCH:

            ' unexpected error, create a message from the error
            Case Else:
                MsgBox "ERROR #" & .Number & ": " & _
                        .Description, _
                        vbExclamation, "ERROR"

        End Select

    End With

End Sub
```

10. Now enter the public function `GetValueFromSetting`, which accepts a variant as an argument and returns either a `Long` or `String` dependent upon the data type of the argument:

```
Public Function GetValueFromSetting( _
        vSetting As Variant) As Variant

    ' if the setting is a number, return a long; otherwise,
    ' return a string

    If (IsNumeric(vSetting)) Then
        GetValueFromSetting = CLng(vSetting)
    Else
        GetValueFromSetting = CStr(vSetting)
    End If

End Function
```

11. The following function returns the default setting for the specified key name. These defaults were obtained from the Visual Basic Books Online and can be changed to your desired settings.

```
Public Function GetDefaultKeySetting(sKey As String) As Variant

    ' return the default key setting for the key specified

    Select Case sKey

        Case "dbPageTimeout":
            GetDefaultKeySetting = 5000

        Case "dbSharedAsyncDelay":
            GetDefaultKeySetting = 0

        Case "dbExclusiveAsyncDelay":
            GetDefaultKeySetting = 2000

        Case "dbLockEntry":
            GetDefaultKeySetting = 20

        Case "dbUserCommitSync":
            GetDefaultKeySetting = "Yes"

        Case "dbImplicitCommitSync":
            GetDefaultKeySetting = "No"

        Case "dbMaxBufferSize":
            GetDefaultKeySetting = 0

        Case "dbMaxLocksPerFile":
            GetDefaultKeySetting = 9500

        Case "dbLockDelay":
            GetDefaultKeySetting = 100
```

```
            Case "dbRecycleLVs":
                GetDefaultKeySetting = 0

            Case "dbFlushTransactionTimeout":
                GetDefaultKeySetting = 500

    End Select

End Function
```

12. Finally, enter the code for the public function `GetParameterFromKey` as shown here. This function returns the corresponding parameter enumeration value for a specified key.

```
Public Function GetParameterFromKey(ByVal sKey As String) As Long

    ' return the correct constant for the given key

    Select Case sKey

        Case "dbPageTimeout":
            GetParameterFromKey = dbPageTimeout

        Case "dbSharedAsyncDelay":
            GetParameterFromKey = dbSharedAsyncDelay

        Case "dbExclusiveAsyncDelay":
            GetParameterFromKey = dbExclusiveAsyncDelay

        Case "dbLockRetry":
            GetParameterFromKey = dbLockRetry

        Case "dbUserCommitSync":
            GetParameterFromKey = dbUserCommitSync

        Case "dbImplicitCommitSync":
            GetParameterFromKey = dbImplicitCommitSync

        Case "dbMaxBufferSize":
            GetParameterFromKey = dbMaxBufferSize

        Case "dbMaxLocksPerFile":
            GetParameterFromKey = dbMaxLocksPerFile

        Case "dbLockDelay":
            GetParameterFromKey = dbLockDelay

        Case "dbRecycleLVs":
            GetParameterFromKey = dbRecycleLVs

        Case "dbFlushTransactionTimeout":
            GetParameterFromKey = dbFlushTransactionTimeout

    End Select

End Function
```

How It Works

This project uses two files for code. The first file, the `frmSetOptions` form, holds the information for displaying and altering the application's Jet engine state information.

The second file used in this project, the `RegistryInformation` module, is designed to be portable and to be added to your own project. By calling the `LoadJetRegistryInformation` and passing the application's name and section, the procedure loads all the state information stored for the Jet in the specified section of the Windows Registry. It then uses the `SetOption` method to temporarily change the parameter values of Jet engine access for the life of your application.

Comments

It is important not to change the values of the actual settings for the Jet in the key Jet\3.5\Engines\Jet 3.5\ because it is very likely this is where the rest of your applications are finding the parameter values for Jet DAO access. If by some chance you decide to change these values and need to set them back to their original values, you can find the default settings from the Microsoft Visual Basic Books Online, in the "Initializing the Microsoft Jet 3.5 Database Engine" section.

For more information on the meaning of the parameters used in this section, see How-To 11.4, "Tune the Jet Database Engine Through Windows Registry Entries."

COMPLEXITY
INTERMEDIATE

11.3 How do I...
Determine which database and report-related files need to be distributed with my applications?

Problem

I am creating an application that uses the Jet database engine and Crystal Reports. How do I determine the files I need to distribute with my application?

Technique

Before Visual Basic 5.0, life was rough. Actually, life is still rough, but we are getting there. Creating distribution disks for your application was a headache up until Microsoft began delivering its Application Setup Wizard with Visual Basic 5.0. With the introduction of Visual Basic 6.0, Microsoft offers us the Package and Deployment Wizard. The Package and Deployment Wizard does everything that the Application Wizard in Visual Basic 5.0 did, but it also adds the ability to create packages for network or Internet distribution. In this How-To, we will concentrate on how the Package and Deployment Wizard can be used to create conventional disk-based packages for our applications.

Steps

Run the Package and Deployment Wizard that comes with Visual Basic 6.0. You will see the wizard as shown in Figure 11.3.

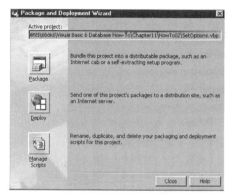

Figure 11.3. The Package and Deployment Wizard.

1. After choosing to create a package, choose a packaging script as shown in Figure 11.4.

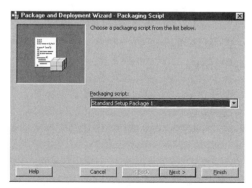

Figure 11.4. Choosing a packaging script.

2. Click the Next button and you will see the panel shown in Figure 11.5. In this panel, you select the type of setup you wish to create.

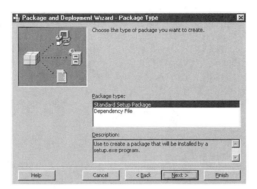

Figure 11.5. Choosing a setup type.

3. After choosing the type of setup, choose the location to build the setup as shown in Figure 11.6.

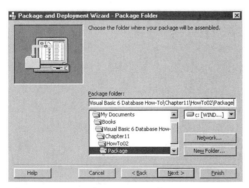

Figure 11.6. Choosing a location to build the setup.

4. If your application uses DAO, you will choose drivers from the list shown in Figure 11.7.

5. Figure 11.8 shows a list of files that have been chosen to be included in your package. In this step, you can deselect or add files for your package.

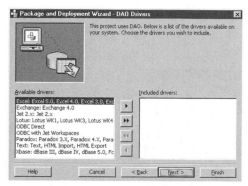

Figure 11.7. Choosing a DAO driver.

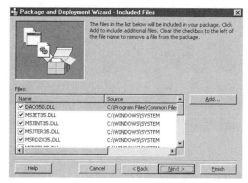

Figure 11.8. Choosing files for the setup.

6. Next, choose whether you would like a single cab or multiple cab files for your installation as shown in Figure 11.9.

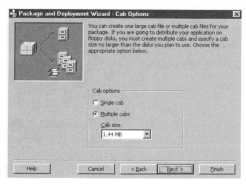

Figure 11.9. Choosing a distribution size.

7. Next, enter the name that should be shown when the setup program for your application is run. This is shown in Figure 11.10.

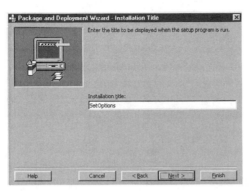

Figure 11.10. Choosing a name for the setup.

8. After entering a setup name for your application, click the Next button to get to the screen shown in Figure 11.11. This screen allows you to select the menu groups and items that should be created once your application is created.

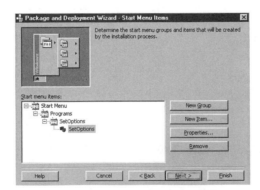

Figure 11.11. Choosing menu groups and Items.

9. The next step, as shown in Figure 11.12, allows you to change the locations in which particular items in your package can be located.

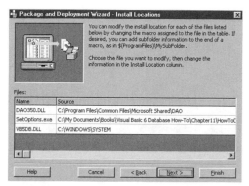

Figure 11.12. Changing the location
of setup components.

10. After you have set the correct location for the files in Figure 11.12, click
the Next button to see Figure 11.13. This screen allows you to indicate
which files in your package are considered shared files.

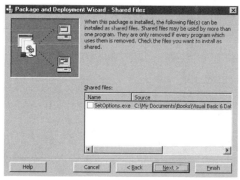

Figure 11.13. Choosing shared files.

11. After completing this, you will see the Finished panel as shown in Figure
11.14. Click Finish to complete the installation setup process.

12. Type a name for the installation script and click Save Script.

13. Click Finish to create your application package.

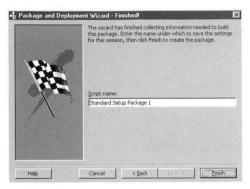

Figure 11.14. Completing the setup.

How It Works

Problems arise sometimes when files become lost or when the Package and Deployment Wizard does not find all the files necessary to be included in our distribution disks. All the files that actually have meaning to us to run our application are considered runtime files.

Runtime Files

There is a check list of standard runtime files that you should work through when creating a set of distribution disks. This checklist is as follows:

- ✔ The program's main executable.

- ✔ Any database (MDB files for Access) or report files (RPT files for Crystal Reports).

- ✔ Any other data files (DAT), text files (TXT), or Registry files (REG). These files are those that will not be found by a wizard, but accessed from within your application.

- ✔ Any ActiveX components (OCX files).

- ✔ The Visual Basic runtime DLL (MSVBVM60.DLL).

- ✔ Any other dependency files (DLL or EXE).

You should be able to know immediately what database, report, data, and ActiveX files you are to add to your setup disks because these are files that you explicitly added to your project. The Visual Basic runtime DLL (MSVBVM60.DLL) is necessary for every Visual Basic application. The trickiest files to find are component dependency files.

Component Dependencies

Component dependencies are files that are necessary in order to use specific ActiveX controls and particular components that are added as references from your application. There are a number of resources, however, to locate the proper dependency files that are important to you.

First, it is important to always consult the documentation on all third-party components, as well as Microsoft components, to see which DLLs are necessary in order to use its product. For instance, the Microsoft Data Reporter requires the MSDBRPT.DLL file. In most cases, REG files are also necessary. These files have registration information, entered into the Windows Registry, that is used to determine the licensing usage available to the user for the particular component.

The second source for finding the appropriate dependency files for your distribution disks is the Visual Basic documentation. All the included components are documented and explain which files are necessary in order for them to work properly. All ActiveX controls will come with DEP files, if they don't already. For example, the Microsoft Data Repeater ActiveX control comes with a file named MSDATREP.DEP, and Crystal Reports comes with CRYSTL32.DEP. These files are used by the Package and Deployment Wizard to determine which files are necessary for installation.

The third and most important source of information is the VB6DEP.INI file. This file replaces the original SWDEPEND.INI file of earlier times and describes the dependencies used by Visual Basic.

The VB6DEP.INI file can be found in the Visual Basic \Wizards\PDWizard directory. This file lists necessary dependencies for all available Visual Basic components. This file is used by the Package and Deployment Wizard to determine the appropriate files necessary to successfully run your application.

Comments

The following is a portion of the MSDATREP.DEP file. It lists the information necessary to successfully incorporate the MSDATREP.OCX ActiveX control that is for the Microsoft Data Repeater.

```
[MSDatRep.ocx]
Dest=$(WinSysPath)
Register=$(DLLSelfRegister)
Version=6.0.80.52
Uses1=ComCat.dll
Uses2=MSStdFmt.dll
Uses3=MSBind.dll
CABFileName=MSDatRep.cab
CABDefaultURL=http://activex.microsoft.com/controls/vb6
CABINFFile=MSDatRep.inf
```

The header of this portion of code, [MSDatRep.ocx], indicates the file in question. The first key, Dest, indicates where the file should be stored on the installation machine (in this case, the Windows System path).

The second parameter, Register, indicates that the file will self-register in the Windows Registry. The Version parameter clearly holds the file's version number to compare with older files during the installation process.

After this, a list of additional dependencies is listed with the parameter form of UsesX, where X is the number of the dependency. These are files that the actual file being installed (MSDATREP.OCX) uses to reference; therefore, they in turn must also be installed. The CABFileName parameter is the name of the installation file for the particular installed file, and CABINFFile is the file that contains the installation information for the installed file.

I skipped the CABDefaultURL parameter, which indicates the default Web site that is used in reference to the installed file for upgrades or more information.

COMPLEXITY
ADVANCED

11.4 How do I...
Tune the Jet database engine through Windows Registry entries?

Problem

My application needs to alter the way the Jet engine is initiated in the Windows Registry in order to obtain better performance. I know I can edit the Windows Registry using RegEdit, but I do not know what to actually do. How do I tune the Jet engine through the Windows Registry?

Technique

When you install the Microsoft Jet engine for the first time, two DLL files are registered in the Windows Registry. These files are MSJET35.DLL and MSRD2X35.DLL. When these files are registered, two entries are created in the HKEY_LOCAL_MACHINES\Software\Microsoft\Jet\3.5\Engines folder. This is done automatically when you install Access 97.

The first of these keys represents the path to the system database file. The typical path for this key would be the system directory of Windows; therefore, no path is necessary because the system directory is usually part of the default path. The following is an example of this SystemDB key:

```
SystemDB = "C:\WINDOWS\SYSTEM\SYSTEM.MDB"
```

The second key that is created is called CompactBYPkey. When this key is set to anything but zero, databases will be compacted in the order of the primary key. If no primary key exists, the database is compacted in base-table order. A value of zero for the CompactBYPkey key will instruct the Jet engine to compact databases in base-table order. The default value for this key is nonzero, as in the following example:

```
CompactBYPkey = 1
```

It should be noted that this setting is good only for databases created with the Microsoft Jet database engine, version 3.0 or later. Any database created from an earlier version will compact by base-table order automatically.

The Microsoft Jet is controlled by keys set in the \HKEY_LOCAL_MACHINES\ Software\Microsoft\Jet\3.5\Engines\Jet 3.5 folder of the Windows Registry. The default settings for these keys are shown in Table 11.4.

Table 11.4. The Jet\3.5\Engines\Jet 3.5 keys and default values.

KEY	DEFAULT
PageTimeout	5000
SharedAsyncDelay	0
ExclusiveAsyncDelay	2000
LockRetry	20
UserCommitSync	Yes
ImplicitCommitSync	No
MaxBufferSize	0
MaxLocksPerFile	9500
LockDelay	100
FlushTransactionTimeout	500
Threads	3

By adjusting these settings, you can manipulate how the Jet engine operates in every program that uses these settings. The keys listed in Table 11.4 are briefly described in the text that follows.

Steps

Run the **RegEdit** application that is in the Windows directory on your machine. Locate the \HKEY_LOCAL_MACHINES\Software\Microsoft\Jet\3.5\Engines\Jet 3.5 section of the Registry, and you should see something similar to what's shown in Figure 11.15.

1. Choose a key in the section that you are now in. Choose Edit | Modify from the RegEdit menu.

2. Edit the value of the key that you selected. For a complete list of the available keys for this section, see the "How It Works" section of this How-To.

3. Click OK to save your changes or Cancel to abort.

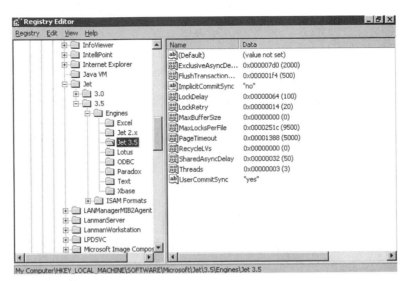

Figure 11.15. The \HKEY_LOCAL_MACHINES\Software\
Microsoft\Jet\3.5\Engines\Jet 3.5 of the Windows Registry.

How It Works

The following is a list of the keys that make up the \HKEY_LOCAL_MACHINES\
Software\Microsoft\Jet\3.5\Engines\Jet 3.5 section of the Windows Registry and a
description of each.

PageTimeout

The `PageTimeout` key is used to indicate the time interval between when data
that is not read-locked is placed in an internal cache and when that data is
invalidated. This key is measured in milliseconds, with a default value of **5000** or
5 seconds.

FlushTransactionTimeout

The `FlushTransactionTimeout` key disables the `ExclusiveAsyncDelay` and
`SharedAsyncDelay` keys with a value of 1. A value of **0** enables these keys. The
`FlushTransactionTimeout` is the value that will start asynchronous writes only
after the amount of time specified has expired and no pages have been added to
the cache. An exception to this statement is if the cache exceeds the
`MaxBufferSize`, the cache will start asynchronous writing even if the time has
expired. For instance, the Microsoft Jet 3.51 database engine will wait 500
milliseconds during non-activity or until the cache size is exceeded before
starting asynchronous writes.

LockDelay

The `LockDelay` key holds a value in milliseconds used to determine the time in between lock requests indicated by the `LockRetry` key. This key was added to prevent "bursting" (overloading of the network) that would occur with certain network operating systems.

MaxLocksPerFile

The `MaxLocksPerFile` key holds a value indicating the maximum number of Microsoft Jet transactions. If the locks in a transaction attempt to exceed the `MaxLocksPerFile` key value, the transaction is split into multiple parts and partially committed. This concept was conceived in order to prevent NetWare 3.1 server crashes when the specified NetWare lock limit was exceeded as well as to improve performance with both NetWare and NT.

LockRetry

The `LockRetry` key indicates the number of times to repeat attempts to access a locked page before returning a lock conflict message. The default value for the `LockRetry` key is `20`.

RecycleLVs

The `RecycleLVs` key is used to indicate whether Microsoft Jet is to recycle long value pages. These include the Memo, Long Binary (OLE object), and Binary data types. With Microsoft Jet 3.0, if the `RecycleLVs` key was not set, these long value pages would be recycled when the last user closed the database. Microsoft Jet 3.51 will start to recycle most long value pages when the database is expanded—in other words, when groups of pages are added. When this feature is enabled, you will notice a performance drop when using long value data types. With Microsoft Access 97, this feature is automatically enabled and disabled.

MaxBufferSize

The `MaxBufferSize` key represents the size of the database engine internal cache. This value is represented in kilobytes. The `MaxBufferSize` key must be an integer greater than or equal to 512. The default value for the `MaxBufferSize` varies depending on the amount of RAM installed on the user's system. The formula for calculating the default is as follows:

```
((RAM - 12MB) / 4) + 512KB
```

Here, *RAM* is the amount of memory on the current system, measured in megabytes (MB). To set the value of the `MaxBufferSize` to the default, simply set the key to zero.

Threads

The `Threads` key represents the number of background threads available to the Microsoft Jet database engine. The default value for the `Threads` key is `3`.

UserCommitSync

The `UserCommitSync` key indicates whether the system should wait for a commit to finish. If the value is `Yes`, which is the default, the system will wait for a commit to finish. If the value is `No`, the system will perform the commit asynchronously.

ImplicitCommitSync

The `ImplicitCommitSync` key represents whether the system will wait for a commit to finish. A default value of `No` will instruct the system to continue without waiting for the commit to finish, whereas a value of `Yes` will cause the system to wait.

ExclusiveAsyncDelay

The `ExclusiveAsyncDelay` key specifies the amount of time (in milliseconds) an asynchronous flush of an exclusive database is to be deferred. The default value for this key is **2000** milliseconds (2 seconds).

SharedAsyncDelay

The `SharedAsyncDelay` key represents the amount of time (in milliseconds) to defer an asynchronous flush of a shared database. The default for the `SharedAsyncDelay` is **0**.

COMPLEXITY
ADVANCED

11.5 How do I...
Tune the ODBC engine using Windows Registry entries?

Problem

My application needs to alter the way in which the ODBC engine is initiated in the Windows Registry in order to obtain better performance. I know I can edit the Windows Registry using RegEdit, but I don't know what to actually do. How do I tune the ODBC engine through the Windows Registry?

Technique

The ODBC engine keys are stored in the Windows Registry in the \HKEY_LOCAL_MACHINE\Software\Microsoft\Jet\3.5\Engines\ODBC section. Table 11.5 lists the available keys and their respective default values.

Table 11.5. The Jet\3.5\Engines\ODBC keys and default values.

KEY	DEFAULT
LoginTimeout	20
QueryTimeout	60
ConnectionTimeout	600
AsyncRetryInterval	500
AttachCaseSensitive	0
AttachableObjects	'TABLE', 'VIEW', 'SYSTEM TABLE', 'ALIAS', 'SYNONYM'
SnapshotOnly	0
TraceSQLMode	0
TraceODBCAPI	0
DisableAsync	1
JetTryAuth	1
PreparedInsert	0
PreparedUpdate	0
FastRequery	0

By adjusting the values of any of these keys, you can affect the way any application that uses the ODBC jet engine accesses data. The following is a brief description of each key represented in Table 11.5.

Steps

Run the **RegEdit** application that is in the Windows directory on your machine. Locate the \HKEY_LOCAL_MACHINE\Software\Microsoft\Jet\3.5\Engines\ODBC section of the Registry, and you should see something similar to Figure 11.13.

1. Choose a key in the section that you are now in. Choose Edit | Modify from the RegEdit menu.

2. Edit the value of the key that you have selected. For a complete list of the available keys for this section, see the "How It Works" section of this How-To.

3. Click OK to save your changes or Cancel to abort.

How It Works

The following sections contain a list of the keys that make up the \HKEY_LOCAL_MACHINE\Software\Microsoft\Jet\3.5\Engines\ODBC section of the Windows Registry, and a description of each.

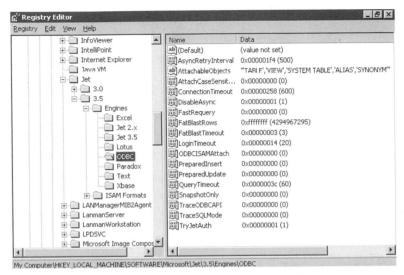

Figure 11.16. The \HKEY_LOCAL_MACHINE\Software\
Microsoft\Jet\3.5\Engines\ODBC of the Windows Registry.

LoginTimeout

The LoginTimout key is used to store the maximum number of seconds a login attempt can take. After the specified time, timing out occurs with an error. The default for LoginTimout is 20 seconds.

QueryTimeout

The QueryTimeout key is used to store the maximum number of seconds the entire processing time can take to run a query before actually timing out. The default value for this key is 60 seconds. If the DisableAsync key is set to its default of 0, the QueryTimeout key is used to indicate the time in seconds waited for a response from the server between polls for the completion of a query.

ConnectionTimeout

The ConnectionTimeout key is used to store the maximum amount of seconds a cached connection may remain idle before timing out. The default value for the ConnectionTimeout key is 600 seconds (10 minutes).

AsyncRetryInterval

The AsyncRetryInverval is used to measure the time allotted between polls to determine whether the server has completed processing a query. The AsyncRetryInterval key is measured in milliseconds with a default of 500. This key is available only for asynchronous processing.

AttachCaseSensitive

The `AttachCaseSensitive` key is used to determine what type of matching is enabled for linking tables. A default value of `0` indicates that the linking process is not case sensitive whereas a value of `1` indicates that the tables must match according to case.

AttachableObjects

The `AttachableObjects` key holds a list of server object types that are allowed to be linked. The default value for this key is `'TABLE'`, `'VIEW'`, `'SYSTEM TABLE'`, `'ALIAS'`, `'SYNONYM'`.

SnapshotOnly

The `SnapshotOnly` key indicates whether `Recordsets` objects must be snapshots (default value of `0`); they may also be dynasets (value of `1`).

TraceSQLMode

The `TraceSQLMode` key is equivalent to the `SQLTraceMode` key. It indicates whether a trace of SQL statements will be recorded in `SQLOUT.TXT` that is sent to an ODBC data source. The default value for the `TraceSQLMode` key is `0`, or no. A value of `1` indicates yes.

TraceODBCAPI

The `TraceODBCAPI` key indicates whether ODBC API calls are traced in the `ODBCAPI.TXT` file. A value of `0` indicates no, and `1` indicates yes. The default for this key is no.

DisableAsync

The `DisableAsync` key is an indicator of whether to force synchronous query execution. This key can either be set to its default of `1` for a force of synchronous query execution, or `0` for using asynchronous query execution if possible.

JetTryAuth

The `JetTryAuth` key indicates whether the Microsoft Access user name and password are to be used to log in to the server before prompting. The default value is yes (`1`). A value of `0` indicates no.

PreparedInsert

The `PreparedInsert` key is used to determine whether to use a prepared `INSERT` statement that inserts data in all columns. The default value for this key is `1`, which indicates using a prepared `INSERT` statement. A value of `0` would indicate using a custom `INSERT` statement that inserts only non-null values. By using prepared `INSERT` statements, nulls can overwrite server defaults. In addition, triggers can execute on columns that were not inserted explicitly.

PreparedUpdate

The `PreparedUpdate` key is used to determine whether to use a prepared `UPDATE` statement that updates data in all the available columns. A value of `0` is the default and this indicates that a custom `UPDATE` statement is to be used and sets only columns that have changed. A value of `1` is used to use a prepared `UPDATE` statement.

FastRequery

The `FastRequery` key is used to indicate whether to use a prepared `SELECT` statement for parameterized queries. The default value is no, or `0`. A value of `1` indicates yes.

ACTIVEX AND AUTOMATION

12

ACTIVEX AND AUTOMATION

How do I...

12.1 Use ActiveX Automation to edit pictures, documents, and spreadsheets embedded in an application's database?

12.2 Provide access to database files through a private class module?

12.3 Publish my ActiveX private class so that others can use it?

12.4 Provide controlled access to an encrypted, password-protected database using an ActiveX EXE server?

12.5 Use Microsoft Access as an ActiveX server to print reports from Visual Basic?

12.6 Use Microsoft Access queries containing user-defined functions from Visual Basic?

12.7 Convert database data to a spreadsheet form that can be used to edit and analyze data?

12.8 Include an editable report writer in a Visual Basic application?

12.9 Work with the Windows Registry for my ActiveX classes?

12.10 Create my own custom data control?

12.11 Create my own data bound control?

12.12 Use the DataRepeater control with custom Data Bound controls?

ActiveX Overview

ActiveX is the umbrella name Microsoft applies to developer technology that implements the *component object model* (COM). At its heart, COM allows applications to communicate with each other and use each other's features without regard to the original development language, date of development, or version compatibility. The component object model started from the concepts of *object-oriented programming* (OOP) and extended that model into the operating system to allow any COM program object to communicate successfully with any other COM object supporting the desired interfaces.

OBJECT-ORIENTED PROGRAMMING

Object-oriented programming provides disciplines and methods for source code re-use and recycling. OOP engineering concepts define an environment in which program objects model "real-world" objects. Each object is responsible for its own data, program logic, lifetime, and interfaces to the outside world. Formally, the academic experts tell us that "true" objects must support *encapsulation*, *inheritance*, and *polymorphism*.

Encapsulation means that each object provides a safe container (or capsule) for its *properties* (data) and *methods* (code). The object defines which properties and methods it will allow other objects to see (*public*) and which ones remain only inside the object (*private*).

Inheritance means that a new object can be defined as a "kind of" another object and gain all the "parent" object's properties and methods without doing any work.

Polymorphism is the capability of a derived object to change or override the inherited methods of its parents. You can have a dog object with a method to bark, and you can then have a big dog and a little dog inherited from the parent dog, each with a bark— but those two barks can be different (woof, and WOOF WOOF, for example) if that method is overridden in the new object.

COM Has Its Roots in OOP

The *component object model* (COM) and the *distributed component object model* (DCOM) extend the object-oriented programming (see sidebar) paradigm to allow preexisting software applications and objects to interact through a published, stable specification. Microsoft's first widely published implementation of the component object model was *Object Linking and Embedding* (OLE). This technology allowed previously compiled programs to embed or link their objects (Word documents or Excel spreadsheets) into new documents or forms.

Unfortunately, VB6 does not fully implement object-oriented programming. In particular, polymorphism is given short shrift. In traditional OOP, an object can inherit methods from a parent and then change or override only selected methods without having to re-implement all the parent's methods. With VB6, the programmer must implement all inherited methods of a parent object even if only one method is to be changed. By using the **Implements** keyword, a programmer tells the VB6 compiler that the class is implementing an interface derived from another class. The "bird" object "flies on" feathered wings. The "airliner" object "flies on" metal wings. In VB6, both the bird and the airliner classes would be declared to *implement* the **FlyingThing** class in order to encapsulate the **FlyingThing**'s properties and methods. Both birds and airliners are flying objects, and both implement a "flies on" property, but they appear to share similar properties and behaviors even though they are different objects.

ActiveX and Visual Basic 6

Visual Basic 6 provides several ways to incorporate ActiveX technologies in applications, determined primarily by how the calling application fits into the ActiveX component's environment:

✔ Code components serve as a library of objects available to calling applications. Built as Visual Basic class modules, the services can be built as *dynamic link libraries* (DLLs), can be separate EXE files, or can be statically bound into the calling application. The remainder of this chapter focuses on ActiveX code components.

✔ ActiveX controls are functionally equivalent to the visual controls you put on your forms. They differ from other ActiveX components in that they talk back to the calling application by raising events whose responses can modify the behavior of the control. ActiveX controls run in the caller's process space and communicate directly through memory.

✔ ActiveX documents are forms designed to appear within Internet browser windows. They are very similar to ActiveX controls because they must be used within a browser container. They are similar to code components in that they can be implemented as DLL or EXE files and run either within the calling process environment (DLL) or as a separate process (EXE).

The three ActiveX methods share the use of the component object model as the operating-environment glue that allows successful communication between components.

Building and Using Code Components

As developers, we build all our ActiveX code components as *class modules*. At the simple, practical level, Visual Basic 6 treats class modules as objects implementing properties and methods in just the same manner in which we can use the Visual Basic label control from our code. We can set the `Caption` property and then invoke the `Refresh` method to ensure that the caption is displayed immediately. Visual Basic will help us write the code with its code completion features and will show us as we type the defined properties and methods for each object in the application. As a result, programmers will reuse existing code more often, develop systems faster, and produce more reliable systems. The use of classes to develop our features and functions helps keep other programmers from using our code in ways we did not intend.

ActiveX code components publish properties and methods that are available for use in your application. An ActiveX code component can be included in an application by referencing a component from the Project menu in the development environment. When included, component properties and methods can be invoked from the calling application as though the calling application had all the component application's functionality. For example, an application referencing a Microsoft Office EXE component can use the Visual Basic for Applications (VBA) methods to manipulate the Office component's properties to create powerful business solutions.

Visual Basic 4 called code components *object linking and embedding*, which is used to embed or link another application's object within the calling application. The calling application is called the container. A Visual Basic application acting as the container can use the `OLE Container` control to display linked or embedded objects belonging to server applications. The type of object depends on the server. A spreadsheet program typically provides worksheet objects and graph objects. A word processing program provides document objects. A graphics program provides picture objects.

As mentioned previously, the balance of this chapter pertains to ActiveX code components. The specific How-To's consist of the following tasks.

12.1 Use ActiveX Automation to Edit Pictures, Documents, and Spreadsheets Embedded in an Application's Database

You can use the OLE `Object` field type in a Microsoft Access database file to store linked or embedded objects, and then display those objects on a Visual Basic form. Users can view or edit the object from within the Visual Basic application. This How-To shows you how to use an `OLE Container` control linked to a data control to accomplish this task.

12.2 Provide Access to Database Files Through a Private Class Module

The first step to creating an ActiveX code component is to create and debug a private class module that implements all the desired properties and methods. This How-To shows you a simple class-based replacement for the data control that implements core functions.

12.3 Publish My ActiveX Private Class so That Others Can Use It

After you build a useful class module for simple data access, other members of your workgroup or corporation might find it useful. Company policy, however, requires that your class module's functions only be distributed as object code—you can't share your source. This How-To shows how to convert your class module into an ActiveX DLL that can be used by other applications.

12.4 Provide Controlled Access to an Encrypted, Password-Protected Database Using an ActiveX EXE Server

Visual Basic 6.0 has given the language a much stronger and more useful set of object-oriented features with ActiveX. This How-To demonstrates a method of creating an ActiveX EXE component in Visual Basic that can be used from other applications or even from other machines while hiding the details of its operation and encapsulating its data.

12.5 Use Microsoft Access as an ActiveX Server to Print Reports from Visual Basic

The application design requires that all reports be centrally administered, and the Access database has been selected as the report repository. This How-To demonstrates using Microsoft Access from Visual Basic to print reports defined within the database.

12.6 Use Microsoft Access Queries Containing User-Defined Functions from Visual Basic

Sometimes, an application needs to take advantage of Access database functions that are not available directly to Visual Basic 6.0. This How-To demonstrates using Microsoft Access as a component to use a query containing a user-defined function.

12.7 Convert Database Data to a Spreadsheet Form That Can Be Used to Edit and Analyze Data

Although Visual Basic is an extremely powerful and flexible tool and environment, it lacks many specialized functions for financial, statistical, and scientific analyses of data in a database. This How-To shows how you can use the specialized statistical functions from Microsoft Excel to make statistical calculations on any database accessible to Visual Basic.

12.8 Include an Editable Report Writer in a Visual Basic Application

One of the biggest advantages of using ActiveX code components with Visual Basic applications is that you can use the functionality of other applications in Visual Basic. In this How-To, you will see how you can use all the power of Microsoft Word in Visual Basic, eliminating the need to duplicate the programming in your own code.

12.9 Work with the Windows Registry for My ActiveX Classes

ActiveX code components bring lots of power and flexibility to your applications, but they rely on correct registration in order for other programs to find them. This How-To shows the use of the registration server to register and "unregister" your controls.

12.10 Create My Own Custom Data Control

The data control provided with Visual Basic 6 is a powerful tool for building many applications, but it can add tremendous amounts of processing overhead because it is a general-purpose tool with methods and events that no one needs for most projects. This How-To shows you how to build a custom data control purpose-built for a single table using data access objects.

12.11 Create My Own Data Bound Control

The data bound list box provided with Visual Basic is quite powerful, but using a data control to populate can add a lot of unnecessary overhead to an application. This How-To shows you a data bound combo box control that loads a specific code value type such as HAIRCOLOR from a specified database.

12.12 Use the DataRepeater Control with Custom Data Bound Controls

The DataRepeater control, new in Visual Basic 6, takes your custom data bound control and duplicates it so that your custom control acts like a line in a list box. This How-To shows you how to use the DataRepeater control with your custom bound control to build a database application that can browse and edit many records at the same time.

COMPLEXITY
INTERMEDIATE

12.1 How do I...
Use ActiveX Automation to edit pictures, documents, and spreadsheets embedded in an application's database?

Problem

I'm creating a customer service database with a table that documents contacts with customers. When the customer is sent a letter, I'd like to put a copy of the actual word processing document into the table. How can I do this with Visual Basic?

Technique

Microsoft Access provides the OLE `Object` field type into which you can place either a linked or an embedded OLE object. An embedded object is actually stored in the database. Linked objects are not stored in the database; rather, the database stores a reference to the file containing the object.

The Visual Basic `OLE Container` control is a control used to place an OLE object onto a form. The `OLE Container` control is then bound to an `OLE Object` field in a Microsoft Access database through a data control. The data control and `OLE Container` control together manage the retrieval and updating of the `OLE Object` field and the display of the field's contents on the form.

Visual Basic can insert a new object into a Microsoft Access database `OLE Object` field in two ways. The `OLE Container` control's `InsertObjectDlg` box displays the Insert Object dialog box. The dialog box enables the user to choose to create a new object from any application on the system that can act as an OLE Server. This creates an embedded object. The dialog box also gives the user the means to select a file containing an OLE object and to designate that the object be stored as an embedded or linked object.

If the Clipboard contains an object created by an OLE Server application, and if the current control is an `OLE Container`, Visual Basic can paste the contents of the Clipboard into the control. The `OLE Container`'s `Paste` method pastes the object into the control in the default format (which depends on the type of object). The `PasteSpecial` method displays a dialog box that lets the user select the format for those object types that support more than one format.

Steps

Open the project Embedded.VBP. If necessary, edit the **DatabaseName** property of the **datObjects** control to point to a copy of Chapter12.MDB. Then run the project. The form shown in Figure 12.1 appears. Use the record navigation buttons of the data control to page through the records. As you display a record, the application shows you the contents of the **OLE Object** field, the type of object, and the name of the object. Double-click the object, and Paintbrush opens with the object displayed. Edit the object in Paintbrush, and then choose File | Exit from the Paintbrush menu. When the dialog box appears asking whether you want to update the link to the Visual Basic application, click Yes.

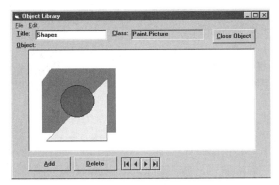

Figure 12.1. The Object Library form.

On the form, click the Add button. Click the **OLE Container** control, and then choose Edit | Insert Object. The Insert Object dialog box appears, as shown in Figure 12.2. To create a new embedded object from one of the listed applications, choose the object from the list and click OK. To create an object from a file, choose the Create from File option. When the Insert Object dialog box changes in appearance (see Figure 12.3), either enter a filename or click Browse and select a file from the File Open dialog box that appears. If you want to select a linked object, click the Link check box. To create an embedded object, leave the Link check box blank.

1. Create a new project called Embedded.VBP. Use **Form1** to create the objects and properties listed in Table 12.1, and save the form as OBJLIB.FRM. If you have moved the files installed by the distribution disk, edit the **DatabaseName** property of the data control on **Form1** to point to the current location of Chapter12.MDB.

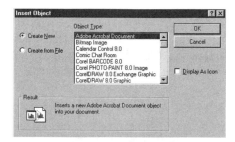

Figure 12.2. The Insert Object dialog box.

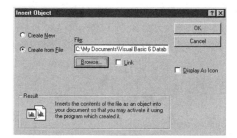

Figure 12.3. The Insert Object dialog box with the Create from File option selected.

Table 12.1. Objects and properties for the Object Library form.

OBJECT	PROPERTY	SETTING
Form	Name	Form1
	Caption	"Object Library"
Name	CommandButton	cmdClick
	Caption	"&Close Object"
Name	CommandButton	cmdDelete
	Caption	"&Delete"
Name	CommandButton	cmdAdd
	Caption	"&Add"
Name	TextBox	txtTitle
	DataField	"Title"
	DataSource	"datObjects"
Name	Data	datObjects
	Connect	"Access"
	DatabaseName	"C:\Code\Chapter12\Chapter12.mdb"

continued on next page

continued from previous page

OBJECT	PROPERTY	SETTING
	RecordsetType	1 'Dynaset
	RecordSource	"ObjectLibrary"
Name	Label	lblClass
	DataField	"Object Type"
	DataSource	"datObjects"
Name	OLE	oleObject
	DataField	"Object"
	DataSource	"datObjects"
	SizeMode	3 'Zoom
Name	Label	Label1
	AutoSize	-1 'True
Name	Label	Label2
	AutoSize	-1 'True

2. Use the Visual Basic menu editor to create the menu shown in Table 12.2.

Table 12.2. Menu specifications for the Object Library form.

CAPTION	NAME	SHORTCUT KEY
&File	mnuFile	
----E&xit	mnuFileExit	
&Edit	mnuEdit	
----&Paste	mnuEditPaste	Ctrl+V
----Past&e Special	mnuEditPasteSpecial	
---- ----	mnuEditSep	
----&Insert Object	mnuEditInsertObject	

3. Add the following code to the declarations section of `Form1`. This variable tracks deletions in progress when, during `cmdDelete_Click` processing, the data control fires a reposition event in response to the issued `MoveNext`.

```
Private mblnDeleting As Boolean
```

4. Enter the following code as the `Click` event for `cmdAdd`:

```
Private Sub cmdAdd_Click()
    Data1.Recordset.AddNew
End Sub
```

5. Enter the following code as the `Click` event for `cmdDelete`:

```
Private Sub cmdDelete_Click()

    On Error GoTo DeleteError
    mblnDeleting = True
    datObjects.Recordset.Delete
    'oleObject.Class = ""
    datObjects.Recordset.MoveNext
    ' Handle the "no current record" case.
    If datObjects.Recordset.EOF Then
        ' Handle the special case of deleting the
        ' last record
        datObjects.Recordset.MoveLast
    End If
    mblnDeleting = False

    ' Reset the error handler
    On Error GoTo 0
    Exit Sub

DeleteError:
    If Err.Number = 3021 Then              ' No current record
        Resume Next
    End If

End Sub
```

6. Enter the following code as the `Click` event for `mnuEdit`. If the Edit menu is opened when the `OLE Container` control is the active control, the Edit menu's Insert Object item is enabled. The procedure looks at the `PasteOK` property of the OLE Container control. If `PasteOK` is `True`, the object currently on the Windows Clipboard supports OLE, so the Paste and PasteSpecial items are enabled. If `PasteOK` is `False`, the item on the Clipboard cannot be an OLE object, so Paste and PasteOK are disabled. If the active control is anything other than the `OLE Container` control, all the Edit menu choices are disabled.

```
Private Sub mnuEdit_Click()
    If Me.ActiveControl.Name = "oleObject" Then
        mnuEditPaste.Enabled = oleObject.PasteOK
        mnuEditPasteSpecial.Enabled = oleObject.PasteOK
        mnuEditInsertObject.Enabled = True
    Else
        mnuEditPaste.Enabled = False
        mnuEditPasteSpecial.Enabled = False
        mnuEditInsertObject.Enabled = False
    End If
End Sub
```

7. Enter the following code as the `Click` event of the Edit menu's Insert Object item. This code calls the `InsertObjDlg` method of the OLE object. That method displays the Insert Object dialog box and manages the actual

insertion of the object designated by the user. If the user inserts a new
object, the procedure then gets the **Class** property of the **OLE Container**
control and displays it in the Class label on the form.

```
Private Sub mnuEditInsertObject_Click()
    OLE1.InsertObjDlg
    If OLE1.DataChanged Then
        lblClass.Caption = OLE1.Class
    End If
End Sub
```

8. Enter the following code as the **Click** event for **mnuPaste**. When the user
chooses this menu item, the code pastes the object currently on the
Clipboard into the **OLE Container** control and updates the Class label on
the form.

```
Private Sub mnuEditInsertObject_Click()
    oleObject.InsertObjDlg
    If oleObject.DataChanged Then
        lblClass.Caption = oleObject.Class
    End If
End Sub
```

9. Enter the following code as the **Click** event for **mnuPasteSpecial**. When
the user chooses this menu item, the code invokes the **PasteSpecialDlg**
method of the **OLE Container** control. This method displays the Paste
Special dialog box, which allows the user to choose the format and linkage
type to be used for the object.

```
Private Sub mnuEditPasteSpecial_Click()
    oleObject.PasteSpecialDlg
    lblClass.Caption = oleObject.Class
End Sub
```

10. Enter the following code as the **Click** event for **cmdCloseObject** to update
the Access database OLE Object database field:

```
Private Sub cmdCloseObject_Click()

    ' Save the updated object
    If oleObject.DataChanged Or txtTitle.DataChanged Then
        datObjects.UpdateRecord
    End If

End Sub
```

11. Enter the following code as the **Click** event for **mnuFileExit**:

```
Private Sub mnuFileExit_Click()

    If oleObject.DataChanged Or txtTitle.DataChanged Then
        datObjects.UpdateRecord
    End If
```

```
        Unload Me

    End Sub
```

12. Enter the following code as the **Reposition** event for **datObject**. This procedure checks to see whether we are in the middle of a delete operation before referencing a potentially non-existent data-bound **oleObject**. The **mblnDeleting** variable controls accidentally re-entering the validation event when the data control is positioned at "No current record" after deletion of the last record.

```
Private Sub datObjects_Reposition()

    If Not mblnDeleting Then
        ' Update the label for the oleObject class if the
        ' reposition is not a MoveNext after deletion of
        ' the last record. The change to the lblClass value
        ' forces another validation and record update
        ' attempt. The update attempt after the deletion of
        ' the last record causes a "no current record" error
        If lblClass.Caption = "" Then
            lblClass.Caption = oleObject.Class
        End If
    End If

End Sub
```

13. Enter the following code for the **Form_Load** event. This procedure sets the database name for the data control to be the database in the application directory.

```
Dim strDbName As String
    Dim strResponse As String

    On Error GoTo LoadError

    ' Set the database of the data control
    strDbName = App.Path
    strDbName = strDbName & "\Chapter14.mdb"
    datObjects.DatabaseName = strDbName

    ' Indicate that we are not currently deleting a
    ' record
    mblnDeleting = False

    Exit Sub

LoadError:
    MsgBox Err.Description & Chr(13) & "from " & Err.Source _
            & " -- Number: " & CStr(Err.Number)
    Unload Me

End Sub
```

How It Works

The `OLE Container` control contains the image of the data you are storing, the name of the application used to manipulate the data, and the actual object data (embedded) or a reference to the actual object data (linked). For example, when you embed a spreadsheet in the `OLE Container` control, the display image of the spreadsheet, the application name (usually Excel), and the spreadsheet data itself are stored in the `OLE Container` control.

The data control is responsible for storing the embedded object in the Access OLE object database field. You might notice the "extra" work required to deal with the case of record movement after deleting the last record. The form uses a control variable (`mblnDeleting`) to determine whether a delete operation is in progress. The variable is checked in the `Reposition` event to prevent use of the `oleObject.Class` field when the last record has been deleted from the recordset and the unfortunate `No current record` error. There are 12 data validation constants for the data control to meet every programmer's potential needs, but they can cause unfortunate extra work if a reference to control data is required during a different event's firing. In this case, the `Reposition` event needs to check a field value, forcing a validation event before the `Reposition` event is complete.

The `OLE Container` control does almost all the work for this application for us by managing the properties and methods exposed by the ActiveX Automation components registered on the application's computer. Simply double-click the `OLE Container` control, and people using the application have almost all the capabilities of the embedded or linked component. The only limitation is that embedded or linked document saving occurs through the OLE container rather than through the application.

Comments

The properties of the `OLE Container` control give you a great deal of control over how the control works in your application. Two of the most useful properties are the edit-in-place property—actually a setting of the `MiscFlags` property—and the `SizeMode` property. More details on other `OLE Container` control properties can be found in the Visual Basic 6 documentation.

Editing in Place

If an ActiveX Automation application implements in-place editing, the user can edit an object right from your Visual Basic form. When the user double-clicks the `OLE Container` control, the menu bar changes to the one used by the server application that created the object, and any toolbars associated with the server application appear. The full facilities of the server application are available to the containing application. When the user moves the focus off the `OLE Container` control, the menus are restored to those of the client (Visual Basic) application.

Unless you specify otherwise, editing in-place is active for those server applications that support it. To disable editing in-place, set the MiscFlags property to the built-in constant value of 2 (or use the constant vbOLEMiscFlagDisableInPlace).

Controlling the Size

Windows gives the user the ability to resize forms. You might not always know in advance the size of the object that will be stored in a database; therefore, Visual Basic enables you to control how the OLE Container or the object it contains is sized. This is implemented through the settings of the SizeMode property, which are shown in Table 12.3. The default for the SizeMode property is 2 (Autosize).

Table 12.3. Settings for the SizeMode property of the OLE Container control.

SETTING	MEANING
0 - vbOLESizeClip	The object is displayed actual size. If the object is larger than the control, the image is clipped by the control.
1 - vbOLESizeStretch	The object's image is sized to fill the control. May not maintain the original proportions.
2 - vbOLESizeAutoSize	The control is resized to display the entire object. Maintains proportions, but requires that the OLE Container control resize event be handled to change the size of the form or the container.
3 - vbOLESizeZoom	The object is resized to fill as much as possible of the control while maintaining the original proportions.

COMPLEXITY

INTERMEDIATE

12.2 How do I...
Provide access to database files through a private class module?

Problem

I'm writing a companywide expense reporting system and need to control the data access to the expense detail table to ensure that all data is correctly edited before insertion. How do I create a private class module with properties and methods to manage and protect the contents of the expense detail table?

Technique

For this How-To, consider an expense detail table (contained in Expense.MDB). The fields of this table are listed in Table 12.4.

Table 12.4. Expense detail table definition.

FIELD	TYPE
ExpenseID	Long—Auto increment
EmployeeId	Text
ExpenseType	Text
AmountSpent	Currency
Description	Text
DatePurchased	Date/Time
DateSubmitted	Date/Time

The people in the accounting department are very concerned that any entries made to this table always pass certain edit checks. They are most concerned that the submission date always be set to the current date. They want no back-dated submissions to make it look as though they're working slowly. We have decided to manage the expense detail table with a Visual Basic class module to encapsulate the table properties and enforce the critical submission-date requirement.

Class Modules Form the Object Core

Visual Basic class modules implement program objects and are the core building block of all ActiveX code components. Each class implements public or private properties and methods. Properties are data items such as an expense amount. Methods are code procedures that act on the properties. Public items are exposed outside the class to the calling application. Private items are restricted to access by members of the class unless you choose to expose selected methods as *friends* to be invoked directly by code contained within the same project.

The expense detail class will be constructed to have properties (data items) corresponding to each table field plus an additional property to contain the Access database filename. The class assumes that the table is named Expenses. All properties are implemented with the `Private` keyword to ensure that callers cannot access the data directly. A private declaration limits access to a variable or function to code contained within the same module. Access to properties is through the `Property Let` and `Property Get` methods. These special-purpose, public method procedures assign values to and retrieve values from their properties. As values are set and retrieved, the `Let` and `Get` procedures can perform simple edits or complex calculations.

Linking Forms and Classes

The easiest way to link a simple form and its maintenance class is through two subroutines, one for setting the object's values and the other for getting changed object values. These subroutines transfer values between the form's controls and the object's properties by means of the `Property  Let` and `Property  Set` methods. The subroutines are called before any of the object's data movement methods are called.

Building Class Modules

In Visual Basic 6, you can build class modules by typing the entire program module or by using the Class Builder utility. This add-in speeds initial class module construction by automating property variable naming and construction of all required skeleton methods. Unfortunately, the Class Builder cannot delete classes after they are created. The most efficient way to use the Class Builder is to use it for initial definition of most of the class and then use manual editing for the remainder of the code maintenance.

The principal benefit of using the Class Builder utility is that it automatically makes all properties private and creates public **Property Let** and **Property Get** methods to allow calling applications to manipulate the object's properties. Although this approach incurs some additional processing overhead, especially in a private class module used only in your application, it automatically provides placeholders where you can later add code to manipulate properties as they are set.

Steps

Open the project ActiveXExpense.VBP and run the project. The form shown in Figure 12.4 appears. Experiment with the form to understand its simple behavior. The class module implements the most common data control methods.

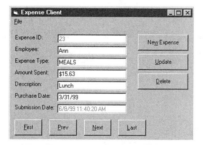

Figure 12.4. The Expense Client form.

1. Create a new project in your work area named ActiveXExpense.VBP, and use **frmExpClient** to create the objects and properties listed in Table 12.5.

Table 12.5. Objects and properties for the Expense client form.

OBJECT	PROPERTY	SETTING
Form	Name	frmExpClient
	Caption	"Expense Client"
CommandButton	Name	cmdLast
	Caption	"&Last"
CommandButton	Name	cmdNext
	Caption	"&Next"
CommandButton	Name	cmdPrev
	Caption	"&Prev"
CommandButton	Name	cmdFirst
	Caption	"&First"
CommandButton	Name	cmdDelete
	Caption	"&Delete"
CommandButton	Name	cmdUpdate
	Caption	"&Update"
CommandButton	Name	cmdNewExpense
	Caption	"Ne&w Expense"
MaskEdBox	Name	mskAmountSpent
	Format	"$#,##0.00;($#,##0.00)"
TextBox	Name	txtSubmitDate
TextBox	Name	txtPurchaseDate
TextBox	Name	txtDescription
TextBox	Name	txtExpenseType
TextBox	Name	txtEmployeeId
TextBox	Name	txtExpenseId
Label	Name	Label1
	Caption	"Expense ID:"
Label	Name	Label2
	Caption	"Employee:"
Label	Name	Label3
	Caption	"Expense Type:"
Label	Name	Label4
	Caption	"Amount Spent:"
Label	Name	Label5
	Caption	"Description:"

OBJECT	PROPERTY	SETTING
Label	Name	Label6
	Caption	"Purchase Date:"
Label	Name	Label7
	Caption	"Submission Date:"

2. Use the Visual Basic Menu Editor to create the menu shown in Table 12.6.

Table 12.6. Menu specifications for the Expense client form.

CAPTION	NAME	SHORTCUT KEY
&File	mnuFile	
----E&xit	mnuFileExit	

3. Enter the following code into the declarations section of frmExpClient. This line declares a private ExpenseDetail class variable to manage the expense details.

```
Private expDetailClass As New ExpenseDetail
```

4. Enter the following code as the Click event of the cmdNewExpense button. The ExpenseDetail class does error trapping for us, so the command button handlers can manage the object as a modal function modifying the database. The strResponse variable provides any required feedback for immediate display.

```
Private Sub cmdNewExpense_Click()

    Dim strResponse As String
    strResponse = SetObjectValues

    If "OK" = strResponse Then
        strResponse = expDetailClass.Insert
        If "OK" <> strResponse Then
            MsgBox strResponse
            Exit Sub
        End If
        Call ReadObjectValues
    Else
        MsgBox strResponse
    End If

End Sub
```

5. Enter the following code as the **Click** event of the **cmdUpdate** button:

```
Private Sub cmdUpdate_Click()
' Updates current record with form values

    Dim strResponse As String
    strResponse = SetObjectValues

    If "OK" = strResponse Then
        strResponse = expDetailClass.Update
        If "OK" <> strResponse Then
            MsgBox strResponse
            Exit Sub
        End If
        Call ReadObjectValues
    Else
        MsgBox strResponse
    End If

End Sub
```

6. Enter the following code as the **Click** event of the **cmdDelete** button:

```
Private Sub cmdDelete_Click()
' Deletes current record from database

    Dim strResponse As String

    strResponse = expDetailClass.Delete
    If "OK" <> strResponse Then
        MsgBox strResponse
    Else
        Call ReadObjectValues
    End If

End Sub
```

7. Enter the following code for the **Click** events of the movement buttons. With the exception of the invoked class methods, these event procedures are virtually identical—they invoke a class method, check the result, and display an error message or data.

```
Private Sub cmdFirst_Click()
' Positions to first record in recordset and displays
' values

    Dim strResponse As String

    strResponse = expDetailClass.MoveFirst
    If "OK" <> strResponse Then
        MsgBox strResponse
    Else
        Call ReadObjectValues
    End If
```

```
                   End Sub

                   Private Sub cmdLast_Click()
                   ' Positions to last record in recordset and displays values

                       Dim strResponse As String

                       strResponse = expDetailClass.MoveLast
                       If "OK" <> strResponse Then
                           MsgBox strResponse
                       Else
                           Call ReadObjectValues
                       End If

                   End Sub

                   Private Sub cmdNext_Click()
                   ' Positions to Next record in recordset and displays values

                       Dim strResponse As String

                       strResponse = expDetailClass.MoveNext
                       If "OK" <> strResponse Then
                           MsgBox strResponse
                       Else
                           Call ReadObjectValues
                       End If

                   End Sub

                   Private Sub cmdPrev_Click()
                   ' Positions to Previous record in recordset and displays
                   ' values

                       Dim strResponse As String

                       strResponse = expDetailClass.MovePrev
                       If "OK" <> strResponse Then
                           MsgBox strResponse
                       Else
                           Call ReadObjectValues
                       End If

                   End Sub
```

8. Enter the following code for the procedure `SetObjectValues`. This function invokes the Expense Detail class's public methods to set the object's property values. The expense type is limited by the object to values of TRAVEL, MEALS, OFFICE, AUTO, or TOLL/PARK. The `strSetExpenseType` method converts the input to uppercase characters and checks for a valid value. Invalid input results in the method returning an informative display message.

```
Private Function SetObjectValues() As String
' Sets related object values from form fields

    Dim strResponse As String

    strResponse = expDetailClass. _
        strSetExpenseType(txtExpenseType.Text)

    On Error GoTo TypeError

    If "OK" = strResponse Then
        expDetailClass.strEmployeeId = txtEmployeeId.Text
        expDetailClass.strDescription = txtDescription.Text
        expDetailClass.dtmDatePurchased = txtPurchaseDate.Text
        expDetailClass.curAmountSpent = CCur(mskAmountSpent.Text)
    End If

    SetObjectValues = strResponse
    Exit Function

TypeError:
    If Err.Number = 13 Then
        expDetailClass.curAmountSpent = 0
        Resume Next
    End If

End Function
```

9. Enter the following code for the procedure **ReadObjectValues**. Note that the form code doesn't have to deal with any potential null values from the database; it just displays the results.

```
Private Sub ReadObjectValues()
' Read the object values into the form fields

    txtExpenseId.Text = CStr(expDetailClass.lngExpenseId)
    txtEmployeeId.Text = expDetailClass.strEmployeeId
    txtExpenseType.Text = expDetailClass.strExpenseType
    txtDescription.Text = expDetailClass.strDescription
    mskAmountSpent.Text = CStr(expDetailClass.curAmountSpent)
    txtPurchaseDate.Text = CStr(expDetailClass.dtmDatePurchased)
    txtSubmitDate.Text = CStr(expDetailClass.dtmDateSubmitted)

End Sub
```

10. Enter the following code for the **Form_Load** event. The invocation of the class's **strDbName Property Let** method causes the object to open the specified database and position its hidden recordset to the first record. An error handler is required in this procedure because **Property Let** procedures cannot return a signal value but can raise errors.

```
Private Sub Form_Load()
' Get the ActiveX object to open its database and position
' to the first record
    Dim strDbName As String
    Dim strResponse As String
```

```
        On Error GoTo LoadError

        strDbName = App.Path
        strDbName = strDbName & "\Expense.mdb"
        expDetailClass.strDbName = strDbName
        strResponse = expDetailClass.MoveFirst
        If "OK" <> strResponse Then
            MsgBox strResponse
        Else
            Call ReadObjectValues
        End If

    Exit Sub

    LoadError:
        MsgBox Err.Description & Chr(13) & "from " & Err.Source _
                & " -- Number: " & CStr(Err.Number)
        Unload Me

    End Sub
```

11. Enter the following code for the **Form_Unload** event. Although this client is using the expense detail class as a private module whose memory will be released when the form is unloaded, EXE and DLL objects will usually not release resources until no caller is making references. Setting an object to the value **Nothing** is the caller's way of tearing down the object connection gracefully.

```
Private Sub Form_Unload(Cancel As Integer)

    Set expDetailClass = Nothing

End Sub
```

12. Enter the following code for the **Click** event of **mnuFileExit**:

```
Private Sub mnuFileExit_Click()

    Unload Me

End Sub
```

13. Use the VB Class Builder to create the skeleton of the Expense Detail class. Select Project | Add Class Module. Double-click VB Class Builder to start the Class Builder add-in. Select File | New | Class, and then name the new class **ExpenseDetail**.

14. Select the newly created **ExpenseDetail** class. Select File | New | Property, and create a property named **lngExpenseId** with Long data type, as shown in Figure 12.5. Continue adding properties until you have defined everything listed in Table 12.7.

Table 12.7. Properties and data types for the `ExpenseDetail` class.

PROPERTY	DATA TYPE
lngExpenseID	Long
strEmployeeId	String
strExpenseType	String
curAmmountSpent	Currency
strDescription	String
dtmDatePurchased	Date
dtmDateSubmitted	Date
strDbName	String

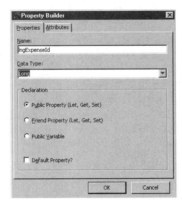

Figure 12.5. The VB
Property Builder.

15. Click the Methods tab of the Class Builder utility to define the methods
and return types listed in Table 12.8. Be sure to define a return data type.
Update the project and exit the Class Builder.

Table 12.8. Methods and data types for the `ExpenseDetail` class.

METHOD	RETURN DATA TYPE
Delete	String
Insert	String
Update	String
MoveFirst	String
MoveNext	String
MovePrev	String
MoveLast	String

16. Add the variables in bold type to the declarations section of your class module. The other variables were created by the Property Builder. The class needs database and recordset variables to perform its work, and it uses the `RecSetOpen` Boolean variable to force closing the recordset and database if a running version of the class is passed a new database name.

```
Option Explicit

'local variable(s) to hold property value(s)
Private mvarlngExpenseId As Long        'local copy
Private mvarstrEmployeeId As String     'local copy
Private mvarstrExpenseType As String    'local copy
Private mvarcurAmountSpent As Currency  'local copy
Private mvarstrDescription As String    'local copy
Private mvardtmDatePurchased As Date    'local copy
Private mvardtmDateSubmitted As Date    'local copy
Private mvarstrDbName As String         'local copy
' Database variables needed to keep track of current
' database condition
Private mdbExpense As Database
Private mrecExpense As Recordset
Private mblnRecSetOpen As Boolean
```

17. Remove the `Property Let` procedures for `lngExpenseId` and `dtmDateSubmitted` from the class module. The Access database engine automatically assigns the `ExpenseId`, and the `Insert` method assigns the date submitted. A class module designed to protect the database can't allow these changes.

18. Modify the `Property Let` procedure for the `strDbName` property as shown next. Whenever the database name property is changed, we need to close an open recordset and database and then open the desired database and recordset.

```
Public Property Let strDbName(ByVal vData As String)
'used when assigning a value to the property, on the left
'side of an assignment.
'Syntax: X.strDbName = 5

    On Error GoTo OpenError

    If mblnRecSetOpen Then
        mrecExpense.Close
        mdbExpense.Close
    End If
    mvarstrDbName = vData
    Set mdbExpense = DBEngine.Workspaces(0). _
        OpenDatabase(mvarstrDbName)
    Set mrecExpense = mdbExpense.OpenRecordset("Expenses")
    mblnRecSetOpen = True

    Exit Property
```

continued on next page

continued from previous page

```
OpenError:
    ' Because we are designing this class for
    ' potential unattended operation, we'll have to raise
    ' an error on our own
    Err.Raise Number:=Err.Number
    Err.Clear
    Exit Property

End Property
```

19. Prepare the `Class Initialize` and `Class Terminate` procedures as shown next. The `Initialize` procedure ensures that all critical variables have their *initial values* set correctly even if we programmers think that they are already set. The `Terminate` procedure cleans up any messes we might have made along the way.

```
Private Sub Class_Initialize()

    ' Indicate that the database is not yet open
    mblnRecSetOpen = False
    ' Clear all object variables
    Call ClearObject

End Sub

Private Sub Class_Terminate()

    ' We don't really care about errors when cleaning up.
    On Error Resume Next
    ' Close the recordset
    mrecExpense.Close
    ' Close the expense database
    mdbExpense.Close
    ' Reset the error handler
    On Error GoTo 0
    Exit Sub

End Sub
```

20. Define the private `ClearObject` procedure to clear the object's properties to known safe values that won't cause database errors and that will look "empty" to anyone reading the values from a caller's form:

```
Private Sub ClearObject()
' Clears all object variables

    mvarlngExpenseId = 0
    mvarstrEmployeeId = ""
    mvarstrExpenseType = ""
    mvarcurAmountSpent = 0
    mvarstrDescription = ""
    mvardtmDatePurchased = CDate("1/1/1980")
    mvardtmDateSubmitted = CDate("1/1/1980")

End Sub
```

21. Define the procedures to map the recordset field values to the object's variables. Note the use of the `With` construct to improve runtime performance and code readability. The `With` construct tells Visual Basic to add the `With` reference to the front of any ambiguous variable references. The source code is easier to read because it is more succinct. Performance is improved because the runtime library doesn't have to search all possible reference values for each assignment statement. In effect, the `With` shorthand works equally well for the programmer and the runtime application.

```
Private Sub SetRecordset(recExp As Recordset)
' Copies current values to Recordset

    With recExp
        !EmployeeId = mvarstrEmployeeId
        !ExpenseType = mvarstrExpenseType
        !AmountSpent = mvarcurAmountSpent
        !Description = mvarstrDescription
        !DatePurchased = mvardtmDatePurchased
        !DateSubmitted = mvardtmDateSubmitted
    End With

End Sub

Private Sub GetRecordset(recExp As Recordset)
' Copies current values to Recordset

    With recExp
        mvarlngExpenseId = 0 + !ExpenseID
        mvarstrEmployeeId = "" & !EmployeeId
        mvarstrExpenseType = "" & !ExpenseType
        mvarcurAmountSpent = 0 + !AmountSpent
        mvarstrDescription = "" & !Description
        mvardtmDatePurchased = !DatePurchased
        mvardtmDateSubmitted = !DateSubmitted
    End With

End Sub
```

22. Create the special expense-type assignment method to provide editing and message response capabilities. This code checks that the assigned value is one of the defined values and responds with an error message if the value is not acceptable. The object supports no other method to set the expense type, so the table is protected.

```
Public Function strSetExpenseType(ByVal vData As String) As String

' Sets the expense type to an allowed value
    Dim strTemp As String
    strTemp = UCase$(vData)

    If strTemp = "TRAVEL" _
    Or strTemp = "MEALS" _
```

continued on next page

continued from previous page

```
            Or strTemp = "OFFICE" _
            Or strTemp = "AUTO" _
            Or strTemp = "TOLL/PARK" Then
                mvarstrExpenseType = strTemp
                strSetExpenseType = "OK"
            Else
                strSetExpenseType = "Expense type must be TRAVEL, MEALS, " _
                                & "OFFICE, AUTO, or TOLL/PARK"
            End If

End Function
```

23. Create the `Insert`, `Update`, and `Delete` methods. These methods closely mimic the interaction of the data control and its recordset, but they do not suffer from the intervening events that make direct programming with the data control problematic.

```
Public Function Insert() As String
' Inserts a brand-new record into the database and leaves
' the newly inserted values as the current object values.

    On Error GoTo InsertError
    With mrecExpense

        .AddNew
        mvardtmDateSubmitted = Now
        Call SetRecordset(mrecExpense)
        .Update
        'Move to the most recently modified record
        .Bookmark = .LastModified
        Call GetRecordset(mrecExpense)
    End With

    Insert = "OK"

    Exit Function

InsertError:
    ' Return the error description
    Insert = Err.Description
    Err.Clear
    Exit Function

End Function

Public Function Update() As String
' Updates Expenses table from current object values
Dim strSql As String

    On Error GoTo UpdateError
    With mrecExpense
        .Edit
        Call SetRecordset(mrecExpense)
```

```
                    .Update
                    .Bookmark = .LastModified
                    Call GetRecordset(mrecExpense)
                End With
                Update = "OK"

                Exit Function

        UpdateError:
            ' Return the error description
            Update = Err.Description
            Err.Clear
            Exit Function
        End Function

        Public Function Delete() As String
        ' Deletes the expense detail record whose value is current
        ' from the database

                On Error GoTo DeleteError

                With mrecExpense
                    .Delete
                    If 0 = .RecordCount Then
                        Call ClearObject
                    Else
                        .MoveNext
                        If .EOF Then
                            Call ClearObject
                        Else
                            Call GetRecordset(mrecExpense)
                        End If
                    End If
                End With

                Delete = "OK"

                Exit Function

        DeleteError:
            ' Return the error description
            Delete = Err.Description
            Err.Clear
            Exit Function

        End Function
```

24. Create the **Move** methods to mimic the data control's movement methods. Note that these four procedures are nearly identical.

```
        Public Function MoveFirst() As String
        ' Retrieve the first record

                On Error GoTo MoveError
                With mrecExpense
```

continued on next page

continued from previous page

```
                    If True = .BOF _
            And True = .EOF Then
                ' Empty recordset
                MoveFirst = "BOF"
            Else
                ' Move to the first record
                .MoveFirst
                Call GetRecordset(mrecExpense)
                MoveFirst = "OK"
            End If
        End With

        Exit Function

MoveError:
        ' Return the error description
        MoveFirst = Err.Description
        Err.Clear
        Exit Function
End Function

Public Function MoveNext() As String
' Moves to next Expenses table record and sets current
' object values

        On Error GoTo MoveError

        With mrecExpense
            If True = .BOF _
            And True = .EOF Then
                ' Empty recordset
                MoveNext = "EOF"
            Else
                ' Move to the next record
                .MoveNext
                If mrecExpense.EOF Then
                    MoveNext = "EOF"
                Else
                    Call GetRecordset(mrecExpense)
                    MoveNext = "OK"
                End If
            End If
        End With

        Exit Function

MoveError:
        ' Return the error description
        MoveNext = Err.Description
        Err.Clear
        Exit Function
End Function

Public Function MovePrev() As String
' Retrieve the record prior to the current one
```

```
    On Error GoTo MoveError

    With mrecExpense

        If True = .BOF _
        And True = .EOF Then
            ' Empty recordset
            MovePrev = "BOF"
        Else
            ' Move to the previous record
            .MovePrevious
            If .BOF Then
                MovePrev = "BOF"
            Else
                Call GetRecordset(mrecExpense)
                MovePrev = "OK"
            End If
        End If


    End With

    Exit Function

MoveError:
    ' Return the error description
    MovePrev = Err.Description
    Err.Clear
    Exit Function
End Function

Public Function MoveLast() As String
' Retrieve the last record

    On Error GoTo MoveError

    With mrecExpense
        If True = .BOF _
        And True = .EOF Then
            ' Empty recordset
            MoveLast = "EOF"
        Else
            ' Move to the last record
            .MoveLast
            Call GetRecordset(mrecExpense)
            MoveLast = "OK"
        End If
    End With

    Exit Function

MoveError:
    ' Return the error description
    MoveLast = Err.Description
    Err.Clear
    Exit Function
End Function
```

How It Works

On `Form_Load` (step 10), the client application sets the database name for the class, causing the database and recordset to open in the class module. The `MoveFirst` method positions the class's recordset at the first record and populates the object's properties. The `ReadObjectValues` procedure copies the object values to the display fields. Each command button on the form invokes a method very similar to a data control method without the data control's performance overhead or frequently annoying events.

Comments

The use of a private class to manage your objects or tables is the starting of the *n-tier* architecture for your applications. In n-tier architectures, presentation (or input/output) is managed by one set of components, business rules by a second tier (class modules), and data by another tier (rules and triggers contained in the database management system). The advantage of objects in this environment is that underlying technology can be changed without affecting the callers as long as the interfaces remain stable.

Finally, you can easily convert class modules to ActiveX DLLs or ActiveX EXEs by including them in a different project and recompiling. You can test and debug a new class as a private module and then convert it to an EXE or a DLL. How-To 12.2 converts the `ExpenseDetail` class to an ActiveX DLL.

COMPLEXITY
BEGINNING

12.3 How do I...
Publish my ActiveX private class so that others can use it?

Problem

The staff in the accounting department loves the new `ExpenseDetail` class and the concept of "black box" interfaces, but they are very worried that employees using the private class in source-code form might compromise the class's security by modifying the code to inflate their own expense reimbursements. How can I prevent access to my class's source code while letting other projects take advantage of the `ExpenseDetail` class?

Technique

There are several ways to publish your class's properties and methods without revealing the source code. After all, major software publishers do it every day. The technique is to convert the class module into an ActiveX DLL or EXE. This

How-To demonstrates using the `ExpenseDetail` class module in an ActiveX DLL.

Steps

To preview the `ExpenseDetail` DLL on your system, you first need to register the code component in your system registry. Visual Basic will register the component for you automatically if you compile once. Open the ActiveXDll.VBP project. Select File | Make ActiveX.DLL to compile the component. Open the ActiveXExpense.vbp project and run it. You should see the form shown in Figure 12.6, which is the same form shown earlier in Figure 12.4 because the form file is identical; only the project composition was changed for the main application program.

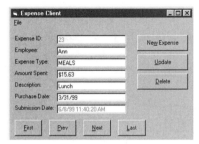

Figure 12.6. The Expense Client form, now using an ActiveX DLL.

1. Create a new project in Visual Basic and specify an ActiveX DLL project when prompted. In the project window, right-click the highest-level project item, and edit the project properties as shown in Figure 12.7. The **Project Name** field is used within Visual Basic and must contain no spaces or hyphens. The project description is stored in your system registry and provides the reference to your code component.

2. Select Project | Add File and add ExpenseDetail.cls to your project. This file is identical to the ExpenseDetail.cls file you wrote in How-To 12.2.

3. Select ExpenseDetail.cls in the project window. Ensure that the **Instancing** property is set to **5-Multi-use**. A *Public, Multiuse* class can be created by an external reference, such as the Expense Client form, and can be used by multiple programs simultaneously.

4. Select File | Make ActiveX.DLL to compile your ActiveX DLL.

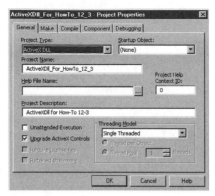

Figure 12.7. Setting the ActiveX
DLL project properties.

5. Open the ActiveXExpense.vbp project. Select Project | References to
display the form shown in Figure 12.8. Be sure to check the reference for
the ActiveX DLL you just created.

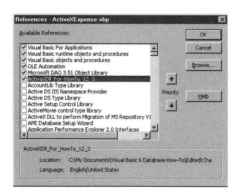

Figure 12.8. Adding a reference to
the ActiveX DLL.

6. Run the Expense Client project to observe the same behavior you saw in
How-To 12.2.

How It Works

The Expense Client with an ActiveX DLL class works the same way as the bound
class because the programs are identical. The power of the component object
model is letting the various pieces work together without the Expense Client
form needing to know how the class code works. It needs only the names and

calling parameters for the public methods and properties exposed by the ActiveX DLL. The exposed interfaces to the ActiveX DLL are made available on your computer when you compile the ActiveX DLL by virtue of Visual Basic 6 automatically registering the DLL in your system registry.

Comments

As you work more with building your own code components, plan to develop a test-and-debug strategy. In How-To 12.2, we developed (and probably tested and debugged) a test client form and a class module linked directly into the project. This approach to class modules simplifies development by allowing you to use the Visual Basic debugger. After the ActiveX DLL is compiled, you can use only the Visual C++ debugger.

Be aware that the use of ActiveX components on your system can eventually lead to excessive Registry entries, especially if you periodically delete and move your development DLL files. How-To 12.9 discusses two Registry utilities from Microsoft that can help keep your Registry under control.

COMPLEXITY
BEGINNING

12.4 How do I...
Provide controlled access to an encrypted, password-protected database using an ActiveX EXE server?

Problem

I have a highly sensitive, protected database for which I must strictly control access—hiding even the details of its format, source, and location, and giving controlled access to sections of the data. How can I create a Visual Basic object that can be used in other applications while protecting the database?

Technique

By creating an ActiveX EXE with a public class object, you can control everything about the database—hiding the details about the database itself, and giving the container application (the application creating and using the object) only limited access to the contents of any or all tables. Because the class methods that access the data are defined by your class module, you can limit access to only one or a few tables, only certain records or a limited number of records, or whatever constraints you choose to place on the database. As far as the container application is concerned, the data could be coming from a network, another program, or anywhere else.

Steps

Open the Visual Basic SECURED.VBP project. Start the application by selecting Run | Start from the Visual Basic main menu, pressing F5, or clicking the Start button on the Visual Basic toolbar. Minimize that instance of Visual Basic. Start Microsoft Excel from the Windows Program Manager and open the SECURED. XLS workbook. Run the Main macro application by selecting Tools | Macro | Macros, selecting the Main macro, and clicking Run. Main creates a spreadsheet with the contents of the database table and then releases the database object. Exit Excel and stop the Visual Basic SECURED application.

1. Start Visual Basic and create a new project in your work area. Select ActiveX EXE as the project type from the new project window, as shown in Figure 12.9. Save the project as SECURED.VBP.

Figure 12.9. The New Project window.

2. This How-To uses Visual Basic's data access objects, so they must be available to the project. Select Project | References from the Visual Basic main menu, and make sure that the Microsoft DAO 3.51 Object Library is checked.

3. Copy the ExpenseDetail.cls file from How-To 12.3 to your work area and rename it ExeExpenseDetail.cls. Remove the default Class1.cls file. Add the ExeExpenseDetail.cls file to your project. Set the properties of the class as shown in Table 12.9.

Table 12.9. Objects and properties for class module ExeExpenseDetail.cls.

PROPERTY	SETTING
Instancing	3—Single Use
Name	ExeExpenseDetail

4. Enter the following code in the **Initialize** event procedure for the class. The **Initialize** event is the rough equivalent to a form's **Load** event procedure, doing all the work needed when a new instance of a class is created by the calling application. In this case, all that is done is to set the location of the hidden database. This code assumes that Chapter12.MDB is in the application path; set this location to whatever drive, path, and file you want to use.

```
Private Sub Class_Initialize()

    On Error GoTo OpenError

    ' Put all the required security code here where it is
    ' protected by compilation.
    mvarstrDbName = App.Path & "\Expense.mdb"
    Set mdbExpense = DBEngine.Workspaces(0). _
        OpenDatabase(mvarstrDbName)
    Set mrecExpense = mdbExpense.OpenRecordset("Expenses")
    mblnRecSetOpen = True

    Exit Sub

OpenError:
        ' Because we are designing this class for
        ' potential unattended operation, we'll have to raise
        ' an error on our own
        Err.Raise Number:=Err.Number
        Err.Clear
        Exit Sub

End Sub
```

5. Enter the following code in the **Class Terminate** procedure. We suppress errors because we're trying to shut down anyway.

```
Private Sub Class_Terminate()

        ' We don't really care about errors when cleaning up.
        On Error Resume Next
        ' Close the recordset
        mrecExpense.Close
        ' Close the expense database
        mdbExpense.Close
        ' Reset the error handler
        On Error GoTo 0
        Exit Sub

End Sub
```

6. Enter the following code in the `FieldCount` and `GetField` procedures. These procedures define the public methods of the class.

```
Public Function FieldCount() As Integer
    FieldCount = 7
End Function

Public Function GetField(intColumn As Integer) As Variant
' Return the requested field
    Select Case intColumn
        Case 0
            GetField = mvarlngExpenseId
        Case 1
            GetField = mvarstrEmployeeId
        Case 2
            GetField = mvarstrExpenseType
        Case 3
            GetField = mvarcurAmountSpent
        Case 4
            GetField = mvarstrDescription
        Case 5
            GetField = mvardtmDatePurchased
        Case 6
            GetField = mvardtmDateSubmitted

    End Select

End Function

Public Property Get BOF() As Boolean
    BOF = rs.BOF
End Property

Public Property Get EOF() As Boolean
    EOF = rs.EOF
End Property

Property Get FieldCount() As Long
    FieldCount = rs.Fields.Count
End Property

Property Get RecordCount() As Long
    Dim bm As String

    'Save our location in the recordset
    bm = rs.Bookmark
    rs.MoveLast
    RecordCount = rs.RecordCount

    'Return to the starting position in the recordset
    rs.Bookmark = bm
End Property
```

7. Change all the `Public Property` procedures to `Private Property` procedures to prevent inadvertent access to the class properties. Change the `Public` functions for insert, update, and delete to `Private` functions. Remove the `Property Let` procedure for `strDbName`.

8. Insert a new code module into the project by selecting Insert | Module from the Visual Basic main menu. Set the name of the module to `modSecuredAccess`, and save the file as SECURED.BAS.

9. Enter the following code in the `Sub Main` procedure. No specific initialization code is required here, but there needs to be at least one empty `Sub Main` to provide an entry point for OLE when another application uses this class.

```
Sub Main()
End Sub
```

10. Set the project options to make the application act as an ActiveX EXE component. Select Project | Properties from the menu. The project properties are shown in Table 12.10.

The `Project Name` is particularly important; this is the application name used in the Windows Registry entry for the application. The object created by this application will then be referred to as

`VBHTOpenSecuredDB.SecuredDatabase`

in programs that use the object.

Table 12.10. Project properties for SECURED.VBP.

PROPERTY	SETTING
Startup Object	Sub Main
Project Name	VBHTOpenSecuredDB
Project Description	Open Secured and Encrypted Chapter14.MDB

11. Because the operating system needs an executable file to extract information about the class, select File | Make EXE from the Visual Basic main menu. Name the program SECURED.EXE and compile the application. Correct any errors that the compiler flags.

12. Execute the application by selecting Run | Start from the main menu, pressing F5, or clicking the Start button on the Visual Basic toolbar. The program loads and then waits for another application to create an object. This approach allows us to debug the standalone EXE file from the Visual Basic environment while a different application invokes our program's services.

13. Start Microsoft Excel. Create a new workbook by selecting File | New from the main menu or by clicking the New Workbook icon on the toolbar. Save the file by selecting File | Save As from the main menu or by clicking the Save icon on the toolbar. Save the file as SECURED.XLS.

14. Insert a new macro module in the workbook by selecting Tools | Macro | Visual Basic Editor from the Excel main menu. Once in the Visual Basic Editor, select Insert | Module to create a new VBA module. Insert the following Visual Basic code into the module. This procedure starts by creating an instance of the `SecuredDatabase` object and then uses the object's properties and methods to move through the database and enter the records into a new worksheet. Note that the Excel application is unaware of where the information is coming from or even how the database is being accessed. All those details are hidden in the SECURED.EXE file.

```
Option Explicit

Sub main()
    Dim numFields As Long
    Dim strResponse As String

    Dim objExpenseDetail As Object
    Set objExpenseDetail = _
        CreateObject("VBHTOpenSecuredDB.ExeExpenseDetail")

    Dim i As Long
    Dim j As Integer

    numFields = objExpenseDetail.FieldCount
    Sheets.Add

    'Format the column headings
    ActiveSheet.Cells(1, 1).Select
    Selection.ColumnWidth = 5
    ActiveCell.FormulaR1C1 = "ID"
    Selection.Font.FontStyle = "Bold"
    Selection.HorizontalAlignment = xlCenter

    ActiveSheet.Cells(1, 2).Select
    Selection.ColumnWidth = 10
    ActiveCell.FormulaR1C1 = "Employee"
    Selection.Font.FontStyle = "Bold"
    Selection.HorizontalAlignment = xlCenter

    ActiveSheet.Cells(1, 3).Select
    Selection.ColumnWidth = 8
    ActiveCell.FormulaR1C1 = "Type"
    Selection.Font.FontStyle = "Bold"
    Selection.HorizontalAlignment = xlCenter

    ActiveSheet.Cells(1, 4).Select
    Selection.ColumnWidth = 10
    ActiveCell.FormulaR1C1 = "Amount"
    Selection.Font.FontStyle = "Bold"
    Selection.HorizontalAlignment = xlCenter

    ActiveSheet.Cells(1, 5).Select
    Selection.ColumnWidth = 15
```

```
    ActiveCell.FormulaR1C1 = "Description"
    Selection.Font.FontStyle = "Bold"
    Selection.HorizontalAlignment = xlCenter

    ActiveSheet.Cells(1, 6).Select
    Selection.ColumnWidth = 10
    ActiveCell.FormulaR1C1 = "Purchased"
    Selection.Font.FontStyle = "Bold"
    Selection.HorizontalAlignment = xlCenter

    ActiveSheet.Cells(1, 7).Select
    Selection.ColumnWidth = 15
    ActiveCell.FormulaR1C1 = "Submitted"
    Selection.Font.FontStyle = "Bold"
    Selection.HorizontalAlignment = xlCenter


    'Put the records into the worksheet
    i = 0
    strResponse = objExpenseDetail.MoveFirst
    Do While "OK" = strResponse
        i = i + 1
        For j = 0 To numFields - 1
            ActiveSheet.Cells(i + 1, j + 1).Select
            ActiveCell.FormulaR1C1 = objExpenseDetail.GetField(j)
        Next
        strResponse = objExpenseDetail.MoveNext
    Loop

    ActiveSheet.Cells(1, 1).Select

    'Clean up by releasing the memory used for objExpenseDetail
    Set objExpenseDetail = Nothing
End Sub
```

15. Run the Main Excel procedure by selecting Tools|Macro|Macros from the main menu, selecting the Main macro from the list, and clicking the Run button, or by clicking the Run Sub/UserForm button from the Macro toolbar while the cursor is within the Main procedure.

How It Works

Visual Basic uses class modules to create objects that can be exposed to other applications. This is essentially the same process used by the Jet engine to expose data access objects or by Microsoft Excel to expose Worksheet or Chart objects.

This How-To has focused on the details of the ActiveX interface between Visual Basic and Excel. Note the comments in the code where you might include parameters for opening secured databases. That information is completely hidden from Excel. For more information about using secured databases, see Chapter 10, "Security and Multiuser Access."

By defining `Property Get`, `Property Let`, and `Public Sub` and `Function` procedures, you can precisely define the information that the class reveals to the outside world and the actions that it takes in response to demands placed on it by outside applications.

The most important part of setting up the class so that it is visible to outside applications is setting the project's properties. The fact that this is a separate EXE code component makes debugging somewhat tricky. The easiest way to debug an ActiveX EXE under development is to start by doing most of the work with the class module bound into an application EXE. After the class module has been debugged, add it into an Active EXE project. You can still debug the class within an ActiveX EXE by running a copy of Visual Basic dedicated to the class.

Comments

This class was defined to be what is called *single-use* in ActiveX terminology in order to ensure that different callers would not affect other callers' data stored within the class. In this ActiveX EXE, the database name, recordset position, and property values contain state, or context, information that is related to the calling program. For example, the correct invocation of the `MoveNext` method assumes that the class properties are correctly set for the caller. If we allowed two different programs to access the ActiveX EXE, Caller A's `MoveNext` would cause Caller B's `MovePrev` to return an erroneous result. A multiuse ActiveX EXE class requires that all the information necessary for a successful method invocation is contained in the method's parameters and return values. If more than one invocation is required to retrieve the required data, the class should be defined to be single-use.

COMPLEXITY
BEGINNING

12.5 How do I...
Use Microsoft Access as an ActiveX server to print reports from Visual Basic?

Problem

The database provided for my Visual Basic project has already been developed, and the prototyping phase developed several Access reports that we want to use again in the final application. Because all workstations will have Access installed, we want to use this technique. How do I invoke an Access report from within a Visual Basic 6 application?

Technique

Microsoft Access is an ActiveX EXE code component. It exposes its Visual Basic for Applications properties and methods just as any other ActiveX EXE does. The most powerful command for use in automating Access as a code component is the `DoCmd` method of the Access Application object. `DoCmd` allows your program to issue most commands within Access that a person sitting at the keyboard can do with a mouse and keyboard.

Steps

Open the project AccessReport.vbp. The form shown in Figure 12.10 appears. Click the command button. Switch to the Access application to view and print the prepared report (see Figure 12.11).

Figure 12.10. The Invoke Access Report form.

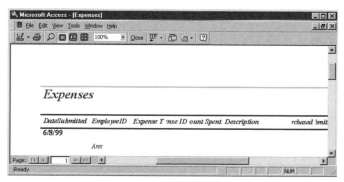

Figure 12.11. The Access Expense report.

1. Create a new project named AccessReport.vbp in your work area. Create the objects and properties listed in Table 12.11.

Table 12.11. Objects and properties for the Access Expense form.

OBJECT	PROPERTY	SETTING
Name	Form	frmInvokeAccessReport
	Caption	"Invoke Access Report"
Name	CommandButton	cmdInvokeReport
	Caption	"&Invoke Access Report"

2. Be sure to select OLE Automation and the Microsoft Access Object Library in the Project References menu. OLE Automation supports the program's capability to create and communicate with Access. The Microsoft Access 8.0 Object Library enables you to use symbolic constant names for Access-defined constants.

3. Insert the following code for the `Click` event of `cmdInvokeReport`:

```
Private Sub cmdInvokeReport_Click()
' Invokes an Access report in Print Preview mode
' Get the ActiveX object to open its database and position
' to the first record
    Dim strDbName As String
    Dim objAccess As Object

    On Error GoTo LoadError

    strDbName = App.Path
    strDbName = strDbName & "\Expense.mdb"
    Set objAccess = CreateObject("Access.Application")
    With objAccess
        .OpenCurrentDatabase FilePath:=strDbName
        .DoCmd.OpenReport ReportName:="ExpenseReport", _
            View:=Access.acPreview
End With

    ' Give up CPU control
    DoEvents

    Set objAccess = Nothing

    Exit Sub

LoadError:
    MsgBox Err.Description & Chr(13) & "from " & Err.Source & _
        " -- Number: " & CStr(Err.Number)
Unload Me

End Sub
```

How It Works

When you click the command button, the Visual Basic `CreateObject` method starts Access. The reference to `"Access.Application"` is resolved by the

Windows operating system through the system registry. The two commands given to the Access application object open the database and prepare the report in Print Preview mode. The report can then be printed within Access.

Inspection of this code shows that using another application to do your bidding is straightforward; the difficult part is discovering which methods and properties are exposed by the object. For Access and the other Microsoft Office applications, the easiest way to discover the available properties and methods is to use that application's Help files. Use the Help contents to find a reference to Visual Basic, switch to the linked Help file, and then search the Help index for the application object. The various methods and properties of the application object should lead you to the commands you need in order to get your job done.

Comments

Although requiring a person to print the report to the printer might seem like an extra step, it takes advantage of the print preview capabilities of Access and provides quite a bit of program polish with very little development work. Before deploying an automated application such as this one, you probably want to enforce some degree of security on the database as discussed in Chapter 10, "Security and Multiuser Access."

COMPLEXITY
INTERMEDIATE

12.6 How do I...
Use Microsoft Access queries containing user-defined functions from Visual Basic?

Problem

Sometimes you will need to use Access user-defined functions within your Visual Basic programs. Unfortunately, Access user-defined functions can be run only by Access. How can I use Access to return data from a query containing a user-defined function?

Technique

To use an Access query containing a user-defined function, you first need an Access-based recordset. Because Access exposes its object methods and properties, we can directly manipulate Access recordsets from Visual Basic by using the Visual Basic for Applications methods exposed by Access. The VBA syntax for working with recordsets is identical to Visual Basic 6 syntax, so no learning curve is required. It is important to remember, however, that the Access recordset is running in a different process, and the performance is likely to be much slower than a native recordset. Both Visual Basic and Access recordsets can be included in the same application. In this way, the slower ActiveX Automation recordset is used only when required for the user-defined function query.

This application uses two Access queries to provide required data. The first provides a list of employees who have submitted expense reports:

```
SELECT DISTINCT EmployeeID
FROM Expenses;
```

The second query is parameter-driven and invokes the user-defined function MyUpper to force the employee name to all uppercase letters:

```
PARAMETERS EmpToFind Text;
SELECT Expenses.ExpenseID, MyUpper([EmployeeID]) AS Expr1,
    Expenses.ExpenseType, Expenses.AmountSpent, Expenses.Description,
    Expenses.DatePurchased, Expenses.DateSubmitted
FROM Expenses
WHERE (((MyUpper([EmployeeID]))=[EmpToFind]))
ORDER BY Expenses.ExpenseID;
```

The EmpToFind parameter limits the query records to only one employee.

Steps

Open the AccessParams.vbp project. If necessary, modify the database location for the database grid's data control to point to your installation directory. Run the application by pressing F5. Then Select an employee and click the Set Employee button to limit the view of expense details to only one employee, as shown in Figure 12.12. Use the data movement buttons to view the selected employee's expenses.

Figure 12.12. The Access User-Defined Function form.

1. Create a new project named AccessParams.vbp in your work area. Copy the ExpenseDetail.cls file from How-To 12.2 to this new project as ExpDetailParam.cls.

2. Select Project | References from the main Visual Basic menu, and select the references shown here:

Ole Automation

Microsoft DAO 3.51 Object Library

Microsoft Access 8.0 Object Library

3. Select Project | Components from the main Visual Basic menu, and select the following components:

Microsoft Masked Edit Control 6.0

Microsoft FlexGrid Control 6.0

4. Modify the declarations section of ExpDetailParam.cls as follows. The new object variables allow direct control of the Access recordset. Declaring **mobjAccess** as an Access.Application object enables Visual Basic's code-completion features in the editor for lazy typists.

```
Option Explicit

'local variable(s) to hold property value(s)
Private mvarlngExpenseId As Long 'local copy
Private mvarstrEmployeeId As String 'local copy
Private mvarstrExpenseType As String 'local copy
Private mvarcurAmountSpent As Currency 'local copy
Private mvarstrDescription As String 'local copy
Private mvardtmDatePurchased As Date 'local copy
Private mvardtmDateSubmitted As Date 'local copy
Private mvarstrDbName As String 'local copy
Private mvarstrEmpToQuery As String 'local copy

Private mblnQueryOpen As Boolean

Private mobjAccess As New Access.Application
Private mobjRecSetExpense As Object
```

5. Modify the **strDbName Property Let** procedure to open the Access query rather than a Visual Basic recordset:

```
Public Property Let strDbName(ByVal vData As String)
'used when assigning a value to the property, on the left
'side of an assignment.
'Syntax: X.strDbName = 5

    On Error GoTo OpenError

    If mblnQueryOpen Then
        mobjAccess.CloseCurrentDatabase
    End If
    mvarstrDbName = vData
    mobjAccess.OpenCurrentDatabase mvarstrDbName
    mobjAccess.Application.Visible = False
```

continued on next page

continued from previous page

```
        mobjAccess.DBEngine.Workspaces(0).Databases(0). _
                QueryDefs("ExpForOneEmployee"). _
                                Parameters("EmpToFind"). _
                Value = mvarstrEmpToQuery
        Set mobjRecSetExpense = mobjAccess.DBEngine.Workspaces(0). _
                Databases(0).QueryDefs("ExpForOneEmployee"). _
                OpenRecordset()

    mblnQueryOpen = True

    Exit Property


OpenError:
    ' Because we are designing this class for
    ' potential unattended operation, we'll have to raise
    ' an error on our own
    Err.Raise Number:=Err.Number
    Err.Clear
    Exit Property

End Property
```

6. Add a new **Property Let** procedure for the name of the employee to query. This procedure closes an open recordset, changes the employee name, and issues a new query.

```
Public Property Let strEmpToQuery(ByVal vData As String)
'used when assigning a value to the property, on the left
'side of an assignment.
'Syntax: X.strEmpToQuery = 5
    mvarstrEmpToQuery = vData
    On Error GoTo OpenError

    If mblnQueryOpen Then
        mobjRecSetExpense.Close
    End If
    mobjAccess.DBEngine.Workspaces(0).Databases(0). _
            QueryDefs("ExpForOneEmployee"). _
                            Parameters("EmpToFind"). _
            Value = mvarstrEmpToQuery
    Set mobjRecSetExpense = mobjAccess.DBEngine.Workspaces(0). _
            Databases(0).QueryDefs("ExpForOneEmployee"). _
            OpenRecordset()
    mblnQueryOpen = True

    Exit Property


OpenError:
    ' Because we are designing this class for
    ' potential unattended operation, we'll have to raise
    ' an error on our own
    Err.Raise Number:=Err.Number
    Err.Clear
    Exit Property

End Property
```

7. Remove the `Delete`, `Update`, and `Insert` methods from the class. Remove the `SetRecordSet` subroutine from the class.

8. Change all code references from `mrecExpense` to `mobjRecSetExpense` throughout the class module.

9. Add the new class property to the `ClearObject` procedure:

```
Private Sub ClearObject()
' Clears all object variables

    mvarlngExpenseId = 0
    mvarstrEmployeeId = ""
    mvarstrExpenseType = ""
    mvarcurAmountSpent = 0
    mvarstrDescription = ""
    mvardtmDatePurchased = CDate("1/1/1980")
    mvardtmDateSubmitted = CDate("1/1/1980")
    mvarstrEmpToQuery = ""

End Sub
```

10. Replace the `Class Initialize` and `Terminate` procedures. We force termination of the Access code component in the `Terminate` procedure.

```
Private Sub Class_Initialize()

    ' Indicate that the database is not yet open
    mblnQueryOpen = False
    ' Clear all object variables
    Call ClearObject

End Sub

Private Sub Class_Terminate()

    ' Close the recordset
    mobjRecSetExpense.Close
    mobjAccess.CloseCurrentDatabase
    mobjAccess.Quit

End Sub
```

11. Create a form to test the `ExpDetailParam` class with the objects properties shown in Table 12.12. Show only the `Employee ID` column for the database grid. Inspection of the Access database used in this project will show that the `ExpEmployeeNames` is an Access query, not a table. Visual Basic can use queries for recordsets and will display queries in the data control's `RecordSource` pull-down list.

Table 12.12. Objects and properties for the Access Params form.

OBJECT	PROPERTY	SETTING
Form	Name	frmExpClient
	Caption	"Expense Client"
Data	Name	datExpEmployees
	Caption	"Exp Employees"
	DatabaseName	"C:\Code\Chapter12\HowTo06\Expense.mdb"
	RecordsetType	2 'Snapshot
	RecordSource	"ExpEmployeeNames"
MSFlexGrid	Name	dbgExpEmployee
	DataSource	datExpEmployees
CommandButton	Name	cmdSetEmployee
	Caption	"&Set Employee"
CommandButton	Name	cmdLast
	Caption	"&Last"
CommandButton	Name	cmdNext
	Caption	"&Next"
CommandButton	Name	cmdPrev
	Caption	"&Prev"
CommandButton	Name	cmdFirst
	Caption	"&First"
MaskEdBox	Name	mskAmountSpent
	Format	"$#,##0.00;($#,##0.00)"
	PromptChar	"_"
TextBox	Name	txtSubmitDate
TextBox	Name	txtPurchaseDate
TextBox	Name	txtDescription
TextBox	Name	txtExpenseType
TextBox	Name	txtEmployeeId
TextBox	Name	txtExpenseId
Label	Name	Label1
	Caption	"Expense ID:"
Label	Name	Label2
	Caption	"Employee:"
Label	Name	Label3
	Caption	"Expense Type:"
Label	Name	Label4
	Caption	"Amount Spent:"

OBJECT	PROPERTY	SETTING
Label	Name	Label5
	Caption	"Description:"
Label	Name	Label6
	Caption	"Purchase Date:"
Label	Name	Label7
	Caption	"Submission Date:"

12. Use the Visual Basic menu editor to create the menu shown in Table 12.13.

Table 12.13. Menu specifications for the Access Params form.

CAPTION	NAME	SHORTCUT KEY
&File	mnuFile	
----E&xit	mnuFileExit	

13. Add the following code to the `Click` event of `cmdSetEmployee`. This procedure obtains the employee name from the selected database grid row, sets the class module's `strEmpToQuery` value, and moves to the first expense for the selected employee.

```
Private Sub cmdSetEmployee_Click()
' Sets Employee ID textbox and initiates new query for
' expenses for the selected employee
    Dim strResponse As String

    On Error GoTo QueryError

    txtEmployeeId.Text = dbgExpEmployee.Text
    expDetailParam.strEmpToQuery = dbgExpEmployee.Text
    strResponse = expDetailParam.MoveFirst
    If "OK" <> strResponse Then
        MsgBox strResponse
    Else
        Call ReadObjectValues
    End If

    Exit Sub

QueryError:
    MsgBox Err.Description & Chr(13) & "from " & Err.Source & _
        " -- Number: " & CStr(Err.Number)
    Exit Sub

End Sub
```

14. Add the following code to the `Click` event for the movement buttons:

```
Private Sub cmdFirst_Click()
' Positions to first record in recordset and displays values

    Dim strResponse As String

    strResponse = expDetailParam.MoveFirst
    If "OK" <> strResponse Then
        MsgBox strResponse
    Else
        Call ReadObjectValues
    End If

End Sub

Private Sub cmdLast_Click()
' Positions to last record in recordset and displays values

    Dim strResponse As String

    strResponse = expDetailParam.MoveLast
    If "OK" <> strResponse Then
        MsgBox strResponse
    Else
        Call ReadObjectValues
    End If

End Sub

Private Sub cmdNext_Click()
' Positions to Next record in recordset and displays values

    Dim strResponse As String

    strResponse = expDetailParam.MoveNext
    If "OK" <> strResponse Then
        MsgBox strResponse
    Else
        Call ReadObjectValues
    End If


End Sub

Private Sub cmdPrev_Click()
' Positions to Previous record in recordset and displays
' values

    Dim strResponse As String

    strResponse = expDetailParam.MovePrev
    If "OK" <> strResponse Then
        MsgBox strResponse
    Else
        Call ReadObjectValues
```

```
        End If

    End Sub
```

15. Define a `ReadObjectValues` procedure to transfer data from the class properties:

```
Private Sub ReadObjectValues()
' Read the object values into the form fields

    txtExpenseId.Text = CStr(expDetailParam.lngExpenseId)
    txtEmployeeId.Text = expDetailParam.strEmployeeId
    txtExpenseType.Text = expDetailParam.strExpenseType
    txtDescription.Text = expDetailParam.strDescription
    mskAmountSpent.Text = CStr(expDetailParam.curAmountSpent)
    txtPurchaseDate.Text = CStr(expDetailParam.dtmDatePurchased)
    txtSubmitDate.Text = CStr(expDetailParam.dtmDateSubmitted)

End Sub
```

16. Create `Form Load` and `Unload` procedures to initialize and tear down the application:

```
Private Sub Form_Load()
' Get the ActiveX object to open its database and position
' to the first record
    Dim strDbName As String
    Dim strResponse As String

    On Error GoTo LoadError

    strDbName = App.Path
    strDbName = strDbName & "\Expense.mdb"
    expDetailParam.strDbName = strDbName
    strResponse = expDetailParam.MoveFirst
    If "OK" <> strResponse Then
        MsgBox strResponse
    Else
        Call ReadObjectValues
    End If

    Exit Sub
LoadError:
    MsgBox Err.Description & Chr(13) & "from " & _
        Err.Source & " -- Number: " & CStr(Err.Number)
    Unload Me
End Sub

Private Sub Form_Unload(Cancel As Integer)

    Set expDetailParam = Nothing

End Sub
```

17. Add the following code to the `Click` event of `mnuFileExit`:

```
Private Sub mnuFileExit_Click()

    Unload Me

End Sub
```

How It Works

When the form loads, the application sets the database name of the class using the `Property Let strDBName` procedure (step 5). This first reference to an `Access.Application` object causes a new Access process to start for our work on behalf of the class. The Access application is made invisible to minimize confusion on the application screen. The query parameter is set to retrieve an employee, and the recordset is created within the class. The class's navigation methods are, in turn, connected to the navigation buttons on the form.

When the `cmdSetEmployee` button is clicked, the class's employee name property is set from the current record on the grid. The class is notified of the employee name change through the `strEmpToQuery Property Let` procedure. The query parameter is changed, and the recordset is reopened to display expenses for a different employee.

This How-To illustrates a generic programming technique frequently used to logically "partition" data displays on forms. For example, you might want to display payment histories for multiple customers in a service bureau application. The use of a grid to display possible customer choices with a detail form for the payments is an example of a partitioning form.

Comments

More and more complex Visual Basic applications are being designed with n-tier architectures relying on different tiers to perform different functions. In this How-To, we are using a classic three-tier architecture consisting of the form, the class, and the Access queries. This approach helps make program code maintenance easier over the long term because interfaces are clear. The use of the Access `ExpEmployee` query to show only one row per employee uses the power inherent in the database engine to preprocess data before using precious bandwidth sending multiple rows and forcing the client to eliminate duplicates.

COMPLEXITY
INTERMEDIATE

12.7 How do I...
Convert database data to a spreadsheet form that can be used to edit and analyze data?

Problem

I have a table with numeric results on which I need to perform some statistical analyses to make the data meaningful. Visual Basic doesn't have an easy way to analyze complex data, nor does it have many statistical analysis functions. How can I do the analyses that I need using a spreadsheet so that I can massage the data?

Technique

Although Visual Basic is missing many of the standard statistical and financial functions that many business and scientific applications need, Microsoft Excel has a rich source of such functions. Using ActiveX Automation, it is relatively easy to create an Excel spreadsheet, populating it with the data from a database, and entering whatever Excel formulas are needed for analysis.

You will need Excel for this How-To, although this same technique can be used with most of the popular spreadsheet applications available for Windows. All that any such spreadsheet needs is support for OLE 2 or later, as well as some way of discovering the objects that the application makes visible to OLE Automation. Microsoft provides a program with many of its other products, including the OLE SDK and some of its programming languages, called OLE2VIEW, that examines an application and presents a list of the objects available and their properties and methods.

Steps

Open the Visual Basic DataAnal.VBP project. Start the application by selecting Run | Start from the Visual Basic main menu, by pressing F5, or by clicking the Start button on the Visual Basic toolbar. Click the Select Database button, and select any Access .MDB file. Select a table from the Table combo box, and then click Load Spreadsheet to select the numeric fields from the table and enter them into an Excel spreadsheet. When the spreadsheet is finished loading (see Figure 12.13), click the down arrow on the Results combo box to examine the average, median, and standard deviation for each field in the table. Double-click the spreadsheet to edit it or examine a cell's contents.

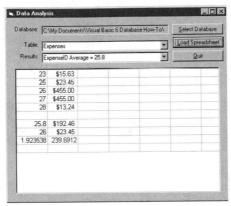

Figure 12.13. The Data Analysis result screen for the DataAnal.vbp project.

1. Start Visual Basic and create a new project. Save the default form as DATAANAL.FRM, and save the project as DATAANAL.VBP. This project uses the Microsoft Common Dialog control, so select Project | Components from the main Visual Basic menu and make sure that the control is selected in the list.

2. This How-To uses Visual Basic's data access objects, so they must be available to the project. Select Project | References from the Visual Basic main menu, and make sure that the Microsoft DAO 3.51 Object Library is checked, as shown in Figure 12.14.

3. Because this application uses the Microsoft Excel 5.0 Object Library, you need to make sure that Visual Basic has access to that library. Select Tools | References from the Visual Basic main menu, and make sure that the box in front of the Excel object library is checked. If it doesn't appear in the list, click the Browse button and add the file XL5EN32.OLB in the Excel program directory, probably C:\Program Files\Office. Normally, however, the Excel installation program activates the object library in the Windows Registry.

If you attempt to run this program without Excel installed, the `cmdLoadSS_Click` event procedure traps the error and shows a message box about the error.

4. Start Microsoft Excel and minimize the application. Having Excel running during development speeds programming because you don't have to wait for Excel to load every time you start the project.

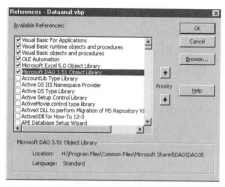

Figure 12.14. Setting object references for DataAnal.vbp.

5. Place controls on the form as shown in Figure 12.13, setting properties as shown in Table 12.14. Note that the Common Dialog control is invisible at runtime, so you can place it anywhere on the form that is convenient. Also note that the menu Raisan can be called anything you like; it is necessary only to allow the Excel menu to appear on the form when the OLE object is activated.

Table 12.14. Objects and properties for DATAANAL.FRM.

OBJECT	PROPERTY	SETTING
Form	Name	frmDataAnal
	Caption	"Data Analysis"
	NegotiateMenus	True
ComboBox	Name	lstResults
CommandButton	Name	cmdLoadSS
	Caption	"&Load Spreadsheet"
	Enabled	0 'False
ComboBox	Name	lstTables
CommandButton	Name	cmdQuit
	Caption	"&Quit"
	Default	-1 'True
CommandButton	Name	cmdSelectDB
	Caption	"&Select Database"
TextBox	Name	txtFileName
	BackColor	&H00C0C0C0& (Light gray)

continued on next page

continued from previous page

OBJECT	PROPERTY	SETTING
Label	Name	Label3
	Alignment	1 'Right Justify
	Caption	"Results:"
OLE	Name	oleExcel
	OLETypeAllowed	1 'Embedded
Label	Name	Label2
	Alignment	1 'Right Justify
	Caption	"Table:"
CommonDialog	Name	cdSelectFile
	DefaultExt	"MDB"
	DialogTitle	"Open Database File"
	Filter	"Access Db (*.mdb)¦*.mdb¦All Files
		(*.*)¦*.*"
Label	Name	Label1
	Alignment	1 'Right Justify
	Caption	"Database:"
Menu	Name	mnuRaisan
	Caption	"Raisan"
	Visible	0 'False

6. Enter the following code into the declarations section of the form. **dbSS** is used as a global database object, and the two constants control the actions of the OLE custom control.

```
'This project makes use of an Excel 5.0 worksheet,
'so the Excel 5.0 Object Library must be specified
'in the VB Tools Reference menu.

Dim dbSS As Database

Const OLE_CreateEmbed As Integer = 0
Const OLE_Activate As Integer = 7
```

7. Enter the following code in the **cmdSelectDB Click** event procedure. This procedure sets up and shows the file open common dialog box for a database to analyze. If a database is selected, it extracts the names of all the tables, and populates the lstTables combo box.

```
Private Sub cmdSelectDB_Click()
    'Select a new database file to analyze
    Dim strFileName As String
    Dim X As TableDef
    Dim saveCursor
```

```
            'Open the file open common dialog
            cdSelectFile.InitDir = App.Path
            cdSelectFile.ShowOpen
            If Len(cdSelectFile.filename) Then
                saveCursor = Me.MousePointer
                Me.MousePointer = vbHourglass

                txtFileName = cdSelectFile.filename

                'Open the database
                Set dbSS = OpenDatabase(txtFileName)

                'Load the lstTables combo box
                lstTables.Clear
                If dbSS.TableDefs.Count Then
                    For Each X In dbSS.TableDefs
                        'Exclude system tables
                        If Not X.Name Like "MSys*" Then
                            lstTables.AddItem X.Name
                        End If
                    Next
                    lstTables.ListIndex = 0
                End If
                Me.MousePointer = saveCursor
            Else
                MsgBox "No file selected."
            End If
        End Sub
```

8. Add this code to the **cmdLoadSS Click** event procedure. When the user clicks the Load Spreadsheet button, the selected table is examined for all the numeric fields, and the names of those fields are put in the **fieldTypes** array. At the end of the **For Each...Next** loop, the variable **i** will contain the number of numeric fields. If there are no numeric fields, the user is shown a message and the procedure exits. (For simplicity, the number of fields is limited to 26 so that you don't have to deal with double-lettered column names such as "AA," "AB," and "BB.") Then the table is opened, and the data from each record for each numeric field is placed in the spreadsheet. After that process is complete, formulas to calculate the average, median, and standard deviation are inserted at the bottom of each column. The columns are assigned unique names so that you can read the values and put them in the **lstResults** combo box.

```
Private Sub cmdLoadSS_Click()
    'If button is enabled, we can start
    Dim rsTable As Recordset
    Dim fld As Field
    Dim fieldTypes() As String
    Dim i As Integer, j As Integer
    Dim rowNo As Integer
    Dim cellRange As String
    Dim cellValue As Variant
```

continued on next page

continued from previous page

```
Dim cellPlace As String
Dim cellName As String
Dim totalRows As Integer
Dim nameExcel As String
Dim temp As String
Dim ssName As String
Dim saveCursor

saveCursor = Me.MousePointer
Me.MousePointer = vbHourglass

'Create an array of all numerical fields to include in
'the spreadsheet
i = 0
For Each fld In dbSS.TableDefs(lstTables.Text).Fields
    If fld.Type = dbInteger Or _
            fld.Type = dbLong Or _
            fld.Type = dbCurrency Or _
            fld.Type = dbSingle Or _
            fld.Type = dbDouble Then
        i = i + 1
        ReDim Preserve fieldTypes(i)
        fieldTypes(i) = fld.Name
    End If
Next

If i = 0 Then
    MsgBox "There are no numeric columns in the table. Exiting
            ➡procedure."
Me.MousePointer = saveCursor
    Exit Sub
End If

'For convenience, limit the number of columns to 26 so
'we don't have to do anything fancy to columns AA, AB,
'and so on
i = IIf(i > 26, 26, i)

'Open the recordset of the table
Set rsTable = dbSS.OpenRecordset(lstTables.Text)

On Error GoTo OLError
oleExcel.CreateEmbed "", "Excel.Sheet.8"
On Error GoTo 0
ssName = oleExcel.object.Name

Do While Not rsTable.EOF
    rowNo = rowNo + 1
    For j = 1 To i
        cellValue = rsTable(fieldTypes(j))
        oleExcel.object.Worksheets(1).Cells(rowNo, j).Value _
            = cellValue
    Next
    rsTable.MoveNext
Loop
```

```
'Insert the formulas to calculate the average, median, and
'standard deviation, and name the cells
totalRows = rowNo
rowNo = totalRows + 2
For j = 1 To i
    cellRange = ColName(j) & "1:" & ColName(j) _
        & Trim(Str(totalRows))
    cellValue = "=AVERAGE(" & cellRange & ")"
    cellPlace = "=Sheet1!$" & ColName(j) & "$" _
        & Trim(Str(rowNo)) _
                & ":$" & ColName(j) & "$" & Trim(Str(rowNo))
    oleExcel.object.Worksheets(1).Cells(rowNo, j).Value _
        = cellValue
    cellName = "average" & Trim(Str(j))
    oleExcel.object.Parent.Names.Add Name:=cellName, _
        RefersTo:=cellPlace
Next
rowNo = rowNo + 1
For j = 1 To i
    cellRange = ColName(j) & "1:" & ColName(j) _
        & Trim(Str(totalRows))
    cellValue = "=MEDIAN(" & cellRange & ")"
    cellPlace = "=Sheet1!$" & ColName(j) & "$" _
        & Trim(Str(rowNo)) _
                & ":$" & ColName(j) & "$" & Trim(Str(rowNo))
    oleExcel.object.Worksheets(1).Cells(rowNo, j).Value _
        = cellValue
    cellName = "median" & Trim(Str(j))
    oleExcel.object.Parent.Names.Add Name:=cellName, _
        RefersTo:=cellPlace
Next
rowNo = rowNo + 1
For j = 1 To i
    cellRange = ColName(j) & "1:" & ColName(j) _
        & Trim(Str(totalRows))
    cellValue = "=STDEV(" & cellRange & ")"
    cellPlace = "=Sheet1!$" & ColName(j) & "$" _
        & Trim(Str(rowNo)) _
                & ":$" & ColName(j) & "$" & Trim(Str(rowNo))
    oleExcel.object.Worksheets(1).Cells(rowNo, j).Value _
        = cellValue
    cellName = "stdev" & Trim(Str(j))
    oleExcel.object.Parent.Names.Add Name:=cellName, _
        RefersTo:=cellPlace
Next

'Lastly, put the results in the lstResults control
lstResults.Clear
For j = 1 To i
    nameExcel = "average" & Trim(Str(j))
    lstResults.AddItem fieldTypes(j) & " Average = " _
        & oleExcel.object.Worksheets(1).Range(nameExcel).Value
Next
For j = 1 To i
    nameExcel = "median" & Trim(Str(j))
```

continued on next page

continued from previous page

```
            lstResults.AddItem fieldTypes(j) & " Median = " _
                & oleExcel.object.Worksheets(1).Range(nameExcel).Value
        Next
        For j = 1 To i
            nameExcel = "stdev" & Trim(Str(j))
            lstResults.AddItem fieldTypes(j) _
                " & " Standard Deviation = " _
                & oleExcel.object.Worksheets(1).Range(nameExcel).Value
        Next
        lstResults.ListIndex = 0

        Me.MousePointer = saveCursor
        Exit Sub

OLError:
        MsgBox "An OLE error occurred, probably because Excel is not
            ➥installed on this computer."
        Unload Me
End Sub
```

9. Add the following code to the **ColName** procedure. This function provides an easy way to convert a column number to its equivalent letter value.

```
Private Function ColName(colNo As Integer)
    Dim alpha As String

    alpha = "ABCDEFGHIJKLMNOPQRSTUVWXYZ"
    ColName = Mid$(alpha, colNo, 1)
End Function
```

10. Add this code to the **lstTables Click** event procedure. When the form first loads, the **cmdLoadSS** command button is disabled because there is no database table selected from which to load data. After the user has selected a database and a table, it is possible to load the spreadsheet.

```
Private Sub lstTables_Click()
    If Len(lstTables.Text) Then
        cmdLoadSS.Enabled = True
    Else
        cmdLoadSS.Enabled = False
    End If
End Sub
```

11. Enter this code for the **cmdQuit Click** event procedure. The **Set** statement releases the **dbSS** database object, and then the program ends.

```
Private Sub cmdQuit_Click()
    Set dbSS = Nothing
    End
End Sub
```

How It Works

An ActiveX Automation object can be either linked or embedded in an OLE control. If all you want to do is see the object, linking is the way to go because the object isn't stored in the application. If you want to visually edit your Visual Basic application, however, you must embed the object. Then you can "activate" the object for editing by double-clicking it at runtime. Double-clicking is the default for activation, but the default can be changed by setting the `AutoActivate` property of the control.

The key to using the OLE control with visual editing is to make sure that it is properly configured for the object, in this case an Excel spreadsheet. For embedded objects, the control's `OLETypeAllowed` must be either `1` (`Embedded`) or `2` (`Either`). The object is then created using this line in `cmdLoadSS_Click()`:

```
oleExcel.CreateEmbed "", "Excel.Sheet.8"
```

If you want the embedded object's application menus to appear when you activate the object, you need to have a menu as part of the form. If your application doesn't otherwise need a menu, create a dummy menu as you did here, name it anything you like, and set the `Visible` property of the single menu item to `False`. That way, the object's menu will appear. If your application does use a menu, create it as you normally would, but set the `NegotiatePosition` property of each menu item to `None`, `Left`, `Middle`, or `Right`, to indicate to Visual Basic how you want to sort the various menu items between the two menus.

Comments

ActiveX Automation is a powerful tool for your programming arsenal, but it might not always be the appropriate tool given the power of the macro languages, such as Visual Basic for Applications, that are now embedded in many applications. For use by an analyst who uses Excel for much of the day, this task might have been better programmed in VBA from Excel. If the analyst later wants to change something, the VBA macro is right there in the spreadsheet. For use as part of an Executive Information System (EIS), where several spreadsheets and Access reports might be required for the complete solution, driving the spreadsheet from Visual Basic might make more sense. Keeping all the custom code for an EIS in one place can simplify application maintenance.

COMPLEXITY
INTERMEDIATE

12.8 How do I...
Include an editable report writer in a Visual Basic application?

Problem

I want to give the users of my application the ability to edit the appearance of the reports generated by my application. Neither Crystal Reports nor Microsoft Data Report allows that. How can I produce a report based on a database and let the users edit it?

Technique

Using Visual Basic with Microsoft Word and the other Microsoft Office applications gives enormous flexibility to your applications. Instead of taking all the time and effort needed to program a mini–word processor or other application, you can use all the power of Microsoft Word. Even using one of the many custom controls available for Visual Basic works only if you can find one that has the particular features you need at a reasonable cost. Why not use the tools you already have?

This How-To uses a WordBasic object to create a database report, which is then embedded in an OLE custom control on a form. The user can make any changes needed, using Word's own menus and toolbars.

Steps

Open the Visual Basic RPTWRITE.VBP project. Start the application by selecting Run | Start from the Visual Basic main menu, by pressing F5, or by clicking the Start button on the Visual Basic toolbar. Click the Create Report button, and select any Access .MDB file. After the data is processed and the report is created, the file is presented in the OLE control, as shown in Figure 12.15. The report is saved to a temporary file, TEMPRPT.DOC, in the application directory. Double-click the report window to activate visual editing and make any changes required. Because a toolbar is not provided with this application, any active Word toolbars appear as floating toolbars. When you are finished editing, click the Save File button to save the report as a Word document of your choice.

1. Start Visual Basic and create a new project. Save the default form as RPTWRITE.FRM, and save the project as RPTWRITE.VBP. This project uses the Microsoft Common Dialog control, so select Tools | Custom Controls from the main Visual Basic menu, and make sure that the control is selected in the list.

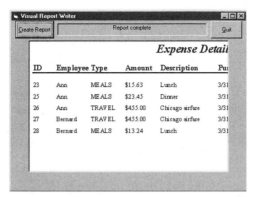

Figure 12.15. The Visual Report Writer form.

2. Start Microsoft Word and minimize the application. Having Word running during development speeds programming because you don't have to wait for Word to load every time you start the project.

3. Place controls on the form as shown in Figure 12.15, setting the properties as shown in Table 12.15. Note that the Common Dialog control is invisible at runtime, so you can place it anywhere on the form that is convenient. Note too that the menu `mnuFratsaBlatz` can be called anything you like; it is necessary to allow the Word menu to appear on the form only when the OLE object is activated.

Table 12.15. Objects and properties for RPTWRITE.FRM.

OBJECT	PROPERTY	SETTING
Form	Name	frmReportWriter
	Caption	"Visual Report Writer"
	NegotiateMenus	True
PictureBox	Name	picHead
	Align	1 'Align Top
	Appearance	0 'Flat
	BackColor	&H00C0C0C0&
	BorderStyle	0 'None
CommandButton	Name	cmdSave
	Caption	"&Save File"
CommandButton	Name	cmdQuit
	Caption	"&Quit"

continued on next page

continued from previous page

OBJECT	PROPERTY	SETTING
CommandButton	Name	cmdReport
	Caption	"&Create Report"
	Default	-1 'True
Label	Name	lblStatus
	Alignment	2 'Center
	BorderStyle	1 'Fixed Single
CommonDialog	Name	cdBiblio
	CancelError	-1 'True
	DefaultExt	"MDB"
	DialogTitle	"BIBLIO.MDB Location"
	FileName	"biblio.mdb"
	Filter	"BIBLIO Database
		(biblio.mdb)¦biblio.mdb¦All Files
		(*.*)¦*.*¦"
OLE	Name	oleWord
	OLETypeAllowed	1 'Embedded
Menu	Name	mnuFratsaBlatz
	Caption	"&FratsaBlatz"
	NegotiatePosition	1 'Left
	Visible	0 'False

4. Enter the following code into the declarations section of the form. The `ColumnTabs`, `ColumnHeaders`, and `ColumnWidths` arrays are used to store report formatting information so that any modifications can be made in one place rather than in several different procedures. The OLE constants are activation and deactivation methods for the OLE control.

```
Option Explicit

Dim mobjWord As Object

Dim strColumnTabs(6) As String
Dim strColumnHeaders(7) As String
Dim strColumnWidths(7) As String

'OLE Control Constants
Const OLE_Activate As Integer = 7
Const OLE_Deactivate As Integer = 9
```

5. Enter the following code in the form's **Load** event procedure. After a status message is put on the form, the Word object used throughout this application is created. The creation of that object starts Word running, so minimize it to get it out of the way. (Unfortunately, the **AppMinimize** command doesn't always work. You can manually minimize it, although it is interesting to watch the report being generated!) Finally, the column names and tab arrays are initialized and the column widths calculated.

```
Status "Creating a Word object"
    Me.Show
    Me.Refresh

    'Create a Microsoft Word object
    Set mobjWord = GetObject("", "Word.Basic")
    mobjWord.AppMinimize ("Microsoft Word")

    cmdReport.Enabled = True
    cmdQuit.Enabled = True

    'Set up standard layout information
    Call SetColumns

    Status "Click on Create Report to create the report."
End Sub
```

6. Enter the following code into the form's **Resize** event procedure. When you use an OLE control containing an object that presents text to the user, you should allow the user to resize the form to see as much or as little of the data as wanted. In this case, the report can go on for many pages, so allowing resizing enables the user to examine and edit the report even in full screen if desired. In this case, resizing is keyed to a couple of static values, the lefthand location of the Create Report button and the height of the picture box at the top. This helps to keep the form in aesthetically pleasing proportion. Note that enough of a border must be kept around the OLE control to allow for Word's rulers at the top and left side of the control; these rulers extend outside the bounds of the control itself.

```
Private Sub Form_Resize()
    Dim intBorder As Integer
    Dim intWindowWidth As Integer

    intBorder = picHead.Height
    intWindowWidth = Me.ScaleWidth

    cmdReport.Height = intBorder
    cmdQuit.Height = intBorder

    cmdQuit.Left = intWindowWidth - cmdQuit.Width - cmdReport.Left
    lblStatus.Width = cmdQuit.Left - lblStatus.Left _
        - cmdReport.Left
    lblStatus.Top = (picHead.Height - lblStatus.Height) / 2
```

continued on next page

continued from previous page

```
        oleWord.Left = intBorder
        oleWord.Width = Me.ScaleWidth - 2 * intBorder
        oleWord.Height = Me.ScaleHeight - oleWord.Top - intBorder

End Sub
```

7. Enter the cmdReport `Click` event procedure in the code section of the form. When the user clicks the Create Report button, this procedure opens the database and prepares it for producing the report. After the database is opened, the procedure calls the `Print` procedures to insert headers, footers, titles, and column headers into the report. A table is inserted into the report and formatted, and then the data is entered into the table using a `Do While` loop. On completion, the report is saved to a temporary file in the application directory and is shown in the OLE control as an embedded object.

```
Private Sub cmdReport_Click()
    Dim strTitle As String
    Dim intIdx As Integer
    Dim strInsertText As String
    Dim strFileName As String
    Dim uexpExpDetail As New ExpenseDetail
    Dim strResponse As String

    Status "Opening database table"

    On Error GoTo ExpDetailError

    ' Use the common dialog to open a database.
    cdExpenseFile.InitDir = App.Path
    cdExpenseFile.ShowOpen

    uexpExpDetail.strDbName = cdExpenseFile.filename

    Status "Creating a new Word document"

    mobjWord.FileNew
    strTitle = "Expense Details"

    Status "Inserting header and footer information"
    PrintHeader strTitle, strColumnTabs(), strColumnHeaders()
    PrintFooter "Enlighthened Software, Inc."
    PrintReportTitle strTitle
    PrintColHeaders strColumnTabs(), strColumnHeaders()

    'Start printing the report
    Status "Adding data to report"
    mobjWord.TableInsertTable NumColumns:=7, _
        NumRows:=2, _
        InitialColWidth:="2 in"
    For intIdx = 0 To 7
        With mobjWord
            .TableSelectColumn
```

```
                .TableColumnWidth ColumnWidth:=strColumnWidths(intIdx)
                .NextCell
                .NextCell
            End With
        Next

        'Format the paragraph height
        mobjWord.TableSelectTable
        mobjWord.FormatParagraph Before:="6 pt"

        'Select the first cell in the table
        'mobjWord.TableSelectColumn
        mobjWord.NextCell

        strResponse = uexpExpDetail.MoveFirst

        Do While "EOF" <> strResponse
            With mobjWord
                strInsertText = CStr(uexpExpDetail.lngExpenseId)
                .Insert strInsertText
                .NextCell
                strInsertText = uexpExpDetail.strEmployeeId
                .Insert strInsertText
                .NextCell
                strInsertText = uexpExpDetail.strExpenseType
                .Insert strInsertText
                .NextCell
                strInsertText = _
                    Format$(uexpExpDetail.curAmountSpent, "Currency")
                .Insert strInsertText
                .NextCell
                strInsertText = uexpExpDetail.strDescription
                .Insert strInsertText
                .NextCell
                strInsertText = _
                    Format$(uexpExpDetail.dtmDatePurchased, _
                        "General Date")
                .Insert strInsertText
                .NextCell
                strInsertText = _
                    Format$(uexpExpDetail.dtmDateSubmitted, _
                        "General Date")
                .Insert strInsertText
                .NextCell
                .TableInsertRow
            End With
            strResponse = uexpExpDetail.MoveNext
        Loop

        'Save the Word document
        mobjWord.ToolsOptionsSave SummaryPrompt:=0

        strFileName = App.Path & "\TempRpt.doc"
        'Word won't let us save a file over an existing document
        If Len(Dir(strFileName)) Then
```

continued on next page

continued from previous page

```
            Kill strFileName
        End If
        mobjWord.FileSaveAs Name:=strFileName

        oleWord.CreateEmbed strFileName
        oleWord.Refresh

        Status "Report complete"

        Exit Sub

ExpDetailError:
    If Err.Number = 70 Then
        Resume Next
    Else
        MsgBox Err.Description & Chr(13) & "from " & Err.Source _
            & " -- Number: " & CStr(Err.Number)
        Exit Sub
    End If

End Sub
```

8. Enter this code in the **SetColumns Sub** procedure. Using the tab settings in the **ColumnTabs** array, this procedure calculates the distance between tab settings. These widths will be used to size the Word table's column widths so that the data appears below the corresponding column header. The **If...Then...Else...End If** structure is used because the first column width will be the actual setting for the first tab. This procedure counts on the tabs being in ascending order, or from left to right on the page.

```
Sub SetColumns()
    Dim intIdx As Integer

    strColumnHeaders(0) = "ID"
    strColumnTabs(0) = "0.5"
    strColumnHeaders(1) = "Employee"
    strColumnTabs(1) = "1.25"
    strColumnHeaders(2) = "Type"
    strColumnTabs(2) = "2.0"
    strColumnHeaders(3) = "Amount"
    strColumnTabs(3) = "2.75"
    strColumnHeaders(4) = "Description"
    strColumnTabs(4) = "4.0"
    strColumnHeaders(5) = "Purchased"
    strColumnTabs(5) = "5.0"
    strColumnHeaders(6) = "Submitted"
    strColumnTabs(6) = "6.5"

    For intIdx = LBound(strColumnTabs) To UBound(strColumnTabs)
        If intIdx Then
            strColumnWidths(intIdx) = _
                Str$(Val(strColumnTabs(intIdx)) - _
                Val(strColumnTabs(intIdx - 1)))
```

```
            Else
                strColumnWidths(intIdx) = strColumnTabs(intIdx)
            End If
        Next
    End Sub
```

9. Enter the following code in the **PrintColHeaders Sub** procedure of the form. This procedure inserts the column headings into the report. Note that this procedure is used twice: once for the first page of the report under the report title, and again in the Word Header so that the headings appear on all subsequent pages. Note that the WordBasic command **ViewHeader** is used twice, acting as a toggle between showing and closing the header.

```
Sub PrintColHeaders(Tabs() As String, ColHeaders() As String)
    Dim intIdx As Integer

    'Assumes cursor is at the beginning of the proper location
    mobjWord.InsertPara
    mobjWord.LineUp
    mobjWord.FormatParagraph Before:="12 pt", _
        After:="6 pt"
    For intIdx = 0 To UBound(Tabs)
        mobjWord.FormatTabs Position:=Tabs(intIdx) + Chr$(34), _
            Align:=0
    Next
    For intIdx = 0 To UBound(ColHeaders) - 1
        mobjWord.Insert ColHeaders(intIdx) + Chr$(9)
    Next

    With mobjWord
        .StartOfLine
        .SelectCurSentence
        .CharRight 1, 1
        .FormatFont Points:="12", _
            Font:="Times New Roman", _
            Bold:=1
        .FormatBordersAndShading ApplyTo:=0, _
            BottomBorder:=2
        .LineDown
    End With
End Sub
```

10. Enter the following code in the **PrintFooter Sub** procedure to insert page footers into the report. Note that the WordBasic command **ViewFooter** is used twice, acting as a toggle between showing and closing the footer.

```
    'Insert the report footer
    mobjWord.ViewFooter
    mobjWord.FormatTabs ClearAll:=1
    mobjWord.FormatTabs Position:="7.0" + Chr$(34), _
        DefTabs:="0.5" + Chr$(34), _
        Align:=2, _
        Leader:=0
```

continued on next page

continued from previous page

```
        mobjWord.StartOfLine
        mobjWord.Insert Company + Chr$(9) + "Page "
        mobjWord.InsertPageField
        mobjWord.SelectCurSentence
        mobjWord.FormatFont Points:="12", _
            Font:="Times New Roman", _
            Bold:=1

        mobjWord.ViewFooter
    End Sub
```

11. Add the following code to the **PrintReport Sub** procedure. Continuing the use of WordBasic commands through OLE, a title is passed to this procedure, entered on the report, and formatted with a larger font and a drop-shadow box. The box does not appear on the report shown in the OLE control, but it will appear when the report is printed.

```
Sub PrintReportTitle(Title As String)
    With mobjWord
        .StartOfDocument
        .InsertPara
        .StartOfDocument
        .Insert Title
        .StartOfLine
        .SelectCurSentence
        .FormatFont Points:="18", _
            Font:="Times New Roman", _
            Bold:=1, _
            Italic:=1
        .CenterPara

        .FormatBordersAndShading ApplyTo:=0, _
            Shadow:=0

        'Leave the cursor on the following line
        .LineDown
    End With
End Sub
```

12. Enter the following code into the **PrintHeader Sub** procedure. The calling procedure passes a report title to this procedure, along with the **Tabs** and **ColHeaders** arrays. The first page of the report will be different from the rest of the report. It will have the page title, but the subsequent pages will have the report title at the top of the page and will be left justified. The column headings are added to the header so that they show on all pages. Recall that the column headings were placed on the first page of the report, under the report title, as well.

```
Sub PrintHeader(Title As String, Tabs() As String, _
    ColHeaders() As String)
    Dim intIdx As Integer
```

```
    With mobjWord
        'For now, set DifferentFirstPage to no
        .FilePageSetup TopMargin:="0.8" + Chr$(34), _
            BottomMargin:="0.8" + Chr$(34), _
            LeftMargin:="0.75" + Chr$(34), _
            RightMargin:="0.75" + Chr$(34), _
            ApplyPropsTo:=4, _
            DifferentFirstPage:=0
    End With

    'Insert the report header
    With mobjWord
        .ViewHeader
        .FormatTabs ClearAll:=1
        .FormatTabs Position:="7.0" + Chr$(34), _
            DefTabs:="0.5" + Chr$(34), _
            Align:=2
        .StartOfLine
        .SelectCurSentence
        .CharRight 1, 1
        .FormatFont Points:="12", _
            Font:="Times New Roman", _
            Bold:=1
        .StartOfLine
        .Insert Title + Chr$(9)
        .InsertDateTime DateTimePic:="d' 'MMMM', 'yyyy", _
            InsertAsField:=0
        .InsertPara
        .InsertPara
    End With

    PrintColHeaders Tabs(), ColHeaders()

    mobjWord.ViewHeader    'Closes if it is open

    'Now set DifferentFirstPage
    mobjWord.FilePageSetup DifferentFirstPage:=1

End Sub
```

13. Enter the following code in the **Status Sub** procedure in the form. By passing a string to this procedure, you can keep the user up-to-date on the progress of the report, because it can take some time to generate the report if the data source is large. A useful enhancement of this might be to add a progress gauge or an accumulated record count to show actual progress through the table.

```
Sub Status(txtCaption)
    lblStatus.Caption = txtCaption
    lblStatus.Refresh
End Sub
```

14. Enter the following code in the `cmdQuit Click` and `Unload` event procedures. When the Quit button is clicked, a final status message is shown and the application ends. When the form is unloaded, the `objWord` object is released by being set to `Nothing`.

```
Private Sub cmdQuit_Click()
    Status "Ending application"
    Unload Me
End Sub

Private Sub Form_Unload(Cancel As Integer)
    'Shut down Word
    Set objWord = Nothing
End Sub
```

How It Works

This How-To uses many of the formatting and inserting commands available in WordBasic. If you are going to modify the code in this How-To, you should have a copy of the Word Developer's Kit, which has lots of detailed information about WordBasic and, of course, Word itself.

The easiest way to become familiar with WordBasic is to use the macro recorder in Word. Before creating a document or formatting it, turn the recorder on by selecting Tools | Macro | Record New Macro, enter a unique name for the macro, and then click Record. Word then records all your steps, not as individual keystrokes but as fully formed commands using VBA. When you are finished making changes, simply click the button with the blue square in the floating Macro Recorder toolbar. You can then open the macro using Tools | Macro | Visual Basic Editor, and you can examine or even cut and paste it into your application. You'll need to reformat the code to conform to Visual Basic's named arguments syntax, and you'll need to enclose the code with `With` *<object name>*...`End With` so that Visual Basic knows which object to apply the commands to. Alternatively, you can append the object name to the front of the WordBasic command for individual lines. Both methods are demonstrated throughout the code in this How-To.

A Word table was used to contain the data in the report. Not only does this make it easy to line up the different fields in the report, but it also simplifies the problem of having fields too long to fit in the width allocated on a single line of the report. By changing the paragraph formatting in the table's cells, you can achieve virtually any appearance you want. Alternatively, you could use the `ColumnTabs` array to put data on the report the same way the column headers were. This approach might be easier if a record's fields will be on multiple lines on the report, but you can also use Word's Merge Cells and other table formatting to achieve different effects on the different lines of a record.

Remember that it is easiest to design the report in Word first and then translate the design into a Visual Basic program, with or without the macro recorder.

If you want the embedded object's application menus to appear when you activate the object, you need to have a menu as part of the form. If your application doesn't otherwise need a menu, create a dummy menu, name it anything you like, and set the **Visible** property of the single menu item to **False**. That way, the object's menu will appear. If your application does use a menu, create it as you normally would, but set the **NegotiatePosition** property of each menu item to **None**, **Left**, **Middle**, or **Right** to give Visual Basic an indication of how you want to sort the various menu items between the two menus.

COMPLEXITY
INTERMEDIATE

12.9 How do I...
Work with the Windows Registry for my ActiveX classes?

Problem

All this work I am doing with ActiveX components means that my development computer is going to require some maintenance. How do I keep my Windows Registry neat and tidy?

Technique

All ActiveX components must be registered in order to work correctly. The Windows Registry contains information about each ActiveX component available on your system and the location of the files required to use the component. ActiveX EXE files created by Visual Basic 6 automatically include the code to register themselves in the system registry. Visual Basic will also register ActiveX DLL files on your development machine. You will need to register your DLLs on machines to which you distribute your programs. The RegSvr32.EXE program is designed to add and remove Registry entries for your components.

Steps

1. Start a DOS command box and change to your Windows System32 directory, usually C:\WINDOWS\SYSTEM32 on Windows 95 and C:\WINNT\SYSTEM32 on Windows NT.

2. Invoke REGSVR32, passing the name of the ActiveX.DLL file from How-To 12.3:

```
C:\WINDOWS\SYSTEM32> REGSVR32 C:\CODE\CHAPTER12\HOWTO03\ACTIVEX.DLL
```

Figure 12.16 shows the results.

Figure 12.16. RegSvr32 run results.

How It Works

Every Windows system has a Registry containing information about nearly everything on the system. The Registry is divided into **HKEY** classes for the current configuration, current user, users, machine, and root. For the purposes of keeping our ActiveX components running, we are concerned with the **HKEY_CLASSES_ROOT** section of the Registry. The component object model uses the Registry in two ways to resolve ActiveX component references—by name and CLSID. The name for a component is assigned by you in the Project Properties dialog box. **ActiveXDll_For_HowTo_12_3.ExpenseDetail** was assigned as the full name for How-To 12.3. Component names are in the form *<Application>.<Object>* in the event that a single DLL or EXE file contains more than one public object. The CLSID is generated by Windows as a GUID (globally unique identifier). The GUID is a 16-byte unique key presented on the screen by Windows as a formatted hexadecimal string. A typical CLSID might look like **{3CF0F563-0DC0-11D1-9AF0-004033373A8F}**.

Windows uses the name of a component as a key into the Registry to find the associated CLSID. The CLSID can then be used to find all the required information about the component so that Windows can run it. The information for the ActiveX.DLL from How-To 12.3 includes

- ✔ The InProcServer32 filename to load to run the component.

- ✔ The ProgID set as the project name on the project properties page (the same as the registered name).

- ✔ The TypeLib identifying the interface defined by the component (so that incompatible client programs will not be allowed to invoke the component).

- ✔ The version number identifying the version of the component program installed (relative to the version number requested by the calling program).

You can manually inspect and modify the Windows Registry by invoking the RegEdt32.EXE program from your Windows system directory.

In this How-To, RegSvr32 loads the specified DLL and invokes **DllRegisterServer** to cause the DLL to be registered on the system. Whenever you use Visual Basic to create an object, the runtime library looks in the Registry for the logical name you supplied, and then loads the associated implementing file. For example, when you request an **Access.Application** object, the Registry is accessed to determine which program on which drive should be started to provide the required services.

Comments

RegSvr32 can also be used to unload DLL files from the Registry with the following syntax:

```
REGSVR32 /U <FileName>.DLL
```

Sometimes, manually unregistering and then reregistering a component can help convince an otherwise balky application to run. Frequently, the cause of application run failure is a missing DLL file called by one of your components. Running RegSvr32 for each component can sometimes help isolate missing DLL files.

In addition to RegSvr32, Microsoft has a program called RegClean available from its Web site. RegClean audits the Registry on a machine and removes entries for which the enabling component is missing. Suppose, for example, that you manually purged all the files for Excel from your system without running the uninstall program. All your registered DLLs would be gone, but the Registry entries would still be there, pointing to non-existent files. ActiveX components for Excel will then fail to run correctly. RegClean cleans up the Registry entries to remove these "dangling" entries pointing to non-existent files. The program also leaves behind an "undo" file when you are finished to help restore mistaken removals.

COMPLEXITY
INTERMEDIATE

12.10 How do I...
Create my own custom data control?

Problem

I like the power of the Visual Basic 6 Data control, but I want something with more speed and a different user interface. How can I mimic the data control's functions but make it run faster?

Technique

Building a data control is simpler than it sounds, but the debug and test environment is more complex than a form-based project because an ActiveX control must run in both the design-time and the runtime environments. Design-time code runs when controls are dropped onto the form, when objects are resized, and when control properties are changed.

In outline, ActiveX controls are developed in the following general sequence:

✔ Plan the control's properties, methods, events, and visual interface.

✔ Create the development and test environment.

✔ Design and develop the visual and design-time interfaces.

✔ Add the code for the data control's functions.

Most of the time spent developing an ActiveX control is spent on the visual interface and the design-time requirements of a visual control.

Plan the Control

Control planning is the easiest and hardest part of development—easiest because everyone knows what a data control needs to do, and hardest because we also have to handle "nasty" things that might be thrown up in our development or support paths. Nobody wants to support a control that crashes every time somebody does something unexpected. Fortunately, Visual Basic's object-oriented features help us expect and prevent errors.

The goal of the simple data control is to provide many of the conveniences of the Visual Basic data control with fast performance and complete source code availability. This data control will support four movement operations (first, previous, next, and last) and three data change operations (add new, update, and delete). The visual implementation of all operations will be *constituent control* buttons placed on the control. A constituent control is one we will place on top of our control to deliver a desired function. Any existing ActiveX control that has been designed to be placed on another control can be a constituent control for another project. All the common controls that shipped with Visual Basic 6 can be used as constituent controls, including text boxes, buttons, frames, list boxes, pictures, labels, and shapes. The OLE Automation control cannot be used as a constituent control. If you plan to distribute your control to others, even at no charge, be sure to check your license agreements and the Visual Basic 6 Books Online carefully.

Build the Development and Test Environment

The development and test environment for an ActiveX control is different from that of standard EXE projects because ActiveX controls have both design-time and runtime code attributes that can be different. The most important distinction is the way in which the control stores design-time property values. Properties such as the captions, data sources, and database names must be stored at design time if they are specified.

The development and test environment is implemented as a project group in order to have the ActiveX control project and the test form project available simultaneously. Whenever the control's object (visual design) window is closed, the control is placed into design-time Run mode, and the design-time code can be debugged within a single Visual Basic programming session.

Develop the Visual and Design-Time Interfaces

Your control's visual interface is the most obvious part of your work because the visual behavior is what everyone will notice. At design time, we deal with the resize event for managing constituent control sizes and control properties that need to be saved with the form. In the case of our private data control, we worry about saving the database location.

Develop the Core Functions

Finally, we can develop the core functions and events for the data control. The core operations displayed by the buttons are directly implemented with the underlying data access object (DAO) methods. The public events notify the form of changes in the underlying data and of validation required prior to new, updated, or deleted records. The validation event is not fired when the data changes through control movement.

Steps

Open the project ExpDataControl.vbg. The form shown in Figure 12.17 appears. Experiment with the form and its buttons to get a feel for how this data control works.

Figure 12.17. The DataControl Test form.

1. Create a new ActiveX control project in your work area. Name the default User Control object `ctlExpenseDetail`. Select Project | References from the main menu, and include a reference to the Microsoft DAO 3.51 Object Library. Make sure that the OLE Automation library is not selected.

2. Select Project | Project1 properties from the Visual Basic 6 main menu, or right-click Project1 in the Project Explorer window and select properties from the Object menu. Name the project `ExpDetailControl`. Set the project description to `Expense Detail ActiveX Control`, as shown in

Figure 12.18. The description will be saved to your Windows system Registry when you compile your project. Save the control and project files.

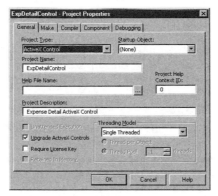

Figure 12.18. The Project Properties window.

3. Add a new project to your work area by selecting File | Add Project from the main menu. The Add Project window appears. Select Standard EXE from the New tab.

4. Name the default form `TestDataControl` and the default project `prjTestDataControl`. Save the project and project group. When prompted, name the project group `ExpDataControl.vbg`. Project groups help you debug related projects from a single Visual Basic 6 session.

5. Add seven command buttons and two frames to the control as shown in Figure 12.19. Don't worry about exact placement because the resize event will manage final placement and sizing. (These visual elements are almost the same as those in How-To 12.2.)

Figure 12.19. Expense data control visual elements.

6. Set the properties of the control elements as shown in Table 12.16.

Table 12.16. Objects and properties for the Expense Data control.

OBJECT	PROPERTY	SETTING
UserControl	Name	ExpDataControl
Frame	Name	fraBorder
	Caption	"Expense Data Control"
Frame	Name	fraNavigate
	Caption	"Navigate"
CommandButton	Name	cmdFirst
	Caption	"&First"
CommandButton	Name	cmdPrev
	Caption	"&Prev"
CommandButton	Name	cmdNext
	Caption	"&Next"
CommandButton	Name	cmdLast
	Caption	"&Last"
Frame	Name	fraMaintain
	Caption	"Maintain"
CommandButton	Name	cmdNew
	Caption	"Ne&w"
CommandButton	Name	cmdUpdate
	Caption	"&Update"
CommandButton	Name	cmdDelete
	Caption	"&Delete"

USING DEBUG.PRINT TO TRACE CONTROL BEHAVIOR

One of the most challenging parts of developing an ActiveX control is determining which events will fire and in what order. This How-To employs Debug.Print statements to trace control behavior, especially during design time. The first statement in most of the control's event procedure is usually this:

```
Debug.Print "Event Name" & Extender.Name
```

At both design time and runtime, this statement causes a debug trace in the immediate window of all control behaviors. The Extender object reflects the control's container into your code in order to access important information about the control's environment. Standard Extender properties for a control include Name,

continued on next page

continued from previous page

Visible, Enabled, Top, Left, Height, and Width. These properties exist in your container's object but can be of value to your code for resizing and property initialization. You can use the trace information to learn more about design-time events and their effect on your control.

7. Add the following code to the UserControl_Resize event of your control:

```
Private Sub UserControl_Resize()
' Resize constituent controls to look "nice"
Dim intMargin As Integer
Dim intHeight As Integer
Dim intWidth As Integer

    ' Trace our behavior
    Static intCountResized As Integer
    intCountResized = intCountResized + 1
    Debug.Print Extender.Name & " Resized " _
        & Str$(intCountResized) & " times"

    ' Adjust the placement of the border frame
    fraBorder.Move 0, 0, ScaleWidth, ScaleHeight

    ' Calculate the standard margin as a proportion of
    ' the total control width.
    intMargin = ScaleWidth / 36

    ' Calculate and adjust the sizes of the internal frames.
    intHeight = (ScaleHeight - (1.5 * intMargin) - intMargin) / 2
    intWidth = ScaleWidth - (2 * intMargin)
    fraMaintain.Move intMargin, (intMargin * 2), _
        intWidth, intHeight
    fraNavigate.Move intMargin, _
        (fraMaintain.Top + fraMaintain.Height), _
        intWidth, intHeight

    ' Adjust the maintenance button sizes and locations
    ' based on the number of buttons and margins required.
    ' We need an extra margin in the height because the frame
    ' caption takes about one margin.
    intHeight = fraMaintain.Height - (3 * intMargin)
    intWidth = (fraMaintain.Width - (4 * intMargin)) / 3
    cmdNew.Move intMargin, _
        2 * intMargin, _
        intWidth, intHeight
    cmdUpdate.Move cmdNew.Left + intWidth + intMargin, _
        2 * intMargin, _
        intWidth, intHeight
    cmdDelete.Move cmdUpdate.Left + cmdUpdate.Width + intMargin, _
        2 * intMargin, _
        intWidth, intHeight
```

```
' Adjust the movement button sizes and locations based on
' the number of buttons and margins required.
intHeight = fraNavigate.Height - (3 * intMargin)
intWidth = (fraNavigate.Width - (5 * intMargin)) / 4
cmdFirst.Move intMargin, _
    2 * intMargin, _
    intWidth, intHeight
cmdPrev.Move cmdFirst.Left + intWidth + intMargin, _
    2 * intMargin, _
    intWidth, intHeight
cmdNext.Move cmdPrev.Left + intWidth + intMargin, _
    2 * intMargin, _
    intWidth, intHeight
cmdLast.Move cmdNext.Left + intWidth + intMargin, _
    2 * intMargin, _
    intWidth, intHeight

End Sub
```

Although lengthy, the **Resize** event code just works from the outside of the control inward, making sure that everything fits on the control with pleasing margins.

8. Set a breakpoint at the beginning of the **Resize** event procedure. Run the design-time environment of your control by closing the control's object design window (where you add buttons and frames). Notice that the Toolbox button for your UserControl, shown in Figure 12.20, has changed from gray to color.

**Figure 12.20.
The Visual
Basic Toolbox
with the user
control active.**

9. Get ready to test your **Resize** event procedure. Select View | Immediate Window from the main menu. Open the **TestDataControl** form design window. Select your new UserControl button from the Visual Basic 6 Toolbox, and draw a control on the form. Don't be surprised when your **Resize** event breakpoint is fired; every time the control is dropped onto a form or resized, this event occurs. Take a moment to walk through the resize code and get a feel for its behavior. Don't forget to clear the breakpoint when you are done.

10. Close the form's design window and stop the design-time instance of the UserControl by opening the UserControl design window.

DEBUGGING AND TESTING USERCONTROL OBJECTS

Debugging `UserControl` objects is straightforward when all the rules are clear. The Visual Basic development environment automatically runs the control's design-time instance whenever the UserControl's object design window is closed. The UserControl's icon is then activated on the Toolbox palette. Any breakpoints or Debug object statements in the UserControl code are then activated, and you can debug design-time code as you manipulate the UserControl on forms or set properties.

However, you might find the instance of your control on the form hatched over (not running in design mode) when you want to test with no apparent way to get the design-time code running. This turn of events is usually caused by a runtime compile-on-demand error, forcing a project reset and premature (in the programmer's mind) return to the design environment. Try manually compiling all the projects in the group to correct this error. Select File | Make Project Group from the Visual Basic main menu. Usually, recompiling the UserControl's .OCX file clears up the design-time environment. Alternatively, you can turn off the Compile On Demand check box on the General tab of the Options dialog box found on the Tools menu.

11. From the UserControl Code window, add a `Caption` property by selecting Tools | Add Procedure from the main menu. Name the procedure `Caption`, and declare it as a public property (see Figure 12.21). Click OK.

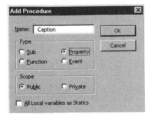

Figure 12.21. Use the Visual Basic Add Procedure window to declare the `Caption` property.

12. Modify the `Caption Property Let` and `Property Get` procedures as shown next. Be sure to change the variant declarations to string declarations.

```
Public Property Get Caption() As String

    Caption = fraBorder.Caption

End Property

Public Property Let Caption(ByVal strNewValue As String)

    ' Place the caption in the border frame.
    fraBorder.Caption = strNewValue
    ' Notify the container so that the property
    ' window may be updated
    PropertyChanged "Caption"

End Property
```

13. Add the following code to the `UserControl_InitProperties` event. Every time the control is placed onto a form, the caption will be set to the control's name. (Remember that referencing a property from within a class causes the `Property Let` function to be called.)

```
Private Sub UserControl InitProperties()
    ' Trace behavior.
    Debug.Print Extender.Name & ": InitProperties"
    ' Set the Caption property
    Caption = Extender.Name

End Sub
```

14. Add the following code to the `UserControl WriteProperties` procedure. The `WriteProperties` event is called whenever the form is saved.

```
Private Sub UserControl_WriteProperties(PropBag As PropertyBag)

    ' Trace behavior.
    Debug.Print Extender.Name & ": WriteProperties"
    'Save the caption property to the property bag.
    PropBag.WriteProperty "Caption", Caption, _
        Extender.Name

End Sub
```

15. Add the following code to the `UserControl ReadProperties` event to retrieve the saved properties:

```
Private Sub UserControl_ReadProperties(PropBag As PropertyBag)

    ' Trace behavior.
    Debug.Print Extender.Name & ": ReadProperties"
```

continued on next page

continued from previous page

```
        'Retrieve the caption
        Caption = PropBag.ReadProperty("Caption", _
                    Extender.Name)

    End Sub
```

16. Compile the entire project by selecting File | Make Project Group from the main menu. Close the UserControl design window and open the test form design window. Place a `UserControl` object on the test form. Experiment with the `Caption` property from the Visual Basic properties window in Design mode. Try saving, closing, and reopening the form, and observe what happens in the Immediate window.

17. Add the following declarations to the UserControl to define our recordset and the fields to be managed:

```
' Variables to define and control the recordset
Private mblnRecSetOpen As Boolean
Private mdbExpense As Database
Private mrecExpense As Recordset
Private mstrDbName As String

' Module variables to hold property value(s)
Private mlngExpenseId As Long
Private mstrEmployeeId As String
Private mstrExpenseType As String
Private mcurAmountSpent As Currency
Private mstrDescription As String
Private mdtmDatePurchased As Date
Private mdtmDateSubmitted As Date
```

18. Define property procedures for the expense detail table by selecting Tools | Add Procedure from the main menu when the UserControl code is active onscreen. Name the property `strDatabaseName` and declare it to be a public property. Modify the generated `Property Get` and `Let` procedures as shown next. This property can be set only at runtime because we don't want to bother with opening and closing recordsets during form design. The `Let` procedure checks to see whether the recordset is already open and closes it before opening it again.

```
Public Property Get strDatabaseName() As String
' Returns the database name to the container
    strDatabaseName = mstrDbName

End Property

Public Property Let strDatabaseName(ByVal strNewValue As String)
' Assigns database name to control and closes and opens the
' control's recordset

    ' Trace behavior.
    Debug.Print Extender.Name & ": Let strDatabaseName"
```

```
        ' Don't allow database to be set at design time
        If Ambient.UserMode = False Then
            Err.Raise Number:=31013, _
                Description:= _
                "Property is read-only at design time."
            Exit Property
        End If

        On Error GoTo OpenError

        If mblnRecSetOpen Then
            mrecExpense.Close
            mdbExpense.Close
        End If
        mstrDbName = strNewValue
        Set mdbExpense = _
            DBEngine.Workspaces(0).OpenDatabase(mstrDbName)
        Set mrecExpense = mdbExpense.OpenRecordset("Expenses")
        mblnRecSetOpen = True

        Exit Property

OpenError:
        ' Because we are designing this class for potential unattended
        ' operation, we'll have to raise an error on our own
        Err.Raise Number:=Err.Number
        Err.Clear
        Exit Property

End Property
```

19. Add some code to initialize the state control variables of the control so that the recordset open and close logic works correctly:

```
Private Sub UserControl_Initialize()
' Initialize control's core variables

        ' Trace behavior, but we can't use the name because
        ' the extender object is not available
        Debug.Print "Initialize"

        mblnRecSetOpen = False

End Sub
```

20. Add a **Terminate** event procedure to close the database and recordset. Note that the Visual Basic documentation states very clearly that control terminate event handlers *must* manage their own errors because there is usually nothing in the container application on the call stack to handle an error. For the same reason, never raise an error from a terminate event. For tracing purposes, the **Extender** object is no longer available for retrieving the control's name.

```
Private Sub UserControl_Terminate()

    ' Trace behavior.
    Debug.Print "UserControl_Terminate"

    ' We don't really care about errors when cleaning up.
    On Error Resume Next
    ' Close the recordset
    mrecExpense.Close
    ' Close the expense database
    mdbExpense.Close
    ' Reset the error handler
    On Error GoTo 0
    Exit Sub

End Sub
```

21. The control will expose two events to its container—one for data changes and the other for validation. Add the following code to the declarations section of the **UserControl**:

```
' Data changed event for data control movement
    ' or internally generated change tells the container
    ' that the control's view of the data has changed
    Public Event DataChanged()

    ' Action enum for validate event eases container
    ' code development
    Public Enum EXP_CHANGE_TYPE
        expAddNewValidate
        expUpdateValidate
        expDeleteValidate
    End Enum

    ' Validate response enum tells the control whether to
    ' proceed with the data change
    Public Enum EXP_RESPONSE_TYPE
        expOK
        expCancel
    End Enum

    ' Validate event for data control
    Public Event ValidateData(ByRef Response As EXP_RESPONSE_TYPE, _
            ByVal Change As EXP_CHANGE_TYPE)
```

The **DataChanged** event will tell the containing form that the underlying data has changed and that the container should refresh its view of the data. The public **Enum** declarations assist the developer of the containing form in understanding the event parameters. The **ValidateData** event will tell the containing form that a data change is about to take place and provide an opportunity for cancellation by the container.

22. Implement three helper subroutines to move data between record fields and the control data variables and to clear the object variables:

```
Private Sub SetRecordset(recExp As Recordset)
' Copies current values to Recordset

    With recExp
        !EmployeeId = mvarstrEmployeeId
        !ExpenseType = mvarstrExpenseType
        !AmountSpent = mvarcurAmountSpent
        !Description = mvarstrDescription
        !DatePurchased = mvardtmDatePurchased
        !DateSubmitted = mvardtmDateSubmitted
    End With

End Sub

Private Sub GetRecordset(recExp As Recordset)
' Copies current values to Recordset

    With recExp
        mvarlngExpenseId = 0 + !ExpenseID
        mvarstrEmployeeId = "" & !EmployeeId
        mvarstrExpenseType = "" & !ExpenseType
        mvarcurAmountSpent = 0 + !AmountSpent
        mvarstrDescription = "" & !Description
        mvardtmDatePurchased = !DatePurchased
        mvardtmDateSubmitted = !DateSubmitted
    End With

End Sub

Private Sub ClearObject()
' Clears all object variables

    mlngExpenseId = 0
    mstrEmployeeId = ""
    mstrExpenseType = ""
    mcurAmountSpent = 0
    mstrDescription = ""
    mdtmDatePurchased = CDate("1/1/1980")
    mdtmDateSubmitted = CDate("1/1/1980")

End Sub
```

23. Implement the core data movement operations by providing code to work for the movement button clicks:

```
Private Sub cmdFirst_Click()
' Move to the first record

    On Error GoTo MoveError
    If mblnRecSetOpen Then
        With mrecExpense
            If Not (True = .BOF _
```

continued on next page

continued from previous page

```
                    And True = .EOF) Then
                        ' Dataset is not empty.
                        ' Move to the first record.
                        .MoveFirst
                        Call GetRecordset(mrecExpense)
                        RaiseEvent DataChanged
                    End If
            End With
        End If

        Exit Sub

MoveError:
        ' Return the error description
        Err.Raise Number:=Err.Number, Source:=Err.Source, _
            Description:=Err.Description
        Err.Clear
        Exit Sub

End Sub

Private Sub cmdLast_Click()
' Move to the last record

    On Error GoTo MoveError
    If mblnRecSetOpen Then
        With mrecExpense
            If Not (True = .BOF _
            And True = .EOF) Then
                    ' Dataset is not empty.
                    ' Move to the last record.
                    .MoveLast
                    Call GetRecordset(mrecExpense)
                    RaiseEvent DataChanged
            End If
        End With
    End If

    Exit Sub

MoveError:
        ' Return the error description
        Err.Raise Number:=Err.Number, Source:=Err.Source, _
            Description:=Err.Description
        Err.Clear
        Exit Sub

End Sub

Private Sub cmdNext_Click()
' Move to the next record

    On Error GoTo MoveError
    If mblnRecSetOpen Then
        With mrecExpense
            If True = .BOF _
            And True = .EOF Then
```

```
                    .MoveLast
            Else
                ' Dataset is not empty.
                ' Move to the previous record.
                .MoveNext
                If .EOF Then
                    .MoveLast
                End If
            End If
            Call GetRecordset(mrecExpense)
            RaiseEvent DataChanged
        End With
    End If

    Exit Sub

MoveError:
    ' Return the error description
    Err.Raise Number:=Err.Number, Source:=Err.Source, _
        Description:=Err.Description
    Err.Clear
    Exit Sub

End Sub

Private Sub cmdPrev_Click()
' Move to the previous record

    On Error GoTo MoveError

    If mblnRecSetOpen Then
        With mrecExpense
            If True = .BOF _
            And True = .EOF Then
                .MoveFirst
            Else
                ' Dataset is not empty.
                ' Move to the previous record.
                .MovePrevious
                If .BOF Then
                    .MoveFirst
                End If
            End If
            Call GetRecordset(mrecExpense)
            RaiseEvent DataChanged
        End With
    End If

    Exit Sub

MoveError:
    ' Return the error description
    Err.Raise Number:=Err.Number, Source:=Err.Source, _
        Description:=Err.Description
    Err.Clear
    Exit Sub

End Sub
```

24. Implement the data maintenance operations by adding `Click` event procedures for the New, Update, and Delete buttons:

```
Private Sub cmdNew_Click()
' Inserts a brand-new record into the database and leaves the
' newly inserted values as the current object values.

Dim uexpResponse As EXP_RESPONSE_TYPE

    On Error GoTo InsertError
    RaiseEvent ValidateData(uexpResponse, expAddNewValidate)
    If expOk = uexpResponse Then
        With mrecExpense
            .AddNew
            mdtmDateSubmitted = Now
            Call SetRecordset(mrecExpense)
            .Update
            'Move to the most recently modified record
            .Bookmark = .LastModified
            Call GetRecordset(mrecExpense)
            RaiseEvent DataChanged
        End With
    End If

    Exit Sub

InsertError:
    ' Return the error description
    Err.Raise Number:=Err.Number, Source:=Err.Source, _
        Description:=Err.Description
    Err.Clear
    Exit Sub

End Sub

Private Sub cmdUpdate_Click()
' Updates Expenses table from current object values
Dim uexpResponse As EXP_RESPONSE_TYPE

    On Error GoTo UpdateError
    RaiseEvent ValidateData(uexpResponse, expAddNewValidate)
    If expOk = uexpResponse Then
        With mrecExpense
            .Edit
            Call SetRecordset(mrecExpense)
            .Update
            'Move to the most recently modified record
            .Bookmark = .LastModified
            Call GetRecordset(mrecExpense)
            RaiseEvent DataChanged
        End With
    End If
```

```
        Exit Sub

UpdateError:
    ' Return the error description
    Err.Raise Number:=Err.Number, Source:=Err.Source, _
        Description:=Err.Description
    Err.Clear
    Exit Sub

End Sub

Private Sub cmdDelete_Click()
' Deletes the expense detail record whose value is
' current from the database

Dim uexpResponse As EXP_RESPONSE_TYPE

    On Error GoTo DeleteError

    RaiseEvent ValidateData(uexpResponse, expAddNewValidate)
    If expOk = uexpResponse Then
        With mrecExpense
            .Delete
            If 0 = .RecordCount Then
                Call ClearObject
            Else
                .MoveNext
                If .EOF Then
                    Call ClearObject
                Else
                    Call GetRecordset(mrecExpense)
                End If
            End If
        End With
    End If
    RaiseEvent DataChanged

    Exit Sub

DeleteError:
    ' Return the error description
    Err.Raise Number:=Err.Number, Source:=Err.Source, _
        Description:=Err.Description
    Err.Clear
    Exit Sub

End Sub
```

25. Provide **Property Get** and **Let** procedures for the core data variables implemented by the control. Note that cutting and pasting the property procedures one pair at a time is much easier than using the Add Procedure dialog box from step 18.

```
Public Property Get curAmountSpent() As Currency
    ' Return the control's current amount
    curAmountSpent = mcurAmountSpent

End Property

Public Property Let curAmountSpent(ByVal curNewValue As Currency)
    ' Set the amount spent
    mcurAmountSpent = curNewValue

End Property

Public Property Get dtmDatePurchased() As Date
    ' Return the control's current purchase date
    dtmDatePurchased = mdtmDatePurchased

End Property

Public Property Let dtmDatePurchased(ByVal dtmNewValue As Date)
    ' Set the purchase date
    mdtmDatePurchased = dtmNewValue

End Property

Public Property Get dtmDateSubmitted() As Date
    ' Return the control's current submitted date.
    ' There is no property Let procedure because the
    ' value is set only when the record is created.
    dtmDateSubmitted = mdtmDateSubmitted

End Property

Public Property Get lngExpenseId() As Long
    ' Return the database-assigned ExpenseID.
    ' Note that there is no Property Let procedure
    ' because the database makes the key assignment.

    lngExpenseId = mlngExpenseId

End Property

Public Property Get strDescription() As String
    ' Return the control's current description
    strDescription = mstrDescription

End Property

Public Property Let strDescription(ByVal strNewValue As String)
    ' Set the expense description
    mstrDescription = strNewValue

End Property

Public Property Get strEmployeeId() As String
    ' Return the control's current employee ID
    strEmployeeId = mstrEmployeeId
```

```
End Property

Public Property Let strEmployeeId(ByVal strNewValue As String)
    ' Set the employee ID
    mstrEmployeeId = strNewValue

End Property

Public Property Get strExpenseType() As String
     ' Return the control's current expense type
    strExpenseType = mstrExpenseType

End Property

Public Property Let strExpenseType(ByVal strNewValue As String)
' Sets the expense type to an allowed value
    Dim strTemp As String

    strTemp = UCase$(strNewValue)
    If strTemp = "TRAVEL" _
    Or strTemp = "MEALS" _
    Or strTemp = "OFFICE" _
    Or strTemp = "AUTO" _
    Or strTemp = "TOLL/PARK" Then
        mstrExpenseType = strTemp
    Else
        Err.Raise Number:=31013, _
            Description:="Expense type must be TRAVEL, MEALS, " _
                        & "OFFICE, AUTO, or TOLL/PARK"
        'Err.Clear
        Exit Property
    End If

End Property
```

The `strExpenseType Property Let` procedure illustrates raising a field-level validation error from a User Control. The `lngExpenseId` and `dtmDateSubmitted` properties do not have `Let` procedures because these properties are set by the database and insert code.

26. The actual data properties should be available only at runtime and should not appear on the control's property page. Select Tools | Procedure Attributes from the main menu. Click Advanced. Select each data property in turn from the Name list box, check Don't Show in Property Browser, and click the Apply button. Figure 12.22 shows the advanced Procedure Attributes dialog box.

27. Complete the Test Data Control form so that it looks like Figure 12.23, and set the form's control attributes as shown in Table 12.17. Note that the **Amount** field is stored in a masked edit control.

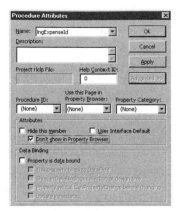

Figure 12.22. The advanced Procedure Attributes dialog box.

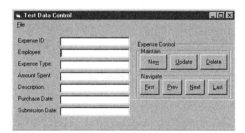

Figure 12.23. Layout of the Test Data Control form.

Table 12.17. Objects and properties for the Test Data Control form.

OBJECT	PROPERTY	SETTING
Form	Name	TestDataControl
	Caption	"Test Data Control"
ExpDetailControl	Name	expControl
	Caption	"Expense Control"
MaskEdBox	Name	mskAmountSpent
	Format	"$#,##0.00;($#,##0.00)"
	PromptChar	"_"
TextBox	Name	txtSubmitDate
TextBox	Name	txtPurchaseDate
TextBox	Name	txtDescription
TextBox	Name	txtExpenseType

OBJECT	PROPERTY	SETTING
TextBox	Name	txtEmployeeId
TextBox	Name	txtExpenseId
Label	Name	Label1
	Caption	"Expense ID:"
Label	Name	Label2
	Caption	"Employee:"
Label	Name	Label3
	Caption	"Expense Type:"
Label	Name	Label4
	Caption	"Amount Spent:"
Label	Name	Label5
	Caption	"Description:"
Label	Name	Label6
	Caption	"Purchase Date:"
Label	Name	Label7
	Caption	"Submission Date:"

28. Use the Visual Basic menu editor to create the menu shown in Table 12.18.

Table 12.18. Menu specifications for the Object Library form.

CAPTION	NAME	SHORTCUT KEY
&File	mnuFile	
----E&xit	mnuFileExit	

29. Add the following code to the **DataChanged** event for the expense user control. Whenever the control notifies the form that a change has been made, the helper routine updates the displayed values.

```
Private Sub expControl_DataChanged()

    ' The data has changed in the control, so update the form
    Call ReadObjectValues

End Sub
```

30. Add the `ReadObjectValues` helper routine to display the control's values:

```
Private Sub ReadObjectValues()
' Read the object values into the form fields

    txtExpenseId.Text = CStr(expControl.lngExpenseId)
    txtEmployeeId.Text = expControl.strEmployeeId
    txtExpenseType.Text = expControl.strExpenseType
    txtDescription.Text = expControl.strDescription
    mskAmountSpent.Text = CStr(expControl.curAmountSpent)
    txtPurchaseDate.Text = CStr(expControl.dtmDatePurchased)
    txtSubmitDate.Text = CStr(expControl.dtmDateSubmitted)

End Sub
```

31. Add the following code to the `Validate` event of the user expense control. The control raises this event when one of the data maintenance buttons is clicked. The error handler is needed to capture errors raised by the control's **Property Let** routines. The **Property Let** routines are called by `SetObjectValues`.

```
Private Sub expControl_ValidateData _
    (Response As ExpDetailControl.EXP_RESPONSE_TYPE, _
    ByVal Change As ExpDetailControl.EXP_CHANGE_TYPE)
' A command button has been pushed; update the control's
' data if needed

    On Error GoTo ValidateError

    Select Case Change
        Case expAddNewValidate, expUpdateValidate
            Call SetObjectValues
            Response = expOk
        Case expDeleteValidate
            Response = expOk
        Case Else
            Response = expCancel
    End Select

    Exit Sub
ValidateError:
    MsgBox Err.Description & " from " _
        & Err.Source & " -- " _
        & CStr(Err.Number)
    Response = expCancel
    Exit Sub

End Sub
```

32. Add the following helper routine to update the control's data values from the form fields:

```
Private Sub SetObjectValues()
' Sets related object values from form fields
```

```
        expControl.strExpenseType = txtExpenseType.Text
        expControl.strEmployeeId = txtEmployeeId.Text
        expControl.strDescription = txtDescription.Text
        expControl.dtmDatePurchased = txtPurchaseDate.Text
        expControl.curAmountSpent = CCur(mskAmountSpent.Text)

        Exit Sub

    End Sub
```

33. Add the following Form_Load procedure to initialize the control's recordset:

```
Private Sub Form_Load()
' Get the ActiveX object to open its database
    Dim strDbName As String
    Dim strResponse As String

    On Error GoTo LoadError

    strDbName = App.Path
    strDbName = strDbName & "\Expense.mdb"
    expControl.strDatabaseName = strDbName

    Exit Sub

LoadError:
    MsgBox Err.Description & Chr(13) & "from " & Err.Source _
            & " -- Number: " & CStr(Err.Number)
    Unload Me

End Sub
```

34. Add the following procedure to the mnuFileExit Click event to exit the program:

```
Private Sub mnuFileExit_Click()

    Unload Me

End Sub
```

How It Works

The hand-crafted data control works by encapsulating recordset movement commands and visual controls in a simple wrapper exposing the database name, two events, and the data value properties (fields). The control itself manages all recordset navigation and the screen interface buttons.

The control begins useful functions when the **strDatabaseName** property is set and the recordset is opened. The **strDatabaseName** property is created to be read-only at design time. Changing it at design time results in an error message being displayed in the development environment.

The control's constituent buttons provide the heart of the user control. Whenever a movement button is clicked, the recordset is moved to a valid record, and the **DataChanged** event is raised to cause the containing application to retrieve current field values from the control's property values. When a database maintenance button is clicked, the control raises the **ValidateData** event to allow the containing form to update the control's copy of the data and to perform any display operations before the database is changed.

The data values of the control are implemented in runtime only and are hidden from the design-time properties window of the container. The **strExpenseType** control raises a private error event to indicate an invalid type together with an explanatory message. The **Property Let** procedure was not implemented for the **lngExpenseId** property because it is assigned by the database when a new record is inserted in the database.

Constituent Controls

Constituent controls are preexisting ActiveX controls placed onto ActiveX controls being developed. In this How-To, frame and button constituent controls were placed onto the simple data control. The caption of the data control was visually displayed as the caption of the surrounding frame. Although we didn't use the technique here, it is possible to expose individual constituent control events as events of the control. For example, if we wanted to raise a **CommandFirstClick** event from the control when the constituent **cmdFirst** button click event occurred, we would declare a new event in the declarations section and add a **RaiseEvents** call in the button click event.

```
Option Explicit

Public Event CommandFirstClick()

Private Sub cmdFirst_Click()
' Move to the first record

' ... Useful, productive code

    ' Tell the container about the click
    RaiseEvent CommandFirstClick

End Sub
```

Debugging ActiveX Controls

Most of the debugging for an ActiveX control project can be accomplished with the simple project group approach shown in this How-To. Unfortunately, errors raised from **Property Let** procedures cannot be debugged in this way. Visual Basic seems to assume that all errors raised by the **Property Let** procedure must be handled by the Visual Basic End or Debug dialog box before the calling container gets a chance to handle the error. The workaround for this problem is to compile the control to its .OCX file and open just the test form's project from Visual Basic. Then the error will be trapped in the containing test form.

Comments

This control was built entirely by hand to illustrate the nuts and bolts of making a data control work within the ActiveX control environment. An ActiveX control skeleton can also be built quickly using the ActiveX Control Interface Wizard available as a Microsoft-supplied add-in to the Visual Basic 6 environment. The Wizard generates all the code required for managing most "standard" ActiveX properties and events, which were ignored in this How-To in the interest of keeping the core data control code more readable. You should use this add-in to develop robust controls that might receive wider distribution through your programming team or corporation.

You can also implement a specialized ActiveX data control function by placing a standard data control on an ActiveX control as a constituent control. This approach would certainly provide more rapid development than starting from button pasting, but at a potential cost in performance and complexity.

COMPLEXITY
INTERMEDIATE

12.11 How do I...
Create my own data bound control?

Problem

I've created a database table for providing code values for list boxes. How can I write a data-bound ActiveX list box control to quickly populate itself from the code value table and be data bound to a control on my form?

Technique

This How-To shows the creation of an enhanced combo box control that fills itself with allowed choices from a code value table contained in the application's database. The CodeValue.mdb database is located in the Chapter12\HowTo10 directory on the CD-ROM. The main Subject data table contains information on criminal suspects, and the Code10 table contains possible values for suspect attributes such as hair color and eye color. The table is called Code10 because it returns 10-character fields based on 10-character code types. Table 12.19 describes the suspect table, and Table 12.20 describes the Code10 table.

Table 12.19. The Suspect table.

FIELD
SuspectId
LastName
FirstName
MiddleName
Alias
EyeColor
HairClr
Religion
MaritalStatus

Table 12.20. The Code 10 table.

FIELD	DESCRIPTION
CodeType10	Type of code values to return—for example, HAIRCOLOR.
CodeValue10	Data value to populate in combo boxes for the code type—for example, Blond.
CodeDesc	Description of this particular type-value pair.

The new control will function almost the same as a standard combo box with the addition of a *code type* to load and an open database object to use for creating the recordset. The ActiveX Control Interface Wizard will write most of the code for this control based on its dialog inputs.

Steps

1. Open the project group TestBoundGroup.vbg and run the application. The form in Figure 12.24 appears. Become familiar with the application, especially the combo box behavior.

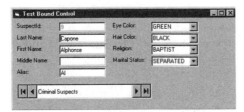

Figure 12.24. The Test Bound Control form.

2. Create a new ActiveX control project in your work area. Place a single ComboBox on the control and name it `cmbCodeValue`. Name the project `BoundComboControl` and the control `ctlBoundCombo`. Save the project.

3. Select Add-Ins|Add-In Manager from the main menu, and load the VB 6 ActiveX Ctrl Interface Wizard. Click OK to close the dialog box.

4. Select Add-Ins|ActiveX Control Interface Wizard from the main menu. Click Next to begin defining the `BoundComboControl` interface.

5. Declare the standard properties, events, and methods in the control's interface. Add the Change event from the Available names list to the Selected Names list by selecting Change on the left and clicking the > button. Similarly, add the `ListCount`, `ListIndex`, `Style`, and `Text` properties to the interface. Figure 12.25 shows the Select Interface Members dialog box. Click Next to proceed.

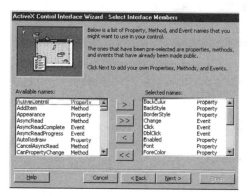

Figure 12.25. The ActiveX Control Interface Wizard - Select Interface Members dialog box.

6. Click New to add the properties, methods, and events listed in Table 12.21. Click Next to proceed.

Table 12.21. The properties and method for the Bound Combo control.

TYPE	NAME	DESCRIPTION
Property	objDatabase	Object variable to contain the open database object from which the combo box should be loaded.
Property	strCodeType	Value for code type to select—for example, HAIRCOLOR.
Method	Reload	Reloads the list box from the database.

7. Use the Set Mapping dialog box (see Figure 12.26) to map most of the public interface properties, methods, and events to the constituent combo box control. Select most of the public names from the lefthand list box and then select `cmbCodeValue` from the Control pull-down list. *Do not map the `objDatabase` and `strSqlWhere` properties nor the `Refresh` method.* Click Next to proceed.

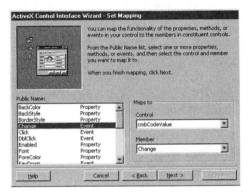

Figure 12.26. The Control Interface Wizard - Set Mapping dialog box.

8. Set the attributes of the unmapped interface members using the Set Attributes dialog box shown in Figure 12.27. The attribute values are shown in Table 12.22.

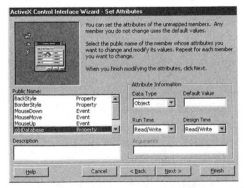

Figure 12.27. The Control Interface Wizard - Set Attributes dialog box.

Table 12.22. Members and properties for the Bound Combo control.

MEMBER	DATA TYPE	RUNTIME	DESIGN-TIME	DESCRIPTION
objDatabase	Object	Write Only	Not Avail.	Open database object supplied at runtime by container.
strCodeType	String	Read/Write	Read/Write	Code value type to retrieve.

9. Add the following code for the UserControl Resize event:

```
Private Sub UserControl_Resize()
' Resize the combo box to the size of the control

' The height can't be changed for certain styles, so
    ' we won't support any height changes.
    Height = cmbCodeValue.Height
    ' Resize the combo box without using the Move method.
    cmbCodeValue.Top = 0
    cmbCodeValue.Left = 0
    cmbCodeValue.Width = ScaleWidth

End Sub
```

10. Make the UserControl project by selecting File|Make BoundComboControl.ocx from the main menu. Correct any compilation errors you find before proceeding.

11. Select File|Add Project from the main menu. Select Standard EXE from the Add Project dialog box. Name the default form frmTestBoundCombo and the project prjTestBoundCombo. Save the project group and name the group TestBoundGroup when prompted.

12. Close the cmbBoundControl design window to activate the control in Design mode. Test the resize event code by resizing the control on the form.

13. Define the Text property to be a data-bound field on the form. Make the control's code the active window in Visual Basic by opening and clicking in the window. Select Tools|Procedure Attributes from the main menu, and select Text as the name. Click Advanced to show more options. Check all options in the Data Binding frame except Update immediate (see Figure 12.28).

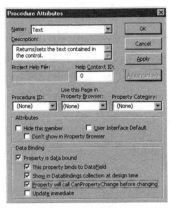

Figure 12.28. The
Procedure Attributes for
a data-bound property.

14. Modify the **Text Property Let** procedure to look like the following code.
The **CanPropertyChange** function asks the container whether the specified
value can be changed and the return value should be observed, even
though Visual Basic always returns **True**.

```
Public Property Let Text(ByVal New_Text As String)
    If CanPropertyChange("Text") Then
        cmbCodeValue.Text() = New_Text
        PropertyChanged "Text"
    End If
End Property
```

15. Add the following code to the **Change** event of **cmbDataBound** to make sure
that the container knows that something changed:

```
Private Sub cmbCodeValue_Change()

    ' Notify the container of data change
    PropertyChanged "Text"

End Sub
```

16. Add a **PropertyChanged** call to the **Click** event of **cmbDataBound**:

```
Private Sub cmbCodeValue_Click()
    RaiseEvent Click
    PropertyChanged "Text"
End Sub
```

17. Modify the wizard-generated **Reload** method to be a procedure (**Sub**)
rather than a function, and add the following code to fill the combo box:

```
Public Sub Reload()
' Reload the combo box
Dim strSql As String
Dim rsCodes As Recordset

    cmbCodeValue.Clear
    ' If the code type has been set
    If "" <> strCodeType Then
        ' Build a SQL statement.
        strSql = "SELECT CodeValue10 FROM Code10 WHERE " _
                    & "CodeType10 = '" & strCodeType _
                    & "' ORDER BY CodeValue10"
        'Get a recordset.
        Set rsCodes = objDatabase.OpenRecordset(strSql, _
                    vbRSTypeSnapShot, dbForwardOnly)
        Do While Not rsCodes.EOF
            ' Add the items.
            cmbCodeValue.AddItem "" & rsCodes("CodeValue10")
            rsCodes.MoveNext
        Loop
    End If

    'Close the recordset
    rsCodes.Close

    Exit Sub

End Sub
```

18. Modify the `objDatabase` Property Set routine to invoke the `Reload` method:

```
Public Property Set objDatabase(ByVal New_objDatabase As Object)

    Set m_objDatabase = New_objDatabase
    PropertyChanged "objDatabase"

    ' Set the object database and invoke the Reload method to
    ' put data into the combo box
    If "" <> strCodeType Then
        Call Reload
    End If

End Property
```

19. Finish building the `TestBoundControl` form by adding fields, labels, and a data control until it looks like Figure 12.29. Table 12.23 lists the form's objects and properties.

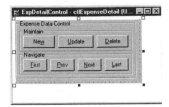

Figure 12.29. Layout for the TestBoundControl form.

Table 12.23. Objects and properties for the Test Bound Control form.

OBJECT	PROPERTY	SETTING
Form	Name	frmTestBoundCombo
	Caption	"Test Bound Control"
Data	Name	dtaSuspects
	Caption	"Criminal Suspects"
	Connect	"Access"
	DatabaseName	"C:\Code\Chapter12\Howto10\CodeValues.mdb"
	RecordSource	"Subject"
ctlBoundCombo	Name	usrEyeBound
	DataField	"EyeColor"
	DataSource	"dtaSuspects"
	strCodeType	"EYECOLOR"
ctlBoundCombo	Name	usrHairBound
	DataField	"HairClr"
	DataSource	"dtaSuspects"
	strCodeType	"HAIRCOLOR"
ctlBoundCombo	Name	usrReligionBound
	DataField	"Religion"
	DataSource	"dtaSuspects"
	strCodeType	"RELIGION"
ctlBoundCombo	Name	usrMarStatBound
	DataField	"MaritalStatus"
	DataSource	"dtaSuspects"
	strCodeType	"MAR STAT"
TextBox	Name	txtSuspectId
	DataField	"SuspectId"
	DataSource	"dtaSuspects"
	Enabled	0 'False
TextBox	Name	txtLastName

OBJECT	PROPERTY	SETTING
	DataField	"LastName"
	DataSource	"dtaSuspects"
TextBox	Name	txtFirstName
	DataField	"FirstName"
	DataSource	"dtaSuspects"
TextBox	Name	txtMiddleName
	DataField	"MiddleName"
	DataSource	"dtaSuspects"
TextBox	Name	txtAlias
	DataField	"Alias"
	DataSource	"dtaSuspects"
Label	Name	Label1
	AutoSize	-1 'True
	Caption	"SuspectId:"
Label	Name	Label2
	AutoSize	-1 'True
	Caption	"Last Name:"
Label	Name	Label3
	AutoSize	-1 'True
	Caption	"First Name:"
Label	Name	Label4
	AutoSize	-1 'True
	Caption	"Middle Name:"
Label	Name	Label5
	AutoSize	-1 'True
	Caption	"Alias:"
Label	Name	Label6
	AutoSize	-1 'True
	Caption	"Eye Color:"
Label	Name	Label7
	AutoSize	-1 'True
	Caption	"Hair Color:"
Label	Name	Label8
	AutoSize	-1 'True
	Caption	"Religion:"
Label	Name	Label9
	AutoSize	-1 'True
	Caption	"Marital Status:"

20. Add the following code to the **Form_Load** event:

```
Private Sub Form_Load()

    dtaSuspects.DatabaseName = App.Path & "\CodeValues.mdb"
    dtaSuspects.Refresh
    ' Initialize the bound combo controls
    Set usrEyeBound.objDatabase = dtaSuspects.Database
    Set usrHairBound.objDatabase = dtaSuspects.Database
    Set usrReligionBound.objDatabase = dtaSuspects.Database
    Set usrMarStatBound.objDatabase = dtaSuspects.Database

End Sub
```

How It Works

When the form loads, the **Set** statements for the bound combo boxes cause the combo boxes to be filled. Any time the combo box contents are changed by a click or change event, **PropertyChanged** is called to inform the containing form that a bound control has changed. The container, in turn, notifies the **dtaSuspects** data control. Most of the control code was generated by the ActiveX Control Interface Wizard to propagate constituent control properties to the bound control.

The ActiveX Interface Control Wizard provides a capable tool for building and extending your own component library. This bound combo box control for displaying code values runs faster than a **DBCombo** control and reduces the visual clutter of its containing form at design time. With a little more work, it could be extended to include a single property page to browse for the Code Types through design-time SQL statements, as well as setting the underlying combo box style.

Comments

The advantage of working with The ActiveX Interface Control Wizard is in the robustness and automated checklist it gives you in the creation of your control. The wizard reminds the developer about *all* the properties and methods of constituent controls in order to ensure that the properties and methods expected by a developer are seamlessly implemented into the control's behavior.

COMPLEXITY
BEGINNING

12.12 How do I...
Use the DataRepeater control with custom Data Bound controls?

Problem

I've created a custom data bound control for editing records in the corporate database, but the users want to be able to see and edit multiple records at the same time. How can I give them a multirecord view and still keep my code investment in the custom data bound control?

Technique

This How-To shows you how to use the DataRepeater control with your custom data bound control to create a multirecord view of the data. By keeping your existing custom data bound control, you reuse tested, working code and keep your business rules in one place. The DataRepeater control takes a bound control and repeats it like a list box of controls. Figure 12.30 shows a record set displayed with a DataRepeater and a custom data bound control.

Figure 12.30. The DataRepeater control.

Steps

1. Create a new ActiveX control project. Name the project RepeaterTestControl and the control ctlAddress. Save the project.

2. Add six text box controls and six labels to ctlAddress. Set the properties according to Table 12.24. Arrange the text boxes and labels so that your interface looks like Figure 12.31.

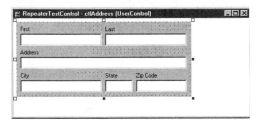

Figure 12.31. The layout for ctlAddress.

Table 12.24. Objects and properties for the ctlAddress control.

OBJECT	PROPERTY	SETTING
Text	Name	txtFirstName
	Text	""
Text	Name	txtLastName
	Text	""
Text	Name	txtAddress
	Text	""
Text	Name	txtCity
	Text	""
Text	Name	txtState
	Text	""
Text	Name	txtZip
	Text	""
Label	Name	lblFirstName
	Caption	"First Name"
Label	Name	lblLastName
	Caption	"Last Name"
Label	Name	lblAddress
	Caption	"Address"
Label	Name	lblCity
	Caption	"City"
Label	Name	lblState
	Caption	"State"
Label	Name	lblZip
	Caption	"Zip Code"

3. This control has a fixed size, so update the Resize event to match the following code. Depending on how you laid out the text boxes and labels, you may have to adjust the values for height and width.

```
Private Sub UserControl_Resize()
    If Height <> 2325 Then
        Height = 2325
    End If
    If Width <> 5445 Then
        Width = 5445
    End If
End Sub
```

4. Select Add-Ins | Add-In Manager from the main menu, and load the VB 6 ActiveX Ctrl Interface Wizard. Click OK to close the dialog box.

5. Select Add-Ins | ActiveX Control Interface Wizard from the main menu. Click Next to begin defining the **ctlAddress** interface.

6. Remove all the items from the Selected Names list and click next to proceed.

7. Use the New button to add six new custom properties: **FirstName**, **LastName**, **Address**, **City**, **State**, and **Zip**. Click the Next button to move to the Set Mapping screen.

8. For each of the new properties, map the property to the corresponding Text control's Text property. Figure 12.32 shows the Address property mapped to the txtAddress's Text property. Click Next and then click Finish to exit the ActiveX Control Interface Wizard.

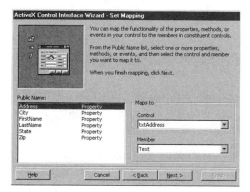

Figure 12.32. Mapping properties to constituent control properties.

9. Select Tools | Procedure Attributes to open the Procedure Attributes dialog box. Click the Advanced button to expose the entire dialog box. For the custom property added in the ActiveX Control Interface Wizard, choose the Property is Data Bound and Show in DataBindings Collection at Design Time options. Figure 12.33 shows the settings for the **Address** property. Click OK and save the project.

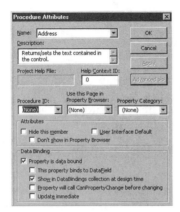

Figure 12.33. Setting the procedure attributes for the Address property.

10. Compile the RepeaterTestControl.OCX. ctlAddress is now a simple bound control for displaying a person's name and address.

11. Add a new Standard EXE project by selecting File | Add Project. Name the new project DataRepeaterTest.

12. Copy the Addresses.MDB file from the Chapter12\HowTo12 directory on the CD to the working directory of the project.

13. Select Project | Components to show the Components dialog box. Select Microsoft ADO Data Control 6.0 and Microsoft DataRepeater Control 6.0. Click OK to add the controls to your project.

14. Add a DataRepeater and ADO Data control to the default form. Set the properties according to Table 12.25.

Table 12.25. Objects and properties for the Data Repeater Test form.

OBJECT	PROPERTY	SETTING
Form	Name	frmDataRepeaterTest
	Caption	"Data Repeater How To"
DataRepeater	Name	datarepAddresses
	Caption	"Addresses"
	DataSource	adodcAddresses
	RepeatedControlName	RepeaterTestControl.ctlAddress
ADO Data Control	Name	adodcAddresses
	Caption	"Addresses"
	ConnectionString	"Provider=Microsoft.Jet.OLEDB.3.51;
		DataSource=Addresses.mdb"
RecordSource	"Addresses"	

15. Right-click the DataRepeater control and select DataRepeater Properties. Using the RepeaterBindings tab, match the PropertyNames with DataFields. First select the property in the PropertyName combo box and then select the field from the DataField combo box. Click the Add button to add the selections to the list. Do this for FirstName, LastName, Address, City, State, and Zip. This step binds the fields in the RecordSource of the ADO Data control to the bound fields of the ctlAddress. Click OK to change the properties.

How It Works

The aptly named DataRepeater control creates multiple instances of your custom bound control and shows them in a list style view. With this tool you can move a single record view to a multiple record view with little or no code change. This particular use of the DataRepeater allows the user to browse and edit a list of people and addresses in Addresses.mdb. To navigate through the list use the scrollbars on the DataRepeater or the classic data buttons on the ADO Data control.

Comments

The DataRepeater control can only be used with the ADO Data control; unfortunately, it doesn't work with the regular Data control or the RemoteData control. However, for existing applications, conversions should be fairly straightforward. ADO can access all the data sources available to the Data control and the RemoteData control.

CHAPTER 13

ADVANCED DATABASE TECHNIQUES

13

ADVANCED DATABASE TECHNIQUES

How do I...

13.1 Search for database records by using a Soundex algorithm?

13.2 Back up selected database objects at a set schedule?

13.3 Replicate a database by using the Jet engine?

13.4 Omit specified objects from replicas?

13.5 Create a nonreplicated version of a replicated database?

Many times, there's just one more thing that needs to be done for everything to work correctly. The How-To's in this chapter cover various advanced features of database programming that help polish your applications. The database back-up and replication features are particularly valuable because they can help you reduce support time and costs for your applications. A simple automated backup program in the Windows startup group can save hours of headaches after your application or customer has made a serious mistake.

13.1 Search for Database Records by Using a Soundex Algorithm

The Soundex feature available in many database management systems (DBMS) enables you to search for names of people, places, or streets without knowing the exact spelling. This How-To demonstrates using the Soundex function and points out some common problems with its use.

13.2 Back Up Selected Database Objects at a Set Schedule

The `SQL SELECT...INTO` statement provides a smooth way to perform a very selective online backup. This How-To uses an enhanced ActiveX timer control to periodically back-up selected database objects.

13.3 Replicate a Database by Using the Jet Engine

Access and the Jet engine enable you to copy databases and keep their contents synchronized in different locations. This How-To demonstrates creating and synchronizing a replicated database.

13.4 Omit Specified Objects from Replicas

By default, replication makes copies of everything in your database. This How-To demonstrates keeping some objects local when making a replica set.

13.5 Create a Nonreplicated Version of a Replicated Database

Strictly speaking, you cannot make a nonreplicated version of a replicated database, but you can remove a replica from the replica set and change the replica so that its structure can be modified. This How-To changes a replica database into a standalone database.

COMPLEXITY
BEGINNING

13.1 How do I...
Search for database records by using a Soundex algorithm?

Problem

The people answering the telephones in the order entry department sometimes have a difficult time understanding the names of individuals who call in. How can I write more forgiving SQL queries to look up names?

Technique

This How-To uses the Soundex function of Microsoft SQL Server. The sample SQL statements should also work with Sybase databases. Soundex is an encoding method for converting character strings into four digit codes. The goal is to provide a fuzzier search pattern for people trying find name-based data.

Steps

1. Connect to a SQL database from your workstation using a SQL command processor such as ISQL/W.

2. Issue the following commands to set up a test environment and open the file SOUNDEX.SQL from the How-To directory:

```
if exists (select * from sysobjects
    where id = object_id('dbo.SoundexText') and sysstat & 0xf = 3)
    drop table dbo.SoundexTest
GO

CREATE TABLE dbo.SoundexTest (
    LastName char (20) NULL ,
    FirstName char (20) NULL
)
GO

INSERT INTO SoundexTest VALUES ('Brown', 'Laura')
INSERT INTO SoundexTest VALUES ('Browne', 'Laura')
INSERT INTO SoundexTest VALUES ('Brun', 'Laura')
INSERT INTO SoundexTest VALUES ('Braun', 'Laura')
INSERT INTO SoundexTest VALUES ('Broom', 'Laura')

INSERT INTO SoundexTest VALUES ('Harper', 'Bill');
INSERT INTO SoundexTest VALUES ('Harpster', 'Bill');
INSERT INTO SoundexTest VALUES ('Hahpah', 'Bill');
INSERT INTO SoundexTest VALUES ('Hobber', 'Bill');
INSERT INTO SoundexTest VALUES ('Hopper', 'Bill');
INSERT INTO SoundexTest VALUES ('Hooper', 'Bill');

INSERT INTO SoundexTest VALUES ('Kennedy', 'Dennis');
INSERT INTO SoundexTest VALUES ('Kenney', 'Dennis');
INSERT INTO SoundexTest VALUES ('Kennealy', 'Dennis');
INSERT INTO SoundexTest VALUES ('Kenney', 'Dennis');
```

3. Issue the following **SELECT** statement to verify that all rows were inserted into the database. All rows should be retrieved and displayed as in Table 13.1.

```
SELECT * FROM SoundexTest ORDER BY LastName, FirstName
```

Table 13.1. *SELECT* all rows results.

LAST NAME	FIRST NAME
Braun	Laura
Broom	Laura
Brown	Laura
Browne	Laura
Brun	Laura
Hahpah	Bill
Harper	Bill
Harpster	Bill
Hobber	Bill
Hooper	Bill
Hopper	Bill
Kennealy	Dennis
Kennedy	Dennis
Kenney	Dennis
Kenney	Dennis

4. Issue a **SOUNDEX SELECT** to find *Brown*. Table 13.2 shows all five Laura's.

```
SELECT * FROM SoundexTest
WHERE SOUNDEX (LastName) = SOUNDEX ('Brown')
ORDER BY LastName, FirstName
```

Table 13.2. *SELECT SOUNDEX ('Brown')* results.

LAST NAME	FIRST NAME
Braun	Laura
Broom	Laura
Brown	Laura
Browne	Laura
Brun	Laura

5. Use Soundex to find the various Harper records. Table 13.3 shows the results for various search targets.

```
SELECT * FROM SoundexTest
WHERE SOUNDEX (LastName) = SOUNDEX ('Harper')
ORDER BY LastName, FirstName

SELECT * FROM SoundexTest
```

```
WHERE SOUNDEX (LastName) = SOUNDEX ('Harp')
ORDER BY LastName, FirstName

SELECT * FROM SoundexTest
WHERE SOUNDEX (LastName) = SOUNDEX ('Hopper')
ORDER BY LastName, FirstName
```

Table 13.3. *SELECT SOUNDEX* results with different keys.

TARGET	LAST NAME	FIRST NAME
Harper	Harper	Bill
Harp	No records returned	
Hopper	Hobber	Bill
	Hooper	Bill
	Hopper	Bill

How It Works

The Soundex algorithm was established by the United States government to provide name searching for the Social Security Administration and the National Archives. The Soundex code is created by taking the first letter of the string and then adding values according to Table 13.4.

Table 13.4. Soundex coding guide.

CODE DIGIT	LETTER
0	All others or word too short
1	B, P, F, V
2	C, S, G, J, K, Q, X, Z
3	D, T
4	L
5	M, N
6	R

Table 13.5 shows the generated Soundex code and the last name for the sample data. Usually, Soundex will give a reasonable result, but it can make some interesting mistakes if the R is missed in a query. Notice in particular that the Soundex for *Harper* and *Hopper* don't match. Soundex can also be problematic if too few letters are provided for coding. Because all vowels and the silent letters H, Y, and W are dropped from the coding digits, a Soundex search for *BR* will not return any of our *B* names.

Table 13.5. Soundex coding results.

SOUNDEX CODE	LAST NAME
B650	Brown
B650	Browne
B650	Brun
B650	Braun
B650	Broom
H616	Harper
H612	Harpster
H100	Hahpah
H160	Hopper
H160	Hobber
H160	Hooper
K530	Kennedy
K500	Kenney
K540	Kennealy

Comments

This sample showed a way to use the SOUNDEX function in queries. Unfortunately, these SELECT statements are very inefficient because they force the database manager to examine each row of the table. If SOUNDEX makes sense for your application, try to create a column whose value is the SOUNDEX of the target column, and then create an index on the SOUNDEX column.

COMPLEXITY
INTERMEDIATE

13.2 How do I...
Back up selected database objects at a set schedule?

Problem

There are several tables in my database that need to be automatically backed up periodically. How can I force an automatic backup on a periodic basis?

Technique

The solution to this problem requires two core components: an enhanced timer and a database backup routine. The enhanced timer will be implemented as an ActiveX control that supports a "time to trigger" property and notification event.

The database backup routine will create a new database and use a SELECT...INTO statement to implement the selective backup. The remainder of the project is a test form.

The extended timer control is required because the standard Visual Basic control only supports timers of approximately one minute in length. The extended timer control is driven by the `TimeToTrigger` property and will raise its `ExtendedTimerPop` event once per day at the specified time. The standard Visual Basic timer is used repeatedly and enabled until the time to trigger is within one minute of the current time. Then the Visual Basic timer is set to the precise number of seconds required to meet the `TimeToTrigger` property exactly.

Steps

Open the Backup.vbg project group to preview this project. Compile the enhanced timer control and then the Backup Test project. Run the Backup Test project (see Figure 13.1). Enter a near future time in the Trigger Time field and click the Start Timer button. Wait patiently until your system clock is one minute past the trigger time. Close the form and check in the application directory for a newly created backup copy of the Expense.MDB file whose name begins with the letters *BU* (for backup).

Figure 13.1. The Backup
Test Form dialog box.

1. Create a new ActiveX Control project. Name the control `ctlEnhancedTimer` and the project `prjEnhancedTimer`.

2. Select the `ctlEnhancedTimer` control and set its `InvisibleAtRunTime` property to true.

3. Draw a single timer control on the object and name it `tmrCheckIt`. Save the project.

4. Select Add-Ins|Add-In Manager from the main menu and make sure that the VB 6 ActiveX Ctrl Interface Wizard is available in your environment by selecting it and checking Loaded/Unloaded in the Load Behavior frame. Select Add-Ins|ActiveX Control Interface Wizard from the main menu.

5. Click the Next button to proceed to the Select Interface Members dialog box (see Figure 13.2). Remove all names except the enabled property from the Selected Names window on the right.

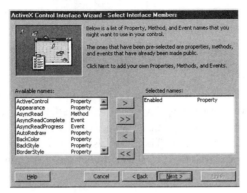

Figure 13.2. The Select Interface
Members dialog box.

6. Click Next to proceed to Create Custom Interface Members. Add the
single property and event listed in Table 13.6 to the control.

Table 13.6. Properties, methods, and events for the extended timer
control.

TYPE	NAME	DESCRIPTION
Property	TimeToTrigger	Date/Time variable to contain the desired trigger time for timer.
Event	ExtendedTimerPop	Notifies the container that the TimeToTrigger has arrived.

7. Click Next to proceed to the wizard's Set Mapping dialog box. Select the
public name Enabled and map it to the timer control's Enabled member, as
shown in Figure 13.3.

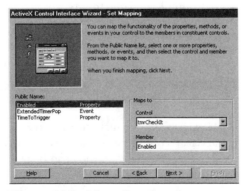

Figure 13.3. Mapping the timer
control member.

8. Click Next to set attributes for the extended timer control. Use the wizard's dialog box to set the `TimeToTrigger` property to be a Date variable with Read/Write capabilities at both runtime and design time.

9. Click Finish to have the wizard complete the skeleton code.

10. Add a Boolean to control variable to the Declarations section of the user control. This variable determines whether the last internal timer has been set for final event notification to the container.

```
Option Explicit
'Default Property Values:
Const m_def_TimeToTrigger = 0
'Property Variables:
Dim m_TimeToTrigger As Date
'Event Declarations:
Event ExtendedTimerPop()


' Private control variable
Private m_bLastInternalTimer As Boolean
```

11. Add the `SetTimer` helper procedure to set the internal timer control's interval property:

```
Private Function SetTimer() As Integer
' Determine if this is should be the last internal
' timer call
    Dim lDifference As Long

    lDifference = DateDiff("s", TimeValue(Now()), _
                     TimeValue(TimeToTrigger))
    If lDifference < 30 And lDifference > 0 Then
        ' This is the last timer to use
        m_bLastInternalTimer = True
        SetTimer = CInt(lDifference) * 1000
    Else
        ' Set timer for 30 more seconds
        m_bLastInternalTimer = False
        SetTimer = 30000
    End If

End Function
```

12. Add the following code to the timer event of the contained timer to implement a continuous, event-fired loop to achieve the desired long timer:

```
Private Sub tmrCheckIt_Timer()
' Handle the internal timer pop

    If m_bLastInternalTimer Then
        ' Notify the container
        tmrCheckIt.Enabled = False
        RaiseEvent ExtendedTimerPop
    Else
```

continued on next page

continued from previous page

```
                ' Wait a while longer
                tmrCheckIt.Interval = SetTimer()
                tmrCheckIt.Enabled = True
            End If

        End Sub
```

13. Add the following boldface code to the `UserControl_InitProperties` procedure to set the initial timer value:

```
Private Sub UserControl_InitProperties()
' Set up the timer variables

    ' Set the timer
    If Ambient.UserMode = True Then
        tmrCheckIt.Interval = SetTimer()
    End If

    m_TimeToTrigger = m_def_TimeToTrigger

End Sub
```

14. Add the following boldface code to the `Property Let Enabled` procedure. The interval must be set correctly for the container to enable the extended timer control at runtime.

```
Public Property Let Enabled(ByVal New_Enabled As Boolean)
    If Ambient.UserMode = True Then
        tmrCheckIt.Interval = SetTimer()
    End If
    tmrCheckIt.Enabled() = New_Enabled
    PropertyChanged "Enabled"
End Property
```

15. Add the following code to the `Property Let TimeToTrigger` procedure. The check for a valid date is required to prevent invalid calculations.

```
Public Property Let TimeToTrigger(ByVal New_TimeToTrigger As Date)

    ' Check that the new value is a valid date.
    If Not IsDate(New_TimeToTrigger) Then
        Err.Raise 380
        Err.Clear
        Exit Property
    End If

    m_TimeToTrigger = New_TimeToTrigger
    PropertyChanged "TimeToTrigger"
End Property
```

16. Add the following code to the `UserControl_Resize` procedure to keep the control approximately the same size as the timer control:

```
Private Sub UserControl_Resize()
' Resize the user control to a fixed size
```

```
          Size 420, 420

     End Sub
```

17. Select File | Make EnhancedTimer.ocx from the Visual Basic main menu to compile the control. Correct any compilation errors.

18. Select File | Add Project from the main menu and add a new Standard EXE project to your Visual Basic environment. Name the default form `frmBackupTest`. Name the new project `prjBackupTest`. Save the project group and all its components. Name the project group `Backup` when prompted.

19. Test the design-time behavior of the control by drawing the control on the form and experimenting with resizing the control.

20. Add a text box, label, and command button to the test form and set the properties as listed in Table 13.7.

Table 13.7. Objects and properties for the Backup Test form.

OBJECT	PROPERTY	SETTING
Form	Name	frmBackupTest
	Caption	Backup Test Form
CommandButton	Name	cmdStartTimer
	Caption	&Start Timer
TextBox	Name	txtTriggerTime
ctlEnhancedTimer	Name	ctlEnhancedTimer1
Label	Name	Label1
	AutoSize	-1 'True
	Caption	Trigger Time:

21. Add the following code to the `cmdStartTimer_Click` procedure to set the time to trigger and to enable the control:

```
Private Sub cmdStartTimer_Click()
' Start the timer

    If Not IsDate(txtTriggerTime.Text) Then
        MsgBox "Invalid time format"
    Else
        ctlEnhancedTimer1.TimeToTrigger = txtTriggerTime.Text
        ctlEnhancedTimer1.Enabled = True
    End If

End Sub
```

22. Add the following code to the `ctlEnhancedTimer1_ExtendedTimerPop` procedure to allow for control testing before beginning on the database backup code:

```
Private Sub ctlEnhancedTimer1_ExtendedTimerPop()

    Debug.Print "Extended timer pop"

End Sub
```

23. Compile and test the form. Be sure to save the project group.

24. In the project group window, make the **prjBackupTest** project active by highlighting it with the mouse. Select Project | Add Class Module from the Visual Basic main menu. When the Add Class Module dialog box appears, as in Figure 13.4, select VBCLASS.

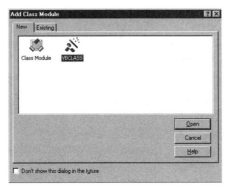

Figure 13.4. The Add Class Module dialog box.

25. Select File | New Class from the Class Builder menu. Name the class **clsBackupTable** and click OK.

26. Highlight **clsBackupTable** in the Class Builder Classes window. Add the properties listed in Table 13.8 to the class by selecting File | New Property from the Class Builder menu or by right-clicking in the properties tab. Figure 13.5 shows the completed Properties tab.

Table 13.8. Properties for the *clsBackupTable* module.

NAME	DATA TYPE	DECLARATION
TableName	String	Public Property
DatabaseObject	Object	Public Property

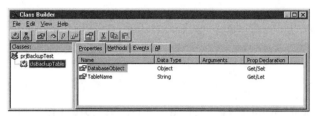

Figure 13.5. The completed Properties tab for
clsBackupTable.

27. Click on the Class Builder Methods tab. Add a new method by selecting
File | New method from the Class Builder menu or by right-clicking on the
Methods tab. Name the method **DoBackup** and give it no arguments and
no return data type.

28. Exit from Class Builder by selecting File | Exit from the menu. Update the
project with your changes. Save the project group.

29. Add a reference to Data Access Objects by selecting Project | References
from the Visual Basic main menu and checking Microsoft DAO 3.51
Object Library. Click OK to close the dialog box.

30. Add the following code to the **DoBackup** procedure to actually implement
the table backup by creating a new .MDB file and copying the data:

```
Public Sub DoBackup()
Dim strDbName As String, strSql As String
Dim dbNew As Database

    On Error GoTo DbError
    ' Format a database name from the current time
    strDbName = Format(Now, "Buyyyymmmddhhnnss") & ".mdb"
    strDbName = App.Path & "\" & strDbName
    ' Make sure there isn't already a file with the name of
    ' the new database.
    If Dir(strDbName) <> "" Then Kill strDbName

    ' Create the new database
    Set dbNew = Workspaces(0).CreateDatabase(strDbName, _
            dbLangGeneral)
    ' Create a SQL command string to create the backup
    strSql = "SELECT " & TableName & ".* INTO " _
            & TableName & " IN '" & strDbName _
            & "' FROM " & TableName
    mvarDatabaseObject.Execute strSql

    Exit Sub

DbError:
```

continued on next page

continued from previous page

```
        Err.Raise Err.Number, Err.Source, Err.Description
        Err.Clear
        Exit Sub

End Sub
```

31. Add the following declarations to the **frmBackupTest** form. These variables are required for the backup class.

```
Option Explicit

Private usrBackupTable As New clsBackupTable
Private dbOpenDb As Database
```

32. Add a **Form_Load** procedure to initialize the backup class:

```
Private Sub Form_Load()
Dim strDbName As String

    On Error GoTo DbError
    strDbName = App.Path & "\Expense.mdb"
    ' Open a database for the Backup class to use
    Set dbOpenDb = Workspaces(0).OpenDatabase(strDbName)
    Set usrBackupTable.Database = dbOpenDb
    usrBackupTable.TableName = "Expenses"
    Exit Sub

DbError:
    MsgBox Err.Description & " from " & Err.Source _
        & " Number = " & CStr(Err.Number)
    End

End Sub
```

33. Complete the **ctlEnhancedTimer1_ExtendedTimerPop** procedure by adding an invocation of the **DoBackup** procedure. Don't forget the error handler.

```
Private Sub ctlEnhancedTimer1_ExtendedTimerPop()

    On Error GoTo BackupError

    Debug.Print "Extended timer pop"
    usrBackupTable.DoBackup
    ' Restart the timer
    ctlEnhancedTimer1.Enabled = True
    Exit Sub

BackupError:
    MsgBox Err.Description & " from " & Err.Source _
        & " Number = " & CStr(Err.Number)
    Exit Sub

End Sub
```

How It Works

The first half of this How-To focuses on creating a timer control to support the backup application. In this case, the standard timer control does not provide the functionality needed to wake up at a specific time. This control's timeliness can be attributed to the SetTimer function specified in step 11. Every thirty seconds the control wakes up and checks to see how soon it should fire its event. If there is less than 30 seconds, the internal timer is adjusted to exactly the amount of time needed so that it wakes up on time.

On the application side of the How-To, a backup class handles the work of backing up a table. When the timer pops, the `clsBackupTable`'s `DoBackup` method is invoked, and the timer is restarted. The `Form_Load` procedure initializes the backup class, and the button click starts the timer.

Comments

In addition to solving a particular problem, this How-To demonstrated the use of component programming to promote code reuse. The `BackupTable` class can have many uses outside of this project, especially if it was modified to allow multiple table names instead of just one. A variation on the `BackupTable` class could also be used in programs placed in the Windows Startup program group to provide an automatic backup every time Windows is restarted.

The enhanced timer control can simplify many aspects of your current timer programs because is works reliably for more than a minute. You might want to consider adding a schedule table to the enhanced timer control to allow for multiple events or a schedule such as daily, weekly, or monthly.

COMPLEXITY
INTERMEDIATE

13.3 How do I...
Replicate a database by using the Jet engine?

Problem

The sales representatives in our company like to enter their expense reports on their laptop computers. How can I capture the expenses they enter in the field into the main expense database file?

Technique

Jet database replication enables you to create database copies and keep them synchronized. Both database design and contents are copied whenever the databases are synchronized. Replication creation requires that you make one database your Design Master and then invoke the `MakeReplica` method to create additional database copies. Use the `Synchronize` method to make the data consistent between two databases.

Steps

Open the project Replicate.vbp. Use the Browse buttons and select a source and replica database name (see Figure 13.6). Choose a database that can be modified; this How-To will make extensive changes. Click Create Replica to create a replica database. Use the VisData data maintenance utility (in the VB6 directory) to change a record in one of the databases. Click Synchronize. Use VisData to verify the change was propagated to the other database.

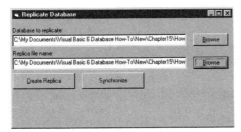

Figure 13.6. The Replicate Database form.

1. Create a new Standard EXE project in your workspace. Name the default form frmReplicate and the project prjReplicate. Save the form and project to disk.

2. Select Project | Components from the main menu and check Microsoft Common Dialog Control 6.0 (see Figure 13.7). Select Project | References from the Visual Basic main menu and activate the Microsoft DAO 3.51 Object Library by checking its box in the selection list.

3. Draw text boxes, labels, command buttons, and a Common Dialog control on the form as shown in Figure 13.6. Set the form's objects and properties as listed in Table 13.9.

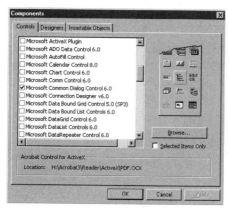

Figure 13.7. Selecting the Microsoft Common Dialog Control 6.0.

Table 13.9. Objects and properties for the Replicate Database form.

OBJECT	PROPERTY	SETTING
Form	Name	frmReplicate
	Caption	Replicate Database
CommandButton	Name	cmdOpenTo
	Caption	&Browse
CommandButton	Name	cmdSynchronize
	Caption	S&ynchronize
CommandButton	Name	cmdCreateReplica
	Caption	&Create Replica
CommandButton	Name	cmdOpenFrom
	Caption	&Browse
TextBox	Name	txtReplicaDbName
TextBox	Name	txtDbNameFrom
CommonDialog	Name	cdOpenFile
	Filter	Access Files (*.mdb)¦*.mdb
Label	Name	Label1
	AutoSize	-1 'True
	Caption	Database to replicate:
Label	Name	Label2
	AutoSize	-1 'True
	Caption	Replica file name:

4. Add the following code to the Browse button procedures:

```
Private Sub cmdOpenFrom_Click()
' Open the Replicate from database file
    cdOpenFile.InitDir = App.Path
    cdOpenFile.ShowOpen
    txtDbNameFrom.Text = cdOpenFile.filename

End Sub

Private Sub cmdOpenTo_Click()
' Open the Replicate to database file
    cdOpenFile.InitDir = App.Path
    cdOpenFile.filename = "Replica.mdb"
    cdOpenFile.ShowOpen
    txtReplicaDbName.Text = cdOpenFile.filename

End Sub
```

5. Add the `MakeReplicable` procedure to the form's code. This procedure checks for the existence of the `Replicable` property, adds it, if needed, and sets the value to `T` to make the `from` database a Design Master.

```
Function MakeReplicable(ByRef dbMaster As Database) As Boolean
' Makes the passed database replicable
Dim prpReplicable As Property
Dim intIdx As Integer
Dim bFound As Boolean

    On Error GoTo DbError

    ' Check for existence of the replicable property
    For intIdx = 0 To (dbMaster.Properties.Count - 1)
        If dbMaster.Properties(intIdx).Name = "Replicable" Then
            bFound = True
            Exit For
        End If
    Next

    If Not bFound Then
        ' Create the property
        Set prpReplicable = dbMaster.CreateProperty( _
            "Replicable", dbText, "T")
        ' Append it to the collection
        dbMaster.Properties.Append prpReplicable
    End If

    ' Set the value of Replicable to true.
    dbMaster.Properties("Replicable").Value = "T"

    MakeReplicable = True

    Exit Function

DbError:
```

```
        MsgBox Err.Description & " From: " & Err.Source _
                & "Number: " & Err.Number
        MakeReplicable = False
        Exit Function

    End Function
```

6. Add the `CopyReplica` helper function. This function actually creates a replica database using the `from` database as a source.

```
Function CopyReplica(ByRef dbMaster As Database, strRepName As _
    String) As Boolean
' Makes a replica database from the passed master

    On Error GoTo DbError

    ' If the target file exists, purge it
    If Dir(strRepName) <> "" Then Kill strRepName

    dbMaster.MakeReplica strRepName, "Replica of " & dbMaster.Name

    CopyReplica = True

    Exit Function

DbError:
    MsgBox Err.Description & " From: " & Err.Source _
            & "Number: " & Err.Number
    CopyReplica = False
    Exit Function

End Function
```

7. Add the following code to the `cmdCreateReplica_Click` procedure. This procedure gains exclusive control of the database, makes it a Design Master, and creates the specified replica. The `bContinue` Boolean prevents proceeding past an error.

```
Private Sub cmdCreateReplica_Click()
' Create a replica from the named database
Dim dbMaster As Database
Dim bContinue As Boolean

    On Error GoTo DbError

    ' Open the database in exclusive mode
    Set dbMaster = Workspaces(0).OpenDatabase(txtDbNameFrom.Text _
        True)

    ' Make the database the Design Master
    bContinue = MakeReplicable(dbMaster)

    ' Make the replica
    bContinue = CopyReplica(dbMaster, txtReplicaDbName.Text)
```

continued on next page

continued from previous page

```
        dbMaster.Close

        Exit Sub

    DbError:
        MsgBox Err.Description & " From: " & Err.Source _
                & "Number: " & Err.Number
        Exit Sub

    End Sub
```

8. Add the code for the **cmdSynchronize_Click** procedure. This procedure synchronizes the contents of two databases in the same replica set.

```
Private Sub cmdSynchronize_Click()

Dim dbMaster As Database

    On Error GoTo DbError

    ' Open the database in non-exclusive mode
    Set dbMaster = Workspaces(0).OpenDatabase(txtDbNameFrom.Text _
        False)

    ' Synchronize the databases
    dbMaster.Synchronize txtReplicaDbName.Text, _
                    dbRepImpExpChanges

    dbMaster.Close

    Exit Sub

DbError:
    MsgBox Err.Description & " From: " & Err.Source _
            & "Number: " & Err.Number
    Exit Sub

End Sub
```

How It Works

When you replicate databases, Jet modifies the database properties and the structure of your tables substantially in order to track record and design changes. The **Synchronize** method uses these additional structures to track database design and data changes and apply the changes consistently over many databases.

The core concept of replication is the replica set governed by a single Design Master database. The Design Master is the place where all design changes must occur for all replicas. A database is a member of a replica set if it was created as a replica of the Design Master or as a replica of an existing replica. Any member of the replica set may synchronize data with any other member of the replica set. Figure 13.8 shows the basic relationships.

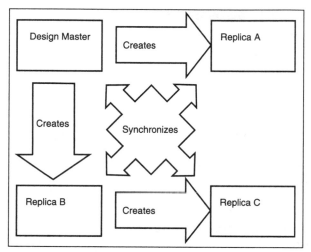

Figure 13.8. Replica set showing creation and synchronization.

Database Modifications

Jet makes several database modifications when you make a database replicable. When these changes are made, most of them are permanent.

The new database properties are `Replicable`, `ReplicaID`, and `DesignMasterID`. The `Replicable` property indicates that the database can be replicated and that the table structures have been modified. Once a database has been made replicable with the addition of the `Replicable` property, the `ReplicaID` is a unique identifier for this database file.

The `DesignMasterID` is a unique identifier specifying the database that can initiate all design changes for the replica set. Jet replication uses GUIDs (globally unique identifiers) wherever it needs a unique key for a database or field value. A *GUID* is a 16-byte generated value designed to be unique no matter where or when it is assigned. GUID values are usually displayed in hexadecimal notation with added hyphens for visual clarity. The database that is the Design Master has the same values for `ReplicaID` and `DesignMasterID`. Figure 13.9 shows the important database properties for a Design Master database as viewed by VisData application that ships with Visual Basic. Figure 13.10 shows the same properties for a replica. Note that the `DesignMasterID` GUID is the same as the `ReplicaID` GUID for the Design Master database. The replica database in Figure 13.10 has the `ReplicaID` of the Design Master database as its `DesignMasterID`. Equal values for `ReplicaID` and `DesignMasterID` are what define a database as a Design Master.

Figure 13.9. Database properties for a Design Master.

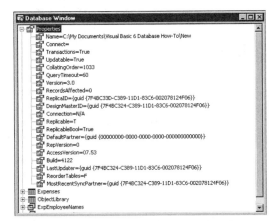

Figure 13.10. Database properties for a replica.

In addition to database property changes, making a database replicable adds about a dozen system tables to the database to track the Design Master, other replicas, table aliases, schema design problems, synchronization system errors, local replica-to-replica exchange logs, data conflicts, schedules, deleted records, and generation history. Because of all the property and system table changes, making a database replicable is a permanent operation. After the `Replicable` database property is set to `T`, it cannot be changed.

Table Modifications

In addition to database modifications, replication changes the table structures by adding three columns: a unique identifier, a generation identifier, and a lineage indicator. The unique identifier is stored in the s_GUID column and contains a globally unique identifier for this record in any replica.

The generation identifier is used to speed up incremental synchronization so that only changed records need to be sent to other replicas. Each time a record is changed, the generation number is set to zero. At synchronization time, all records with generation number zero are sent. The generation number is then set at both databases to one higher than the last generation number assigned. In addition, records with higher generation numbers are sent because they reflect more recent changes. Record additions and deletions are also reconciled between the two databases.

The lineage indicator is used to help resolve conflicts between simultaneous updates to data in different databases. When the same record is updated in two different replicas, a conflict can result. The Synchronize method resolves this conflict by using the s_Lineage field to determine which record will be placed into both databases. The losing database will have a copy of the losing record in a table named *table_name*_Conflict, where *table_name* is the original table name. For example, a conflict-losing record from the Expenses table would be saved at the losing location only into the Expenses_Conflict table.

Comments

Replication is a powerful tool in your database programming kit, but will require careful planning to implement successfully. Design considerations for replicated databases can become problematic because of our friend Murphy, whose famous law states, "If anything can go wrong, it will go wrong and at the worst possible time." I believe that Murphy might have been an optimist when it comes to complex replication schemes. Microsoft's core replication technology does a marvelous job of managing *one-way* replication. *One-way* implies that the data will be changed in only one location. With central administration, one-way data is the contents of list boxes, zip code tables, and product definitions that you want to push out to field laptops. For data collection, *one-way* means that a central site is collecting from multiple remote sites.

Two-way replication increases programming requirements because of the need to design and develop conflict-resolution programs and procedures. The placement of conflict losing records into only one database may make it difficult to implement conflict resolution programs in the desired location. For example, a sales automation application may want all conflict resolutions managed at the home office, but the Synchronize method might place a conflict notification into a sales rep's laptop in East Podunk. Hand-crafted code may then be required to find the remote conflicts and transport them back to the home office. One way to avoid conflicts is to use one-way replication only and separate tables into databases, depending on direction of data movement.

In addition to the synchronization itself, you should consider carefully your approach to how and when you plan to compact databases and run the RepairDatabase method. Compaction physically removes all deleted records from the database and assists with compaction of the generations of tables whose designs have changed. The `RepairDatabase` method inspects all system areas and tables for correctness and discards any incorrect data. A database that was open for write operations during a power failure or system crash can be left in a possibly corrupt state that should be repaired by the `RepairDatabase` method.

COMPLEXITY
INTERMEDIATE

13.4 How do I...
Omit specified objects from replicas?

Problem

Replication is working great for my data collection application, but the experimental tables in the Design Master database keep getting replicated to the field. How can I omit undesired objects from the replicas?

Technique

The Jet `KeepLocal` property was designed to prevent database objects from being propagated during replication. Just set value `KeepLocal` to `T` in the database's property collection, and the object won't be replicated.

Steps

Open the project Replicate.vbp in the How-To04 directory (refer to Figure 13.06). Use the Browse buttons and select Expenses.mdb as the master database name and Replica.mdb as the replica database name. Click Create Replica to create a replica database. Use the VisData data maintenance utility (in the VB6 directory) to inspect the structures of the original and replica databases to verify that the replica contains only the Expenses table.

1. Start with the completed form from How-To 13.3.

2. Add the `SetKeepLocal` helper function to the form's code:

```
Function SetKeepLocal(dbTarget As Database, strCollName _
    As String, strObjectName As String) As Boolean
' Sets KeepLocal to "T" for the passed object.

    Dim intIdx As Integer
    Dim blnFound As Boolean
    Dim tdfTableDef As TableDef
    Dim prpProperty As Property
    Dim docDocument As Document
    Dim qdfQueryDef As QueryDef
```

```
On Error GoTo ErrorHandler

Select Case strCollName

    Case "Forms", "Reports", "Modules", "Scripts"
        Set docDocument = dbTarget.Containers(strCollName). _
            Documents(strObjectName)
        blnFound = False
        For intIdx = 0 To docDocument.Properties.Count - 1
            If docDocument.Properties(intIdx).Name _
            = "KeepLocal" Then
                blnFound = True
                Exit For
            End If
        Next intIdx
        If Not blnFound Then
            Set prpProperty = docDocument.CreateProperty _
                ("KeepLocal", dbText, "T")
            docDocument.Properties.Append prpProperty
        Else
            docDocument.Properties("KeepLocal").Value = "T"
        End If

    Case "TableDefs"
        Set tdfTableDef = dbTarget.TableDefs(strObjectName)
        blnFound = False
        For intIdx = 0 To tdfTableDef.Properties.Count - 1
            If tdfTableDef.Properties(intIdx).Name _
            = "KeepLocal" Then
                blnFound = True
                Exit For
            End If
        Next intIdx
        If Not blnFound Then
            Set prpProperty = tdfTableDef.CreateProperty _
                ("KeepLocal", dbText, "T")
            tdfTableDef.Properties.Append prpProperty
        Else
            tdfTableDef.Properties("KeepLocal").Value = "T"
        End If

    Case "QueryDefs"
        Set qdfQueryDef = dbTarget.QueryDefs(strObjectName)
        blnFound = False
        For intIdx = 0 To qdfQueryDef.Properties.Count - 1
            If qdfQueryDef.Properties(intIdx).Name _
            = "KeepLocal" Then
                blnFound = True
                Exit For
            End If
        Next intIdx
        If Not blnFound Then
            Set prpProperty = qdfQueryDef.CreateProperty _
                ("KeepLocal", dbText, "T")
            qdfQueryDef.Properties.Append prpProperty
        Else
```

continued on next page

continued from previous page

```
                                qdfQueryDef.Properties("KeepLocal").Value = "T"
                    End If

            End Select

            SetKeepLocal = True
            Exit Function


        ErrorHandler:
            MsgBox Err.Description & " From: " & Err.Source _
                    & "Number: " & Err.Number
            SetKeepLocal = False
            Exit Function

        End Function
```

3. Remove the dbMaster.Synchronize call and add the following boldface code to the `cmdCreateReplica_Click` procedure:

```
Private Sub cmdCreateReplica_Click()
' Create a replica from the named database
Dim dbMaster As Database
Dim bContinue As Boolean

    On Error GoTo DbError

    ' Open the database in exclusive mode
    Set dbMaster = Workspaces(0).OpenDatabase(txtDbNameFrom.Text _
        True)

    ' Keep everything but the expenses table local
    bContinue = SetKeepLocal(dbMaster, "QueryDefs", _
                "ExpEmployeeNames")
    If bContinue Then _
        bContinue = SetKeepLocal(dbMaster, "QueryDefs", _
                    "ExpForOneEmployee")
    If bContinue Then _
        bContinue = SetKeepLocal(dbMaster, "TableDefs", _
                    "ObjectLibrary")

    ' Make the database the Design Master
    If bContinue Then _
        bContinue = MakeReplicable(dbMaster)

    ' Make the replica
    If bContinue Then _
        bContinue = CopyReplica(dbMaster, txtReplicaDbName.Text)

    dbMaster.Close

    Exit Sub
```

```
DbError:
    MsgBox Err.Description & " From: " & Err.Source _
            & "Number: " & Err.Number
    Exit Sub

End Sub
```

How It Works

When the `KeepLocal` property is set to `T`, the `CreateReplica` method doesn't create a replica of the database object. If you later want to replicate an object that was originally kept local, change its `Replicable` property to `T` in the Design Master and synchronize the replicas to propagate the additions. The VisData utility that shipped with Visual Basic can be used to make many of these changes.

Comments

In addition to the `KeepLocal` property, partial replication enables replicas to contain only part of the Design Master's data. To make a partial replica:

✔ Specify the `dbRepMakePartial` option on the `MakeReplica` method.

✔ Use the `TableDefs ReplicaFilter` property and `Relations PartialReplica` property to specified the desired records.

✔ Invoke the `Database PopulatePartial` method to move the desired data into the replica.

COMPLEXITY
INTERMEDIATE

13.5 How do I...
Create a nonreplicated version of a replicated database?

Problem

I've created a set of replica databases, but I want to allow one copy to be modified by another developer in her test environment. How can I cut a replica out of the replica set so that it can be changed independently of the others?

Technique

Within a set of replicas, only one database is allowed to have design changes, such as table creation or field size changes. All other replicas must have their design changes made at the Design Master database and synchronized through the replica set. This strict requirement ensures that the Data Access Objects Synchronize method can adequately track and implement changes. After all, "Too many cooks spoil the broth." But there are times when a replica needs to be cut out of the replica set. The reasons might include testing a new replication schema without affecting the existing replica set, quality assurance testing of the replication methods, or a major application design change. The core technique for returning design independence to a replica database for structure changes is to make the replica into a new Design Master.

Steps

Open the project BreakReplica.vbp (see Figure 13.11). Select Replica.mdb as your database. Click Break Replica. Verify so that you can modify table definitions using the VisData utility.

Figure 13.11. The Break Replica Set form.

1. Create a new Standard EXE project in your workspace. Name the default form frmBreakReplica and the project prjBreakReplica. Save the form and project to disk.

2. Select Project|Components from the main menu and check Microsoft Common Dialog Control 6.0. Select Project|References from the Visual Basic main menu and activate the Microsoft DAO 3.51 Object Library by checking its box in the selection list.

3. Draw controls on the form so that it looks like Figure 13.12. Don't forget to add a Common Dialog control. Set the form's objects and properties as listed in Table 13.10.

Table 13.10. Objects and properties for the Break Replica Set form.

OBJECT	PROPERTY	SETTING
Form	Name	frmBreakReplica
	Caption	Break Replica Set
CommandButton	Name	cmdBreakReplica
	Caption	&Break Replica

OBJECT	PROPERTY	SETTING
CommandButton	Name	cmdOpenFrom
	Caption	&Browse
CommonDialog	Name	cdOpenFile
	Filter	Access Files (*.mdb)|*.mdb
TextBox	Name	txtDbNameFrom
Label	Name	Label1
	AutoSize	-1 'True
	Caption	Database to remove from set:

4. Add the following code to the **cmdOpenFrom_Click** procedure to select a filename:

```
Private Sub cmdOpenFrom_Click()
' Open the Replicate from database file
    cdOpenFile.InitDir = App.Path
    cdOpenFile.ShowOpen
    txtDbNameFrom.Text = cdOpenFile.filename

End Sub
```

5. Add the following code to the **cmdBreakReplica_Click** procedure to set the selected database's **DesignMasterID** to itself:

```
Private Sub cmdBreakReplica_Click()
Dim dbReplica As Database

    On Error GoTo DbError

    ' Open the database in exclusive mode
    Set dbReplica = Workspaces(0).OpenDatabase(txtDbNameFrom.Text _
        True)

    dbReplica.DesignMasterID = dbReplica.ReplicaID

    dbReplica.Close

    Exit Sub

DbError:
    MsgBox Err.Description & " From: " & Err.Source _
            & "Number: " & Err.Number
    Exit Sub

End Sub
```

How It Works

To remove a database from the restrictions placed on replicas, you simply need to make the database replica its own Design Master by setting the **DesignMasterID** to the `ReplicaID` as shown in step 5. The database will be immediately cut out of the replica set and will no longer be easily able to synchronize data structure or content changes with its previous replica siblings. In other words, breaking a database out of a replica set should be considered permanent. In a production environment, the break-up could be very inconvenient if done incorrectly.

Replicated databases remain replicated with all the extra properties and system tables after the database's `Replicable` property is set to `T`. How-To 13.3 discusses the changes made to the database when it is converted to a replica. Breaking a database out of a replica set will not make the database nonreplicable; it will allow only its own design changes. All the extra data will still be in the database.

Comments

Replication is a fairly permanent decision, but it can be a powerful tool, especially with the use of the partial replication methods to propagate design changes with very little coding effort. A package being distributed to many locations can use replication to propagate design changes while never transmitting any data. Field database design changes can be managed by distributing a new, empty member of the replica set with the required design changes and synchronizing with a replica filters set to pass no records.

A

SQL REFERENCE

With the use of commands, predicates, clauses, operators, aggregate functions, and joins, the Structured Query Language (SQL) can successfully compose a query that returns a specified range of fields.

SQL is a language that ties in closely with the Microsoft Jet Engine and Data Access Object (DAO). By indicating relations between tables and other queries of a database, through SQL, records are temporarily created and passed back to the recordset object of the database object in Visual Basic.

This appendix serves as a quick reference and introduction to SQL. Using this reference, you should be able to create your own SQL statements in Visual Basic to better exploit the power of the Microsoft Jet Engine and its components.

SQL Statement Classifications

SQL statements are broken into two distinct classifications, both of which are discussed in detail in this appendix. The first classification, the Data Definition Language (DDL), is used to create, modify, or remove the actual definitions in a particular database. The second classification, the Data Manipulation Language (DML), is used to create, modify, remove, or gather information that resides in the structure of the database. In other words, you would use DDL to create tables, fields, and indexes, and you would use DML to populate, alter, and retrieve the information that resides in the tables and field.

Table A.1 lists the seven available SQL commands that are the basis of any SQL statement. These commands indicate what kind of query the SQL statement actually is. Table A.1 also indicates the classification of each command listed, either definition (DDL) or manipulation (DML). A SQL command is used together with other components of a SQL statement to create either an action query or a selection query. Action queries are those that begin with a SQL command other than **SELECT**. As you might guess, a query beginning with **SELECT** is a selection query.

Table A.1. SQL commands.

COMMAND	CLASSIFICATION	DESCRIPTION
CREATE	Definition	Create a table, a field, or an index.
ALTER	Definition	Modify a table by adding a field or changing a field definition.
DROP	Definition	Drop a table or an index.
SELECT	Manipulation	Query a database with given parameters.
INSERT	Manipulation	Insert multiple records with one operation.
UPDATE	Manipulation	Change information throughout a range with given parameters.
DELETE	Manipulation	Remove records from the table.

When using queries, you will use various clauses that are implemented in the SQL statement. Table A.2 lists and describes the available clauses for SQL used by the Microsoft Jet Engine.

Table A.2. SQL clauses.

CLAUSE	DESCRIPTIONS
FROM	Specifies the table from which data is queried
WHERE	Specifies the condition(s) for the query
GROUP BY	Specifies the group(s) for the selected information
HAVING	Specifies the condition(s) for each group in the query
ORDER BY	Specifies the order of the query

The first of these clauses, FROM, is used to indicate the table or query used to gather the information for the SQL statement. More than one table or query can be listed in the statement, using the FROM clause. When doing so, you are creating at least one join in your query. Joins are discussed later in this appendix.

The second clause, WHERE, lists the condition or conditions that must be met for a record to be included in the query results. Each condition is evaluated using conditional operators. Multiple conditions are listed using logical operators. Table A.3 lists available conditional and logical operators.

Table A.3. SQL operators.

OPERATOR	TYPE	CONDITION IS MET WHEN
AND	Logical	Both expressions are true.
OR	Logical	Either expression is true.
NOT	Logical	The expression is false.
<	Comparison	The first expression is *less than* the second expression.
<=	Comparison	The first expression is *less than or equal to* the second expression.

OPERATOR	TYPE	CONDITION IS MET WHEN
>	Comparison	The first expression is *greater than* the second expression.
>=	Comparison	The first expression is *greater than or equal to* the second expression.
=	Comparison	The first expression is *equal to* the second expression.
<>	Comparison	The first expression is *not equal to* the second expression.
BETWEEN	Comparison	The value belongs to a specified set of values.
LIKE	Comparison	The value matches the pattern specified.
IN	Comparison	The record belongs to a particular group in a database.

The third SQL clause, GROUP BY, is used to group the query's result set. GROUP BY uses at least one field name from a table or query listed in the statement's FROM clause to evaluate the records and group like values. You can also use an aggregate function in a SQL statement to create summaries of the groups in the recordset. The list of available aggregate functions is shown in Table A.4.

Table A.4. SQL aggregate functions.

FUNCTION	DESCRIPTION
AVG	Returns the average value of a specified field
COUNT	Returns the number of records in a query
SUM	Returns the sum of the values in a specified field
MAX	Returns the largest value in a specified field
MIN	Returns the smallest value in a specified field

The fourth SQL clause, HAVING, specifies conditions (of the same syntax used for the WHERE clause) the groups must meet to be included in the resulting recordset.

The last SQL clause, ORDER BY, uses field names to order the result set in a specified manner. More information on all the SQL commands and clauses is presented in detail throughout this appendix.

Data Definition Language

DDL statements are used to create, alter, or remove tables, fields, and indexes from a database. The three SQL commands used to do so are CREATE, DROP, and ALTER. All three are action queries.

Action queries in Visual Basic can be initiated in one of two ways. The first method of invoking an action query is by using a QueryDef object. The second is by using the Execute method of the database object, as shown here:

```
db.Execute sSQLStatement
```

This assumes that db is a database object variable successfully set to a valid database, and sSQLStatement is a valid string variable containing a valid action SQL statement.

The CREATE **Command**

The CREATE command is used to create tables and indexes in a specified database. To create a table in a given database, use the CREATE TABLE statement with the syntax shown here:

```
CREATE TABLE table (fld1 type [(sz)] [NOT NULL] [idx1] [, fld2 type [(sz)]
        [NOT NULL] [idx2] [, ...]] [, CONSTRAINT MFidx [, ...]])
```

In the preceding syntax, the table name succeeds the actual CREATE TABLE statement and is followed by a comma-delimited list of field definitions that are used to create the specified table. At least one field must be listed in parentheses as shown. Any valid database type can be used to indicate the type of field to be created, and a size (sz) can be specified for text and binary fields.

The following example creates a new table in the db database with three fields:

```
db.Execute "CREATE TABLE Customers (CustNum INTEGER, " _
        & "CustName TEXT (25), Address TEXT (30))"
```

The new table created is called Customers. It contains an integer field named CustNum and two text fields named CustName and Address.

Using the NOT NULL optional parameter, you can specify that the field can never have a NULL value. If a NULL value is assigned to a field created with this option, a runtime error will occur. The following example is a more bulletproof table definition:

```
db.Execute "CREATE TABLE Customers (CustNum INTEGER NOT NULL, " _
        & "CustName TEXT NOT NULL (25), Address TEXT (30))"
```

This version of the CREATE TABLE action query specifies that the Number and CustName field values cannot consist of any NULL values. The Address field, however, can.

You can also use the CONSTRAINT clause in a CREATE TABLE statement to create an index either on an individual field or on multiple fields. The following example creates an index in a new table:

```
db.Execute "CREATE TABLE Customers (" _
        & "CustNum INTEGER CONSTRAINT CustNumIndex PRIMARY, " _
        & "CustName TEXT (25), Address TEXT (30))"
```

This example creates a table with three fields as shown before, but it also adds an index named CustNumIndex for the CustNum field.

To create an index on multiple fields, you can also use the CONSTRAINT clause as shown in this example:

```
db.Execute "CREATE TABLE Customers (CustNum INTEGER, " _
        & "CustName TEXT (25), Address TEXT (30), " _
        & "CONSTRAINT CustIndex UNIQUE (CustNum, CustName))"
```

Notice that the new index created by the CONSTRAINT clause, named CustIndex, is composed of both the CustNum and the CustName fields described in the SQL statement. The difference between creating an individual field index and creating a multiple field index with the **CREATE TABLE** statement is that, with the individual fields, you indicate the **CONSTRAINT** clause after the given field, without a comma. Creating indexes of multiple fields with the **CONSTRAINT** clause, you specify the index after the fields in the index are created, separated by a comma, listing the individual fields, as shown in the last example. More information on the **CONSTRAINT** clause can be found in the "Using the **CONSTRAINT** Clause" section, later in this appendix.

You do not necessarily have to create indexes in the **CREATE TABLE** statement—you can also explicitly create indexes using the **CREATE INDEX** statement as shown in this example:

```
db.Execute "CREATE UNIQUE INDEX CustIndex ON Customers (CustNum, CustName)"
```

This statement leads to the same results as derived by the last **CREATE TABLE** statement.

The syntax for the **CREATE INDEX** statement is as follows:

```
CREATE [UNIQUE] INDEX idx ON table (fld1 [ASC¦DESC]
     [, fld2 [ASC¦DESC], ...])
     [WITH {PRIMARY ¦ DISALLOW NULL ¦ IGNORE NULL}]
```

When using the **CREATE INDEX** statement, specifying the **UNIQUE** option as shown in the preceding example, you are telling the Jet Engine that no two combinations, for the values of the fields listed, are to be allowed, thus creating a unique index on the fields. By default, indexes are created in ascending order (**ASC** keyword), but you can specify to list the order of the values of an index in descending order by using the **DESC** keyword after the corresponding field name.

The last portion of the **CREATE INDEX** statement allows you to specify, in more detail, how an index is to be handled. You do this with the **WITH** clause of the **CREATE INDEX** statement. To create a primary key on the table indicated, use the **WITH PRIMARY** statement. This statement creates a unique index that is now the primary key. Only one primary key can exist per table; attempting to create an additional one will result in a runtime error.

You can also prohibit the use of **NULL** values in an index, with the **WITH DISALLOW NULL** statement, or you can allow **NULL** values with the **WITH IGNORE NULL** statement.

The ALTER **Command**

The second command belonging to the SQL Data Definition Language is **ALTER**. You can use the **ALTER TABLE** statement to complete four distinct tasks:

✔ Add a new field to a table.

✔ Delete a field from a table.

✔ Add a new index to a table.

✔ Delete an index from a table.

You can add or delete only one field or index with each **ALTER TABLE** statement. The syntax for **ALTER TABLE** is shown here:

```
ALTER TABLE table {ADD {COLUMN fld type[(size)] [NOT NULL] [CONSTRAINT idx]
          ¦ CONSTRAINT MFidx} ¦ DROP {COLUMN fld ¦ CONSTRAINT indexname}}
```

The following example creates a new field in an existing table named Customers:

```
db.Execute "ALTER TABLE Customers ADD COLUMN PhoneNum TEXT (12)"
```

Just as you can add a field to a table, you can delete one, as shown in this example:

```
db.Execute "ALTER TABLE Customers DROP PhoneNum"
```

You can also specify new indexes just as you did with **CREATE TABLE**, except that you can add the index after the table is already created, as shown here:

```
db.Execute "ALTER TABLE Customers " _
     & "ADD CONSTRAINT NameAndPhoneIndex (CustName, PhoneNum)"
```

Now you can delete that index with this final example:

```
db.Execute "ALTER TABLE Customers DROP CONSTRAINT NameAndPhoneIndex"
```

Using the CONSTRAINT **Clause**

So far you have seen the **CONSTRAINT** clause in both the **CREATE** and the **ALTER** SQL commands. Now take a closer look at this clause and discover how powerful it really is.

In its simplest form, a constraint is an index. Not only does the **CONSTRAINT** clause allow you to create or remove indexes as shown in the **CREATE** and **ALTER** command sections, but it also allows you to create primary and foreign keys to define relations and enforce referential integrity.

As shown earlier, by example, there are two versions of the **CONSTRAINT** statement, one for individual field indexes and one for multiple field indexes. The syntax for a single field index is shown here:

```
CONSTRAINT name {PRIMARY KEY ¦ UNIQUE ¦ NOT NULL ¦
     REFERENCES foreigntable
          [(foreignfield1, foreignfield2)]}
```

The syntax for a multiple field index **CONSTRAINT** is this:

```
CONSTRAINT name
     {PRIMARY KEY (primary1[, primary2 [, ...]]) ¦
     UNIQUE (unique1[, unique2 [, ...]]) ¦
     NOT NULL (notnull1[, notnull2 [, ...]]) ¦
     FOREIGN KEY (ref1[, ref2 [, ...]])
       REFERENCES foreigntable
          [(foreignfield1 [, foreignfield2 [, ...]])]}
```

The name of the index to be created is specified directly after the **CONSTRAINT** keyword. In either version, you can create three types of indexes:

✔ A **UNIQUE** index. A unique index has no two fields, as indicated in the **CONSTRAINT** clause, with the same values.

✔ A PRIMARY KEY index. A primary key is, by definition, unique. This means that all the fields included in the primary key definition must also be unique.

✔ A FOREIGN KEY index. A foreign key is an index that uses another table to create an index on the current one.

You can create a foreign key to create a relationship between multiple fields as in the following example:

```
db.Execute "ALTER TABLE Customers " _
    & "ADD CONSTRAINT NewIndex " _
    & "FOREIGN KEY (CustNum) REFERENCES Orders (CustNum)"
```

This example creates a relation between the Customers table and the Orders table of the **db** database object. A new index is created, NewIndex, that links the two tables based on the CustNum field name.

The DROP Command

The DROP command comes in two flavors: DROP TABLE and DROP INDEX. As you might easily guess, the DROP TABLE statement removes an existing table from a database as shown here:

```
db.Execute "DROP TABLE Customers"
```

The DROP INDEX statement works similarly to the DROP TABLE statement, except that it removes an index from a given table as shown in this example:

```
db.Execute "DROP INDEX CustNumIndex ON Customers"
```

For reference, the syntax of the DROP command is as follows:

```
DROP {TABLE table | INDEX idx ON table}
```

Data Manipulation Language

DML commands create a mix of action and selection queries. The commands SELECT, INSERT, UPDATE, and DELETE are used to quickly and efficiently, through the use of the Jet Engine performance, manipulate the data residing in specified tables.

The SELECT Command

The SELECT command differs from all other SQL commands in that it is a part of a selection query rather than an action query. When you're using a selection query in a Visual Basic application, it is most commonly set in a recordset object of a given database. Assuming that **rs** is a valid recordset object and **db** is a database object already set to a valid database file, you can use the following statement to gather all the records in the Customers table of the **db** object:

```
Set rs = db.OpenRecordset("SELECT * FROM Customers")
```

This example uses the most generic and basic form of a SELECT statement. This section explains the various components of the SELECT statement and describes how the programmer can use each component to effectively sort and filter records according to his or her needs.

The syntax for the **SELECT** statement is as follows:

```
SELECT [predicate]
       { * ¦ table.* ¦
         [table.]field1 [AS alias1] [, [table.]field2 [AS alias2] [, ...]]}
FROM   tableexpression [, ...] [IN externaldatabase]
[WHERE... ]
[GROUP BY... ]
[HAVING... ]
[ORDER BY... ]
```

It is quite understandable to be overwhelmed by this declaration, but not all the clauses included in this syntax are necessarily used together—although they could be.

Take the following **SELECT** statement, for example:

```
SELECT DISTINCT CustNum, CustName
FROM Customers
WHERE (CustNum >= 100) AND (CustNum <= 120)
ORDER BY CustName;
```

This statement retrieves only the fields **CustNum** and **CustName** from the Customers table. The **WHERE** clause in this statement shows two conditions. The first condition says that the **CustNum** field values must be greater than or equal to 100. The second condition states that the **CustNum** field values must be less than or equal to 120. So far, you can see that the **SELECT** statement shown previously will return the **CustNum** and **CustName** for all records with a customer number between 100 and 120. The last part of this statement says to order the records returned by the query by the **CustName** field—in other words, in alphabetical order. You can also request the records to be returned in reverse alphabetical order by placing the **DESC** keyword after the **ORDER BY CustName** clause.

You can use multiple conditions in a **SELECT** statement as shown in this statement. For a complete list of operators for conditions, both logical and comparison, see Table A.4 at the beginning of this section.

It is important to note that the **DISTINCT** keyword following the **SELECT** command is called a predicate. This keyword indicates that only distinct (unique) combinations of fields will be returned. In this example, if you had three records in the Customers table with the same customer number and name, but with different addresses, only one record would be returned. If you were to add the **Address** field to the list of fields in the **SELECT** statement, you would receive three records for the same customer number and name because the combination (number, name, and address) is unique for each record returned.

The **DISTINCT** keyword is not the only predicate available in a **SELECT** statement. Table A.5 lists the four available predicates for a **SELECT** statement.

Table A.5. *SELECT* predicates.

PREDICATE	DESCRIPTION
ALL	Returns all records, even duplicates
DISTINCT	Returns only unique records, based on fields specified in the statement
DISTINCTROW	Returns only unique records, based on all fields in the specified table(s), even those not listed in the SELECT statement
TOP	Returns the first *n* records or the top *p* percentage of records of the selected recordset

The default predicate used in SELECT statements not indicating a predicate is ALL. ALL returns all records that meet the conditions of the selection query.

The TOP predicate is used in conjunction with the ORDER BY clause of a SELECT statement. It can be used in one of two ways:

✔ TOP *n* returns the first n records.

✔ TOP *p* PERCENT returns the top p percentage of the entire recordset.

Following is an example of the TOP predicate:

```
SELECT TOP 10 PERCENT OrderNum, OrderPrice
FROM Orders
ORDER BY OrderPrice;
```

This statement would return the top 10% of records in the Orders table, based on the OrderPrice field. If you were to order the recordset returned by this statement by the OrderNum field, you would get the top 10% of records based on the OrderNum, which would probably not make a whole lot of sense.

It is worth pointing out that if there are identical values for the ORDER BY field that is specified, there is a chance that more than the desired number of records will be returned. Assume, for instance, that I wanted to get the top 10 parts based on quantity ordered. If there were 9 distinct quantity amounts that topped the list and 2 others that followed, with the same value, I would have 11 records in all when I only wanted 10. The same is true for the TOP *p* PERCENT format. If I wanted to retrieve the top 2% of part prices with my selection query, I would use the following statement:

```
SELECT TOP 2 PERCENT PartName
FROM Orders
ORDER BY PartPrice;
```

This example returns the names of the items priced in the top 2%. If I have numerous items all with the same price, they are considered one item, so I can very easily retrieve more records than I expected. It is also important to understand what you are asking for when using the TOP predicate. For instance, it might be easy to think that you are getting the top 10 customers based on moneys spent, but you must specifically state that you want the selection to be made on a field such as TotalMoneySpent as compared to TotalOrderPrice.

You can also group records that are returned from a query by using the GROUP
BY clause in a SELECT statement, as in the following example:

```
SELECT PartName, Count(PartName)
FROM Orders
WHERE (PartPrice > 10)
GROUP BY PartName;
```

This SELECT statement gathers and groups all the records from the Orders
table whose PartPrice field values are greater than 10. These records are then
grouped by the PartNum field only, and a count of the number of each type of
part sold is returned. In other words, the resulting recordset contains the distinct
names of parts that cost over $10 and a count of the number of orders for each
part.

The function COUNT, in this example, is called an aggregate function. Other
aggregate functions include AVG, SUM, MAX, and MIN. Table A.4 is a list of
aggregate functions and their descriptions.

Another example of using an aggregate function is shown here:

```
SELECT PartName, SUM(PartPrice)
FROM Orders
WHERE (PartPrice > 10)
GROUP BY PartName
HAVING (SUM(PartPrice) > 1000) AND (PartName LIKE "WIDGET*");
```

This example introduces the HAVING clause. This clause acts very similarly to
the WHERE clause, except that it tests the condition specified after the grouping
has occurred, unlike the WHERE clause, which tests conditions of records to be
included in the groups. The preceding SELECT statement gathers distinct part
names and a sum of the total prices sold from the Orders table. The only
condition for records to be included in this grouping is that the price of each
part be greater than 10.

After the groups have been created by the Jet Engine, only the groups with a
total PartPrice summary of more than 1,000 are included. In addition to this
condition, you can see the use of the LIKE keyword. You can use the LIKE
keyword anywhere you can specify a condition. LIKE uses pattern matching to
check whether a field should be included in a resulting recordset. In this
example, only groups with a PartName field value beginning with the characters
WIDGET will be included in the recordset.

Joins

Joins are a very commonly used function of a SELECT statement. Joins are used
to create temporary relationships between tables when evaluating a selection
query. Following is the syntax for using joins in a SELECT statement:

```
SELECT ...
FROM table1 [LEFT ¦ RIGHT] JOIN table2 ON (table1.fld1 CompOp table2.fld2)
```

CompOp is a comparison operator (refer to Table A.4). A join effects the FROM
clause of a SELECT statement as shown in the preceding syntax declaration.

Left and right joins mirror each other in definition. A left join (called a left outer join) includes all records from table1, even if no related records are found in table2. A right join (called a right outer join) includes all records from table2, even if no related records are found in table1. Take the following statement, for example:

```
SELECT Customers.*, Orders.*
FROM Customers LEFT JOIN Orders ON (Customers.CustNum = Orders.CustNum);
```

This example returns all fields from the Customers table and only the fields from the Orders table that have matching `CustNum` fields. In other words, the resulting recordset from this statement would include all the customers and information on orders for those customers that did order.

To create a join that returns only records that are included in both tables (inner join), you do not have to use the `JOIN` clause at all, as shown in this example:

```
SELECT Customers.*, Orders.*
FROM Customers, Orders
WHERE (Customers.CustNum = Orders.CustNum);
```

This statement would return a shorter recordset than the earlier statement, given that there are customers who did not place orders. In this `SELECT` statement, only the customers who placed orders qualify to be returned in the recordset.

Although it is unnecessary to do so, there is a SQL clause to specify inner joins, as shown in this example:

```
SELECT Customers.*, Orders.*
FROM Customers INNER JOIN Orders ON (Customers.CustNum = Orders.CustNum);
```

This statement is the equivalent to the preceding one, and in many cases it is actually easier to read and comprehend at a glance.

You might also care to specify more than one condition in any of your joins, as shown in this example:

```
SELECT Customers.*, Orders.*
FROM Customers INNER JOIN Orders
ON ((Customers.CustNum = Orders.CustNum)
AND (Customers.Flag = Orders.Flag));
```

If you really want to go overboard, and many times you might find that you need to, you can nest joins within each other as shown in the following example:

```
SELECT Customers.*, Orders.*, Tax.*
FROM Customers INNER JOIN
  (Orders INNER JOIN Tax ON (Orders.State = Tax.State))
    ON (Customers.CustNum = Orders.CustNum));
```

This `SELECT` statement returns all the records in which there is a customer number from the Customers table and Orders table and a state in the Orders table and the Tax table.

You can nest either a LEFT JOIN or a RIGHT JOIN inside an INNER JOIN; however, you cannot nest an INNER JOIN inside either a LEFT JOIN or a RIGHT JOIN.

The INSERT **Command**

The INSERT command is used in the INSERT INTO statement to create an append query, a type of action query. You can use this command to add single or multiple rows to a table. This is the syntax for adding a single row using the INSERT INTO statement:

```
INSERT INTO table [(fld1[, fld2[, ...]])]
VALUES (val1[, val2[, ...])
```

Using this syntax, you can add single rows to a table. You must specify each field and its value that you want to add. If you leave out a field and its corresponding value, a NULL value is automatically inserted into the field. The new records are appended to the end of the table. Following is an example of how to add a row onto a specific table:

```
INSERT INTO Customers (CustNum, CustName)
VALUES (1, "Kimberly");
```

If other fields are in the Customers table, they are assigned a NULL value.

The syntax for adding multiple rows differs slightly:

```
INSERT INTO table2 [(fld1[, fld2[, ...]])]
SELECT [table1.]fld1[, fld2[, ...]
FROM ...
```

This syntax takes a specified selection of records from table1 and inserts them into table2. The number of fields for both tables must be the same and in the correct order. The following example demonstrates the INSERT INTO statement:

```
INSERT INTO Delivered (CustNum, DelPart, PriceCharged)
SELECT CustNum, PartName, PartPrice
FROM Orders
WHERE (Delivered = True);
```

This example inserts all the delivered orders from the Orders table into the corresponding fields of the Delivered table.

The INSERT INTO statement appends records at the end of an existing table, but you can also use a similar statement and selection of records to create a new table, as in this example:

```
SELECT CustNum, PartName, PartPrice
INTO DeliveredBackup
FROM Orders
WHERE (Delivered = True);
```

This example creates a new table called DeliveredBackup, with the identical fields and properties of the fields listed in the SELECT clause from the Orders table. The new table would include all the records with the Delivered field value of True.

The UPDATE **Command**

The UPDATE command is used to set information in a current table to a new value. The syntax for the UPDATE command is as follows:

```
UPDATE table
SET value
WHERE criteria
```

The value of the SET clause in the UPDATE statement is an assignment expression that will alter the current value of the selected records of the table specified. Here is an example of the UPDATE statement:

```
UPDATE Orders
SET OrderTotal = (PartPrice * Quantity);
```

If no WHERE clause is specified, as in this example, the UPDATE query makes the necessary changes to all the records in the specified table. In this example, the OrderTotal field is calculated based on the PartPrice and Quantity field values for the corresponding record.

With a single SQL UPDATE query, it's possible to update multiple fields for each record, as shown in this next example:

```
UPDATE Orders
SET OrderTotal = (PartPrice * Quantity),
    Discount = (PartPrice * .05) * Quantity
WHERE (OrderDate < #1/1/1998#);
```

This example gives a new value to both the OrderTotal field and the Discount field for all records whose OrderDate field value is before January 1, 1998. Notice the use of the number signs (#) before and after the date criteria in the WHERE clause. This is the correct notation for specifying dates in a condition.

Notice that you cannot reverse UPDATE queries and must take care to ensure that the correct records are selected for the update. To check which fields are going to be updated before the execution of the UPDATE statement, create a selection query with the same criteria as the UPDATE query.

The DELETE **Command**

The DELETE command is used to perform bulk deletions of records within a specified table in one operation. You can specify conditions to select the records from a table to delete. When you use the DELETE command, entire records are deleted, not individual fields. The syntax for the DELETE command is shown here:

```
DELETE table.*
FROM table
WHERE ...
```

Following is an example of a DELETE statement:

```
DELETE *
FROM Customers
WHERE (LastOrderDate <= #6/20/73#);
```

This example deletes all the records in the Customers table in which the last order date was June 20, 1973, or earlier (You don't need their business anyway!).

You can use the DELETE command to delete all the data in a particular table while maintaining the actual structure and definition of the table, as shown in this example:

```
DELETE * FROM Orders;
```

This command could obviously be very dangerous; therefore, use this form of the DELETE command with extreme caution.

Comments

SQL is a convenient, effective, and easy way to organize data for your applications. By using the commands described in this appendix, you can select, filter, order, and group records in any way you need. The SQL is much more involved than is described in this brief reference, but by knowing just these basic commands and functions, you can create just about any desired recordset from your raw data.

B

DATA ACCESS OBJECT REFERENCE

The Data Access Object (DAO) model provides you with an object-oriented interface to all the data manipulation techniques inherent in Microsoft Jet Database files. Figure B.1 shows the entire DAO object model in its hierarchical form.

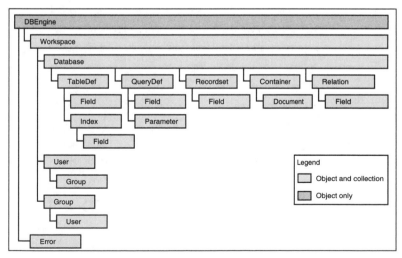

Figure B.1. The Data Access Object model.

This appendix is designed as a reference to all the objects included in the DAO object model. The collections and objects are listed in alphabetical order with tables indicating and describing all the available methods and properties available to each.

Containers **Collection,** Container **Object**

The `Containers` collection contains all the `Container` objects that are part of a database. A container name can be `Database`, `Tables`, or `Relations`. Table B.1 shows the method of the `Containers` collection; Table B.2 shows its property. Table B.3 lists the properties of the `Container` object.

Table B.1. *Containers* collection method.

METHOD	DESCRIPTION
Refresh	Updates the contents of the collection to reflect the current status of the database

Table B.2. *Containers* collection property.

PROPERTY	DESCRIPTION
Count	The number of objects in the collection

Table B.3. *Container* object properties.

PROPERTY	DESCRIPTION
AllPermissions	Returns all permissions for the user named by UserName, including those that are inherited from the user's group as well as the user's specific permissions
Inherit	Sets or returns a value that indicates whether the document will receive a default Permissions property setting
Name	Sets a user-defined name for the DAO object
Owner	Sets the owner of the current Container object
Permissions	Sets the permissions available for the user, of the current Container object, named by UserName
UserName	Indicates the name of the user for the current Container object

Databases **Collection,** Database **Object**

The `Database` object is a member of the `Databases` collection. The `Database` object is a means of access to an open database file. Table B.4 shows the method of the `Databases` collection; Table B.5 shows its property. Table B.6 lists the methods of the `Database` object, and Table B.7 lists the properties.

Table B.4. *Databases* collection method.

METHOD	DESCRIPTION
Refresh	Updates the contents of the collection to reflect the current status of the database

Table B.5. *Databases* collection property.

PROPERTY	DESCRIPTION
Count	Returns the number of objects in the collection

Table B.6. *Database* object methods.

METHOD	DESCRIPTION
Close	Closes the current Database object
	Creates a new Property object
	Creates a new QueryDef object and adds it to the QueryDefs collection
CreateRelation	Creates a new Relation object and adds it to the Relations collection
CreateTableDef	Creates a new TableDef object and adds it to the TableDefs collection
Execute	Executes the specified SQL action query
MakeReplica	Makes a new replica from another database replica
NewPassword	Assigns a new password to the Database object
OpenRecordset	Creates a new Recordset object and adds it to the Recordsets collection
PopulatePartial	Synchronizes changes in a partial replica with the full replica and repopulates the partial replica based on the current replica filters
Synchronize	Synchronizes two replicas

Table B.7. *Database* object properties.

PROPERTY	DESCRIPTION
CollatingOrder	Returns the sequence of the sort order in text and string comparison
Connect	Returns information about the source
Connection	Returns a connection object corresponding to the current Database object
Name	Sets a user-defined name for the DAO object
QueryTimeout	Indicates the number of seconds to wait until an error is reported when executing a query
RecordsAffected	Indicates the number of records that were affected by the last call of the Execute method
Replicable	Indicates whether the current Database object can be replicated
ReplicaID	Returns a 16-byte value that uniquely identifies a database replica

continued on next page

continued from previous page

PROPERTY	DESCRIPTION
Transactions	Indicates whether an object supports transactions
Updatable	Indicates whether an object can be updated
V1xNullBehavior	Indicates whether zero-length strings in Text or Memo fields are converted to NULL values
Version	Indicates the DAO version currently in use

Documents **Collection,** Document **Object**

The Documents collection contains all the Document objects for a specific type of Microsoft Jet Database object (Database, Table or Query, or Relationship). Table B.8 shows the method of the Documents collection, and Table B.9 shows its property. Table B.10 shows the Document object method; Table B.11 lists its properties.

Table B.8. *Documents* collection method.

METHOD	DESCRIPTION
Refresh	Updates the contents of the collection to reflect the current status of the database

Table B.9. *Documents* collection property.

PROPERTY	DESCRIPTION
Count	Returns the number of objects in the collection

Table B.10. *Document* object methods.

METHOD	DESCRIPTION
CreateProperty	Creates a new user-defined Property object

Table B.11. *Document* object properties.

PROPERTY	DESCRIPTION
AllPermissions	Indicates all the permissions belonging to the current user of the document that are specific as well as inherited from its group
Container	Returns the name of the Container object to which the current Document object belongs
DateCreated	Returns the date and time the current object was created
LastUpdated	Returns the date and time the current object was last modified
KeepLocal	Indicates that the current object is not to be replicated
Name	Sets a user-defined name for the DAO object

PROPERTY	DESCRIPTION
Owner	Returns the user that is considered the owner of the current Document object
Permissions	Returns the permissions specific to the current user of the document
Replicable	Indicates whether the current Document object can be replicated
UserName	Returns the name of the current user of the document

DBEngine **Object**

DBEngine is the only part of the DAO object model that is not a collection; rather it is only an object that contains and controls all the other components of the DAO object model. Table B.12 lists the methods of the **DBEngine** object; Table B.13 lists the properties.

Table B.12. *DBEngine* object methods.

METHOD	DESCRIPTION
BeginTrans	Begins transaction for the database engine
CommitTrans	Commits changes since the last call to the BeginTrans method
Rollback	Rolls back to the state before the call to the BeginTrans method
CompactDatabase	Compacts an existing database into a new database
CreateDatabase	Creates a new Database object, saves it to disk, and returns the opened Database object
CreateWorkspace	Creates a new Workspace object and appends it to the Workspaces collection
Idle	Allows the Jet engine to complete any pending tasks by suspending data processing
OpenConnection	Opens a connection to an ODBC data source
OpenDatabase	Opens a database and returns a Database object that represents it
RegisterDatabase	Enters connection information for an ODBC data source in the Windows Registry
RepairDatabase	Tries to repair a corrupt Jet database
SetOption	Temporarily overrides values in the Windows Registry for the Microsoft Jet database engine

Table B.13. *DBEngine* object properties.

PROPERTY	DESCRIPTION
DefaultType	Sets the type of Workspace object to be used when the next Workspace object is created
DefaultUser	Sets the username of the default Workspace object to be created
DefaultPassword	Sets the password used to create the default Workspace object when it is initiated
IniPath	Indicates the path of the information used from the Windows Registry about the Jet database engine
LoginTimeout	Returns the number of seconds before an error occurs when attempting to log on to an ODBC data base
SystemDB	Returns the path and name of the current workgroup information file
Version	Indicates the DAO version currently in use

Errors **Collection,** Error **Object**

The Errors collection is a collection of Error objects pertaining to individual DAO operation failures. Table B.14 shows the Errors collection method, and Table B.15 shows its property. Table B.16 lists the properties of the Error object.

Table B.14. *Errors* collection method.

METHOD	DESCRIPTION
Refresh	Updates the contents of the collection to reflect the current status of the database

Table B.15. *Errors* collection property.

PROPERTY	DESCRIPTION
Count	Returns the number of objects in the collection

Table B.16. *Error* object properties.

PROPERTY	DESCRIPTION
Description	Indicates the description of the current error
HelpContext	Returns the context ID for a topic in a Windows Help file
HelpFile	Returns the name of a Windows Help file
Number	Indicates the number referring to the current error
Source	Indicates the source of the current error

Fields **Collection,** Field **Object**

The Fields collection belongs to the Index, QueryDef, Relation, and TableDef objects. The collection is composed of all the Field objects of the corresponding object. The Field object is used to access the value of that field and its definition. Table B.17 lists the methods of the Fields collection, and Table B.18 shows its property. Table B.19 lists the Field object's methods, and Table B.20 lists its properties.

Table B.17. *Fields* collection methods.

METHOD	DESCRIPTION
Append	Adds a new object to the collection
Delete	Removes an object from the collection
Refresh	Updates the contents of the collection to reflect the current status of the database

Table B.18. *Fields* collection property.

PROPERTY	DESCRIPTION
Count	Indicates the number of objects in the collection

Table B.19. *Field* object methods.

METHOD	DESCRIPTION
AppendChunk	Appends a string to a Memo or Long Binary field
CreateProperty	Creates a new user-defined Property object
GetChunk	Returns a portion of a Memo or Long Binary field

Table B.20. *Field* object properties.

PROPERTY	DESCRIPTION
AllowZeroLength	Indicates whether a zero-length value can be stored in the field
Attributes	Returns information containing characteristics of an object
CollatingOrder	Returns the sequence of the sort order in text and string comparison
DataUpdatable	Indicates whether the object's data can be updated
DefaultValue	Returns a default value given to the field if no other value is specified
FieldSize	Indicates the number of bytes used in the database for a Memo or Long Binary field
ForeignName	Returns the name of a Field object in a foreign table that corresponds to a field in a primary table for a relationship
Name	Sets a user-defined name for the DAO object
OrdinalPosition	Indicates a numbered position of the current field in the Fields collection
OriginalValue	Returns the value of the field when the last batch update began
Required	Indicates whether the field must be given a value
Size	Returns the size in length of the field
SourceField	Indicates the name of the field that is the original source of the data for the current Field object
SourceTable	Sets the name of the table that is the original source of the data for a Field object
Type	Returns the operational type of object
ValidateOnSet	Indicates whether a Field object value is indicated when its Value property is set
ValidationRule	Returns the value that validates data in a field as it is changed or added to a table
ValidationText	Indicates the message that your application displays if the value of the Field object does not satisfy the validation rule
Value	Returns the actual data stored in the field
VisibleValue	Returns the value that is newer than the OriginalValue property as determined by a batch update conflict

Groups **Collection,** Group **Object**

The `Groups` collection contains `Group` objects of a workspace or user. A `Group` object is a group of users who have common access permissions. Table B.21 lists the methods of the `Groups` collection, and Table B.22 shows its property. Table B.23 shows the `Group` object's method, and Table B.24 lists its properties.

Table B.21. *Groups* collection methods.

METHOD	DESCRIPTION
Append	Adds a new object to the collection
Delete	Removes an object from the collection
Refresh	Updates the contents of the collection to reflect the current status of the database

Table B.22. *Groups* collection property.

PROPERTY	DESCRIPTION
Count	Indicates the number of objects in the collection

Table B.23. *Group* object method.

METHOD	DESCRIPTION
CreateUser	Creates a new user object for the current group

Table B.24. *Group* object properties.

PROPERTY	DESCRIPTION
Name	Sets a user-defined name for the DAO object
PID	Returns a group personal identifier

Indexes **Collection,** Index **Object**

The `Indexes` collection contains all the `Index` objects pertaining to a particular `TableDef` object. The `Index` object specifies the order of the records in a table. Table B.25 lists the `Indexes` collection methods, and Table B.26 shows the `Indexes` collection property. Table B.27 lists the `Index` object methods, and Table B.28 lists the `Index` object properties.

Table B.25. *Indexes* collection methods.

METHOD	DESCRIPTION
Append	Adds a new object to the collection
Delete	Removes an object from the collection
Refresh	Updates the contents of the collection to reflect the current status of the database

Table B.26. *Indexes* collection property.

PROPERTY	DESCRIPTION
Count	Indicates the number of objects in the collection

Table B.27. *Index* object methods.

METHOD	DESCRIPTION
CreateField	Creates a Field object and appends it to the Fields collection
CreateProperty	Creates a Property object

Table B.28. *Index* object properties.

PROPERTY	DESCRIPTION
Clustered	Indicates whether the Index object is a clustered index
DistinctCount	Indicates the number of unique values for the Index object
Foreign	Indicates whether the current Index object represents a foreign key
IgnoreNulls	Indicates whether NULL values in the fields of the current Index object are allowed
Name	Sets a user-defined name for the DAO object
Primary	Indicates that the current index is the primary key
Required	Indicates that the values of the Field objects that make up the current Index object must be specified
Unique	Indicates that the combination of the Field object values that make up the current Index object are unique

Parameters **Collection,** Parameter **Object**

The **Parameters** collection contains all the **Parameter** objects of a **QueryDef** object. A **Parameter** object contains a value that is passed to a **QueryDef** object. Table B.29 shows the **Parameters** collection method, and Table B.30 shows its property. Table B.31 lists the **Parameter** object properties.

Table B.29. *Parameters* collection method.

METHOD	DESCRIPTION
Refresh	Updates the contents of the collection to reflect the current status of the database

Table B.30. *Parameters* collection property.

PROPERTY	DESCRIPTION
Count	Indicates the number of objects in the collection

Table B.31. *Parameter* object properties.

PROPERTY	DESCRIPTION
Direction	Indicates whether the object represents an input, an output, both, or the return value from the procedure
Name	Sets a user-defined name for the DAO object
Type	Indicates the operational type of object
Value	Sets the value of the Parameter object

QueryDefs **Collection,** QueryDef **Object**

The QueryDefs collection holds all QueryDef objects for a database. The QueryDef object is a stored definition of a query in a Jet database file or a temporary definition in an ODBCDirect workspace. Table B.32 lists the methods of the QueryDefs collection, and Table B.33 shows its property. Table B.34 lists the methods of the QueryDef object, and Table B.35 lists its properties.

Table B.32. *QueryDefs* collection methods.

METHOD	DESCRIPTION
Append	Adds a new object to the collection
Delete	Removes an object from the collection
Refresh	Updates the contents of the collection to reflect the current status of the database

Table B.33. *QueryDefs* collection property.

PROPERTY	DESCRIPTION
Count	Indicates the number of objects in the collection

Table B.34. *QueryDef* object methods.

METHOD	DESCRIPTION
Cancel	Cancels execution of an asynchronous method call
Close	Closes the current recordset
CreateProperty	Creates a new user-defined Property object
Execute	Executes the current query definition
OpenRecordset	Creates a new Recordset object and appends it to the Recordsets collection

Table B.35. *QueryDef* object properties.

PROPERTY	DESCRIPTION
CacheSize	Returns the number of locally cached records that will be received from an ODBC data source
Connect	Indicates the information about the source of an open connection
DateCreated	Returns the date and time the current object was created
LastUpdated	Returns the date and time the current object was last modified
KeepLocal	Indicates that the current object is not to be replicated
LogMessages	Indicates whether messages from an ODBC data source are recorded
MaxRecords	Indicates the maximum return from the query
Name	Sets a user-defined name for the DAO object
ODBCTimeout	Returns a number, indicating the number of seconds to wait before a timeout error occurs when a QueryDef is executed on an ODBC database
Prepare	Indicates whether the query should be prepared on the server as a temporary stored procedure
RecordsAffected	Indicates the number of records affected by the last call to the Execute method
Replicable	Indicates whether the current object can be replicated
ReturnsRecords	Indicates whether a SQL pass-through query returns records
SQL	Sets the SQL statement that composes the current query
StillExecuting	Indicates whether an asynchronous operation has finished executing
Type	Returns the operational type of object
Updatable	Indicates whether the QueryDef object can be updated

Recordsets **Collection,** Recordset **Object**

The Recordsets collection contains all open Recordset objects of a database. Through the Recordset object, data can be manipulated and accessed. Recordset types include Table, Dynaset, Snapshot, Forward-only, and Dynamic. All recordsets are accessed by rows (records) and columns (fields). Table B.36 shows the method of the Recordsets collection, and Table B.37 shows its property. Table B.38 lists the methods of the Recordset object, and Table B.39 lists its properties.

Table B.36. *Recordsets* collection method.

METHOD	DESCRIPTION
Refresh	Updates the contents of the collection to reflect the current status of the database

Table B.37. *Recordsets* collection property.

PROPERTY	DESCRIPTION
Count	Indicates the number of objects in the collection

Table B.38. *Recordset* object methods.

METHOD	DESCRIPTION
AddNew	Adds a new record to the current recordset
Cancel	Cancels operation of an asynchronous operation
CancelUpdate	Cancels any pending updates
Clone	Creates a duplicate of the current Recordset object
Close	Closes the current recordset
CopyQueryDef	Returns a QueryDef object that is a copy of the QueryDef used to create the current Recordset object
Delete	Deletes the current record
Edit	Prepares the current record for editing by Visual Basic code
FillCache	Fills all or part of a Recordset object that contains data from an ODBC data source
FindFirst	Finds the first record that matches specified criteria
FindLast	Finds the last record that matches specified criteria
FindNext	Finds the next record that matches specified criteria
FindPrevious	Finds the previous record that matches specified criteria
GetRows	Returns multiple rows from the current Recordset object
Move	Moves the position of the current record in the current Recordset object
MoveFirst	Moves to the first record of the recordset
MoveLast	Moves to the last record of the recordset
MoveNext	Moves to the next record of the recordset
MovePrevious	Moves to the previous record of the recordset
NextRecordset	Returns the next set of records returned by a multipart selection query in an OpenRecordset call
OpenRecordset	Sets the recordset to a new selection of records
Requery	Performs the specified query again to update the recordset with the current database information
Seek	Finds a match to a specific criteria by using an index of the current recordset
Update	Saves changes specified to the recordset from the AddNew or Edit method

Table B.39. *Recordset* object properties.

PROPERTY	DESCRIPTION
AbsolutePosition	Sets the record pointer position within the Recordset object
BatchCollisionCount	Indicates the number of records that did not complete the last batch update
BatchCollisions	Returns an array of bookmarks indicating which rows generated collisions in the last batch update operation
BatchSize	Indicates the number of statements sent back to the server in each batch
BOF	Returns the beginning-of-file indicator
EOF	Returns the end-of-file indicator
Bookmark	Returns the bookmark for a record position
Bookmarkable	Returns a Boolean stating the capability to create bookmarks
CacheSize	Indicates the number of locally cached records that will be received from an ODBC data source
CacheStart	Returns a bookmark to the first record in a Recordset object containing data to be locally cached from an ODBC data source
Connection	Sets the Connection object that owns the current Recordset object
DateCreated	Returns the date and time the current object was created
LastUpdated	Returns the date and time the current object was last modified
EditMode	Indicates the state of editing for the current record
Filter	Sets a filter to determine the records included in a subsequently opened Recordset object
Index	Sets the current index for the Recordset object
LastModified	Returns a bookmark to the last edited or new record of the current Recordset object
LockEdits	Indicates the type of locking that is in effect while editing
Name	Sets a user-defined name for the DAO object
NoMatch	Indicates whether a record was found after using either the Seek method or a Find method
PercentPosition	Returns an approximate percentage of the current record position as compared to the entire record population of the current Recordset object
RecordCount	Indicates the number of records in the current Recordset object
RecordStatus	Returns the update status of a current record that is part of a batch update
Restartable	Indicates whether the current object supports the ReQuery method
Sort	Sets the order for records in the current Recordset object
StillExecuting	Indicates whether an asynchronous operation has finished
Transactions	Indicates whether the object supports transactions
Type	Indicates the operational type of the object

continued on next page

continued from previous page

PROPERTY	DESCRIPTION
Updatable	Indicates whether the current object can be updated
UpdateOptions	Indicates the way in which batch updates are executed
ValidationRule	Returns the value that validates data in a field as it is changed or added to a table
ValidationText	Sets a message that your application displays if the value of the Field object does not satisfy the validation rule

Relations **Collection,** Relation **Object**

The Relations collection contains all the Relation objects stored in a database. A Relation object indicates the relationship between fields and tables or queries of a Jet database. Table B.40 lists the methods of the Relations collection, and Table B.41 shows its property. Table B.42 shows the method of the Relation object, and Table B.43 lists its properties.

Table B.40. *Relations* collection methods.

METHOD	DESCRIPTION
Append	Adds a new object to the collection
Delete	Removes an object from the collection
Refresh	Updates the contents of the collection to reflect the current status of the database

Table B.41. *Relations* collection property.

PROPERTY	DESCRIPTION
Count	Indicates the number of objects in the collection

Table B.42. *Relation* object method.

METHOD	DESCRIPTION
CreateField	Creates a Field object and appends it to the Fields collection

Table B.43. *Relation* object properties.

PROPERTY	DESCRIPTION
Attributes	Returns characteristics of the current Relation object
ForeignTable	Sets the name of the current Relation object's foreign table
Name	Sets a user-defined name for the DAO object

PROPERTY	DESCRIPTION
PartialReplica	Indicates whether the Relation object should be included in a partial replica
Table	Returns the name of the current Relation object's primary table
ValidationText	Sets a message that your application displays if the value of the Field object does not satisfy the validation rule

TableDefs **Collection,** TableDef **Object**

The TableDefs collection contains all TableDef objects for a given database. The TableDef object is used to access and manipulate a tables definition. Table B.44 lists the methods of the TableDefs collection, and Table B.45 shows its property. Table B.46 lists the methods of the TableDef object, and Table B.47 lists its properties.

Table B.44. *TableDefs* collection methods.

METHOD	DESCRIPTION
Append	Adds a new object to the collection
Delete	Removes an object from the collection
Refresh	Updates the contents of the collection to reflect the current status of the database

Table B.45. *TableDefs* collection property.

PROPERTY	DESCRIPTION
Count	Indicates the number of objects in the collection

Table B.46. *TableDef* object methods.

METHOD	DESCRIPTION
CreateField	Creates a new Field object for the current TableDef and appends it to the Fields collection
CreateIndex	Creates a new Index object for the current TableDef object and appends it to the Indexes collection
CreateProperty	Creates a new user-defined Property object for the current TableDef object
OpenRecordset	Creates a new Recordset object and appends it to the Recordsets collection
RefreshLink	Updates the connection information for a linked table

Table B.47. *TableDef* object properties.

PROPERTY	DESCRIPTION
Attributes	Indicates the characteristics of the current `TableDef` object
ConflictTable	Returns the name of a conflict table containing the database records that conflicted during the synchronization of two replicas
Connect	Sets information about the source of an open connection
DateCreated	Returns the date and time the current object was created
LastUpdated	Returns the date and time the current object was last modified
KeepLocal	Indicates that the object is not to be replicated with replication of the database
Name	Sets a user-defined name for the DAO object
RecordCount	Indicates the number of records in a table
Replicable	Indicates whether the object is replicable
ReplicaFilter	Indicates what subset of records is replicated from a full replica
SourceTableName	Indicates the name of a linked table or the name of a base table
Updatable	Indicates whether you can change the DAO object
ValidationRule	Sets a value that validates data in a field as it is changed or added to a table
ValidationText	Sets a message that your application displays if the value of the `Field` object does not satisfy the validation rule

Workspaces **Collection,** Workspace **Object**

The `Workspaces` collection contains all active `Workspace` objects that are not hidden. A `Workspace` object defines how the Visual Basic application interacts with data. Table B.48 lists the methods of the `Workspaces` collection, and Table B.49 shows its property. Table B.50 lists the methods of the `Workspace` object, and Table B.51 lists its properties.

Table B.48. *Workspaces* collection methods.

METHOD	DESCRIPTION
Append	Adds a new object to the collection
Delete	Removes an object from the collection
Refresh	Updates the contents of the collection to reflect the current status of the database

Table B.49. *Workspaces* collection property.

PROPERTY	DESCRIPTION
Count	Indicates the number of objects in the collection

Table B.50. *Workspace* object methods.

METHOD	DESCRIPTION
BeginTrans	Begins transaction for the workspace
CommitTrans	Commits changes since the last call to the BeginTrans method
Rollback	Rolls back to the workspace state before the call to the BeginTrans method
Close	Closes the Workspace object
CreateDatabase	Creates a new Database object
CreateGroup	Creates a new Group object
CreateUser	Creates a new User object
OpenConnection	Opens a connection object for an ODBC data source
OpenDatabase	Opens a database with the current workspace

Table B.51. *Workspace* object properties.

PROPERTY	DESCRIPTION
DefaultCursorDriver	Returns the type of cursor driver used on the connection created by the call to OpenConnection or OpenDatabase
IsolateODBCTrans	Indicates whether multiple transactions that involve the same Jet-connected ODBC data source are isolated
LoginTimeout	Indicates the number of seconds before an error occurs while attempting to log on to an ODBC database
Name	Sets a user-defined name for the DAO object
Type	Indicates the operational type of object
UserName	Returns the owner of the current workspace object

Users **Collection,** User **Object**

A Users collection contains all User objects belonging to a particular Workspace or Group object. The User object refers to a specific user account with various permissions. Table B.52 lists the methods of the Users collection, and Table B.53 shows its property. Table B.54 lists the methods of the User object, and Table B.55 lists its properties.

Table B.52. *Users* collection methods.

METHOD	DESCRIPTION
Append	Adds a new object to the collection
Delete	Removes an object from the collection
Refresh	Updates the contents of the collection to reflect the current status of the database

Table B.53. *Users* collection property.

PROPERTY	DESCRIPTION
Count	Indicates the number of objects in the collection

Table B.54. *User* object methods.

METHOD	DESCRIPTION
CreateGroup	Creates a new Group object for the current user
NewPassword	Changes the password of the current user

Table B.55. *User* object properties.

PROPERTY	DESCRIPTION
Name	Sets the name of the current User object
Password	Sets the password for the current User object
PID	Returns a personal identifier for the current User object

REMOTE DATA
OBJECT REFERENCE

The remote data object (RDO) model provides you with an object-oriented interface to open database connectivity (ODBC) datasources. Figure C.1 shows the entire RDO object model in its hierarchical form.

This appendix is designed as a reference to all the objects included in the RDO object model. The collections and objects are listed in alphabetical order with tables indicating and describing all the available methods and properties available to each.

rdoColumns Collection, rdoColumn Object

The rdoColumns collection contains all the columns in a rdoResultset or rdoTable. Table C.1 shows the method for the rdoColumns collection, and Table C.2 lists the properties for the rdoColumns collection. Table C.3 lists the events, Table C.4 lists the methods, and Table C.5 lists the properties for the rdoColumn object.

Table C.1. rdoColumns collection method.

METHOD	DESCRIPTION
Refresh	Updates the contents of the collection to reflect the current status of the database

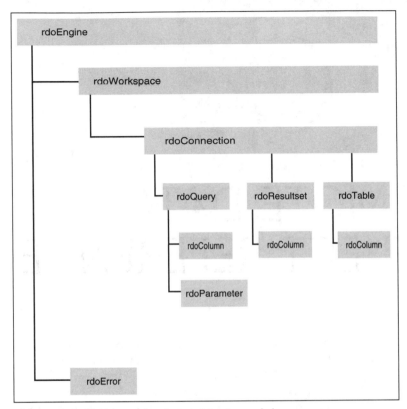

Figure C.1. The remote data object model.

Table C.2. rdoColumns collection properties.

PROPERTY	DESCRIPTION
Count	The number of objects in the collection
Item	Returns the specified object from the collection

Table C.3. rdoColumn object events.

EVENT	DESCRIPTION
DataChanged	Fired when a column's data changes
WillChangeData	Fired before a column's data is changed

Table C.4. rdoColumn object methods.

METHOD	DESCRIPTION
AppendChunk	Appends data to an rdoColumn
ColumnSize	The number of bytes in an rdoColumn's value
GetChunk	Returns a portion of an rdoColumn's value

Table C.5. rdoColumn object properties.

PROPERTY	DESCRIPTION
AllowZeroLength	Indicates whether a zero-length string is acceptable in the Value property
Attributes	Returns attributes of an rdoColumn
BatchConflictValue	Returns the value currently in the database during an optimistic batch update conflict
ChunkRequired	Indicates that GetChunk and AppendChunk must be used with this rdoColumn
KeyColumn	Returns or sets whether this column is part of the primary key
Name	Returns the name of the remote data object
OrdinalPosition	Returns the relative position in the collection
OriginalValue	Returns the value of a column when it was fetched from the database
Required	Indicates whether a column requires a non-NULL value
Size	Returns the size of an rdoColumn
SourceColumn	Returns the object's original source column name
SourceTable	Returns the object's original source table name
Status	Returns or sets the column buffer state
Type	Returns the data type of the object
Updatable	Indicates whether changes can be made to the object
Value	Returns or sets the value of the object when ChunkRequired is False

rdoConnections **Collection,** rdoConnection **Object**

The rdoConnections collection manages all the connections in an rdoEnvironment. Table C.6 lists the methods and Table C.7 lists the properties of the rdoConnections collection. Table C.8 lists the events, Table C.9 lists the methods, and Table C.10 lists the properties of the rdoConnection object.

Table C.6. rdoConnections collection methods.

METHOD	DESCRIPTION
Add	Adds an item to the collection
Remove	Removes an item from the collection

Table C.7. rdoConnections collection properties.

PROPERTY	DESCRIPTION
Count	The number of objects in the collection
Item	Returns the specified object from the collection

Table C.8. rdoConnection object events.

EVENT	DESCRIPTION
BeforeConnect	Fired before the ODBC call to SQLDriverConnect
Connect	Fired after the connection is made to the ODBC datasource
Disconnect	Fired after a connection has been closed
QueryComplete	Fired after an asynchronous query is completed
QueryTimeout	Fired after a query has exceeded the QueryTimeout property
WillExecute	Fired before a query is executed

Table C.9. rdoConnection object methods.

METHOD	DESCRIPTION
BeginTrans	Begins a transaction
Cancel	Cancels an asynchronous query or pending results
Close	Closes the connection
CommitTrans	Commits a transaction
EstablishConnection	Connects to a datasource
Execute	Executes a query
OpenResultset	Creates a new rdoResultset
RollbackTrans	Rolls back a transaction

Table C.10. rdoConnection object properties.

PROPERTY	DESCRIPTION
AsyncCheckInterval	Keeps track of how often checks are done on asynchronous queries
Connect	Returns information about the open connection
CursorDriver	Returns or sets where the cursor is to be created
hDbc	The ODBC connection handle for use with the ODBC API
LastQueryResults	The last resultset returned on a prepared statement
LoginTimeout	Returns or sets the login timeout, measured in seconds
LogMessages	Returns or sets the ODBC trace file pathname
Name	The name of the object

PROPERTY	DESCRIPTION
QueryTimeout	Returns or sets the query timeout
rdoQueries	The prepared statements collection
rdoResultsets	The result sets collection
rdoTables	The tables collection
RowsAffected	The number of rows affected by the last query
StillConnecting	Indicates a connection is still attempting to connect
StillExecuting	Indicates an asynchronous query is still executing
Transactions	Indicates whether a cursor supports transactions
Updatable	Indicates whether a cursor is updatable
Version	Returns the version of the ODBC driver

rdoEngine **Object**

The **rdoEngine** is the parent object of the RDO object model. It does not need to be created. Table C.11 shows the event of the **rdoEngine** object. Table C.12 lists the methods of the **rdoEngine**, and Table C.13 lists its properties.

Table C.11. rdoEngine object event.

EVENT	DESCRIPTION
InfoMessage	Fired when an rdoError is added to the rdoErrors collection

Table C.12. rdoEngine object methods.

METHOD	DESCRIPTION
rdoCreateEnvironment	Creates a new rdoEnvironment
rdoRegisterDataSource	Registers a new ODBC datasource

Table C.13. rdoEngine object properties.

PROPERTY	DESCRIPTION
rdoDefaultCursorDriver	Returns or sets the default of where cursors are created for connections
RdoDefaultErrorThreshold	Returns or sets the default error threshold
rdoDefaultLoginTimeout	Returns or sets the timeout value for connecting to a datasource
rdoDefaultPassword	Returns or sets the default password for any new rdoEnvironment
rdoDefaultUser	Returns or sets the default user for any new rdoEnvironment
rdoEnvironments	The collection of all the active rdoEnvironments
rdoErrors	The collection of all the rdoErrors
rdoLocaleID	The locale ID used for loading resources
rdoVersion	The version of the RDO library

rdoEnvironments Collection, rdoEnvironment Object

The rdoEnvironment is a grouping of connections for a particular user. The rdoEnvironments collection is the collection of all those rdoEnviroment objects. Table C.14 lists the methods and Table C.15 lists the properties for the rdoEnvironments collection. Table C.16 lists the events, Table C.17 lists the methods, and Table C.18 lists the properties for the rdoEnvironment object.

Table C.14. rdoEnvironments collection methods.

METHOD	DESCRIPTION
Add	Adds an item to the collection
Remove	Removes an item from the collection

Table C.15. rdoEnvironments collection properties.

PROPERTY	DESCRIPTION
Count	The number of objects in the collection
Item	Returns the specified object from the collection

Table C.16. rdoEnvironment object events.

EVENT	DESCRIPTION
BeginTrans	Fired after the BeginTrans method is completed
CommitTrans	Fired after the CommitTrans method is completed
RollbackTrans	Fired after the RollbackTrans method is completed

Table C.17. rdoEnvironment object methods.

METHOD	DESCRIPTION
BeginTrans	Begins a transaction
Close	Closes the object
CommitTrans	Commits a transaction
OpenConnection	Adds an item to the rdoConnections collection
RollbackTrans	Rolls back a transaction

Table C.18. rdoEnvironment object properties.

PROPERTY	DESCRIPTION
CursorDriver	Returns or sets where cursors are created
hEnv	Returns the handle to the ODBC environment
LoginTimeout	Returns or sets the login timeout
Name	Returns the name of the object
Password	Returns or sets the password
rdoConnections	The collection of rdoConnections in this environment
UserName	Returns or sets the username

rdoErrors **Collection,** rdoError **Object**

The rdoErrors collection manages errors returned by RDO operations. For each operation there might be multiple rdoError objects. Table C.19 shows the method of the rdoErrors collection, Table C.20 lists the properties of the rdoErrors collection, and Table C.21 lists the properties of the rdoError object.

Table C.19. rdoErrors collection method.

METHOD	DESCRIPTION
Clear	Clears the collection

Table C.20. rdoErrors collection properties.

PROPERTY	DESCRIPTION
Count	The number of objects in the collection
Item	Returns the specified object from the collection

Table C.21. rdoError object properties.

PROPERTY	DESCRIPTION
Description	Returns the description of the error
HelpContext	Returns a help context ID associated with the error
HelpFile	Returns a help file associated with the error
Number	Returns the error number
Source	Returns the source of the error
SQLRetcode	Returns the return value from the most recent RDO operation
SQLState	Returns the type of error as specified by the X/Open and SQL Access Group SQL

rdoParameters **Collection,** rdoParameter **Object**

The rdoParameters collection manages the list of rdoParameter objects for an rdoQuery. Table C.22 lists the properties for the rdoParameters collection. Table C.23 shows the method and Table C.24 lists the properties for the rdoParameter object.

Table C.22. rdoParameters collection properties.

PROPERTY	DESCRIPTION
Count	The number of objects in the collection
Item	Returns the specified object from the collection

Table C.23. rdoParameter object method.

METHOD	DESCRIPTION
AppendChunk	Appends data to the object's data property

Table C.24. rdoParameter object properties.

PROPERTY	DESCRIPTION
Direction	Returns or sets how a parameter is passed to or from a procedure
Name	Returns or sets the name of the object
Size	Returns or sets the size of the object
Type	Returns or sets the data type of the object
Value	Returns or sets the value of the object

rdoQueries **Collection,** rdoQuery **Object**

An rdoQuery object is used to manage Structured Query Language (SQL) queries where there are input or output parameters. The rdoQueries collection is made up of the rdoQuery objects for an rdoConnection. Table C.25 lists the properties for the rdoQueries collection. Table C.26 lists the methods and Table C.27 lists the properties for the rdoQuery object.

Table C.25. rdoQueries collection properties.

PROPERTY	DESCRIPTION
Count	The number of objects in the collection
Item	Returns the specified object from the collection

Table C.26. rdoQuery object methods.

METHOD	DESCRIPTION
Cancel	Cancels an asynchronous query or pending result
Close	Closes the object
Execute	Executes the query
OpenResultset	Creates a new rdoResultset

Table C.27. rdoQuery object properties.

PROPERTY	DESCRIPTION
ActiveConnection	Returns a reference to the parent rdoConnection
BindThreshold	Returns or sets the size of the largest column automatically bound under ODBC
CursorType	Returns or sets the type of cursor
hStmt	Returns the handle to the ODBC statement
KeysetSize	Returns or sets the number of rows in the keyset buffer
LockType	Returns or sets the type of concurrency handling
MaxRows	Returns or sets the maximum number of rows in the resultset
Name	Returns the name of the object
Prepared	Returns or sets whether the query should be prepared
QueryTimeout	Returns or sets the query timeout
rdoColumns	Returns the set of columns in the query
rdoParameters	Returns the set of parameters in the query
RowsAffected	Returns the number of rows affected by the most recent Execute method
RowsetSize	Returns or sets the number of cursor rows in memory
SQL	Returns or sets the SQL statement for the query
StillExecuting	Returns whether an asynchronous query is still executing
Type	Returns the type of the object

rdoResultsets **Collection,** rdoResultset **Object**

An **rdoResultset** object is the object used by the RDO to manage results from data retrieval operations. The **rdoResultsets** collection is used by **rdoConnection** objects to manage all the resultsets on that connection. Table C.28 lists the properties of the **rdoResultsets** collection. Table C.29 lists the events, Table C.30 lists the methods, and Table C.31 lists the properties of the **rdoResultset** object.

Table C.28. `rdoResultsets` collection properties.

PROPERTY	DESCRIPTION
Count	The number of objects in the collection
Item	Returns the specified object from the collection

Table C.29. `rdoResultset` object events.

EVENT	DESCRIPTION
Associate	Fired after a new connection is associated with the object
Dissociate	Fired after the associated connection is set to nothing
ResultsChanged	Fired after the current rowset is changed
RowCurrencyChange	Fired after the resultset is moved to a new row or no row
RowStatusChanged	Fired after the current row's state changes
WillAssociate	Fired before a new connection is associated with the object
WillDissociate	Fired before the associated connection is set to nothing
WillUpdateRows	Fired before the updated rows are applied to the server

Table C.30. `rdoResultset` object methods.

METHOD	DESCRIPTION
AddNew	Creates a new copy buffer for a new row
BatchUpdate	Performs a batched optimistic update
Cancel	Cancels an asynchronous query or pending result
CancelBatch	Cancels uncommitted changes in a batch
CancelUpdate	Cancels pending updates
Close	Closes the object
Delete	Deletes the current row
Edit	Copies the current row to a copy buffer for editing
GetClipString	Retrieves multiple rows into a string
GetRows	Retrieves multiple rows into an array
MoreResults	Moves to the next resultset
Move	Repositions the current row
MoveFirst	Moves to the first row
MoveLast	Moves to the last row
MoveNext	Moves to the next row
MovePrevious	Moves to the previous row
Requery	Requeries the resultset
Resync	Retrieves the batch update conflict values for the current row
Update	Saves the copy buffer to the database

Table C.31. rdoResultset object properties.

PROPERTY	DESCRIPTION
AbsolutePosition	Returns the row number of the rdoResultset object's current row
ActiveConnection	Returns a reference to the parent rdoConnection
BatchCollisionCount	Returns the number of rows with collisions in a batch update
BatchCollisionRows	Returns an array of rows with collisions in a batch update
BatchSize	Returns or sets the number of rows in a batch update
BOF	Returns whether the current row precedes the first row
Bookmark	Returns or sets a bookmark identifying the current row
Bookmarkable	Returns whether an rdoResultset supports bookmarks
EditMode	Returns the editing state of the current row
EOF	Returns whether the current row is after the last row
hStmt	Returns the ODBC statement handle
LastModified	Returns the bookmark of the last modified row
LockEdits	Returns whether locking is in effect while editing
LockType	Returns or sets the type of concurrency handling
Name	Returns the name of the object
PercentPosition	Returns or sets the position in the rdoResultset by percentage
rdoColumns	Returns the rdoColumn objects in the rdoResultset
Restartable	Returns whether the object supports the Requery method
RowCount	Returns the number of rows in the object
Status	Returns or sets the status of the current row
StillExecuting	Returns whether an asynchronous query is still executing
Transactions	Returns whether the object supports transactions
Type	Returns the type of the object
Updatable	Returns whether the object is updatable
UpdateCriteria	Returns or sets how the WHERE clause is constructed for each row during an optimistic batch update
UpdateOperation	Returns or sets whether, during an optimistic batch update, to use an UPDATE or a DELETE/INSERT combination

rdoTables **Collection,** rdoTable **Object**

The rdoTables collection manages the table in an rdoConnection. The rdoTable object manages a table in an ODBC datasource. Table C.32 lists the properties of the rdoTables collection. Table C.33 shows the method for the rdoTable object, and Table C.34 lists the properties for the rdoTable object.

Table C.32. rdoTables collection properties.

PROPERTY	DESCRIPTION
Count	The number of objects in the collection
Item	Returns the specified object from the collection

Table C.33. rdoTable object method.

METHOD	DESCRIPTION
OpenResultset	Creates a new rdoResultset

Table C.34. rdoTable object properties.

PROPERTY	DESCRIPTION
Name	Returns the name of the object
rdoColumns	Returns the rdoColumn objects in the table
RowCount	Returns the number of rows in the object
Type	Returns the type of object
Updatable	Indicates whether changes can be made to the object

ACTIVEX DATA
OBJECTS REFERENCE

The ActiveX Data Objects provide you with an interface to OLE DB data sources. Figure D.1 shows the entire ADO object model.

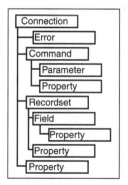

Figure D.1. The ActiveX Data Objects object model.

This appendix is designed as a reference to all the objects that are included in the ADO object model. The collections and objects are listed in alphabetical order with tables indicating and describing all the methods and properties available to each.

Command **Object**

The Command object contains the properties and methods necessary to execute SQL commands using ADO. Tables D.1 and D.2 summarize the methods and properties of the Command object.

Table D.1. Command Object Methods

METHOD	DESCRIPTION
Cancel	Cancels an asynchronously executing command
CreateParameter	Creates a new Parameter object
Execute	Executes the command

Table D.2. Command Object Properties

PROPERTY	DESCRIPTION
ActiveConnection	Returns or sets the active Connection object
CommandText	Returns or sets the command text
CommandTimeout	Returns or sets the timeout in seconds
CommandType	Returns or sets the command type
Name	Returns the name of the object
Parameters	Returns the parameters for this command
Prepared	Returns or sets whether to compile this command before executing
Properties	Returns the dynamic properties of object
State	Returns the current state of the object

Connection **Object**

The Connection object manages a data provider connection in ADO. Table D.3 describes the Connection object events, Table D.4 summarizes the Connection object methods, and Table D.5 lists the Connection object properties.

Table D.3. Connection Object Events

EVENT	DESCRIPTION
BeginTransComplete	Fired after the BeginTrans method is completed
CommitTransComplete	Fired after the CommitTrans method is completed
ConnectComplete	Fired after the Open method is completed
Disconnect	Fired after the Close method is completed
ExecuteComplete	Fired after the Execute method is completed
InfoMessage	Fired when an information message comes from the data provider

EVENT	DESCRIPTION
RollbackTransComplete	Fired after the `RollbackTrans` method is complete
WillConnect	Fired before a connection is made
WillExecute	Fired before the `Execute` method is performed

Table D.4. Connection Object Methods

METHOD	DESCRIPTION
BeginTrans	Begins a transaction
Cancel	Cancels an asynchronous operation
Close	Closes an object
Execute	Executes a SQL statement or query
Open	Open the connection
OpenSchema	Returns a `Recordset` object filled with database information
RollbackTrans	Rolls back a transaction

Table D.5. Connection Object Properties

PROPERTY	DESCRIPTION
Attributes	Indicates characteristics of the object
CommandTimeout	Returns or sets the timeout for the Execute method
ConnectionString	Returns or sets the connection string
ConnectionTimeout	Returns or sets the timeout to establish a connection
CursorLocation	Returns or sets where the cursor is created
DefaultDatabase	Returns or sets the default database
Errors	Returns the collection of `Error` objects raised by data providers
IsolationLevel	Returns or set the level of isolation for transactions
Mode	Returns the available permissions for modifying data
Properties	Returns the dynamic properties for the object
Provider	Returns the name of the data provider
State	Returns the current state of the object
Version	Returns the ADO version number

Errors **Collection,** Error **Object**

The **Errors** collection and **Error** object manage the data provider generated errors for a **Connection** object. Tables D.6 and D.7 list the methods and properties for the **Errors** collection. Table D.8 lists the properties for the **Error** object.

Table D.6. Errors Collection Methods

METHOD	DESCRIPTION
Clear	Clears the collection
Refresh	Refreshes the items in the collection

Table D.7. Errors Collection Properties

PROPERTY	DESCRIPTION
Count	Returns the number of items in the collection
Item	Returns the specified object from the collection

Table D.8. Error Object Properties

PROPERTY	DESCRIPTION
Description	Returns the description of the error
HelpContext	Returns a Help Context Id if a HelpFile is available
HelpFile	Returns the name of a help file where help on the error is available
NativeError	Returns the error number reported by the underlying API or interface
Number	Returns the error number
Source	Returns the name of the source of the error
SQLState	Returns the five-character ANSI standard error

Fields **Collection,** Field **Object**

The **Fields** collection and **Field** object are the columns or fields returned in a **Recordset** object. Table D.9 summarizes the methods of the **Fields** collection. Table D.10 describes the properties of the **Fields** collection. Tables D.11 and D.12 lists the methods and properties of the **Field** object.

Table D.9. Fields Collection Methods

METHOD	DESCRIPTION
Append	Appends an object to the collection
Delete	Deletes an object from the collection
Refresh	Refreshes the items in the collection

Table D.10. Fields Collection Properties

PROPERTY	DESCRIPTION
Count	Returns the number of items in the collection
Item	Returns the specified object from the collection

Table D.11. Field Object Methods

METHOD	DESCRIPTION
AppendChunk	Appends data to the object's value
GetChunk	Returns a portion of data from the object's value

Table D.12. Field Object Properties

PROPERTY	DESCRIPTION
ActualSize	Returns the size of the field
Attributes	Indicates characteristics of the object
DataFormat	Returns or sets the stdDataFormat object
DefinedSize	The defined size of the field
Name	The name of the object
NumericScale	Returns or sets the number of decimal places to which numeric values will be resolved
OriginalValue	Returns the values of the field when the Recordset was first opened
Precision	Returns or sets the maximum number of digits used to represent values
Properties	Returns the dynamic properties for the object
Type	Returns the datatype
UnderlyingValue	Returns the object's current value in the database
Value	Returns the object's current value in the Recordset

Parameters **Collection,** Parameter **Object**

The **Parameters** collection and **Parameter** object are used with the **Command** object to execute stored procedures. Tables D.13 and D.14 list the methods and properties for the **Parameters** collection. Table D.15 lists the method for the **Parameter** object, and Table D.16 lists the properties of the **Parameter** object.

Table D.13. Parameters Collection Methods

METHOD	DESCRIPTION
Append	Appends an object to the collection
Delete	Deletes an object from the collection
Refresh	Refreshes the items in the collection

Table D.14. Parameters Collection Properties

PROPERTY	DESCRIPTION
Count	Returns the number of items in the collection
Item	Returns the specified object from the collection

Table D.15. Parameter Object method

METHOD	DESCRIPTION
AppendChunk	Appends data to the object's value.

Table D.16. Parameter Object Properties

PROPERTY	DESCRIPTION
Attributes	Indicates characteristics of the object
Direction	Returns or sets the direction of the parameter
Name	The name of the object
NumericScale	Returns or sets the number of decimal places to which numeric values will be resolved
Precision	Returns or sets the maximum digits used to represent values
Properties	Returns the dynamic properties for the object
Size	Returns the maximum size of the object
Type	Returns the datatype
Value	Returns the object's value

Properties **Collection,** Property **Object**

The Properties collection and the Property object manage dynamic characteristics for an ADO object. Tables D.17 and D.18 list the methods and properties of the Properties collection. Table D.19 lists the properties of the Property object.

Table D.17. Properties Collection Method

METHOD	DESCRIPTION
Refresh	Refreshes the items in the collection

Table D.18. Properties Collection Properties

PROPERTY	DESCRIPTION
Count	Returns the number of items in the collection
Item	Returns the specified object from the collection

Table D.19. Property Object Properties

PROPERTY	DESCRIPTION
Attributes	Indicates characteristics of the object
Name	The name of the object
Type	Returns the datatype
Value	Returns the object's value

Recordset **Object**

The Recordset object handles the rows returned from an opened table or executed query. Tables D.20, D.21, and D.22 describe the events, methods, and properties of the Recordset object.

Table D.20. Recordset Object Events

EVENT	DESCRIPTION
EndOfRecordset	Fired when the end of the Recordset is reached
FetchComplete	Fired when the entire Recordset is fetched
FetchProgress	Fired to indicate the progress of the data fetch
FieldChangeComplete	Fired after a field is changed
MoveComplete	Fired after the Recordset moves to another record
RecordChangeComplete	Fired after a record is changed
RecordsetChangeComplete	Fired after the Recordset is changed
WillChangeField	Fired before a field's value is changed
WillChangeRecord	Fired before a record is changed.
WillChangeRecordset	Fired before the Recordset is changed.
WillMove	Fired before the Recordset moves to another record.

Table D.21. Recordset Object Methods

METHOD	DESCRIPTION
AddNew	Adds a new record to the object
Cancel	Cancels an asynchronously executing command
CancelBatch	Cancels changes before BatchUpdate has been called
CancelUpdate	Cancels changes before an Update has been called
Clone	Returns a duplicate Recordset
Close	Closes the object
CompareBookmarks	Compares two bookmarks

continued on next page

continued from previous page

METHOD	DESCRIPTION
Delete	Deletes from the Recordset
Find	Finds a record in the Recordset
GetRows	Retrieves records into an array
GetString	Retrieves records into a string
Move	Moves the position of the current record
MoveFirst	Moves to the first record of the Recordset
MoveLast	Moves to the last record of the Recordset
MoveNext	Moves to the next record of the Recordset
MovePrevious	Moves to the previous record of the Recordset
NextRecordset	Clears current Recordset and moves to the next Recordset
Open	Opens the object
Requery	Refreshes the Recordset by re-executing the underlying query
Resync	Refreshes the Recordset to the current database values
Save	Saves the Recordset to a file
Supports	Returns whether the object supports a particular function
Update	Saves the changes to the current row to the database
UpdateBatch	Saves the changes of the current batch to the database

Table D.22. Recordset Object Properties

PROPERTY	DESCRIPTION
AbsolutePage	Returns or sets the page of the current record
AbsolutePosition	Returns or sets the current record position by ordinal
ActiveCommand	Returns the command object that created the Recordset
ActiveConnection	Returns the active connection used by the Recordset
BOF	Returns whether the current record position is before the beginning of the Recordset
Bookmark	Returns or sets a bookmark for the current record
CacheSize	Returns or sets the number records that will be cached in local memory
CursorLocation	Returns or sets where the cursor will be created
CursorType	Returns or sets the type of cursor
DataMember	Returns or sets the data member to retrieve from the object referenced by the datasource property
DataSource	Returns or sets the object containing data the Recordset represents
EditMode	Returns the editing status of the current record
EOF	Returns if the current record position is past the end of the Recordset
Fields	Returns the collection of Field object's in the Recordset
Filter	Returns or sets the filter for data

PROPERTY	DESCRIPTION
LockType	Returns or sets the locking strategy
MarshalOptions	Returns or sets how the Recordset should be marshaled using DCOM
MaxRecords	Returns or sets the maximum number of records to return
PageCount	Returns the number of pages the Recordset contains
PageSize	Returns or sets the size of the pages
Properties	Returns the dynamic properties for the object
RecordCount	Returns the number of records
Sort	Returns or sets the sort criteria
Source	Returns or sets the source of the data
State	Returns the current state of the object
Status	Returns the status with regards to batch updates
StayInSync	Returns or sets whether the parent row should change when underlying child rows change in a hierarchical Recordset

A SHORT
INTRODUCTION
TO VISUAL BASIC
OBJECTS

The introduction of Visual Basic 5 made object-oriented programming much easier. This appendix defines and discusses objects as well as illustrates how to use them.

Object Overview

The biggest selling point of object-oriented programming is *encapsulation*. Encapsulation means that both the data and the means of transforming or altering that data is wrapped up into one easy-to-use shell called an *object*. In its simplest form, an object is a group of data describing a particular item that cannot be described by a single number or string.

For instance, imagine that you want to make yourself the object in which to store your application. With a single variable, you can give yourself a name. Most likely you need much more information than this to describe yourself. You might want to indicate your age and possibly your address. It is possible to incorporate all this information into one structure that represents you. Take, for example, the following type declaration:

```
Private Type Person
    Name As String
    Age As Integer
    Address As String
    City As String
    State As String
    ZipCode As String
End Type
```

This declaration creates a new data type called Person that can hold a person's name, age, address, city, state, and zip code. To create a new person, you would use something similar to the following declaration:

```
Private Steven As Person
```

This data structure was acceptable to Visual Basic programmers until version 6, when developers suddenly demanded more (and we have the right!).

Now, in Visual Basic 6, you can include much more in a data structure than just the data. Using encapsulation, you can add methods and events. The data, as we know it, becomes properties. Properties are user-interface variables or variable objects. With these interfaces, you can cleanly access the data for what is now called a class.

The concept of classes was not developed for Visual Basic; it was developed a long time ago for much older languages. (If I quote a language that invented classes or object-oriented programming, I know I will receive hate mail telling me of an earlier programming language, so I'll be vague in my history.) What's important is that you have the ability to use classes now in Visual Basic.

A class is similar to a type declaration in that it is a framework or a shell used to hold and manipulate data; however, no data or manipulation occurs in the class itself. To work with this structure, you must create an instance of the class by declaring a variable—an object variable:

```
Private m_oNewPerson As New Person
```

Here, **Person** is no longer the name of a data structure but rather the name of a class that would hold properties called **Name**, **Age**, **Address**, and so on. You would also have methods within this class to manipulate this information. For instance, you might have a method that is part of the **Person** class that would load a person's information from a file. In this case, you might have a **Load** method, as in this example:

```
m_oNewPerson.Load "Steven"
```

This example accepts a string as an argument to determine the name of the person to load.

There have always been objects in Visual Basic, even if you haven't realized it. Take, for instance, the TextBox control. This is an object—an instance of the text box class. You can use object-oriented programming to access the properties of a TextBox control as shown in this procedure:

```
Private Sub DoSomethingSenseless()

    Text1.Enabled = True
```

```
    Text1.Text = "Hello Mommy!"
    Text1.SelStart = 0
    Text1.SelLength = Len(Text1.Text)

End Sub
```

This example simply sets various properties of the TextBox control to what you have specified. You also read one of the properties from the TextBox control (`Text1.Text`), as shown in the last line.

You can call methods of this control in a fashion similar to this:

```
Text1.SetFocus
```

In this example, you simply called the **SetFocus** method that puts the focus of the window to the TextBox control.

The **DoSomethingSenseless** routine shown previously takes advantage of a great interface to the TextBox control. However, there is an even more object-oriented approach you can choose to take, as shown in this newly revised **DoSomethingSenseless** routine:

```
Private Sub DoSomethingSenseless()

    With Text1
        .Enabled = True
        .Text = "Hello Mommy!"
        .SelStart = 0
        .SelLength = Len(.Text)
        .SetFocus
    End With

End Sub
```

This routine uses a statement called **With**. **With** uses the **Text1** control to access its public members.

Many objects have default properties. The TextBox control's default property is the **Text** property. The following example shows how you can access the default property:

```
Private Sub DoMoreThings()

    ' declare a new object and call it oNewObject
    Dim oNewObject As Object

    ' all objects can be set to the 'root' type of Object
    Set oNewObject = Text1

    ' the following are equivalent
    oNewObject.Text = "Hello Dad!"
    oNewObject = "Hello Dad!"

    Text1.Text = "Hello Dad!"
    Text1 = "Hello Dad!"

End Sub
```

Notice the declaration of a new object variable in the beginning of this routine. All objects can be assigned to the Object data type. This means that all objects implement the object class. After you have the new object, you can set it to the **Text1** control (actually, just give it a reference to the control). This step allows you to access your **Text1** control using the **oNewObject** object variable. Also notice that the **Text** property does not have to be entered to assign the property its value because it is the object's default value.

Your Own Object

You can create your own object definition, or class, using Visual Basic 6. To do so, first create a new project. Along with **Form1**, which should already be part of your new project, add a class module. Name the class **Person**, and add the following code to the declarations section of the class module:

```
Option Explicit

Private m_sFirstName As String
Private m_sLastName As String
```

These two member variables of the **Person** class are private variables—they cannot be accessed by anybody outside of your class.

Now add your public properties, which serve as your user interface to retrieve information from the user:

```
Public Property Let FirstName(ByVal sNewValue As String)
    m_sFirstName = sNewValue
End Property

Public Property Let LastName(ByVal sNewValue As String)
    m_sLastName = sNewValue
End Property
```

Please note that there are no **Property Get** routines for the **FirstName** and **LastName** properties. This means that the properties are write-only and cannot be read.

Now create a property that allows the user to retrieve the entire name of the **Person** class as shown here:

```
Public Property Get FullName() As String
    FullName = m_sFirstName & " " & m_sLastName
End Property
```

This is a **Property Get** routine, and there is no **Property Let** routine, so this property is read-only.

You can now use your new class in a routine to create a new **Person** object:

```
Private Sub CreatePerson()

    Dim oNewPerson As New Person

    With oNewPerson
```

```
' retrieve information from the user
.FirstName = InputBox$("Enter first name:")
.LastName = InputBox$("Enter last name:")

' display the full name for the user
MsgBox "Person's full name: " & .FullName

End With

End Sub
```

This routine declares a new instance of the **Person** class that you wrote earlier. The user is then asked for the first and last name of the new person, and both strings are stored in the corresponding property. Finally, the **FullName** property is called to show the user the full name of the new person.

Collections of Objects

Collections are used to group related data objects into a single set. In DAO, collections are everywhere—from the **Workspaces** collection to the **Fields** and **Indexes** collections.

A collection is a good place to keep a list of objects. For instance, take the **Person** class shown previously. Suppose you want to add many people to a group or list. In this case, it would be good to use the **Collection** class to keep track of the people. Take the following event, for example:

```
Public Persons As New Collection


Private Sub cmdAddPerson_Click()

    ' initiate a new person object
    Dim oNewPerson As New Person

    With oNewPerson

        ' get new name from the user
        .FirstName = InputBox$("Enter first name:")
        .LastName = InputBox$("Enter last name:")

        ' add the person to the persons collection
        Persons.Add .FullName

    End With

End Sub
```

This event fires when a person presses a command button. First, a new **Person** object is initiated from the **Person** class. Next, the person's first and last names are filled. Finally, the person is added to the collection using the **Add** method of the **Persons** collection.

The **Collection** class stores all items as Variant data types. Therefore, you can add any data type to a collection object, with the exception of user-defined types. This also means that you can add different types to the same collection because the **Collection** class cannot tell the difference anyway.

Table E.1 shows the property and three methods of the **Collection** class.

Table E.1. The *Collection* class.

METHOD OR PROPERTY	DESCRIPTION
Count property	Returns the number of items belonging to the current collection object
Add method	Adds a new item to the current collection object
Item method	Returns an item, by an index or a key, from the current collection object
Remove method	Removes an item from the current collection, by an index or a key

As you can see, the **Collection** class is pretty straightforward. Although arrays are more efficient memory managers than collection objects, they cannot compete with other advantages. For one, you never need to use **ReDim** with a collection object—it takes care of its size for you. Also, the **Collection** class can access its items very quickly using the **Item** method, whereas an array does not have this built-in functionality.

An item of a collection is retrieved, removed, or added to a collection object, using a key and an index. A *key* is a string used during the **Add** method call, whereas an index is usually determined after each object is added to a collection. An *index* is a long value that can be determined by using the **before** and **after** parameters; however, the index can change after another object is added to the collection.

You can use the index to iterate through a collection to access each item, as shown in this example:

```
Dim nCount As Integer

With Persons

    For nCount = 1 To .Count
        Debug.Print .Item(nCount).FullName
    Next nCount

End With
```

This code uses the **Count** property of the **Persons** collection to determine an upper bound for the **For...Next** loop. For each item in the collection object **Persons**, the **FullName** property is printed to the Immediate Window.

An easier and more efficient way to iterate through a collection is to use the **For Each...Next** statement instead of the **For...Next**, as shown in this code:

```
Dim oPerson As Person

For Each oPerson In Persons
    Debug.Print oPerson.FullName
Next nCount
```

This code declares a new object variable called oPerson as a Person object. Using this variable, the For Each oPerson In Persons line of code sets oPerson to each Persons.Item(index) object in the collection. Now you can use the oPerson object to access the collection object.

Adding an Item to a Collection Object

To add items to a collection, you would use the Add method with the following syntax:

```
Sub Add (item As Variant [, key As Variant] [, before As Variant]
                                          [, after As Variant])
```

The first parameter to the routine is the actual object you are to add to the collection, and the second is a key that would be used to quickly search for the given object. The following statements demonstrate the use of keys in a collection:

```
Persons.Add oNewPerson, oNewPerson.FullName
Persons.Add oNewPerson, "Jason"
```

The other two parameters for the Add method are the before and after parameters. By using one of these two parameters, you can specify the ordinal position of your item in the collection object as shown in these examples:

```
Persons.Add oNewPerson, "Jason", 1          ' adds as first item
Persons.Add oNewPerson, "John", before:=3   ' adds as second item
Persons.Add oNewPerson, "Kimberly", after:=6  ' adds as seventh item
```

As you can see, the Add method supports named arguments.

Removing an Item from a Collection Object

To delete an item from a collection, you must know the index or the key of the item intended for deletion. The syntax for the Remove method is as follows:

```
Sub Remove (index As Variant)
```

The *index* argument in the Remove method can be either the item's key or the item's index number.

Following are a couple examples of the Remove method:

```
Persons.Remove 5
Persons.Remove "Jason"
```

Accessing Items in a Collection Object

To access items in a collection, you can use the Item method. The syntax for the Item method is as follows:

```
Function Item (index As Variant) As Variant
```

You must use the Set statement when the Item being returned is an object variable. The *index* argument is either the key or the index of the item in the collection object, as shown in these examples:

```
Set oNewPerson = Persons.Item(6)
Set oNewPerson = Persons.Item("Jason")
Set oNewPerson = Persons(6)
Set oNewPerson = Persons("Jason")
```

Notice the last two statements. The **Item** method is omitted because it is the default method for the **Collection** class.

INDEX

Symbols

* (asterisk), 151
[ ] (brackets), 134
% (percent sign), 374
? (question mark), 151, 469
" (quotation marks), 136
_ (underscore), 374
1NF (first normal form), 240-241
lstRoyalty_Click procedure, 518
lstTables list box, 196
1stTables_Click procedure, 305
lstTablesAndQueries_Click procedure, 692, 704-705
1stVendors_Click procedure, 326
lstUsers_Click procedure, 692
2NF (second normal form), 240-242
3NF (third normal form), 240-244
3027 error message, 677
3167 error message, 677
3186 error message, 677
3197 error message, 677
3260 error message, 677
3261 error message, 677
3262 error message, 677
3356 error message, 677

A

AbsolutePage property (Recordset object), 990
AbsolutePosition property
    rdoResultset object, 981
    Recordset object, 965, 990
access control
    Access database files, 677
        defaults, 679-681
        permissions, 678
        sample project, 682-686
        secured systems, 679-681
        sessions, 682
        SIDs, 679
        unsecured systems, 679
        workspaces, 682

ActiveX, 825-832
    encryption, 745-751
    exclusive access
        databases, 651-658
        tables, 658-667
    ownership
        changing, 701-706
        default owners, 701
    passwords
        changing, 706-712
        database passwords, 712-719
    permissions, 686-687
        assigning, 688-700
        property values, 687-688
        SIDs, 679
    record locking, 667-677
    user activity, tracking, 738-744
    user groups
        adding/deleting users, 731-738
        defining, 725-730
        permissions, 678
Access databases
    as ActiveX servers, 832-835
    attached tables
        creating, 309-317
        limitations, 308
    compacting, 352
    creation dates, retrieving, 301-308
    encryption, 745-751
    graphics, saving
        OLE Container control, 336
        PictureBox control, 335-340
    last-modified dates, retrieving, 301-308
    ownership
        changing, 701-706
        default owners, 701
    parameter queries
        example, 356-363
        overview, 355-356
    passwords, 712-719
        changing, 706-712
    permissions, 686-687

assigning, 688-700
  property values, 687-688
  SIDs, 679
records, counting, 301-308
repairing, 351-354
security, 677
  defaults, 679-681
  permissions, 678
  sample project, 682-686
  secured systems, 679-681
  sessions, 682
  SIDs, 679
  unsecured systems, 679
  workspaces, 682
text files, importing, 317-335
transactions
  canceling, 341
  committing, 341
  defined, 341
  error handling, 342
  integrity, 341
  starting, 341
  Transact project example, 342-351
user groups
  adding/deleting users, 731-738
  creating, 725-730
  permissions, 678
users
  activity, tracking, 738-744
  adding, 719-725
see also databases
Access queries, 835-844
accessing
  collections, 999-1000
  databases, 805-822
  recordsets, 493-496
  Registry entries, 757-763
AccessParams project, 836
  movement buttons, 842-843
  objects/properties, 839-841
  procedures
    ClearObject, 839
    cmdSetEmployee_Click, 841
    Form_Load, 843
    Form_Unload, 843
    ReadObjectValues, 843
    strDbName Property Let, 837-838
    strEmpToQuery Property Let, 838

AccessReport project
  cmdInvokeReport_Click procedure, 834
  form objects/properties, 833
ActiveConnection property
  Command object, 984
  rdoQuery object, 979
  rdoResultset object, 981
  Recordset object, 990
ActiveX controls, see controls
ActiveX technology, 792-794
  controlled database access, 825-832
  databases, converting to spreadsheets,
    845-853
  debugging, 890
  documents, 793
  editable report writers, 854-865
    cmdReport_Click procedure, 858-860
    columns, 860-861
    controls, 855-856
    footers, 861-862
    formatting, 856
    headers, 861
    progress bars, 863
    resizing, 857-858
    titles, 862-863
  editing
    embedded objects, 797-804
    in-place editing, 804-805
  private classes
    creating, 805-822
    linking, 806
    publishing, 822-825
  Registry settings, 865-867
  servers, 832-835
  see also ADO; controls
ActiveXExpense project
  ExpenseDetail class
    intialization, 816
    methods, 814
    properties, 813-814
    variables, 815
  menu specifications, 809
  Move functions, 819-821
  movement buttons, 810-811
  objects/properties, 807-809
  procedures
    ClearObject, 816
    cmdDelete_Click, 810

cmdNewExpense_Click, 809
cmdUpdate_Click, 810
Delete, 819
Form_Load, 812-813
Form_Unload, 813
Insert, 818
ReadObjectValues, 812
SetObjectValues, 811-812
SetRecordset, 817
strSetExpenseType, 817-818
Update, 818
Active Data Objects, see ADO
ActualSize property (Field object), 987
ADD COLUMN clause, 216
ADD CONSTRAINT clause, 216
Add procedure, 973, 998-999
AddAndDelete project (HT204), 83
IsNew property, 89
mblnIsNew flag, 87-88
menu specifications, 84
procedures
AddNewRecord, 88
DeleteRecord, 89-90
Form_Load event, 84-85
mnuData_Click event, 85-87
NewRecord, 89
SaveRecord, 90
AddDeleteBound project, 21
menu specifications, 22
procedures
datEmployees_Validate, 22-24
mnuDataAdd_Click, 24
mnuDataDelete_Click, 25
mnuDataSave_Click, 25
mnuEditUndo_Click, 24
mnuFileExit_Click, 25
mnuFormUnload_Click, 26
AddField project
form objects/properties, 216-217
procedures
cmdAddField_Click, 220-221
cmdClose_Click, 224
cmdRemoveField_Click, 223
FillFieldList, 218-219
FillTypeList, 219-220
Form_Load, 218
LegalName, 221-223

AddGroup project
form objects/properties, 726, 732
procedures
AddUserToGroup, 737
cmdAddGroup_Click, 727-729
cmdClose_Click, 729, 735
cmdMove_Click, 734-735
FillAvailableUserList, 735-736
FillGroupCombo, 735-736
FillGroupList, 729
FillIncludedUsers, 735-736
Form_Load, 727, 733-734
GetNewPID, 730
RemoveUserFromGroup, 737
AddIndex procedure, 264-265
AddNew procedure, 21, 33, 437, 964, 980, 989
AddNewRecord procedure, 88
AddRecord procedure, 440, 450
AddRelation procedure, 278
AddRules procedure, 292-295
AddSpaces procedure, 398
AddTable procedure, 256-257
AddToGrid procedure, 333
AddUser project
form objects/properties, 720
procedures
cmdAddUser_Click, 721-723
FillUserList, 724
Form_Load, 721
GetNewPID, 724-725
AddUserToGroup procedure, 737
Administer permissions, 678
Administrator (ODBC), 375
data sources
maintaining, 377-380
name types, 377
property pages, 378
starting, 377-378
ADO (ActiveX Data Objects), 484, 983
business objects
incorporating into MTS, 542-547
middle-tier, 531-542
Command object, 984
Connection object
events, 984-985
methods, 985
properties, 985

data retrieval, 493-496
databases, browsing, 486-489
error handling, 547-551
Error objects, 986
Errors collection, 985-986
Field object, 987
Fields collection, 986-987
Parameter object, 988
Parameters collection, 987-988
Properties collection, 988
Property object, 989
records, creating/deleting, 489-492
recordsets
 batch updates, 523-528
 editing, 496-507
 remote updates, 528-531
Recordset object
 events, 989
 methods, 989-990
 properties, 990-991
SQL Server objects, editing, 520-522
stored procedures
 executing, 512-515
 parameters, 516-520
transaction processing, 507-511
ADODC project, 487-489, 529
 Form_Load procedure, 530-531
 Form_Unload procedure, 530-531
 ShowADOError procedure, 531
ADODC2 project
 form objects/properties, 490-491
 procedures
 mnuDelete_Click, 492
 mnuExit_Click, 492
 mnuNew_Click, 492
 mnuSave_Click, 492
 Save, 491
aggregate procedures, 167-168, 941, 948
algorithms, Soundex, 910
 coding guide, 913
 coding results, 913-914
 example, 911-913
ALL keyword, 947
AllowZeroLength property, 289
 Field object, 959
 rdoColumn object, 973
AllPermissions property
 Container object, 954
 Document object, 956

ALTER statement, 940
ALTER TABLE statement, 216, 943-945
AlterObjects project
 buttons, 522
 form objects/properties, 521
AND keyword, 135-136, 174
AND logical operator, 940
APIConnect procedure, 400
apk prefix, 262
Append procedure, 260, 986
append queries, creating, 950
Append.frm project
 objects/properties, 201-202
 procedures
 cmdAppendRecords_Click, 205-206
 cmdCancel_Click, 208
 cmdCreateTable_Click, 204
 cmdDeleteRecords_Click, 206-207
 cmdDropTable_Click, 205
 cmdOK_Click, 208
 FillList, 204
 Form_Load, 203-204
 GetPublisher, 209
AppendChunk procedure, 959, 973, 987-988
appending records, 199-200
architecture of ODBC, 368-370
arguments
 CreateDatabase procedure, 232-233
 search pattern arguments, 374
 SQLGetFunctions procedure, 421
 SQLGetInfo procedure, 420
assigning permissions, 688-689
 form-level declarations, 690
 procedures
 1stTablesAndQueries_Click, 692
 1stUsers_Click, 692
 chkPermission_Click, 693-694
 cmdSave_Click, 694-696
 FillTableAndQueriesList, 697
 FillUserList, 697
 ReadPermissions, 698-700
 UnCheckAll, 697
asterisk (*), 151
AsynchCheckInterval property (rdoConnection
 object), 974
AsyncRetryInterval Registry key, 786

ATTACH project, 309
  form objects/properties, 310-311
  procedures
    1stBox_DblClick, 316
    cmdAttach_Click, 311-312
    cmdCancel_Click, 316
    cmdDetach_Click, 312-313
    cmdOK_Click, 316
    Display, 315-316
    ExtractPath, 314
    GetFileName, 311
    GetMDBFile, 313-314
    ListTables, 314-315
AttachableObjects Registry key, 787
AttachCaseSensitive Registry key, 787
attached tables, 308
  creating, 309-311
    cmdAttach_Click procedure, 311-312
    cmdDetach_Click procedure, 312-313
    Display procedure, 315-316
    ExtractPath procedure, 314
    GetFileName procedure, 311
    GetMDBFile procedure, 313-314
    ListTables procedure, 314-315
  limitations, 308
attributes argument (RegisterDatabase
    function), 391
Attributes property
  Field object, 959, 987
  Connection object, 985
  Parameter object, 988
  rdoColumn object, 973
  Relation object, 966
  TableDef object, 301, 968
auditing Registry, 867
Authors application, *see* BatchUpdate project
Authors project
  custom properties, 587
  data validation, 588-589
  fields, 584
  form objects/properties, 586-587
  procedures
    cmdQuit_Click, 589
    Form_Load, 587
  report title, 584
  smart links, 583

AuthorsDR project, 564-566
automation, *see* ActiveX
Avg procedure, 168, 941

B

Backup project, 915
  BackupTable class module, 920
  enhanced timer control, 915
    Boolean variable, 917
    compiling, 919
    enabling, 918
    event-fired loops, 917
    initial values, 918
    properties, 916
    sizing, 918
  procedures
    cmdStartTimer_Click, 919
    DoBackup, 921-922
    ExtendedTimerPop, 920
    Form_Load, 922
    SetTimer, 917
    TimeToTrigger, 918
backups, scheduling, 914-923
  backup procedures, 919-922
  extended timer control, 915-919
banding reports, 604
batch updates, 523-528
BatchCollisionCount property
  rdoResultset object, 981
  Recordset object, 965
BatchCollisionRows property (rdoResultset
    object), 981
BatchCollisions property (Recordset object),
    965
BatchConflictValue property (rdoColumn
    object), 973
BatchSize property
  rdoResultset object, 981
  Recordset object, 965
BatchUpdate project (Authors application),
    523
  column headers, 524
  objects/properties, 524, 527
  procedures
    cmdApply_Click, 526
    Form_Load, 525
    Form_Unload, 525
    listAuthors_DblClick, 525

BatchUpdate procedure, 980
BeforeReadingRecords procedure, 603
BeginTrans procedure, 341, 957, 974-976, 985
BeginTransComplete event, 984
Between operator, 151, 941
BINARY data type, 186
BindThreshold property (rdoQuery object), 979
BIT data type, 186
BitMask procedure, 417
bitmasks, 417
blank lines, preventing (Crystal Reports), 627-634
blnFormIsDirty flag, 350
BOF property
    rdoResultset object, 981
    Recordset object, 965, 990
BOFAction property (data control), 27
Bookmark property
    rdoResultset object, 981
    Recordset object, 965, 990
Bookmarkable property
    rdoResultset object, 981
    Recordset object, 965
bound controls
    bound lists, creating, 28-36
    creating, 891-900
    data validation, 12-16
    DataRepeater, 901-905
    DBCombo, 28
        focus, 35
        properties, 29
    DBList, 28-29, 35
    defined, 6, 11
    records
        adding, 20-27
        browsing, 8-12
        deleting, 20-27
    undoing changes, 16-20
bound grid cells, editing, 42-46
BoundColumn property (DBList control), 29
BoundComboControl project
    compiling, 895
    procedures
        cmbCodeValue_Click, 896
        objDatabase Property Set, 897
        Reload, 896-897
        TextPropertyLet, 896

properties, 893-895
    sizing, 895
    TestBoundControl form, 897-899
brackets ([ ]), 134
breaking replicas out of replica sets, 935-938
    cmdBreakReplica_Click procedure, 937
    cmdOpenFrom_Click procedure, 937
    objects/properties, 936
BreakReplica project, 936-937
BrowseBound project, 10-11
browsing
    databases
        ADO Data control, 486-489
        RDC, 433-437
    recordsets
        bound controls, 8-12
        DAO, 59-61
        Move methods, 61-62
        RDO, 445-452
buffers (ODBC), 370
bulk mailings, 591-592
    bulk mail report, 592
        formula fields, 594, 597-598
        group sections, 595
        hidden fields, 596
        page footer, 599-602
        previewing, 602
        sort order, 598
    form letters, 613-614
        body, 615-617
        dates, 614
        margins, 615
        page headers, 619-620
        salutations, 615
    mailing labels, 609-610
        graphics, 611
        sizing, 612
        text fields, 612
        types, 610
bulk updates, 181-185
business objects
    incorporating into MTS, 542-547
    middle-tier, 531-542
business rules
    enforcing, 288-296
    overview, 288
BYTE data type, 186

C

CacheSize property
  QueryDef object, 963
  Recordset object, 965, 990
CacheStart property (Recordset object), 965
calculated fields, creating
  Crystal Reports, 591-604
  Data Reports, 567-571
Cancel procedure, 974, 984-985, 989
CancelBatch procedure, 980, 989
Cancelled property, 268
CancelUpdate procedure, 33, 964, 980, 989
CanPropertyChange procedure, 896
cascading deletes, 275
cascading updates, 275
catalog functions, 374
cbInfoValueMax argument (SQLGetInfo
  function), 420
cboFieldDataType_Click procedure, 254
cboFieldName_Click procedure, 285
cboForeignName_Click procedure, 285
cboTableDefName_Click procedure, 270, 284
CDBExplorer class module, 251
  indexes, 264
  table relations, 278, 282
ChangePassword procedure, 471-472, 711
changing
  ownership, 701-706
  passwords, 471-472, 706-712
  see also editing
CheckDatabaseVersion procedure, 359-360
CheckForLogoField procedure, 338-339
chkPermission_Click procedure, 693-694
ChunkRequired property (rdoColumn
  object), 973
classes
  instantiating, 994
  private classes
    creating, 805-822
    linking, 806
    publishing, 822-825
  Registry settings, 865-867
Class_Initialize procedure
  UnboundBrowser project, 65-66
  Seek project, 102
Class_Terminate procedure, 65-66

clauses (SQL), 940
  ADD COLUMN, 216
  ADD CONSTRAINT, 216
  CONSTRAINT
    ALTER TABLE statement, 944
    CREATE TABLE statement, 942
  DROP COLUMN, 216
  DROP CONSTRAINT, 216
  FROM
    DELETE statement, 200
    INNER JOIN keyword, 159-160
    INSERT INTO statement, 200
    SELECT INTO statement, 210
    SELECT statement, 948
  GROUP BY, 172, 948
  HAVING, 172-173, 948
  SET, 181, 951
  WHERE
    DELETE statement, 200
    SELECT statement, 154-155
    UPDATE statement, 181
  WITH, 943
  see also keywords; statements
Clear procedure, 986
ClearControls procedure, 462
ClearForm procedure, 349
ClearObject procedure, 816, 839
Clone procedure, 964, 989
Close procedure, 974-976, 985, 989
Clustered property (Index object), 961
cmdAddField_Click procedure, 271
cmdAddGroup_Click procedure, 727-729
cmdAddRecord_Click procedure, 662-663
cmdAddRules_Click procedure, 292
cmdAddUser_Click procedure, 721-723
cmdAdd_Click procedure, 254
cmdAppendRecords button, 209
cmdApply_Click procedure, 526
cmdAttach_Click procedure, 311-312
cmdChangeFile_Click procedure, 306
cmdChangePassword_Click procedure, 717
cmdCloseDatabase_Click procedure, 653-654
cmdCloseTable_Click procedure, 663
cmdConnect_Click procedure, 396-397, 443
cmdCopyConnect_Click procedure, 399
cmdCreateDB_Click procedure, 236
cmdCreateDSN_Click procedure, 388
cmdDecryptDatabase_Click procedure, 749

cmdDeleteRecords button, 209
cmdDetach_Click procedure, 312-313
cmdEncryptDatabase_Click procedure, 749
cmdGetConnect_Click procedure, 398
cmdGetInfo_Click procedure, 411-413
cmdImport_Click procedure, 322-324
cmdInvokeReport_Click procedure, 834
cmdListVendors_Click procedure, 325
cmdLoadSS_Click procedure, 849-852
cmdMove_Click procedure, 71-72
cmdNewExpense_Click procedure, 809
cmdOpenExclusive_Click procedure, 654
cmdOpenTable_Click procedure, 661-662
cmdSelectDB_Click procedure, 848
cmdSetEmployee_Click procedure, 841
cmdVendorDetails_Click procedure, 327-328
CollatingOrder property
    Database object, 955
    Field object, 959
Collection class, 997-998
collections, 997-999
    Containers, 954
    Databases, 955
    Documents, 956
    Errors, 115, 958, 985-986
    Fields, 958, 986-987
    Groups, 960
    Indexes, 961
    iterating through, 998
    objects, accessing, 998-1000
    Parameters, 962, 987-988
    Properties, 988
    QueryDefs, 962
    rdoColumns, 446, 971
    rdoConnections, 973-974
    rdoEnvironments, 976
    rdoErrors, 473, 977
    rdoParameters, 468, 978
    rdoQueries, 978
    rdoResultsets, 980
    rdoTables, 982
    Recordsets, 964
    Relations, 966
    TableDefs, 301, 967
    Users, 969
    Workspaces, 968
ColName procedure, 852
columns, see fields

ColumnSize procedure, 973
ColumnsToControls procedure, 461
COM (component object model), 793
combining duplicate values
    GROUP BY clause, 172
    HAVING clause, 172-173
    IN subqueries, 173-174
    sample project, 174-177
Command object, 984
commands, see statements
CommandText property (Command
    object), 984
CommandTimeout property
    Command object, 984
    Connection object, 985
CommandType property (Command
    object), 984
committing transactions, 341
CommitTrans procedure, 341, 957, 974-976
CommitTransComplete event, 984
CompactBYPkey Registry key, 780
CompactDatabase procedure, 352, 957
compacting databases, 352, 931
CompareBookmarks procedure, 989
comparison operators, 135, 940
compatibility of databases, 9
component dependencies, 778-779
component object model (COM), 793
concatenating strings, 626
configuring Crystal Reports Designer, 557
ConflictTable property (TableDef object), 968
conformance levels
    ODBC drivers, 371
    SQL grammar conformance levels, 373-374
Connect project, 393
    error handling, 399-400
    objects/properties, 395
    procedures
        AddSpaces, 398
        cmdConnect_Click, 396-397
        cmdCopyConnect_Click, 398
        cmdGetConnect_Click, 398
        Form_Load, 395-396
Connect property
    Database object, 955
    QueryDef object, 963
    rdoConnection object, 974
    TableDef object, 968

connect strings, 370
CONNECT.VBP project file, 393
ConnectComplete event, 984
connection handle (hDbc), 370
Connection object
  events, 984-985
  methods, 985
  properties, 985
connection pools, 543
Connection property
  Database object, 955
  Recordset object, 965
ConnectionString property (Connection object), 985
ConnectionTimeout property (Connection object), 985
ConnectionTimeout Registry key, 786
Const statement, 195, 207
constants
  dbEncrypt, 234
  dbLangArabic, 233
  dbLangChineseSimplified, 233
  dbLangChineseTraditional, 233
  dbLangCyrillic, 233
  dbLangCzech, 233
  dbLangDutch, 233
  dbLangGeneral, 233
  dbLangGreek, 233
  dbLangHebrew, 233
  dbLangHungarian, 233
  dbLangIcelandic, 233
  dbLangJapanese, 233
  dbLangKorean, 233
  dbLangNordic, 233
  dbLangNorwDan, 233
  dbLangPolish, 233
  dbLangSlovenian, 233
  dbLangSpanish, 233
  dbLangSwedFin, 233
  dbLangThai, 233
  dbLangTurkish, 233
  dbVersion10, 234
  dbVersion11, 234
  dbVersion20, 234
  dbVersion30, 234
  rptKeyHTML, 576
  rptKeyUnicodeHTML_UTF8, 576
  rptKeyUnicodeText, 576

constituent controls, 890
CONSTRAINT clause
  ALTER TABLE statement, 944
  CREATE TABLE statement, 942
constraints, 258-259
Container object, 954
Container property (Document object), 956
Containers collection, 954
controls
  ADO Data control
    browsing databases, 486-489
    creating records, 489-492
    deleting records, 489-492
  bound controls
    adding records, 20-27
    bound lists, 28-36
    browsing recordsets, 8-12
    creating, 891-900
    data validation, 12-16
    defined, 6, 11
    deleting records, 20-27
    undoing changes, 16-20
  constituent controls, 890
  custom controls
    core procedures, 869
    creating, 867
    planning, 868
    test environment, 868-869
    visual interface, 869
  Data, 430
    ODBC applications, 380, 383-385
    SQL statements, 136
  DataRepeater, 901-905
  DBCombo, 28
    focus, 35
    properties, 29
  DBGrid
    applications, 42
    design-time properties, 37
    editing cells, 42-46
  DBList, 28, 139
    focus, 35
    properties, 29
  debugging, 890
  EnhancedTimer, 915
    Boolean variable, 917
    compiling, 919
    enabling, 918

event-fired loops, 917
initial values, 918
properties, 916
SetTimer procedure, 917
sizing, 918
TimeToTrigger procedure, 918
ExpDataControl, 869
   captions, 874-875
   compiling, 876
   data maintenance, 882-883
   data movement operations, 879-881
   data updates, 887-888
   data validation, 878
   error handling, 888
   exiting, 889
   objects/properties, 871
   property procedures, 883-885
   resizing, 872-873
   Test Data Control form, 885-887
OLE Container
   embedded objects, 797-804
   in-place editing, 804
   sizing, 805
PictureBox, 335-340
RDC, 430
   adding records, 437-440
   browsing databases, 433-437
   deleting records, 437-440
rptFunction, 571
TextBox, 994
Treeview, 246
unbound, 61-62
ControlsToColumns procedure, 462
converting
   data types, 373
   databases to spreadsheets, 845-853
CopyQueryDef procedure, 964
CopyReplica procedure, 927
Core level conformance (ODBC), 371
Core SQL grammar conformance level, 373
corrupted databases, repairing, 351-354
Count procedure, 168, 941
   arguments, 171
   duplicate recordsets, 172
Count property
   Collection class, 998
   Databases collection, 955
   Fields collection, 959

Groups collection, 960
Indexes collection, 961
Parameters collection, 962
QueryDefs collection, 962
rdoColumns collection, 972
rdoConnections collection, 974
Recordsets collection, 964
Relations collection, 966
Users collection, 970
Workspaces collection, 968
COUNTER data type, 186
counting records, 106-110, 301-308
Create Relation form, 276
CREATE statements, 940-942
   CREATE DATABASE, 236
   CREATE INDEX, 943
   CREATE TABLE, 186, 942-943
CreateAuthor procedure, 348
CreateDatabase procedure, 957
   arguments, 232-233
   locale constants, 233
   option constants, 234
CreateDB procedure, 235
CreateField procedure, 961, 966-967
CreateGroup procedure, 970
CreateIndex procedure, 260, 272-273
CreateIndex project (HT403), 260-262
   command buttons, 266
   general declarations, 267
   menu controls, 262
   procedures
      AddIndex, 264-265
      DeleteIndex, 264-265
      cboTableDefName_Click, 270-271
      cmdAddField_Click, 271
      cmd_Click, 272
      CreateIndex, 272-273
      EnableIndex, 268
      EnableOK, 268
      Form_Load, 270
      GetFields, 269
      GetTables, 269
      Initialize, 268
      mnuIndex_Click, 263-264
   properties, 265-266
   TableDefName property, 268
CreateIndex procedure, 967
CreateNewDSN procedure, 389-390

CreateParameter procedure, 984
CreateProperty procedure, 956, 959, 967
CreatePublisher procedure, 348-349
CreateQuery procedure, 468
CreateQueryDef procedure, 157
CreateRelation procedure, 274, 286-287
CreateRelation project (HT404), 276
   Database property, 282
   general declarations, 281
   procedures
      AddRelation, 279
      cbdFieldName_Click, 285
      cbdForeignName_Click, 285
      cboTableDefName_Click, 284-285
      cmd_Click, 286
      CreateRelation, 286-287
      DeleteRelation, 277-278
      EnableOK, 282
      EnableRelation, 282
      Form_Load event, 283-284
      GetFields, 283
      GetTables, 283
      mnuRelation_Click, 277
      txtRelation_Change, 285
   properties, 279-281
   Relation menu, 277-279
CreateRelation procedure, 955
CreateReplica procedure, 934-935
CreateRules project (HT405)
   business rules, 290-291
   declarations, 292
   objects/properties, 291-292
   procedures
      cmdAddRules_Click, 292-295
      GetOpenDBName, 293-294
      mnuFileExit_Click, 293
      mnuFileOpen_Click, 292
CreateTable project (HT201), 247-248
   CDBExplorer class module, 251
   controls, 248
   Database property, 257
   declarations, 253
   procedures
      AddTable, 256-257
      cboFieldDataType_Click, 254
      cmdAdd_Click, 254-255
      cmd_Click, 256
      Form_Load, 253-254
      frmCreateTAbleDef, 252-253

      mnuFileNew_Click, 249-250
      mnuFileOpen_Click, 249-250
      tvTreeView_Expand, 250-251
      tvTreeView_NodeClick, 250-251
      txtTableDefName_Change, 255-256
CreateTableDef procedure, 955
CreateUser procedure, 960
CreateWorkspace procedure, 682, 957
cross-tab reports, 634-638
crosstab queries, 225, 228
Crosstab.vbp project, 226-228
Crystal Format Number dialog box, 586
Crystal Info, 559
Crystal Reports, 556
   advantages, 558
   Crystal Info, 559
   Crystal Reports Professional 6, 559
   Designer, 557
   form letters, 613-614
      body text, 615-618
      dates, 614-615
      detail sections, 618
      margins, 615
      page headers, 619-620
      salutations, 615
      text fields, 621
   mailing labels, 609-610
      graphics, 611
      sizing, 612
      text fields, 612
      types, 610
   Report Designer, 559
   reports
      banding, 604
      blank lines, 627-634
      calculated fields, 591-604
      cross-tab reports, 634-638
      formula formats, 590
      print order, 605-609
      printing, 557-558, 582-589
      user-entered variables, 638-646
   string manipulation, 622-626
   see also Data Reports
CTitles class module
   declarations, 64-65
   procedures
      Class_Initialize, 65-66
      Class_Terminate, 65-66

GetCurrentRecord, 67
RaiseClassError, 66
Update, 67
ctlEnhancedTimer control, 915
  Boolean variable, 917
  compiling, 919
  enabling, 918
  event-fired loops, 917
  initial values, 918
  properties, 916
  SetTimer procedure, 917
  sizing, 918
  TimeToTrigger procedure, 918
CURRENCY data type, 186
CursorDriver property
  rdoConnection object, 974
  rdoEnvironment object, 977
CursorLocation property
  Connection object, 985
  Recordset object, 990
cursors, 446
CursorType property
  rdoQuery object, 979
  Recordset object, 990
CUSTDIR project, 622-624
custom data controls
  creating, 867-869
  ExpDataControl example, 869
    captions, 874-875
    compiling, 876
    data maintenance operations, 882-883
    data movement operations, 879-881
    data updates, 887-888
    data validation, 878
    error handling, 888
    exiting, 889
    objects/properties, 871
    property procedures, 883-885
    resizing, 872-873
    Test Data Control form, 885-887
  planning, 868
  test environment, 868-869
cutting replicas from replica set, 935-938
  cmdBreakReplica_Click procedure, 937
  cmdOpenFrom_Click procedure, 937
  objects/properties, 936

D

DAO (Data Access Objects), 58, 430
  Container object, 954
  Containers collection, 954
  Database object, 955-956
  Databases collection, 955
  databases, opening, 61
  data validation, 75-79
    class declarations, 76-77
    IsValid property, 77-78
    RaiseClassError procedure, 77
    SaveRecord procedure, 78-79
  DBEngine object, 957
  Document object, 956-957
  Documents collection, 956
  error handling, 110-116
    class modules, 113
    multiuser environments, 112-113
    On Error statement, 110
    sample project, 114-116
  Error object, 958
  Errors collection, 115, 958
  Excel worksheet access, 116-124
    cmdCancel_Click procedure, 123
    cmdEdit_Click procedure, 120-121
    cmdRefresh_Click procedure, 122
    Excelpath procedure, 121
    form properties, 117-119
    Form_Activate procedure, 120
    Form_Unload procedure, 122
    PopulateListView procedure, 124-125
  Field object, 959
  Fields collection, 958
  generic lookup forms, 91
    FSearchResults form, 93-97
    menu specifications, 92
    mnuDataFindPublisher_Click
      procedure, 92-93
  Group object, 960
  Groups collection, 960
  hierarchy, 60
  Index object, 961
  Indexes collection, 961
  Parameter object, 962
  Parameters collection, 962
  QueryDef object, 963
  QueryDefs collection, 962

records
  adding, 82-91
  browsing, 59-61
  counting, 106-110
  deleting, 82-91
  finding, 97-105
  navigating, 61-62
  undoing changes, 79-82
  updating, 62-75
Recordset object
  methods, 964
  properties, 965-966
Recordsets collection, 964
Relation object
  creating, 274
  methods, 966
  properties, 966-967
Relations collection, 966
tables, creating, 247
TableDef object
  methods, 967
  properties, 968
TableDefs collection, 967
temporary Registry settings, 763-772
User object, 970
Users collection, 969
Workspace object, 969
Workspaces collection, 968
Data control, 6, 430
  custom data controls
    core procedures, 869
    creating, 867
    planning, 868
    test environment, 868-869
    visual interface, 869
  databases, browsing, 486-489
  dtaData, 144
  events, 13
  ExpDataControl example, 869
    captions, 874-875
    compiling, 876
    data maintenance operations, 882-883
    data movement operations, 879-881
    data updates, 887-888
    data validation, 878
    error handling, 888
    exiting, 889
    objects/properties, 871
      property procedures, 883-885
      resizing, 872-873
      Test Data Control form, 885-887
  ODBC applications, 380, 383-385
  properties, 27
  records, creating/deleting, 489-492
  SQL statements, 136
  see also controls
Data Definition Language, see DDL
data integrity, 341
Data Manipulation Language, see DML
Data Reports, 556
  advantages, 558
  query parameters, 579-582
  reports
    calculated fields, 567-571
    creating, 563-567
    exporting, 572, 575-578
    previewing, 572-574, 578
    printing, 572-575, 578
  see also Crystal Reports
data source names (DSNs), 370, 377
data sources (ODBC)
  connecting to
    SQLBrowseConnect procedure, 402-403
    SQLConnection procedure, 401
    SQLDriverConnect procedure, 401-402
  creating, 385-393
    CreateNewDSN procedure, 389-390
    errors, 391-392
    GetODBCdrvs procedure, 389
    ODBCDSNList procedure, 388
    Register objects/properties, 386-387
    RegisterDatabase procedure, 391
  defined, 369
  DSNs, 370, 377
  maintaining, 377-380
  name types, 377
data types
  BINARY, 186
  BUT, 186
  BYTE, 186
  COUNTER, 186
  CURRENCY, 186
  DATETIME, 186
  DOUBLE, 186
  LONG, 186
  LONGBINARY, 186

LONGTEXT, 186
ODBC
   grammar conformance levels, 373-374
   numeric precision conversion, 373
   Visual Basic equivalents, 372-373
SHORT, 186
SINGLE, 186
TEXT, 186
data validation
  bound controls, 12-16
  DAO, 75-79
   class declarations, 76-77
   IsValid property, 77-78
   RaiseClassError procedure, 77
   SaveRecord procedure, 78-79
data-bound grid cells, editing, 42-46
DATAANAL project, 846
  objects/properties, 847-848
  procedures
   1stTables_Click, 852
   cmdLoadSS_Click, 849-852
   cmdQuit_Click, 852
   cmdSelectDB_Click, 848-849
   ColName, 852
database administrators (DBAs), 432
Database object
  methods, 955
  properties, 955-956
  variables, 150
DatabaseCreator project (HT401)
  objects/properties, 234
  procedures
   cmdCreateDB_Click, 236
   CreateDB, 235
   GetDBName, 235
DatabaseError procedure, 656
DatabasePassword project
  objects/properties, 713
  procedures
   cmdChangePassword_Click, 717-718
   cmdCloseDatabase_Click, 718
   cmdExit_Click, 718
   cmdOpenDatabase_Click, 715-717
   Form_Load, 714-715
   Form_Unload, 715
databases, flat-file, 238-239

databases, relational
  Access, *see* Access databases
  access control
   ActiveX, 825-832
   private class modules, 805-822
  as ActiveX servers, 832-835
  attached tables
   creating, 309-317
   limitations, 308
  backups, scheduling, 914-923
  browsing, 486-489
  business rules
   enforcing, 288-296
   overview, 288
  compacting, 352, 931
  compatibility, 9
  converting to spreadsheets, 845-853
  creating
   CREATE DATABASE statement, 236
   CreateDatabase procedure, 232-234
   sample project, 234-236
  creation dates, 301-308
  data retrieval, 493-496
  embedded objects, editing, 797-804
  encryption, 745-751
  exclusive access, 651-658
  fields
   defining, 246-258
   naming conventions, 241
   overview, 237-238
  graphics, saving
   OLE Container control, 336
   PictureBox control, 335-340
  indexes
   adding, 260
   constraints, 258-259
   defining, 260-273
   limitations, 260
   naming conventions, 262
   performance indexes, 258-260
  last-modified dates, 301-308
  models, 236-237
  normalization
   first normal form, 240-241
   limitations, 239-240
   second normal form, 240-242
   third normal form, 240-244
  opening, 61

passwords
    changing, 706-712
    creating, 712-719
queries, 355-363
records
    adding, 437-442
    browsing, 433-437
    connecting to, 442-445
    counting, 301-308
    deleting, 437-442, 951-952
    editing, 452-464
    locking, 667-677
recordsets
    batch updates, 523-528
    browsing, 8-12
    editing, 496-507
    navigating, 445-452
    remote updates, 528-531
relationships, 274-288
repairing, 351-354
replicas
    breaking out of replica set, 935-938
    creating, 923-928
    database modifications, 929-930
    one-way, 931
    partial replication, 932-935
    table modifications, 930-931
    two-way, 931
searching, 910-914
tables, 237-238
    creating, 942-943
    defining, 246-258
    deleting, 945
    editing, 943-945
    joins, 948-950
    naming conventions, 241
    primary keys, 242
    relationships, 244-246
text files, importing, 317-335
transaction processing
    ADO, 507-511
    canceling, 341
    committing, 341
    deadlocks, 511
    defined, 341
    error handling, 342
    integrity, 341

    starting, 341
    Transact project example, 342-351
user activity, tracking, 738-744
user groups
    adding/deleting users, 731-738
    defining, 725-730
    permissions, 678
users, adding, 719-725
see also ODBC
Databases collection, 955
DataChanged event (rdoColumn object), 972
DataField property (DBList control), 29
DataFormat property (Field object), 987
DataProject project, 568, 579
    control functions, 571
    objects/properties, 568-570, 581
DataRepeater control, 901-905
DataSource property (DBList control), 29
DataUpdatable property (Field object), 959
DateCreated property
    Document object, 956
    QueryDef object, 963
    Recordset object, 965
    TableDef object, 968
    TableDefs object, 301
DATETIME data type, 186
datObjects_Reposition procedure, 803
DBAs (database administrators), 432
DBCombo control, 28
    focus, 35
    properties, 29
dbEncrypt constant, 234
DBEngine object, 957
dbfBiblio variable (Database object), 150
DBGrid control
    applications, 42
    cells, editing, 42-46
    design-time properties, 37
dbLangArabic constant, 233
dbLangChineseSimplified constant, 233
dbLangChineseTraditional constant, 233
dbLangCyrillic constant, 233
dbLangCzech constant, 233
dbLangDutch constant, 233
dbLangGeneral constant, 233
dbLangGreek constant, 233
dbLangHebrew constant, 233
dbLangHungarian constant, 233

dbLangIcelandic constant, 233
dbLangJapanese constant, 233
dbLangKorean constant, 233
dbLangNordic constant, 233
dbLangNorwDan constant, 233
dbLangPolish constant, 233
dbLangSlovenian constant, 233
dbLangSpanish constant, 233
dbLangSwedFin constant, 233
dbLangThai constant, 233
dbLangTurkish constant, 233
DBList control, 28, 139
    focus, 35
    properties, 29
dbname argument (RegisterDatabase
    function), 391
DBPath procedure, 660
dbVersion10 constant, 234
dbVersion11 constant, 234
dbVersion20 constant, 234
dbVersion30 constant, 234
DCOM (distributed component object
    model), 793
DDL (Data Definition Language), 941
    ALTER statement, 943-945
    CREATE statement, 942
    CREATE INDEX statement, 943
    CREATE TABLE statement, 942-943
    DROP INDEX statement, 945
    DROP TABLE statement, 945
deadlocks, 511
Debug.Print statement, 871
debugging
    controls, 890
    ODBC, 372
Declare statement, 372
default object properties, 995-996
DefaultCursorDriver property (Workspace
    object), 969
DefaultDatabase property (Connection
    object), 985
DefaultPassword property (DBEngine
    object), 957
DefaultType property (DBEngine object), 957
DefaultUser property (DBEngine object), 957
DefaultValue property (Field object), 959
DefinedSize property (Field object), 987

defining
    fields
        DAO, 247
        sample project, 247-258
        SQL, 246
    indexes
        Append procedure, 260
        CreateIndex procedure, 260
        sample project, 260-273
        SQL, 273
    objects, 996-997
    table relations
        cascading deletes, 275
        cascading updates, 275
        Relation objects, 274-275
        sample project, 276-288
    tables
        DAO, 247
        sample project, 247-258
        SQL, 246
Delete Data permissions, 678
Delete procedure, 21, 819, 986, 990
DELETE statement, 200, 940, 951-952
DeleteAuthor procedure, 534, 545
DeleteIndex procedure, 264-265
DeleteRecord procedure, 89-90, 440
DeleteRelation functions, 277
DeleteRow procedure, 460
DeleteSetting statement, 758
deleting
    fields, 944
    indexes, 944-945
    objects from collections, 999
    records, 951-952
        ADO Data control, 489-492
        bound controls, 20-27
        DAO, 82-91
        SQL, 200
    Registry keys, 758
    replicas from replica sets, 935-938
    tables, 187, 945
    user passwords, 706-712
    users from groups, 731-738
deploying applications, 779-780
    component dependencies, 778-779
    Package and Deployment Wizard, 772-773
    runtime files, 778

Description property
    Error object, 958, 986
    rdoError object, 977
designing databases, 237
    fields, 238
    flat-file, 238-239
    indexes, 258-260
    normalization, 239-244
    tables, 238
DesignMasterID identifier, 929
detail records, displaying, 36-42
dialog boxes
    Change Password, 469
    Crystal Format Number, 586
    ODBC login, hiding, 393-400
    Procedure Attributes, 904
    Select Data Source, 396
    Set Mapping, 894
Direction property
    Parameter object, 962, 988
    rdoParameter object, 978
DisableAsync Registry key, 787
Disconnect event, 984
displaying master-detail records, 36-42
DisplayRecord procedure, 674
DISTINCT keyword, 140, 207, 946
DistinctCount property (Index object), 961
DISTINCTROW keyword, 144-145, 947
distributed component object model
    (DCOM), 793
distributing applications, 779-780
    component dependencies, 778-779
    Package and Deployment Wizard, 772-773
    runtime files, 778
DML (Data Manipulation Language)
    DELETE statement, 951-952
    INSERT statement, 950
    SELECT statement, 945
        FROM clause, 948
        GROUP BY clause, 948
        HAVING clause, 948
        LIKE keyword, 948
        predicates, 946
        syntax, 946
    UPDATE statement, 951
DoBackup procedure, 921
Document object, 956-957
Documents collection, 956

DOUBLE data type, 186
driver argument (RegisterDatabase
    function), 391
Driver Manager (ODBC), 369
driver-defined escape characters, 374
drivers (ODBC), 369, 371-372
DROP statement, 940
    DROP COLUMN, 216
    DROP CONSTRAINT, 216
    DROP INDEX, 945
    DROP TABLE, 187, 214, 945
drop-down lists
    creating, 28-29
    sorting, 35
DSNs (data source names), 370, 377
dtaData recordset, 167
duplicate values, combining
    GROUP BY clause, 172
    HAVING clause, 172-173
    IN subqueries, 173-174
    sample project, 174-177
dynasets, counting records in, 106-110

E

editable report writers, 854-865
    cmdReport_Click procedure, 858-860
    columns, 860-861
    controls, 855-856
    footers, 861-862
    formatting, 856
    headers, 861
    progress bars, 863
    resizing, 857-858
    titles, 862-863
editing
    DBGrid cells, 42-46
    embedded objects
        ActiveX Automation, 797-804
        in-place editing, 804-805
    records, 452-464
    recordsets, 496-507
    SQL Server objects, 520-522
    tables
        ALTER TABLE statement, 943-945
        table structure, 215-225
    see also changing

EditMode property
   rdoResultset object, 981
   Recordset object, 965, 990
embedded objects, editing
   ActiveX Automation, 797-804
   in-place editing, 804-805
Embedded project
   menu specifications, 800
   objects/properties, 798-800
   procedures
      cmdAdd_Click, 800
      cmdCloseObject_Click, 802
      cmdDelete_Click, 801
      datObjects_Repostion, 803
      mnuEditInsertObject_Click, 802
      mnuEdit_Click, 801
      mnuFileExit_Click, 802
      mnuPasteSpecial_Click, 802
EnableIndex procedure, 268
EnableOK procedure, 268, 282
EnableRelation procedure, 282
enabling timer control, 918
encapsulation, 792, 993-994
encrypted databases
   access control, 825-832
   creating, 745-751
Encryptor procedure, 749-750
Encryptor project
   objects/properties, 746
   procedures
      cmdClose_Click, 749
      cmdCreateDatabase_Click, 747-748
      cmdDecryptDatabase_Click, 749
      cmdEncryptDatabase_Click, 749
      Encryptor, 749-750
      Form_Load, 746-747
End statement, 51, 113
EndOfRecordset event, 989
enforcing business rules, 288-296
EnhancedTimer control, 915
   Boolean variable, 917
   compiling, 919
   enabling, 918
   event-fired loops, 917
   initial values, 918
   properties, 916
   SetTimer procedure, 917
   sizing, 918
   TimeToTrigger procedure, 918

enumerations
   advantages, 69
   defined, 65
environment handle (hENV), 370
EOF property
   rdoResultset object, 981
   Recordset object, 965, 990
EOFAction property (data control), 27
Erl procedure, 51
Err object, 51
Err.Clear statement, 51, 113
error handling, 46-47
   ADO, 547-551
   class modules, 113
   clearing errors, 113
   database-locking error messages, 677
   Err object, 51
   error locations, finding, 50
   error types, 49
   Errors collection, 115
   Errors project, 52-54
   examples, 110-111, 114-116
   Expense data control, 888
   multiuser environment, 49-50, 112-113
   On Error statement, 110
      example, 47-48
      On Error Goto, 48
      On Error Resume Next, 49
   procedures
      DatabaseError, 656-657
      LegalName, 192
      RecordError, 675-676
      ShowADOError, 506, 531
      SQLError, 399-400
      TableError, 664-666
   RDO
      rdoErrors collection, 473
      sample project, 476-479
      tips, 474-475
   runtime errors, 26
   terminating error handlers, 51
   text import procedures, 325
   transactions, 342
Error object, 958, 986
Errors collection, 115, 958, 985-986
Errors project
   error handling, 53-54
   form properties, 52

Errors property (Connection object), 985
escape characters, 374
EstablishConnection procedure, 442, 974
events
    BeginTransComplete, 984
    CommitTransComplete, 984
    ConnectComplete, 984
    Disconnect, 984
    EndOfRecordset, 989
    ExecuteComplete, 984
    FetchComplete, 989
    FetchProgress, 989
    FieldChangeComplete, 989
    InfoMessage, 984
    MoveComplete, 989
    rdoColumn objects, 972
    rdoConnection objects, 974
    rdoEnvironment objects, 976
    rdoResultset objects, 980
    RecordChangeComplete, 989
    RecordsetChangeComplete, 989
    RollbackTransComplete, 985
    RowStatusChanged, 452
    Validate, 13-15
    WillChangeField, 989
    WillChangeRecord, 989
    WillChangeRecordset, 989
    WillConnect, 985
    WillExecute, 985
    WillMove, 989
Excel spreadsheets
    accessing with DAO, 116-126
    converting databases to, 845-853
ExcelDAO project
    declarations, 119
    objects/properties, 117-119
    OK button, 122-123
    procedures
        cmdCancel_Click, 123
        cmdEdit_Click, 120-121
        cmdRefresh_Click, 122
        Form_Activate, 120
        Form_Unload, 122
        HideBottomForm, 123
        PopulateListView, 124-125
        ExcelPath, 121
        ShowBottomForm, 123
ExcelPath procedure, 121

exclusive access
    databases, 651-658
    tables, 658-667
Exclusive project
    constant declarations, 653
    error handling, 656-657
    objects/properties, 652-653
    procedures
        cmdCloseDatabase_Click, 653-654
        cmdExit_Click, 654
        cmdOpenExclusive_Click, 654
        OpenDB, 655-656
ExclusiveAsyncDelay Registry key, 784
Execute procedure, 955, 974, 984-985
    ALTER TABLE statement, 216
    DROP TABLE statement, 187
    INSERT INTO statement, 200
    SELECT...INTO statement, 210
    temporary tables, 194
ExecuteComplete event, 984
executing
    batch updates, 523-528
    stored procedures
        ADO, 512-520
        RDO, 464-472
Exit statement, 51, 113
expControl_ValidateData procedure, 888
ExpDataControl, 869
    captions, 874-875
    compiling, 876
    data maintenance operations, 882-883
    data movement operations, 879-881
    data updates, 887-888
    data validation, 878
    error handling, 888
    exiting, 889
    objects/properties, 871
    property procedures, 883-885
    resizing , 872-873
    Test Data Control form, 885-887
ExpenseDetail class
    initialization, 816
    methods, 814
    properties, 813-814
    variables, 815
ExploreDatabase procedure, 249
exporting reports, 572, 575-578
ExportReport procedure, 572, 576-578

Extended SQL grammar conformance, 374
ExtendedTimerPop procedure, 920-922
ExtractField procedure, 329
ExtractStatusData procedure, 306

F

FastRequery Registry key, 788
FetchComplete event, 989
FetchProgress event, 989
fFunction argument (SQLGetFunctions function), 421
Field object, 959, 987
FieldChangeComplete event, 989
FieldCount function, 828
fields, 237-238
    adding, 943
    calculated fields
        Crystal Reports, 591-604
        Data Reports, 567-571
    defining
        DAO, 247
        sample project, 247-258
        SQL, 246
    deleting, 944
    multiple, 135
    naming conventions, 241
    repeating groups, 240
    selecting, 140-145
Fields collection, 218, 958, 986-987
Fields property (Recordset object), 990
FieldSize property (Field object), 959
File DSN, 377
files
    MSDATREP.DEP, 779-780
    ODBC trace logs, 372
    text files, importing, 317-335
FillAvailableUserList procedure, 735
FillCache procedure, 964
FillFieldList procedure, 218-219
FillGroupCombo procedure, 735
FillGroupList procedure, 729
FillIncludedUsers procedure, 735
FillInvoiceList procedure, 326-327
FillList procedure, 204, 344-345
FillRoyalty procedure, 518
FillTableAndQueriesList procedure, 704
FillTypeList routine, 218
FillUserList procedure, 697, 704, 710, 724

Filter property (Recordset object), 965, 990
Find procedure, 990
FindFirst procedure, 964
finding records
    by index values, 97-105
    Soundex algorithm, 910-914
FindLast procedure, 964
FindNext procedure, 964
FindPrevious procedure, 964
fInfoType argument (SQLGetInfo function), 420
first normal form (1NF), 240-241
First procedure, 168
flags
    blnFormIsDirty, 350
    mblnCancel, 267
    mblnInRefresh, 72-74
    mblnIsDirty, 69
    mblnIsNew, 87
    see also constants
flat-file databases, 238-239
    see also databases
FlushTransactionTimeout Registry key, 782
focus, 35
footers (report writer application), 861-862
foreign keys, 945
Foreign property (Index object), 961
ForeignName property (Field object), 959
ForeignTable property (Relation object), 966
form letters, creating, 613-614
    body text, 615-618
    dates, 614-615
    detail sections, 618
    margins, 615
    page headers, 619-620
    salutations, 615
    text fields, 621
    see also bulk mailings
FormatError procedure, 548
FORMLTR project, 613-614
    body, 615-617
    dates, 614
    margins, 615
    page headers, 619-620
    salutations, 615
Formulas property (Crystal Reports custom control), 645
formulas, *see* calculated fields

frmODBC_Load procedure, 387-388
frmPublisherSelect command, 207
FROM clause, 159, 940
    DELETE statement, 200
    INNER JOIN keyword, 159-160
    INSERT INTO statement, 200
    multitable recordsets, 160
    outer joins, 164
    SELECT INTO statement, 210
    SELECT statement, 948
FSearchResults form (generic lookup form)
    declarations, 94
    procedures
        cmd_Click, 94
        KeyValue property procedure, 95
        lvwResults_ItemClick, 95
        Search, 95-97
    properties, 93
functions, see procedures

G

generation identifiers, 931
generic lookup form (DAO)
    declarations, 94
    procedures
        cmd_Click, 94
        KeyValue property procedure, 95
        lvwResults_ItemClick, 95
        Search, 95-97
    properties, 93
GetAllSettings statement, 757
GetChunk procedure, 959, 973, 987
GetClipString procedure, 980
GetCurrentRecord procedure, 67
GetData procedure, 74
GetDatabase procedure, 304-307
GetDBName procedure, 235
GetField function, 828
GetFields procedure, 269, 283
GetFileName procedure, 311
GetList procedure, 533, 545-546
GetNewPID procedure, 724, 730
GetODBCdbs procedure, 388, 405
GetODBCdvrs procedure, 389
GetOpenDBName procedure, 293
GetPrimaryKey procedure, 664, 743
GetPrivateProfileString procedure, 64

GetPubID procedure, 148
GetPublisher procedure, 206, 209
GetRows procedure, 964, 980, 990
GetSetting statement, 757
GetStates procedure, 451, 459
GetString procedure, 990
GetTables procedure, 269, 283
globally unique identifiers (GUIDs), 929
grammar conformance levels, 373-374
granting permissions, 688-700
    form-level declarations, 690
    objects/properties, 688-689
    procedures
        1stTablesAndQueries_Click, 692
        1stUsers_Click, 692
        chkPermission_Click, 693-694
        cmdSave_Click, 694-696
        FillTableAndQueriesList, 697
        FillUserList, 697
        ReadPermissions, 698-700
        UnCheckAll, 697
graphics
    mailing labels, 611
    saving to database files
        OLE Container control, 336
        PictureBox control, 335-340
grid cells (bound), editing, 42-46
GridChange project
    menu specifications, 44
    objects/properties, 43-44
    procedures
        cmdChangeGridCell_Click, 45
        datProducts_Reposition, 45
        mnuFileExit_Click, 46
GridLister project
    menu specifications, 39
    objects/properties, 37-39
    procedures, 40-41
grids, see DBGrid control
GROUP BY clause, 172, 940-941, 948
Group object, 960
groups
    defining, 725-730
    permissions, 678
    users, adding/deleting, 731-738
Groups collection, 960
GUIDs (globally unique identifiers), 929

H

handles (ODBC)
    hDbc, 370
    hEnv, 370
    hStmt, 371
handling errors, *see* error handling
HAVING clause, 172-173, 940-941, 948
hDbc handle (connection handle), 370
hDbc property (rdoConnection object), 974
headers (report writer application), 861
HelpContext property
    Error object, 958, 986
    rdoError object, 977
HelpFile property
    Error object, 958, 986
    rdoError object, 977
hEnv handle
    environment handle, 370
    rdoEnvironment object, 977
hiding ODBC login dialog box, 395-400
hStmt property, 371
    rdoQuery object, 979
    rdoResultset object, 981
HT201 project, *see* UnboundBrowser project
HT202 project, *see* Validating Browser project
HT203 project, *see* UndoBrowser project
HT204 project, *see* AddAndDelete project
HT205 project, *see* LookupBrowser project
HT206 project, *see* Seek project
HT207 project, *see* RecordCounts project
HT401 project, *see* DatabaseCreator project
HT402 project, *see* CreateTable project
HT403 project, *see* CreateIndex project
HT404 project, *see* CreateRelation project
HT405 project, *see* CreateRules project
HT701-HT707, *see* Publishers database project

I

Idle procedure, 957
IDs (identifiers)
    DesignMasterID, 929
    generation identifiers, 931
    GUIDs, 929
    PIDs, 679
    ReplicaID, 929
    SIDs, 679

idx prefix, 262
IgnoreNulls property (Index object), 961
IIf procedure, 153
images, *see* graphics
Implements keyword, 793
ImplicitCommitSync Registry key, 784
importing text files, 317-321, 326-328,
    334-335
    error handling, 325
    procedures
        AddToGrid, 333
        cmdImport_Click, 322-324
        cmdListVendors_Click, 325
        ExtractField, 329
        FillInvoiceList, 326-327
        InitializeGrid, 322
        Retrieve, 332-333
        StoreNewItem, 329-330
        WriteItem, 330-332
IN operator, 941
IN subqueries
    NOT keyword, 177
    overview, 173-174
in-place editing, 804-805
incorporating business objects into MTS,
    542-547
Index object, 961
Index property (Recordset object), 104, 965
indexes, 998
    constraints, 258-259
    creating
        ALTER TABLE statement, 944-945
        Append procedure, 260
        CreateIndex procedure, 260, 943
        sample project, 260-273
        SQL, 273
    deleting, 944-945
    limitations, 260
    naming conventions, 262
    performance indexes, 258-260
    searching, 97-105
    unique, 944
Indexes collection, 961
IndexName property, 104
InfoMessage event (rdoEngine object), 975,
    984
Inherit property (Container object), 954
inheritance, 792

IniPath property (DBEngine object), 957
Initialize procedure, 268
InitializeGrid procedure, 322
INNER JOIN keyword, 159
inner joins, creating, 159-160, 163, 949
Insert Data permissions, 678
Insert procedure, 818
INSERT statement, 940, 950
INSERT...INTO statement, 199-200, 209
instantiating classes, 994
intAction procedure, 221
integrity (data), 341
IsNew property, 89
IsolateODBCTrans property (Workspace
    object), 969
IsolationLevel property (Connection object),
    985
IsValid property, 77
Item property
    rdoColumns collection, 972
    rdoConnections collection, 974
Item procedure, 999
iterating through collections, 115, 998

J

Jet engine
    business rules, enforcing, 288-296
    crosstab queries, 225
    database replication, 923-924
        breaking replicas out of replica set, 935-938
        Browse button procedures, 926
        database modifications, 929-930
        object omissions, 932
        one-way replication, 931
        partial replication, 932-935
        procedures, 926-928
        table modifications, 930-931
        two-way replication, 931
    tuning (Registry), 780-781
        CompactBYPkey, 780
        default values, 781
        ExclusiveAsyncDelay key, 784
        FlushTransactionTimeout key, 782
        ImplicitCommitSync key, 784
        LockDelay key, 783
        LockRetry key, 783
        MaxBufferSize key, 783
        MaxLocksPerFile key, 783

        PageTimeout key, 782
        RecycleLVs key, 783
        SharedAsyncDelay key, 784
        SystemDB key, 780
        Threads key, 783
        UserCommitSync key, 784
JetTryAuth Registry key, 787
joins, 948
    inner joins, 159-160, 163, 949
    left joins, 949
    multifield, 160
    nesting, 949-950
    outer joins, 163-167
    right joins, 949

K

KeepLocal property
    Document object, 956
    QueryDef object, 963
    TableDef object, 968
KeyColumn property (rdoColumn object), 973
keys (index), 998
    foreign, 945
    primary, 242, 945
        constraints, 259
        creating, 943
keys (Registry)
    accessing, 757-763
    deleting, 758
    ExclusiveAsyncDelay, 784
    FlushTransactionTimeout, 782
    ImplicitCommitSync, 784
    Jet engine, 780-781
        CompactBYPkey, 780
        default values, 781
        SystemDB, 780
    LockDelay, 783
    LockRetry, 783
    MaxBufferSize, 783
    MaxLocksPerFile, 783
    ODBC engine
        AsyncRetryInterval, 786
        AttachableObjects, 787
        AttachCaseSensitive, 787
        ConnectionTimeout, 786
        default settings, 784-785
        DisableAsync, 787
        FastRequery, 788

JetTryAuth, 787
LoginTimeout, 786
PreparedInsert, 787
PreparedUpdate, 788
QueryTimeout, 786
SnapshotOnly, 787
TraceODBCAPI, 787
TraceSQLMode, 787
PageTimeout, 782
RecycleLVs, 783
saving, 758
SharedAsyncDelay, 784
temporary DAO settings, 763-772
Threads, 783
UserCommitSync, 784
KeysetSize property (rdoQuery object), 979
keywords
ALL, 947
AND, 135-136
DISTINCT, 140, 946
DISTINCTROW, 144-145, 947
Implements, 793
INNER JOIN, 159
LIKE, 948
NOT, 177
OR, 135-136
PIVOT, 225
TOP, 947
TRANSFORM, 225
WithEvents, 452
see also clauses; statements

L

labels (mailing labels), 609-610
creating, 609
graphics, 611
sizing, 612
text fields, 612
types, 610
Last procedure, 168
LastModified property
rdoResultset object, 981
Recordset object, 965
LastQueryResults property (rdoConnection object), 974
LastUpdated property
Document object, 956
QueryDef object, 963

Recordset object, 965
TableDef object, 301, 968
LCase procedure, 178-179
left joins, 164, 949
LegalName procedure, 191-192, 221
Length procedure, 625
letters (form), 613-614
body text, 615-618
dates, 614-615
detail sections, 618
margins, 615
page headers, 619-620
salutations, 615
text fields, 621
Level 1 conformance (ODBC), 371
Level 2 conformance (ODBC), 371
LIKE clause
SELECT statement, 948
UPDATE statement, 183
Like operator, 151, 941
lineage indicators, 931
linking classes, 806
list boxes, creating, 28-29
ListAuthors project, 493-495
ListAuthors2 project, 497
column headers, 499
declarations, 499
error handling, 506
objects/properties, 498-499
procedures
cmdDelete_Click, 504-505
cmdNew_Click, 501
cmdUpdate_Click, 502-504
Form_Load, 499-500
Form_Unload, 500
listAuthors_ItemClick, 505-506
RecordChanged, 500
listAuthors_DblClick procedure, 525
ListBound project
form properties, 30-31
menu specifications, 31
procedures
datProducts_Validate, 31-32
Form_Unload, 34
mnuDataAdd_Click, 33
mnuDataDelete_Click, 33
mnuDataSave_Click, 34
mnuEditUndo_Click, 33
mnuFileExit_Click, 34

ListField property (DBList control), 29
listing ODBC services
  Services objects/properties, 403
  procedures
    BitMask, 417
    GetODBCdbs, 405
    ODBCConnectDS, 406
    SpecialInt, 414-417
    SpecialLong, 417-418
    SpecialStr, 413-414
    SQLGetFunctions, 421
    SQLGetInfo, 410-412, 419-420
listings
  error handling
    enabling handlers, 110-111
    multiuser environments, 112-113
  multiuser error handler, 49-50
ListRecords subroutine, 184-185
lists
  bound, 28-36
  drop-down lists, 28-29
  focus, 35
  sorting, 35
ListTables subroutine, 196
Load event, 179
Load procedure, 157
LoadGetInfo procedure, 421
locale constants (CreateDatabase method), 233
location of errors, finding, 50
LockDelay Registry key, 783
LockEdits property, 666
  rdoResultset object, 981
  Recordset object, 965
locking
  databases, 651-658
    cmdCloseDatabase_Click procedure, 653-654
    cmdOpenExclusive_Click procedure, 654
    constant declarations, 653
    error handling, 656-657
    OpenDB procedure, 655-656
  records, 667-676
    DisplayRecord procedure, 674
    error handling, 675-677
    form-level variables, 669
    LockEdits property, 672-673
    optimistic locking, 667
    UpdateRecord procedure, 672, 675

  tables, 658-667
    cmdAddRecord_Click procedure, 662-663
    cmdCloseTable_Click procedure, 663
    cmdExit_Click procedure, 664
    cmdOpenTable_Click procedure, 661-662
    DBPath procedure, 660
    error handling, 664-666
    Form_Unload procedure, 661
    GetPrimaryKey procedure, 664
    initialization procedure, 660
LockRetry Registry key, 783
LockType property
  rdoQuery object, 979
  rdoResultset object, 981
  Recordset object, 991
log files (ODBC), 372
logging user activity, 738-744
logical operators, 940
login dialog box (ODBC), hiding, 393-402
LoginTimeout property
  DBEngine object, 957
  rdoConnection object, 974
  rdoEnvironment object, 977
  Workspace object, 969
LoginTimeout Registry key, 786
LogMessages property
  QueryDef object, 963
  rdoConnection object, 974
LONG data type, 186
LONGBINARY data type, 186
LONGTEXT data type, 186
lookup forms (DAO), 91-97
LookupBrowser project (HT205)
  FSearchResults form
    Cancelled property procedure, 95
    cmd_Click procedure, 94
    declarations, 94
    KeyValue property procedure, 95
    lvwResults_ItemClick procedure, 95
    properties, 93
    Search procedure, 95-97
  menu specifications, 92
  mnuDataFindPublisher_Click event, 92-93
LowerCase procedure, 625
lvwResults_ItemClick procedure, 95

M

MAILANAL project, 634-637
mailing labels, creating, 609-610
  graphics, 611
  size, 612
  text fields, 612
  types, 610
MAILLIST project, 638-640
  objects/properties, 640-641
  procedures
    1stReportType_Click, 642
    cmdQuit_Click, 645
    cmdReport_Click, 643-645
    Form_Load, 641
    optPageNoType_Click, 642-643
MakeReplica procedure, 955
MakeReplicable procedure, 926-927
MakeTabl.frm project
  objects/properties, 211
  procedures
    cmdClose_Click, 215
    cmdCreateTable_Click, 213-214
    cmdDropTable_Click, 214-215
    FillList, 213
    Form_Load, 212-213
many-to-many relationships, 244
mapping control properties, 894
MarshalOptions property (Recordset object),
  991
master-detail records, displaying, 36-42
Max procedure, 168, 941
MaxBufferSize Registry key, 783
MaxLocksPerFile Registry key, 783
MaxRecords property
  QueryDef object, 963
  Recordset object, 991
MaxRows property (rdoQuery object), 979
mblnCancel flag, 267
mblnInRefresh flag, 72-74
mblnIsDirty flag, 69
mblnIsNew flag, 87
metacharacters, 374
methods, *see* procedures
Microsoft Access databases, *see* Access
  databases
Microsoft Data Reports, *see* Data Reports
Microsoft Knowledge Base Web site, 478
Microsoft ODBC 3.0 Programmer's Reference
  and SDK Guide, 375

Microsoft SQL Server 6.5, *see* SQL Server
Microsoft Transaction Server (MTS)
  advantages, 542-543
  business objects, incorporating, 542-547
middle-tier business objects, creating, 531-542
MiddleTier project
  DeleteAuthor procedure, 545
  error handling
    FormatError procedure, 548
    On Error Goto statemetns, 548-550
  GetList procedure, 545-546
  NewAuthor procedure, 543
  UpdateAuthor procedure, 544
mimimum SQL grammar conformance level,
  373
Min procedure, 168, 941
mlRowState variable, 456
mnuDataFindPublisher_Click procedure,
  92-93
mnuDataIndexName_Click procedure,
  100-101
mnuDataSaveRecord_Click procedure, 73-74
mnuData_Click procedure, 73-74
mnuEditInsertObject_Click procedure, 802
mnuEditPasteSpecial_Click procedure, 802
mnuRelation_Click procedure, 277
Mode property (Connection object), 985
model databases, 236-237
Modify Design permissions, 678
MoreResults procedure, 446, 980
Move procedure, 68, 964, 990
MoveComplete event, 989
MoveFirst procedure, 61, 460, 964, 980, 990
MoveLast procedure, 62, 460, 964, 980, 990
MoveNext procedure, 61, 461, 964, 980, 990
MovePrevious procedure, 61, 461, 964,
  980, 990
MSDATREP.DEP file, 779-780
MSFlexGrid control, 227
mstrTableDefName variable, 267
MTS (Microsoft Transaction Server)
  advantages, 542-543
  business objects, incorporating, 543-547
multifield joins, 160
multiuser access
  Access database files, 677
    default security, 679-681
    permissions, 678
    sample project, 682-686

secured systems, 679-681
sessions, 682
SIDs, 679
unsecured systems, 679
workspaces, 682
databases
  encryption, 745-751
  exclusive access, 651-658
error handling, 49-50, 112-113
ownership
  changing, 701-706
  default owners, 701
passwords
  changing, 706-712
  creating, 712-719
permissions, 686-687
  assigning, 688-700
  property values, 687-688
  SIDs, 679
record locking, 667-677
tables, 658-667
user activity, tracking, 738-744
user groups
  adding/deleting users, 731-738
  defining, 725-730
  permissions, 678
users, adding, 719-725

N

Name property
  Command object, 984
  Container object, 954
  Database object, 955
  Document object, 956
  Field object, 959, 987
  Group object, 960
  Index object, 961
  Parameter object, 962, 988
  QueryDef object, 963
  rdoColumn object, 973
  rdoConnection object, 974
  rdoEnvironment object, 977
  rdoQuery object, 979
  rdoParameter object, 978
  rdoResultset object, 981
  rdoTable object, 982
  Recordset object, 965
  Relation object, 966

TableDef object, 968, 301
  User object, 970
  Workspace object, 969
naming conventions
  indexes, 262
  tables, 241
NativeError property (Error object), 986
navigating
  records, 21
  RecordSources, 27
nesting
  joins, 949-950
  SELECT statements, 173-174
NewAuthor procedure, 535, 543
NewPassword procedure, 707, 713, 955, 970
NewRecord procedure, 89, 450
NewRow procedure, 459
NewTable.vbp project
  object/properties, 188-190
  procedures
    cmdAddField, 191-192
    cmdClose_Click, 195, 198
    cmdCreateTable_Click, 194-195
    cmdDelete_Click, 197
    cmdRemoveField_Click, 194
    FillTypeList, 190
    Form_Load, 190
    LegalName, 192-194
    ListTables, 196
    TableIsEmpty, 197-198
NextRecordset procedure, 964, 990
NoMatch property (Recordset object), 965
normalization
  first normal form, 240-241
  limitations, 239-240
  second normal form, 240-242
  third normal form, 240-244
NOT keyword, 177
NOT NULL parameter (CREATE TABLE statement), 942
NOT logical operator, 940
Number property
  Error object, 958, 986
  rdoError object, 977
numeric precision conversion (data types), 373
NumericScale property
  Field object, 987
  Parameter object, 988
NumericText procedure, 625

O

object-oriented programming (OOP), 792
objects, 993
    Active Data Objects, *see* ADO
    adding to collections, 999
    collections, 998
    creating, 996-997
    data access objects, *see* DAO
    encapsulation, 993-994
    remote data objects, *see* RDO
    removing from collections, 999
    SQL Server objects, editing, 520-522
ODBC (Open Database Connectivity),
    367-368, 431
    Administrator, 375
        property pages, 378
        starting, 377-378
    architecture, 368-370
    conformance levels, 371
    connect strings, 370
    Data control, 380, 383-385
    data sources
        connecting to, 400-402
        creating, 385-393
        defined, 369
        maintaining, 377-380
        name types, 377
    data types
        grammar conformance levels, 373-374
        numeric precision conversion, 373
        Visual Basic equivalents, 372-373
    debugging, 372
    Driver Manager, 369
    drivers, 369
    handles
        hDbc, 370
        hEnv, 370
        hStmt, 371
    I/O buffers, 370
    login dialog box, hiding, 393-402
    ODBCDirect, 421-424
    performance tuning (Registry), 784-785
        AsyncRetryInterval key, 786
        AttachableObjects key, 787
        AttachCaseSensitive key, 787
        ConnectionTimeout key, 786
        default Registry settings, 784-785
        DisableAsync key, 787
        FastRequery key, 788
        JetTryAuth key, 787
        LoginTimeout key, 786
        PreparedInsert key, 787
        PreparedUpdate key, 788
        QueryTimeout key, 786
        SnapshotOnly key, 787
        TraceODBCAPI key, 787
        TraceSQLMode key, 787
    procedures
        calling, 372
        catalog functions, 374
    SDK, 368
    services, listing available, 403-421
    translators, 370
ODBC Direct, 430
ODBCAPI.BAS file, 372
ODBCConnectDS procedure, 406
ODBCDisconnectDS procedure, 390
ODBCDSNList procedure, 388
ODBCLoadFuncs procedure, 421
ODBCTimeout property (QueryDef
    object), 963
OLE Container control
    embedded objects, 797-804
    in-place editing, 804
    sizing, 805
    see also ActiveX
OLEDB/ADO, 431
omitting objects from replicas
    cmdCreateReplica_Click procedure,
        934-935
    SetKeepLocal procedure, 932-934
On Error statement, 51, 110
    example, 47-48
    On Error Goto, 48, 548-551
    On Error Resume Next, 49
one-to-many relationships, 244
one-to-one relationships, 244-246
one way database replication, 931
OOP (object-oriented programming), 792
Open Database Connectivity, *see* ODBC
Open procedure, 985, 990
OpenConnection procedure, 442-443, 451,
    957, 969, 976
OpenDatabase procedure, 61, 368, 957, 969
OpenDB procedure, 655-656

opening
    connections, 442-443, 451, 957, 969, 976
    databases
        exclusive access, 651-658
        OpenDatabase procedure, 61, 368, 957, 969
    recordsets, 136-137, 158, 658, 955, 964,
        967
    resultsets, 446, 974, 979, 982
    tables, 658-667
OpenRecordset method, 658, 955, 964, 967
    arguments, 136
    parameter queries, 158
    SQL statements, 137
OpenResultset procedure, 446, 974, 979, 982
OpenSchema procedure, 985
operators, 940-941
    Between, 151
    comparison, 135
    Like, 151
optAuthorTitle_Click procedure, 514
optimistic record locking, 667
optimizing performance, *see* performance
    tuning
option constants (CreateDatabase method),
    234
Option Explicit, 436
OR keyword, 135-136
OR logical operator, 940
ORDER BY clause, 940-941
OrdinalPosition property
    Field object, 959
    rdoColumn object, 973
OriginalValue property
    Field object, 959, 987
    rdoColumn object, 973
outer joins, creating, 163-167
OutputType project, 572
    DataReport1, 577-578
    objects/properties, 573-574
    procedures
        cmdExit_Click, 576
        cmdExport_Click, 575-576
        cmdPreview_Click, 574
        cmdPrint_Click, 574-575
        Form_Load, 574
Owner property
    Container object, 954
    Document object, 957

ownership
    changing, 701-706
    default owners, 701
Ownership project
    objects/properties, 701-702
    procedures
        1stTableAndQueries_Click, 704
        cmdClose_Click, 705
        cmdSave_Click, 705
        FillTableAndQueriesList, 704
        FillUserList, 704
        Form_Load, 702-703
        Form_Unload, 703

P

Package and Deployment Wizard, 772-773
PageCount property (Recordset object), 991
PageSize property (Recordset object), 991
PageTimeout Registry key, 782
Parameter object, 962, 988
parameter queries, 155-159, 355-356
    example, 356-363
parameterized stored procedures, executing
    ADO, 516-520
    RDO, 468-472
ParameterQuery project, 356
    objects/properties, 357-358
    procedures
        CheckDatabaseVersion, 359-360
        Form_Load, 362
        RunQuery, 360-361
parameters
    Data Reports, 579-582
    LockEdits, 666
    SQL statements, 155
Parameters collection, 962, 987-988
Parameters property (Command object), 984
ParameterStoredProcedure project, *see*
    RoyaltyList project
partial replication
    cmdCreateReplica_Click procedure,
        934-935
    SetKeepLocal procedure, 932-934
PartialReplica property (Relation object), 967
Password property
    rdoEnvironment object, 977
    User object, 970

passwords
    changing, 470, 706-712
    creating, 712-719
Passwords project
    objects/properties, 707
    procedures
        ChangePassword, 711-712
        cmdChangePassword_Click, 709-710
        cmdClose_Click, 710
        cmdDeletePassword_Click, 710
        FillUserList, 710-711
        Form_Load, 708-709
PasteSpecial procedure, 797
pcbInfoValue argument (SQLGetInfo
    function), 420
percent sign (%), 374
PercentPosition property
    rdoResultset object, 981
    Recordset object, 965
performance indexes, 258-260
performance tuning
    Jet engine
        CompactBYPkey key, 780
        default Registry values, 781
        ExclusiveAsynchDelay key, 784
        FlushTransactionTimeout key, 782
        ImplicitCommitSync key, 784
        LockDelay key, 783
        LockRetry key, 783
        MaxBufferSize key, 783
        MaxLocksPerFile key, 783
        PageTimeout key, 782
        RecycleLVs key, 783
        SharedAsynchDelay key, 784
        SystemDB key, 780
        Threads key, 783
        UserCommitSync key, 784
    ODBC engine
        AsyncRetryInterval key, 786
        AttachableObjects key, 787
        AttachCaseSensitive key, 787
        ConnectionTimeout key, 786
        default Registry settings, 784-785
        DisableAsync key, 787
        FastRequery key, 788
        JetTryAuth key, 787
        LoginTimeout key, 786
        PreparedInsert key, 787
        PreparedUpdate key, 788

        QueryTimeout key, 786
        SnapshotOnly key, 787
        TraceODBCAPI key, 787
        TraceSQLMode key, 787
permissions, 686-687
    Access database files, 678
    assigning, 688-700
        1stTablesAndQueries_Click procedure, 692
        1stUsers_Click procedure, 692
        chkPermission_Click procedure, 693-694
        cmdSave_Click procedure, 694-696
        FillTableAndQueriesList procedure, 697
        FillUserList procedure, 697
        form-level declarations, 690
        ReadPermissions procedure, 698-700
        UnCheckAll procedure, 697
    property values, 687-688
    SIDs, 679
Permissions property
    Container object, 954
    Document object, 957
Permitter project
    form-level declarations, 690
    objects/properties, 688-689
    procedures
        1stTablesAndQueries_Click, 692
        1stUsers_Click, 692
        chkPermission_Click, 693-694
        cmdClose_Click, 696
        cmdSave_Click, 694-696
        FillTableAndQueriesList, 697
        FillUserList, 697
        Form_Load, 690-691
        Form_Unload, 692
        ReadPermissions, 698-700
        UnCheckAll, 697
Person project, 381-383
personal identifiers (PIDs), 679
pessimistic record locking, 667
pfExists argument (SQLGetFunctions
    function), 421
PicLoad project, 337
    objects/properties, 337-338
    procedures
        CheckForLogoField, 338-339
        cmdClose_Click, 340
        cmdLoad_Click, 339-340
        Form_Load, 339

PictureBox control, 335-340
pictures, *see* graphics
PID property
    Group object, 960
    User object, 970
PIDs (personal identifiers), 679
PIVOT keyword, 225
planning custom data controls, 868
polymorphism, 792
PopulateListView procedure, 124, 743-744
PopulatePartial procedure, 955
Precision property
    Field object, 987
    Parameter object, 988
predicates
    ALL, 947
    DISTINCT, 946
    DISTINCTROW, 947
    TOP, 947
Prepare property (QueryDef object), 963
Prepared property
    Command object, 984
    rdoQuery object, 979
PreparedInsert Registry key, 787
PreparedUpdate Registry key, 788
previewing reports, 572-574, 578
primary keys, 242, 945
    constraints, 259
    creating, 943
    duplicate records, 145
Primary property (Index object), 961
PrintColHeaders procedure, 861
PrintFooter procedure, 861-862
PrintHeader procedure, 862-863
printing
    form letters, 613-614
        body text, 615-618
        dates, 614-615
        detail sections, 618
        margins, 615
        page headers, 619-620
        salutations, 615
        text fields, 621
    mailing labels, 609-610
        graphics, 611
        label types, 610
        size, 612
        text fields, 612

reports, 832-835
    Crystal Reports, 557-558, 582-589
    Data Reports, 572-575, 578
    print order, 605-609
PrintReport procedure, 572, 575, 578
PrintReportTitle procedure, 862
private classes
    creating, 805-822
    linking, 806
    publishing, 822-825
Procedure Attributes dialog box, 904
procedures
    lstRoyalty_Click, 518
    1stTables_Click, 305
    lstTablesAndQueries_Click, 692, 704-705
    lstUsers_Click, 692
    1stVendors_Click, 326
    Add, 973, 998-999
    AddIndex, 264-265
    AddNew, 21, 33, 437, 964, 980, 989
    AddNewRecord, 88
    AddRecord, 440, 450
    AddRelation, 278
    AddRules, 292-295
    AddSpaces, 398
    AddTable, 256-257
    AddToGrid, 333
    AddUserToGroup, 737
    aggregate functions, 167-168
    APIConnect, 400
    Append, 260, 986
    AppendChunk, 959, 973, 987-988
    Avg, 168, 941
    BatchUpdate, 980
    BeforeReadingRecords, 603
    BeginTrans, 957, 974-976, 985
    BitMask, 417
    Cancel, 974, 984-985, 989
    CancelBatch, 980, 989
    CancelUpdate, 33, 964, 980, 989
    CanPropertyChange, 896
    catalog functions, 374
    cboFieldDataType_Click, 254
    cboFieldName_Click, 285
    cboForeignName_Click, 285
    cboTableDefName_Click, 270, 284
    ChangePassword, 471-472, 711
    CheckDatabaseVersion, 359-360

CheckForLogoField, 338-339
chkPermission_Click, 693-694
Clear, 986
ClearControls, 462
ClearForm, 349
ClearObject, 816, 839
Clone, 964, 989
Close, 974-976, 985, 989
cmdAddField_Click, 271
cmdAddGroup_Click, 727-729
cmdAddRecord_Click, 662-663
cmdAddRules_Click, 292
cmdAddUser_Click, 721-723
cmdApply_Click, 526
cmdAttach_Click, 311-312
cmdChangeFile_Click, 306
cmdChangePassword_Click, 717
cmdCloseDatabase_Click, 653-654
cmdCloseTable_Click, 663
cmdConnect_Click, 396-397, 443
cmdCopyConnect_Click, 399
cmdCreateDB_Click, 236
cmdCreateDSN_Click, 388
cmdDecryptDatabase_Click, 749
cmdDetach_Click, 312-313
cmdEncryptDatabase_Click, 749
cmdGetConnect_Click, 398
cmdGetInfo_Click, 411-413
cmdImportClick, 322-324
cmdListVendors_Click, 325
cmdLoadSS, 849-852
cmdNewExpense_Click, 809
cmdOpenExclusive_Click, 654
cmdOpenTable_Click, 661-662
cmdSelectDB_Click, 848
cmdSetEmployee_Click, 841
cmdVendorDetails_Click, 327-328
Collection class, 998
ColName, 852
ColumnSize, 973
ColumnsToControls, 461
CommitTrans, 957, 974-976
CompactDatabase, 352, 957
CompareBookmarks, 989
ControlsToColumns, 462
CopyQueryDef, 964
CopyReplica, 927
Count, 168, 171, 941

CreateAuthor, 348
CreateDatabase, 232-234, 957
CreateDB, 235
CreateField, 961, 966-967
CreateGroup, 970
CreateIndex, 260, 272-273, 967
CreateNewDSN, 389-390
CreateParameter, 984
CreateProperty, 956, 959, 967
CreatePublisher, 348-349
CreateQuery, 468
CreateRelation, 274, 286-287, 955
CreateReplica, 934-935
CreateTableDef, 955
CreateUser, 960
CreateWorkspace, 682, 957
DatabaseError, 656
datObjects_Reposition, 803
DBPath, 660
Delete, 21, 819, 986, 990
DeleteAuthor, 534, 545
DeleteIndex, 264-265
DeleteRecord, 89-90, 440
DeleteRelation, 277
DeleteRow, 460
Display, 315-316
DisplayRecord, 674
DoBackup, 921
EnableIndex, 268
EnableOK, 268, 282
EnableRelation, 282
Encryptor, 749-750
Erl, 51
EstablishConnection, 442, 974
ExcelPath, 121
Execute, 955, 974, 984-985
expControl_ValidateData, 888
ExploreDatabase, 249
ExportReport, 572, 576-578
ExtendedTimerPop, 920-922
ExtractField, 329
ExtractPath, 314
ExtractStatusData, 306
FieldCount, 828
FillAvailableUserList, 735
FillCache, 964
FillFieldList, 218-219
FillGroupCombo, 735

FillGroupList, 729
FillIncludedUsers, 735
FillInvoiceList, 326-327
FillList, 204, 344-345
FillRoyalty, 518
FillTableAndQueriesList, 704
FillTypeList, 218
FillUserList, 697, 704, 710, 724
Find, 990
FindFirst, 964
FindLast, 964
FindNext, 964
FindPrevious, 964
First, 168
FormatError, 548
frmODBC_Load, 387-388
GetChunk, 959, 973, 987
GetClipString, 980
GetCurrentRecord, 67
GetData, 74
GetDatabase, 304-307
GetDBName, 235
GetField, 828
GetFields, 269, 283
GetFileName, 311
GetList, 533, 545-546
GetMDBFile, 313-314
GetNewPID, 724, 730
GetODBCdbs, 388, 405
GetODBCdvrs, 389
GetOpenDBName, 293
GetPrimaryKey, 664, 743
GetPrivateProfileString, 64
GetPubID, 148
GetPublisher, 209
GetRows, 964, 980, 990
GetStates, 451, 459
GetString, 990
GetTables, 269, 283
Idle, 957
IIf, 153
Initialize, 268
InitializeGrid, 322
Insert, 818
Item, 999
Last, 168
LCase, 178-179
LegalName, 191-192, 221

Length, 625
listAuthors_DblClick, 525
ListRecords, 184-185
ListTables, 314-315
LoadGetInfo, 421
LowerCase, 625
MakeReplica, 955
MakeReplicable, 926-927
Max, 168, 941
Min, 168, 941
mnuEditInsertObject_Click, 802
mnuEditPasteSpecial_Click, 802
mnuRelation_Click, 277
MoreResults, 446, 980
Move, 68, 964, 990
MoveFirst, 61, 460, 964, 980, 990
MoveLast, 62, 460, 964, 980, 990
MoveNext, 61, 461, 964, 980, 990
MovePrevious, 61, 461, 964, 980, 990
NewAuthor, 535, 543
NewPassword, 707, 713, 955, 970
NewRecord, 89, 450
NewRow, 459
NextRecordset, 964, 990
NumericText, 625
ODBCConnectDS, 406
ODBCDisconnectDS, 390
ODBCDSNList, 388
ODBCLoadFuncs, 421
Open, 985, 990
OpenConnection, 442-443, 451, 957, 969, 976
OpenDatabase, 61, 368, 957, 969
OpenDB, 655-656
OpenRecordset, 136-137, 658, 955, 964, 967
OpenResultset, 446, 974, 979, 982
OpenSchema, 985
optAuthorTitle_Click, 514
PasteSpecial, 797
PopulateListView, 124, 743-744
PopulatePartial, 955
PrintColHeaders, 861
PrintFooter, 861-862
PrintHeader, 862-863
PrintReport, 572, 575, 578
PrintReportTitle, 862

RaiseClassError, 66, 77, 103
rdc_Error, 476
rdoCreateEnvironment, 975
rdoRegisterDataSource, 975
ReadObjectValues, 812, 843, 888
ReadPermissions, 698-700
RecordError, 675
Refresh, 955, 971, 986
RefreshControls, 143
RefreshLink, 967
RefreshList, 514
RefreshLists, 509
RegisterDatabase, 391, 957
Reload, 896
Remove, 973, 999
RemoveUserFromGroup, 737
RepairDatabase, 351-354, 931, 957
ReplicateString, 625
RepopulateKeys, 761-762
Requery, 158, 363, 964, 980, 990
Resync, 980, 990
Retrieve, 332-333
Rollback, 957, 969
RollbackTrans, 974-976, 985
RunQuery, 360-361
Save, 990
SaveRecord, 69, 78, 90, 345-347, 441, 450
SaveRow, 460
Search, 95
Seek, 98, 964
SeekRecord, 104
SetAbort, 546
SetColumns, 860-861
SetComplete, 546
SetExpenseType, 817-818
SetKeepLocal, 932-934
SetObjectValues, 811-812, 888
SetOption, 763, 957
SetRecordset, 817
SetTimer, 917
SetupToolbar, 463
Show, 572, 578
ShowADOError, 506, 531
ShowBottomForm, 123
SpecialInt, 414
SpecialLong, 418
SpecialStr, 413-414
SQLBrowseConnect, 402-403

SQLConnect, 401
SQLDataSources, 388, 406
SQLDriverConnect, 401-402
SQLDrivers, 389
SQLError, 399-400
SQLFreeEnv, 390
SQLGetFunctions, 406, 421
SQLGetInfo, 410-413, 419-420
SQLGetTypeInfo, 374
StDev, 168
StDevP, 168
stored procedures
    defined, 464-465
    disadvantages, 465
    executing, 464-472, 512-520
    spStates, 466
    sp_password, 469
StoreNewItem, 329-330
strNWindDb, 52
Sum, 168, 941
Supports, 990
Synchronize, 955
TableError, 664-666
TableIsEmpty, 197-198
tb_ButtonClick, 456
Terminate, 459
TimeToTrigger, 918
ToNumber, 625
ToText, 625
TrimLeft, 625
TrimRight, 610, 625
txtRelation_Change, 285
txtTableDefName_Change, 255-256
UnCheckAll, 697
UndoRecord, 82
Update, 437, 502, 818, 964, 980, 990
UpdateAuthor, 534-535, 544
UpdateBatch, 523, 990
UpdateControls, 16
UpdateRecord, 67, 675
UpperCase, 625
user-defined procedures, 835-844
UserControl_ReadProperties, 875
UserControl_Resize, 872-873
UserControl_WriteProperties, 875
Var, 168
VarP, 168
WhilePrintingRecords, 603

WhileReadingRecords, 604
WriteItem, 330-332
projects, *see* names of specific projects
properties
    Command object, 984
    Connection object, 985
    Container object, 954
    Crystal Reports custom control, 645
    data control, 27, 136
    Database object, 955-956
    Databases collection, 955
    DBCombo control, 29
    DBEngine object, 957
    DBGrid control, 37
    DBList control, 29
    defined, 6
    Document object, 956-957
    Documents collection, 956
    Error object, 986
    Errors collection, 958, 986
    Errors object, 958
    Field object, 987
    Fields collection, 959, 987
    Fields object, 959
    Group object, 960
    Groups collection, 960
    Index object, 961
    Indexes collection, 961
    OLE Container control, 805
    Parameter object, 962, 988
    Parameters collection, 962, 988
    Properties collection, 988
    Property object, 989
    QueryDef object, 963
    QueryDefs collection, 962
    rdoColumn object, 973
    rdoColumns collection, 972
    rdoConnection object, 974-975
    rdoConnections collection, 974
    rdoEngine object, 975
    rdoEnvironment object, 977
    rdoEnvironments collection, 976
    rdoError object, 977
    rdoErrors collection, 977
    rdoParameter object, 978
    rdoParameters collection, 978
    rdoQueries collection, 978
    rdoQuery object, 979
    rdoResultset object, 981
    rdoResultsets collection, 980
    rdoTable object, 982
    rdoTables collection, 982
    Recordset object, 965-966, 990-991
    Recordsets collection, 964
    Relation object, 966-967
    Relations collection, 966
    TableDef object, 968
    TableDefs collection, 967
    TableDefs objects, 301-302
    User object, 970
    Users collection, 970
    Workspace object, 969
    Workspaces collection, 968
Properties collection, 988
Properties property
    Command object, 984
    Connection object, 985
    Field object, 987
    Parameter object, 988
    Recordset object, 991
    UnboundBrowser project, 68
Property object, 989
property pages (ODBC Administrator), 378
Property Set procedure (UnboundBrowser
    project), 68
Provider property (Connection object), 985
pstrState parameter, 157
PUBLISH project, 605
    fields, 606
    objects/properties, 606-607
    procedures
        cmdQuit_Click, 608
        cmdReport_Click, 607
        Form_Load, 608
Publishers database project (HT701-707), 453
    adding/deleting records, 437-442
        AddRecord procedure, 440
        Data menu controls, 439
        Data menu specifications, 439
        DeleteRecord procedure, 440
        mnuFileExit_Click procedure, 439
        SaveRecord procedure, 439-441
    browsing, 434-437
        declarations, 436
        menu controls, 436
        objects/properties, 434-436

connecting to
   cmdConnect_Click procedure, 443
   objects/properties, 442
   OpenConnection procedure, 444
editing records, 453
   cboState_Change procedure, 456-457
   cboState_Click procedure, 456-457
   ClearControls procedure, 462-463
   ColumnsToControls procedure, 461-462
   ControlsToColumns procedure, 462
   DeleteRow procedure, 460
   Form_Load procedure, 455-456
   GetStates procedure, 459
   Initialize procedure, 458-459
   menu controls, 454
   mnuDataDelete_Click procedure, 458
   mnuDataNew_Click procedure, 457
   mnuDataSave_Click procedure, 458
   mnuFileExit_Click procedure, 457
   MoveFirst procedure, 460-461
   MoveLast procedure, 460-461
   MoveNext procedure, 461
   MovePrevious procedure, 461
   NewRow procedure, 459-460
   SaveRow procedure, 460
   SetupToolbar procedure, 463
   tb_ButtonClick procedure, 456
   Terminate procedure, 459
error handling, 475-478
executing stored procedures, 464-466
   ChangePassword procedure, 471-472
   objects/properties, 470
navigating recordsets, 445-446
   AddRecord procedure, 450
   Form_Load procedure, 449
   GetStates procedure, 451
   menu controls, 449-450
   NewRecord procedure, 450
   OpenConnection procedure, 451
   SaveRecord procedure, 450
publishing private class modules, 822-825

Q

queries, 464
   append, 950
   crosstab, 225, 228
   functions, 145-150
   IN subqueries, 173-174, 177

parameter queries, 155-159, 355-356
   example, 356-363
ranges of values, 150-155
   Between operator, 151
   comparison operators, 151
   sample project, 151-154
   wildcards, 151
Soundex algorithm, 910-914
unique fields, selecting, 140-145
user-defined functions, 835-844
variables, 145-150
wildcards, 150, 153-155
QueryDef object
   methods, 963
   parameter queries, 157
   properties, 963
QueryDefs collection, 962
QueryTimeout property
   Database object, 955
   rdoConnection object, 975
   rdoQuery object, 979
QueryTimeout Registry key, 786
Query_Unload procedure (UnboundBrowser
   project), 71
question mark (?), 151, 469
quotation marks ("), 136

R

RaiseClassError procedure, 66, 77, 103
RAISERROR statement, 474
range of values (queries), 150-155
   Between operator, 151
   comparison operators, 151
   sample project, 151-154
   wildcards, 151
RDC (RemoteData control), 430
   adding records, 437-440
   browsing records, 433-437
   deleting records, 437-440
rdc_Error procedure, 476
RDO (Remote Data Objects), 431
   connection form, 443
   database connections, 442-445
   hierarchy, 444
   error handling
      rdoErrors collection, 473
      sample project, 476-479
      tips, 474-475

rdoColumn object, 972-973
rdoColumns collection, 971
rdoConnection object, 974-975
rdoConnections collection, 973-974
rdoEngine object, 975
rdoEnvironment object, 976-977
rdoEnvironments collection, 976
rdoError object, 977
rdoErrors collection, 977
rdoParameter object, 978
rdoParameters collection, 978
rdoQueries collection, 978
rdoQuery object, 979
rdoResultset object, 980-981
rdoResultsets collection, 980
rdoTable object, 982
rdoTables collection, 982
records
   adding, 442
   deleting, 442
   editing, 452-464
recordsets, navigating, 445-452
SQL Server errors, 479
stored procedures
   executing, 464-468
   parameters, 468-472
rdoColumn object, 972-973
rdoColumns collection, 446, 971
rdoColumns property
   rdoQuery object, 979
   rdoResultset object, 981
   rdoTable object, 982
rdoConnection object
   events, 974
   Execution procedure, 465
   methods, 974
   properties, 974-975
rdoConnections collection, 973-974
rdoConnections property (rdoEnvironment
   object), 977
rdoCreateEnvironment procedure, 975
rdoDefaultCursorDriver property (rdoEngine
   object), 975
RdoDefaultErrorThreshold property
   (rdoEngine object), 975
rdoDefaultLoginTimeout property (rdoEngine
   object), 975

rdoDefaultPassword property (rdoEngine
   object), 975
rdoDefaultUser property (rdoEngine object),
   975
rdoEngine object, 975
rdoEnvironment object, 976-977
rdoEnvironments collection, 976
rdoEnvironments property (rdoEngine
   object), 975
rdoError object, 977
rdoErrors collection, 473, 977
rdoErrors property (rdoEngine object), 975
rdoLocaleID property (rdoEngine object), 975
rdoParameter object, 978
rdoParameters collection, 468, 978
rdoParameters property (rdoQuery object), 979
rdoQueries collection, 978
rdoQueries property (rdoConnection
   object), 975
rdoQuery object, 979
rdoRegisterDataSource procedure, 975
rdoResultset object, 445, 980-981
rdoResultsets collection, 980
rdoResultsets property (rdoConnection
   object), 975
rdoTable object, 982
rdoTables collection, 982
rdoTables property (rdoConnection
   object), 975
rdoVersion property (rdoEngine object), 975
Read Data permissions, 678
ReadObjectValues procedure, 812, 843, 888
ReadPermissions procedure, 698-700
RecordChangeComplete event, 989
RecordCount property
   Recordset object, 965, 991
   TableDef object, 301, 968
RecordCounts project (HT207)
   objects/properties, 107-108
   procedures
      cmdExit_Click, 109
      Form_Load, 108-109
RecordError procedure, 675
RecordLocker project
   error handling, 675-676
   form-level variables, 669
   objects/properties, 668-669
   option button events, 672-673

procedures
  cmdClose_Click, 672
  cmdEdit_Click, 671-672
  cmdMove_Click, 673-674
  cmdRefresh_Click, 672
  cmdUpdate_Click, 672
  DisplayRecord, 674
  Form_Load, 670
  Form_Unload, 671
  UpdateRecord, 675
records
  adding
    bound controls, 20-27
    DAO, 82-91
    RDC, 437-440
    RDO, 442
  browsing
    DAO, 60-61
    RDC, 433-437
    RDO, 445-452
  counting, 106-110, 301-308
  creating, 489-492
  deleting, 951-952
    ADO Data control, 489-492
    bound controls, 20-27
    DAO, 82-91
    RDC, 437-440
    RDO, 442
  editing, 452-464
  finding
    by index values, 97-105
    Soundex algorithm, 910-914
  generic lookup forms, 91-97
  locking, 667-676
    DisplayRecord procedure, 674
    error handling, 675-677
    form-level variables, 669
    LockEdits property, 672-673
    optimistic locking, 667
    pessimistic locking, 667
    UpdateRecord procedure, 672, 675
  master-detail, displaying, 36-42
  navigating, 21, 61-62
  updating
    bulk updates, 181-185
    DAO, 62-75
RecordsAffected property
  Database object, 955
  QueryDef object, 963

Recordset object
  events, 989
  methods, 964, 989-990
  properties, 965-966, 990-991
RecordsetChangeComplete event, 989
recordsets
  accessing, 493-496
  browsing
    bound controls, 8-12
    DAO, 59-61
  creating with SQL, 133-140
    form properties, 137
    Form_Load event, 138-139
    multiple fields, 135
  defined, 6, 11
  duplicate values, combining
    GROUP BY clause, 172
    HAVING clause, 172-173
    IN subqueries, 173-174
    sample project, 174-177
  editing, 496-507
  navigating
    Move methods, 61-62
    RDO, 445-452
  records
    adding, 20-21, 24-28
    counting, 106-110
    deleting, 20-21, 24-28
  SQL, 177-181
  updating
    batch updates, 523-528
    remote updates, 528-531
Recordsets collection, 964
RecordSource property
  crosstab queries, 227
  Data control, 136
RecordSources, 9, 27
RecordStatus property (Recordset object), 965
RecycleLVs Registry key, 783
Refresh procedure, 955, 971, 986
RefreshControls procedure, 143
RefreshLink procedure, 967
RefreshList procedure, 509, 514
RegClean program, 867
Register project, 385
  objects/properties, 386-387
  procedures
    cmdCreateDSN_Click, 388
    CreateNewDSN, 389-390

frmODBC_Load, 387-388
GetODBCdbs, 388
GetODBCdvrs, 389
ODBCDisconnectDS, 390
ODBCDriverList, 389
ODBCDSNList, 388
SQLFreeEnv, 390
RegisterDatabase procedure, 391, 957
registering data sources
    errors, 391
    Register form, 386-389
    procedures
        CreateNewDSN, 389-390
        RegisterDatabase, 385, 391
Registry, 755
    ActiveX class settings, 865-867
    entries, accessing, 757-763
    Jet engine, tuning
        default values, 781
        ExclusiveAsyncDelay key, 784
        FlushTransactionTimeout key, 782
        ImplicitCommitSync key, 784
        LockDelay key, 783
        LockRetry key, 783
        MaxBufferSize key, 783
        MaxLocksPerFile key, 783
        PageTimeout key, 782
        RecycleLVs key, 783
        SharedAsyncDelay key, 784
        SystemDB key, 780
        Threads key, 783
        UserCommitSync key, 784
    ODBC engine, tuning
        AsyncRetryInterval key, 786
        AttachableObjects key, 787
        AttachCaseSensitive key, 787
        ConnectionTimeout key, 786
        default values, 784-785
        DisableAsync key, 787
        FastRequery key, 788
        JetTryAuth key, 787
        LoginTimeout key, 786
        PreparedInsert key, 787
        PreparedUpdate key, 788
        QueryTimeout key, 786
        SnapshotOnly key, 787
        TraceODBCAPI key, 787
        TraceSQLMode key, 787

RegClean program, 867
    restoring, 756
    temporary DAO settings, 763-772
    viewing, 755
RegistryEditor project
    objects/properties, 758-759
    procedures
        1stKeys_Click, 759-760
        cmdClose_Click, 760
        cmdSave_Click, 761
        Form_Load, 759
        RepopulateKeys, 761-762
        txtApplicationName_Change, 760
RegSvr32, 867
Relation object
    creating, 274-275
    methods, 966
    properties, 966-967
relational databases, *see* databases
Relations collection, 966
relationships
    defining
        cascading deletes, 275
        cascading updates, 275
        Relation objects, 274-275
        sample project, 276-288
    many-to-many, 244
    one-to-many, 244
    one-to-one, 244-246
Reload procedure, 896
Remote Data Objects, *see* RDO
remote updates, 528-531
RemoteData control, *see* RDC
Remove procedure, 973, 999
RemoveUserFromGroup procedure, 737
removing, *see* deleting
REPAIR project
    objects/properties, 352-353
    procedures
        cmdClose_Click, 354
        cmdOK_Click, 353-354
RepairDatabase procedure, 351-354
repairing databases, 351-354
RepeaterTestControl project, 901
    objects/properties, 902
    sizing, 903
    test form, 905
repeating groups (fields), 240

Replica project
  cmdCreateReplica_Click procedure,
    934-935
  SetKeepLocal procedure, 932-934
Replicable property
  Database object, 955
  Document object, 957
  QueryDef object, 963
  TableDef object, 968
ReplicaFilter property (TableDef object), 968
ReplicaID identifier, 929, 955
replicas (databases)
  breaking out of replica set, 935-938
  creating
    database modifications, 929-930
    Jet engine, 923-928
    one-way replication, 931
    table modifications, 930-931
    two-way replication, 931
  partial replication, 932-935
    cmdCreateReplica_Click procedure, 934-935
    SetKeepLocal procedure, 932-934
Replicate project, 924
  objects/properties, 924-925
  procedures
    Browse button procedures, 926
    cmdCreateReplica_Click, 927-928
    cmdSynchronize_Click, 928
    CopyReplica, 927
    MakeReplicable, 926-927
ReplicateString procedure, 625
RepopulateKeys procedure, 761-762
reports
  Crystal Reports, 556
    advantages, 558
    banding, 604
    blank lines, 627-634
    calculated fields, 591-604
    cross-tab reports, 634-638
    Crystal Info, 559
    Crystal Reports Professional 6, 559
    Designer, 557-559
    form letters, 613-621
    formula formats, 590
    mailing labels, 609-612
    print order, 605-609
    printing, 557-558, 582-589
    string manipulation, 622-626
    user-entered variables, 638-646

Data Reports, 556
  advantages, 558
  calculated fields, 567-571
  creating, 563-567
  exporting, 572, 575-578
  previewing, 572-574, 578
  printing, 572-575, 578
  query parameters, 579-582
editable report writers, 854-865
  cmdReport_Click procedure, 858-860
  columns, 860-861
  controls, 855-856
  footers, 861-862
  formatting, 856
  headers, 861
  progress bars, 863
  resizing, 857-858
  titles, 862-863
  printing, 832-835
Requery procedure, 157-158, 363, 964, 980,
  990
Required property
  Field object, 289, 959
  rdoColumn object, 973
  Required property, 961
resizing forms, 805
Restartable property
  rdoResultset object, 981
  Recordset object, 965
restoring Registry, 756
Resultset object, 437
Resume statement, 51, 113
Resync procedure, 980, 990
Retrieve procedure, 332-333
return values
  SQLDriverConnect procedure, 402
  SQLGetInfo procedure, 420
ReturnsRecords property (QueryDef
  object), 963
rgbInfoValue argument (SQLGetInfo
  function), 420
right joins, 164, 949
Rollback procedure, 342, 957, 969
RollbackTrans procedure, 974-976, 985
RollbackTransComplete event, 985
routines, *see* procedures
RowCount property
  rdoResultset object, 981
  rdoTable object, 982

RowData dynamic array, 419
rows, *see* records
RowsAffected property
    rdoConnection object, 975
    rdoQuery object, 979
RowsetSize property (rdoQuery object), 979
RowSource property (DBList control), 29
RowStatusChanged event, 452
RoyaltyList project (parameterized stored
    procedures)
    column headers, 518
    objects/properties, 517
    procedures
        1stRoyalty_Click, 518-519
        FillRoyalty, 518
        Form_Load, 518
rptFunction control, 571
rptKeyHTML constant, 576
rptKeyText constant, 576
rptKeyUnicodeHTML_UTF8 constant, 576
RPTWRITE project
    formatting, 856
    objects/properties, 855-856
    procedures
        cmdQuit_Click, 864
        cmdReport_Click, 858-860
        Form_Load, 857
        Form_Resize, 857-858
        PrintColHeaders, 861
        PrintFooter, 861-862
        PrintHeader, 862-863
        PrintReportTitle, 862
        SetColumns, 860-861
        Status, 863
rules (business), 288-296
RunQuery procedure, 360-361
runtime errors, 26
    see also error handling
runtime files, 778

S

Save procedure, 990
SaveRecord procedure, 69, 78, 90, 345-347,
    441, 450
SaveRow procedure, 460
SaveSetting statement, 758

saving
    graphics to database files
        OLE Container control, 336
        PictureBox control, 335-340
    Registry settings, 758
scheduling database backups, 914-923
    Backup Test form, 919-920
    BackupTable class module, 920
    extended timer control, 915-919
    procedures
        DoBackup, 921-922
        Form_Load, 922
search pattern arguments, 374
Search procedure, 95
searching
    databases, 910-914
    indexes, 97-105
second normal form (2NF), 240-242
Secure project
    objects/properties, 683
    procedures
        cmdCancel_Click, 685
        cmdOK_Click, 684-685
        Form_Load, 683-684
SECURED project
    compiling, 829
    executing, 829
    macro module, 830-831
    objects/properties, 826
    procedures
        Class_Terminate, 827
        FieldCount, 828
        GetField, 828
        initialization procedures, 827
secured systems (Access), accessing, 681-686
security
    Access database files, 677, 825-832
        defaults, 679-681
        permissions, 678
        Secure project, 682-686
        secured systems, 679-681
        sessions, 682
        SIDs, 679
        unsecured systems, 679
        workspaces, 682
    encryption, 745-751
    exclusive access
        databases, 651-658
        tables, 658-667

ownership
  changing, 701-706
  default owners, 701
passwords
  changing, 706-712
  creating, 712-719
permissions, 686-687
  assigning, 688-700
  property values, 687-688
  SIDs, 679
record locking, 667-677
user activity, tracking, 738-744
user groups
  adding/deleting users, 731-738
  defining, 725-730
  permissions, 678
users, adding, 719-725
Security IDs (SIDs), 679
Seek project (HT206)
  CTitles class declarations, 101-102
  Index property, 104
  IndexName property, 104
  menu specifications, 99
  procedures
    Class_Initialize, 102-103
    mnuDataIndexName_Click, 100-101
    mnuDataSeek_Click, 100-101
    mnuData_Click, 100
    RaiseClassError, 103-104
    SeekRecord, 104-105
Seek procedure, 98, 964
SeekRecord procedure, 104
Select 10 project
  objects/properties, 178-179
  procedures
    Form_Load, 179-180
    cmdClose_Click, 180
Select 5 project
  objects/properties, 156
  procedures
    cmdClose_Click, 158
    cmdSearch_Click, 157-158
Select 6 project
  declarations, 162
  objects/properties, 161-162
  procedures, 162
Select 8 project
  objects/properties, 169-170
  procedures, 171

Select 9 project
  objects/properties, 174-175
  procedures
    cmdClose_Click, 177
    Form_Load, 175-176
Select Data Source dialog box, 397
SELECT INTO statement, 210-211
Select Publisher form, 202
SELECT statement, 6, 940, 945
  bulk updates, 184
  clauses
    ALL, 947
    AND, 135-136
    DISTINCT, 140, 946
    DISTINCTROW, 144-145, 947
    FROM, 159-160, 948
    GROUP BY, 172, 948
    HAVING, 172-173, 948
    LIKE, 948
    OR, 135-136
    TOP, 947
    WHERE clause, 154-155
  crosstab queries, 226
  nesting, 173-174
  parameter queries, 155
  syntax, 134, 946
Select1 project, 137
  objects/properties, 138
  procedures, 138-139
Select2 project, 141
  objects/properties, 142
  procedures
    cmdClose_Click, 144
    cmdShowAll_Click, 143
    cmdShowUnique_Click, 143
    RefreshControls, 143
Select3 project
  objects/properties, 146-147
  procedures
    dlstPublishers_Click, 147-148
    Form_Load, 147
Select4 project, 151
  objects/properties, 152
  procedures
    cmdClose_Click, 154
    cmdLookup_Click, 153-154
SelectionFormula property (Crystal Reports
  custom control), 645

servers
  ActiveX
    controlled database access, 825-832
    Microsoft Access, 832-835
  MTS
    advantages, 542-543
    business objects, 543-547
services (ODBC), listing
  Services objects/properties, 403
  procedures
    BitMask, 417
    GetODBCdbs, 405
    ODBCConnectDS, 106
    SpecialInt, 414-417
    SpecialLong, 417-418
    SpecialStr, 413-414
    SQLGetFunctions, 421
    SQLGetInfo, 410-412, 419-420
Services project
  GetInfo form
    BitMask procedure, 417
    cmdCancel_Click procedure, 418
    cmdGetInfo_Click procedure, 410-413
    cmdSelection_Click procedure, 418
    Form_Load procedure, 410
    properties, 409-410
    SpecialInt procedure, 414-417
    SpecialLong procedure, 418
    SpecialStr procedure, 413-414
  Services form
    cmdProperties_Click procedure, 408
    GetODBCdbs procedure, 405
    ODBCConnectDS procedure, 406
    properties, 404-405
SET clause, 181, 951
Set Mapping dialog box, 894
SetAbort procedure, 546
SetColumns procedure, 860-861
SetComplete procedure, 546
SetExpenseType procedure, 817-818
SetKeepLocal procedure, 932-934
SetObjectValues procedure, 811-812, 888
SetOption procedure, 763, 957
SetOptions project
  general declarations, 765
  objects/properties, 763-765
  procedures
    cboKeys_Click, 766-767
    cmdClose_Click, 767
    cmdDelete_Click, 768
    cmdSave_Click, 767-768
    Form_Load, 765-766
    GetDefaultKeySetting, 770-771
    GetParameterFromKey, 771
    GetValueFromSetting, 770
    LoadJetRegistryInformation, 768-769
SetRecordset procedure, 817
SetTimer procedure, 917
SetupToolbar procedure, 463
SharedAsyncDelay Registry key, 784
SHIPLBL project, 609-610
  graphics, 611
  label types, 610
  sizing labels, 612
  text fields, 612
  TrimRight procedure, 610
SHORT data type, 186
Show procedure, 572, 578
ShowADOError procedure, 506, 531
ShowBottomForm procedure, 123
SIDs (Security IDs), 679
silent argument (RegisterDatabase
  function), 391
SINGLE data type, 186
Size property
  Field object, 959
  Parameter object, 988
  rdoColumn object, 973
  rdoParameter object, 978
SizeMode property (OLE Container
  control), 805
sizing
  forms, 805
  timer control container, 918
snapshot-type recordsets, counting records in,
  106-110
SnapshotOnly Registry key, 787
Sort property (Recordset object), 965, 991
SortFields property (Crystal Reports custom
  control), 645
sorting lists, 35
Soundex algorithm, 910-914
  coding guide, 913
  coding results, 913-914
  example, 911-913
Source property
  Error object, 958, 986
  rdoError object, 977
  Recordset object, 991

SourceColumn property (rdoColumn object), 973

SourceField property (Field object), 959

SourceTable property
Field object, 959
rdoColumn object, 973

SourceTableName property (TableDef object), 301, 968

SpecialInt procedure, 414

SpecialLong procedure, 418

SpecialStr procedure, 413-414

spreadsheets
accessing with DAO, 116-126
converting databases to, 845-853

spStates stored procedure, 466

sp_password stored procedure, 469

sp_password system stored procedure, 469

SQL (Structured Query Language), 130, 939
aggregate functions, 167-168, 941, 948
bulk updates, 181-185
case sensitivity, 135
clauses, *see* clauses
comparison operators, 135
data types, 186
enclosure syntax requirements, 134
joins, 159-160, 163
multifield, 160
outer joins, 163-167
grammar conformance levels, 373-374
operators, 151, 940-941
processing speed, 141
queries, 464
crosstab, 225, 228
functions, 145-150
IN subqueries, 173-174, 177
parameter queries, 155-159
ranges of values, 150, 153-155
selecting unique fields, 140-145
Soundex algorithm, 910-914
variables, 145-150
wildcards, 150, 153-155
records
appending, 199-200
deleting, 200
recordsets,creating, 133-140
duplicate values, 172-177
form properties, 137
Form_Load event, 138-139

multiple fields, 135
special formatting, 177-181
statement classifications, 939-940
statements, *see* statements
stored procedures
executing with ADO, 512-515
parameterized, 516-520
tables
creating, 185-186, 210-215
deleting, 187
modifying structure, 215-225
see also SQL Server databases

SQL property
QueryDef object, 963
rdoQuery object, 979

SQL Server databases
browsing
ADO Data control, 486-489
RemoteData control, 433-437
connecting to, 442-445
data retrieval, 493-496
objects, editing, 520-522
records
adding, 437-442
creating, 489-492
deleting, 437-442, 489-492
editing, 452-464
recordsets
editing, 496-507
navigating, 445-452
stored procedures
executing, 464-468
parameters, 468-472
transaction processing
ADO, 507-511
deadlocks, 511
see also databases

SQLBrowseConnect procedure, 402-403

SQLConnect procedure, 401

SQLDataSources procedure, 388, 405-406

SQLDriverConnect function
connection options, 401-402
return values, 402

SQLDriverConnect procedure, 401

SQLDrivers procedure, 389

SQLError procedure, 399-400

SQLFreeEnv procedure, 390

SQLGetFunctions procedure, 406
  arguments, 421
  syntax, 420
SQLGetInfo procedure, 410-413
  arguments, 420
  return values, 419-420
SQLGetTypeInfo procedure, 374
SQLRetcode property (rdoError object), 977
SQLState property
  Error object, 986
  rdoError object, 977
SQL_DRIVER_COMPLETE return value, 402
SQL_DRIVER_COMPLETE_REQUIRED return
  value, 402
SQL_DRIVER_NOPROMPT return value, 402
SQL_DRIVER_PROMPT return value, 402
starting
  ODBC Administrator, 377-378
  transactions, 341
State property
  Command object, 984
  Connection object, 985
  Recordset object, 991
statement handle (hStmt), 371
statements, 939-940
  ALTER TABLE, 216, 943-945
  BeginTrans, 341
  case sensitivity, 135
  CommitTrans, 341
  Const, 195
  CREATE, 942
    CREATE DATABASE, 236
    CREATE INDEX, 943
    CREATE TABLE, 186, 942-943
  Debug.Print, 871
  Declare, 372
  DELETE, 200, 951-952
  DeleteSetting, 758
  DROP
    DROP INDEX, 945
    DROP TABLE, 187, 945
  enclosure syntax requirements, 134
  End, 51, 113
  Err.Clear, 51, 113
  Exit, 51, 113
  INSERT, 950
  INSERT INTO, 199-200

On Error, 51, 110
  example, 47-48
  On Error Goto, 48, 548-551
  On Error Resume Next, 49
OpenRecordset procedure, 136-137
  parameters, 155
RAISERROR, 474
Resume, 51, 113
SaveSetting, 758
SELECT, 6, 945-946
  AND keyword, 135-136
  DISTINCT keyword, 140
  DISTINCTROW keyword, 144-145
  FROM clause, 159-160, 948
  GROUP BY clause, 172, 948
  HAVING clause, 172-173, 948
  LIKE keyword, 948
  nesting, 173-174
  OR keyword, 135-136
  syntax, 134, 946
  WHERE clause, 154-155
SELECT INTO, 210-211
UPDATE, 181, 951
Visual Basic functions within, 177-181
Status property
  rdoColumn object, 973
  rdoResultset object, 981
  Recordset object, 991
StDev procedure, 168
StDevP procedure, 168
StillConnecting property (rdoConnection
  object), 975
StillExecuting property
  QueryDef object, 963
  rdoConnection object, 975
  rdoQuery object, 979
  rdoResultset object, 981
  Recordset object, 965
stored parameter queries
  example, 356-363
  overview, 355-356
stored procedures
  defined, 464-465
  disadvantages, 465
  executing
    ADO, 512-515
    RDO, 464-472

parameterized, 516-520
spStates, 466
sp_password, 469
StoredProcedure project, 512
    objects/properties, 513
    procedures
        optAuthroTitle_Click, 514
        RefreshList, 514-515
StoreNewItem procedure, 329-330
strDatabaseName property (Expense data
    control), 876-877
strings
    concatenating, 626
    converting, 625
    wildcards, 151
strNWindDb procedure, 52
Structured Query Language, see SQL
Style property (DBCombo control), 29
subroutines, see procedures
subtotals, calculating (Crystal Reports),
    591-604
Sum procedure, 168, 941
Supports procedure, 990
Synchronize procedure, 955
synchronizing databases, 928
System DSN, 377
SystemDB property (DBEngine object), 957
SystemDB Registry key, 780

T

Table property (Relation object), 967
TableData project, 302
    clsTableData module, 306
    objects/properties, 303
    procedures
        1stTables_Click, 305
        cmdChangeFile_Click, 306
        ExtractStatusData, 306
        GetDatabase, 304-305
        istTables_Click, 305
TableDef objects
    creating, 256-257
    methods, 967
    properties, 301-302, 968
TableDefName property, 268
TableDefs collection, 196, 301, 967
TableError procedure, 664-666
TableIsEmpty procedure, 197-198

TableLocker project
    error handling, 664-666
    objects/properties, 659
    procedures
        cmdAddRecord_Click, 662-663
        cmdCloseTable_Click, 663
        cmdExit_Click, 664
        cmdOpenTable_Click, 661-662
        DBPath, 660
        Form_Unload, 661
        GetPrimaryKey, 664
        initialization procedure, 660
tables, 237-238
    attached tables
        creating, 309-317
        limitations, 308
    bound lists, 28-36
    creating
        CREATE TABLE statement, 942-943
        DAO, 247
        from existing tables, 210-215
        sample project, 247-258
        SQL, 185-186, 246
    creation dates, retrieving, 301-308
    data-bound grid cells, editing, 42-46
    deleting, 187, 945
    editing, 215-225, 943-945
    exclusive access, 658-667
    fields
        adding, 943
        deleting, 944
    joins, 948
        creating, 949
        inner joins, 159-160, 163
        left, 949
        multifield, 160
        nesting, 949-950
        outer joins, 163-167
        right, 949
    last-modified dates, retrieving, 301-308
    naming conventions, 241
    primary keys, 242, 943
    relationships
        defining, 274-288
        many-to-many, 244
        one-to-many, 244
        one-to-one, 244-246
    structure, 222

temporary, 185-187, 211
see also records; recordsets
tb_ButtonClick procedure, 456
temporary tables
  creating, 185-186
  deleting, 187
Terminate procedure, 459
TEXT data type, 186
text files, importing, 317-321, 326-328,
  334-335
  error handling, 325
  procedures
    AddToGrid, 333
    cmdImport_Click, 322-324
    cmdListVendors_Click, 325
    ExtractField, 329
    FillInvoiceList, 326-327
    InitializeGrid, 322
    Retrieve, 332-333
    StoreNewItem, 329-330
    WriteItem, 330-332
TextBox control, 994
TextImport project, 318
  error handling, 325
  objects/properties, 319-321
  procedures
    1stVendors_Click, 326
    AddToGrid, 333
    cmdImport_Click, 322-324
    cmdListVendors_Click, 325
    cmdVendorDetails_Click, 327-328
    ExtractField, 329
    FillInvoiceList, 326-327
    Form_Load, 321
    InitializeGrid, 322
    Property Let DelimitedString, 328-332
    Retrieve, 332-333
    StoreNewItem, 329-330
    WriteItem, 330-332
third normal form (3NF), 240-244
Threads Registry key, 783
three-tier architecture
  business objects, 542-547
  middle-tier objects, 531-542
ThreeTier project, 532
  column headers, 536
  Details dialog box, 540-541
  objects/properties, 536

procedures
  Class_Initialize, 533
  Class_Terminate, 533
  cmdDelete_Click, 537
  cmdEdit_Click, 537-538
  cmdNew_Click, 538-539
  DeleteAuthor, 534
  Form_Load, 536
  Form_Unload, 537
  GetList, 533
  NewAuthor, 535
  UpdateAuthor, 534-535
timer controls
  database backups, 915
  EnhancedTimer, 915
    Boolean variable, 917
    compiling, 919
    enabling, 918
    event-fired loops, 917
    initial values, 918
    properties, 916
    SetTimer procedure, 917
    sizing, 918
    TimeToTrigger procedure, 918
TITLES project, 627-628
  description field, 629
  detail section, 629
  group footer, 631
  margins, 628
  page numbers, 633
  summary fields, 631
titles, printing (report writer application),
  862-863
ToNumber procedure, 625
TOP predicate, 947
ToText procedure, 625
trace logs, 372
TraceODBCAPI Registry key, 787
TraceSQLMode Registry key, 787
tracing control behavior, 871
Tracker project
  objects/properties, 739
  procedures
    cmdAddRecord_Click, 741-742
    cmdClose_Click, 742
    Form_Load, 740-741
    Form_Unload, 741
    GetPrimaryKey, 743
    PopulateListView, 743-744

tracking user activity, 738-744
TRANSACT project
    error handling, 348
    general declarations, 344
    objects/properties, 343-344
    procedures
        Change, 350
        ClearForm, 349
        cmdClose_Click, 349-350
        CreateAuthor, 348
        CreatePublisher, 348-349
        FillList, 344-345
        Form_Load, 344
        SaveRecord, 345-347
transaction processing
    ADO, 507-511
    deadlocks, 511
Transaction project
    declarations, 509
    objects/properties, 508-509
    procedures
        cmdTransfer_Click, 510-511
        Form_Load, 509
        Form_Unload, 509
        RefreshLists, 509-510
transactions
    canceling, 341
    committing, 341
    defined, 341
    error handling, 342
    integrity, 341
    starting, 341
    see also TRANSACT project
Transactions property
    Database object, 956
    rdoConnection object, 975
    rdoResultset object, 981
    Recordset object, 965
TRANSFORM keyword, 225
translators (ODBC), 370
trapping errors, *see* error handing
Treeview control, 246
TrimLeft procedure, 625
TrimRight procedure, 610, 625
troubleshooting
    data source registration, 391
    deadlocks, 511
    see also error handling

tuning performance, *see* performance tuning
two-way database replication, 931
txtRelation_Change procedure, 285
txtTableDefName_Change procedure, 255-256
txt_Change procedure, 72-73
Type property
    Field object, 959, 987
    Parameter object, 962, 988
    QueryDef object, 963
    rdoColumn object, 973
    rdoParameter object, 978
    rdoQuery object, 979
    rdoResultset object, 981
    rdoTable object, 982
    Recordset object, 965
    Workspace object, 969

U

UDA (Universal Data Access), 484
udx prefix, 262
unbound controls, navigating records
    with, 61-62
UnboundBrowser project (HT201), 62
    Ctitles declarations, 64-65
    menu specifications, 63
    objects/properties, 62-63
    procedures
        Class_Initialize, 65-66
        Class_Terminate, 65-66
        cmdMove_Click, 71-72
        Form_Load, 70
        GetCurrentRecord, 67
        GetData, 74
        GetPrivateProfileString, 64
        IsDirty Property Get, 68
        mnuDataSaveRecord_Click, 73-74
        mnuData_Click, 73-74
        mnuFileExit_Click, 73
        Move, 69
        Property Get, 68
        Property Let, 68
        Query_Unload, 71
        RaiseClassError, 66
        SaveRecord, 69
        UpdateRecord, 67
        txt_Change, 72-73
UnCheckAll procedure, 697
UnderlyingValue property (Field object), 987

underscore (_), 374
UndoBound project
    objects/properties, 17
    procedures
        datEmployees_Validate, 17-19
        Form_Unload, 19
        mnuEditUndo_Click, 19
        mnuExit_Click, 19
UndoBrowser project (HT203), 80
    Edit menu specifications, 80
    procedures
        mnuEditUndo_Click, 81
        mnuEdit_Click, 81
        UndoRecord, 82
undoing changes
    bound controls, 16-20
    DAO, 79-82
        Edit menu specifications, 80
        mnuEditUndo_Click event, 81
        mnuEdit_Click event, 81
        UndoRecord procedure, 82
UndoRecord procedure, 82
unique indexes, 944
Unique property (Index object), 961
Universal Data Access (UDA), 484
unsecured systems (Access), 679
Updatable property
    Database object, 956
    QueryDef object, 963
    rdoColumn object, 973
    rdoConnection object, 975
    rdoResultset object, 981
    Recordset object, 966
    TableDef object, 301, 968
Update Data permissions, 678
Update procedure, 437, 502, 818, 990
UPDATE statement, 181, 940, 951
Update procedure, 964, 980
Update.vbp project
    objects/properties, 182
    procedures
        cmdClose_Click, 185
        cmdRestore_Click, 183-184
        cmdUpdate_Click, 183
        ListRecords, 184-185
UpdateAuthor procedure, 534-535, 544
UpdateBatch procedure, 523, 990
UpdateControls procedure, 16

UpdateCriteria property (rdoResultset
    object), 981
UpdateOperation property (rdoResultset
    object), 981
UpdateOptions property (Recordset object),
    966
UpdateRecord procedure, 67, 675
updating
    records
        bulk updates, 181-185
        DAO, 62-75
    recordsets
        ADO, 496-507
        batch updates, 523-528
        remote updates, 528-531
upgrading Crystal Reports, 559
UpperCase procedure, 625
User DSN, 377
User object, 970
user-defined procedures, 835-844
user-entered variables (Crystal Reports),
    638-646
UserCommitSync Registry key, 784
UserControl ReadProperties procedure, 875
UserControl_InitProperties procedure, 918
UserControl_Resize procedure, 872-873
UserControl_WriteProperties procedure, 875
UserName property
    Container object, 954
    Document object, 957
    rdoEnvironment object, 977
    Workspace object, 969
users
    adding, 719-725
    groups
        adding users to, 731-738
        defining, 725-730
        permissions, 678
        removing users from, 731-738
    tracking, 738-744
Users collection, 969

V

V1xNullBehavior property (Database
    object), 956
Validate event
    arguments, 13
    example, 14-15

ValidateBound project
    form, 13
    procedures
        Form_Unload, 15
        mnuExit_Click, 15
        Validate, 14-15
ValidateOnSet property (Field object), 959
validating data
    bound controls, 12-16
    Crystal Reports, 588-589
    DAO, 75-79
        class declarations, 76-77
        IsValid property, 77-78
        RaiseClassError procedure, 77
        SaveRecord procedure, 78-79
ValidatingBrowser project (HT202), 76
    class declarations, 76-77
    IsValid property, 77-78
    procedures
        RaiseClassError, 77
        SaveRecord, 78-79
ValidationRule property, 289-291
    Field object, 959
    Recordset object, 966
    TableDef object, 302, 968
ValidationText property, 289
    Field object, 959
    Recordset object, 966
    Relation object, 967
    TableDef object, 302, 968
Value property
    Field object, 959, 987
    Parameter object, 962, 988
    rdoColumn object, 973
    rdoParameter object, 978
Var procedure, 168
variables
    Database object, 150
    mlRowState, 456
    mstrTableDefName, 267
    SQL query criteria, 145-150
    user-defined variables, 638-646
VarP procedure, 168
VBSQL, 431
Version property
    Connection object, 985
    Database object, 956
    DBEngine object, 957

rdoConnection object, 975
RegisterDatabase procedure, 393
viewing
    available ODBC services, 403
        BitMask procedure, 417
        GetODBCdbs procedure, 405
        ODBCConnectDS procedure, 406
        Services objects/properties, 404-405
        SpecialInt procedure, 414-417
        SpecialLong procedure, 418
        SpecialStr procedure, 413-414
        SQLGetFuntions procedure, 421
        SQLGetInfo procedure, 410-413, 419-420
    Registry, 755
VisibleValue property (Field object), 959

W-Z

Web sites, Microsoft Knowledge Base, 478
WHERE clause, 155, 940
    bulk updates, 185
    DELETE statement, 200
    SELECT statement, 154
    UPDATE statement, 181
WhilePrintingRecords procedure, 603
WhileReadingRecords procedure, 604
wildcards
    Count procedure, 171
    SQL queries, 150, 153-155
WillChangeData event, 972
WillChangeField event, 989
WillChangeRecord event, 989
WillChangeRecordset event, 989
WillConnect event, 985
WillExecute event, 985
WillMove event, 989
Windows Registry, *see* Registry
WITH clause, 943
WithEvents keyword, 452
wizards, Package and Deployment Wizard,
    772-773
worksheets (Excel)
    accessing with DAO, 116-126
    converting databases to, 845-853
workspaces
    Access databases, 682
    Workspace object, 969
    Workspaces collection, 968, 997
WriteItem procedure, 330-332

The Waite Group's Visual Basic 6 How-To

Eric Brierley, Anthony Prince, and David Rinaldi

Visual Basic 6 How-To is a programmer-oriented, problem-solving guide that teaches readers how to enhance their Visual Basic skills. Chapters are organized by topic and divided into how-tos. Each how-to describes a problem, develops a technique for solving the problem, presents a step-by-step solution, furnishes relevant tips, comments, and warnings, and presents alternative solutions where applicable. *Visual Basic 6 How-To* offers illustrated solutions and complete working code. Whenever possible, the code is modularized and fully encapsulated for easy transplant into other applications. *Visual Basic 6 How-To* demonstrates how to take advantage of new interface options and Windows APIs, and contains all-new How-Tos on building multi-tier Web-based applications, Advanced Data Objects (ADO), and much more. *Visual Basic How-To* has sold over 50,000 copies to date and won the *Visual Basic Programmer's Journal* Reader's Choice Award 1995. It contains expanded coverage of Visual Basic 6, including Internet topics and lots of all new How-Tos. It is written in The Waite Group's proven question and answer format.

$39.99 US/$57.95 CDN	*Programming - Intermediate*	
1-57169-153-7	*800 pp.*	
1 CD	*Waite Group*	

The Waite Group's Visual Basic 6 Client/Server How-To

Noel Jerke, et al

Visual Basic 6 Client/Server How-To is a practical step-by-step guide to implementing multi-tiered distributed client/server solutions using the tools provided in Microsoft's Visual Basic. It addresses the needs of programmers looking for answers to real-world questions and assures them that what they create really works. It also helps simplify the client/server development process by providing a framework for solution development. Save hundreds of hours of programming time by providing step-by-step solutions to more than 75 Visual Basic 6 client/server problems. Covers topics like OOP, ODBC, OLE, RDO, distributed computing, and *n*-tier client/server development. Addresses the issues associated with deploying business rules on an intermediate, centralized server.

$49.99 US/$71.95 CDN	*Programming: Intermediate - Advanced*	
1-57169-154-5	*1,000 pp.*	
1 CD	*Sams*	

Dan Appleman's Developing COM/ActiveX Components with Visual Basic 6

Dan Appleman

Developing COM Components with Visual Basic 6 is a focused tutorial for learning component development. It teaches the reader the programming concepts and the technical steps needed to create ActiveX components. Dan Appleman is the author whom Visual Basic programmers recommend to their friends and colleagues. He consistently delivers on his promise to break through the confusion and hype surrounding Visual Basic and ActiveX. Appleman goes beyond the basics to show readers common pitfalls and practical solutions for key problems. Dan Appleman revises a successful title with new information on Visual Basic 6. Appleman is one of the foremost developers in the Visual Basic community and the author of *Visual Basic 5.0 Programmer's Guide to the Win32 API*. The book comes complete with a new CD and all new material.

$49.99 US/$71.95 CDN	*Programming - Intermediate*
1-56276-576-0	*850 pp.*
1 CD	*Que*

Doing Objects in Visual Basic 6

Deborah Kurata

Doing Objects in Microsoft Visual Basic 6 is an intermediate level tutorial which begins with the fundamentals of OOP. It advances to the technical aspects of using the VB IDE to create objects and interface with databases, Web sites, and Internet applications. This revised edition features more technical information than the last edition. It specifically highlights the features of the new release of Visual Basic. This is a revised edition of *Doing Objects in Microsoft Visual Basic 5.0*, the #1 OOP title for Visual Basic programmers and developers. The text focuses on the technical aspects of developing objects and covers the Internet and database programming aspects of Visual Basic 6.

$49.99 US/$46.18 CDN	*Programming: Intermediate - Expert*
1-56276-577-9	*560 pp.*
1 CD	*Que*

Visual Basic 6 Unleashed

Rob Thayer

Visual Basic 6 Unleashed provides comprehensive coverage of the most sought-after topics in Visual Basic programming. *Visual Basic 6 Unleashed* provides a means for a casual level Visual Basic programmer to quickly become productive with the new release of Visual Basic. This book provides the reader with a comprehensive reference to virtually all the topics that are used in today's leading-edge Visual Basic applications. This book takes advantage of the past success of the Unleashed series along with the extremely large size of the Visual Basic market. The integration of the text and CD-ROM makes this an invaluable tool for accomplished Visual Basic programmers—everything they need to know as well as the tools and utilities to make it work. It includes topics important to developers including creating and using ActiveX controls, creating Wizards, adding and controlling RDO, tuning and optimization, and much more. It is targeted towards the beginning to intermediate level programmer who needs additional step-by-step guidance in learning the more detailed features of Visual Basic. The reader can use this book as a building block to step to the next level from *Sams Teach Yourself Visual Basic 6 in 21 Days*.

$49.99 US/$71.95 CDN	*Programming: Advanced - Expert*
0-672-31309-X	*1,000 pp.*
Sams	

Add to Your Sams Library Today with the Best Books for Programming, Operating Systems, and New Technologies

To order, visit our Web site at www.mcp.com or fax us at

1-800-835-3202

ISBN	Quantity	Description of Item	Unit Cost	Total Cost
1-571-69153-7		The Waite Group's Visual Basic 6 How-To	$39.99	
1-571-69154-5		The Waite Group's Visual Basic 6 Client/Server How-To	$49.99	
1-56276-576-0		Dan Appleman's Developing COM/ActiveX Components with Visual Basic 6	$49.99	
1-56276-577-9		Doing Objects in Visual Basic	$49.99	
0-672-31309-X		Visual Basic 6 Unleashed	$49.99	
		Shipping and Handling: See information below.		
		TOTAL		

Shipping and Handling

Standard	$5.00
2nd Day	$10.00
Next Day	$17.50
International	$40.00

201 W. 103rd Street, Indianapolis, Indiana 46290   1-800-835-3202 — FAX

Book ISBN 1-57169-152-9

WHAT'S ON THE DISC

The companion CD-ROM contains all of the authors' source code and samples from the book and many third-party software products.

Windows 95/NT4 Installation Instructions

1. Insert the CD-ROM disc into your CD-ROM drive.

2. From the Windows 95 desktop, double-click the My Computer icon.

3. Double-click the icon representing your CD-ROM drive.

4. Double-click the icon titled SETUP.EXE to run the installation program.

5. Installation creates a program group named "VB6 DB How To." This group will contain icons to browse the CD-ROM.

NOTE

If Windows 95 is installed on your computer, and you have the AutoPlay feature enabled, the SETUP.EXE program starts automatically when you insert the disc into your CD-ROM drive.